SOA Using
Java™ Web Services

SOA Using
Java™ Web Services

Mark D. Hansen

PRENTICE
HALL

**Upper Saddle River, NJ • Boston • Indianapolis • San Francisco
New York • Toronto • Montreal • London • Munich • Paris • Madrid
Capetown • Sydney • Tokyo • Singapore • Mexico City**

This Book Is Safari Enabled

The Safari® Enabled icon on the cover of your favorite technology book means the book is available through Safari Bookshelf. When you buy this book, you get free access to the online edition for 45 days.

Safari Bookshelf is an electronic reference library that lets you easily search thousands of technical books, find code samples, download chapters, and access technical information whenever and wherever you need it.

To gain 45-day Safari Enabled access to this book:

- Go to http://www.prenhallprofessional.com/safarienabled
- Complete the brief registration form
- Enter the coupon code Q0CN-0ABE-9QIA-M4E8-NUJ3

If you have difficulty registering on Safari Bookshelf or accessing the online edition, please e-mail customer-service@safaribooksonline.com.

Visit us on the Web: www.prenhallprofessional.com

Library of Congress Cataloging-in-Publication Data

Hansen, Mark D.
   SOA Using Java Web Services / Mark D. Hansen.
     p. cm.
   Includes bibliographical references and index.
   ISBN 978-0-13-044968-9 (pbk. : alk. paper) 1. Web services.
   2. Java (Comput0er program language) 3. Computer network architectures. I.
Title.
   TK5105.88813.H35 2007
   006.7'6—dc22

                                 2007009650

ISBN-13: 978-0-13-044968-9
ISBN-10:   0-13-044968-7

Text printed in the United States on recycled paper at RR Donnelley in Crawfordsville, Indiana.
First printing, April 2007

To my wife, Lorraine, and our children, Elizabeth, Eric, and Emily.

Contents

Foreword

Pat Helland, formerly of Microsoft, has a great acronym he likes to use when talking about interoperability: HST, or "Hooking Stuff Together." (Actually, he uses an altogether different word there in the middle, but I'm told this is a family book, so I paraphrased.) No matter how much you dress it up in fancy words and complex flowcharts, interoperability simply means "Hooking Stuff Together"—something Web Services are all about.

Ever since the second computer came online, True Interoperability remains the goal that still eludes us. IT environments are home to a wide array of different technologies, all of which serve some useful purpose (or so I'm told). Despite various vendors' attempts to establish their tool of choice as the sole/dominant tool for building (and porting) applications, the IT world has only become more—not less—diverse. Numerous solutions have been posited as "the answer" to the thorny problem of getting program "A" to be able to talk to program "B," regardless of what language, platform, operating system, or hardware the two programs are written in or running on. None had proven to be entirely successful, either requiring an "all-or-nothing" mentality, or offering only solutions to handle the simplest situations and nothing more.

In 1998, Don Box and Dave Winer, along with a couple of guys from Microsoft, IBM, and Lotus, sat down and wrote a short document describing an idea for replicating a remote procedure call stack into an XML message. The idea was simple: If all of the various distributed object toolkits available at the time—DCOM, Java RMI, and CORBA being the principal concerns—shared a common wire format, it would be a simple matter to achieve the Holy Grail of enterprise IT programming: True Interoperability.

In the beginning, SOAP held out the prospect of a simpler, better way to Hook Stuff Together: XML, the lingua franca of data, passed over HTTP, the Dark Horse candidate in the Distributed Object wars, with all the semantics of the traditional distributed object programming model surrounding it. It seemed an easy prospect; just slip the XML in where nobody would see it, way down deep in the distributed object's generated code. What we didn't realize at the time, unfortunately, was that this vision was all too simplistic, and horribly naïve. It might work for environments that were remarkably similar to one another (à la Java and .NET), but even there, problems would arise, owing to differences XML simply couldn't wash away. Coupled with the fact that none of the so-called standards was, in fact, a standard from any kind of legitimate standards body, and that vendors were putting out "WS-Foo" specifications every time you turned around, the intended simplicity of the solution was, in a word, absent. In fact, to put it bluntly, for a long time, the whole Web Services story was more "mess" than "message."

In Chapter 1 of this book, Mark Hansen writes, "Web Services are not easy." Whatever happened to the "Simple" in "SOAP?"

Ironically, even as Web Services start to take on "dirty word" status, alongside EJB and COBOL, the message is becoming increasingly clear, and the chances of "getting it right" have never been higher. Distractions such as the SOAP versus REST debate aside (which really isn't a debate, as anyone who's really read the SOAP 1.2 spec and the REST dissertation can tell), the various vendors and industry groups are finally coming to a point where they can actually Hook Stuff Together in more meaningful ways than just "I'll pass you a string, which you'll parse...."

As an instructor with DevelopMentor—where I taught Java, .NET, and XML—I had the privilege of learning about SOAP, WSDL, and Web Services from the very guys who were writing the specs, including Don Box and Martin Gudgin, our representative to the W3C, who helped coauthor the SOAP and Schema specs, among others. As an industry consultant focused on interoperability between Java, .NET, and other platforms, I get a unique first-person view of real-world interoperability problems. And as an independent speaker and mentor, I get to study the various interoperability toolkits and see how well they work.

Not everybody gets that chance, however, and unless you're a real low-level "plumbing" wonk like I am, and find a twisted joy in reading through the myriad WS-*-related specifications, things like SOAP and WSDL remain arcane, high-bar topics that seemingly nobody in his or her right mind would attempt to learn, just to get your Java code to be able to talk to other platforms. That's okay; quite honestly, you shouldn't have to. If you have to absorb every level of detail in a given programming environment in order to use it, well, something is wrong.

The JAX-WS and JAXB standards were created to help you avoid having to know all those low-level, byzantine details of the Web Services plumbing, unless and until you want to. Mark's book will help you navigate through the twisty parts of JAX-WS and JAXB because he's been there. He had to fight his way through the mess to get to the message, and now he's going to turn around and act as your guide—Virgil to your Dante, if you will—through the rocky parts.

Because in the end, all of this is supposed to be about Hooking Stuff Together.

—Ted Neward
Java, .NET, XML Services
Consulting, Teaching, Speaking, Writing
www.tedneward.com

Preface

Java became a powerful development platform for Service-Oriented Architecture (SOA) in 2006. Java EE 5, released in May 2006, significantly enhanced the power and usability of the Web Services capabilities on the application server. Then Java SE 6, released in December 2006, incorporated the majority of those capabilities into the standard edition of the Java programming language.

Because robust Web Services technology is the foundation for implementing SOA, Java now provides the tools modern enterprises require to integrate their Java applications into SOA infrastructures.

Of course, Java has had basic Web Services capabilities for some time. JAX-RPC 1.0 was released in June 2002. J2EE 1.4, finalized in November 2003, included JAX-RPC 1.1. So what is significant about the latest versions of the Java Web Services (JWS) APIs?

The answers are power and ease of use. Programmers will find it much easier to build enterprise-class applications with Web Services in Java EE 5 than in J2EE 1.4. Evidence of that is contained in Chapters 9 and 10, which describe an application I developed to integrate online shopping across eBay, Yahoo! Shopping, and Amazon. It's a pure Java EE 5 application, called SOAShopper, that consumes REST and SOAP services from those shopping sites. SOAShopper also provides its own SOAP and REST endpoints for cross-platform search, and supports an Ajax front-end. SOAShopper would have been a struggle to develop using J2EE 1.4 and JAX-RPC. With the new Java Web Services standards, it was a pleasure to write.

This book focuses on the following standards comprising the new Java Web Services:

- JAX-WS 2.0 [JSR 224]—The Java API for XML-Based Web Services. The successor to JAX-RPC, it enables you to build and consume Web services with Java.
- JAXB 2.0 [JSR 222]—The Java Architecture for XML Binding. Tightly integrated with JAX-WS, the JAXB standard controls how Java objects are represented as XML.

- WS-Metadata [JSR 181]—Web Services Metadata for the Java Platform. WS-Metadata provides annotations that facilitate the flexible definition and deployment of Java Web Services.
- WSEE 1.2 [JSR 109]—Web Services for Java EE. WSEE defines the programming model and run-time behavior of Web Services in the Java EE container.

These standards contain a few big improvements and many little enhancements that add up to a significantly more powerful Web Services programming platform. New annotations, for example, make it easier to write Web Services applications. And the delegation, in JAX-WS 2.0 [JSR 224], of the Java/XML binding to JAXB 2.0 [JSR 222] greatly improves the usability of JAX-WS as compared with JAX-RPC. The deployment model has been greatly simplified by WS-Metadata 1.0 [JSR 181] and an improved 1.2 release of WSEE [JSR-109].

Chapters 1 and 2 review these JWS standards in detail and describe how they improve on the previous set of JWS standards. Chapters 3 through 10 focus on writing code. To really understand the power and ease of use of the new Java Web Services, you need to start writing code. And that is primarily what this book is about. Chapters 3 through 10 are packed with code examples showing you how to best take advantage of the powerful features, avoid some of the pitfalls, and work around some of the limitations.

Chapter 11 looks to the future and offers some ideas, along with a prototype implementation, for a WSDL-centric approach to creating Web Services that might further improve JWS as a platform for Service-Oriented Architecture.

I started writing this book in 2002, when JAX-RPC first appeared on the scene. I soon ran into trouble, though, because I wanted it to be a book for programmers and I had a hard time writing good sample code with JAX-RPC. Four years later, when I started playing around with beta versions of the GlassFish Java EE 5 application server, I noticed that things had significantly improved. It was now fun to program Web Services in Java and I recommitted myself to finishing this book.

The result is a book with lots of code showing you how to deal with SOAP, WSDL, and REST from inside the Java programming language. Hopefully this code, and the writing that goes with it, will help you master Java Web Services and enable you to start using Java as a powerful platform for SOA.

About This Book

An Unbiased Guide to Java Web Services for SOA

My primary goal in this book is to offer an unbiased guide to using the Java Web Services (JWS) standards for SOA. Of course, any author has a bias, and I admit to believing that the JWS standards are quite good. Otherwise, I would not have written this book.

Having admitted my bias, I also freely admit that JWS has weaknesses, particularly when it comes to the development approach known as *Start from WSDL and Java*. As you will see described in many different ways in this book, the JWS standards present a Java-centric approach to Web Services. That approach can be troublesome when you need to work with established SOA standards and map your Java application to existing XML Schema documents and WSDLs.

In such situations, it's helpful to be able to take a WSDL-centric approach to Web Services development. In this area, JWS is less strong. Throughout the book, I point out those shortcomings, and offer strategies you can use to overcome them. Chapter 11 even offers a prototype framework, called SOA-J, that illustrates an alternative, WSDL-centric approach to Java Web Services.

Written for Java Developers and Architects

This is a book for people who are interested in code—primarily the developers who write systems and the architects who design them. There are a lot of coding examples you can download, install, and run.

Being a book for Java programmers working with Web Services, the discussion and examples provided within assume you have a working knowledge of Java and a basic understanding of XML and XML Schema. You don't need to know a lot about SOAP or WSDL to dive in and start learning. However, as you go along in the book, you might want to browse through an introductory tutorial on WSDL and/or XML Schema if you need to firm up your grasp on some of the Web Services basics. Throughout the book, I offer references to Web sites and other books where you can brush up on background material.

Knowledge of J2SE 5.0 Is Assumed

This book assumes you have a basic understanding of J2SE 5.0—particularly the Java language extensions generics and annotations. If you are not familiar with generics or annotations, you can learn all you need to know from the free documentation and tutorials available at http://java.sun.com.

Don't be intimidated by these topics. Generics and annotations are not hard to master—and you need to understand them if you are going to do Web Services with Java EE 5 and Java SE 6. The reason I have not written an introduction to generics and annotations as part of this book is that there is so much good, free information available on the Web. My focus in this book is to go beyond what is freely available in the online tutorials and documentation.

Why GlassFish?

All the code examples presented in this book have been developed and tested using the GlassFish [GLASSFISH] open source Java EE 5 reference implementation. At the time I wrote this, it was the only implementation available. Now that the book is going to press, there are more, and the code should run on all these platforms without change. The only changes that will need to be made have to do with the build process where GlassFish specific tools (e.g., the `wsimport` WSDL to Java compiler, the `asadmin` deployment utility) are used.

I plan to test the example code on other platforms as they become available and to post instructions for running them on JBoss, BEA, IBM, and so on, as these vendors support the JWS standards. Check the book's Web site (http://soabook.com) for updates on progress with other platforms.

If you haven't tried GlassFish, I suggest you check it out at https://glassfish.dev.java.net. It supports the cutting edge in Java EE and the community is terrific. In particular, I've had good experiences getting technical support on the mailing lists. It's not uncommon to post a question there and have one of the JSR specification leads respond with an answer within minutes!

Why Some Topics Aren't Covered

Both SOA and Web Services are vast topics. Even when restricting the discussion to Java technology, it is impossible to cover everything in one book. Faced with that reality, I decided to focus on what I consider to be the core issues that are important to Java developers and architects. The core issues involve creating, deploying, and invoking Web Services in a manner that enables them to be composed into loosely coupled SOA applications.

In narrowing the book's focus, it is inevitable that I will have disappointed some readers because a particular topic of interest to them isn't covered. Some of these topics, pointed out by my reviewers, are listed here, along with the reasons why I didn't include them.

SOA Design Principles

This is not a book that covers the concepts and design philosophy behind SOA. It is a how-to book that teaches Java developers to code SOA components using Java Web Services. For a thorough introduction to SOA concepts and design, I recommend Thomas Erl's *Service-Oriented Architecture* [Erl].

UDDI

UDDI is very important. And Java EE 5 includes the JAX-R standard interface to UDDI repositories. But JAX-R hasn't changed since J2EE 1.4. And it is covered well in many other books and online tutorials. So, in an effort to keep this book to a manageable size, I have left it out.

Enterprise Messaging

I wish I could have included a chapter on Enterprise Messaging. After all, it is a cornerstone of SOA. However, this book restricts itself to the capabilities provided by JWS. JWS does not support WS-Reliable Messaging [WS-RM] or any other SOAP/WSDL-oriented reliable messaging mechanism. Of course, Java EE 5 includes support for the Java Message Service API (JMS). And JMS is a useful tool for implementing SOA applications. But by itself, JMS isn't a Web Services tool. So, in the interest of focus, I have left it out.

WS-Addressing, WS-Security, and the Many Other WS-* Standards

Explaining the myriad standards for the Web Services stack would require many thousands of pages. Since these WS-* standards are not yet part of JWS, I have not covered them. In addition, my sense is that most Java developers are still mastering SOAP over HTTP. The need for a programmer's guide to WS-* is probably several years away.

Fonts and Special Characters

Courier font is used for Java types, XML Schema components, and all code examples included in the text. For example:

```
java.lang.String—a Java class (fully qualified)
MyPurchaseOrder—a Java class
xs:string—an XML Schema type
po:billTo—an XML Schema global element
```

Courier font is also used to signify software-environment-specific items (e.g., paths, directories, environment variables) and text interactions with the computer. For example:

```
JAVA_HOME—an environment variable
$JAVA_HOME/bin—a directory
mvn install—an instruction typed into the console
```

Italics indicate that a term is defined in the glossary. I don't always use italics—only when a term may not have been used before and I think the reader might want to know it is defined in the Glossary. For example, Chapter 2 uses this sentence:

> When a *service implementation bean* (SIB) with minimal source code annotations is deployed, the resulting WSDL is based on this default mapping.

In this usage, the term "service implementation bean" has not yet been defined.

Italics may also be used for emphasis, as in this example:

> However, while the standard mapping makes it easy to deploy a Web Service, it is not clear that the result is a *useful* Web Service.

<> indicates an environment specific directory location. For example:

```
<AppServer>—the location where the Java EE 5 application server is
```
installed
```
<book-code>—the location where the book example code is installed
```

Code Fragments in Text

The text contains lots of code fragments to illustrate the discussion. At the bottom of each code fragment is the file path showing where it came from. So, for example, the following code fragment comes from <book-code>/ chap03/eisrecords/src/xml/order.xml. Moreover, the line numbers on the left show you the line number in the file where the code comes from.

```
 4  <Order xmlns="http://www.example.com/oms"
 5    xmlns:xsi="http://www.w3.org/2001/XMLSchema-instance"
 6    xsi:schemaLocation="http://www.example.com/oms
 7    http://soabook.com/example/oms/orders.xsd">
 8    <OrderKey>ENT1234567</OrderKey>
 9    <OrderHeader>
10      <SALES_ORG>NE</SALES_ORG>
11      <PURCH_DATE>2005-12-09</PURCH_DATE>
12      <CUST_NO>ENT0072123</CUST_NO>
13      <PYMT_METH>PO</PYMT_METH>
14      <PURCH_ORD_NO>PO-72123-0007</PURCH_ORD_NO>
15      <WAR_DEL_DATE>2005-12-16</WAR_DEL_DATE>
16    </OrderHeader>
17    <OrderItems>
18      <item>
19        <ITM_NUMBER>012345</ITM_NUMBER>
20        <STORAGE_LOC>NE02</STORAGE_LOC>
21        <TARGET_QTY>50</TARGET_QTY>
22        <TARGET_UOM>CNT</TARGET_UOM>
23        <PRICE_PER_UOM>7.95</PRICE_PER_UOM>
24        <SHORT_TEXT>7 mm Teflon Gasket</SHORT_TEXT>
25      </item>
26      <item>
27        <ITM_NUMBER>543210</ITM_NUMBER>
28        <TARGET_QTY>5</TARGET_QTY>
29        <TARGET_UOM>KG</TARGET_UOM>
30        <PRICE_PER_UOM>12.58</PRICE_PER_UOM>
31        <SHORT_TEXT>Lithium grease with PTFE/Teflon</SHORT_TEXT>
32      </item>
33    </OrderItems>
34    <OrderText>This order is a rush.</OrderText>
35  </Order>
```

book-code/chap03/eisrecords/src/xml/order.xml

Acknowledgments

I could not have written this book without help and support from many talented people. In particular, I am indebted to everybody in the Project GlassFish community for providing valuable insights that appear throughout this book. In particular, I'd like to recognize Stephen DiMilla, Jerome Dochez, Joseph Fialli, Mike Grogan, Doug Kohlert, Kohsuke Kawaguchi, Jitendra Kotamraju, Bhakti Mehta, Carla Mott, Dhiru Pandey, Vivek Pandey, Dinesh Patil, Eduardo Pelegri-Llopart, Vijay Ramachandran, and Kathy Walsh. From among this list, additional thanks are owed to Vijay Ramachandran and Doug Kohlert at Sun Microsystems for reviewing the chapters on WS-Metadata, WSEE, and JAX-WS.

I first considered this project when Professor Stuart Madnick invited me to be a visiting scholar at MIT where I conducted research on process and data integration using Web Services technology. Working with him and his research team sparked my interest in Java Web Services and eventually led to this book.

Bruce Scharlau, Art Sedighi, and Matt Anderson reviewed early versions of this book and provided many helpful comments that have been incorporated.

I would also like to acknowledge my friends in Bangalore, India—Kishore Gopalakrishna and his team: Rohit Agarwal, Vinit Sharma, and Rohit Choudhary. They provided invaluable contributions to the SOA-J project described in Chapter 11.

Ted Neward provided insightful comments and graciously agreed to write the Foreword. It is a great privilege to have him associated with this project.

This book could never have happened without the patient guidance of my editor, Greg Doench, at Prentice Hall. His wisdom and experience were invaluable. I'd also like to thank Michelle Housley, Julie Nahil, Dmitri Korzh, and all the staff at Prentice Hall for shepherding this book through the publication process.

On the home front, my children, Elizabeth, Eric, and Emily, provided lots of hugs and playful interruptions that helped keep me going while I was writing. Lastly, and most importantly, it was the love and support of my wife, Lorraine, that made this book possible. Without her patience and understanding, this task would have been impossible.

About the Author

Mark D. Hansen, Ph.D., is a software developer, consultant, and entrepreneur. His company, Javector Software, provides consulting and software application development focused on Web Services. Mark is also a content developer for Project GlassFish and has developed the open source SOA-J application framework for WSDL-centric Web Services development.

Previously, Mark was a visiting scholar at MIT researching applications for process and data integration using Web Services technology. Before that, Mark was an executive vice president for Xpedior, Inc., a leading provider of eBusiness consulting services. He joined Xpedior when they acquired his consulting firm—Kinderhook Systems.

Mark founded Kinderhook in 1993 to develop custom Internet solutions for Fortune 500 firms. Prior to founding Kinderhook Systems, Hansen was a founder and vice president of technology for QDB Solutions, Inc., a Cambridge, Massachusetts, based software firm providing tools for data integrity management in corporate data warehouses. QDB Solutions was acquired by Prizm Technologies in 1997.

Mark's work has been featured in publications such as the *Wall Street Journal, Information Week, Computer World, Database Management, Database Programming and Design, Business Communications Review, EAI Journal*, and *IntelligentEnterprise*.

Mark earned a Ph.D. from the MIT Laboratory for Computer Science, a masters degree from the MIT Sloan School of Management, a master's degree in mathematics from the University of Chicago, and a bachelor's degree in mathematics from Cornell University.

Mark and his wife, Lorraine, live in suburban New York, with their three children, Elizabeth, Eric, and Emily.

CHAPTER 1

Service-Oriented Architecture with Java Web Services

Modern enterprise Java applications need to support the principles of Service-Oriented Architecture (SOA). The foundation of most SOA applications is Web Services. So, if you are an enterprise Java developer, you probably want to master the Web Services standards included with Java EE 5 and Java SE 6. These standards include JAX-WS (formerly JAX-RPC) [JSR 224], JAXB [JSR 222], Web Services Metadata (WS-Metadata) [JSR 181], SOAP with Attachments API for Java (SAAJ) [JSR 67], and Web Services for Java EE (WSEE)[1] [JSR 109]. I call these standards, taken together, Java Web Services (JWS).

SOA applications are constructed from loosely coupled Web services. Therefore, naturally, as enterprise Java developers, we turn to JWS tools for creating SOA applications. Furthermore, the leading enterprise Java vendors hold out JWS technologies as the development platform of choice for SOA applications.

So, the JWS standards are very important. They are the foundation for SOA development with enterprise Java. And loosely coupled SOA applications are critical to corporate competitiveness because they enable business processes to be flexible and they adapt to rapidly changing global markets.

Unfortunately, if you are like me, you may have found the Java Web Services learning curve a little steep. It seems that lots of powerful and complex machinery is required just to deploy a Java class as a Web service or create a simple client to consume such services. Sure, you can get the simple "Hello World" application from the Java EE 5 tutorial to work.

---

1. As the deployment standard for EE containers, WSEE is supported only in Java EE, not Java SE.

However, when you need to deploy your purchase ordering system, things suddenly seem to get much more complicated. Either the WSDL you start with gets compiled into myriad bizarre classes that have to be manually wrapped and mapped into your real purchasing system, or, if you start from your Java classes, the WSDL that gets produced doesn't turn out the way you need it to. If you have been frustrated by problems like these, I sympathize with you. So have I, and that is what motivated me to write this book.

1.1   Am I Stupid, or Is Java Web Services Really Hard?

At first, I just thought I was stupid. Prior to getting involved with Java Web Services, I had been running a consulting business. I figured that since I'd been a manager for the past several years, the technologist side of my brain had atrophied. "Keep working at it!" I said to myself, "and you'll master this stuff." That was three years ago, and as I wrestled with JWS annotations, deployment descriptors, WSDL proxies, schema compilers, and so on, I've compiled my "lessons learned" into this book.

During these past three years, I've mastered topics such as Java generics, reflection, persistence, and concurrency. I've studied the Apache Axis [AXIS, AXIS2] source code—and even submitted a few patches. I've convinced myself that I'm not stupid. Yet, it was a long struggle for me to develop an intuitive understanding of the JWS standards. And I'm not the only one who has experienced this.

Richard Monson-Haefel, a distinguished technologist, published a 960-page book [Monson-Haefel] on the J2EE 1.4 versions of these Java Web Services specifications in late 2003. Nine hundred sixty pages! That fact alone indicates that a significant learning curve is associated with JWS. It's not that any one particular topic is very difficult. Sure, it takes a little while to figure out what the JAX-WS API does. However, the real difficulty is getting your mind around all these APIs and how they relate to the underlying Web Services standards (e.g., XML, WSDL, and SOAP), the HTTP protocol, and the other Java EE container services (e.g., dependency injection). Trying to mentally connect what's going on at the Java level with the underlying WSDL, SOAP, XML, and HTTP can make working with the JWS standards feel awkward and unnatural.

During the past two years, a chorus of technologists—Monson-Haefel among them—has been bashing the Java Web Services standards. Their view is based on experiences they had working with the older, J2EE 1.4 versions, of JWS. And I agree that it is difficult to do useful SOA-style development work with those older APIs. However, I have trouble agreeing that the specifications themselves, especially the latest versions embedded in Java EE 5 and Java SE 6, are the real problem. Instead, I suspect the problem itself—creating a general-purpose framework for Java Web Services development—is just plain complicated.

Richard Monson-Haefel posted this e-mail on his blog April 22, 2006. It summarizes pretty well how many of us feel after having spent a lot of time working on Java Web Services:

Dave Podnar's Five Stages of Dealing with Web Services

1. Denial—It's Simple Object Access Protocol, right?
2. Over Involvement—OK, I'll read the SOAP, WSDL, WS-I BP, JAX-RPC, SAAJ, JAX-P ... specs. Next, I'll check the Wiki and finally follow an example showing service and client sides.
3. Anger—I can't believe those #$%&*@s made it so difficult!
4. Guilt—Everyone is using Web Services, it must be me, I must be missing something.
5. Acceptance—It is what it is, Web Services aren't simple or easy.

One thesis of this book, simply stated, is that Web Services are hard. We need to accept that fact and move on. Web Services are hard because they are a form of distributed computing, and distributed computing is just about the hardest problem in computer science.

So, this book doesn't hype the JWS standards and tell you that they make building SOA-style applications easy. Instead, this book helps you navigate JWS and understand the strengths and weaknesses of its component technologies. Along the way, I share with you the lessons I have learned, showing how JWS can be used to build powerful SOA-style applications that deploy and consume Web Services effectively. The culmination of this journey is the construction of the sample SOAShopper application, in Chapters 9 and 10, which implements a consolidated shopping engine integrated with eBay, Amazon, and Yahoo! Shopping. SOAShopper publishes both REST and SOAP endpoints, consumes both REST and SOAP endpoints, and provides an Ajax front end.

1.1.1 Don't Drink That Kool-Aid

In early 2001, when Ariba, IBM, and Microsoft published WSDL 1.1 as a W3C Note [WSDL 1.1], Web Services were envisioned as a way to make distributed computing *easier*. No longer would developers need to understand CORBA to create cross-platform, distributed applications. Even better, Web Services were envisioned as a technology to make distributed computing over the Internet possible.

Like me, most Java developers bought into this early Web Services vision. It made sense given our experience with the Internet during the 1990s. HTML over HTTP had fueled the astonishing growth of the World Wide Web—a distributed computing platform for people. We believed that standards (like SOAP and WSDL) for XML over HTTP would fuel similar growth for Web Services—a distributed computing platform for business applications.

We all drank that Kool-Aid. We believed that Web Services would make distributed computing easy.

The leaders of the Enterprise Java industry set to work implementing the Web Services vision. Along the way to realizing this vision, the Java industry discovered that they had created some pretty daunting specifications. The people who read the early JAX-RPC, JAXB, and other specifications—including myself—became alarmed. We figured that something must have gone wrong. We assumed that the Expert Groups leading these specifications had gotten off-track. We became disillusioned and bitter about the lost promise of Web Services. We started bickering among ourselves about SOAP versus REST and who is to blame for the complexity of the Java Web Services specifications.

But the complexity problem isnt a result of choosing the SOAP framework instead of REST. It's not a result of overengineering on the part of the Expert Groups. As the Expert Groups got down to brass tacks—trying to make the Web Services vision happen—they rediscovered that distributed computing really is a daunting challenge. SOAP, WSDL, XML, and even REST are not going to make distributed computing easy.

Certainly, the JWS specifications are flawed. But that is to be expected—new technologies often come out with quirks and idiosyncrasies that make them difficult to work with (look at EJB). These problems are corrected as enhancements are made in subsequent versions[2] of the technology.

---

2. Note that EJB 3.0 continues to improve and implements the advanced Aspect Oriented Programming and Inversion of Control features its many detractors have been calling for.

As one example of how the JWS specifications have improved, consider JAX-WS 2.0. Chapters 6 and 7 describe that specification in detail, so for now, I'm just going to give a preview of why I think it's such a big improvement over JAX-RPC 1.1. For starters, the JAX-RPC data binding has been removed and the specification has been simplified to focus on the WSDL to Java mapping along with support for REST endpoints. The XML Schema to Java data binding from JAX-RPC has been replaced with JAXB 2.0, a much superior and widely used technology. Second, JAX-WS lets you use annotations to control the shape of the WSDL generated from a Java interface. The use of annotations in this manner simplifies and in some cases eliminates the need for the deployment descriptors required to deploy a JAX-RPC service. Third, JAX-WS provides interfaces (`Dispatch` on the client side and `Provider` on the server side) that enable programmers to directly access and work with XML—effectively bypassing the JAXB data binding when they don't want to use it.

For certain, JAX-WS 2.0 could still be improved. The biggest improvement I can think of would be to provide an alternative binding (in addition to JAXB) that lets the developer work directly with the native XML types that are specified in a WSDL and its associated schema. Some type of XML extension to Java, like XJ [XJ], might do the job. Much of the complexity and confusion developers experience when working with JAX-WS relate to the difficulty of determining how the JAX-WS/JAXB-generated classes created by the JAX-WS WSDL compiler map to the XML messages specified in the WSDL. However, that is a whole research area (creating a language that makes it simple to program directly with native XML types) unto itself where we are all still waiting for some breakthroughs. My point here is not that JAX-WS is ideal, but simply that is has improved on JAX-RPC, much as EJB 3.0 has improved on EJB 2.1.

To summarize, in the years since the WSDL specification came out, the Enterprise Java community has created from scratch a Java-centric platform for distributed computing based on Web Services technologies. This has been a Herculean task and it shouldn't surprise anyone that the specifications are difficult to understand! Viewed from this perspective, the JWS standards are not bad at all. In fact, they are a huge step toward enabling Java to become an SOA development platform. These standards give us the APIs we need to wrestle with the complexities of Web Services development.

So why are we disillusioned? What lesson should we be learning as we wallow in our disillusionment? I think it is the same lesson we learn over and over again in this business—"Don't drink the Kool-Aid"! If we didn't start out by assuming that Web Services were going to be a silver bullet for distributed computing, we wouldn't be disillusioned. Instead, we would be optimistic.

1.1.2 JWS Is a Toolset, Not an Application Framework

Realizing that Web Services are intrinsically difficult forced me to rethink my assumptions about the JWS specifications. I no longer believed that these specifications could be significantly simplified. I accepted their complexity as the natural expression of the complexity of the underlying distributed computing problem.

Instead of viewing JWS as an application framework for SOA-style development, I recognized it as a toolset for consuming and deploying Web Services—the components of an SOA-based distributed computing environment. My problem had not been stupidity, but expecting too much from my tools. Creating SOA applications with the JWS technologies requires some discipline and design savvy. Throughout this book, I offer examples of good design that make application development with JWS easier.

For example, in Chapter 4 I discuss the use of centralized XML Schema libraries as a mechanism to promote *separation of concerns*. Such libraries separate the type definition process (a necessary part of creating SOA application with Web Services) from the interface definition process (i.e., creating WSDL representations of individual SOA components). As another example, Chapter 5 shows how to isolate the JWS generated classes from the rest of your application by introducing a type mapping layer into your SOA systems. This technique is then used in the Chapter 9 implementation of SOAShopper.

One way to encourage good design and make programming easier is to use an application framework. For example, the Apache Struts [STRUTS] framework encourages Web applications development based on the Model 2 or Model View Controller (MVC) framework. Frameworks offer a layer of abstraction on top of complex toolsets. The layer of abstraction encourages you to program in a certain way. By restricting your programming choices to a subset of proven patterns, the framework makes your job easier and less confusing.

Application frameworks can also encourage good design. A good SOA framework, therefore, should encourage the use of XML Schema libraries and promote the reuse of schema across WSDL documents. A good SOA framework should separate compiled schemas and WSDL from the rest of the application classes.

Application frameworks employ toolsets, but they also go beyond toolsets. They encourage a particular manner of using toolsets. Struts, for example, employs servlets and JavaServer Pages (JSP), among other toolsets. On top of these toolsets, Struts provides a framework of classes (e.g., `Action`, `ActionMapping`) for building applications according to the MVC framework.

Thinking through the Struts analogy to Web Services, I realized that JWS provides a toolset but not an application framework. To develop SOA business applications, I really wanted an application framework like Struts—not just the underlying toolset. Because SOA is WSDL-centric (i.e., WSDL defines the interfaces for communicating with services), ideally, I wanted a framework that allowed me to do WSDL-centric development.

Unfortunately, as of this writing, no popular application frameworks, analogous to Struts, have emerged for Java Web Services. I've taken a first pass at developing one, called SOA-J. For curious readers, an overview of SOA-J is included in Chapter 11.

1.1.3 Epiphany

Understanding that JWS is a toolset and not an application framework was my epiphany. Once I got past that, I realized that to be successful with JWS, I would need to spend a lot of time getting intimately familiar with how the toolset operates. This book passes those experiences on to you. It is filled with lots of examples of how to accomplish various tasks (e.g., publish a REST endpoint, replace the JAXB binding with something else like Castor, consume a Web service with no WSDL, etc.). So, if you like lots of code examples, you will not be disappointed.

Before digging in to the code, however, I need to introduce some common terminology to discuss the different components common to any platform that enables the development and deployment of Web Services.[3] I call any such platform a Web Services platform. The next section introduces what I call the Web Services Platform Architecture (WSPA), which provides the common terminology that is used throughout this book for discussing Web Services platforms. Think of the WSPA as our reference architecture. As we discuss Java Web Services, we will refer to the WSPA to discuss its strengths and weaknesses.

---

3. Some other platforms, in addition to Java EE 5, for deploying Web services include Axis [AXIS] [AXIS2], Systinet Server [SYSTINET], and XFire [XFIRE].

1.2   Web Services Platform Architecture

A Web Services platform is a set of tools for invoking and deploying Web Services using a particular programming language. Although my focus is Java, the concepts described in this section apply across languages.

The platform has server-side components and client-side components. The server-side components are usually packaged within some type of container (e.g., a Java EE application server or a servlet engine). The client-side components are usually packaged as tools for accessing Java interface instances that are bound to Web Services. Any Web Services platform, whether Apache Axis, XFire, Systinet Server [SYSTINET], JWS, or something else, has to provide three core subsystems: Invocation, Serialization,[4] and Deployment. To get started, a basic discussion of these subsystems, in the abstract, will help us understand what JWS is designed to do and give us some terminology for discussing its behavior.

1.2.1 Invocation

There are invocation mechanisms on both the server side and the client side. On the server side, the invocation mechanism is responsible for:

Server-Side Invocation

1. Receiving a SOAP message from a transport (e.g., from an HTTP or JMS endpoint).
2. Invoking handlers that preprocess the message (e.g., to persist the message for reliability purposes, or process SOAP headers).
3. Determining the message's target service—in other words, which WSDL operation the message is intended to invoke.
4. Given the target WSDL operation, determining which Java class/method to invoke. I call this the Java target. Determining the Java target is referred to as *dispatching*.
5. Handing off the SOAP message to the Serialization subsystem to deserialize it into Java objects that can be passed to the Java target as parameters.
6. Invoking the Java target using the parameters generated by the Serialization subsystem and getting the Java object returned by the target method.

---

4. I use the term "Serialization" as shorthand for "Serialization and Deserialization."

7. Handing off the returned object to the Serialization subsystem to serialize it into an XML element conformant with the return message specified by the target WSDL operation.
8. Wrapping the returned XML element as a SOAP message response conforming to the target WSDL operation.
9. Handing the SOAP response back to the transport for delivery.

At each stage in this process, the invocation subsystem must also handle exceptions. When an exception occurs, the invocation subsystem often must package it as a SOAP fault message to be returned to the client. In practice, the invocation process is more nuanced and complex than this. However, the steps outlined here offer a good starting point for our discussion of Java Web Services architecture. Later chapters go into greater detail—particularly Chapters 6 and 7 where I examine JAX-WS, and Chapter 11 where the SOA-J[5] invocation mechanism is described.

As you can see, the invocation process is nontrivial. Part of its complexity results from having to support SOAP. We'll look at a simpler alternative, known as REST (Representational State Transfer), in Chapter 3. Even with REST, however, invocation is complicated. It's just not that easy to solve the generalized problem of mapping an XML description of a Web service to a Java target and invoking that target with an XML message.

On the client side, the invocation process is similar if you want to invoke a Web service using a Java interface. This approach may not always be the most appropriate way to invoke a Web service—a lot depends on the problem you are solving. If your client is working with XML, it might be easier to just construct a SOAP message from XML and pass it to the Web service. On the other hand, if your client is working with Java objects, as JWS assumes, the client-side invocation subsystem is responsible for:

Client-Side Invocation

1. Creating an instance of the Web service endpoint implementing a Java interface referred to (JWS terminology) as the *service endpoint interface* (SEI). The invocation subsystem has one or more factories for creating SEI instances. These instances are either created on the fly, or accessed using JNDI. Typically, SEI instances are implemented using Java proxies and invocation handlers. I cover this fascinating topic in depth in Chapter 6.
2. Handling an invocation of the SEI instance.

---

5. SOA-J is introduced in Section 1.5 as an application framework built on top of JWS.

3. Taking the parameters passed to the SEI and passing them to the Serialization subsystem to be serialized into XML elements that conform to the XML Schema specified by the target service's WSDL.

4. Based on the target service's WSDL, wrapping the parameter elements in a SOAP message.

5. Invoking handlers that post-process the message (e.g., to persist the message for reliability purposes, or set SOAP headers) based on Quality of Service (QoS) or other requirements.

6. Handing off the message to the transport for delivery to the target Web service.

7. Receiving the SOAP message response from the transport.

8. Handing off the SOAP message to the Serialization subsystem to deserialize it into a Java object that is an instance of the class specified by the SEI's return type.

9. Completing the invocation of the SEI by returning the deserialized SOAP response.

Again, for simplicity of presentation, I have left out a description of the exception handling process. In general, client-side invocation is the inverse of server-side invocation. On the server side, the invocation subsystem front-ends a Java method with a proxy SOAP operation defined by the WSDL. It executes the WSDL operation by invoking a Java method. Conversely, on the client side, the invocation subsystem front-ends the WSDL-defined SOAP operation with a proxy Java interface. It handles a Java method call by executing a WSDL operation. Figure 1–1 illustrates this mirror image behavior.

One interesting point to make here is that only the middle part of Figure 1–1, the SOAP request/response, is specified by the WSDL. The Java method invocations at either end are completely arbitrary from a Web Services perspective. In fact, you have one Java method signature on the client side and a completely different method signature on the server side. In most cases, the method signatures are different, and the programming languages used are different, because if both sides were working with the same Java class libraries, this invocation could occur via Java RMI.

Also keep in mind that Figure 1–1 simply illustrates the mirror-image nature of invocation on the client and server sides. In practice, one side of this diagram or the other is probably not doing a Java method invocation. For example, Web Services enable us to have a Java client invoking a CICS transaction over SOAP/HTTP. In that scenario, you have a Java invocation subsystem only on the client side and something else that converts SOAP to CICS on the server side.

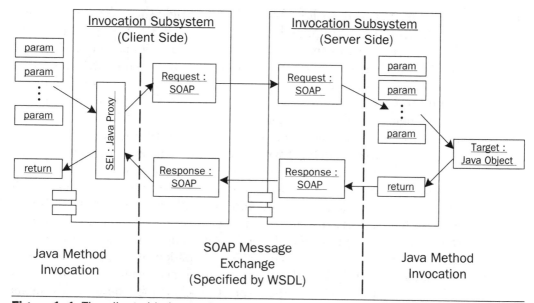

Figure 1–1 The client-side invocation subsystem translates a method call on the SEI proxy into a SOAP request/response and, vice versa, the server-side invocation subsystem translates the SOAP request/response into a method call on the Java target.

1.2.2 Serialization

Serialization is the process of transforming an instance of a Java class into an XML element. The inverse process, transforming an XML element into an instance of a Java class, is called deserialization. In this book, I often refer to both serialization and deserialization as simply "serialization."

Serialization is arguably the most important component of any platform for Java Web Services. Figure 1–2 illustrates the problem serialization solves. I'm going to dive into some details about how serialization relates to WSDL and SOAP here to explain this figure.[6] The details are necessary (even in Chapter 1!) to understand exactly what the serialization subsystem of the WSPA is doing.

Hosted within a Web Services container may be many SOAP endpoints—each corresponding to a group of Web services. An endpoint has an associated WSDL interface that defines the operations that can be performed on the endpoint.

---

6. Don't worry if you need a better understanding of WSDL and SOAP to understand this explanation. I cover it in more detail in Chapter 4. For now, just focus on getting the general idea.

In Figure 1–2, the callout box in the lower right shows a snippet of such a WSDL interface. Examine this snippet and notice the `<types>` element. This element contains the XML Schema type definitions that are used in the Web services defined by the rest of the WSDL document. The snippet shows the definition for an element named `customerPurchase`. The qualified name of this element is `wrapper:customerPurchase`. As you can see, that element is used as the single part in the message definition for `onCustomerPurchase`. Looking further down in the snippet, the `portType` named `CustomerPurchase` is defined with an operation named `processCustomerPurchase` that uses the `onCustomerPurchase` message as its input.

So, the snippet defines a Web service, `processCustomerService`, which requires an input message containing a single instance of the element `wrapper:customerPurchase`. Invoking this Web service, therefore, requires constructing a SOAP message containing an instance of `wrapper:customerPurchase`. Notice that the definition of `wrapper:customerPurchase` in the WSDL snippet references the two elements `imported:customer` and `imported:po`. The schema for these two elements is not shown, but from the name of the prefix (`imported`), we can assume that they are imported into the WSDL elsewhere. So, constructing the SOAP message requires creating instances of `imported:customer` and `imported:po`.

Now, examine the Java snippet in the callout box in the lower-left side of Figure 1–2 and notice the imported classes `com.soabook.sales.Customer` and `com.soabook.purchasing.PurchaseOrder`. These classes are used as the parameter classes for the method `newPurchase`. The Web service proxy shown in Figure 1–2 binds the Java interface method `newPurchase` to the WSDL operation `processCustomerPurchase`. This proxy was created by the invocation subsystem. It invokes the WSDL operation deployed at the SOAP endpoint by sending it a SOAP message. So, the Web service proxy's implementation of the method `newPurchase` must invoke some machinery that takes instances of `com.soabook.sales.Customer` and `com.soabook.purchasing.PurchaseOrder` and creates an instance of `wrapper:customerPurchase` that can be embedded in the body of a SOAP message.

That machinery is the serialization subsystem of the Web Services Platform Architecture (WSPA). The Serialization subsystem is responsible for the following steps in the invocation process:

Serialization Subsystem's Role during Invocation

1. Receiving the parameters from the Web service proxy
2. Serializing the parameter `cust` (an instance of `com.soabook.sales` `.Customer`) into an instance of `imported:customer`

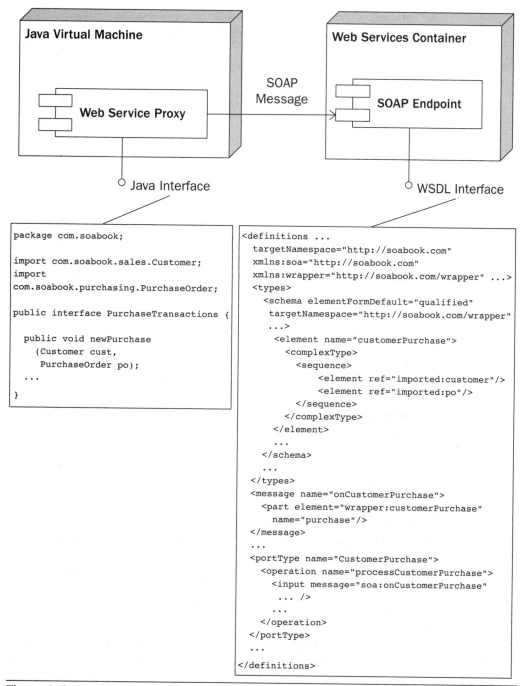

Figure 1–2 Serialization translates a Java instance into an XML document for transport via SOAP to a Web service.

3. Serializing the parameter `po` (an instance of `com.soabook.purchasing.PurchaseOrder`) into an instance of `imported:po`
4. Combining these two elements into an instance of `wrapper:customerPurchase`
5. Handing off the instance of `wrapper:customerPurchase` to the Web service proxy to be embedded in a SOAP message and sent to the SOAP endpoint

As this simple example illustrates, the serialization subsystem is central to the process of invoking a Web service via a Java interface. The serialization subsystem translates the parameters (passed to the interface proxy) from instances of their respective Java classes into instances of the target XML Schema—in this case, the target is `wrapper:customerPurchase`. These mappings—from Java classes to target XML Schema components—are called *type mappings*. To accomplish this translation, the serialization engine needs a set of *mapping strategies* (as illustrated in Figure 1–3) that tell it how to implement the type mappings; in other words, how to serialize the instances of the Java classes into instances of the XML Schema components.

A mapping strategy associates a Java class, its target XML Schema type, and a description of a serializer (or deserializer) that can transform instances of the class to instances of the Schema type (or vice versa). A *serialization context* is a set of mapping strategies that can be used by the serialization subsystem to implement the type mappings used by a particular Web service deployment.

Different Web Services platforms provide different mechanisms for specifying the mapping strategies that make up a serialization context. In many cases, multiple methods are used. Some of these mechanisms are:

Mechanisms for Implementing Type Mappings

- Standard binding. The mappings are predefined by a standard binding of Java classes to XML Schema. Each Java class has a unique representation as an XML Schema. JWS starts from this approach and allows customizations. The standard binding is described by the JAXB and JAX-WS specifications.
- Source code annotations. JWS uses this approach to provide customizations on top of the standard binding. Annotations in the source code of a target Java class modify the standard binding to specify how the class maps to XML Schema components and how the WSDL description of the Web service is shaped.

- Algorithmic. The mappings are embedded in the algorithms executed by the serialization subsystem. JAX-RPC 1.1 and Axis 1.x [AXIS] take this approach.

- Rule-based. The mappings are specified as rules that can be created and edited independent of the serialization subsystem. The rules are interpreted by the serialization subsystem. SOA-J (introduced in Section 1.5) uses a rule-based approach for mapping. The Castor [CASTOR] serialization framework also supports this approach with its mapping files mechanism.

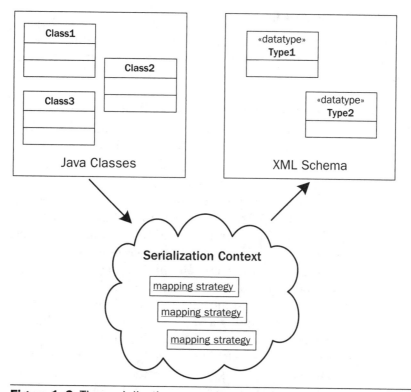

Figure 1–3 The serialization context contains mapping strategies used by the Serialization subsystem to perform serialization.

Each of these approaches has advantages and disadvantages. JWS has introduced source code annotations as a mechanism to make it easier for Java programmers to specify how a Java target should be represented as a WSDL operation. I happen to like the rule-based approach because it enables end users to map preexisting Java classes to preexisting XML Schema types—something that is very useful if you are using Web Services to do enterprise integration in a loosely coupled, SOA style where there are lots of legacy classes and schemas to work with.

Serialization is a rich and fascinating topic. Different approaches are better suited to different types of tasks (e.g., legacy integration versus Greenfield development). That is why there are and probably always will be a number of different approaches to serialization competing in the market-place. I look at JAXB 2.0 serialization in depth in Chapter 5.

1.2.3 Deployment

The deployment subsystem supplies the tools for setting up a Java target so that it can be invoked as a Web service via SOAP messages. At a high level, the deployment subsystem needs to handle:

Deployment Subsystem Responsibilities

- Deploying the Java target(s). This task varies greatly depending on the Java container where invocation takes place. For an EJB container, it may mean deploying a stateless session bean. In other situations, it simply means making each Java target's class definition available to the class loader employed by the invocation subsystem.
- Mapping WSDL operation(s) to a Java target(s). This involves configuring the Web Services platform so that the invocation subsystem can properly associate an incoming SOAP message with its Java target. This association (or binding) is stored as meta-data which the invocation subsystem can access from the deployment subsystem to determine the Java target that should be invoked. In addition to associating a WSDL operation with a Java method, the deployment subsystem must help the invocation system to properly interpret the SOAP binding (e.g., rpc versus document style, wrapped versus unwrapped parameters) of an incoming message.
- Defining a serialization context. The deployment subsystem configures the serialization subsystem with the serialization context (see Figure 1–3) needed to bind the XML Schema types from the WSDL with the parameter and return classes from the Java target(s). This serialization context is used by the serialization subsystem to implement the binding of WSDL operation(s) to Java target(s).
- Publishing the WSDL. The deployment subsystem associates a Java target with the WSDL document containing the WSDL operation it is bound to. This WSDL document is made available to the

Web service's clients as a URL or in another form (e.g., within a UDDI registry).

- Configuring SOAP handlers. The deployment subsystem configures the necessary SOAP handlers needed to provide QoS pre- or post-invocation of the Java target. These handlers provide services such as authentication, reliability, and encryption. Although the invocation subsystem invokes the handlers, they are configured and associated with a Web service by the deployment subsystem.
- Configuring an endpoint listener. The deployment subsystem configures the container so that there is a SOAP message transport listener at the URI specified by the WSDL port. In some Web Services platforms, the WSDL is supplied without an endpoint being defined, and the endpoint is "filled in" by the deployment subsystem from a deployment descriptor.

As you can see from this description, the deployment subsystem needs to do a lot of rather nonglamorous tasks. To handle a wide variety of situations (e.g., QoS requirements, custom Java/XML bindings, configurable endpoint URLs, etc.), the deployment descriptors (XML files used by the deployment subsystem) quickly grow complicated and difficult to manage without visual tools.[7] Figure 1–4 shows the possible deployment descriptors used by a Web Services platform and their relationships to the underlying containers.

As shown in Figure 1–4, the Web Services platform may span multiple containers. Here, I am showing you the application server container (e.g., Java EE) and a Web Services directory container (e.g., UDDI). The directory may be included in the application server container. Arrows show the dependencies. As you can see, each of the objects deployed in the container depends on container-specific deployment descriptors. The endpoint listener, SOAP handlers, and Java target may also be described in the WSDL/Java mapping descriptor. The multiple references reflect the multiple roles of the objects. For example, the Java target is deployed both as an object in the container and in the Web Services platform.

To summarize, the Web Services Platform Architecture (WSPA) defines three subsystems: invocation, serialization, and deployment. As the exploration of Java Web Services unfolds through the rest of the book, I refer to

---

7. Historically, the proliferation of deployment descriptors has been a common complaint when working with EJB 2.1. With Web Services in J2SE 1.4, the deployment descriptors grow even more complex! Luckily, in Java EE 5, the need for deployment descriptors has been greatly reduced.

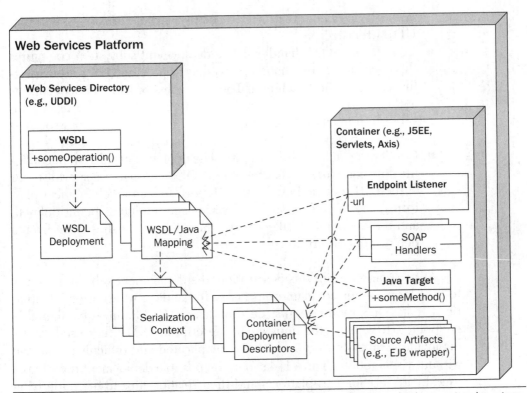

Figure 1–4 Many possible deployment descriptors can be used by a deployment subsystem.

these subsystems and their details, to discuss the roles that various components of JWS play in the overall WSPA specified by Java EE and Java SE.

1.3   Java Web Services Standards: Chapters 2 through 8

As mentioned, the primary purpose of this book is to provide you with a detailed technical understanding of how to use Java Web Services in your SOA application development. Since real technical understanding only comes with hands-on coding, this book provides many software examples for you to examine and play with. The first step toward developing a detailed technical understanding is to explore the JWS APIs in depth, examining their strengths and limitations. Chapter 2 provides a high-level overview of the JWS APIs. Chapters 3–8 provide detailed examples of how to write and deploy Web services with these APIs. These examples go well beyond the usual "Hello World" tutorials provided by vendors. Rather, they provide detailed, real-world implementations. In addition to simply showing you how to program with these APIs, I use the examples to relate them back to the Web Services Platform Architecture described in Section 1.2. Here is a summary of these chapters and how they work together.

Chapter 2: An Overview of Java Web Services—A high-level overview of the features, strengths, and weaknesses of the major Java Web Services APIs is provided, including JAX-WS 2.0 [JSR 224], JAXB 2.0 [JSR 222], WS-Metadata 2.0 [JSR 181], and Web Services for Java EE 1.2 [JSR-109]. I explore where each of these APIs fits into the Web Services Application Framework. The SOAP with Attachments API for Java (SAAJ) [JSR 67] is not discussed here, but investigated in Chapters 6 and 7 within the context of the JAX-WS discussions on SOAP processing.

Chapter 3: Basic SOA Using REST—The technical examples start by looking at the simplest approach to Web Services: Representational State Transfer (REST). I show how to implement RESTful services using plain old HTTP, and JWS. I also discuss the limitations of REST as an approach to SOA integration. Understanding these limitations provides the motivation for introducing SOAP and WSDL in the next chapter.

Chapter 4: The Role of WSDL, SOAP, and Java/XML Mapping in SOA—This chapter starts by discussing why WSDL and SOAP are needed for SOA. Then, it moves into a detailed description of how SOAP and WSDL are used in real-world SOA integration scenarios. I relate SOAP and WSDL to the Web Services Platform Architecture described in Section 1.2 to show how the dispatching of a SOAP request depends on the structure of the WSDL. Some limitations of the JAX-WS 2.0 dispatching mechanism are pointed out. Lastly, this chapter discusses how the XML carried by a SOAP request should be mapped to the Java classes that implement a Web service. JAXB 2.0 is introduced as a tool for implementing such a mapping, and some of its limitations and workarounds are described.

Chapter 5: The JAXB 2.0 Data Binding—JAXB 2.0 is described in depth and compared with other approaches for mapping XML to Java. Lots of detailed technical examples are provided that demonstrate the JAXB 2.0 standard Java/XML binding, the schema compiler, and the annotations generated by the schema compiler. I also describe how the JAXB runtime performs serialization and deserialization based on the annotations, and how you can use your own annotations to customize the behavior of the JAXB serialization and deserialization processes. I relate JAXB 2.0 back to the serialization subsystem of the Web Services Platform Architecture—the reference architecture used in this book. Some JAXB 2.0 limitations are explored in detail—in particular, I discuss the difficulty of abstracting out type mappings from a serialization subsystem based on JAXB 2.0, and how this violates separation of concerns and negatively impacts change management. Workarounds to these limitations are demonstrated, including detailed examples of how to use advanced JAXB 2.0 features like the `XmlAdapter` class and how to custom-build your own recursive serialization subsystem based on JAXB 2.0. The custom serialization scheme introduced here is further elaborated on in Chapter 11 where the prototype SOA-J serialization subsystem is introduced.

Chapter 6: JAX-WS 2.0—Client-Side Development—The client-side APIs from JAX-WS 2.0 are described in detail. I explain how to invoke a Web service using a JAX-WS 2.0 proxy class that provides a Java interface to the target service. In these examples, I show you how to use the JAX-WS WSDL compiler (e.g., the GlassFish `wsimport` utility[8]) to create Java interfaces from WSDL at compile time, and then how to use those interfaces to create JAX-WS proxy class instances that can invoke Web services at run-time. In addition to these nuts-and-bolts examples, Chapter 6 provides an in-depth discussion of the JAX-WS 2.0 WSDL to Java mapping. Under-standing this mapping is critical to understanding how to use the classes generated by the JAX-WS WSDL compiler. The annotations used by JAX-WS on the generated interface classes are described, and I demonstrate how these annotations shape the SOAP messages that are sent and received by a JAX-WS 2.0 proxy. This chapter also discusses exception handling and how JAX-WS maps SOAP fault messages to Java `Exception` class instances. Having covered the basics, I then come back to the REST model intro-duced in Chapter 3 and explore in more depth how to do XML messaging (without SOAP) using JAX-WS. This leads to a discussion of how you can replace the default binding and use JAX-WS (via the `Dispatch` API) to invoke Web services using a variety of bindings, including custom annotated JAXB classes and Castor [CASTOR]. Detailed technical "how-to" examples are also provided to illustrate JAX-WS asynchronous invocation and SOAP message handlers.

Chapter 7: JAX-WS 2.0—Server-Side Development—This chapter is the second half of the JAX-WS 2.0 discussion, and focuses on the server-side APIs. The discussion starts with a description of the JAX-WS server-side architecture and how it maps to the Web Services Platform Architec-ture reference design discussed in Section 1.2. This description gives you a detailed understanding of how the various JAX-WS pieces fit together, including the SOAP protocol binding, fault processing, message handlers,

---

8. As discussed in the Preface to this book, all the examples have been developed and tested using GlassFish [GLASSFISH]. However, the underlying code will run on any JAX-WS implementation. The IBM, JBoss, BEA, and Oracle tools for JAX-WS, for example, will all implement the same WSDL to Java mapping and generate similar classes.

JAXB binding interface, WSDL generation, and dispatching services. After this description, I introduce a series of examples that illustrate how to deploy Web services using both the `@WebService` and `@WebServicePro-vider` annotations. Resource injection of the `WebServiceContext` is explored as a mechanism to access the HTTP request headers delivered with a SOAP request. I also go through a detailed example of how to deploy a Web service using Castor [CASTOR] as an alternative binding mechanism to JAXB 2.0. The chapter ends with discussions of validation and fault processing, and an example of how to implement server-side handlers and how to do container-less deployment using the `javax.xml.ws.Endpoint` class for Web Services deployment in J2SE.

Chapter 8: Packaging and Deployment of SOA Components (JSR-181 and JSR-109)—This chapter wraps up the detailed discussion of the JWS standards by focusing on the nuts and bolts of how Web services are packaged and deployed. I cover the WS-Metadata [JSR 181] annotations and give examples of how to use them to deploy Web services as EJB and servlet endpoints. You learn how to deploy Web services without using any deployment descriptors (yes, it is possible with Java EE 5!), and when and where it makes sense to use deployment descriptors to override the defaults and annotation-based deployment mechanisms. This chapter includes a description of the WAR structure required for servlet endpoint deployment, and the EJB JAR/EAR structure used with EJB endpoints. In addition, I give a detailed overview of how a Java EE 5 container implements the deployment processing (i.e., how the container goes from annotated package components to a deployed Web service). Like the other JWS API descriptions, this discussion relates back to the Web Services Platform Architecture reference design discussed in Section 1.2 to critique the pluses and minuses of the Java EE 5 Web Services deployment subsystem. There are many variations in how you can do packaging and deployment, so this chapter includes ten different packaging examples illustrating the appropriate use of each variation. Lastly, as an advanced topic, I cover the support for OASIS XML Catalogs [XML Catalog 1.1] provided in Java EE 5.

1.4   The SOAShopper Case Study: Chapters 9 and 10

Chapters 9 and 10 pull together all the technologies and techniques described in Chapters 2 through 8 and demonstrate how to build an SOA integration application using JWS. The SOAShopper application is an online shopping system that integrates eBay, Amazon, and Yahoo! Shopping. It is a Web Services consumer since it is a client of those shopping sites. It is also a Web Services provider since it deploys REST and SOAP endpoints that provide search services across the three shopping sites.

Chapter 9: SOAShopper: Integrating eBay, Amazon, and Yahoo! Shopping—Although SOAShopper is a demo application, the techniques it demonstrates are powerful. In this chapter, you will see all the tools of the previous chapters come together to create a real SOA integration system. The discussion and examples in this chapter include code for consuming and deploying RESTful services, consuming and deploying WSDL/SOAP services, implementing type mappings with JAXB, WSDL-centric service integration, and support for Ajax clients.

Chapter 10: Ajax and Java Web Services—Chapter 10 uses the SOAShopper application developed in Chapter 9 and shows how to build an Ajax front-end that consumes the RESTful services it provides. The focus in this chapter is on how JWS can be used to support Ajax clients.

1.5   SOA-J and WSDL-Centric Development: Chapter 11

Readers who only want to learn Java Web Services (JWS) can skip Chapter 11. However, if you are interested in exploring how to implement a Web Services Platform Architecture (WSPA) that is WSDL-centric and uses the tools provided by JWS, you should read Chapter 11. This final chapter provides a detailed walkthrough of SOA-J.

The term "WSDL-centric" means creating a Web service by building its WSDL and annotating that WSDL document with references to the Java elements that implement it. Such a WSDL-centric approach is intended for situations[9] where you need to create Web services that integrate into a standard corporate or eBusiness framework (i.e., where there are standard schemas and message descriptions).

SOA-J is a prototype application framework. I created it as a proof-of-concept to explore the viability of WSDL-centric SOA development with JWS. The source code (open source) for SOA-J is included with the code examples you can download with this book.[10] You can also find the latest version of SOA-J at http://soa-j.org.

---

9. Such situations are discussed in Chapter 4.
10. See Appendix B for instructions on how to download, install, and configure the book software.

Chapter 11: WSDL-Centric Java Web Services with SOA-J—This chapter walks you through how SOA-J is designed as an application framework on top of JWS. I show how it provides a straightforward mechanism for composing an SOA component by constructing its WSDL. There are many UML diagrams in this chapter, because I go through the architecture of SOA-J in some detail. This discussion should be useful for anybody who has ever wondered how a Web Services engine (aka "SOAP server") works. The principles used here are summarized in the WSPA[11] and are employed by products such as Axis and XFire. My motivation for including the implementation details goes back to my early experiments with Apache Axis. The first time I looked at the Axis source code, I felt completely lost. After reading my description of SOA-J, hopefully you will not feel as lost when and if you ever find yourself looking at the source code for another Web Services engine.

---

11. See Section 1.2.

CHAPTER 2

An Overview of Java Web Services

This chapter provides an overview of the capabilities provided by the Java Web Service (JWS) standards supported by Java EE 5 and Java SE 6. The discussion starts (Section 2.1) by looking at the role of JWS in SOA application development. Next (Section 2.2), some of the Java EE 5 "ease-of-use" features are covered. Making the programming process easier was stated as the number-one goal for the release of Java EE 5 Web Services, so right up front there is a quick review of these ease-of-use design decisions and their impact on development.

The main discussion in this chapter (Sections 2.3–2.5) groups each JWS capability according to the Java Specification Request[1] (JSR) that defines it. As each of the JSRs is reviewed, its features are related back to the reference platform—the Web Services Platform Architecture described in Chapter 1, Section 1.2. The primary JSRs discussed here, and throughout the book, are JAX-WS 2.0 [JSR 224], JAXB 2.0 [JSR 222], WS-Metadata 2.0 [JSR 181], and Web Services for J2EE 1.2 [JSR 109]—often abbreviated WSEE.

The chapter concludes (Section 2.7) by looking at some of the other Java EE 5 innovations that are not specifically part of the Web Services JSRs, but have an impact on Web Services development. This discussion covers capabilities such as dependency injection and EJB 3.0.

This chapter provides an appreciation for the big picture and sets the stage to dive into the design and programming details described in Chapters 3 through 11.

---

1. The Java community defines new features for the language using JSRs. JSRs are defined and approved as part of the Java Community Process described at www.jcp.org.

2.1 The Role of JWS in SOA Application Development

Basically, JWS comprises a set of enabling technologies for consuming and creating Web services using Java. To begin the discussion of where the JWS enabling technologies fit in SOA development, a hypothetical SOA application is examined.

2.1.1 A Hypothetical SOA Application

Figure 2–1 shows the hypothetical SOA application used in this discussion. It is an Order Management application for processing customer orders. It receives customer orders as SOAP requests and returns order confirmations as SOAP responses.

The Order Management application at the center of Figure 2–1 is labeled a "SOA Composite App" to emphasize that it is constructed as a composite of underlying services. On page 46 of [Erl], Thomas Erl writes, "services exist as independent units of logic. A business process can therefore be broken down into a series of services, each responsible for executing a portion of the process." Describing this example in Erl's language, one would say that the SOA composite application is automating the order management business process. That business process is broken down into the following steps as labeled in Figure 2–1.

Order Management Business Process

1. A customer sends a Customer Order containing, among other information, a PO Number and a list of Order Items—the products and quantities being ordered.
2. The PO Number and Order Items are passed to the Purchase Order System. It checks the Purchase Order to determine whether it covers the items being ordered and what payment terms are required.
3. If the PO covers the Order Items, an Authorization and a description of the required Payment Terms are returned.
4. Next, the Order Items are forwarded to the Inventory Management System to determine whether they are in stock and what the likely delivery dates are.
5. This information—the Item Availability—is returned.
6. Lastly, a response message is sent back to the customer—the Order Confirmation—detailing the payment terms and the anticipated delivery dates for the items.

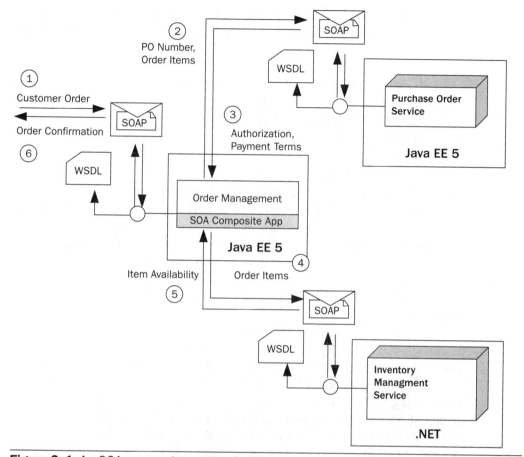

Figure 2–1 An SOA composite application for order management.

Using Erl's terminology, this business process can be broken down into two "independent units of logic"—the Purchase Order Service and the Inventory Management Service. As services participating in an SOA composite application, these "units of logic" can be described in terms of their input and output messages. The Purchase Order Service (upper-right corner of Figure 2–1) is responsible for providing the following service:

Purchase Order Service

Input Message: A PO number and a list of items being ordered.
Processing: Determine whether the Purchase Order covers the items being ordered and what payment terms are required.

Output Message: An authorization for the items being ordered and a description of the payment terms required for those items.

As indicated in Figure 2–1, the Purchase Order Service is implemented using Java EE 5. The other service composed by the Order Management System is the Inventory Management System. It is responsible for providing the following service:

Inventory Management Service

Input Message: A list of the items being ordered.

Processing: Determines whether the items are in stock and when they will be available to ship.

Output Message: A list of the items and their estimated ship dates—referred to as Item Availability.

As indicated in Figure 2–1, the Inventory Management Service is implemented using .NET.

The Order Management System, pictured in the center of Figure 2–1, is described as an SOA composite application because it is a composite of the underlying services provided by the Purchase Order Service and the Inventory Management Service. It processes the incoming Customer Order by invoking first the Purchase Order Service and then the Inventory Management Service, and combining the information received from those services to create the Order Confirmation. Notice that this Order Management System itself can be considered a service. In fact, to the sender of the Customer Order, it is treated exactly as any other service. Hence, using SOA, services can be composed of underlying services. The Order Management Service thus constructed can be described as follows:

Order Management Service

Input Message: A Customer Order containing, among other information, a PO Number and a list of Order Items—the products and quantities being ordered.

Processing: Determines whether the customer is authorized to purchase the requested items under the specified PO, and if so, what the payment terms are and when the items will be available to ship.

Output Message: Order Confirmation—detailing the payment terms and the anticipated delivery dates for the items.

As indicated in Figure 2–1, the Order Management Service is implemented using Java EE 5.

2.1.2 JWS Enables SOA Development

When thinking about this Order Management design, it is clear that composite SOA applications require that the underlying services they invoke have well-defined interfaces. For example, for the Order Management System to request authorization and payment terms from the Purchase Order System, it must know exactly what form that request should take. It must also know how to encapsulate that request in a message with a format that can be received and understood by the Purchase Order Service. In this example, Web Services standards provide the structure necessary to define the required interfaces. Although not required for SOA, Web Services provide a set of interface and messaging standards that facilitate building SOA applications in a platform-neutral manner. In the example just discussed, the Purchase Order Service is implemented on Java EE 5 and the Inventory Management Service is implemented on .NET. However, since both Java EE 5 and .NET support Web Services, it is possible to construct the Order Management by invoking those underlying applications using their Web Services interfaces.

When using Web Services, interface definitions are defined using WSDL [WSDL 1.1, WSDL 2.0]. Hence, each of the services pictured in Figure 2–1 is illustrated as being associated with a WSDL document. WSDL is expressed using XML. It defines the input and output parameters of a Web service in terms of XML Schema[2] [XSD Part 0]. The input parameters are delivered to a Web service using a messaging structure. Likewise, the output parameters are received in a message. Again, SOA does not force any particular message structure, but an obvious choice is the SOAP [SOAP 1.1, SOAP 1.2] standard. SOAP messages can be used to carry the input and output parameters specified by the WSDL interface definition. So, Web Services provide two key ingredients needed for SOA development: an interface definition language (WSDL) and a messaging standard (SOAP).

SOAP messages can be exchanged over a variety of transports (e.g., HTTP, SMTP, and JMS). In the Order Management example described previously, HTTP is the transport that is used. HTTP GET requests are issued to retrieve the WSDL interface definitions from services, and HTTP

---

2. This is just a quick overview. The use of WSDL and SOAP in Web Services is discussed in detail in Chapter 4.

POST is used to handle the SOAP request/response exchanges. That is how a basic Web Services framework (i.e., WSDL with SOAP/HTTP) is used for SOA application development.

The JWS standards provide tools for working with WSDL and SOAP/HTTP from within the Java programming language. There are server-side tools for enabling Java methods to be invoked with SOAP and for publishing the related WSDL interface definitions. Likewise, there are client-side tools for reading WSDL documents and sending/receiving SOAP messages. Figure 2–2 shows how the various Java Web Services standards (JSRs) support the server side of the equation. To explain the roles of these various JSRs on the server side, the deployment and invocation of a service is traced using the numerical labels in Figure 2–2. This discussion now becomes much more detail-oriented, dropping down from the 10,000-foot SOA level to the 100-foot level where the JWS standards start to be discussed in depth.[3]

To understand what Figure 2–2 is illustrating, start at the bottom with the folder labeled "Port Component." This represents a packaged Web service that is being deployed to the Java EE 5 container. The box in the center, labeled "Web Service Application," represents the run-time classes (after deployment) that implement a Web service. Above that are some boxes labeled "Java Parameters," and a single box labeled "Java Return." The parameter boxes represent run-time instances of the Java objects being passed to a method of one of the classes inside the "Web Service Application." Thinking back to the Purchase Order Service example (Figure 2–1), these parameters could be the PO Number and Order Items. Likewise, the boxes above these, labeled "XML Parameters" and "XML Return," represent the XML form of these parameters and return value. Continuing up the figure, near the top is a circle labeled "Endpoint." That represents the URL where the Web Service Application receives HTTP GET requests for its WSDL interface definition document, and HTTP POST requests for exchanging SOAP input and output messages.

The shaded bars in Figure 2–2 illustrate which JSRs correspond to the various stages of the Web service deployment and invocation. Tracing through labels 1–10 in Figure 2–2, the role of these JSRs at each stage is explained:

Server-Side Deployment and Invocation of a Web Service

1. JWS defines the *Port component* (sometimes referred to as Port) as the server view of a Web service. A Port component can be packaged

---

3. In subsequent chapters, the discussion drops down to the 10-foot level and examines detailed coding examples.

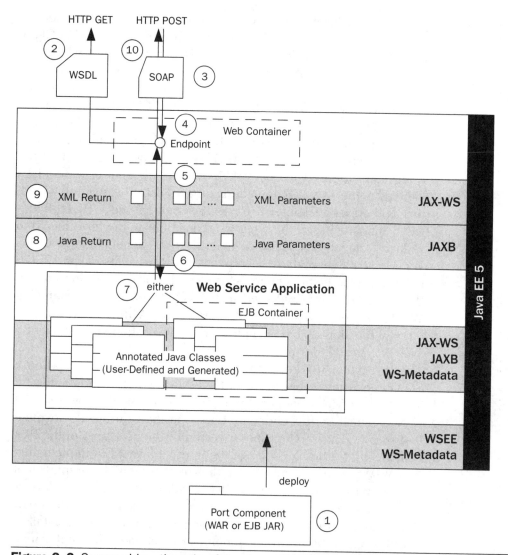

Figure 2–2 Server side—the role of the Java EE 5 Web Services JSRs.

as a WAR (for deployment as a servlet endpoint) or as an EJB JAR (for deployment as an EJB endpoint). WSEE [JSR 109] is the primary standard defining the deployment process and the packaging structure (including the deployment descriptors). WS-Metadata [JSR 181] describes how annotations on the packaged classes shape the deployment (e.g., the WSDL interface representing a Port component can be customized using WS-Metadata annotations). Deployment of a

Java EE 5 Port component corresponds to a function of the deployment subsystem in the WSPA reference system introduced in Chapter 1. Chapter 8 provides an in-depth discussion of deployment.

2. Moving to the top of Figure 2–2, this description now traces the invocation of the Web service deployed by the Port component described in step 1. The endpoint supports HTTP GET requests for the WSDL describing the Web service. The structure of this WSDL is determined by the JAX-WS WSDL/Java mapping. This mapping is described in detail in Chapter 6. This mapping can be customized using annotations defined by JAX-WS, JAXB, and WS-Metadata. Generally, the JAX-WS annotations manipulate the style of WSDL that is used (see Chapter 4 for a discussion of the WSDL styles). JAXB annotations, on the other hand, manipulate the representation of Java parameters and return types as XML Schema components. WS-Metadata annotations manipulate the particulars of the WSDL interface (e.g., the target namespace and the local names for many of the XML elements contained in the WSDL document). Handling WSDL requests is not officially part of the WSPA;[4] however, it is often a function that is included in the invocation subsystem of a Web Services Platform.

3. The invocation of the deployed Web service is initiated when a SOAP request is received, via an HTTP POST, at the endpoint.

4. The Web service's endpoint is typically implemented by a servlet class listening at the endpoint URL specified during deployment (see step 1). This servlet is not specified by the developer of the Port component. Rather, it is part of the internal Java EE 5 implementation of JWS. During deployment, the annotations and/or deployment descriptors are read by the WSEE runtime, the endpoint URL is determined, and the container's internals are configured to deploy the listener at that endpoint. This process is described in detail in Chapter 8. Setting up the endpoint is a function of the deployment subsystem in the WSPA.

5. Step 5 illustrates that the SOAP request has become a set of XML parameters—instances of the XML Schema components specified as parameters in the WSDL. The JAX-WS runtime is responsible for

---

4. That is because in practice, there are a number of ways the client can get a WSDL description. Oftentimes, WSDL documents are accessed through a UDDI directory. In such cases, the request for a WSDL is simply forwarded to the directory and not actually handled by the Web Services Platform. UDDI is not covered in this book; I explain why in the Preface.

extracting these parameters from the SOAP message. It is a fairly nontrivial transformation that is discussed in detail in Chapter 4. This extracting of the XML parameters is defined to be a part of the dispatching process handled by the invocation subsystem in the WSPA.

6. Next, the XML parameters are deserialized into Java parameters. This deserialization is handled by the JAXB runtime. Deserialization is controlled (i.e., the type mappings are defined) by the annotations on the target Java classes. The JAXB runtime uses introspection to examine the annotations on the target classes, and that information (together with the standard Java/XML binding defined by JAXB) is used to generate instances of the target parameters. JAXB serialization and annotations are described in Chapter 5. This step maps to the serialization subsystem in the WSPA.

7. Once the parameters have been created, the target Java class/ method is invoked. In the WSPA, this is a responsibility of the invocation subsystem. Within Java EE 5, it is handled by the JAX-WS runtime. The class providing the method for invocation can be either an EJB or a POJO. Figure 2–2 shows that JAX-WS, JAXB, and WS-Metadata all play a role in defining the annotated Java classes that comprise the Web service application. That is because annotations from each of these JSRs are used in these classes. The class that is invoked (called the service implementation bean) must be marked by a WS-Metadata annotation (e.g., `@WebService`) indicating that it implements a Web service. The classes representing the parameter and return types most likely have many JAXB annotations. In addition, some JAX-WS annotations may have been used on the service implementation bean to control the style of the WSDL.

8. After the invocation, the steps in this process run in reverse. That Java return type class is handed off for JAXB serialization to become an XML return type instance. This serialization (like the deserialization described in step 6) is controlled by the annotations on the Java return class.

9. Next, the JAX-WS runtime takes the XML return type instance and wraps it in a SOAP response.

10. Finally, the SOAP response is sent back to the requester as the payload of the HTTP response.

Some steps have been left out of this description (e.g., server-side handler invocation). However, it provides more than enough detail to convey an idea of what is going on inside the Java EE 5 container when a Web service is deployed and invoked. All the information presented in these steps is explained in greater detail in subsequent chapters, so don't get discouraged if it feels a little overwhelming at this point. Remember Dave Podnar's fifth stage for dealing with Web Services:[5] "Acceptance—It is what it is, Web Services aren't simple or easy."

Figure 2–3 shows how the various JWS standards (JSRs) support the client-side of the Web services equation. This discussion applies to client-side implementations using either Java SE 6 or Java EE 5. As in the server-side description, the roles of these various JSRs are explained by tracing through the process of reading a WSDL and invoking a service following the numerical labels provided in Figure 2–3.

The overlapping shaded areas in Figure 2–3 show where the various JSRs come into play on the client side.

Client-Side Invocation of a Web Service

1. The first step in client-side invocation of a Web service typically involves the generation of a service endpoint interface (SEI) using a WSDL to Java mapping tool. The SEI provides a Java representation of the Web service to be invoked. The SEI is generated prior to compiling the client application, as its interface definitions are used in the client application.[6] Figure 2–3 shows that generating the SEI involves JAXB, JAX-WS, and WS-Metadata. JAXB maps the XML parameters and return types described in the WSDL to Java parameters and a return type used in the SEI. WS-Metadata annotations adorn the SEI to document the mapping from `wsdl:operations` to Java methods. JAX-WS, meanwhile, provides the standard mapping from WSDL to Java that is captured in the structure of the SEI and documented with the WS-Metadata annotations.

2. At runtime, an instance of the JAX-WS `javax.xml.ws.Service` class is used to provide the client view of the Web service to be invoked. One of the `Service.getPort` methods is used to obtain a run-time instance of the SEI generated in the previous step. The run-time instance is implemented using Java proxy technology and is represented in Figure 2–3 as Proxy Instance. As shown in the figure, the Proxy Instance implements the service endpoint interface (SEI).

---

5. See Chapter 1, Section 1.1.
6. It is also possible to invoke a Web service without generating a SEI by simply sending XML directly to the Web service. This approach uses the JAX-WS `Dispatch` interface, which is described in detail in Chapter 6.

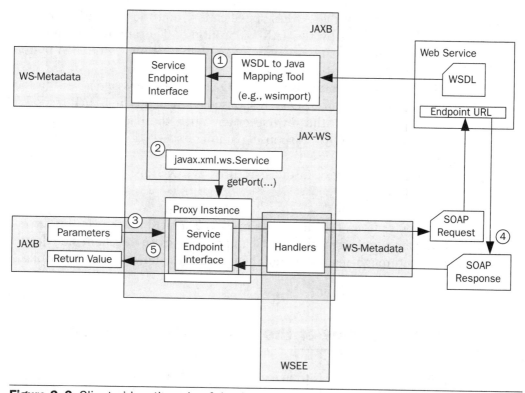

Figure 2–3 Client side—the role of the Java Web Services JSRs.

3. Next, the Web service invocation is started by invoking one of the SEI methods on the Proxy Instance. The parameters passed to the SEI method are instances of classes that are generated during creation of the SEI (step 1). These classes are defined by the JAXB mapping from the schemas included in the WSDL. Figure 2–3 indicates that the SEI implemented by the Proxy Instance also makes use of WS-Metadata and JAX-WS. There are annotations on the SEI that are defined by both of those JSRs—however, these annotations do not impact the user's call to the SEI method. These annotations are used by the JAX-WS runtime to translate from the JAXB parameters and method invocation to the SOAP request that is sent to the Web service. Once the SOAP request has been generated by the JAX-WS runtime, and before it is sent to the Web service endpoint, the handlers (if any) are invoked. Handlers are defined by the user, and can manipulate the SOAP request/ response messages. The process of packaging client-side handlers

is defined by the WSEE specification[7] and the invocation of handlers is done by the JAX-WS runtime. The annotations used to attach handlers to an endpoint implementation are defined by the WS-Metadata specification.

4. After handler processing, the SOAP request message is sent to the Web service and a SOAP response is returned. The SOAP response is processed in the reverse order. First, the handlers are applied. Then, the SOAP response parameters are deserialized (via the JAXB runtime).

5. Lastly, the proxy instance returns a JAXB instance as the return value.

As you can see, the client-side process is a bit simpler than the server-side deployment and invocation. Chapter 6 focuses on the client-side details and goes through many programming examples showing how to invoke a Web service.

2.2 A Quick Overview of the Ease-of-Use Features

A primary goal of JWS is to make it easier for Java developers to create and deploy Web Services. As stated in the Java Specification Request for Java EE 5 [JSR 244], "The major theme for the next version of Java EE is ease of development."

To make a programming framework easy to use, the architects must make design decisions that involve trade-offs. For example, the JavaServer Pages Standard Tag Library (JSTL) [JSR 52] makes it easier to create and maintain JavaServer Pages (JSP) [JSR 152] by standardizing common functions such as accessing URL-based resources and XML processing. However, this ease of use is paid for with functionality trade-offs. For example, the XML processing in JSTL doesn't support the Simple API for XML (SAX), for processing XML documents.

A good trade-off provides lots of ease of use with few limitations. Most JSP authors don't need SAX processing capabilities, so the trade-off in this example is a good one for them. Furthermore, a good trade-off lets you "opt out" when necessary. For example, JSP 2.0 lets you opt out of JSTL and use scriptlets, or custom tags, as needed to handle situations

---

7. Only supported with Java EE 5 or Java SE 6 clients.

that don't fit within the JSTL framework. So, if you need to use SAX, you still can.

In this section, I take a brief look at the "ease-of-use" design decisions implicit in JWS and how they impact the usefulness of the platform. I briefly discuss whether these design decisions are "good trade-offs," but most of that discussion is interspersed throughout Chapters 3–8.

As demonstrated by the Web Services Platform Architecture overview from Chapter 1, Section 1.2, deploying Web Services with Java is inherently rather complicated. A primary design goal of a Web Services platform should be to hide this complexity—particularly the deployment complexity—from the developer. You shouldn't need to worry about multiple deployment descriptor files in order to set up a simple, or even moderately complex, SOA-style application based on Web Services.

A tried-and-true approach to reducing that complexity is to simplify the problem by restricting its generality. JWS has several mechanisms that attempt to reduce complexity by imposing constraints on how Web Services are created and deployed. Chief among these are source code annotations, a standard WSDL/Java mapping, a standard serialization context (i.e., JAXB), and the "Start from Java" development mode.

2.2.1 Source Code Annotations

The JWS designers have introduced source code annotations for Web Services to help reduce deployment complexity. Annotations are defined by JAX-WS [JSR 224], WS-Metadata [JSR 181], and JAXB [JSR 222]. These annotations are used within all three subsystems defined by the WSPA: invocation, serialization, and deployment.

For example, in many cases using WS-Metadata annotations allows one to bypass the complex deployment descriptors required for deploying JAX-RPC services, and instead simply annotate the class being deployed to describe how it should map to a Web service. Using this approach, the JWS deployment subsystem generates the descriptors required by the container and Web Services platform. As a developer, you don't need to worry about the descriptors—just the annotations.

Of course, this leads to more-complex and difficult-to-read source code. And if you want to publish SOA-style Web Services interfaces for existing Java classes using this approach, you are going to have to either create wrapper classes with the necessary annotations or add annotations to the existing classes. Only time and real-world programming experience will determine whether annotations are easier to manage than deployment descriptors.

2.2.2 Standard WSDL/Java Mapping

JAX-WS defines a standard mapping of WSDL to/from Java. When a *service implementation bean*[8] (SIB) with minimal source code annotations is deployed, the resulting WSDL is based on this default mapping. Having a default mapping certainly makes it easier for a Java programmer, who may not understand much about WSDL or XML, to deploy a Web service. And it is part of the larger goal of building Web Services support directly into the Java programming language.

However, while the standard mapping makes it easy to deploy a Web service, it is not clear that the result is a *useful* Web service. The problem with the standard mapping is that it isn't helpful if your Web service needs to conform to an existing WSDL contract. Granted, the annotations discussed earlier allow you to "shape" the resulting WSDL, but there are limitations on how far you can go with such customizations. For example, you can't map two operations on the same WSDL port to methods from two different SIBs. So, if you have a `wsdl:port` with the operations `foo` and `bar`, both `foo` and `bar` must be mapped to methods on the same Java class or interface. One cannot map `foo` to `MyClass.doFoo()` and `bar` to `AnotherClass.doBar()`.[9]

Even more basic, you can't map a WSDL port to anything but a SIB—there is no capability to deploy a nonannotated class as a Web service.[10]

Again, time will tell how useful the standard WSDL/Java mapping turns out to be. It is premature to either praise it or criticize it. At this point, your best bet is to understand it well enough to determine whether it meets your needs.

Having said that the jury is still out on the standard WSDL/Java mapping, I must also say that the simple fact that Java has a standard mapping for WSDL is incredibly important. The standard mapping, despite its limitations, makes it possible to easily deploy Java classes as Web services. It also makes it possible to automatically generate service endpoint interfaces (SEIs), as illustrated in Figure 2–3, from an existing WSDL.

---

8. A service implementation bean is the type of class that can be deployed as a Web service endpoint. It can be either a POJO or a stateless session bean and must meet certain criteria discussed in Chapter 8, Section 8.1.

9. This limitation is discussed further in Chapter 4, Section 4.3.6.

10. According to Section 3.1 of [JSR 181], an implementation of a SIB is required to have an `@WebService` annotation.

2.2.3 Standard Serialization Context

A standard serialization context simplifies development by removing the need to specify type mappings and serializers along with a Web Services deployment. In other words, when using a standard serialization context, you do not have to define the XML to which their Java classes are mapped. A default mapping is provided by the standard serialization context. JWS accomplishes this by delegating serialization to JAXB. JAXB has standard rules for (de)serializing XML Schema components to/from Java objects. Using JAXB limits the types of mappings that are supported, but greatly simplifies the specification of a Web service.

This is definitely an area where simplification is welcome and JAXB provides a solid framework for Java/XML binding. Again, difficulties creep in when we start to look at how useful the results of such a standard serialization framework are in practice. To be specific, when we compile an XML Schema using JAXB, the Java classes that are produced often don't resemble any of our existing classes. So, for example, if you want to deploy a Web service that uses some XML Schema type for a purchase order (e.g., `imported:po`) using the JAXB framework, you are not going to be able to use your existing `PurchaseOrder` class. You will have to use the `Po` class generated by JAXB from `imported:po`.

Using the generated JAXB classes is fine if you are starting application development from scratch. That is because when you are starting from scratch, for example, it is not a problem to use the generated `Po` class that JAXB maps to `imported:po`. However, if you are deploying a Web service based on existing classes (e.g., your `PurchaseOrder` class), JAXB may have less value. There are two ways to deal with this problem—both discussed in detail in Chapter 5. First, you can customize the standard JAXB mapping to "shape" the resulting classes. Using this approach, you may be able to add annotations to your `PurchaseOrder` class so that JAXB maps it to `imported:po`. As you will see in Chapter 4, however, using annotations in this way is challenging, and many times, it is impossible to produce the mapping desired. Second, you can use wrappers to map your familiar classes to the JAXB-generated code. Using the wrapper approach, you would write Java code to translate between the generated `Po` class and your existing `Purchase-Order` class. Wrappers work, but if you write them, you must maintain that code. The wrapper approach essentially boils down to storing your Java/XML mappings as Java code—something that is not generally recommended because it is difficult to debug and complicates change management. For example, if the `imported:po` schema changes, the generated class `Po` also changes, and you will then need to update your wrapper code.

Previous experience with JAX-RPC 1.1 offers a cautionary tale. JAX-RPC 1.1 taught us that simplification achieved by restricting the supported type mappings makes the platform impractical. In JAX-RPC 1.1 (taken together with JSR-109 Version 1.1—the original deployment specification for J2EE Web Services), the serialization context is defined in the JAX-RPC mapping file. This mapping file can be automatically generated by a deployment tool, or it can be hand-coded to allow the type mappings to be "shaped." In this framework, mapping rules can be defined, but only to/from simple Java types such as `java.lang.String`, arrays of simple types, or a special type of Java Bean defined in Section 5.4 of the JAX-RPC 1.1 specification called the "JAX-RPC Value Type." This restriction is imposed to simplify serialization for JAX-RPC 1.1 implementations. Unfortunately, for a great many use-case scenarios, Web services need to be deployed with type mappings for classes that are not "JAX-RPC Value Types." This limitation has restricted the usefulness of JAX-RPC 1.1 as a Web Services platform. Analogously, the standard JAXB type mapping mechanism based on annotations, while certainly much easier to use than the JAX-RPC 1.1 approach, still restricts the structure of the XML that can be deployed in a Web service and may, therefore, restrict the usefulness of JAXB as a standard serialization framework for Web Services deployment.

On the whole, however, my feeling is that JAXB 2.0 is not overly restrictive and strikes the right balance between simplification and functionality. It has been embraced by a great many developers as their Java/XML binding tool of choice.

2.2.4 Development Models

JWS is designed to help make Web Services development easier for Java developers. As a result, it is biased toward the "Start from Java" development mode. "Start from Java" assumes that you create a Web service by starting with the development of a Java class. In fact, all you need to do to deploy that class as a Web service, for the most part, is to annotate it with `@WebService`. The JAX-WS and JAXB run-time engines will map that class to a WSDL document using the standard WSDL/Java and XML/Java mappings. In the "Start from Java" development mode, if you need to tweak the shape of your WSDL or XML types, that can be done by adding annotations to your class. "Start from Java" is the only development mode that is required by WS-Metadata implementations.

Alternatively, JWS also defines the "Start from WSDL" development mode. Using this approach, you take a preexisting WSDL and use a WSDL compiler (provided as part of the JAX-WS implementation) to generate a set of Java program elements that implement the WSDL. Using this approach, you get a set of SEIs that map to the WSDL. Your job is to implement the SEIs with the appropriate business logic to implement the Web services defined by the WSDL.

Finally, the JWS specifications[11] also mention a "Start from WSDL and Java" development mode. Using this approach, you reference a preexisting WSDL from the @WebService annotation on the Java class intended to implement it. The annotations on this class must map the class to the referenced WSDL. If there is a mismatch, failure will occur at some point in the development or deployment process. Practically speaking, I think that this approach will prove tricky for the majority of programmers because it requires you to be intimately familiar with how the annotations shape the WSDL. In addition, you may even unwittingly start out with a Java class that is simply impossible to map to the referenced WSDL using the annotations. Making this approach work will require vendors to provide good tools that give programmers intelligent feedback on how to best use annotations to map the Java class to the referenced WSDL.

As you can see, when doing "Start from WSDL and Java," the deployment problem becomes a matter of mapping the WSDL structure to the Java methods and parameters of your existing classes. In my experience, this is the problem most commonly faced by developers who are using Web Services for systems integration—either internally or with business partners. Developers doing integration often start with a WSDL contract that needs to be implemented (e.g., a specification for a business partner's e-Business interface or an SOA service needed for an internal EAI project). Developers doing integration also usually start with some existing classes (e.g., the purchasing system). The programming challenge is to front-end the existing system with a Web service that conforms to the WSDL.

Note that you can't really solve the "Start from WSDL and Java" problem elegantly without a highly customizable serialization subsystem. In "Start from WSDL and Java" development mode, you have preexisting XML schema types that must map to preexisting Java objects (parameters and return type). So, almost any Web Services platform that attempts to simplify the serialization problem (e.g., by defining a standard serialization context such as JAX-RPC 1.1) ends up introducing the need for wrapper code in order to solve "Start from WSDL and Java" problems. The wrapper code is needed to take you from the standard Java representations of the existing WDSL and XML Schema document to your existing classes. In practice, that is the approach most commonly used to solve the "Start from

---

11. See [JSR 181] Section 2.0.

WSDL and Java" problem. Developers use the JAX-WS WSDL compiler to generate a SEI from the existing WSDL, following the "Start from WSDL" development mode. Then, this SEI is mapped to the existing classes using wrappers.

On the other hand, there is a case to be made that the "Start from WSDL and Java" development mode is actually the easiest to deal with because when both the WSDL and the Java are defined, the developer does not need to do any design work. That is, the developer doesn't need to design a flexible and useful WSDL or a good Java API. This may be true from a designer's point of view, but from a developer's point of view, "Start from WSDL and Java" is the most difficult problem to solve using the JWS tools. JWS can generate valid WSDL from your Java, and it can compile Java classes from your XML Schema, but it can't help you very much when it comes to mapping existing Java to existing XML Schema and WSDL.

Precisely because of the difficulties it presents to the JWS tools, I feel strongly that the best way to understand Web Services development and deployment is to assume that you have existing WSDL and Java artifacts to work with. As a developer, if you learn to solve "Start with WSDL and Java" problems, the other two development modes are much easier to deal with. That is because doing "Start with WSDL and Java" forces you to learn the details of JWS Java/XML binding (JAXB) and Java/WSDL mapping (JAX-WS). In addition, you will learn to recognize the limitations of "Start with Java" and "Start with WSDL," so you can avoid creating Web Services architectures that can cause problems down the road.

2.2.5 JWS Trade-Offs

As discussed previously, each of the JWS simplifications trade off against the capability of the Web Services platform to create and deploy useful Web Services. For example, the JWS "Start from Java" development mode makes it easy to deploy a Web service, but how useful is that Web service? Is it compliant with your enterprise or industry XML Schema standard types? I discuss these trade-offs—for JAX-WS, JAXB, WS-Metadata, and WSEE—throughout Chapters 3–10. In Chapter 11, I look at another design approach to dealing with these trade-offs that focuses on making "Start from WSDL and Java" and change management problems easier to solve by employing what I call "WSDL-centric" development.

Before diving into Chapters 3–10, and heading further down the path of explaining and critiquing JWS details, I spend the rest of this chapter taking a step back to give you an overview of the JWS programming model as it relates to the general Web Services Platform Architecture described in

Chapter 1, Section 1.2. There is a lot of powerful machinery inside JWS, and the better you understand it, the more tools you will have to bring to bear on your own Web Services development challenges. The remainder of this chapter provides a quick tour of that machinery.

2.3 JAX-WS 2.0

JAX-WS 2.0 specifies the invocation subsystem of JWS, part of the deployment subsystem, and even a little bit of the serialization subsystem. It is a follow-on specification to JAX-RPC 1.1 and offers many improvements to that specification.

JAX-WS provides a lot of features, and Table 2–1 shows where some of them fit into the Web Services Platform Architecture described in Chapter 1, Section 1.2. This section describes each of the features cataloged in Table 2–1.

Table 2–1 JAX-WS Feature Map

Invocation	Serialization	Deployment
Dynamic and Static Clients	WSDL Styles—Support for RPC/Literal and Document/Literal Wrapped	Java/WSDL Mapping Static WSDL
Invocation with Java Interface Proxies		XML Service Providers
Invocation with XML		XML Catalogs
Message Context		Run-time Endpoint Publishing (Java SE Only)
Handler Framework		
SOAP Binding		
HTTP Binding		
Converting Exceptions to SOAP Faults		
Asynchronous Invocation		
One-Way Operations		
Client Side Thread Management		
Pseudo Reference Passing		

2.3.1 Java/WSDL Mapping

The JAX-WS 2.0 specification [JSR 224] defines a standard Java/WSDL mapping. This standard Java/WSDL mapping is part of the JWS deployment subsystem. It determines how WSDL operations are bound to Java methods—in other words, when a SOAP message invokes a WSDL operation, the Java/WSDL mapping determines which Java method gets invoked and how that SOAP message is mapped to the method's parameters. Conversely, the mapping also determines how the method's return value gets mapped to the SOAP response.

This standard mapping allows one to start with a Java class, pass it through a JAX-WS processor (usually a utility called something like `java2wsdl` or `wsgen`), and generate a WSDL description of a Web service endpoint. A developer can influence the shape of the generated WSDL by annotating the Java source code as described in the WS-Metadata discussion in Section 2.5. The generated WSDL always conforms to the WS-I Basic Profile 1.1 [WS-I BP 1.1]. This is referred to as the "Start from Java" development mode.

Conversely, one can start with a WSDL document and generate Java classes and interfaces. The standard mapping can be customized by either using embedded binding declarations (annotations to the WSDL source that are made using the `jaxws:bindings` extension element) or supplying an external binding file that contains the declarations. The Java classes that one gets this way are wrapper classes, and the developer needs to fill in the business logic required to implement the Web service. The classes generated in this manner include source code annotations that describe the WSDL/Java mapping. Deploying these classes, with the generated annotations, results in a Web service that "faithfully reflects[s] the information in the WSDL document(s) that were given as input to the mapping processes ...."[12] So, when developers deploy those generated classes, they might not get exactly the same WSDL they started with, but it should be functionally equivalent. This is referred to as the "Start from WSDL" development mode.

If you've noticed that the "Start from WSDL" development mode is really the same as "Start from Java" once you get to deployment, you are right. JWS is a Java-centric approach to Web Services. Even when you start with the WSDL, you use JAX-WS to translate that WSDL into annotated Java source that becomes the JWS implementation's internal definition of your Web service. JAX-WS treats WSDL as an interface definition language

---

12. JAX-WS 2.0 specification, Chapter 2 [JSR 224].

(IDL) from which Java classes are generated. The actual WSDL that is displayed at runtime is derived from the annotations.

Although the annotations give you a great deal of flexibility in determining the shape of the WSDL (e.g., you can even force some of a Java method's parameters to be mapped to SOAP header elements), some basic principles of this WSDL/Java mapping are not flexible:

- **WSDL port types map to Java interfaces:** A `wsdl:portType` element is mapped to a Java interface called the service endpoint interface (SEI). This is a granularity constraint. You cannot map individual operations within a port type to different Java interfaces. The JWS model enforces a 1–1 correspondence between a SEI and a port type. To implement a port type, you must deploy a SEI.
- **Parameter and return type mappings must be compatible with JAXB:** The annotations let you specify specific type mappings for the SEI parameters and return type. However, these type mappings must be compatible with JAXB 2.0. That is, the classes used for the SEI parameters and return type must use JAXB annotations to specify the XML Schema components to which they are mapped.

2.3.2 Static WSDL

JAX-WS lets the developer specify a static WSDL document that can bypass the automatic generation of WSDL that is based on the standard WSDL/Java and XML/Java (JAXB) mappings. This is an important capability when you need to publish a Web service that conforms to a specific WSDL—the most common use case when you are doing SOA-style systems integration.

This capability also makes it possible for you to publish WSDL based on existing schemas (e.g., your existing `po:purchaseOrder` element definition) rather than JAXB-generated types. The static WSDL approach is used in the "Start from WSDL and Java" development mode (see Section 2.2.4).

2.3.3 Dynamic and Static Clients

JAX-WS Web Service clients are instances of `javax.xml.ws.Service`. An instance of `Service` corresponds to a `wsdl:service` element of the target Web service's WSDL document. `Service` instances can be created dynamically or statically. For dynamic generation, the `Service` is created at runtime by one of the `Service.create` factory methods. Alternatively, during development, one can generate a subclass of `Service` from a WSDL document using the JAX-WS processing tool (e.g., `wsimport` for GlassFish) provided by the JAX-WS vendor.

2.3.4 Invocation with Java Interface Proxies

Both dynamically and statically generated `Service` instances can create a proxy for invoking a Web service using a *service endpoint interface* (SEI). One of the `Service.getPort` methods is used to create an instance of the SEI that is bound to the target `wsdl:port`. Of course, the SEI used must be consistent with the JAX-WS Java/WSDL mapping and JAXB XML/Java mapping. For this reason, when SEI proxies are used, it is usually with a statically generated `Service` instance that is created along with the SEI when the JAX-WS processing tool (e.g., `wsimport` from GlassFish) compiles the target WSDL prior to runtime.

2.3.5 Invocation with XML

As an alternative to invocation with Java interface proxies, a `Service` instance can be used to invoke a Web service by sending and receiving XML messages. In this case, the `Service` provides an instance of `javax.xml.ws.Dispatch` using one of the `createDispatch` methods. This can be a useful feature for when you want to bypass the JAXB serialization process.[13] It lets you construct your own SOAP message and send it directly to a Web service. It also enables you to interact with a Web service directly via XML without having to translate in and out of Java. Often, when doing Web Services programming, you will find that working directly with the XML is the most natural way to get things done. Kudos to the JAX-WS architects for putting this in (it was left out of JAX-RPC)!

2.3.6 XML Service Providers

Just as you can invoke a Web service using XML messages (see Section 2.3.5), so it is possible to deploy a service that simply sends and receives XML messages without providing any automated binding to JAXB annotated classes. JAX-WS provides this capability through the `javax.xml.ws.Provider` interface. When a service is created using the `Provider` interface, it doesn't use a SEI—bypassing the JAX-WS Java/WSDL mapping and the JAXB Java/XML mapping. The `Provider` interface lets you write services that work directly

---

13. Chapter 6 provides an example of how to use `Dispatch` to bypass JAXB serialization.

with the XML request and response messages. I illustrate how to use this approach to deploy services that make use of non-JAXB type mappings in Chapter 7.

2.3.7 Handler Framework

JAX-WS defines request and response handlers that can be used on both the client side and the server side. Handlers provide pre- and post-processing of messages. For example, a handler could be used to post-process a client message, adding authentication headers, before it is sent to a target Web service. On the server side, a handler could be used to preprocess the message, checking those authentication headers, before the message is dispatched to invoke the target service.

JAX-WS handlers are organized into an ordered list known as a handler chain and are invoked in order. Handlers have read/write access to the XML message and the message's context (see Section 2.3.8)—both on the client side and on the server side. Handler chains are configured using deployment metadata (i.e., `@javax.jws.HandlerChain`). Alternatively, on the client side, handler chains can be configured at runtime using the `HandlerResolver` interface.

Handler chains are defined at the port level—so all methods defined by a SEI must use the same handler chain. This is true for both client- and server-side invocation.

JAX-WS defines two types of handlers: logical and protocol. Logical handlers are concerned with the processing of the XML message and are independent of the protocol binding. Protocol handlers, on the other hand, are designed for processing related to the protocol binding (e.g., SOAP). The protocol handler for SOAP,[14] for example, has access to the SOAP structure of a message via the SAAJ API [JSR 67]. A logical handler[15] on the same chain provides access to the message payload as a `javax.xml.transform.Source` or JAXB annotated class instance, but not via the SAAJ API.

Configuration files, termed "handler chain files," are required for the deployment of handlers specified using the `@HandlerChain` annotation. WSEE [JSR-109] specifies the deployment model for handlers, including the use of these handler chain files.

---

14. `javax.xml.ws.handler.soap.SOAPHandler<T extends SOAPMessageContext>`
15. `javax.xml.ws.handler.LogicalHandler<C extends LogicalMessageContext>`

2.3.8 Message Context

JAX-WS enables handlers, endpoints, and clients to manipulate a message context (`javax.xml.ws.handler.MessageContext`) that travels along with the XML request/response messages. This is a useful tool that enables, for example, communication between request handlers, endpoint implementation, and response handlers. To understand how a message context can be used, suppose you want to implement some type of message sequencing (e.g., as in Web Services ReliableMessaging [WS-RM]) and you have a request handler that pulls a message's order in a particular sequence out of a SOAP header element. In this case, the endpoint, which is processing messages concurrently, might not want to send the response until all previous messages in the sequence have been processed. The ordering of the responses, or even the endpoint processing, can be controlled based on the sequence information the request handler has put in the message context.

Endpoint implementations can get access to the message context using dependency injection (see Section 2.7.1).

Clients can access the message context using the `getRequestContext` and `getResponseContext` methods of the `BindingProvider` interface. This capability can be used to facilitate initialization of protocol-specific features. While, strictly speaking, this is outside of the Web Services stack, it can be very useful. For example, this feature enables you to work with HTTP authentication by specifying the username and password in the client message context.

2.3.9 SOAP Binding

JAX-WS 2.0 specifies a SOAP binding for SOAP message processing. This includes `mustUnderstand` processing, and support for the SOAP 1.2 next[16] and `ultimateReceiver`[17] roles. The SOAP binding also supports SOAP handlers (an extension of protocol handlers—see Section 2.3.3) for SOAP header processing. The SOAP binding maps handler and service exceptions to SOAP fault messages (see Section 2.3.11). WS-Metadata annotations (see Section 2.5.2) can be used to customize this SOAP binding.

JAX-WS implementations must support the SOAP HTTP binding, SOAP With Attachments, and SOAP MTOM.

---

16. Or, equivalently, the SOAP 1.1 next actor.
17. Or, equivalently in SOAP 1.1, the omission of the actor attribute.

2.3.10 HTTP Binding

In addition to the traditional SOAP binding, JAX-WS provides an XML/HTTP binding to enable the deployment and consumption of Web services defined using the REST framework [Fielding]. Such services, often called RESTful, send and receive XML over the HTTP transport, without using SOAP. The HTTP binding enables JAX-WS to deploy and consume RESTful services. Chapter 3 describes how to implement RESTful services using JAX-WS and the HTTP binding.

2.3.11 Converting Exceptions to SOAP Faults

The JAX-WS mapping of Java `java.lang.Exception` to SOAP fault messages (WSDL faults) is very useful. Even when one deploys a RESTful service using the `Provider` interface (see Section 2.3.6), the JAX-WS runtime can convert `Exception` instances into SOAP fault messages that are returned to the client. The mapping from Java exceptions to WSDL faults is controlled by the `WebFault` annotation. This feature saves you a lot of time and energy by eliminating the need to write code that maps your service exceptions to SOAP faults. Of course, if you want to customize the fault handling process, you can do so with JAX-WS handlers.[18] I take advantage of this JAX-WS fault handling in SOA-J, even though I bypass the entire Java/WSDL mapping and JAXB serialization mechanisms.

There has been criticism of the JAX-WS approach for turning Java exceptions into SOAP faults. The main criticism seems to be that it inserts Java-related implementation details into the Web Services stack, potentially confusing Web Services consumers that are not implemented in Java and have nothing to do with Java. This criticism strikes me as misguided. Java exceptions thrown because a Web service gags on a badly constructed SOAP message—or a message with bad content—are not Java-specific exceptions. Translating these into WSDL fault messages makes a lot of sense. On the other hand, if you throw an exception because of some kind of Java run-time problem (e.g., a class cast exception), that should not make its way out into a WSDL fault message.

So, you still need to write good code, and catch the exceptions that are Java internal issues—reinterpreting them as SOAP fault messages that are not Java-specific. On the other hand, it is safe to pass along application-specific exceptions to the SOAP fault mechanism of JAX-WS.

---

18. Chapter 7, Section 7.5, provides programming examples showing how to implement SOAP fault processing with handlers.

2.3.12 Asynchronous Invocation

JAX-WS adds asynchronous support to the invocation model defined by JAX-RPC 1.1. This is a big step forward for enterprise Java, since asynchrony is a fundamental requirement for SOAP.

Even better, however, is the fact that JAX-WS supports two models for asynchronous request-response messaging: polling and callback. Polling enables client code to repeatedly check a response object to determine whether a response has been received. Alternatively, the callback approach defines a handler that processes the response asynchronously when it is available. Asynchronous callback is much like defining a listener on a Java Message Service (JMS) [JSR 914] temporary message queue to handle responses that come in asynchronously. The listener is invoked when the responding service "calls back" with the response. Polling is analogous to checking the temporary queue periodically as you wait for the response to arrive.

2.3.13 One-Way Operations

JAX-WS 2.0 supports mapping Java methods to WSDL one-way operations. This is an important feature because it enables "fire and forget" style messaging similar to JMS, but based on SOAP over HTTP. One-way operations pave the way for developers to add support for reliable messaging protocols (e.g., Web Services Reliable Messaging [WS-RM]). Reliable messaging would enable JWS to be used as a platform for creating loosely coupled applications based on messaging-style Web Services—a key goal of SOA design.

2.3.14 Client-Side Thread Management

An instance of `java.util.concurrent.Executor` can be set on a JAX-WS client (i.e., an instance of `javax.xml.ws.Service`) to provide custom thread control. This allows the developer to control thread creation and usage when doing asynchronous Web service invocation. One use case for this capability is to implement custom thread pooling to enhance performance. See Section 2.3.12 for more on asynchronous invocation.

2.3.15 WSDL Styles—Support for RPC/Literal and Document/Literal Wrapped

JAX-WS delegates serialization to JAXB. However, to package the serialized parameters into a SOAP message, JAXB needs some guidance from JAX-WS. That guidance depends on the WSDL style used by the deployed Web service—and that style is determined when the service is deployed. For example, the parameters could be packaged as individual children of the SOAP body element (unwrapped), or they could be wrapped into a single element child of the body (wrapped).

JAX-WS supports the two most popular, WS-I-compliant, WSDL styles: rpc/literal and document/literal wrapped.[19] The rpc/literal style is called "RPC" by the JAX-WS specification.[20] It is specified by using a `javax.jws.SOAPBinding` annotation with the following properties: a `style` of RPC, a `use` of LITERAL, and a `parameterStyle` of WRAPPED. The document/literal wrapped style is called "Document Wrapped" by the JAX-WS specification.[21] It is specified by using a `javax.jws.SOAPBinding` annotation with the following properties: a `style` of DOCUMENT, a `use` of LITERAL, and a `parameterStyle` of WRAPPED.

WSDL style is a confusing topic that is critical for interoperability of Web Services across multiple platforms (e.g., Java and .Net). This topic is described in depth in Chapter 4, Section 4.3.

Based on the style of WSDL being employed, JAX-WS defines two beans for each method: a request bean and a response bean. These beans are essentially wrappers for the request parameters and response value. When serialized by JAXB, the request bean and response bean produce the correct SOAP request message body and SOAP response message body, respectively.

2.3.16 XML Catalogs

JAX-WS provides support for XML Catalogs—including the OASIS XML Catalogs 1.1 specifications. This is a great feature because, as discussed in Chapter 4, it's helpful for WSDL documents to import external schemas so that you don't have to keep duplicating the same schema information in each WSDL document whenever you use standard types. The challenge to importing schemas is being able to find them at runtime. Should you deploy the schemas on some local HTTP server? You could, but if that URL ends up as http://localhost/myschema.xsd, it's not going to resolve properly on another machine.

An XML Catalog lets you map external references to imported schemas to local instances of such schemas. If you do your packaging properly (e.g., adding schemas to the application jar files), these local instances should be

19. It also supports document/literal/bare, which is not WS-I-compliant.
20. See Section 3.6.2.3 of [JSR 224].
21. See Section 3.6.2.1 of [JSR 224].

accessible by the context class loader at runtime. Chapter 8, Section 8.7, provides a programming example illustrating how to use XML Catalogs.

2.3.17 Pseudoreference Passing (Holder<T> for Out and In/Out Parameters)

Java method invocations pass object references by value. When you pass an instance of PurchaseOrder in a Java method invocation, the value the receiving object gets is a reference to that PurchaseOrder—not a copy of that PurchaseOrder. Web Services do not work this way. When a PurchaseOrder is passed to a Web service, a serialized copy of the instance is wrapped in a SOAP message and transmitted over the wire.

Passing references is useful because sometimes you would like to invoke a method that changes the state of your PurchaseOrder instance (e.g., normalizes the billing address). JAX-WS 2.0 provides a pseudoreference passing mechanism based on the Holder class. Of course, one can't really pass a reference to a PurchaseOrder residing in a local address space using SOAP, but JAX-WS can make it appear as though you are doing just that. This is accomplished by using a Holder<PurchaseOrder> class as a reference to your PurchaseOrder. During the invocation of the Web service, JAX-WS sends a copy of your PurchaseOrder to the target, and gets back a modified version of it (e.g., with the billing address normalized). Under the covers, JAX-WS updates the Holder<PurchaseOrder> instance so that it references the PurchaseOrder instance received from the Web service.

This mechanism works, but I think it has dubious value and can even be dangerous. Suppose that you have other objects referencing your PurchaseOrder instance. These object references are not updated as a result of the Web service invocation—only the Holder class instance gets updated. Therefore, these references are now invalid and you will have to manually update them. In my opinion, the Holder concept (along with in/out and out parameters other than a return value) is misguided. You can't pass an object reference to a Web service, and trying to make it seem as though you are leads to confusing and error-prone code.

2.3.18 Run-time Endpoint Publishing (Java SE Only)

JAX-WS provides a capability that enables the publishing of Web Services endpoints at runtime.[22] There is a simple API (javax.xml.ws.Endpoint) that you can use to assign an instance of a Web service implementation to a URL.

---

22. Typically, creating an endpoint that can be invoked requires a deployment step.

Run-time endpoint publishing is awesome—in my opinion, it is one of the coolest features in JAX-WS. Unfortunately, it isn't allowed within the Java EE 5 container per WSEE [JSR 109]. Section 5.3.3 of WSEE states, "The use of this functionality is considered non-portable in a managed environment. It is required that both the servlet and the EJB container disallow the publishing of the Endpoint dynamically ...."

I wish the Expert Groups could have gotten together to figure out how to support this terrific feature within the Java EE 5 container, particularly since it is so consistent with the "ease-of-use" goals set out for Java EE 5. Hopefully, we will see it in a future version of Java EE.

In any event, the good news is that the JAX-WS specified dynamic endpoint publishing mechanism is supported in Java SE—starting with version 6.[23] I provide a detailed programming example of how to use this feature of Java SE 6 in Chapter 7, Section 7.7.

The following code snippet gives you an idea of the power and simplicity of the Endpoint API:

```
MyServiceImpl myWebService = ... // construct your Web service
Endpoint myEndpoint = Endpoint.publish("http://javector.com/myService",
  myWebService);
```

The JAX-WS runtime takes care of creating the necessary server infrastructure. That includes creating the HTTP context and listening for SOAP requests on the specified URL. When using this simple approach, the WSDL contract for the endpoint is created dynamically based on the source code annotations included in `MyServiceImpl` or the metadata documents deployed using the `Endpoint.setMetadata` method. The default location for the WSDL is `http://javector.com/myService?wsdl`.

Additional Endpoint methods enable you to customize the binding (if you want something other than SOAP1.1/HTTP) and the server context. JAX-WS also lets you set custom `java.util.concurrent.Executor` instances per endpoint to control how concurrent requests are serviced. This is a nice feature if you need to optimize threading for concurrency or performance objectives.

---

23. Java SE 6 can be downloaded from http://java.sun.com/javase/6.

2.4 JAXB 2.0

Section 2.3 highlighted what I consider the most interesting and important features of the JAX-WS specification. Each of these features will be covered in depth in the coming chapters—particularly Chapters 6 and 7, which focus on the JAX-WS client side and server side, respectively.

In this section, the focus is on the important and interesting features of JAXB 2.0. JAXB 2.0 defines a standard Java/XML binding from Java representations to XML Schema components and vice versa. It tackles a tough problem. XML Schema is a complex and expressive language. So is Java. Implementing a standard binding between these languages is a big, complex task. It is no wonder the specification weighs in at more than 370 pages!

JAX-RPC defined its own Java/XML binding—independent of JAXB 1.0. JAX-WS 2.0 (the successor to JAX-RPC) no longer defines a Java/XML binding. That task has been delegated to JAXB 2.0.

My goal in this book is not to provide a comprehensive programmer's guide to JAXB 2.0. Rather, this book focuses narrowly on its application to Web Services—on its role as the Java/XML binding framework for JAX-WS 2.0. This section of Chapter 2 talks about what kinds of problems JAXB can solve and how it fits into the Web Services Platform Architecture described in Chapter 1, Section 1.2. Along the way, I highlight those features of JAXB 2.0 that define its character—that is, the features that make it good at some things and not so good at others. Chapters 4 and 5 provide much more detail and programming examples related to JAXB 2.0.

To start the discussion about JAXB 2.0, it is helpful to clearly define how I use the term *Java/XML binding* and the related terms *Java/XML map* and *type mapping*.[24] I define a type mapping to be a relationship between a Java programming element and an XML Schema component— for example, `corp:AddressType` and `samples.Address`. A type mapping is implemented by a serializer and a deserializer. The serializer converts instances of the Java class into XML instances that conform to the schema. The deserializer does the reverse. A type mapping can be expressed simply as a pair: <J, X>, where J is a Java program element and X is an XML Schema component. By itself (i.e., without the serializer and deserializer), a type mapping says nothing about how it is implemented.

---

24. As far as I can tell, there is no consistent usage of these terms in the general literature— not even in the Java specifications. The usage described here is what I developed for this book to try to bring some order to the terminology.

I define a Java/XML map to be a set of type mappings. It is not necessarily a function—in other words, the same Java class could be mapped to two different XML Schema types. If a Java/XML map sends each Java programming element to a unique XML Schema component (i.e., it defines a function), I call it a Java/XML binding.

Beyond this definition of a binding as a map where each Java class uniquely represents a schema component, is a difference in the way a binding framework encourages you to think about serialization versus how a type mapping framework encourages you to think. Programmers working with bindings tend to think of the Java class as a representation of some schema type or element. That is, from the binding perspective, the Java class represents the schema it is bound to. And that binding is thought of as a higher-level API (e.g., higher-level than DOM) for manipulating schema instances.

On the contrary, programmers working with a type mapping framework are not encouraged to think of the Java classes as representing (or bound to) particular schema components. Rather, the type mappings simply represent a bridge to the XML world from the Java world. In this mindset, the Java classes do not exist simply to represent a corresponding XML schema component. Rather, they perform a function within an existing system (e.g., purchasing) and when needed, they can be serialized to/from an appropriate XML form to exchange data with another system.

Using this terminology, JAXB 2.0 is best thought of as a Java/XML binding tool. That is because the annotations on the Java classes used by JAXB 2.0 define a binding. Each class maps to a unique XML Schema component based on its annotations.[25] Chapter 5, Section 5.1, discusses the distinction between binding and mapping in more detail.

As you read this section, keep in mind that the JAXB 2.0 specification provides a Java binding of an XML schema to make it easy for Java programmers to work with XML instances of the schema. The goal of JAXB 2.0 is to provide a higher level of abstraction than Java implementations of SAX, DOM, XPath, or other approaches to manipulating XML in the Java programming language. The binding provides this mechanism by associating a set of Java classes with an XML schema so that schema instances are manipulated using Java methods.

---

25. This is slightly untrue in the case of the `@XmlRootElement` annotation. Classes so annotated may define both an XML Schema type and a global element of that type. The basic concept holds true, however. There is no way to apply two sets of annotations (and hence define two type mappings) on a single Java class.

The JAXB 2.0 authors envision two scenarios from which bindings arise:

- **Start from Java:** In this scenario, the Java classes exist first and are used to generate an XML schema via a JAXB 2.0 schema generator. The classes need not be explicitly annotated, because JAXB 2.0 defines defaults to supply implied annotations wherever needed.
- **Start from XML Schema:** In this scenario, the schema(s) exists first and the Java classes in the data binding are created using a JAXB 2.0 schema compiler.

Notice that neither case is designed to deal with the "Start from XML and Java" situation commonly faced when approaching the problem of SOA-style integration. In that scenario, you typically have an XML schema—or at least some corporate standard XML types—which you need to make use of. You also have a set of existing Java classes that need to be front-ended with Web Services interfaces. So, the challenge is to map existing XML schema to existing Java classes[26]—the "Start from XML and Java" problem. In the integration scenario, you are interested in defining a Java/XML *map* (and the serializers to implement its *type mappings*), rather than applying an existing Java/XML binding—such as the one defined by JAXB 2.0. One difference is that you may have multiple Java classes that need to map to a single XML schema. Another difference is that you cannot rely on a schema compiler or generator to automatically create the mappings needed for SOA-style integration. The mappings must be specified by the developer. In some cases, the mappings might not even be possible to implement using JAXB 2.0 annotations. Section 1.3 of the JAXB 2.0 specification [JSR 222] states that "The JAXB annotation mechanism is not sophisticated enough to enable mapping an arbitrary class to all XML schema concepts."

This "Start from Schema and Java" problem is not solved directly by JAXB 2.0, but you can use JAXB 2.0 as a tool for solving that problem. Some ad hoc approaches using JAXB 2.0 to solve the "Start from Schema and Java" problem are described in Chapter 5. A more general and sophisticated approach is described in Chapter 11 where the SOA-J serialization subsystem is analyzed.

Like JAX-WS, JAXB provides many features, and Table 2–2 shows how those features I regard as the most important or interesting map to the invocation, serialization, and deployment subsystems of the Web Services Plat-

26. This is similar to the "Start from WSDL and Java" development mode described in Section 2.2.4.

form Architecture described in Chapter 1, Section 1.2. The remainder of this section describes each of the features cataloged in Table 2–2.

Table 2–2 JAXB Feature Map

Invocation	Serialization	Deployment
	Binding Runtime Framework (Marshal/Unmarshal)	Binding XML Schema to Java Representations
	Mapping Annotations	Mapping Java Types to XML Schema
	Validation	Mapping Annotations
	Marshal Event Callbacks	Binding Language
	Partial Binding	Portability
	Binary Data Encoding (MTOM or WS-I)	

2.4.1 Binding XML Schema to Java Representations

As discussed previously, the JAXB 2.0 specification provides a standard Java/XML binding that represents XML Schema components (e.g., elements, types, attributes) as Java content (e.g., classes, bean properties). This binding forms the part of the JWS deployment subsystem that maps the WSDL message parts to Java method parameters and return types that are used during invocation of a Web service.

JAXB 2.0 implementations provide a *schema compiler* that generates JAXB schema-derived Java program elements from an XML schema. In general, the schema-derived program elements generated from complex types are referred to as Java *value classes*. Each value class provides access to the content of its corresponding schema component using get/set properties. So, the elements and attributes of a complex type are mapped to properties of a Java value class. The superficial characteristics of the value classes (e.g., names of the bean properties) can be customized by using the JAXB Binding Language (see Section 2.4.4). However, the basic structure of a value class is determined by its source schema component. For example, an element that occurs multiple times, such as

```
<xs:element name="foo" type="Bar" maxOccurs="unbounded"/>
```

can be mapped to a `List<Bar>` or `Bar[]`, but either way, the structure is basically the same.

Now, suppose you want to map an XML schema component representing a phone number as separate area code and local number, to a Java property that is a single string (see Example 2–1).

Example 2–1 Mapping Two Attributes to a Single Bean Property

```
<xs:element name="phone">
  <xs:complexType>
    <xs:attribute name="area" type="xs:string"/>
    <xs:attribute name="localnum" type="xs:string"/>
  </xs:complexType>
</xs:element>

String getPhone();  // returns area+"-"+localnum
void setPhone(String s); // where s = area+"-"+localnum
```

To do this with JAXB, you have to resort to writing a custom mapping class by extending `javax.xml.bind.annotation.adapters.XmlAdapter` (see Section 2.4.3).

In contrast to complex types, simple types—and particularly the built-in XML Schema types like `xs:string`—are mapped to the corresponding Java primitives or holder classes (e.g., `java.lang.String`, `java.lang.Integer`, `int`).

Outside of their use in the JWS framework, JAXB value classes can be a great tool for manipulating XML instances at a high level of abstraction. Along with these classes, the schema compiler generates factories for creating element instances. These factories and value classes enable you to easily create valid XML instances from a schema. Working with a lower-level API—like DOM—makes writing programs that create valid schema instances much harder. Using DOM, for instance, the programmer assembles an infoset and then must run it through a JAXP `Validator` to catch errors. Alternatively, using JAXB (or similar schema-compiler tools like XmlBeans [XMLBeans]) makes it much easier to write code that produces valid XML.

The primary drawback of the JAXB Java representation of XML Schema is that it does not help us serialize existing Java objects to valid instances of existing schema components. As discussed in Section 2.2.4, this "Start from WSDL and Java" (SFJW) problem is important for SOA-style integration. The consequence of this JAXB limitation is that when you deploy a Web service using an existing WSDL (or build a WSDL from some existing schema(s)), the Java interfaces that are generated (i.e., the SEIs) have parameters and return types that are JAXB value classes. To use these classes with your existing Java applications, you need to write mapping code to go from your existing classes to the JAXB value classes. That is almost as much work as writing your own serializers!

2.4.2 Mapping Java Types to XML Schema

The JAXB 2.0 Java/XML binding also provides a standard map from Java classes to XML Schema. JAX-WS 2.0 uses this map to generate WSDL from a Java class deployed as a Web service. This "Start from Java" (SFJ) approach to Web Services (see Section 2.2.4) is the primary use case for the JAXB Java to XML Schema standard mapping.

When doing SFJ, the parameters and return type of a Java method being deployed as a `wsdl:operation` determine the schema components in the `wsdl:types` section. WSDL structure is explained in detail in Chapter 4, but for now it suffices to understand that the `wsdl:types` section contains XML Schema element and type definitions used in the WSDL interface definitions describing the Web service.

JAXB implementations provide a *schema generator* that creates schema from existing classes using the standard map. The schema generator looks for JavaBeans style properties and maps them to attributes and elements. If the class you start with doesn't look like a JavaBean, not much XML Schema can be generated from it. However, if your class has lots of properties, the JAXB schema generator will be able to create useful schema from it. However, the defaults may not come up with names you like—nor map properties to elements versus attributes in a way you would like. To get past these problems, mapping annotations are provided (see Section 2.4.3) that enable you to tell the schema generator how to match fields and classes with XML Schema components. In theory, this approach could be used to map an existing Java interface to an existing port type. But again, this is almost as much work as writing a custom serializer. Another drawback is that you can't provide multiple sets of annotations to provide bindings to more than one schema component.

2.4.3 Mapping Annotations

Mapping annotations are the mechanism used by JAXB 2.0 for customizing the standard Java/XML binding. The schema generator discussed in Section 2.4.2 actually requires two inputs: a set of classes and a set of mapping annotations. The schema generator, however, assumes defaults for everything, so if there are no annotations, the schema generated is based entirely on the default Java/XML binding.

Example 2–2 shows how a mapping annotation is used to map the JavaBean property defined by get/set `PurchaseOrderNumber` to the schema element named `orderNum`:

Example 2–2 Customizing the Default Mapping of a Property's Name

```
public class PurchaseOrder {
  // ...
  @XmlElement(name="orderNum")})
  String getPurchaseOrderNumber();
  void setPurchaseOrderNumber();
};


<xs:element name="orderNum" type="xs:string"/>
```

Besides allowing the developer to customize the Java/XML binding, these annotations are also generated by the schema compiler when mapping in the reverse direction. That is, when you are working in the "Start from XML" (SFX) development mode, the code that JAXB generates from your schema contains annotations that document the XML components from which the program elements were mapped. These generated annotations are used at runtime to marshal JAXB classes to/from an XML infoset representation. A JAXB implementation can actually figure out how to marshal an instance of a generated class—created by another implementation of JAXB—based on these annotations. That is the key to portability discussed in Section 2.4.7.

Yet another use for mapping annotations is controlling a binary data encoding—i.e., how binary data such as images are encoded. This is discussed in Section 2.4.10.

As you can see, mapping annotations comprise part of the serialization subsystem and the deployment subsystem for a JWS implementation. These annotations are used in serialization because they guide the marshalling of Java value classes to XML infosets that are serialized in/out of SOAP messages before and after invocation. In addition, the annotations are used during deployment (in the "Start from Java" development mode) to define the XML schema for the WSDL message parts corresponding to the parameters and return types of a deployed Java interface. These two uses go hand in hand. The annotations define a set of type mappings (deployment) and serve as the marshalling instructions for implementing those type mappings (serialization).

Combining the type mapping specification language and the marshalling instructions into a single mechanism—annotations—has the following implications for Web Services developers:

- Creating the type mappings is a programming task that parallels the creation of the Java classes. You can't declaratively specify the type mappings separately from their implementation.
- The type mappings cannot be determined without running the schema generator against the Java classes (or using some other form of reflection to examine the annotations).

One of the goals for JWS is to make it easy to build a Web service from a Java class. Annotations enable the Java programmer to specify the type mappings and serialization mechanism in one language, right along with the Java code that implements the Web service. So, for the pure Java programmers, annotations probably do make Web Services easier.

However, the impact of this annotation-centric design in other areas may be less beneficial. It certainly makes the "Start from WSDL and Java" (SFWJ) development mode more complex. For example, one obvious limitation with annotations is that they force you to adopt a one-to-one correspondence between schema components and Java classes. What happens, for example, if you need to map the `PurchaseOrder` class to different XML schema types for different Web services you need to deploy? If the binding is captured in the `PurchaseOrder` annotations, you can't do it without creating multiple versions of `PurchaseOrder`.

SFWJ development mode also requires type mappings that are not supported by JAXB 2.0 annotations. These situations are very common, as illustrated by the simple phone number case in Example 2–1. Unfortunately, the `@XmlJavaTypeAdapter` method provided by JAXB is a cumbersome mechanism for handling such situations. Using `@XmlJavaTypeAdapter` requires that one:

- Annotate the source Java class, and implement an adapter class extending `javax.xml.bind.annotation.adapters.XmlAdapter`.
- Create an adapter that must translate the class being mapped (i.e., the bound type) to a value type that the JAXB 2.0 annotations can map to the target XML schema component. So, in addition to writing the translation class, you still need to write the annotations.

The @XmlJavaTypeAdapter approach gives you a lot of power to control the serialization process, but it is a lot of work.

2.4.4 Binding Language

Section 2.4.3 described the annotation features that enable customization of the JAXB Java/XML binding process. The JAXB 2.0 *binding language* provides an analogous feature for annotating XML that enables you to customize the Java representation of XML Schema described in Section 2.4.1.

The binding language is part of the deployment subsystem within the JWS framework. It is used to shape the form of the Java types that become the parameters and return types of the SEIs. Unlike mapping annotations, the binding language declarations are not used by the JAXB runtime for marshalling. So, the binding language is purely part of the deployment subsystem and is not used by the serialization subsystem. The annotations that are generated by the schema compiler, however, are derived from the source schema together with its binding declarations. So, the binding declarations are used to design the mapping annotations that ultimately control (together with the standard XML/Java binding) the serialization subsystem, but they are not part of the serialization subsystem.

Unlike annotations, which are always inline with the Java source code, the binding language customizations, called *binding declarations*, can be provided either inline with the XML schema (i.e., inline annotated schema) or in a separate configuration file (i.e., external binding declaration).

Binding declarations have scope. For example, a binding declaration can be global, as in Example 2–3.

Example 2–3 A Binding Declaration with Global Scope

```
<jaxb:globalBindings>
  <jaxb:javaType name="long" xmlType="xs:date"
    parseMethod="pkg.MyDatatypeConverter.myParseDate"
    printMethod="pkg.MyDatatypeConverter.myPrintDate"/>
  </jaxb:javaType>
</jaxb:globalBindings>
```

Such a declaration applies to all schemas being compiled. In this case, it means that the XML instances of type xs:date should be mapped to a Java `long` rather than following the default binding to `javax.xml.datatype.XMLGregorianCalendar`. The `parseMethod` and `printMethod` attributes tell JAXB where to find the methods that can marshal this type mapping. Note that the `xmlType` specified here must be an XML atomic datatype derived from restriction. So this approach cannot be used to specify nonstandard type mappings in general.

Alternatively, a binding may have component scope when it appears within an `<xs:appinfo>` element inside the component's schema definition. Example 2–4 shows a binding declaration inside an element declaration.

Example 2–4 A Binding Declaration with Component Scope

```
<xs:complexType name="foo">
  <xs:sequence>
    <xs:element name="po" type="javector:PurchaseOrder"
      maxOccurs="unbounded"/>
      <xs:annotation><xs:appinfo>
        <jaxb:dom/>
      </xs:appinfo></xs:annotation>
    </xs:element>
  </xs:sequence>
</xs:complexType>
```

The binding declaration part of this schema appears in bold. Such a declaration applies only to the local component. In this case, it means that the element named `po` gets mapped to a DOM—specifically, an instance of `org.w3c.dom.Element`. Mapping to a DOM can be useful when you don't want to use the JAXB 2.0 binding. It provides an ad hoc method for integrating other serialization mechanisms with JAXB. In this example, if you have a custom serializer for `javector:PurchaseOrder`, you could get the DOM from JAXB in this manner and then pass it to your serializer.

In between global and component scope are two other levels: definition scope and schema scope.

Binding declarations can also be provided in an external bindings file. Such external bindings use XPath expressions to refer back to their associated schema. Example 2–5 shows how the binding declaration from Example 2–4 looks as part of an external binding file.

Example 2–5 An External Binding File That References Its Associated Schema Using XPath Expressions

```
<jaxb:bindings xmlns:jaxb="http://java.sun.com/xml/ns/jaxb"
  xmlns:xs="http://www.w3.org/2001/XMLSchema" version="1.0">
  <jaxb:bindings schemaLocation=".../mySchema.xsd">
    <jaxb:bindings node="//xs:complexType[@name='foo']">
      <jaxb:bindings node=".//xs:element[@name='po']">
        <jaxb:dom/>
      </jaxb:bindings>
    </jaxb:bindings>
  </jaxb:bindings>
</jaxb:bindings>
```

It is important to be able to put the binding declarations in an external file because many Web Services developers doing "Start from WSDL" do not want to "pollute" their WSDL with implementation-specific XML. After all, the entire point of Web Services is to provide technology- and platform- independent access to business processes. Not only is it bad form for such JAXB implementation-specific XML to creep into the WSDL, but also it makes the WSDL harder for human readers to understand. In addition, some developers and architects are concerned about security in this area. Putting Java implementation information in the WSDL gives malicious hackers some information about your internal systems that might help them exploit security holes. Whether or not you share those security concerns, somebody in your organization might, and it could become an impediment to getting your Web services deployed.

Unfortunately, the XPath-based approach to creating an external bindings file is difficult to use. First, it requires a Web Services developer to be comfortable with XPath. Most Java developers are not. Second, the external bindings file is difficult to debug. You have to rerun the schema compiler and test the resulting Java classes each time you change the binding declarations. For this mechanism to be useable, the JAXB provider is going to have to give you a nice set of visual development tools to create, edit, and test these bindings.

Wrapping up this discussion of the binding language, I want to point out that it is not possible to specify custom type mappings and serializations using this approach. By comparison, when you are using the "Start from Java" development mode to generate XML schema from an annotated POJO, as discussed in Section 2.4.3, you can use the @XmlJavaTypeAdapter to insert a custom type mapping. No such equivalent mechanism exists for going the other way, starting with an XML schema and binding declarations. As a result, if you use the "Start from WSDL" development mode, you need to apply a workaround to employ custom serialization.

One such workaround involves the `<jaxb:dom>` declaration shown in Example 2–4 and Example 2–5. This binding declaration effectively "exempts" an XML schema component from the standard mapping and binds it to a DOM element. Within the generated program elements, the schema component is represented as an instance of `org.w3c.dom.Element`. Your application code can then pass this `Element` instance to a custom deserializer. However, before marshalling back to XML, you must make sure you invoke your custom serializer to get a DOM, and then pass this DOM using the generated program elements. Once this is done, you invoke the JAXB marshal operation.

To conclude this short analysis of the binding language, I'd say that it is mostly useful for tweaking the structure of the Java program elements that are generated by the schema compiler. There is not much support for custom serialization. The usefulness of the binding language is further hampered by the fact that it is very difficult to use in an external binding file. To avoid these difficulties, you are forced to put the binding declarations inline with your WSDL. So, if you don't want to pollute your WSDL with implementation-specific XML, you have to keep two separate copies of the WSDL—one for internal use with JAXB and one for external publication. Neither of these options is particularly appealing.

2.4.5 Binding Run-time Framework (Marshal/Unmarshal)

The JAXB 2.0 *binding run-time framework* is the heart of the serialization subsystem for a JWS implementation. The binding run-time framework implements the *marshal* and *unmarshal* operations.

JAXB uses the terms "marshal/unmarshal" rather than "serialize/deserialize." "Marshal" is more descriptive because the result of marshaling a Java program element could be a DOM—for example—which is still not serialized. So, marshalling is really the process of converting instances of JAXB-annotated classes to an XML infoset representation (e.g., an XML document stored in a file, a DOM) according to the JAXB 2.0 standard Java/XML binding as customized by the annotations. Likewise, unmarshalling is the process of converting an XML infoset representation (e.g., an XML document stored in a file, a DOM) to a tree of *content objects*. The conversion is defined by the infoset's associated XML schema together with the JAXB 2.0 *standard Java/XML mapping* as customized by any *mapping annotations* specified in the program element definitions of the target content objects. The content objects' Java program elements are either JAXB 2.0 schema-derived program elements or existing program elements mapped to the schema by the schema generator.

The following steps indicate how the binding run-time framework interfaces with the JAX-WS 2.0 invocation architecture to invoke a Web service deployed in a JWS-compliant application:

1. The JWS application receives a SOAP message at a deployed endpoint.
2. Based on the configuration of the SOAP binding (`javax.xml.ws.soap.SOAPBinding`) for the endpoint, JAX-WS prepares an instance of the message context (`javax.xml.ws.handler.soap.SOAPMessageContext`), which includes a SAAJ representation of the message.
3. JAXB may be required to provide MTOM/XOP[27] processing in order to create the SAAJ representation of the message. Such processing may be deferred until required. That is, for performance reasons, MTOM processing may be deferred until an application actually requests access to a part of the SOAP message requiring MTOM processing to be realized as a SAAJ instance.
4. JAX-WS invokes the handlers. During handler processing, the application has SAAJ interface access to the SOAP message contents. As discussed in the preceding step, SAAJ access may trigger MTOM processing, which is handled by the JAXB run-time binding framework.
5. After the request handlers are finished, the JAXB runtime unmarshals the SOAP message contents into a request bean (see Section 2.3.14). Although the request bean is defined by JAX-WS, based on the parameter and return type packaging of the deployment, JAXB implements the binding of the request bean to the SOAP message request.
6. The request bean, constructed by the JAXB runtime, contains the Java objects that are passed as parameters to the Java method that implements the Web service. JAX-WS invokes the method using these parameters.
7. JAX-WS hands off the Java object returned from the method invocation and uses it to create an instance of the response bean (see Section 2.3.14).
8. JAXB marshals the response bean.

27. See Section 2.4.10 for a description of MTOM/XOP.

9. As in step 2, based on the SOAP binding configuration for the end-point, JAX-WS updates the message context to include a SAAJ representation of the response. This is a SAAJ interface on top of the response bean.
10. JAX-WS invokes the response handlers.
11. Prior to transmitting the response message, JAX-WS invokes the JAXB runtime as necessary to provide MTOM processing for the message.
12. JAX-WS hands off the response message to the protocol transport.

There are a few issues here to point out that will help our understanding of the JWS specifications. First, two sets of deserialization activities occur during an invocation. Initially, the JAX-WS implementation deserializes the serialized form of the request message coming off the wire into an infoset representation with a SAAJ interface. Because SAAJ is DOM-oriented, the underlying infoset representation may be a DOM implementation, but it could also be STaX or some other type of *pull parser* that provides "as-needed" access to the infoset.[28] The subsequent set of serialization activities occurs when the JAXB runtime unmarshals the infoset representation into JAXB-annotated program elements.

Second, although MTOM processing is actually part of the first serialization (creating an infoset representation from the serialized wire format), it is handled by the JAXB runtime on behalf of JAX-WS.

Third, all handler processing occurs before JAXB unmarshalling and after JAXB marshalling from/to the infoset representation of the SOAP message. As a result, programmers do not have access to the JAXB-annotated program elements within the handlers by default. Of course, if you want to do JAXB marshalling inside a handler, you can use that approach to get access to the infoset via the JAXB binding. However, that approach introduces yet another marshalling step into the process, which could degrade performance.

Figure 2–4 illustrates this two-stage deserialization process. A SOAP request starts in an "on-the-wire" format—shown here as a MIME package. The first stage converts the wire format to an XML infoset and provides SAAJ access. This form of the request is used by the handler framework.

---

28. While not a JWS implementation, Axis2 (http://ws.apache.org/axis2/) provides an example of this approach. Its AXIOM object model provides a performance-oriented interface to SOAP messages. With AXIOM, the SOAP message remains in its serialized form until the application (e.g., a handler) requests access to a part of it. When access is requested, only as much of the message as is needed gets deserialized.

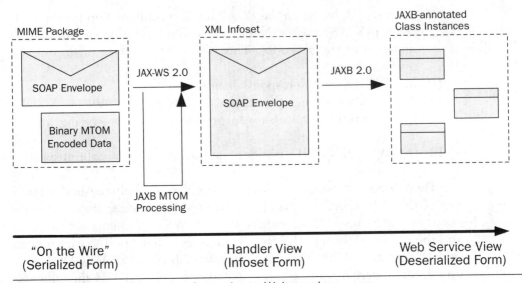

Figure 2–4 JWS serialization—from wire to Web service.

The second stage unmarshals the infoset into Java program elements. These elements are used by the Java Web service as parameters for the method invocation.

In addition to supporting this two-stage (de)serialization framework for invocation of a Java Web service, the JAXB runtime provides the `javax.xml.bind.*` APIs giving programmers access to the following capabilities (among others):

- **Marshalling:** Application-level programs can marshal between JAXB-annotated class instances and various XML infoset forms.
- **Object factories and constructors:** Factories and constructors are provided for creating instances of JAXB-annotated classes. This provides programmers with a convenient method for creating instances of XML schema components: Create an instance of the corresponding JAXB-annotated class using the object factory or constructor. Set the Java properties as needed. Then, marshal the instance to get the XML.

From my perspective, JAXB 2.0 surpasses JAXB 1.0 and other schema compilation frameworks (e.g., XmlBeans [XMLBEANS]) for Java/XML binding primarily because it provides for marshalling to/from POJOs and not just schema-derived program elements. This capability is central to the "Start from Java" development mode for creating and deploying Web services.

My biggest criticism has nothing to do with the JAXB runtime per se, but rather the fact that it is the only Java/XML binding framework supported within JWS. As illustrated in Figure 2–4, there are two distinct components to the serialization process: (1) creating the XML infoset; and (2) marshalling between the infoset and the Java objects that implement the Web service.

It would not be difficult for the JWS specifications to accommodate pluggable alternatives to the JAXB 2.0 run-time binding framework. Currently, the transition from the XML infoset view to the JAXB program elements occurs "behind the scenes." This unmarshalling happens after the request handlers have finished and before the invocation of the deployed Java object. It is carried out by the JAX-WS 2.0 implementation and is not part of the standard API—at least in this 2.0 release. It is easy to imagine how a few more APIs could be exposed to allow the Web Services deployment system to specify the run-time binding framework.

2.4.6 Validation

Validation is a key component of the serialization subsystem. In order to implement Web Services, you need to be able to control how invalid XML gets handled. By invalid, I mean XML that is not valid with respect to the WSDL/XML Schema that defines the Web service. Oftentimes, it is desirable to let some types of invalid XML get by. For example, whether or not a particular attribute is set may have no bearing on the invocation of the Web service that is the target of a particular SOAP message.

Unlike with JAXB 1.0, the unmarshalling of invalid XML is allowed by JAXB 2.0—in fact, that is the default behavior. JAXB-annotated value classes require the use of JAXB 2.0's *flexible unmarshalling mode* that allows certain invalid conditions (e.g., out-of-order elements, missing or unexpected elements) to get by the unmarshal validation process.

This is a big improvement because it allows flexibility in the handling of invalid data. However, if validation is required, it can be turned on. JAXB 2.0 validation during unmarshalling can be activated by providing an instance of a JAXP 1.3 `javax.xml.validation.Schema` to the `Unmarshaller.setSchema()` method.

When validation is enabled, the default behavior is to throw an unchecked exception when the first error is encountered. However, one can change this behavior by defining and setting a `javax.xml.bind.ValidationEventHandler` using the `Unmarshaller.setEventHandler()` method. Using this approach, when a validation error occurs, the event handler is called. The event handler can be written so that it aggregates all the errors reported during unmarshalling and reports them at once. Actually, a default implementation for this type of validation is provided by `javax.xml.bind.util.ValidationEventCollector`. This can be very useful for debugging. It is also useful when there are certain types of errors you don't want to have thrown as unchecked exceptions.

JAXB 2.0 also supports fail-fast validation, although it is optional for implementations of the 2.0 release. Presumably, in later releases it will be required. When supported, fail-fast validation gives you run-time checking of all manipulations to a Java content tree. Any manipulations that result in the underlying XML infoset becoming invalid with respect to the associated schema throw an exception. Fail-fast validation is implemented using predicates. Predicates are code fragments that apply schema validation rules to program element properties. When fail-fast validation is supported, a JAXB value type's property setters are generated with predicates that apply the validation rules specified in the source schema.

In addition, you can still use the more rigid structural unmarshalling mode that was the only approach available under JAXB 1.0. However, if you choose to use this approach, you have to work with a JAXB *Java content interface* rather than value classes. That means, for one thing, working with object factories rather than constructors. The only reason I can see to use the older JAXB 1.0 approach is if you want to map multiple occurrences of an element name to different JAXB properties. This can be useful, for example, if you have something like multiple `street` elements representing multiple lines of an address, and you want to map them to Java properties like `street1`, `street2`, and so on. However, I've never run into a situation where this kind of capability was really required.

2.4.7 Portability

JAXB 2.0 portability is achieved using the mapping annotations described in Section 2.4.3. The run-time marshaller from any JAXB implementation must be able to serialize a JAXB-annotated class to an instance of its target schema. Likewise, the run-time unmarshaller must be able to deserialize a schema instance to an instance of the JAXB-annotated class.

This is important because it means that one can deploy a Web service built from JAXB-annotated classes to any JAXB 2.0 platform (e.g., SAP Netweaver, JBoss, GlassFish) without having to recompile the schema and/or refactor the Web service to use vendor-specific implementation classes.

2.4.8 Marshal Event Callbacks

Callbacks enable application-specific processing during serialization.[29] You can define processing to occur either before serialization (just after target creation) or immediately after serialization. This is a useful feature for setting properties outside of the serialization process.

One use case I've encountered involved unmarshalling XML into an existing POJO that combines data from multiple sources. For example, you could have a customer object that you annotate so that it can be unmarshalled from a SOAP message containing customer information. However, if not all of the customer data (e.g., transaction history) is available in the SOAP message, you may want to load the rest of the object's data from another source (e.g., SAP). In such situations, you can use an event callback to load the SAP data after the unmarshalling is finished.

2.4.9 Partial Binding

The `javax.xml.bind.Binder` class supports partial binding of an XML document. This enables one, for example, to create a JAXB binding of a SOAP header without processing the body. Potentially, this capability could be very useful from a performance perspective if you could harness it to only update a particular SOAP header element when doing handler processing.

Imagine, for example, that one wants to create a handler to mark a SOAP header element named `myapp:persisted` as `true` to indicate that the entire SOAP message has been persisted to permanent storage. The following indicates how that might be accomplished with the partial binding mechanism:

```
org.w3c.dom.Element persistedElt = ... // get from SOAP header
Binder<org.w3c.dom.Node> myBinder = jaxbContext.createBinder();
PersistedValueClass perVC = (PersistedValueClass)
myBinder.unmarshal(persistedElt);
perVC.setPersisted(true);
myBinder.updateXML(perVC); // updates the XML infoset
```

Manipulating the SOAP header infoset inside handlers is much easier this way because you don't have to deal with navigating and updating via the

---

29. The term *serialization* here is used to mean either serialization or deserialization. This is how it is used throughout the book.

DOM interface. It is also less error-prone. If you have ever spent hours debugging DOM code that introduces bad data into an XML infoset, you will appreciate the improved rigor provided with this type of partial binding approach. If fail-fast validation (see Section 2.4.6) is supported by the underlying JAXB implementation, and it is turned on, the validity of the XML after handler processing is guaranteed.

2.4.10 Binary Data Encoding (MTOM or WS-I)

The JWS programming model supports the optimization of binary data transmission with SOAP messages. Such optimization involves encoding binary data (e.g., an image file as `xsd:base64Binary`), moving it out of the SOAP envelope, attaching a compressed version to the MIME package, and placing references to the encoded parts in the SOAP envelope. Binary optimization support, part of the serialization subsystem, is provided by the JAXB run-time implementation. JAXB provides the services that "unpackage" the binary data prior to unmarshalling (see Figure 2–4) and "package" it after marshalling as part of serializing a SOAP message onto the wire. JAXB 2.0 supports two types of binary data encoding: MTOM/XOP and WSIAP.

MTOM is the W3C standard titled "SOAP Message Transmission Optimization Mechanism" (see www.w3.org/TR/soap12-mtom/). It describes a standard procedure for taking content out of the XML infoset, compressing it, packaging it as a MIME attachment, and replacing it with a reference in the infoset. The packaging encoding used with MTOM is XOP, another W3C recommendation titled "XML-binary Optimized Packaging" [XOP]. XOP replaces base64-encoded content with a `xop:include` element that references the respective MIME part encoded as a binary octet stream. If data is already available as a binary octet stream, it can be placed directly in an XOP package.

WSIAP is the WS-I Attachments Profile Version 1.0 [WSIAP]. WSIAP clarifies SOAP Messages with Attachments (SwA) [SwA]. SwA was the industry's first attempt to standardize an approach to treating binary data as SOAP message attachments. Support for WSIAP is built into a number of products, so it is important for JWS to support it. However, the industry now seems to be converging on MTOM/XOP as the primary standard.

JAXB uses annotations to specify which Java properties in a class should be serialized using MTOM or WSIAP. For MTOM, the `@XmlMimeType` annotation lets you specify how a binary (e.g., `java.awt.Image`) Java property gets bound to a schema element decorated with the `xmime:content-Type` attribute. The `xmime:contentType` attribute [XMIME] is used to indicate the content type of an XML element with type `xs:base64Binary` or `xs:hexBinary`. For WSIAP, the `@XmlAttachmentRef` annotation plays the same role.

When working with a JAXB implementation, the MTOM and WSIAP support is provided by extending the abstract classes `AttachmentMarshaller` and `AttachmentUnmarshaller`. For example, a JAX-WS implementation provides general MIME processing. However, to handle MTOM or WSIAP packaging, it plugs into the JAXB implementation at runtime. This is accomplished by having the JAX-WS runtime register its `AttachmentMarshaller` and `Attachment-Unmarshaller` using the `Marshaller.setAttachmentMarshaller` and `Unmarshaller.setAttachmentUnmarshaller` methods.

MTOM processing is an important component of a Web Services platform. Given the structure of JWS, with MIME processing handled by JAX-WS and attachment unmarshalling handled by JAXB, it is clear that attempting to use the MTOM capabilities while substituting a non-JAXB serialization subsystem would require some workarounds. The reason for caring about that problem is, again, handling the "Start from WSDL and Java" development mode that doesn't get addressed very well by JAXB. The situation with MTOM is similar to that with SOAP fault processing (see Section 2.3.11). I like the JWS SOAP fault mechanism, but would like to be able to use it without necessarily buying into the entire JWS programming model. The same is true with MTOM. It would be nice to be able to access the MTOM processing services without using the whole JWS architecture.

2.5 WS-Metadata 2.0

Section 2.4 provided a high-level tour of the JAXB 2.0 specification, focusing particularly on the features relevant to SOA development and deployment. JAXB 2.0 is covered in detail in Chapter 5 where numerous programming examples are provided that illustrate how to handle SOA challenges using JAXB. Taken together, JAX-WS and JAXB provide most of the JWS framework for invocation and serialization.

In this section, the focus is on deployment, and particularly, how JWS uses annotations to facilitate the deployment of Java classes as Web services. WS-Metadata 2.0 defines the standard annotations that are used to develop and deploy Web Services using Java SE 6 and within a Java EE 5 run-time container. A primary goal of this specification is "ease of use"—making it easier to write, deploy, and consume a Web service. This goal is part of the larger "ease-of-use" goal for Java EE 5.

Annotations are at the center of the "ease-of-use" features that permeate Java EE 5. For example, annotations are also used heavily in EJB 3.0 as a mechanism to reduce or eliminate the need for deployment descriptors and add functionality such as dependency injection (see Section 2.7.1) for stateless session beans.

I agree that annotations make it much easier to develop and deploy a Web service when you are starting from a Java class. The bias of WS-Metadata is the "Start from Java" development mode. As demonstrated in the code examples from Chapter 8, you need to do a lot less work to deploy a Web service using Java EE 5 than J2EE 1.4.

In general, I think the WS-Metadata annotations are a huge step forward. However, there is one area where I think it may be possible to come up with something better—the "Start from WSDL and Java" development mode. For "Start from WSDL and Java," the impact of annotations is mixed. To get you thinking about the impact of annotations on the full life cycle of a "Start from WSDL and Java" application, consider this example.

Suppose you have a `PurchaseOrder` class and you want to deploy the `createPurchaseOrder()` method as a Web service operation. Furthermore, suppose your organization needs to publish this Web service using a standard WSDL interface your business partners all use to front-end their purchasing processes. In this scenario, you have an existing operation, `ns:createPO`, and you need to use that operation, including the standard `ns:PurchaseOrder` element defined by the XML schema your business partners have agreed on.

To use WS-Metadata, you are going to have to edit your `PurchaseOrder` class to include the necessary annotations. That may or may not be possible, depending on whether you have access to the source code (e.g., there are licensing issues if it is third-party software). Even if you have the source code, it might be part of a large application and you may not have the authority within your organization, for this project, to recompile and redeploy the application with your annotations.

But for the sake of argument, assume you can add the necessary annotations and recompile/redeploy the application. Then, you still have the issue of mapping the `PurchaseOrder` program elements to the `ns:PurchaseOrder` element using the JAXB annotations (see Section 2.4.3). It may be impossible to get JAXB to implement this mapping[30]—even with extensive mapping customizations.

---

30. Many Java/XML mappings are impossible to implement using JAXB annotations. See Section 2.4 and Chapter 5 for details.

Again, for the sake of argument, assume there is a mapping that can be expressed using annotations. How do you find this mapping? You have to make some annotations, run the WSDL/schema generator, and look at the resulting WSDL to see whether it matches the standard WSDL agreed on by your business partners. That process is kind of like trying to do assembly language programming by writing C code, compiling it, and looking at the bytes to see whether it produced what you want. Not a very efficient process!

But, again, for the sake of argument, assume you have persevered and were able to come up with annotations that generate the necessary WSDL. Now, what happens if your business partners make a change to the WSDL? In this case, you are back at square one, editing the annotations, running the WSDL/schema generator, and trying to get things lined up again. Once you have the correct annotations figured out (assuming it's even possible), again, you have to recompile and redeploy the code with the new annotations.

Hopefully, this example has convinced you that annotations may have some limitations with respect to the "Start from WSDL and Java" development mode. Faced with these issues, most programmers will choose to create a wrapper for the `PurchaseOrder` class. This can best be accomplished by running the WSDL/schema compiler on your business partners' standard WSDL. You can take the resulting Java classes and turn them into wrappers that invoke your real classes. Annotations let you delimit your modification to the generated classes, so you can "refresh" them if the WSDL changes and not lose the modifications you put in to invoke your existing `PurchaseOrder.createPurchaseOrder()` method.

In this overview of WS-Metadata, I take the point of view of a programmer who is using this *wrapper-based integration* approach to "Start from WSDL and Java" development mode. That is not to say that I believe the wrapper-based integration approach is the best way to approach the "Start from WSDL and Java" development mode. It may be, but I think it is worth exploring some other possibilities. For example, in Chapter 11, I use SOA-J to demonstrate a different approach to "Start from WSDL and Java" and SOA-style systems integration. But at this point, I am reviewing the JWS programming model, where wrapper-based integration is probably the best approach to "Start from WSDL and Java" development.

As shown in Table 2–3, the WS-Metadata features discussed here are all related to Web Services deployment. The remainder of this section provides an overview of these features. Chapter 8 examines WS-Metadata and WSEE (JSR-109) in detail and provides many deployment examples.

Before looking at each of these features one by one, examine Figure 2–5, which shows how WS-Metadata can be used to shape the deployment of a Web

Table 2–3 WS-Metadata 2.0 Feature Map

Invocation	Serialization	Deployment
		WSDL Mapping Annotations
		SOAP Binding Annotations
		Handler Annotations
		Service Implementation Bean
		Start from WSDL and Java
		Automatic Deployment

service. The code and WSDL in Figure 2–5 illustrate a variety of WS-Metadata annotations working together. This example is taken from the WS-Metadata 2.0 specification—Section 4.7.3 (Example 3—the document/literal wrapped example).

The WS-Metadata annotations are numbered 1–8 and the red lines show where, in the WSDL, the annotation has its effect. The following items give you a general idea of what these annotations are doing without a lot of detail. I discuss these annotations in detail in Chapter 8. The various styles of WSDL are described in Chapter 4.

1. @WebService marks this Java class as a Web service so that the JWS implementation will understand that it is to be deployed.
2. @SOAPBinding indicates that this Web service uses the SOAP protocol.
3. The @SOAPBinding.style element indicates that this Web service should be deployed using the document style. This annotation sets the WSDL soap:binding element's style attribute as shown.
4. The @SOAPBinding.use element indicates that the messages for this Web service should be sent using the literal format (as opposed to encoded). This annotation affects the soap:body element's use attribute as shown.
5. The @SOAPBinding.parameterStyle element indicates that the messages for this Web service should use wrapped parameters. As a result, the element name of the parameter wrapper becomes "SubmitPO"—the same as the operation name of the Web service.

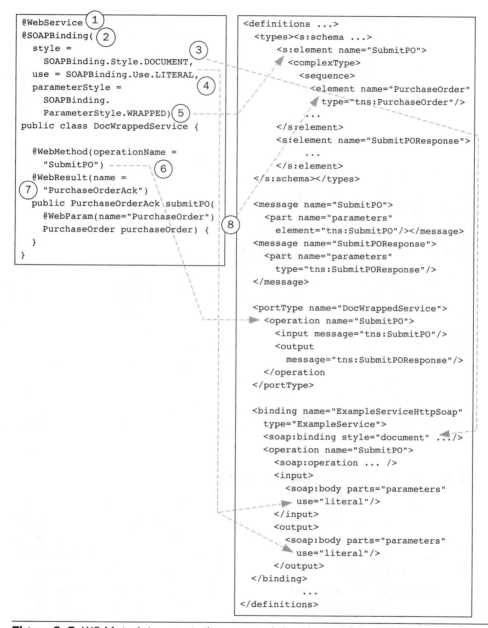

```
@WebService (1)
@SOAPBinding( (2)
  style =                          (3)
    SOAPBinding.Style.DOCUMENT,
  use = SOAPBinding.Use.LITERAL,
  parameterStyle =                 (4)
    SOAPBinding.
    ParameterStyle.WRAPPED) (5)
public class DocWrappedService {

  @WebMethod(operationName =
    "SubmitPO") --------- (6)
  @WebResult(name =
(7)  "PurchaseOrderAck")
  public PurchaseOrderAck submitPO(
    @WebParam(name="PurchaseOrder")    (8)
    PurchaseOrder purchaseOrder) {
  }
}
```

```
<definitions ...>
  <types><s:schema ...>
    <s:element name="SubmitPO">
      <complexType>
        <sequence>
          <element name="PurchaseOrder"
            type="tns:PurchaseOrder"/>
          ...
      </s:element>
      <s:element name="SubmitPOResponse">
        ...
      </s:element>
  </s:schema></types>

  <message name="SubmitPO">
    <part name="parameters"
      element="tns:SubmitPO"/></message>
  <message name="SubmitPOResponse">
    <part name="parameters"
      type="tns:SubmitPOResponse"/>
  </message>

  <portType name="DocWrappedService">
    <operation name="SubmitPO">
      <input message="tns:SubmitPO"/>
      <output
        message="tns:SubmitPOResponse"/>
    </operation>
  </portType>

  <binding name="ExampleServiceHttpSoap"
    type="ExampleService">
    <soap:binding style="document" .../>
    <operation name="SubmitPO">
      <soap:operation ... />
      <input>
        <soap:body parts="parameters"
          use="literal"/>
      </input>
      <output>
        <soap:body parts="parameters"
          use="literal"/>
      </output>
    </operation>
  </binding>
      ...
</definitions>
```

Figure 2–5 WS-Metadata annotations control the shape of the WSDL.

6. The `@WebMethod.operationName` element specifies that the WSDL operation name should be "SubmitPO."

7. The `@WebResult.name` element specifies that the response message should be an element named "PurchaseOrderAck." Note that this element is not shown here, but would be enclosed in the response wrapper named "SubmitPOResponse."

8. The `@WebParam.name` element specifies that the name for the request parameter mapping to the Java parameter `purchaseOrder` be named "PurchaseOrder." Like the response, this element is also enclosed in a wrapper.

In this example from Figure 2–5, you can also see the impact of the JAX-WS default WSDL/Java mapping. For example, the `portType`'s name, `DocWrappedService`, is the same as the Java class name.

2.5.1 WSDL Mapping Annotations

The WS-Metadata 2.0 WSDL mapping annotations, belonging to the `javax.jws` package, enable you to shape the WSDL/Java mapping by specifying information such as the WSDL operation name assigned to a particular Java method. These annotations enable you to customize the default WSDL/Java mapping discussed in Section 2.3.1. In Figure 2–5, the following annotations are classified as WSDL Mapping Annotations: `@WebService`, `@WebMethod`, `@WebResult`, and `@WebParam`.

If you are doing "Start from WSDL" or "Start from WSDL and Java," the `WebService.wsdlLocation` element is essential. It enables you to specify the location of your predefined WSDL.

2.5.2 SOAP Binding Annotations

The WS-Metadata 2.0 SOAP binding annotations, belonging to the `javax.jws.soap` package, give you the power to customize the SOAP binding style, use, and parameter style. These annotations are used to customize the default JAX-WS SOAP binding described in Section 2.3.9. The JAX-WS default for the binding style/use/parameter is document/literal wrapped. However, using the `javax.jws.SOAPBinding` annotation, you can specify other possibilities such as rpc/literal and document/literal bare. SOAP binding style and parameter wrapping has been a source of much confusion and interoperability problems. In this area, WS-Metadata and JAX-WS shine, making it easy and intuitive for Java developers to understand and shape the SOAP bindings of their Web services. SOAP binding style and parameter wrapping is described in detail in Chapter 4, Section 4.3.

2.5.3 Handler Annotations

The deployment of handlers, as discussed in Section 2.3.7, is specified using WS-Metadata annotations. The `javax.jws.HandlerChain` annotation is used to associate a Web service with an externally defined handler chain defined in a file referenced by the `@HandlerChain.file` member value.

The `javax.jws.soap.SOAPMessageHandlers` annotation described in WS-Metadata 2.0 has been deprecated, for JAX-WS endpoints cannot be used as a mechanism for deploying SOAP handlers when using JAX-WS.

2.5.4 Service Implementation Bean

WS-Metadata 2.0 (Section 3.1) defines the requirements for deploying a Java class as a Web service. Classes that meet these requirements are called service implementation beans (SIBs). While JAX-RPC required services to be implemented using service endpoint interfaces (SEIs) that had to extend `java.rmi.Remote`, that requirement no longer applies with JAX-WS and WS-Metadata. In addition, both POJOs and EJBs that conform to the service implementation bean requirements can be deployed as Web services. This is a big improvement over J2EE 1.4, which has two different bean specifications—one for EJB deployment (which requires a Web service to be implemented with the stateless session bean interfaces) and one for Web container (servlet) deployment.

The JSR-181 processor (see Section 2.5.5) creates different artifacts depending on the target container—including EJB 2.1 interfaces if the target is a J2EE 1.4 EJB container. However, annotations enable the developer to work at a higher level of abstraction and avoid being sucked into the time-consuming and tedious details of container-specific deployment. The artifacts that are generated by the JSR-181 processor are defined by WSEE 1.2, which describes the portability requirements for Java Web Services.

2.5.5 Start from WSDL and Java

The "Start from WSDL and Java" development mode is supported by using annotations to map constructs on an existing Java class or interface to constructs on a WSDL document. For example, the `@WebMethod.operation-Name` annotation can be used to associate a method with a predefined `wsdl:operation`. The pros and cons of this approach are discussed in the introduction to this discussion of WS-Metadata (see Section 2.5).

Some of the problems pointed out in that discussion are addressed by the specification's requirement that implementations of JSR-181 that support

"Start with WSDL and Java" must provide feedback indicating when the Web service implementation diverges from the WSDL contract. You can imagine that a well-implemented tool would guide you through the process of annotating an existing Java source file to conform it to an existing WSDL with a GUI to highlight areas of nonconformance and suggested annotations. You can also imagine a bad tool that just runs the JSR-181 processor and gives you batch output consisting of a series of nonconformance errors.

In any event, the intention of such a feedback mechanism is to help the developer keep his Java code in line with potential changes in the WSDL. This is an important feature.

2.5.6 Automatic Deployment

Automatic deployment, a "drag-and-drop" deployment model, similar to that used by Java Server Pages (JSPs), is envisioned by the WS-Metadata specification (see Section 2.4 of [JSR 181]), but is not required. In such a model, the run-time deployment of a Web service is entirely dependent on its annotations. A vendor-specific deployment tool is not required.

GlassFish—the Java EE 5 implementation used for the examples in this book—provides such a "drag-and-drop" deployment capability.[31] Programming examples are provided in Chapter 8.

2.6   WSEE 1.2

Whereas WS-Metadata 2.0, discussed in the preceding section, defines an annotation-based programming model for creating Java Web services, the WSEE 1.2 specification defines a service architecture and packaging to ensure portability of Web services across Java EE application server implementations.

Many of the complaints related to Web Services in J2EE 1.4 center on the complexity of deployment using WSEE 1.0. This deployment complexity has been greatly reduced through the use of annotations as described in Section 2.5, together with the simplified architecture and packaging described here.

As shown in Table 2–4, the WSEE 1.2 features discussed here are all deployment-related. The remainder of this section provides a brief discussion of these features. Chapter 8 examines WSEE 1.2 [JSR 109] in

---

31. See Appendix B for more details on GlassFish. Also see [GLASSFISH].

detail, along with MS-Metadata [JSR 181], and provides many deployment examples.

Table 2–4 WSEE 1.2 Feature Map

Invocation	Serialization	Deployment
		Port Component
		Servlet Endpoints
		EJB Endpoints
		Simplified Packaging
		Handler Programming Model

2.6.1 Port Component

A *port component* is what gets packaged and deployed to the container to implement a Web service. Defined by WSEE, a port component is an addition to the Java EE platform and can be considered the Web Services counterpart to other familiar deployable components such as servlets and JSPs (Web container) or EJBs (EJB container).

A port component defines the programming model artifacts that make up portable Web service applications, including the service implementation bean (SIB) (see Section 2.5.4). The SIB is the only required artifact—unlike with J2EE, the `webservices.xml` descriptor is not required.

The port component, as defined in WSEE 1.2, is a welcome simplification of the J2EE 1.4 model. In J2EE 1.4, the other artifacts required for deployment include the service endpoint interface (SEI), the Web Services deployment descriptor (`webservices.xml`), and the JAX-RPC mapping deployment descriptor. In WSEE 1.2, the following artifacts may optionally be included in a port component: WSDL document, SEI, and `webservices.xml`. When provided, the `webservices.xml` deployment descriptor overrides any conflicting deployment information provided by annotations.

2.6.2 Servlet Endpoints

WSEE 1.2 specifies that a POJO, as long as it meets the requirement spelled out in WS-Metadata for a SIB, can be used to implement a Web service deployed to the Web container. This is commonly referred to as a servlet endpoint.

2.6.3 EJB Endpoints

WSEE 1.2 specifies that a stateless session bean can be used to implement a Web service to be deployed in the EJB container. This is commonly referred to as an EJB endpoint. The requirements for creating a SIB from a stateless session bean are spelled out in detail in Section 5 of WSEE.

2.6.4 Simplified Packaging

For many common deployment scenarios, no deployment descriptors are required. Furthermore, when they are required, they are much simpler than their counterparts in J2EE 1.4. Detailed examples of various packaging options are provided in Chapter 8.

2.6.5 Handler Programming Model

Handler annotations are defined by WS-Metadata 2.0 (see Section 2.5.3). The programming and run-time model for handlers in Java EE 5 is described in WSEE 1.2. The WS-Metadata `@HandlerChain` annotation associates a handler chain with a port component. WSEE defines the structure of the handler chain deployment descriptor. WSEE also specified such run-time behavior as the capability of handlers to access `<env-entry>` parameters via resource injection. Chapter 7, Section 7.6, and Chapter 8, Section 8.3, provide examples of how to use handlers.

2.7 Impact of Other Java EE 5 Annotation Capabilities

The idea of using WS-Metadata 2.0 annotations (described in Section 2.5) to simplify development and deployment is one example of the broad use of annotations introduced throughout the Java EE 5 specifications. This section briefly mentions a few of the other exciting new annotation capabilities built into the Java EE 5 platform that developers can use when developing Web services applications.

2.7.1 Dependency Injection

Java EE 5 introduces dependency injection mechanisms that simplify the process of instantiating context within various containers. Dependency injection is used to acquire references to resources (e.g., database connections) or other objects (e.g., Web Services clients) when an object is created by the container. Different containers support different types of dependency injection. The Java

EE 5 specification identifies injection support within the EJB, Web, and application client (i.e., main class) containers.

Certain dependency injection patterns for supporting Web Services have been built into the JAX-WS 2.0 specification. For example, the `@Web-ServiceRef` annotation specifies the injection of a reference to a specific Web service. After such a reference is instantiated, it can be used as a client to invoke the referenced Web service. Likewise, the JAX-WS 2.0 `javax.xml.ws.WebServiceContext` can be obtained, inside of a Web service implementation, but using the `@Resource` annotation for dependency injection. Examples of dependency injection being used in this way are provided in Chapters 6 and 7 where JAX-WS is discussed in detail.

2.7.2 Interceptors

An interceptor is a method that intercepts another method's invocation. This is the Java EE 5 implementation of the Aspect Oriented Programming (AOP) interceptor concept. For example, you might have a `submitPur-chaseOrder(PurchaseOrder po)` method where you want to validate the incoming `po` before invoking the method. Such validation could be implemented as an interceptor that is associated with the `submitPurchaseOrder` method using the `javax.interceptor.Interceptors` annotation.

Interceptors make it easier to add additional services to methods when they are deployed as Web Services. Validation, as described previously, is one example. Another is security. Imagine a scenario where a user's credentials are supplied in the SOAP header. You may want to restrict access to individual methods on a `wsdl:port` based on the caller's credentials. Instead of trying to figure out, in a request handler, which method is going to be invoked and applying the security constraint in the handler, it is much easier to store the credentials in the message context. Then, define an interceptor on each method that applies the security rule based on the user's credentials stored in the message context.

2.7.3 POJO Support in EJB 3.0

The EJB 3.0 specification is exciting because it removes a lot of the complexity associated with creating and deploying Enterprise JavaBeans. It is outside the scope of this book to discuss EJB 3.0 in detail, but I would like to point out the impact of POJO support on Web Services.

EJB 3.0 enables developers to deploy POJOs as stateless session beans simply by adding the `@stateless` annotation. You no longer need to provide an `EJBObject`, `EJBLocalObject`, or `java.rmi.Remote` interface. Nor do you need to provide a home interface.

This makes it much easier to deploy existing POJOs to implement Web services within the EJB container. Using the J2EE 1.4 model (EJB 2.1 and JAX-RPC 1.1), if you wanted to deploy an existing POJO as a Web service via the EJB container, you needed to create a stateless session bean wrapper that implemented the necessary interfaces. Lifting this requirement has removed one roadblock to the "Start from WSDL and Java" development approach.

2.8   Conclusions

This chapter provided an overview of the Web Services capabilities provided by JWS. It started at the 10,000-foot level looking at a generic SOA application and describing where Web Services fit in. Then, it descended to the 100-foot level to describe some of the run-time implementation details of Web Services within Java EE 5 and Java SE 6. Then, Sections 2.3–2.7 continued at that 100-foot level to review the development and deployment features of JAX-WS 2.0, JAXB 2.0, WS-Metadata 2.0, WSEE 1.2, and some other specifications related to Web Services. If you have managed to get through all of this, you've had a good overview of Java Web Services. You've also heard some of my thoughts on the pros and cons of JWS as a platform for SOA development. If you just skimmed this chapter, that is also fine. You can come back to it anytime you want a break from the programming examples in the rest of this book and you need to get back to the "big picture."

Chapters 3–8 take you down to the 10-foot level, and provide detailed examples of how to program with Java Web Services. Chapter 3 starts with the REST model for Web services. I start with REST because it is simple and helps you get your feet wet if you are not that familiar with WSDL and/ or SOAP. If you are not interested in REST, or want to jump right into WSDL and SOAP, please feel free to skip ahead to Chapter 4.

2.8.1 Configuring Your Environment to Build and Run the Software Examples

The remaining chapters contain lots of programming examples. I highly recommend that you download, examine, and run these examples as you work through the book. You will learn a lot more from such "hands-on" experience than you will from just reading the text.

Running the code requires that you to set up a build environment. See Appendix B for instructions on setting up that environment and downloading the source code for the examples.

CHAPTER 3

Basic SOA Using REST

In this chapter, I describe the basic tools and techniques for implementing SOA components using the REST paradigm. REST stands for Representational State Transfer. It was first introduced by Roy Fielding[1] in his 2000 doctoral dissertation [Fielding]. For the past several years, a great debate has been going on about the merits of the REST versus SOAP architectural styles for Web Services. It is not my intention, in this book, to weigh in on either side of that debate. My feeling is that both approaches are useful for implementing SOA components. For simple applications, REST is an easy way to get started.

If you are an advanced Java programmer, you might find the first half of this chapter to be very basic. I have intentionally started out with simplistic examples, using only HTTP and servlets, so that readers who are not advanced in Java can come up the learning curve and get a sense of the basics before introducing the Java Web Services (JWS) APIs. If you have a good grounding in HTTP and Java servlets, please feel free to skip the introductory material and focus on the sections dealing with JAX-WS.

3.1 Why REST?

Some readers may wonder why this book starts with REST before discussing SOAP and WSDL-based Web Services. The reason is that REST is easy to understand. By starting with REST, I can describe some of the basic SOA Web Services concepts without getting into the complexities of SOAP and WSDL. Also, the limitations of REST provide the motivation for introducing SOAP and WSDL in Chapter 4. If you are not interested in REST, feel free to skip ahead to Chapter 4.

---

1. Fielding is one of the principal authors of the HTTP specification and a co-founder of the Apache HTTP Server project.

3.1.1 What Is REST?

REST-style services (i.e., RESTful services) adhere to a set of constraints and architectural principles that include the following:

- RESTful services are *stateless*. As Fielding writes in Section 5.1.3 of his thesis, "each request from client to server must contain all the information necessary to understand the request, and cannot take advantage of any stored context on the server."
- RESTful services have a uniform interface. This constraint is usually taken to mean that the only allowed operations are the HTTP operations: GET, POST, PUT, and DELETE.
- REST-based architectures are built from *resources* (pieces of information) that are uniquely identified by URIs. For example, in a RESTful purchasing system, each purchase order has a unique URI.
- REST components manipulate resources by exchanging *representations* of the resources. For example, a purchase order resource can be represented by an XML document. Within a RESTful purchasing system, a purchase order might be updated by posting an XML document containing the changed purchase order to its URI.

Fielding writes that "REST-based architectures communicate primarily through the transfer of representations of resources" (Section 5.3.3). This is fundamentally different from the Remote Procedure Call (RPC) approach that encapsulates the notion of invoking a procedure on the remote server. Hence, RPC messages typically contain information about the procedure to be invoked or action to be taken. This information is referred to as a *verb* in a Web service request. In the REST model, the only verbs allowed are GET, POST, PUT, and DELETE. In the RPC approach, typically many operations are invoked at the same URI. This is to be contrasted with the REST approach of having a unique URI for each resource.

These are the basic principles behind REST. However, when people talk about the benefits of RESTful systems today, they usually are not strictly applying these principles. For example, among REST advocates, keeping shopping cart data on the server and maintaining a session related to the shopping process that is using the cart is acceptable.[2] In fact, the XML/HTTP Binding provided by JAX-WS for implementing RESTful

---

2. Storing session information or shopping cart data on the server is a clear violation of Fielding's original REST concept since it violates the requirement that a service be stateless.

services provides for session management capabilities using cookies, URL rewriting, and SSL session IDs.

More significant deviations from Fielding's definition of REST involve getting around the "uniform interface" constraint by embedding verbs and parameters inside URLs. The Amazom.com REST interface, for example, includes verbs in query strings and doesn't have unique URIs for each resource. Systems like this, although labeled as RESTful, are really starting to look very much like RPC using XML over HTTP without SOAP.

For the purposes of this book, I am not going to wade into a debate on what is or isn't RESTful. I simply define RESTful Web Services in contrast to SOAP Web Services. Table 3–1 illustrates the principal differences.

Table 3–1 RESTful Web Services versus SOAP Web Services

	REST	SOAP
Message Format	XML	XML inside a SOAP Envelope
Interface Definition	none[a]	WSDL
Transport	HTTP	HTTP, FTP, MIME, JMS, SMTP, etc.

a. Some would argue that XML Schema could be used as an interface definition for RESTful services. Not only is that approach possible, but it is used in many practical cases. However, it is not a complete interface solution because many, if not most, RESTful services incorporate HTTP parameters (e.g., URL query strings) in addition to XML as part of their invocation interface. Chapter 9 looks at the Yahoo! Shopping RESTful interface, which uses HTTP parameters in this manner.

This is consistent with common usage in the REST versus SOAP debates. REST uses simple XML over HTTP without a WSDL interface definition.

3.1.2 Topics Covered in This Chapter

In addition to introducing RESTful Web Services, this chapter introduces and reviews some basic techniques for integrating Enterprise Information Systems (EISs) using XML, XSLT, HTTP, and Java. For each example, I demonstrate how to implement it with and without JWS. The versions of the examples without JWS use basic Java HTTP and XML techniques. Both approaches are provided to give you a sense of what is really happening, under the covers, when a Web service is consumed or deployed using JWS. This should give you a better understanding of the mechanisms underlying JWS and when to use them. For simple Web services, often it is easier to work with the basic Java tools than to pull out all the power of JWS. On the other hand, you will see from these examples how things can quickly get complicated and require the power of the JWS technologies.

Since one focus of this book is on SOA-style development for the enterprise, many of the examples deal with EIS—the basic infrastructure of most corporate computing environments. This chapter describes

- Structuring EIS Records as XML documents
- Getting EIS records from a REST service (with and without JWS)
- Posting EIS records to a REST service (with and without JWS)
- Basic SOA-style integration of REST services using XSLT for data transformation
- Deploying a REST service to be used for getting EIS records—in other words, an HTTP GET service (with and without JWS)
- Deploying a REST service to be used for posting EIS records—in other words, an HTTP POST service (with and without JWS)

3.2   XML Documents and Schema for EIS Records

The first step toward implementing an SOA component that consumes or provides EIS records involves formatting the EIS records that need to be exchanged as XML documents. This process is formalized by creating an XML Schema to represent the structure of an XML document for a particular EIS record. This section introduces some simple examples that are used throughout this chapter to illustrate the role of XML and XML Schema in SOA-style applications development based on Web Services. Understanding these examples requires a basic knowledge of XML and XML Schema. If you are new to XML, you should get an introductory text such as *Beginning XML* by David Hunter et al. [Hunter]. For the necessary background on XML Schema, I suggest *Definitive XML Schema* by Priscilla Walmsley [Walmsley]. Alternatively, if you know basic XML, but need to brush up on XML Schema, you can probably find all you need to know for this book by reading through the W3C's "XML Schema Part 0: Primer" [XSD Part 0].

To illustrate how XML is used, I employ an example based on the fictitious XYZ Corporation. The example illustrates real SOA challenges faced by many companies. XYZ Corporation has an Order Management System (OMS) that needs to be integrated with a Customer Service System (CSS). The OMS should be thought of as an EIS, such as SAP, for taking customer orders and tracking them through delivery. The CSS should be thought of as an EIS, such as Oracle's Siebel Customer Relationship Management Applications, that is used by customer service employees as a tool for handling customer inquiries.

XYZ Corporation would like to build an SOA application bridging the OMS and the CSS. Every time a new order is entered in the OMS (or an existing order is updated), the new SOA application should transfer that information to the CSS and add it to the relevant customer's history log. The purpose of this SOA application is to ensure that customer service representatives have fast access, through the CSS, to basic customer order information. If customer service representatives need access to more detailed order information from the OMS, the CSS will contain the keys within the customer history log (updated via the SOA application) to query the OMS and access that detailed information.

Figure 3–1 illustrates what an OMS order record looks like as it might appear on a user interface.

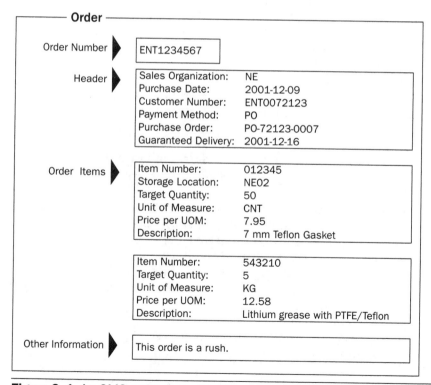

Figure 3–1 An OMS order record as it appears in the user interface.

The structure displayed in the user interface provides a guide to constructing an XML document for the EIS order record. Note that the record is divided into four sections that contain data: Order Number, Order Header, Order Items, and Other Information. Example 3–1 illustrates how this record can be represented as an XML document.

Example 3–1 An XML Representation of the Order Record Appearing in Figure 3–1

```
 4  <Order xmlns="http://www.example.com/oms"
 5    xmlns:xsi="http://www.w3.org/2001/XMLSchema-instance"
 6    xsi:schemaLocation="http://www.example.com/oms
 7    http://soabook.com/example/oms/orders.xsd">
 8    <OrderKey>ENT1234567</OrderKey>
 9    <OrderHeader>
10      <SALES_ORG>NE</SALES_ORG>
11      <PURCH_DATE>2005-12-09</PURCH_DATE>
12      <CUST_NO>ENT0072123</CUST_NO>
13      <PYMT_METH>PO</PYMT_METH>
14      <PURCH_ORD_NO>PO-72123-0007</PURCH_ORD_NO>
15      <WAR_DEL_DATE>2005-12-16</WAR_DEL_DATE>
16    </OrderHeader>
17    <OrderItems>
18      <item>
19        <ITM_NUMBER>012345</ITM_NUMBER>
20        <STORAGE_LOC>NE02</STORAGE_LOC>
21        <TARGET_QTY>50</TARGET_QTY>
22        <TARGET_UOM>CNT</TARGET_UOM>
23        <PRICE_PER_UOM>7.95</PRICE_PER_UOM>
24        <SHORT_TEXT>7 mm Teflon Gasket</SHORT_TEXT>
25      </item>
26      <item>
27        <ITM_NUMBER>543210</ITM_NUMBER>
28        <TARGET_QTY>5</TARGET_QTY>
29        <TARGET_UOM>KG</TARGET_UOM>
30        <PRICE_PER_UOM>12.58</PRICE_PER_UOM>
31        <SHORT_TEXT>Lithium grease with PTFE/Teflon</SHORT_TEXT>
32      </item>
33    </OrderItems>
34    <OrderText>This order is a rush.</OrderText>
35  </Order>
```

book-code/chap03/eisrecords/src/xml/order.xml

Note the use of namespaces in this example. The `Order` element is from the namespace `http://www.example.com/oms`. Note that `http://www.example.com` is the URL used by XYZ Corporation as the base part of its corporate namespaces. The `/oms` indicates, more specifically, the namespace associated with the OMS. When developing SOA systems with XML, it is important to use namespaces, because documents originating from different systems may use the same tags (e.g., "item"), and it is important to interpret the tag in the proper context. For more information on namespaces and how they are used, see the World Wide Web Consortium's (W3C) Recommendation [Namespaces in XML].

In addition to namespaces, when developing SOA systems based on XML, it is important to employ XML Schema to validate documents. Just as a relational database management system allows you to impose constraints on data values and format within the database schema, so XML Schema can be used to validate the integrity of XML documents. XML Schema is important for maintaining data quality and integrity when sharing information among multiple systems.

Notice that the `Order` element of `order.xml` contains the attribute:

```
xsi:schemaLocation="http://www.example.com/oms
   http://soabook.com/example/oms/orders.xsd"
```

This attribute associates `order.xml` with an XML Schema and contains two references. First, `http://www.example.com/oms` gives the namespace to be used for interpreting the schema. Second, `http://soabook.com/example/oms/orders.xsd` is a location where the schema can be found.

Example 3–2 shows just a fragment[3] of the schema used to validate `order.xml`. As indicated by the file reference printed at the bottom of the example, the entire schema document can be found at `com/javector/chap4/eisrecords/order.xsd`. This schema (`order.xsd`) and its instance document (the `order.xml` file) are simplified examples of the SAP XML interface for the business object `SalesOrder` within the Logistics Module.

Although this example is simplified, it illustrates the major issues faced when creating an SOA application that accesses SAP or another EIS.

---

3. Because fragments published in this book correspond directly to the source files in the accompanying download package, sometimes—for XML documents—the closing tags get cut off. Although that can sometimes make the structure look confusing or "off balance," I decided that was better than including the entire XML file in cases where the length could run on for several pages.

Example 3–2 A Fragment of the XML Schema for Validating an Order Document

```
4   <schema targetNamespace="http://www.example.com/oms"
5     xmlns="http://www.w3.org/2001/XMLSchema"
6     xmlns:oms="http://www.example.com/oms" version="1.0"
7     elementFormDefault="qualified">
8     <element name="Orders" type="oms:OrdersType"/>
9     <element name="Order" type="oms:OrderType"/>
10    <complexType name="OrdersType">
11      <sequence>
12        <element ref="oms:Order" maxOccurs="unbounded"/>
13      </sequence>
14    </complexType>
15    <complexType name="OrderType">
16      <annotation>
17        <documentation>A Customer Order</documentation>
18      </annotation>
19      <sequence>
20        <element name="OrderKey">
21          <annotation>
22            <documentation>
23  Unique Sales Document Identifier
24            </documentation>
25          </annotation>
26          <simpleType>
27            <restriction base="string">
28              <maxLength value="10"/>
29            </restriction>
30          </simpleType>
31        </element>
32        <element name="OrderHeader" type="oms:BUSOBJ_HEADER">
33          <annotation>
34            <documentation>
35  Order Header referencing customer, payment, sale organization information.
36            </documentation>
37          </annotation>
38        </element>
39        <element name="OrderItems">
40          <annotation>
41            <documentation>Items in the Order</documentation>
42          </annotation>
43          <complexType>
44            <sequence>
45              <element name="item" type="oms:BUSOBJ_ITEM"
```

```
46                    maxOccurs="unbounded"/>
47              </sequence>
48            </complexType>
49          </element>
```

book-code/chap03/eisrecords/src/xml/orders.xsd

Notice that schemas allow you to restrict values and specify formats for data. For example, the element OrderKey, that is the unique identifier for sales documents, is restricted to being, at most, 10 characters in length. The restriction is accomplished using the restriction element in the simple type definition of OrderKey. Restrictions on simple types like this are known as facets. For further explanation of simple type facets, see [XSD Part 0]. Facets are an important data quality management tool in an SOA environment because they enable you to ensure that the data being shared across systems is properly formatted and can be interpreted by the receiving system.

Next, Figure 3–2 shows the Customer History Record from the Customer Service System (CSS). Consider how it relates to orders and how it is used within the CSS.

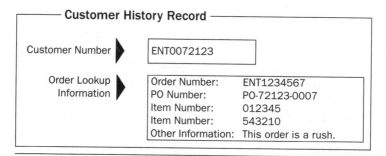

Figure 3–2 A Customer History Record as it appears on a CSS form.

The simple SOA application described in this chapter is responsible for linking the OMS to the CSS to ensure that each time an order is created or modified in the OMS, a corresponding Customer History Record is sent and entered in the Customer History Log within the CSS. The Customer History Log is a record of all transactions the customer has had with XYZ Corporation. It is important to note that not all of the order information is stored in the Customer History Log within the CSS. Only enough is stored so that if a customer calls with a question about an order, the customer service representative can pull up the History Log and drill down to individual order records stored in the OMS to answer the customer's questions. Individual, detailed order records are retrieved from the OMS in real time using the keys stored in the CSS.

The architecture is designed this way to avoid storing lots of redundant data in the CSS and OMS. The problem with redundant data is that it takes up unnecessary disk space, and tends to get out of sync with the original data, creating data quality problems that can be quite difficult to debug and clean up.

The form in Figure 3–2 shows the minimal set of information that needs to be moved from the OMS to the CSS. Example 3–3 shows how that information is structured as an XML record. The OMS sends this type of XML to the CSS each time there is a new order.

Example 3–3 XML Representation of the Screen Pictured in Figure 3–2

```
 4  <css:CustomerHistoryEntry xmlns:css="http://www.example.com/css"
 5    xmlns="http://www.example.com/css"
 6    xmlns:xsi="http://www.w3.org/2001/XMLSchema-instance"
 7    xsi:schemaLocation="http://www.example.com/css
 8    http://soabook.com/example/css/custhistentries.xsd">
 9  <CustomerNumber>ENT0072123</CustomerNumber>
10  <OrderLookupInfo>
11    <OrderNumber>ENT1234567</OrderNumber>
12    <PURCH_ORD_NO>PO-72123-0007</PURCH_ORD_NO>
13    <ITM_NUMBER>012345</ITM_NUMBER>
14    <ITM_NUMBER>543210</ITM_NUMBER>
15    <OrderText>This order is a rush.</OrderText>
16  </OrderLookupInfo>
17  </css:CustomerHistoryEntry>
```

book-code/chap03/eisrecords/src/xml/custhistentry.xml

In this example, the CustomerNumber element uniquely identifies the customer and is referenced by the CUST_NO element, inside the Order-Header element illustrated in Figure 3–1. Likewise, the OrderNumber element inside the OrderLookupInfo element referenced the OrderKey element illustrated in Figure 3–1. These constraints could be enforced within the schema by using the unique, key, and keyref XML Schema Elements (see Section 5 of [XSD Part 0]). However, for simplicity, those types of constraints are left out for now.

Example 3–4 shows a fragment of the schema for validating the Customer History Record. This schema is important for validating the quality of the data being reformatted and exchanged by the SOA application bridge.

Example 3–4 XML Schema for an Entry in the CSS Customer History Log

```
4   <schema targetNamespace="http://www.example.com/css"
5    xmlns="http://www.w3.org/2001/XMLSchema"
6    xmlns:css="http://www.example.com/css" version="1.0"
7    elementFormDefault="qualified">
8    <element name="CustomerHistoryEntries"
       type="css:CustomerHistoryEntriesType"/>
9     <element name="CustomerHistoryEntry" type="css:CustomerHistoryEntryType"/>
10    <complexType name="CustomerHistoryEntriesType">
11      <sequence>
12        <element ref="css:CustomerHistoryEntry" maxOccurs="unbounded"/>
13      </sequence>
14    </complexType>
15    <complexType name="CustomerHistoryEntryType">
16      <sequence>
17        <element name="CustomerNumber">
18          <annotation>
19            <documentation>Unique Customer Identifier</documentation>
20          </annotation>
21          <simpleType>
22            <restriction base="string">
23              <maxLength value="10"/>
24            </restriction>
25          </simpleType>
26        </element>
27        <element name="OrderLookupInfo">
28          <annotation>
29            <documentation>Keys and searchable text that can be used to look
30              up additional order information from the OMS</documentation>
31          </annotation>
32          <complexType>
33            <sequence>
34              <element name="OrderNumber">
35                <annotation>
36                  <documentation>Unique Sales Order Identifier - Key for CSS
37                    lookup of order records</documentation>
38                </annotation>
39                <simpleType>
```

```
40                  <restriction base="string">
41                    <maxLength value="10"/>
42                  </restriction>
43                </simpleType>
44              </element>
```

book-code/chap03/eisrecords/src/xml/custhistentries.xsd

As in Example 3–2, you can see the facets are used to restrict the values for `CustomerNumber` and `OrderNumber`. Notice that schemas allow us to restrict values and specify formats for data. For example, the element `OrderKey`, that is the unique identifier for sales documents, is restricted to being, at most, 10 characters in length. The restriction is accomplished using the restriction element in the simple type definition of `OrderKey`.

3.2.1 No WSDL Doesn't Necessarily Mean No Interfaces

The previous examples show how XML Schema can be used to define structure for XML documents. That structure is critical for defining how applications interact with each other in an SOA-style Web Services infrastructure. It is a fundamental principle of systems integration design that applications must interact across well-defined interfaces. Even in this simple example, as illustrated in Example 3–4, you can see how XML Schema can be used to define the structure of an update record to the CSS Customer History Log. The Customer History schema defines the interface to the Customer History Log. In this manner, any system that needs to update the CSS with customer activity can map whatever form their data is in to the `custhistentry.xsd` schema and send it as a message to the CSS. The following two concepts, illustrated by the simple examples in this section, provide the foundation for SOA-style integration using Web Services:

1. XML documents are used to exchange messages between applications.
2. XML Schema documents define the application interfaces.

Point (2) is important to bear in mind. It tells you that, even when using RESTful services (without WSDL and SOAP), the schema of the XML documents being exchanged between SOA components can be used to define interfaces for the services. Unfortunately, this use of XML Schema to formalize interfaces for RESTful services is not universally accepted as part of the REST framework.[4] If you plan to use REST for your SOA applications, however, I strongly encourage you to provide XML Schema to define the message structure interface for each service.

This section gave you a quick introduction to how EIS records can be represented as XML documents. In the next section, we begin to look at the basics of messaging—sending XML over the Hypertext Transfer Protocol (HTTP).

3.3   REST Clients with and without JWS

A basic capability you often need when implementing an SOA Web service is easily downloading and uploading XML files from/to an HTTP server. For example, suppose that the OMS runs a nightly batch job and writes all new and changed orders from the previous day to a set of XML documents that can be accessed using a Web service named `NewOrders`. The CSS can then, each morning, retrieve those files and update its Customer History. This is a simple, but common and highly practical, form of SOA-style loosely coupled integration.

The next few sections focus on uploading/downloading XML documents with bare-bones RESTful Web Services. I show how to write clients for RESTful services with and without JWS. This material may seem very basic to advanced Java programmers, but it is always good to review the basics before diving into a complex subject like SOA with Java Web Services.

It is a common misconception that implementing Web Services with Java requires lots of heavy machinery like JAX-WS. This is not the case, as even J2SE 1.4 provides powerful tools for HTTP communication and XML processing that enable you to build and consume RESTful Web services. JAX-WS and the other JWS tools provide many advantages, of course, which we discuss later in this section and throughout the rest of this book.

Doing REST without JWS gives you a hands-on appreciation for what HTTP can and cannot do. It quickly becomes clear that, although it is easy to do simple things without the JWS machinery, as you get more ambitious, you start to need some more powerful tools to handle invocation, serialization, and the other components of an SOA Web Services infrastructure.

Since this is a book about Java, I start with the assumption that the EISs have Java APIs for accessing the needed records. The challenge addressed

---

4. Perhaps this is because such interface definitions complicate the REST model, and REST proponents like to position it as simpler than SOAP.

in the next few sections is to deploy a Java API as a Web service or to invoke a Web service using Java.

3.3.1 Getting EIS Records from a REST Service without Using JWS

This section briefly examines how to get an XML document from a RESTful Web service. In this example, the Web service is accessed with an HTTP GET request. The client application needs to issue the HTTP GET, and process the HTTP response stream that contains the XML document. Instead of using the JWS APIs (e.g., JAX-WS), I simply use the `javax.net.HttpURLConnection` class to handle most of the work related to generating the HTTP GET and processing the response.

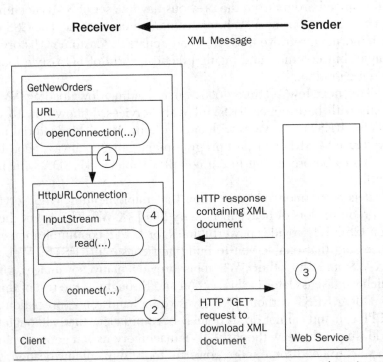

Figure 3–3 The client uses the `HttpURLConnection` class to make an HTTP GET request and receive an HTTP response.

Figure 3–3 illustrates the XML transfer process from the client's side. Note that the client is implemented as the class `GetNewOrders` and that it uses instances of the classes `URL` and `HttpURLConnection`. The following steps show how these classes work together to implement the XML document download protocol.

1. The client uses the `URL.openConnection()` method to create an instance of `HttpURLConnection` representing a connection to the Web service's `URL`.
2. `HttpURLConnection.connect()` sends the HTTP GET request that has been configured using the Web service's URL.
3. The Web service processes the request and writes the appropriate XML document to the HTTP response stream.
4. The `HttpURLConnection`'s `InputStream` is used to read the HTTP response's XML document.

In the implementation of this example, the client simply writes the XML document to the console. You will see it print out on your console when you run it (instructions follow). In a real SOA-style loosely coupled application, the document might be parsed, transformed, and sent to another component of the distributed application. An example of such processing is provided in Section 3.4.

Example 3–5 shows the client-side code for issuing the HTTP GET request and receiving the XML document via the HTTP response. Notice that the `string` used to construct the URL instance is passed to the client as `args[0]`. The `HttpULRConnection`—con—doesn't send the HTTP request until its `connect()` method gets invoked. Before this happens, the `setRequestMethod()` is invoked to specify that a GET request should be sent.

Example 3–5 Implementing a Java Client to Download an XML Document from a RESTful Web Service

```
27    public static void main(String[] args) throws Exception {
28
29      if (args.length != 1) {
30        System.err.println
31        ("Usage: java GetNewOrders <Web Service URL>");
32        System.exit(1);
33      }
34      // Create the HTTP connection to the URL
35      URL url = new URL(args[0]);
36      HttpURLConnection con =
37        (HttpURLConnection) url.openConnection();
38      con.setRequestMethod("GET");
39      con.connect();
```

```
40        // write the XML from the input stream to standard out
41        InputStream in = con.getInputStream();
42        byte[] b = new byte[1024];   // 1K buffer
43        int result = in.read(b);
44        while (result != -1) {
45          System.out.write(b,0,result);
46          result =in.read(b);
47        }
48        in.close();
49        con.disconnect();
50      }
```

book-code/chap03/rest-get/client-http/src/java/samples/GetNewOrders.java

To run this example, do the following:

1. Start GlassFish (if it is not already running).
2. Go to <book-code>/chap03/rest-get/endpoint-servlet.
3. To build and deploy the Web service enter:

       mvn install [5]

   ... and when that command finishes, enter:

       ant deploy

4. Go to <book-code>/chap03/rest-get/client-http.
5. To run the client enter:

       mvn install

6. To undeploy the Web service, go back to <book-code>/chap03/rest-get/endpoint-servlet and enter:

       ant undeploy

In this example, the HttpURLConnection class does all the work. It sends the HTTP GET request to the Web service URL[6] and provides access to the response as an InputStream. Now, let's look at how this is done using JWS.

---

5. mvn is the command to run Maven, the build tool used throughout this book. See Appendix B, Software Configuration Guide, for details about installing and running the examples in this book.

6. In this example, the URL where the RESTful service deployed is http://localhost:8080/rest-get-servlet/NewOrders (assuming your Java EE Web container is running on localhost:8080). You can always see what parameters are used to invoke code in the examples by examining the build.xml file from the directory where you are running the example.

3.3.2 Getting EIS Records from a REST Service with JWS

When using the JAX-WS 2.0 API to create a client that consumes a REST-ful Web service, the `javax.xml.ws.Dispatch<T>`[7] interface does most of the work—performing a role similar to `HttpURLConnection`.

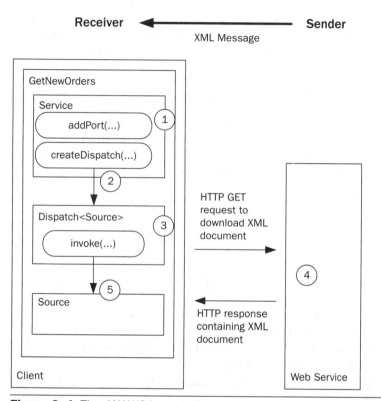

Figure 3–4 The JAX-WS-based client uses an instance of `Dispatch<Source>` to make an HTTP GET request and receive an HTTP response.

Figure 3–4 shows how the JAX-WS-based client works. This time, the class `GetNewOrders` is implemented using the `javax.ws.xml.Service` class. `Service` is an abstraction that provides a client interface to a Web service. First introduced in JAX-RPC 1.0, `Service` is designed to represent a WSDL defined service. Since RESTful services do not have WSDL

---

7. A detailed discussion of the `javax.xml.ws.Dispatch<T>` interface is provided in Chapter 6, Section 6.2, where the JAX-WS client API is explained in depth.

representations, the `Service` API is a little awkward for our purposes here (as you can see in the discussion of the code). However, that is how the JAX-WS API is designed.

In this example, `Service` is used to create an instance of `javax.xml.ws.Dispatch<Source>`, which enables XML message-level interaction with the target Web service. `Dispatch` is the low-level JAX-WS 2.0 API that requires clients to construct messages by working directly with the XML, rather than with a higher-level binding such as JAXB 2.0 schema-derived program elements. For many REST proponents, however, this is exactly the programming paradigm they want—direct access to the XML request and response messages.

The following steps trace the execution of the JAX-WS version of the `GetNewOrders` client illustrated in Figure 3–4.

1. The client uses the `Service.addPort()` method to create a port within the `Service` instance that can be used to access the RESTful Web service.
2. Next, the `Service.createDispatch()` method is invoked to create an instance of `Dispatch<Source>`—a `Dispatch` instance that enables you to work with XML request/response messages as instances of `javax.xml.transform.Source`.
3. The `Dispatch.invoke()` method then packages the XML request—per the JAX-WS 2.0 HTTP Binding—and sends it to the RESTful service. The `invoke()` method waits for the response before returning.
4. The service processes the HTTP GET and sends an HTTP response that includes the XML.
5. The `invoke()` method returns the response XML message as an instance of `Source`.

Example 3–6 shows the code used to implement the JAX-WS version of `GetNewOrders`. Browsing through this code, you can see some of the awkwardness that comes from applying the WSDL-oriented `Service` API in a REST context. First, notice that you have to create `QName` instances for the `Service` instance and the "port" that corresponds to the RESTful Web service. In a SOAP scenario, these qualified names would correspond to the WSDL definitions for the `wsdl:service` and `wsdl:port`. Since there is no WSDL when invoking a RESTful service, these `QName` instances are gratuitous in this example. They are required by the API, but not used to invoke the RESTful service.

Example 3–6 The `GetNewOrders` Client As Implemented with JAX-WS

```
35    public static void main(String[] args) throws Exception {
36      if (args.length != 1) {
37        System.err.println
38        ("Usage: java GetNewOrders <Web Service URL>");
39        System.exit(1);
40      }
41      QName svcQName = new QName("http://sample", "svc");
42      QName portQName = new QName("http://sample", "port");
43      Service svc = Service.create(svcQName);
44      svc.addPort(portQName, HTTPBinding.HTTP_BINDING, args[0]);
45      Dispatch<Source> dis =
46        svc.createDispatch(portQName, Source.class, Service.Mode.PAYLOAD);
47      Map<String, Object> requestContext = dis.getRequestContext();
48      requestContext.put(MessageContext.HTTP_REQUEST_METHOD, "GET");
49      Source result = dis.invoke(null);
50      try {
51        TransformerFactory.newInstance().newTransformer()
52        .transform(result, new StreamResult(System.out));
53      } catch (Exception e) {
54        throw new IOException(e.getMessage());
55      }
56    }
```

book-code/chap03/rest-get/client-jaxws/src/java/samples/GetNewOrders.java

To run this example, do the following:

1. Start GlassFish (if it is not already running).
2. Go to <book-code>/chap03/rest-get/endpoint-servlet.
3. To build and deploy the Web service enter:

   mvn install

   ... and when that command finishes, then enter:

   ant deploy

4. Go to <book-code>/chap03/rest-get/client-jaxws.
5. To run the client enter:

   mvn install

6. To undeploy the Web service, go back to <book-code>/chap03/rest-get/endpoint-servlet and enter:

   ant undeploy

Looking at the code in Example 3–6, you can also see that the `addPort()` method takes a URI parameter that defines the transport binding. The default is SOAP over HTTP, but in this case, the `HTTPBinding.HTTP_BINDING` URI is used to specify the JAX-WS 2.0 HTTP Binding. The final parameter passed to the `addPort()` method is the URL of the RESTful Web service—in this case, `args[0]`.

Once the port for the RESTful service has been added by the `addPort()` method, it can be used to create an instance of `Dispatch<Source>`. The type parameter—in this case, `Source`—is passed as a parameter to the `createDispatch()` method. The type of payload is specified as well. Here, I have specified `Service.Mode.PAYLOAD` (as opposed to `Service.Mode.MESSAGE`). When working with SOAP, the MESSAGE mode indicates that you want to work with the entire SOAP envelope as opposed to just the SOAP body (or payload). In the REST scenario, there is no envelope, so PAYLOAD is the option that makes sense.

Besides `Source`, the other valid type parameters for `Dispatch` are `JAXB` objects, `java.xml.soap.SOAPMessage`, and `javax.activation.DataSource`. In Chapter 6,[8] I look at examples using `JAXB` and `SOAPMessage`. `DataSource` enables clients to work with MIME-typed messages—a scenario I don't cover in this book.

How does this implementation compare with the `HttpURLConnection` version illustrated in Example 3–5? Table 3–2 illustrates some similarities and differences.

Table 3–2 `HttpURLConnection` versus JAX-WS

	HttpURLConnection Version	**JAX-WS Version**
Representation of the RESTful Web service	`java.net.URL`	`javax.xml.ws.Service`
Invocation Object	`java.net.HttpURLConnection`	`javax.xml.ws.Dispatch`
Message Form	`java.io.InputStream`	`javax.xml.transform.Source`

As you can see, the JAX-WS version gives us a much richer interface, although in a simple REST scenario like this, it is not always that useful. A URL is an adequate representation of a RESTful service since there is no

<hr>

8. Chapter 6 is a detailed overview of the JAX-WS client-side API.

associated WSDL to provide further definition anyway. About the only other information that is needed is whether to use HTTP POST or HTTP GET. As we have seen, `Service` is really designed to be a Java representation of WSDL, so it's not particularly helpful here.

The `Dispatch` interface, on the other hand, is better suited for working with XML request/response than `HttpURLConnection`. First, its `invoke()` method captures the request/response semantics of the HTTP Binding better than the `HttpURLConnection.connect()` method. Second, rather than reading and writing streams, the `Dispatch` interface enables us to work directly with XML representations such as `Source`. This is much more natural, as we will see when we start linking RESTful services together and using XSLT for data transformation (Section 3.4).

Having looked at clients that get XML from a RESTful Web service, the next two sections show how to send XML to such a service. These sections also demonstrate how to pass parameters to the RESTful service as part of the URL.

3.3.3 Sending EIS Records to a REST Service without Using JWS

In Section 3.3.1, I used `HttpURLConnection` to implement a "pull" architecture for XML document messaging—in other words, the document is "pulled" by the client from the Web service. In a "pull" architecture, the receiver of the XML document initiates the transfer. In the code example provided, we used the HTTP GET method to serve as the request mechanism.

Sending XML to a RESTful Web service is not much different from getting XML. The main differences for the "push" architecture are that the sender initiates the transfer and the HTTP POST method is used. This architecture is used, for example, when the OMS wants to upload all new and changed orders to the CSS on a regular basis. To implement such an upload process, the CSS would need to provide a Web service where the OMS could post XML documents.

In this example, I implement a "push" architecture using `HttpURLConnection`.

Figure 3–5 illustrates push messaging. As you can see, it is similar to the previous example, except that the client is now the sender of messages and the Web service is the receiver. The following steps are illustrated in the figure:

1. The client uses the `URL.openConnection()` method to create an instance of `HttpURLConnection` representing a connection to the

RESTful Web service's URL. In this example, the URL has a parameter: SourceSystem=OMS. This parameter indicates that the XML document being sent comes from the "OMS" system.

2. HttpURLConnection.connect() begins the HTTP POST request to the Web service's URL.

3. The client writes the XML document to the HTTP request stream, essentially appending it to the POST request that has been started.

4. The RESTful service processes the HTTP POST.

5. The response—a simple "200 OK"—is sent back to the client indicating that the document has been received.

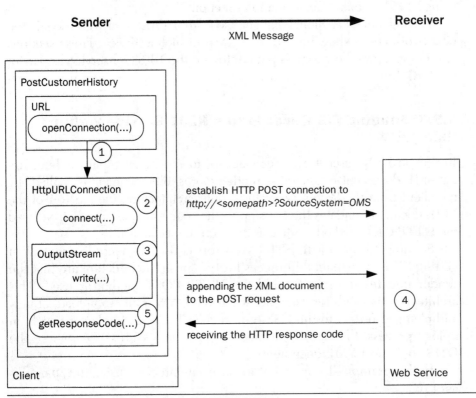

Figure 3–5 Push messaging with HTTP POST.

Example 3–7 shows the client-side code for implementing the HTTP POST with an HttpULRConnection. Notice that we use setRequest-Method("POST") to configure the HTTP request as a POST. After that, the connect() method initiates the HTTP request, and the remaining code writes the XML document (specified by the filename args[0]) to the output stream.

Example 3–7 Client Uses POST to Upload an XML Document to the Web Service

```
28   public static void main(String[] args) throws Exception {
29     if (args.length != 2) {
30       System.err.println
31         ("Usage: java PostCustomerHistory <XML file name> "
32         + "<Web Service URL>");
33       System.exit(1);
34     }
35     FileInputStream in = new FileInputStream(args[0]);
36     URL url = new URL(args[1]);
37     HttpURLConnection con =
38       (HttpURLConnection) url.openConnection();
39     con.setDoOutput(true);
40     con.setRequestMethod("POST");
41     con.connect();
42     OutputStream out = con.getOutputStream();
43     // write the XML doc from file to the HTTP connection
44     byte[] b = new byte[1024];   // 1K buffer
45     int result = in.read(b);
46     while (result != -1) {
47       out.write(b,0,result);
48       result = in.read(b);
49     }
50     out.close();
51     in.close();
52     // write HTTP response to console
53     System.out.println(con.getResponseCode() +
54                        " " + con.getResponseMessage());
55   }
```

book-code/chap03/rest-post/client-http/src/java/samples/
PostCustomerHistory.java

To run this example, do the following:

1. Start GlassFish (if it is not already running).
2. Go to <book-code>/chap03/rest-post/endpoint-servlet.
3. To build and deploy the Web service enter:

```
mvn install
```

... and when that command finishes, then enter:

```
ant deploy
```

4. Go to `<book-code>/chap03/rest-post/client-http`.

5. To run the client enter:

```
mvn install
```

6. To undeploy the Web service, go back to `<book-code>/chap03/`
`rest-post/endpoint-servlet` and enter:

```
ant undeploy
```

What you can't see here is the form of the URL that is passed in as
`args[1]`. To see the URL being used, you can look at the `<book-code>/`
chap03/rest-post/endpoint-servlet/build.xml file containing the goal used to
invoke this service. You will see that the URL has the form:

```
http://<somepath>?SourceSystem=OMS
```

The parameter `SourceSystem` specifies where the XML document (i.e.,
the customer history entry) is coming from. In this example, the only value for
`SourceSystem` that the RESTful Web service accepts is "OMS." Try changing
the URL inside build.xml to specify `SourceSystem=XYZ` and see what happens. You will get an error message indicating the source is not supported yet.

The URL parameter `SourceSystem` is a parameter of the RESTful Web
service. That is one way parameters are passed to RESTful services. Chapter
4 discusses how SOAP services get parameters—they are embedded in the
SOAP message itself. You can also design a RESTful service that receives
parameters in the XML document, but this is kind of like reinventing SOAP.

The REST approach of using URL parameter passing is simple, but it
also has drawbacks. The primary drawback is that there is no interface
description of a RESTful service, so there is no way to determine—without
some other form of documentation—what URL parameters are required.
Some REST purists handle that objection by pointing out that URL parameters are not needed for proper REST systems where resources are uniquely
defined by URIs. In this example, the URL could instead have the form:

```
http://<somepath>/OMS
```

In this case, the convention is that you post customer histories from the
OMS to the `.../OMS` URI, and customer histories from the XYZ system to
the `.../XYZ` URI, and so on.

Other REST advocates, who are slightly less purist, argue that URL
parameters are fine as long as they are *nouns* rather than *verbs*. An example
of a verb parameter would be something like:

```
http://<somepath>/ShoppingCart?action=clear
```

In this case, the `action` parameter specifies an operation to be carried out on the resource—clearing the shopping cart. Specifying verbs like this is a big REST no-no, but you can still find lots of so-called RESTful services out there that are implemented this way.

My perspective on this debate is that, even if we follow the REST purists and do away with URL parameters, we have just changed the syntax, not the semantics. The underlying semantics (and therefore the implementation) defines a resource (Customer History System) that can receive updates from various sources (e.g., OMS, XYZ), and needs to know what the source is.

If you implement that semantics by embedding parameters in the URL path—rather than by using URL parameters—you have only made the system's interface even harder to understand. For example, when you use the URL parameter form (e.g., `http://<somepath>?SourceSystem=OMS`), at least you can tell that the OMS is a parameter designating the source system. However, when you use the normalized version without parameters (e.g., `http://<somepath>/OMS`), you don't get any clues as to the meaning of the "OMS."

But, in either case, REST still provides you with no way to document your interface—in other words, no WSDL. In my opinion, this is the primary reason why SOAP is more appropriate than REST for SOA-style systems integration. Doing systems integration is all about defining the interfaces between systems. If you don't have a language in which to express the interfaces (i.e., no WSDL), it is very hard to be rigorous about defining the interfaces. As indicated in Section 3.2.1, you can try to work around this REST limitation by using XML Schema to define the interface. That approach works, but in addition to not being standard practice, it has other limitations. For example, in the case just discussed, the parameter (`SourceSystem=OMS`) is not part of the XML message received by the RESTful service. So, to define an interface that specifies this parameter, you would have to refactor the RESTful service to accept a parameter inside the XML message that indicates the source system. The basic problem here is that URL parameters, since they are not part of the XML message, cannot be specified in an XML Schema-based interface definition.

This example has shown how to develop an `HttpURLConnection`-based client for sending XML documents to a RESTful service that requires URL parameters. The next section shows you how to do the same thing using JAX-WS 2.0.

3.3.4 Sending EIS Records to a REST Service with JWS

As in Section 3.3.2, the client in this section uses `javax.xml.ws.Service` and `javax.xml.ws.Dispatch` rather than `java.net.URL` and `HttpURLConnection`. The major difference from that section is that here, the XML document is being pushed to the service. To do that, the XML document needs to be stored as an instance of a Java class that can be used by the `Dispatch<Source>` instance. In this case, the type parameter is `Source`, so a `Source` instance must be created from the XML document that is to be sent to the RESTful service.

This example also illustrates how to get HTTP-related information from the `Dispatch` object by accessing its response context. As demonstrated here, a bit more work is needed to get the HTTP status code than with the simple `HttpURLConnection.getResponseCode()` method used in the previous example.

Figure 3–6 illustrates push messaging as implemented with JAX-WS 2.0. There is a little more detail here than shown in the `HttpURLConnection` example from Figure 3–5. The steps are as follows:

1. The client uses the `Service.addPort()` method to create a port within the `Service` instance that can be used to access the RESTful Web service.

2. Next, the `Service.createDispatch()` method is invoked to create an instance of `Dispatch<Source>`—a `Dispatch` instance that enables you to work with XML request/response messages as instances of `javax.xml.transform.Source`.

3. The XML file to be posted to the RESTful service is wrapped in an instance of `javax.xml.transform.stream.StreamSource`. `StreamSource` implements the `Source` type parameter required by `Dispatch<Source>`.

4. The `Dispatch.invoke()` method then packages the XML document into an HTTP POST request—per the JAX-WS 2.0 HTTP Binding—and sends it to the RESTful service. The `invoke()` method waits for the response before returning.

5. The service processes the HTTP POST and sends an HTTP response that includes an HTTP response code.

6. Because the HTTP response code is part of the HTTP message (transport level), and not part of the XML payload, to examine it the client invokes `Dispatch.getResponseContext()` to get the HTTP context for the response.

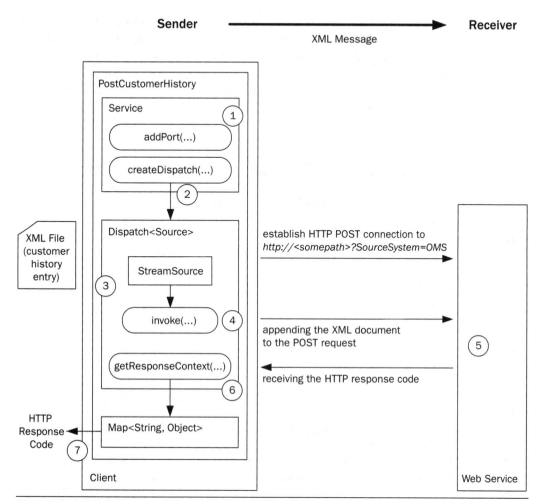

Figure 3–6 Push messaging with HTTP POST and JAX-WS 2.0.

7. The HTTP context is represented as a `Map<String, Object>` instance. This map provides access to the HTTP headers and other information that is outside the XML payload. Here, it is used to access the HTTP response code (i.e., 200 for "OK," 500 for "Server Failure," etc.).

Example 3–8 shows the implementation of `PostCustomerHistory` using JAX-WS. It is similar to Example 3–6, and you should review the discussion of REST and JAX-WS given there.

The main difference here from the `HttpURLConnection` version
(Example 3–7) is that the `Dispach.invoke()` method is invoked with a
`StreamSource` parameter that is constructed from the XML file being
posted to the RESTful Web service. Notice that there is no need to write
the XML out to a stream as in the `HttpURLConnection` example. The `Dis-
patch<Source>` instance lets you deal with the XML request and response
payloads as instances of `Source`.

Example 3–8 The `PostCustomerHistory` Client as Implemented with JAX-WS

```
33    public static void main(String[] args) throws Exception {
34      if (args.length != 2) {
35        System.err.println
36          ("Usage: java XMLUploadSender <XML file name> "
37          + "<Web Service URL>");
38        System.exit(1);
39      }
40      QName svcQName = new QName("http://sample", "svc");
41      QName portQName = new QName("http://sample", "port");
42      Service svc = Service.create(svcQName);
43      svc.addPort(portQName, HTTPBinding.HTTP_BINDING, args[1]);
44      Dispatch<Source> dis =
45            svc.createDispatch(portQName, Source.class, Service.Mode.PAYLOAD);
46      dis.invoke(new StreamSource(new File(args[0])));
47      Map<String, Object> respContext = dis.getResponseContext();
48      Integer respCode =
49        (Integer) respContext.get(MessageContext.HTTP_RESPONSE_CODE);
50      System.out.println("HTTP Response Code: "+respCode);
51    }
```

book-code/chap03/rest-post/client-jaxws/src/java/samples/PostCustomerHistory.java

To run this example, do the following. After the example is run, the
results (customer history entries) are written by the application to a temporary file of the form `${user.home}/tmp/soabook*.xml`. So, you can look to
your `${user.home}/tmp` directory to verify that the example ran properly.

1. Start GlassFish (if it is not already running).
2. Go to `<book-code>/chap03/rest-post/endpoint-servlet`.
3. To build and deploy the Web service enter:

```
mvn install
```

... and when that command finishes, then enter:

```
ant deploy
```

4. Go to `<book-code>/chap03/rest-post/client-jaxws`.

5. To run the client enter:

```
mvn install
```

6. To undeploy the Web service, go back to `<book-code>/chap03/`
`rest-post/endpoint-servlet` and enter:

```
ant undeploy
```

As you can see from this example, getting the HTTP response code from the `Dispatch` instance is a little awkward. First, you need to request the response context. That is because `Dispatch` is not an HTTP-specific interface. So, it doesn't make sense for `Dispatch` to have a convenience method like `HttpURLConnection.getResponseCode()`. The JAX-WS Expert Group envisions scenarios where `Dispatch` is used with non-HTTP bindings. So, the way it works is that the `Dispatch.getResponseContext()` method provides an instance of `Map<String, Object>` that contains context information about the underlying protocol.

The `getResponseContext` method is inherited from the `javax.xml.ws.BindingProvider` interface (of which `Dispatch` is a sub-interface). `BindingProvider` provides a representation of the underlying protocol binding (e.g., XML/HTTP or SOAP/HTTP) being used for Web Services communication. When a `BindingProvider` does a request/response, the request and response messages are embedded in a context that is binding-specific. The message and its context move through a chain of handlers during the invocation process. All this is beyond the scope of our simple discussion here, but it is useful background (see Chapter 6 for a detailed discussion of JAX-WS client-side handlers). The response context represents the final state of the message context after the invocation is completed. So, access to the response context is provided through the JAX-WS handler framework APIs.

The way this handler framework manifests itself here is that the keys that are used to look up information in the response context are provided by `javax.ws.handler.MessageContext`. As shown in the code, `Message-Context.HTTP_RESPONSE_CODE` is the key used to access the HTTP response code.

In the `HttpURLConnection` case, there is no distinction between the message and its context. One works directly with the HTTP requests and responses. So, the processing model is simpler. However, the drawback is that you have to create your own code to extract the XML messaging from the HTTP communications. In these simple examples, that doesn't seem like a big deal. The only manifestation of that extraction process so far has been reading and writing XML to the HTTP input and output streams. However, as the complexity of the processing increases, dealing with messages rather than streams becomes a valuable additional layer of abstraction. For example, when you want to introduce handlers to do Java/XML binding or reliable messaging, you don't want to have to create your own handler framework for pre- and post-processing of the HTTP streams.

That wraps up our basic discussion about how to invoke RESTful Web services. Next, the discussion turns to XSLT—the XML data transformation language—and how it can be used to implement basic SOA-style loosely coupled integration of multiple Web services.

3.4   SOA-Style Integration Using XSLT and JAXP for Data Transformation

Some readers may be wondering why a book about SOA with Java Web Services would include a section on XSLT. The reason is that XLST provides a powerful and efficient data transformation engine that can be used to translate messages from one format to another. When building SOA applications, developers commonly encounter problems where they need to integrate systems that require the same message type (e.g., purchase order) in different formats. XSLT provides a standard mechanism for translating between message formats when messages are represented as XML documents.

The perceding section introduced two Web services:

- The OMS "NewOrders" Web service that provides access to the new orders that have come in during the past day
- The CSS "CustomerHistory" Web service that receives updates to the customer history database

This section shows how to build a simple SOA application that links these two Web services together. I am going to walk through an example that gets the new orders, transforms them into customer history entries, and posts those entries to the CSS. This example introduces data transformation using XSLT—a cornerstone of SOA-style loosely coupled integration.

3.4.1 How and Why to Use XSLT for Data Transformation

A core component of any SOA system is its capability to transform data from one format to another. Often referred to as *data transformation*, this capability is most naturally addressed within the Web Services context using eXtensible Stylesheet Language Transformations (XSLT). We assume the reader is familiar with the basics of XSLT. Our focus is on the application of XSLT to SOA-style loosely coupled integration. To brush up on XSLT, see the W3C's Web site at www.w3.org/Style/XSL/. In addition to the specification (the examples in this book use Version 1.0—see [XSLT 1.0]), the site has links to a variety of helpful tutorials. Another good refresher can be found in Sun's Java/XML Tutorial (http://java.sun.com/webservices/jaxp/dist/1.1/docs/tutorial/xslt/index.html). Sun's tutorial is especially useful because it discusses the JAXP APIs along with XSLT.

Because XSLT is a sophisticated data transformation language, it can take a long time to learn in depth. Fortunately, the data transformations required by most SOA applications need to use only a small part of the XSLT language that does not take a long time to learn. If you are struggling to understand this section of the book, you should have no trouble once you review the Sun tutorial. There is no need to study XSLT in great depth at this point!

XSLT makes sense as the transformation tool of choice within SOA integration frameworks, because it is a universally accepted standard and the transformation engines that interpret XSLT to perform data transformations keep getting better and faster. Although it may be expedient to write some quick and dirty code to perform a simple transformation here and there, it does not make sense to leave the data transformation language and processing unstandardized when developing a framework for SOA integration that will be used across an organization.

To demonstrate how XSLT can be used for data transformation, we consider a scenario where the new orders, accessed from the OMS, are used to create customer history records that update the CSS customer history database. The business reason for doing this is so that users of the CSS have fast access to an up-to-date record of the transactions a customer has made with the company. Such information needs to be available nearly instantly when handling customer care telephone calls, for example. If the customer care representative needs to examine the details of any transaction in the customer history, the information stored there from the OMS provides important keys, such as `OrderKey` and `ITM_NUMBER`, that will enable detailed information to be retrieved from the OMS rapidly.

Figure 3–7 illustrates the data mapping that transforms an OMS order record into a CSS customer history record. The order record and customer history record are introduced in Figure 3–1 and Figure 3–2, respectively.

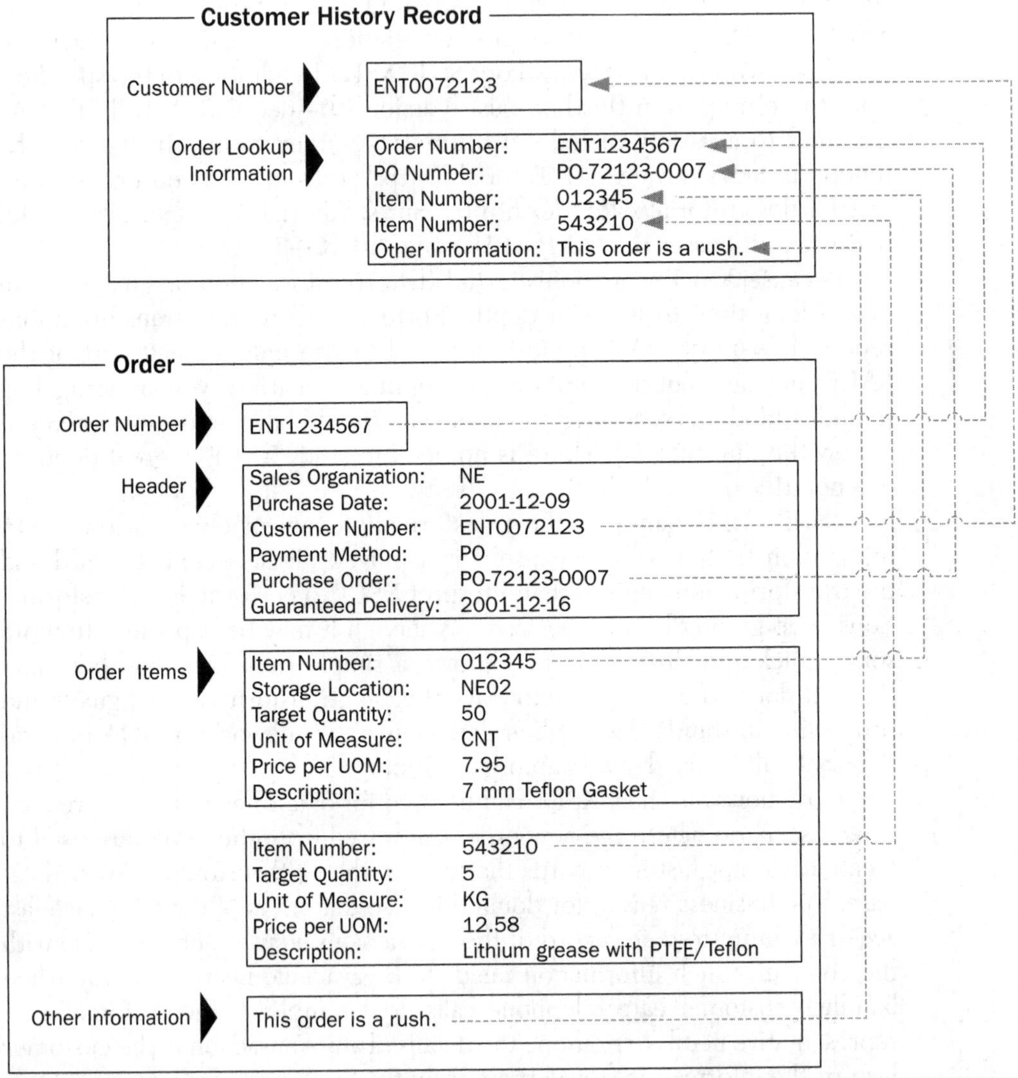

Figure 3–7 A data mapping for the transformation from a sales order to a customer history record.

As illustrated in Figure 3–7, the Customer Number in the Order becomes a foreign key in the Customer History Record, which links it back to other information about the customer. Order Number, PO Number, and Item Number are mapped over because having them in the CSS will enable additional SOA components to be built that provide quick lookups from a customer history record to detailed order, purchase order, and item information in the OMS and other systems. Note that there may be multiple instances of an item number in a customer history record, if an order includes more than one type of item.

The following examples review the XSLT for transforming a set of OMS orders into a set of CSS customer history entries. The set of orders is formatted as an `oms:Orders` element in the schema `http://soabook.com/example/oms/orders.xsd` (Example 3–2). The set of customer histories is formatted as a `css:CustomerHistoryEntries` element in the schema `http://soabook.com/example/css/custhistentries.xsd` (Example 3–4). The XSL transformation from an order to a customer history is represented pictorially in Figure 3–7.

The XSLT language is declarative. It defines transformations of source documents to target documents. An XSL transformation comprises a set of template rules—represented by instances of the `xsl:template` element—that are children of the root `xsl:stylesheet` element. Hence, an XSLT document is often referred to as a stylesheet. The template elements in the stylesheet define the structure of the target document that is created from the source.

XSLT uses the XPath language (see [XPath]) to identify chunks of data in the source document (e.g., `OrderKey`). Together with the template rules, the XPath expressions determine where to place the chunks of data in the target document.

Example 3–9 illustrates a stylesheet for transforming orders to customer histories. This discussion breaks the stylesheet into bite-size chunks. The example shows the beginning of the XSLT document, including the `xsl:stylesheet` namespace declarations and `xsl:output` element.

Example 3–9 XSLT for Customer History—Namespaces and Output Elements

```
4  <xsl:stylesheet version="1.0"
5    xmlns:xsl="http://www.w3.org/1999/XSL/Transform"
6    xmlns:oms="http://www.example.com/oms">
7    <xsl:output method="xml" version="1.0" encoding="UTF-8"/>
```

book-code/chap03/xslt/etc/order_to_history.xslt

As you can see, the prefix oms is used to denote the Order Management System namespace: http://www.example.com/oms. The xsl:output element controls the format of the stylesheet output. The attribute method="xml" indicates that the result should be output as XML. Note that this stylesheet does not specify that the output should be indented (i.e., it does not include the attribute indent="yes"). You should avoid specifying visual formatting such as indentation in the base-level transformation. I recommend using a separate XSLT stylesheet to format XML for human-readable output when necessary. Note that the encoding is specified (encoding="UTF-8"), as it is throughout this book, as UTF-8.

The next portion of the XSLT, shown in Example 3–10, provides the rules for processing the oms:Orders element.

Example 3–10 XSLT for Customer History—Creating the Customer History Entry

```
11    <xsl:template match="oms:Orders">
12      <CustomerHistoryEntries xmlns="http://www.example.com/css"
13        xmlns:xsi="http://www.w3.org/2001/XMLSchema-instance"
14        xsi:schemaLocation="http://www.example.com/css
15        http://soabook.com/example/css/custhistentries.xsd">
16        <xsl:apply-templates/>
17      </CustomerHistoryEntries>
18    </xsl:template>
19    <xsl:template match="oms:Order">
20      <CustomerHistoryEntry xmlns="http://www.example.com/css">
21        <CustomerNumber>
22          <xsl:apply-templates select="./oms:OrderHeader/oms:CUST_NO"/>
23        </CustomerNumber>
24        <OrderLookupInfo>
25          <xsl:apply-templates select="./oms:OrderKey"/>
26          <xsl:apply-templates
27            select="./oms:OrderHeader/oms:PURCH_ORD_NO"/>
28          <xsl:apply-templates
29            select="./oms:OrderItems/oms:item/oms:ITM_NUMBER"/>
30          <xsl:apply-templates select="./oms:OrderText"/>
31        </OrderLookupInfo>
32      </CustomerHistoryEntry>
33    </xsl:template>
```

book-code/chap03/xslt/etc/order_to_history.xslt

At the beginning of the block, you see a template being defined to match the pattern "oms:Orders"—in other words, it matches the `oms:Orders` element in the source document. Inside this template, you see the definition of a `CustomerHistoryEntries` element. The contents appearing inside the template form the output for the target document. So, this template provides the rules for transforming an `oms:Orders` element into a `css:CustomerHistoryEntries` element.

Now, notice that this template has the instruction `<xsl:apply-templates/>` inside it. Inside a template, XML in the `xsl` namespace is interpreted as instructions and not as content to be output to the target document. This particular instruction tells the XSLT processor to apply the other templates in the stylesheet to the children of the `oms:Orders` node and insert the results into the target document. So, that is how the `css:CustomerHistoryEntries` element gets constructed in the target document. Its opening and closing tags are specified in this template. Its children are defined by the results of the `<xsl:apply-templates>` instruction and are inserted between the opening and closing tags.

Continuing to examine Example 3–10, you can see that the bottom half defines another template matching the `oms:Order` element. So, if any children of `oms:Orders` are instances of `oms:Order`, these children will be processed by this template and the results will be inserted the `CustomerHistoryEntries` tags. Looking inside this template for `oms:Order`, you can see that it contains the contents for an element, `CustomerHistoryEntry`, and the two top-level elements `CustomerNumber` and `OrderLookupInfo`. Now, look inside the tags for `CustomerNumber` and you see another `xsl:apply-templates` instruction. However, this one has the attribute:

```
select="./oms:OrderHeader/oms:CUST_NO"
```

This template is providing the instructions for filling in the contents of the `CustomerNumber` element. And the XPath expression `./oms:OrderHeader/oms:CUST_NO` restricts the children of `oms:Order` that this template is applied to. That XPath expression tells the XSLT processor to only apply templates to `oms:CUST_NO` elements that are children of `oms:OrderHeader`. In this manner, the XPath expression reaches into the source document, pulls out the `oms:CUST_NO` element, processes it, and inserts the results inside the `CustomerNumber` tags. That is how `oms:CUST_NO` gets transformed into `css:CustomerNumber` and inserted into the right place in the target document.

Looking at some of the other `xsl:apply-templates` instructions occurring in Example 3–10, you can see that the `<OrderLookupInfo>` element is populated from the source elements specified by the XPath expressions: `./oms:OrderKey`, `./oms:OrderHeader/PURCH_ORD_NO`, `./oms:OrderItems/item/ITM_NUMBER`, and `./oms:OrderText`. Notice that these XPath expressions correspond to the dotted line mappings in Figure 3–7.

Continuing to review this stylesheet, now have a look at Example 3–11, which shows the templates that match these XPath expressions.

Example 3–11 XSLT for Customer History—Detail-Level Templates

```
37   <xsl:template match="oms:CUST_NO">
38     <xsl:value-of select="."/>
39   </xsl:template>
40   <xsl:template match="oms:OrderKey">
41     <OrderNumber xmlns="http://www.example.com/css">
42       <xsl:value-of select="."/>
43     </OrderNumber>
44   </xsl:template>
45   <xsl:template match="oms:PURCH_ORD_NO">
46     <PURCH_ORD_NO xmlns="http://www.example.com/css">
47       <xsl:value-of select="."/>
48     </PURCH_ORD_NO>
49   </xsl:template>
50   <xsl:template match="oms:ITM_NUMBER">
51     <ITM_NUMBER xmlns="http://www.example.com/css">
52       <xsl:value-of select="."/>
53     </ITM_NUMBER>
54   </xsl:template>
55   <xsl:template match="oms:OrderText">
56     <OrderText xmlns="http://www.example.com/css">
57       <xsl:value-of select="."/>
58     </OrderText>
59   </xsl:template>
```

book-code/chap03/xslt/etc/order_to_history.xslt

Here you can see, for example, that the template matching `oms:OrderKey` simply returns the value of that element (the instruction `<xsl:value-of select="."/>` returns the string value of the current node). The net result is that this `stylesheet` maps the value of oms:OrderKey to a subelement in the target document named OrderNumber that is a child of CustomerHistoryEntry.

Having walked through an example of an XSLT, the next section looks at how such transformations are applied using Java.

3.4.2 XSLT Processing Using JAXP

XSLT processing in Java is accomplished using the Java API of XML Processing (JAXP) [JSR 206]. Specifically, the JAXP javax.xml.transform.Transformer class can be used to convert a source document to a target document according to the rules specified in a stylesheet. JAXP provides the foundation from which all Java XML processing is built.

Figure 3–8 shows a simplified architecture diagram illustrating the role of the JAXP API. A variety of different types of Java applications can use the JAXP API, including servlets, JSPs, and EJBs. All of these use JAXP to access the various capabilities that are included in any JAXP implementation, such as a SAX parser, a DOM implementation, and an XSL processor that supports XSLT. The package javax.xml.parsers provides a common factory interface to access different implementations of SAX and DOM (e.g., Xerces) as well as XSLT (e.g., Xalan). The interfaces for SAX and DOM are found in the org.xml.sax and org.w3c.dom packages, respectively. The XSLT APIs are found in the javax.xml.transform packages.

As shown in Figure 3–8, JAXP isolates a Java application (e.g., client, servlets, JSP, EJB) from the implementation of the XSLT transformer, and the SAX and DOM parsers. JAXP defines factory classes that instantiate wrapper objects on the transformer and parser implementations. The transformer/parser implementation classes that are used at runtime are determined by system property and/or classpath settings.

JAXP is an important enabling standard making it feasible to use Java and Web Services for constructing SOA-style systems integration applications. Not only does it integrate the XML parsing and transformation standards with Java, but also it isolates the SOA application components from the SAX, DOM, and XSLT implementations. This is important, because as better and faster implementations come to market, SOA components will be able to take advantage of them to improve the performance without needing to be rewritten.

By using the JAXP architecture and XML for messaging, most of the data transformation work involved in integrating SOA components with Java boils down to writing XSLT. The example used to demonstrate this is illustrated in Figure 3–9. This application reads orders from an OMS Web service, transforms them into customer history updates, and writes these updates to a CSS Web service.

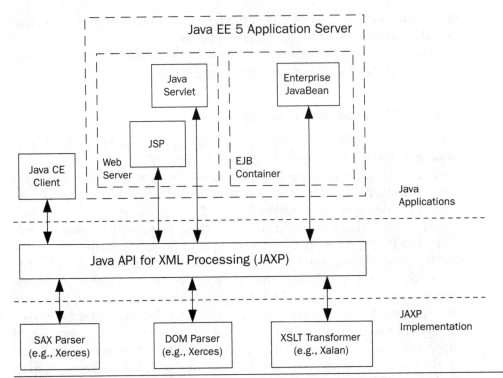

Figure 3–8 Architecture of the Java API for XML Processing (JAXP).

This example is constructed by tying together the examples from Sections 3.3.2 and 3.3.4 and using XSLT in the middle to transform the orders into customer histories. The steps in the process illustrated in Figure 3–9 are:

1. A `Service` instance is used to create two `Dispatch<Source>` instances—one to invoke the OMS Web service, and the other to invoke the CSS Web service.
2. The first `Dispatch<Source>` instance's `invoke` method is used to get the orders from the OMS Web service.
3. The orders (an XML document) are returned from `invoke()` as a `Source` instance.
4. The XSLT stylesheet file (`order_to_history.xslt`) is used, by a `TransformerFactory`, to construct a `Transformer` instance based on the stylesheet.
5. The `Transfomer.transform()` method is invoked to apply the stylesheet rules to the `Source` instance (`orders`). The resulting cus-

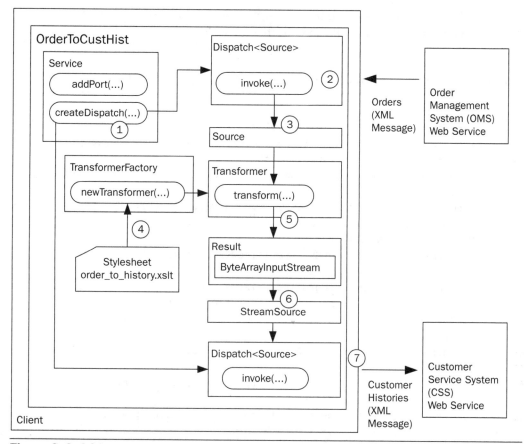

Figure 3–9 SOA-style integration with XSLT for data transformation.

tomer histories (an XML document—see Example 3–3) are written to a `Result` instance that has been created.

6. In this case, the `Result` instance is created as a wrapper from a `ByteArrayInputStream`. So, the XML is extracted from the underlying array and wrapped in a `StreamSource` object that can be consumed by the second `Dispatch` instance.

7. Lastly, as in Figure 3–6, the `Dispatch.invoke()` method is used to post the customer histories XML to the CSS Web service.

The code in Example 3–12 shows how the steps from Figure 3–9 are implemented. The Java used to create and invoke the `Dispatch` instances (to get and send the XML to the RESTful Web services) is the same as in

Example 3–6 and Example 3–8—please see those discussions for an overview of how `Dispatch` works in this scenario.

Example 3–12 Java Code That Applies the XSLT for Customer History

```
51    // Get the new orders
52    Service svc = Service.create(svcQName);
53    svc.addPort(orderQName, HTTPBinding.HTTP_BINDING, newOrdersUrl);
54    Dispatch<Source> getOrdersDispatch =
55      svc.createDispatch(orderQName, Source.class, Service.Mode.PAYLOAD);
56    Source newOrdersSource =
57      getOrdersDispatch.invoke(new StreamSource(new StringReader("<empty/>")));
58    // Instantiate a Transformer using our XSLT file
59    Transformer transformer =
60      TransformerFactory.newInstance().newTransformer
61      (new StreamSource(new File(xsltFile)));
62    // Transform the new orders into history entry files
63    ByteArrayOutputStream ba = new ByteArrayOutputStream();
64    transformer.transform(newOrdersSource, new StreamResult(ba));
65    // Update the customer histories
66    svc.addPort(histQName, HTTPBinding.HTTP_BINDING, addCustHistUrl);
67    Dispatch<Source> postCustomerHistoryDispatch =
68      svc.createDispatch(histQName, Source.class, Service.Mode.PAYLOAD);
69    postCustomerHistoryDispatch
70    .invoke(new StreamSource(new StringReader(ba.toString())));
```

book-code/chap03/xslt/src/java/samples/OrderToCustHist.java

To see how the XSLT is implemented, look to the middle of the example code where an instance of the default `TransformerFactory` is obtained using `TransformerFactory.newInstance()`. Using this factory, a `Transformer` is created by passing the XSLT file (the one discussed previously that implements the mapping illustrated in Figure 3–7) as a `StreamSource` to the `newTransformer()` method. The resulting `Transformer` then applies the XSLT to the `Source` instance obtained by invoking the `getOrdersDispatch` instance. As shown here, the second parameter used in the invocation of `transformer.transform()` is a `StreamResult` wrapping an underlying `ByteArrayOutputStream`. In this manner, the results of the XSL transformation are written to that byte array. The end of the example code shows how that byte array is wrapped inside a `StreamSource` that can be passed to the `postCustomerHistoryDispatch.invoke()` method to post the customer histories to the CSS Web service.

To run this example, do the following. After the example is run, the results (customer history entries) are written by the application to a temporary file of the form `${user.home}/tmp/soabook*.xml`. So, you can look to your `${user.home}/tmp` directory to verify that the example ran properly.

1. Start GlassFish (if it is not already running).
2. Go to `<book-code>/chap03/rest-post/endpoint-servlet`.
3. To build and deploy the Web service enter:

   ```
   mvn install
   ```

   ... and when that command finishes, then enter:

   ```
   ant deploy
   ```

4. Go to `<book-code>/chap03/rest-get/endpoint-servlet`.
5. To build and deploy the Web service enter:

   ```
   mvn install
   ```

   ... and when that command finishes, then enter:

   ```
   ant deploy
   ```

6. Go to `<book-code>/chap03/xslt`.
7. To run the client enter:

   ```
   mvn install
   ```

8. To undeploy the Web service, go back to `<book-code>/chap03/rest-get/endpoint-servlet` and enter:

   ```
   ant undeploy
   ```

9. Do the same in the directory `<book-code>/chap03/rest-post/endpoint-servlet`.

That concludes this brief introduction to data transformation using XSLT with JAXP. XML processing with JAXP is examined in more detail in Chapter 5 where data binding is introduced and JAXB is compared with SAX and DOM. The next two sections of this chapter look at how RESTful services are deployed—with and without the JWS.

3.5 RESTful Services with and without JWS

The focus now switches from client-side consumption of RESTful Web Services to development and deployment of such services themselves. As in Section 3.3, this section examines how to deploy such services both with and without JAX-WS. As before, the purpose here is to compare and contrast the JWS approach with the bare-bones approach of simply working with Java's HTTP servlet tools to build and deploy a simple RESTful service.

Again, the example used to illustrate the concepts in this section is a basic building block of SOA Web Services—the deployment of a simple download service. In this case, it is the "New Orders" service discussed from the client perspective in previous sections. This section examines how to deploy a Java class that provides a `getNewOrders()` method both with and without JAX-WS.

3.5.1 Deploying a REST Service without Using JWS

This section provides the first example in the book of how to deploy a Java method as a Web service. It is the simplest RESTful Web service imaginable—the service consumed by the client in Section 3.3.2. This service simply returns an XML document containing the "new orders."

Example 3–13 shows a *mock object* implementation of the `getNewOrders()` method. This implementation of `OrderManager` is called a mock object because it is a "mock-up" of a real `OrderManager` class. It is a stub implementation of the server side. The `getNewOrders()` method returns the contents of a hard-coded file (`/orders.xml`) instead of providing a live interface to an Order Management System. Throughout this book, mock objects like this are used to illustrate the Java classes that are deployed as Web Services. This strategy provides realistic examples you can actually run, without requiring you to have any actual back-end systems to provide Order Management or Customer Service implementations.

Example 3–13 The `OrderManager.getNewOrders(...)` Method to Be Deployed As a Web Service

```
26  public class OrderManager {
27
28    public Source getNewOrders() throws FileNotFoundException {
29      // get the resource that provides the new orders
30      InputStream src = getClass().getResourceAsStream("/orders.xml");
31      if ( src == null ) {
32        throw new FileNotFoundException("/orders.xml");
33      }
34      return new StreamSource(src);
35    }
36
37  }
```

book-code/chap03/rest-get/endpoint-servlet/src/java/samples/OrderManager.java

Several questions arise when considering how to enable this method as a Web service:

1. How is the class instantiated?
2. How is the `Source` instance returned by `getNewOrders()` converted into an XML stream in an HTTP response message?
3. How is the class deployed as a Web service?

These three questions mirror the three components of a Web Services Platform Architecture outlined in Chapter 1, Section 1.2. Question #1 is about invocation—the first component of a Web Services Platform Architecture. To invoke a Web service, you must be able to get an instance of its implementation class. Question #2 is about serialization—the second component of a Web Services Platform Architecture. The Java object that is returned must be serialized to XML that can be written out "onto the wire." Question #3 is about deployment—the third component of a Web Services Platform Architecture.

This section gives simple answers to these questions, as the example shows how to deploy the Java method as a Web service using a dedicated servlet. However, what is interesting to note is that, even in this simple case, the solutions need to deal with all three of the Web Services Platform Architecture components.

In this example, the Web service is accessed with an HTTP GET request. The servlet needs to handle the HTTP GET request, instantiate the Java class, invoke the `getNewOrders()` method, and write the results out as XML in the HTTP GET response. Figure 3–10 shows the basic architecture.

As illustrated here, this simple architecture deploys a RESTful Web service using the `java.servlet.http.HttpServlet` class. The `GetNewOrders-Servlet` class acts as a front-end to the `OrderManager` that mediates between the HTTP request/response messages and invokes the Java method that implements the Web service. The steps illustrated in the figure are:

1. The client sends an HTTP GET request to the appropriate URL (a URL that has been associated, in the servlet container's configuration, with the `GetNewOrders` class).
2. The servlet container wraps the HTTP request stream in an instance of `HTTPServletRequest` and passes it to the `GetNewOrdersServlet`'s `doGet()` method.
3. The `doGet()` method creates an instance of the `OrderManager` class and invokes the `getNewOrders()` method.

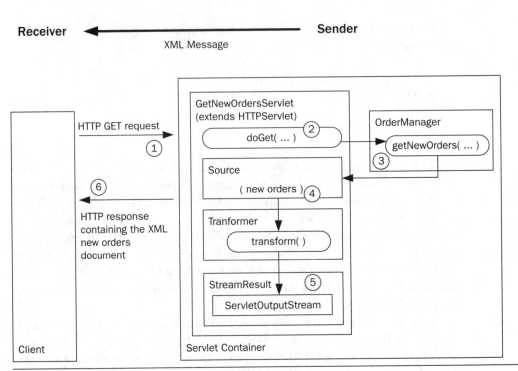

Figure 3–10 RESTful service deployed using `HTTPServlet`.

4. The `getNewOrders()` method returns the new orders XML document as an instance of `javax.xml.transform.Source`.

5. An instance of `javax.xml.transform.Transformer` is used to write the new orders `Source` to the `ServletOutputStream` (wrapped in an instance of `java.xml.transform.stream.StreamResult`).

6. The `getNewOrders()` method returns and the HTTP response containing the new orders XML document is returned to the client.

Example 3–14 shows the code for the `GetNewOrdersServlet`'s `doGet()` method. This code is straightforward, but there are a few items to notice and think about. First, as you can see, the servlet has to instantiate the `OrderManager` class. This assumes that `OrderManager` is available to the class loader. In this example, I accomplish that by bundling the `OrderManager` class in the WAR that is deployed. This is the simplest way to get an instance of a class that needs to be deployed as a Web service, but it is not always feasible. For example, if the class is implemented as an EJB, you will need to request its interface from the EJB container, instead of instantiating an instance. Furthermore, suppose the class requires other container services (e.g., JNDI and a database connection). In the real world, it is not so easy to just deploy a POJO by packaging its class definition into a WAR. Even in this example, using a mock object, the returned data (`orders.xml`) needs to be packaged into the WAR along with the deployed class. How you get an instance of a class being deployed as a Web services is a topic I cover in some detail when we explore the design of the SOA-J in Chapter 11.

Another item to notice is the use of the `HttpServletResponse.setContentType("text/xml")` method to set the content type of the HTTP response. This is important, because many REST clients (including early versions of the GlassFish implementation of `Dispatch`) will fail if the content type is not `"text/xml."` You need to be doubly careful with this, because some of the `HttpServletResponse` methods (e.g., `sendError(int sc, String msg)`), on some servlet containers, change the content type to `"text/xml"` since their error messages are implemented as HTML content.

Lastly, notice the use of the default instance of `Transformer` to simply write XML from a `Source` to a `Result`. Unlike in Section 3.4, here I am not doing any XSL transformation. I am just using the `Transformer` to write the XML returned by the `OrderManager` to the `ServletOutputStream`.

Example 3–14 The `GetNewOrdersServlet doGet(...)` Method

```
33   public void doGet(HttpServletRequest req,
34       HttpServletResponse res)
35   throws IOException, ServletException {
36     // invoke the Java method
37     OrderManager om = new OrderManager();
38     Source src = om.getNewOrders();
39     // write the file to the HTTP response stream
40     ServletOutputStream out = res.getOutputStream();
41     res.setContentType("text/xml");
42     StreamResult strRes = new StreamResult(out);
43     try {
44       TransformerFactory.newInstance().newTransformer()
45       .transform(src, strRes);
46     } catch (Exception e) {
47       throw new IOException(e.getMessage());
48     }
49     out.close();
50   }
```

book-code/chap03/rest-get/endpoint-servlet/src/java/samples
/GetNewOrdersServlet.java

The instructions for deploying and invoking this servlet are included with Example 3–6.

Example 3–15 shows the deployment descriptor for the Web service implemented by the `GetNewOrdersServlet` class (together with `OrderManager`). This is the standard `web.xml` file, which is placed into the `WEB-INF` subdirectory of the WAR package used to deploy this Web service.

Example 3–15 The `web.xml` Deployment Descriptor Bundled in the `GetNewOrdersServlet` WAR

```
 9  <web-app>
10    <servlet>
11      <servlet-name>GetNewOrdersServlet</servlet-name>
12      <servlet-class> samples.GetNewOrdersServlet </servlet-class>
13    </servlet>
14    <servlet-mapping>
15      <servlet-name>GetNewOrdersServlet</servlet-name>
16      <url-pattern>/NewOrders</url-pattern>
17    </servlet-mapping>
18  </web-app>
```

book-code/chap03/rest-get/endpoint-servlet/src/webapp/WEB-INF/web.xml

Notice in Example 3–15 that the servlet `GetNewOrdersServlet` is mapped to the URL pattern `/NewOrders`. The deployment tool you use to deploy the WAR determines the context root for the Web application. In this case, the GlassFish default is being used—and it takes the context root from the name of the WAR file (`chap03-rest-get-endpoint-servlet-1.0.war`). And the base URL for the servlet container is http://localhost:8080 (unless you have customized the profile section of the <bookcode>/pom.xml file when you installed the code example—see Appendix B, Section B.5). So, the URL for this Web service becomes:

http://localhost:8080/chap03-rest-get-endpoint-servlet-1.0/NewOrders

That pretty much wraps up the "how-to" discussion for creating and deploying a simple REST Web service using a servlet to invoke a Java method. As you can see, it is not hard to use servlets for deployment of basic RESTful Web services. The three questions posed at the beginning of the section have been answered as follows:

1. The Web service implementation class (i.e., `OrderManager`) is instantiated using the `no-arg` default constructor. This assumes that such a constructor exists and that the class definition is on the classpath. It also assumes that all resources required by the class are available.
2. The object returned by `getNewOrders()` is converted into an XML stream using a `Transformer`. This is a very simple scenario where the method being deployed returns a result that is already represented as an XML infoset. In most cases, the result will be a Java object that is not an XML infoset representation and requires serialization.
3. The class is deployed by bundling it with a dedicated servlet.

Problems are encountered, however, when you want to deploy multiple services. Using the architecture described in this section, you need to have a servlet for each Web service. That quickly becomes cumbersome and inefficient. What is needed is an invocation subsystem so that a single servlet can be used to invoke more than one service. However, to do that requires a method of mapping URLs to services at a finer granularity than provided by the `web.xml` file. As you can see in Example 3–15, the `web.xml` mapping is from a single URL to a single servlet. So, for a single servlet to handle multiple URLs (and multiple Web services), additional deployment meta-data must be added to this simple architecture that falls outside of the servlet processing model. One way to do this might be to map all base URLs of the form http://example.com/services/* to the servlet. Then, local paths such as `/getNewOrder`, `/addCustomerHistory`, and so on are mapped to individual Web services.

In fact, this approach is used by a variety of Web Services engines, including Apache Axis [AXIS] and the SOA-J engine introduced in Chapter 11. JWS also offers a variation on this approach, which I examine in detail in Chapter 7. For now, I'm going to defer further discussion of deployment issues and move on to the nuts and bolts of how to deploy this "New Orders" example Web service using JAX-WS and JSR-181 annotations.

3.5.2 Deploying a RESTful Service with JWS

This section illustrates how a Web service is deployed using JWS. This is the same service that was deployed in Section 3.5.1. However, the operation of the service—as deployed using JWS—is very different.

The primary difference here is that instead of using a servlet as in Example 3–14, the JWS version uses an instance of `Provider<Source>` to implement the RESTful service. Example 3–16 shows how it is implemented. The `@WebServiceProvider` annotation used in this example is defined by the JAX-WS 2.0 specification. It is used to declare a reference to a Web Service that implements a `Provider<Source>` interface. The `@WebServiceProvider` annotation is required for deploying a RESTful Web service and is discussed in more detail in Chapter 7, which covers JAX-WS server-side development and deployment.

The `Provider<Source>` interface is basically the server-side version of `Dispatch<Source>` discussed in Section 3.3.2. It enables you to create a Web service that works directly with the XML message as an instance of `javax.xml.transform.Source`—rather than a JAXB 2.0 representation of the XML message. Along with `@WebServiceProvider`, the `javax.xml.ws.Provider` interface is explained in greater detail in Chapter 7. In this section, my goal is just to give you a quick example of how a RESTful service can be created and deployed with JAX-WS.

The `@BindingType` annotation (`javax.xml.ws.BindingType`) used in Example 3–16 is also defined by the JAX-WS 2.0 specification and is used to specify the binding that should be employed when publishing an endpoint. The property value indicates the actual binding. In this case, you can see that the value is specified as follow:

```
value=HTTPBinding.HTTP_BINDING
```

This indicates that the XML/HTTP binding should be used, rather than the default SOAP 1.1/HTTP. This is how REST endpoints are specified in JAX-WS 2.0—by setting the `@BindingType`. If one were to leave the `@BindingType` annotation off this example, the Java EE 5 container would deploy it as a service that expects to receive a SOAP envelope, rather than straight XML over HTTP (i.e., REST).

Example 3–16 `GetNewOrdersProvider` Implements `Provider<Source>` to Create a RESTful Web Service

```
21   import javax.xml.transform.Source;
22   import javax.xml.ws.BindingType;
23   import javax.xml.ws.Provider;
24   import javax.xml.ws.WebServiceProvider;
25   import javax.xml.ws.http.HTTPBinding;
26   import javax.xml.ws.http.HTTPException;
27
28   @WebServiceProvider
29   @BindingType(value=HTTPBinding.HTTP_BINDING)
30   public class GetNewOrdersProvider implements Provider<Source> {
31
```

```
32    public Source invoke(Source xml) {
33      OrderManager om = new OrderManager();
34      try {
35        return om.getNewOrders();
36      } catch (Throwable t) {
37        t.printStackTrace();
38        throw new HTTPException(500);
39      }
40    }
41
42  }
```

book-code/chap03/rest-get/endpoint-jaxws/src/java/samples
/GetNewOrdersProvider.java

The `Provider<Source>` interface specifies the `invoke()` method, which receives and returns an instance of `Source`. As shown in this example, inside the `invoke()` message, the `OrderManager` class gets instantiated and the `OrderManager.getNewOrders()` method is invoked to implement the Web service functionality. So, instead of wrapping the `OrderManager` inside an `HttpServlet.doGet()` method, as in Example 3–14, this example wraps the service implementation class inside a `Provider.invoke()` method.

At this point, it is worth asking the same questions posed in Section 3.5.1. In particular:

1. How is the class instantiated?
2. How is the `Source` instance returned by `getNewOrders()` converted into an XML stream in an HTTP response message?
3. How is the class deployed as a Web service?

As you can see from the code, some of these questions get very different answers when a RESTful Web service is implemented as a `Provider<Source>` than when it is implemented using an `HttpServlet`. These differences serve to contrast the JAX-WS 2.0 approach to Web Services deployment with the straightforward servlet implementation of the preceding section.

The answer to the first question is the same in both cases—the class is instantiated each time the service is invoked. However, the answer to the second question is different in this case. Here, the `Source` instance can be returned directly. It does not need to be converted into a stream and written out to the HTTP response message. These details related to the binding of the service to the HTTP transport are handled by the JAX-WS run-time implementation. Lastly, the answer to the third question is also very different. Java EE 5 supports many options for deploying Web services—these are all discussed in Chapter 8. A `web.xml` deployment descriptor can be used (even though this is not a servlet!), but is not required. In fact, it is possible to deploy a JWS Web service without any deployment descriptors. The Java EE 5 container can often deploy a service based entirely on its annotations.

Figure 3–11 shows the architecture supporting the RESTful Web service created and deployed here using JAX-WS 2.0.

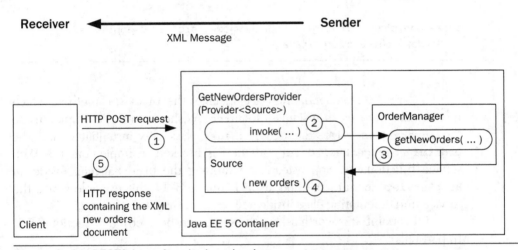

Figure 3–11 RESTful service deployed using `Provider<Source>`.

As illustrated here, this JWS architecture deploys the RESTful Web service using the `java.servlet.http.Provider<Source>` class. The `GetNewOrdersProvider` class acts as a front-end to the `OrderManager` that mediates between the XML request/response messages and invokes the Java method that implements the Web service. The steps illustrated in the figure are:

1. The client sends an HTTP POST request to the appropriate URL (a URL that is specified at deployment time—either in a deployment descriptor or by a deployment tool). Notice that a POST request is used here, rather than a GET request. That is because early implementations of JAX-WS allowed RESTful Web services only to accept POST requests. Recent versions support both POST and GET requests.

2. The JWS container extracts the XML message from the HTTP POST request and passes it to the `GetNewOrders.invoke()` method. This functionality is provided by the JAX-WS runtime.
3. The `invoke()` method creates an instance of the `OrderManager` class and invokes the `getNewOrders()` method.
4. The `getNewOrders()` method returns the new orders XML document as an instance of `javax.xml.transform.Source`.
5. The instance of `Source`—the Web service's return XML message—is inserted into the HTTP response message and returned to the caller. This functionality (i.e., wrapping the XML response message inside the HTTP response message) is provided by the JAX-WS runtime.

In some ways, the JWS implementation of this RESTful Web service is simpler than its servlet-based counterpart discussed in Section 3.5.1. The simplification comes from not having to translate between HTTP request/response messages and the XML request/response messages. JAX-WS handles that translation so that the developer can work directly with the XML messages. In other ways, however, the JWS implementation shown here seems more cumbersome. Two annotations are required—`@WebService-Provider` and `@BindingType`. If you are not used to annotations, these can make the example seem confusing.

To deploy and invoke this RESTful Web service example, do the following:

1. Start GlassFish (if it is not already running).
2. Go to `<book-code>/chap03/rest-get/endpoint-jaxws`.
3. To build and deploy the Web service enter:

```
mvn install
```

... and when that command finishes, then enter:

```
ant deploy
```

4. Go to `<book-code>/chap03/rest-get/client-jaxws`.
5. To run the client enter:

```
ant run-jaxws
```

6. To undeploy the Web service, go back to `<book-code>/chap03/rest-post/endpoint-jaxws` and enter:

```
ant undeploy
```

3.6 Conclusions

In this chapter, I provided a broad introduction to consuming, creating, and deploying RESTful Web Services—using standard `java.net.*` classes and servlets, as well as the JAX-WS 2.0 APIs and annotations. A primary goal of this chapter was to highlight the similarities and differences between traditional Java techniques and the JAX-WS 2.0 approach to Web Services. Another goal was to provide a grounding in some of the basic XML processing techniques used to implement SOA-style integration of RESTful Web services.

In the next chapter, I look at the Java/XML data binding problem and how it can be addressed using traditional JAXP approaches, as well as using JAXB. As I did in this chapter, I compare and contrast the approaches so that you can see the power available to you from the JAXB machinery, but also some of the drawbacks. I help you to determine in which situation JAXB provides the most value and where you are better off using other binding tools.

CHAPTER 4

The Role of WSDL, SOAP, and Java/XML Mapping in SOA

This chapter describes how the core Web Services standards—WSDL and SOAP—are used for implementing SOA in a Java environment. In particular, since a great many Java applications being developed need to integrate with an existing or planned SOA framework, I examine WSDL and SOAP from the perspective of *SOA Integration*. SOA Integration is an approach to systems integration that involves deploying the applications to be integrated as sets of SOA-style services. The integration is accomplished by aggregating the resulting services to create loosely coupled applications built from the underlying services.

The key enabling technology for using WSDL and SOAP with Java is Java/XML mapping. Java/XML mapping technology converts Java instances to XML and vice versa. At the SOA level, systems are defined in terms of XML messages and WSDL operations.[1] Meanwhile, at the Java level, systems are defined in terms of objects and methods. So, to implement SOA components in Java requires translation from Java objects to XML messages and Java methods to WSDL operations.

This chapter is not a detailed introduction to WSDL, SOAP, or XML. I assume you have some basic familiarity with those standards. If not, you should brush up before reading this chapter. A good place to start is with the SOAP and WSDL specifications themselves—see [SOAP 1.1] and [WSDL 1.1]. If you understand XML, these specifications are not difficult to read.

I start this chapter by providing an overview of WSDL and why it is important for SOA. Next, I look at the role of SOAP in SOA and its advantages to REST in this setting. After that, the topic of *dispatching* is discussed.

---

1. And, of course, WSDL is written in XML, so everything at the SOA level boils down to XML.

In a Web Services Platform that is used for SOA, the dispatching mechanism is used to determine which Java method to invoke for a given SOAP request. I show how the dispatching process is governed by the structure of the SOAP message and the style of WSDL used to deploy a Web service. I discuss how JAX-WS 2.0 handles dispatching, some of its limitations, and how to work around these limitations.

Toward the end of this chapter, I provide an introduction to the "Start from WSDL and Java" approach to Java Web Services. This approach is central to SOA. It involves starting with both an XML representation of a service (WSDL) and a Java class. The challenge is to deploy a class/method so that it implements a WSDL that is compliant with enterprise or eBusiness community standards.

I describe why the key to this "Start from WSDL and Java" methodology is a good Java/XML mapping toolset. Then, I look at how well JAXB 2.0 enables you to implement the kinds of Java/XML mappings needed for "Start from WSDL and Java." Lastly, I illustrate some of the techniques that can be used with JAXB 2.0 to implement the kinds of Java/XML mappings that are needed in practice.

To summarize, the material in this chapter describes:

- Why WSDL is essential for SOA.
- Why SOAP is required (i.e., because it is needed to implement WSDL and SOA can't be done without WSDL).
- How dispatching works. Dispatching is a core component of a Web Services Platform's invocation subsystem and it depends heavily on SOAP and WSDL.
- The various JAX-WS 2.0 dispatching alternatives.
- Some of the JAX-WS 2.0 dispatching limitations and how to work around them.
- Why the "Start from WSDL and Java" approach to creating Java Web Services is central to doing SOA with Java.
- How Java/XML mapping enables "Start from WSDL and Java."
- Some of the JAXB 2.0 limitations as a Java/XML mapping tool and how to work around them.

4.1   The Role of WSDL in SOA

WSDL is the *interface definition language* (IDL) that defines the interactions among SOA components. It provides a standard language for describing how to communicate with a component. Without a standard IDL, you must resort to ad hoc documentation to communicate the interfaces for your SOA components.

Enterprise Java developers are usually concerned with how well a technology can scale across enterprise boundaries. In the case of SOA, you must ensure that Web services created in different departments (e.g., order processing and customer service) can interoperate. Whenever you need to design systems that scale and cross boundaries like that, one of the critical success factors is good interface definitions. As a result, you cannot rely on ad hoc documentation to define the interfaces. You must have a standard, and the industry-accepted standard is WSDL 1.1 [WSDL 1.1].

One of the difficulties encountered when trying to use RESTful SOA components on an enterprise scale is that there is no well-accepted industry standard IDL for XML over HTTP without SOAP. WSDL 2.0 [WSDL 2.0], which is in the works, provides support for XML over HTTP without SOAP (see [WSDL 2.0 Part 2]). However, general industry acceptance of WSDL 2.0 is probably many years away.

Figure 4–1 shows the role of WSDL for SOA Integration as described in this book. The figure provides a UML object diagram depicting the relationship of WSDL in an SOA Integration setting. First, notice the Web Services Platform subsystem where deployment takes place. The top-level class depicted in that subsystem is `ServiceDeployment`. Each instance of `ServiceDeployment` corresponds to a Web service that is deployed on this platform. Next, notice that `ServiceDeployment` contains both an operation (taken from the WSDL interface description) and a Java method. In this manner, you see that a Web service deployment defines a relationship between a WSDL interface description and a Java implementation of that description. More specifically, a Web service deployment defines relationships between individual operations in a WSDL and the Java methods that implement them in that particular deployment.

Figure 4–1 shows that a WSDL interface description contains a `types` instance (i.e., the `wsdl:types` element). As you know, this is the top-level element within the `wsdl:definitions` element that describes the XML Schema types used in the WSDL. Here, you can also see that this particular WSDL's `types` instance contains the schema `Orders.xsd` that is part of the XML Schema Library in an Enterprise System. It also incorporates the schema `Faults.xsd` from the Web Services Infrastructure subsystem.

In this manner, SOA envisions that an enterprise maintains libraries of reusable XML Schema definitions that are incorporated in the WSDL definitions used to deploy Web services. I call this concept *reusable schema*.

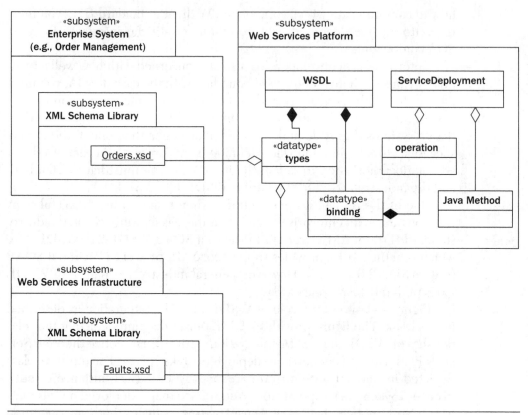

Figure 4–1 The role of WSDL in SOA integration.

Reusable schemas provide the foundation for an enterprise message model that is a cornerstone of SOA. Standard schemas enable standard messages, which in turn enable standard WSDL interfaces to be defined. As I've discussed, WSDL is essential to separation of concerns because clear interface definitions are needed to separate applications into logical units or SOA components. For all the users of the SOA infrastructure to understand those WSDL interfaces, they have to be written in a common language. At one level, XML supplies a common language—but that is just syntax. The datatypes expressed in that language should also be standardized to the extent possible. So, for commonly used types like Address, for example, there should be standard corporate schema definitions that can be reused across SOA components.

The Enterprise System in Figure 4–1 could be the OMS described in Chapter 3, in which case, its schema library would include the orders.xsd schema described there. Other "infrastructure" libraries—like standard schema for fault messages—are also envisioned as part of the SOA framework deployed by an enterprise.

So, as described here, one role of WSDL in the SOA framework is to assemble standard XML types into operations that describe Web services. Another role is as a participant in a Web service's deployment.

4.1.1 A WSDL Example

Figure 4–1 becomes clearer when you look at some actual WSDL. This section provides a simple example to illustrate how WSDL 1.1 is used for SOA Integration. It describes a Web service for getting the orders that have been received during a particular date range.

Example 4–1 shows the `wsdl:types` element from the `GetOrders-Dates.wsdl` sample. This WSDL describes a simple service that takes as input a date range. As output, it provides the orders that were received between those dates.

Example 4–1 The `wsdl:types` Element Integrates Existing Schemas

```
11    <wsdl:types>
12      <xs:schema targetNamespace="http://www.example.com/oms">
13        <xs:include schemaLocation="http://soabook.com/example/oms/orders.xsd"/>
14      </xs:schema>
15      <xs:schema targetNamespace="http://www.example.com/faults">
16        <xs:include schemaLocation="http://soabook.com/example/faults/faults.xsd"
17        />
18      </xs:schema>
19      <xs:schema elementFormDefault="qualified"
20        targetNamespace="http://www.example.com/getord">
21        <xs:element name="getOrdersDates">
22          <xs:complexType>
23            <xs:sequence>
24              <xs:element name="startDate" type="xs:date"/>
25              <xs:element name="endDate" type="xs:date"/>
26            </xs:sequence>
27          </xs:complexType>
28        </xs:element>
29        <xs:element name="getOrdersDatesResponse">
30          <xs:complexType>
31            <xs:sequence>
32              <xs:element name="orders" type="oms:OrdersType"/>
33            </xs:sequence>
```

```
34          </xs:complexType>
35        </xs:element>
36      </xs:schema>
37    </wsdl:types>
```

book-code/chap04/wsdl/GetOrdersDates.wsdl

As you can see, within this `wsdl:types` element, there are `xs:schema` definitions that consist solely of `xs:include` elements that pull in other XML schema. One of these included schemas is located at http://soa-book.com/example/oms/orders.xsd. This is the same `orders.xsd` as described in Chapter 3, Section 3.2. This `xs:include` element is how the relationship, described in Figure 4–1, between the WSDL and the OMS's schema library is implemented. There is another `xs:include` element in Example 4–1—one that pulls in the `faults.xsd` schema that provides the XML Schema definitions for the fault messages used in this WSDL.

Another point to notice about this `wsdl:types` section is that it defines the message elements `getOrdersDates` and `getOrdersDatesResponse`. These are wrapper elements that are used in the document/literal wrapped style of WSDL. WSDL styles are discussed in detail in Section 4.3.

Within the `getOrdersDatesResponse` element, you can see that an element named `orders` is returned that has the type `oms:OrdersType`. This is where the OMS's imported schema gets used. The next example shows where the imported faults get used.

Example 4–2 shows the `wsdl:message` elements and the `wsdl:port-Type` element from the WSDL example.

Example 4–2 The `wsdl:message` and `wsdl:portType` Elements Describe the Message Exchange Interface

```
41    <wsdl:message name="request">
42      <wsdl:part name="parameters" element="getord:getOrdersDates"/>
43    </wsdl:message>
44    <wsdl:message name="response">
45      <wsdl:part name="parameters" element="getord:getOrdersDatesResponse"/>
46    </wsdl:message>
47    <wsdl:message name="inputFault">
48      <wsdl:part name="parameters" element="faults:inputMessageValidationFault"/>
49    </wsdl:message>
```

```
50    <wsdl:portType name="GetOrdersDatesPort">
51      <wsdl:operation name="getOrdersDates">
52        <wsdl:input message="getord:request"/>
53        <wsdl:output message="getord:response"/>
54        <wsdl:fault name="getOrdersInputFault" message="getord:inputFault"/>
55      </wsdl:operation>
56    </wsdl:portType>
```

book-code/chap04/wsdl/GetOrdersDates.wsdl

As you can see, the message named `inputFault` is defined in terms of the element `faults:inputMessageValidationFault`. This is where the `faults.xsd` schema from the Web Services infrastructure (pictured in Figure 4–1) gets used.

SOA is easier if the component Web services use a standard set of faults such as the `faults:inputMessageValidationFault` used here. That is because, when dealing with the Java classes that implement a Web service (or consume it on the client side), JAX-WS 2.0 likes to map a subclass of `java.lang.Exception` to each fault type. If the fault messages are standardized, you can also work with a standard set of exceptions on the Java side.

The schema for this fault message type is listed in Example 4–3.

Example 4–3 The Schema for `faults:inputMessageValidationFault`

```
7    <xs:element name="inputMessageValidationFault"
8      type="faults:InputMessageValidationFaultType"/>
9    <xs:complexType name="InputMessageValidationFaultType">
10     <xs:attribute name="msg" type="xs:string"/>
11   </xs:complexType>
```

book-code/chap04/wsdl/faults.xsd

The next snippet from the sample WSDL, shown in Example 4–4, contains the `wsdl:binding` element that defines the SOAP binding for the `GetOrdersDates` Web service. There are a couple of interesting items to point out here, which I explore in more depth in Section 4.3 where dispatching is discussed.

Example 4–4 The `wsdl:binding` Element Describes the Transport Binding

```
60    <wsdl:binding name="GetOrdersDatesSOAPBinding"
61      type="getord:GetOrdersDatesPort">
62      <soap:binding style="document"
63        transport="http://schemas.xmlsoap.org/soap/http"/>
64      <wsdl:operation name="getOrdersDates">
65        <wsdl:input>
66          <soap:body use="literal"/>
67        </wsdl:input>
68        <wsdl:output>
69          <soap:body use="literal"/>
70        </wsdl:output>
71        <wsdl:fault name="getOrdersInputFault">
72          <soap:fault name="getOrdersInputFault"/>
73        </wsdl:fault>
74      </wsdl:operation>
75    </wsdl:binding>
```

book-code/chap04/wsdl/GetOrdersDates.wsdl

First, the `wsdl:operation` name attribute is `getOrdersDates`, which is the same name used for the request message element. In this case, this is not an accident, but a requirement of the "document/literal wrapped" style discussed in Section 4.3.5. Second, the `soap:binding` style is "document" and the `soap:body` use is "literal." Again, this is a feature of the "document/literal wrapped" style.

Lastly, Example 4–5 shows the `wsdl:service` element. This element describes the endpoint and provides the URL as the `soap:address` location attribute. The Web Services Platform (pictured in Figure 4–1) needs to make sure that the URL provided in the WSDL is synchronized with the address where the endpoint is actually deployed. For this reason, even when doing "Start from WSDL and Java" development, the `location` attribute is often not specified until deployment time, as it is determined by whatever context gets associated with the Web service at that point.

Example 4–5 The `wsdl:service` Element Describes the Endpoint

```
79    <wsdl:service name="GetOrdersDatesService">
80      <wsdl:port name="GetOrdersDatesPort" binding="GetOrdersDatesSOAPBinding">
81        <soap:address location="http://localhost:8080/getorders/getordersdates"/>
```

```
82      </wsdl:port>
83    </wsdl:service>
```

book-code/chap04/wsdl/GetOrdersDates.wsdl

4.2 The Role of SOAP in SOA

The preceding section discusses how SOA requires an interface definition
language (i.e., WSDL) to describe, in a standard way, how to invoke a Web
service component. The WSDL describes an abstract interface (i.e.,
`wsdl:portType` and `wsdl:operation`), and a concrete binding of that interface (i.e., `wsdl:binding`). As shown in Example 4–2, a WSDL operation is
described in terms of abstract messages (i.e., `wsdl:message` elements).
SOAP provides a concrete implementation, or binding for the `wsdl:mes-
sage` elements, thereby defining the XML structure of the messages
exchanged among SOA components in a standard manner. In this book,
SOAP means SOAP Version 1.1 [SOAP 1.1] unless a specific reference is
made to SOAP Version 1.2 [SOAP 1.2].[2]

So, the role of SOAP in SOA is to provide a concrete implementation,
or binding, for the WSDL interfaces. Of course, other bindings are possible. The most popular alternative to SOAP is the REST approach discussed
in Chapter 3. REST proponents argue that it is simpler than SOAP because
it doesn't add any header or body wrapper structure around the SOA messages. In a REST binding for a WSDL operation, the messages could con-
ceivably just be instances of the `wsdl:types`, transmitted over HTTP,
without any envelope. However, as mentioned previously, there is no standard REST binding for WSDL 1.1.

REST proponents also argue that REST is simpler than SOAP because
it does not concern itself with the semantics of SOAP nodes. Along with its
envelope structure, SOAP includes a processing model composed of SOAP
nodes that transmit and receive SOAP messages, and may relay them to
other SOAP nodes. SOAP even goes so far as to prescribe header attributes
such as `env:mustUnderstand` that are used to indicate whether processing
of a SOAP header block is mandatory or optional. Complexity creeps in this
way because if the ultimate receiver node of a SOAP message cannot process a header block that is marked as `env:mustUnderstand`, it must reply

---

2. See Appendix A for more discussion on why SOAP 1.1 is used.

with a SOAP fault. And the SOAP specification describes a standard envelope structure for SOAP faults.

SOAP node semantics and the associated header processing attributes give the REST advocates most of their ammunition for declaring that SOAP is too complicated. I must admit that I have some sympathy for this point of view. However, at this point, the lack of a standard IDL for REST makes it impossible to work with as a standard for enterprise SOA.

In addition to its advantages with WSDL, there is great benefit to the SOAP model of segmenting message data into *header blocks* and a *body*. Generally speaking, headers contain information that is related to the Quality of Service (QoS) provided by the messaging infrastructure—and not the contents of the message being delivered to a particular Web service. Information related to security and reliability, for example, belongs in the header block.

If REST is to support the kind of message processing required by SOA, it is going to have to evolve some kind of data model for separating metadata from message data (e.g., QoS information like guaranteed delivery requirements). The natural way to do that is with headers (e.g., JMS has headers). Likewise, if REST is to support well-defined system interfaces, it must evolve an accepted interface definition language—like a WSDL binding. However, once you add headers and WSDL to REST, you might as well be doing SOAP! The bottom line is that REST is suitable only for the most primitive types of SOA components (like the `GetNewOrders` example illustrated in Chapter 3). To build powerful applications with SOA, a more powerful messaging model, like SOAP, is required. So, in this book, for the most part I stick to SOAP as the messaging standard for SOA.[3]

Example 4–6 shows an example of a SOAP message that could be used to invoke the Web service `GetOrdersDates` described in Section 4.1.1.

Example 4–6 A SOAP Request Message for the `GetOrdersDates` Web Service

```
4   <env1:Envelope xmlns:env1="http://schemas.xmlsoap.org/soap/envelope">
5     <env1:Body>
6       <getord:getOrdersDates xmlns:getord="http://www.example.com/oms/getorders">
7         <getord:startDate>2005-11-19</getord:startDate>
8         <getord:endDate>2005-11-22</getord:endDate>
9       </getord:getOrdersDates>
```

---

3. One interesting exception is in Chapters 9 and 10, where REST is used to integrate with Yahoo! Shopping and to create an Ajax front-end to a JWS application.

```
10    </envl:Body>
11  </envl:Envelope>
```

book-code/chap04/soap/GetOrdersDatesSOAPRequest.xml

You'll notice that this SOAP request message has no headers. Headers are not required, and at this point, I'm leaving them out because I want to focus on the SOAP body and how it is constructed to fit into a framework for SOA.

The SOAP body in Example 4–6 has a single child elements getord:getOrdersDates. This is compliant with the WSDL shown in Example 4–1 (where the element getord:getOrdersDates is defined) and Example 4–2 (where the input message is defined). The getord:startDate and getord:endDate elements provide the range of dates required by the GetOrdersDates Web service. The service is expected to return a SOAP response message that contains the orders received with oms:PURCH_DATE elements that have date values within that range.

Example 4–7 shows a snippet from the SOAP response generated by the GetOrdersDates Web service.

Example 4–7 A SOAP Response Message Returned by the GetOrdersDates Web Service

```
4   <envl:Envelope xmlns:envl="http://schemas.xmlsoap.org/soap/envelope">
5     <envl:Body>
6       <getord:getOrdersDatesResponse
7        xmlns:getord="http://www.example.com/oms/getorders">
8        <Orders xmlns="http://www.example.com/oms"
9         xmlns:xsi="http://www.w3.org/2001/XMLSchema-instance"
10        xsi:schemaLocation="http://www.example.com/oms
11        http://soabook.com/example/oms/orders.xsd">
12        <Order>
13          <OrderKey>ENT1234567</OrderKey>
14          <OrderHeader>
15            <SALES_ORG>NE</SALES_ORG>
16            <PURCH_DATE>2005-11-20</PURCH_DATE>
17            <CUST_NO>ENT0072123</CUST_NO>
18            <PYMT_METH>PO</PYMT_METH>
19            <PURCH_ORD_NO>PO-72123-0007</PURCH_ORD_NO>
20            <WAR_DEL_DATE>2006-12-20</WAR_DEL_DATE>
21          </OrderHeader>
```

book-code/chap04/soap/GetOrdersDatesSOAPResponse.xml

Like the request, the SOAP body in this response message has a single child element. This one is named `getord:getOrdersDatesResponse`. This is compliant with the WSDL shown in Example 4–1 (where the element `getord:getOrdersDatesResponse` is defined) and Example 4–2 (where the output message is defined). Furthermore, the contents of the `getord:getOrdersDatesResponse` element—a single child element, `oms:Orders`—are defined in the schema `http://soabook.com/example/oms/orders.xsd`, which is imported into the WSDL (see Example 4–1). In this manner, the structure of the SOAP body is determined by both the WSDL and the schema library from the OMS subsystem. That is a common pattern in SOA Integration. You should try, as little as possible, to define unique XML types in the WSDL. Rather, XML types should be imported from the relevant subsystems. That is why the WSDL used in these examples imports the schema for `oms:Orders` instead of reproducing it in the `wsdl:types` section. This is an application of the DRY principle (Don't Repeat Yourself) that "Every piece of knowledge must have a single, unambiguous, authoritative representation within a system." [Hunt] The reason for applying the DRY principle in this case is to standardize interfaces (thereby improving interoperability) and reduce maintenance.

Example 4–8 shows what the `GetOrdersDates` Web service returns if it receives invalid input.

Example 4–8 SOAP 1.1 Fault Message Returned by the `GetOrdersDates` Web Service

```
4   <envl:Envelope xmlns:envl="http://schemas.xmlsoap.org/soap/envelope/">
5     <envl:Body>
6       <envl:Fault xmlns:faults="http://www.example.com/faults">
7         <faultcode>envl:Client</faultcode>
8         <faultstring>Bad input message.</faultstring>
9         <detail>
10          <faults:inputMessageValidationFailure
11            msg="The startDate is later than the endDate."/>
12        </detail>
13      </envl:Fault>
14    </envl:Body>
15  </envl:Envelope>
```

book-code/chap04/soap/GetOrdersDatesSOAPFault.xml

This is an example of a SOAP 1.1 fault message. The structure of a SOAP fault is largely determined by the SOAP 1.1 specification [SOAP 1.1]. That specification provides a mechanism to differentiate between the types of faults—the `faultcode` element. As you can see, in this case, the `faultcode` in this example has a value of `env1:Client`—a `QName`. The value a `faultcode` instance can contain is restricted by the SOAP 1.1 specification to four possibilities—see Section 4.4.1 of [SOAP 1.1] for more details. In this case, the `env1:Client` value indicates that something is wrong with the request message and it can't be processed by the Web service.

Looking further down the SOAP fault, you see the `detail` element—used to convey additional information about the nature of the error causing the fault. The contents of the `detail` element are flexible. Here, you can see that `detail` contains a child element, `faults:inputMessageValidation-Failure`—using a `QName` in the namespace of the `Faults` subsystem of the Web Services Infrastructure. So, the element contained in this detail is specified in the centralized schema library. This is another example of the DRY principle discussed with respect to the SOAP response—that, as much as possible, XML types should not be defined directly in the WSDL, but imported from schema library documents that are part of the SOA infrastructure.

Example 4–9 shows a SOAP 1.2 version of this same fault message. I include it here just to give you some of the flavor of the differences between SOAP 1.1 and SOAP 1.2.

Example 4–9 A SOAP 1.2 Version of a Fault Message from Example 4–8

```
4   <env2:Envelope xmlns:env2="http://www.w3.org/2003/05/soap-envelope">
5     <env2:Body>
6       <env2:Fault xmlns:faults="http://www.example.com/faults">
7         <env2:Code>
8           <env2:Value>env2:Sender</env2:Value>
9           <env2:Subcode>
10            <env2:Value>faults:inputMessageValidationFault</env2:Value>
11          </env2:Subcode>
12        </env2:Code>
13        <env2:Reason>
14          <env2:Text xml:lang="en">Bad input message.</env2:Text>
15        </env2:Reason>
16        <env2:Detail>
17          <faults:inputMessageValidationFailure
18          msg="The startDate is later than the endDate."/>
```

```
19          </env2:Detail>
20          </env2:Fault>
21       </env2:Body>
22    </env2:Envelope>
```

book-code/chap04/soap/GetOrdersDatesSOAPFault_SOAP12.xml

One difference from the SOAP 1.1 fault structure is that the type of fault is specified in the `env2:Code` element, instead of using `faultcode`. As you can see, in this case, the `env2:Code` has an `env2:Value` element with the `QName env2:Sender`. The values an `env2:Value` instance can contain are restricted by the SOAP 1.2 specification to five possibilities—see [SOAP 1.2] for more details. In this case, the `env2:Sender` value is roughly equivalent to the SOAP 1.1 `env1:Client` value. The `env2:Subcode` element, appearing immediately after `env2:Value`, provides more information about the cause of the fault. The `env2:Subcode` is optional, and application-specific. Here, it has the value `faults:inputMessageValidationFault`—a `QName` in the namespace of the `Faults` subsystem of the Web Services Infrastructure. This is another application of DRY—using the schema library to define standard fault subcodes.

The `env2:Reason` is roughly equivalent to the SOAP 1.1 `faultstring` element—although with more structure. Likewise, the `env2:Detail` corresponds to the SOAP 1.1 `detail` element.

That concludes a quick tour of SOAP and WSDL within the context of SOA. My goal has been to show you how WSDL and SOAP documents should be constructed from reusable datatypes. A main theme in that regard, related to the DRY principle, is separation of concerns—an important concept whenever one is doing systems integration. In the SOA context, one way in which separation of concerns is expressed is that you want there to be as little overlap as possible across independent SOA components. Since the interface for an SOA component is defined by WSDL, separation of concerns in this context means that the WSDL definitions should overlap as little as possible. One way to accomplish this is to abstract out from the WSDL as many of the type definitions as possible. In the past two sections, I showed how the XML schemas for types—such as `oms:Orders` and `faults:inputMessageValidationFailure`—that get used across an enterprise, should be abstracted out of the SOA component WSDL and placed in schema libraries. One benefit of applying the principle of separation of concerns to an SOA infrastructure comes into play with respect to versioning. If the `Orders.xsd` schema changes, now you don't need to update all the WSDL instances that use `oms:Orders`.

Of course, in such a situation, the WSDL may be automatically updated, but what about the underlying implementation of the SOA component? The implementation is still going to be expecting the old version of `oms:Orders`—regardless of what the WSDL says. If that is what you are thinking, you are a few steps ahead of me at this point. It's an important issue, and I address it in Chapter 5 where I talk about how to maintain the type mappings in our SOA infrastructure.

4.3 Dispatching: How JAX-WS 2.0 Maps WSDL/SOAP to Java Invocation

The past two sections discussed how SOAP and WSDL are interrelated and how they are integrated with schema libraries in an SOA infrastructure. In this section, I start looking at how SOAP and WSDL are related to the implementations of SOA components. One of the key concepts in that regard is *dispatching*.

Dispatching is the mechanism by which a SOAP request message is dispatched to the appropriate Java implementation for execution. It is the heart of the invocation subsystem for a Web Services Platform Architecture. Since Java methods are used to implement WSDL operations, the first step in dispatching is to determine which `wsdl:operation` a given SOAP message should be associated with. That association is determined by the structure of the SOAP message and the style of the WSDL.

4.3.1 Determining the WSDL Port

As noted, the first step in the dispatching process involves associating the SOAP request message with a WSDL operation. But first, you have to know which port a SOAP request should be associated with. Right away, you have problems, because the logical way to do that, based on the WSDL, is to look up the `wsdl:port` based on the `soap:address` the SOAP request was sent to. For example, in Example 4–5, you can see that the address http://localhost:8080/getorders/getordersdates is associated with the `GetOrdersDates wsdl:port`. From there, you get the binding—in this case the `GetOrdersDatesSOAPBinding`. That binding implements a port—the `GetOrdersDatesPort`. So, that is how you decode the port where the operation to be invoked is defined. There is only one problem with that—and it's a big one. The `soap:address` is not required to be included anywhere in the SOAP message.

You might think that you can get the `soap:address` from the underlying HTTP request. This might work, but it isn't guaranteed because multiple URLs might be pointing to the same IP address and context path where the SOA component's Web service is deployed. For example, the HTTP request might be sent to http://myserver.javector.com:8080/getorders/getordersdates instead of http://localhost:8080/getorders/getordersdates.

Web Services Addressing [WS-ADDRESSING 1.0 Core] is the W3C standard designed to solve this problem. Using WS-Addressing, endpoints are unambiguously defined using SOAP header blocks. Unfortunately, wide-scale industry acceptance of WS-Addressing is years away, so this approach cannot be followed as a practical solution for the dispatching problem today.

In practice, a Web Services Platform Architecture typically does look at the underlying HTTP request to identify the intended `soap:address` for a given SOAP message. Usually, a Web service is deployed along with an *endpoint listener*. The endpoint listener associates the URL a request is sent to with a particular `soap:address`. It is usually smart enough to deal with situations where multiple URLs point to the same `soap:address`, and resolves all requests to a canonical representation of the `soap:address`. That canonical representation, ideally, is used as the `soap:address` in the WSDL. So, for example, if `myhost.com` and `anotherhost.com` both resolve to the same IP address, the WSPA should choose one of these as the standard (canonical) representation for use in the WSDL `soap:address`. When a request is received and the HTTP header indicates it was sent to `anotherhost.com`, for the purposes of identifying the `soap:address` the canonical form—`myhost.com`—will be used.

Once the dispatching process has determined the `soap:address`, and therefore the `wsdl:port`, the `wsdl:operation` needs to be determined. For this, you need to look at the SOAP body, and the interpretation of the SOAP body's contents depends on the style of WSDL being used.

When I say "the style of WSDL being used," I mean the values of the `style` (binding style) and `use` attributes. These `style` and `use` attributes are defined by the SOAP Binding (see Section 3.2 of [WSDL 1.1]) extension to WSDL that describes how the Web service maps SOAP messages to its operations. The binding style can either be "rpc" or "document"—and the choice determines the structure of the SOAP `env:Body` as described in the following sections. The `use` can either be "encoded" or "literal"—and the choice determines how the data carried by the SOAP message is serialized. When "literal" is specified, the SOAP message simply carries data that conforms to the XML Schema constraints defined in the WSDL's `types` section. When "encoded" is specified, the data is serialized according to the SOAP Encoding specified in Section 5 of [SOAP 1.1].

In addition to the `style` and `use` attributes, a third characteristic is used to describe the WSDL style that describes how parameters are represented in the SOAP body. In this book, as in the JAX-WS specification, this characteristic is referred to as the parameter style and it can be either "wrapped" or "unwrapped" (unwrapped is also called "bare"). Unlike `style` and `use`, the parameter style does not correspond to any attribute specified in the WSDL description of a Web service.

All this boils down to three alternatives for the style of WSDL being used:[4]

- rpc/literal
- document/literal (also called document/literal unwrapped)
- document/literal wrapped

The parameter style wrapped versus unwrapped distinction refers to how the parameters contained in a SOAP message appear under the SOAP body element. If the parameters are direct children of `env:Body`, that is the unwrapped parameter style. If the parameters appear grouped under a single "wrapper" element, which is the only direct child of the `env:Body`, that is the wrapped parameter style. The following examples should make this clearer. If you get frustrated trying to understand all this, you have my sympathy. It took a long time for this to sink in for me.

As a point of reference, the WSDL and SOAP examples from Sections 4.1.1 and 4.2 use the document/literal wrapped style. That is my preferred style for SOA and the following discussion illustrates why.

4.3.2 The Role of the WS-I Basic Profile

The WS-I Basic Profile (WS-I BP) [WS-I BP 1.1] provides a set of standards related to SOAP, WSDL, and UDDI. It consists "of a set of nonproprietary Web services specifications, along with clarifications, refinements,

---

4. This description of the differences in WSDL styles was derived from e-mail postings by Ann Thomas Manes on the Axis users mailing list, and from a popular article from the IBM developerWorks site titled "Which style of WSDL should I use?" by Russell Butek (www-128.ibm.com/developerworks/webservices/library/ws-whichwsdl/?ca=dgr-devx-WebServicesMVP03).

interpretations, and amplifications of those specifications which promote interoperability."[5] WS-I BP eliminates ambiguities and inconsistencies in the SOAP and WSDL specifications that can cause interoperability problems. So, when organizations adhere to the WS-I BP, it is more likely that their Web services will interoperate. Because of this, it is now considered a best practice to require Web services to be WS-I BP-compliant.

Among the WSDL and SOAP message characteristics prohibited by the WS-I Basic Profile 1.1 are the following:

- The SOAP encoding is prohibited (i.e., the `use` attribute of the `wsdl:binding` must have the value "literal" and never have the value "encoded"). This is because it is very hard to validate a SOAP-encoded message against a WSDL description. The value of an interface definition (i.e., the WSDL) is greatly diminished if one cannot determine whether messages are compliant with the interface.
- A SOAP request message targeting a document/literal style Web service must have, at most, one child element of its `env:Body`.

Of course, there is much more in the WS-I BP specifications than those bulleted items, but those items relate directly to the discussion in the next few sections, so they are highlighted here.

4.3.3 RPC/Literal

The rpc/literal style is always wrapped. It is a style of WSDL that is allowed by WS-I [WS-I BP 1.1]. Its WSDL is distinguished by the following characteristics:

- The input message may have multiple parts.
- Parts are always defined using the `type` attribute (rather than the `element` attribute used for the document binding style).
- The full schema of the message payload is not defined in the `wsdl:types` section. Rather, the types of the input parameters (parts) are defined.
- If a part's `type` attribute specifies a complex type, it must be defined in the `wsdl:types` section.

---

5. Quote from the introduction of [WS-I BP 1.1].

The SOAP message produced in compliance with the rpc/literal WSDL style has the following characteristics:

- The top-level element within the `env:Body` (the wrapper element) has as its local name the `wsdl:operation` name.
- The wrapper element is in the namespace specified by the `namespace` attribute in the `env:Body` definition in the `wsdl:binding`.
- The parameter elements (parts) appear directly underneath the wrapper element and have local names that correspond to the `name` attribute of the `wsdl:part` definition.
- The parameter elements are never namespace-qualified.
- The name of the response element is not defined and is not significant.

Example 4–10 shows how the `wsdl:types` and `wsdl:message` definitions from Section 4.1.1 (Example 4–1 and Example 4–2) look when they are rewritten in the rpc/literal style.

Example 4–10 The rpc/literal WSDL Style

```
11    <wsdl:types>
12      <xs:schema elementFormDefault="qualified"
13        targetNamespace="http://www.example.com/getord">
14        <xs:import schemaLocation="http://www.example.com/oms
15          http://soabook.com/example/oms/orders.xsd"/>
16        <xs:import schemaLocation="http://www.example.com/faults
17          http://soabook.com/example/faults/faults.xsd"/>
18      </xs:schema>
19    </wsdl:types>
20    <wsdl:message name="request">
21      <wsdl:part name="startDate" type="xs:date"/>
22      <wsdl:part name="endDate" type="xs:date"/>
23    </wsdl:message>
24    <wsdl:message name="response">
25      <wsdl:part name="orders" element="oms:getOrdersType"/>
26    </wsdl:message>
```

book-code/chap04/dispatch/GetOrdersDates_rpclit.wsdl

You'll notice that the `wsdl:types` section is much shorter. That is because when using rpc/literal, you don't need to define the full schema of the message payload or the response wrapper. So, you don't need the schema definitions for `getOrdersDates` and `getOrdersDatesResponse`. Also, you can see that in the `wsdl:message` definition for the request, there are two parts. These parameters are no longer defined as children of a wrapper element—although, as you will see, that is how they appear in the SOAP request message.

Example 4–11 shows how the SOAP request message from Section 4.2 (Example 4–6) looks when rewritten for the rpc/literal style.

Example 4–11 An rpc/literal SOAP Request Message

```
 4  <env:Envelope xmlns:env="http://www.w3.org/2003/05/soap-envelope">
 5    <env:Body>
 6      <getOrdersDates>
 7        <startDate>2005-11-19</startDate>
 8        <endDate>2005-11-22</endDate>
 9      </getOrdersDates>
10    </env:Body>
11  </env:Envelope>
```

book-code/chap04/dispatch/GetOrdersDatesSOAPRequest_rpclit.xml

The only difference here is that the namespaces have changed. However, that is a big difference, because if you sent this SOAP message to a Web service expecting the namespaces shown in Example 4–6, it would return a fault.

One benefit of the rpc/literal style of WSDL is that it is relatively easy to read. The biggest drawback is that the contents of the SOAP body are not defined by any XML schema. That is, the wrapper element is generated by convention, and cannot easily be validated. The situation with the response message is even worse—its wrapper element is not even defined by convention, much less a schema. As a result, application clients in an SOA framework that need to consume an rpc/literal service may have trouble digesting the response message. The response needs to be mapped to some Java type, but it is hard to do that if the WSDL doesn't tell you the exact XML representation of the response to expect.

4.3.4 Document/Literal

The document/literal style is unwrapped. As a result, if there are multiple parameters, you can end up with SOAP request messages where the `env:Body` element has multiple children. This is prohibited by WS-I [WS-I BP 1.1]. Hence, this WSDL style is really useful only for messaging—where you don't care about defining parameters.[6] Its WSDL is distinguished by the following characteristics:

- The input message may have multiple parts.
- Parts are always defined using the `element` attribute (rather than the `type` attribute used for the rpc binding style).
- The full schema of the message payload is defined in the `wsdl:types` section. The part's `element` attribute references an element definition in a schema contained in the `wsdl:types` section.

The SOAP message produced in compliance with the document/literal WSDL style has the following characteristics:

- The `wsdl:operation` name does not appear in the SOAP `env:Body`.
- The parameter elements (`parts`) appear directly underneath the `env:Body` and have local names as defined in their corresponding schema found in the `wsdl:types` section.
- The parameter elements are namespace-qualified as specified in their corresponding schema found in the `wsdl:types` section.
- There is no response wrapper element, as the response is unwrapped just like the request.

Example 4–12 shows how the `wsdl:types` and `wsdl:message` definitions from Section 4.1.1 (Example 4–1 and Example 4–2) look when they are rewritten in the document/literal style.

Example 4–12 The document/literal WSDL Style

```
11    <wsdl:types>
12      <xs:schema elementFormDefault="qualified"
13        targetNamespace="http://www.example.com/getord">
14        <xs:import schemaLocation="http://www.example.com/oms
15          http://soabook.com/example/oms/orders.xsd"/>
```

---

6. Some people interpret the WS-I prohibition on multiple `env:Body` children to mean that the document/literal style must use a wrapper element when there are multiple parameters. I find this usage confusing and prefer the usage described here, which may result in SOAP messages that are not WS-I-compliant. My usage is consistent with the terminology in the JAX-WS specification.

```
16          <xs:import schemaLocation="http://www.example.com/faults
17             http://soabook.com/example/faults/faults.xsd"/>
18          <xs:element name="startDate" type="xs:date"/>
19          <xs:element name="endDate" type="xs:date"/>
20          <xs:element name="orders" type="oms:OrdersType"/>
21       </xs:schema>
22     </wsdl:types>
23     <wsdl:message name="request">
24       <wsdl:part name="parameter1" element="getord:startDate"/>
25       <wsdl:part name="parameter2" element="getord:endDate"/>
26     </wsdl:message>
27     <wsdl:message name="response">
28       <wsdl:part name="parameter1" element="getord:orders"/>
29     </wsdl:message>
```

book-code/chap04/dispatch/GetOrdersDates_doclitbare.wsdl

As you can see, the `wsdl:types` section has gotten a little longer than in the rpc/literal case—but it's still not as long as in Example 4–1. That is because the schema now includes the element definitions of the request and response payloads. However, it is not as long as Example 4–1 because there are no wrappers, so you don't need the schema definitions for `getOrdersDates` and `getOrdersDatesResponse`. As in the rpc/literal case, you can see that in the `wsdl:message` definition for the request, there are two parts. This time, however, the parts use the `element` attribute to refer to the global element definitions for the parameters found in the `wsdl:types` section.

Example 4–13 shows how the SOAP request message from Section 4.2 (Example 4–6) looks when rewritten for the document/literal style.

Example 4–13 A document/literal SOAP Request Message

```
4   <env:Envelope xmlns:env="http://www.w3.org/2003/05/soap-envelope">
5     <env:Body xmlns:getord="http://www.example.com/oms/getorders">
6       <getord:startDate>2005-11-19</getord:startDate>
7       <getord:endDate>2005-11-22</getord:endDate>
8     </env:Body>
9   </env:Envelope>
```

book-code/chap04/dispatch/GetOrdersDatesSOAPRequest_doclitbare.xml

The big difference here from the document/literal wrapped case illustrated in Section 4.2 is that there is no wrapper element. Because of this, and the fact that there are two parameters, this SOAP message is not WS-I-compliant.

An advantage of document/literal versus rpc/literal is that the SOAP messages that get produced can be validated against the schemas in the `wsdl:types` section. This is a big advantage because it greatly simplifies real-time validation of messages.

One drawback of the document/literal style of WSDL as compared the rpc/literal style is that it is harder to read because of the schema definitions required. This readability issue gets even worse for document/literal wrapped where the schemas for the wrapper elements have to be included.

The biggest drawback of document/literal is that it produces SOAP messages that are not WS-I-compliant when used with multiple parameters. This is not a surprise, as the original intention of the document/literal style was that it should be used for messaging and not RPC style invocation. And in messaging, there are no parameters.

This drawback is eliminated with the document/literal wrapped style of WSDL discussed in the next section.

4.3.5 Document/Literal Wrapped

Document/literal wrapped is simply document/literal with wrapper elements. Even if you have only one parameter, you still use a wrapper element. And the convention for naming the wrapper element is similar to rpc/literal—the operation name is used as the local part of the wrapper name. Document/literal wrapped style WSDL is distinguished by the following characteristics:

- The input message must have a single part.[7]
- The single part is defined using the `element` attribute (rather than the `type` attribute used for the rpc binding style).
- That single part is a wrapper element. It is the entire message payload and its full schema is defined in the `wsdl:types` section.
- All parameters are immediate children of the wrapper element.

---

7. Actually, you can have additional header parts, but only one body part. Header parts are confusing, however, and I don't encourage their use.

- By convention, the local name of the wrapper element is the `wsdl:operation` name the message is used to invoke.
- A wrapper element is also defined for the output message. By convention, the local name of this response wrapper element is the `wsdl:operation` name suffixed with the string 'Response'.

The SOAP message produced in compliance with the document/literal wrapped WSDL style has the following characteristics:

- The top-level element within the `env:Body` (the wrapper element) has as its local name the `wsdl:operation` name.
- The wrapper element is in the namespace specified in its schema, found in the `wsdl:types` section.
- The parameter elements appear directly underneath the wrapper element. Unlike rpc/literal, their local names do not correspond to the `name` attribute of the `wsdl:part` definition. Rather, they are specified by their schema found in the `wsdl:types` section.
- The parameter elements are namespace-qualified as specified by their schema found in the `wsdl:types` section.

The examples in Section 4.1.1 show WSDL using the document/literal wrapped style. The `types` section of that WSDL is reproduced in Example 4–14.

Example 4–14 A document/literal wrapped Style WSDL Defines Wrapper Elements in the `types` Section

```
11   <wsdl:types>
12     <xs:schema targetNamespace="http://www.example.com/oms">
13       <xs:include schemaLocation="http://soabook.com/example/oms/orders.xsd"/>
14     </xs:schema>
15     <xs:schema targetNamespace="http://www.example.com/faults">
16       <xs:include schemaLocation="http://soabook.com/example/faults/faults.xsd"
17       />
18     </xs:schema>
19     <xs:schema elementFormDefault="qualified"
20       targetNamespace="http://www.example.com/getord">
21       <xs:element name="getOrdersDates">
22         <xs:complexType>
23           <xs:sequence>
24             <xs:element name="startDate" type="xs:date"/>
25             <xs:element name="endDate" type="xs:date"/>
```

```
26                </xs:sequence>
27              </xs:complexType>
28            </xs:element>
29            <xs:element name="getOrdersDatesResponse">
30              <xs:complexType>
31                <xs:sequence>
32                  <xs:element name="orders" type="oms:OrdersType"/>
33                </xs:sequence>
34              </xs:complexType>
35            </xs:element>
36          </xs:schema>
37        </wsdl:types>
```

book-code/chap04/wsdl/GetOrdersDates.wsdl

Note that the element getOrderDates has two children: startDate and endDate. These children are parameters and getOrderDates is a wrapper element. Likewise, the element getOrdersDatesResponse is a wrapper element with a single child. Example 4–15 shows how these wrapper elements are used to define the wsdl:messages used in the wsdl:operation.

Example 4–15 The Wrapper Elements Are the Single wsdl:part Defined for the Request and Response Messages

```
41    <wsdl:message name="request">
42      <wsdl:part name="parameters" element="getord:getOrdersDates"/>
43    </wsdl:message>
44    <wsdl:message name="response">
45      <wsdl:part name="parameters" element="getord:getOrdersDatesResponse"/>
46    </wsdl:message>
47    <wsdl:message name="inputFault">
48      <wsdl:part name="parameters" element="faults:inputMessageValidationFault"/>
49    </wsdl:message>
50    <wsdl:portType name="GetOrdersDatesPort">
51      <wsdl:operation name="getOrdersDates">
52        <wsdl:input message="getord:request"/>
53        <wsdl:output message="getord:response"/>
54        <wsdl:fault name="getOrdersInputFault" message="getord:inputFault"/>
55      </wsdl:operation>
56    </wsdl:portType>
```

book-code/chap04/wsdl/GetOrdersDates.wsdl

The `request` message is defined using the single `wsdl:part` defined by the wrapper element `getOrdersDates`. Likewise, the `response` message is defined by the wrapper element `getOrdersDatesResponse`.

A SOAP message corresponding to this document/literal wrapped WSDL is discussed in Section 4.2 and reproduced in Example 4–16.

Example 4–16 SOAP Request Message for the `getOrdersDates` `wsdl:operation`

```
4   <envl:Envelope xmlns:envl="http://schemas.xmlsoap.org/soap/envelope">
5     <envl:Body>
6       <getord:getOrdersDates xmlns:getord="http://www.example.com/oms/getorders">
7         <getord:startDate>2005-11-19</getord:startDate>
8         <getord:endDate>2005-11-22</getord:endDate>
9       </getord:getOrdersDates>
10    </envl:Body>
11  </envl:Envelope>
```

book-code/chap04/soap/GetOrdersDatesSOAPRequest.xml

Notice that the `env:Body` of this SOAP message contains a single element. It is defined by the wrapper element `getOrdersDates`. The parameters being sent to the Web service are children of `getOrdersDates`—`startDate` and `endDate`.

This style has the advantages of document/literal (primarily the capability to validate SOAP messages against schema), together with the operation name being included as a wrapper element. This makes it a good choice for most purposes.

I went through the other styles here because it is very important to understand how the style of WSDL affects the structure of the SOAP message. Even if you always use document/literal wrapped, you should still understand how its WSDL is structured and what format SOAP messages it produces. The best way to develop that level of understanding is to work through all the various styles shown here.

4.3.6 Summary of the Dispatching Process

At this point, you might be wondering when I am going to get on with the discussion of dispatching. All this talk about WSDL style leads up to that because dispatching requires (in addition to identifying the `wsdl:port`) identifying the `wsdl:operation`, the Java class and method associated with that `wsdl:operation`, and how the input message maps to the parameters of the method. So, the dispatching process involves the following steps:

1. Identify the SOAP message's target `soap:address`.
2. From the `soap:address`, get the `wsdl:port` and `wsdl:portType`.
3. Identify its target `wsdl:operation`.
4. Look up the associated Java class and method.

In this manner, the dispatching process is seen to involve creating the mapping from the SOAP request message to the Java method that will be invoked to process that message. The actual serialization of the message parts into the Java class instances of the respective parameters, and the invocation of the method, are not considered part of the dispatching process. Figure 4–2 illustrates steps 1–4 of this dispatching process.

As illustrated, in step 1, the endpoint listener gets the target URL of the SOAP message from the underlying HTTP transmission. From a Web services point of view, this is "cheating." But, as discussed previously, there is really no alternative unless you use WS-Addressing. This URL is matched against the available WSDLs that have been deployed by the deployment subsystem. Matching against the `soap:address` enables the `wsdl:port` to be identified.

Next, in step 2, the relationships in the WSDL are traced to get from the `wsdl:port`, through the `wsdl:binding`, to the `wsdl:portType`.

Now, in step 3, the invocation subsystem looks at the wrapper element (`getOrdersDates`) from the SOAP message and thereby identifies the `wsdl:operation` of the same name within the `wsdl:portType` identified in step 2.

Lastly, in step 4, the deployment subsystem, which maintains a mapping table (of some kind) that correlates WSDL with Java, looks up the Java class `OrderManager` and method `getOrders(Date, Date)` from the `wsdl:operation`—based on this correlation.

At this point, the invocation subsystem still needs to look inside the SOAP message's wrapper element and correlate (using information from the deployment subsystem) the message parts with the method parameters. I will talk more about that process in Section 4.5.1.

That wraps up my rather detailed discussion of the dispatching process and WSDL styles contained in Sections 4.3.1–4.3.6. I find that going through it in that level of detail really forces you to think through how a Web Services platform works. Armed with this understanding, you are able to see what a given implementation can and cannot do. In the next section, you are going to put that understanding to use as you look at a specific example of a simple dispatching scenario that cannot be implemented using JAX-WS 2.0.

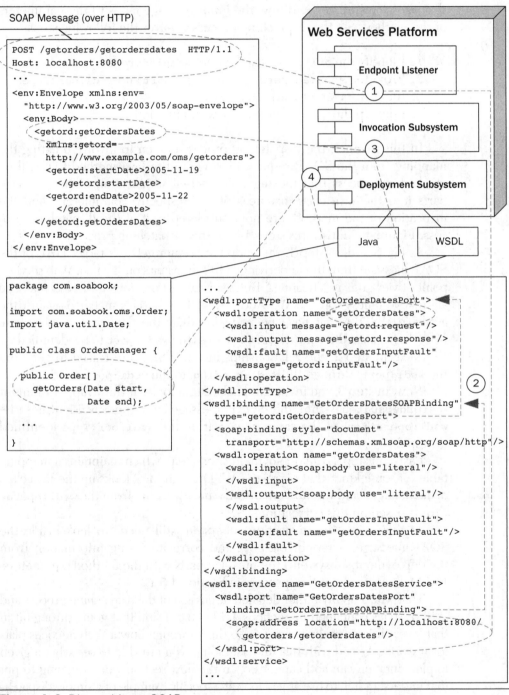

Figure 4–2 Dispatching a SOAP message.

4.3.7 Shortcomings of the JAX-WS 2.0 Dispatching for SOA Integration

As discussed in the previous sections, one role of a Web Services Platform Architecture is to implement a WSDL interface using Java classes and operations. You would assume that you should be able to assemble Java classes and methods however you would like in order to implement the `wsdl:operation` definitions contained in a particular WSDL.

With JAX-WS 2.0 (and its predecessor, JAX-RPC 1.1), it is not always possible to implement a WSDL the way you would like, however. That is because JAX-WS 2.0 uses a standard Java/WSDL mapping that correlates `wsdl:portType` elements with Java classes or interfaces (see Chapter 2, Section 2.2.2). Operations within a single `wsdl:portType` have to be mapped to methods within a single class or interface.

Figure 4–3 This dispatching scenario is not supported by JAX-WS 2.0.

Figure 4–3 shows an example of such a dispatching scenario that is not supported by the JAX-WS 2.0 mapping. As you can see, the WSDL has a `wsdl:portType` description that defines two operations: `getAddress` and `getHistory`. As the diagram shows, I'd like to map them to `Customer.getAddress()` and `CustomerHistory.getCustomerHistory()`, respectively.

But because those methods are in separate classes, JAX-WS 2.0 cannot support such a mapping. Now, it is possible to create some wrapper code that enables you to implement such a scenario. In the next section, I explore how you can do that.

4.4   Working around Some JAX-WS 2.0 Dispatching Limitations

In this section, I walk through a detailed example of how to work around the dispatching difficulties posed by the JAX-WS 2.0 WSDL/Java mapping described in Section 4.3.7. You will see that this example involves creating wrapper code to work with the interfaces generated by the JAX-WS 2.0 WSDL to Java mapping tool provided with your Java EE 5 implementation.

In addition to discussing the workaround, I use this example to point out how JAX-WS uses WS-Metadata annotations to implement the WSDL to Java mapping. This is kind of a prelude to the topic of annotations, which I discuss in depth in Chapter 5.

Example 4–17 shows more of the WSDL from which `wsdl:portType` snippet in Figure 4–3 was taken. Here, I show you all of the WSDL except the `wsdl:binding` and `wsdl:service` definitions. As discussed in the preceding section, I'd like to implement this WSDL by assigning each of the two operations to methods from different classes. You should read through this WSDL now—even though it is a little long—to get familiar with it. It will help you understand the rest of the example.

Example 4–17 WSDL for the `CustomerInformation` Web Service

```
4   <wsdl:definitions targetNamespace="http://www.example.com/css/custinfo"
5     xmlns:wsdl="http://schemas.xmlsoap.org/wsdl/"
6     xmlns:soap="http://schemas.xmlsoap.org/wsdl/soap/"
7     xmlns:xs="http://www.w3.org/2001/XMLSchema"
8     xmlns:xsi="http://www.w3.org/2001/XMLSchema-instance"
9     xmlns:custinfo="http://www.example.com/css/custinfo"
10    xmlns:css="http://www.example.com/css"
```

```
11  xmlns:corp="http://www.example.com/corp"
12  xsi:schemaLocation="http://schemas.xmlsoap.org/wsdl/
13  http://schemas.xmlsoap.org/wsdl/ http://schemas.xmlsoap.org/wsdl/soap/
14  http://schemas.xmlsoap.org/wsdl/soap/">
15  <wsdl:types>
16    <xs:schema elementFormDefault="qualified"
17      targetNamespace="http://www.example.com/css">
18      <xs:include
19        schemaLocation="http://soabook.com/example/css/custhistentries.xsd"/>
20    </xs:schema>
21    <xs:schema elementFormDefault="qualified"
22      targetNamespace="http://www.example.com/corp">
23      <xs:include
24        schemaLocation="http://soabook.com/example/corp/standardtypes.xsd"/>
25    </xs:schema>
26    <xs:schema elementFormDefault="qualified"
27      targetNamespace="http://www.example.com/css/custinfo">
28      <xs:import namespace="http://www.example.com/css"/>
29      <xs:import namespace="http://www.example.com/corp"/>
30      <xs:element name="getAddress">
31        <xs:complexType>
32          <xs:sequence>
33            <xs:element name="custId" type="xs:string"/>
34          </xs:sequence>
35        </xs:complexType>
36      </xs:element>
37      <xs:element name="getAddressResponse">
38        <xs:complexType>
39          <xs:sequence>
40            <xs:element name="address" type="corp:AddressType"/>
41          </xs:sequence>
42        </xs:complexType>
43      </xs:element>
44      <xs:element name="getCustomerHistory">
45        <xs:complexType>
46          <xs:sequence>
47            <xs:element name="custId" type="xs:string"/>
48          </xs:sequence>
49        </xs:complexType>
50      </xs:element>
51      <xs:element name="getCustomerHistoryResponse">
52        <xs:complexType>
53          <xs:sequence>
54            <xs:element name="history" type="css:CustomerHistoryEntriesType"/>
```

```
55              </xs:sequence>
56            </xs:complexType>
57          </xs:element>
58        </xs:schema>
59      </wsdl:types>
60      <wsdl:message name="getAddressRequestMessage">
61        <wsdl:part name="parameters" element="custinfo:getAddress"/>
62      </wsdl:message>
63      <wsdl:message name="getAddressResponseMessage">
64        <wsdl:part name="parameters" element="custinfo:getAddressResponse"/>
65      </wsdl:message>
66      <wsdl:message name="getCustomerHistoryRequestMessage">
67        <wsdl:part name="parameters" element="custinfo:getCustomerHistory"/>
68      </wsdl:message>
69      <wsdl:message name="getCustomerHistoryResponseMessage">
70        <wsdl:part name="parameters" element="custinfo:getCustomerHistoryResponse"/>
71      </wsdl:message>
72      <wsdl:portType name="CustomerInformationPort">
73        <wsdl:operation name="getAddress">
74          <wsdl:input message="custinfo:getAddressRequestMessage"/>
75          <wsdl:output message="custinfo:getAddressResponseMessage"/>
76        </wsdl:operation>
77        <wsdl:operation name="getCustomerHistory">
78          <wsdl:input message="custinfo:getCustomerHistoryRequestMessage"/>
79          <wsdl:output message="custinfo:getCustomerHistoryResponseMessage"/>
80        </wsdl:operation>
81      </wsdl:portType>
```

book-code/chap04/jaxwsworkaround/src/xml/CustomerInformation.wsdl

Here are the salient points to notice about this WSDL:

- It uses the document/literal wrapped style. You can tell that by the presence of the wrapper elements (e.g., custinfo:getAddress and custinfo:getCustomerHistory).
- It includes external schema definitions for css:CustomerHistory-EntriesType and corp:AddressType. The first of these XML types you have seen before in Chapter 3, Section 3.1. The second is the corporate standard schema used to represent addresses. This is another example of the principle discussed in Section 4.1.1—*reusable schema*.

- The operation `getAddress` returns an instance of `corp:AddressType`—the standard reusable schema for `Address`. Likewise, the operation `getCustomerHistory` returns an instance of `css:CustomerHistory-EntriesType`. Of course, both return types are represented as children of their respective wrapper elements.
- Both of the operations—`getAddress` and `getCustomerHistory`—are included in the same `wsdl:portType` with the name `CustomerInformationPort`.

Figure 4–4 illustrates the workaround for mapping this WSDL to methods from two different classes. The `wsdl:portType` named `CustomerInformationPort` is first mapped to a Java interface named `CustomerInformationPort`. In JAX-WS and WS-Metadata terminology, this is called the *service endpoint interface*. It is generated using the standard JAX-WS 2.0 mapping. The two arrows going from the WSDL to the interface show how the `wsdl:operation` definitions map to the method definitions.

Next, the single arrow from the `CustomerInformationPort` interface to the `CustomerInformation` class (lower right-hand corner of Figure 4–4) illustrates my implementation of that interface. In JAX-WS and WS-Metadata terminology, this implementation is called the *service implementation bean*. The `CustomerInformation` class is not generated from the WSDL, but rather is a custom implementation of the `CustomerInformationPort` interface. Normally, the business logic implementing the `wsdl:operation` definitions would go here. However, in this case, the business logic already exists—it is contained in the two classes `Customer` and `CustomerHistory`. As a result, the implementation of the `CustomerInformation` class is a wrapper that is used to invoke the `Customer` and `CustomerHistory` classes that contain the preexisting business logic.

Lastly, the arrows going from `CustomerInformation` to those two classes illustrate how the wrapper is implemented. Each method, `getAddress` and `getCustomerHistory`, uses references to instances of `Customer` and `CustomerHistory`, respectively, to invoke their `getAddress` and `getCustomerHistory` methods. Clearly, this approach works and it is not too difficult to implement. It becomes a problem, however, when it comes to maintenance. In addition to the WSDL and the business logic (i.e., the `Customer` and `CustomerHistory` classes), you now need to maintain this wrapper class.

Example 4–18 shows the code that is generated for the `CustomerInformationPort` interface. All Java EE 5 implementations provide some type of tool that can read WSDL, such as Example 4–17, and generate Java

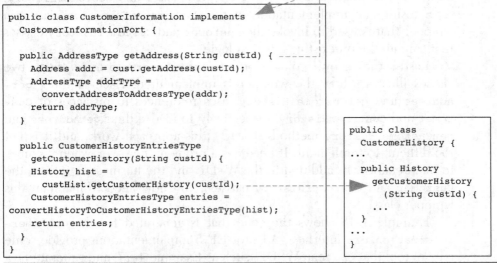

Service Endpoint Interface

```
public interface CustomerInformationPort {

  public AddressType getAddress(String custId);

  public CustomerHistoryEntriesType
    getCustomerHistory(String custId);
}
```

```
<wsdl:portType name="CustomerInformationPort">

  <wsdl:operation name="getAddress">
    <wsdl:input .../>
    <wsdl:output .../>
  </wsdl:operation>

  <wsdl:operation name="getHistory">
    <wsdl:input .../>
    <wsdl:output .../>
  </wsdl:operation>

</wsdl:portType>
```

```
public class Customer {
...
  public Address getAddress(String custId) {
    ...
  }
...
}
```

Service Implementation Bean

```
public class CustomerInformation implements
  CustomerInformationPort {

  public AddressType getAddress(String custId) {
    Address addr = cust.getAddress(custId);
    AddressType addrType =
      convertAddressToAddressType(addr);
    return addrType;
  }

  public CustomerHistoryEntriesType
    getCustomerHistory(String custId) {
    History hist =
      custHist.getCustomerHistory(custId);
    CustomerHistoryEntriesType entries =
convertHistoryToCustomerHistoryEntriesType(hist);
    return entries;
  }
}
```

```
public class
  CustomerHistory {
...
  public History
    getCustomerHistory
      (String custId) {
    ...
  }
...
}
```

Figure 4–4 A workaround for the Section 4.3.7 dispatching scenario.

artifacts that implement the JAX-WS 2.0 WSDL to Java mapping. For this book, I am using the GlassFish implementation of Java EE 5, and the tool provided with GlassFish is called `wsimport`. The code in Example 4–18 was generated using the `wsimport` tool. Like all the examples in this book, you can run this yourself using Maven and/or Ant and generate the code. To do that, follow these steps:

1. Go to `chap04/jaxwsworkaround`.
2. To run the `wsimport` tool, enter `ant gen-java`.
3. The generated artifacts are written to the directory `chap04/jaxws-workaround/target/work/java`.

Example 4–18 The JAX-WS-Generated Code for the `CustomerInformation` Web Service (i.e., the Service Endpoint Interface)

```
19  package com.example.css.custinfo;
20
21  import javax.jws.WebMethod;
22  import javax.jws.WebParam;
23  import javax.jws.WebResult;
24  import javax.jws.WebService;
25  import javax.xml.ws.RequestWrapper;
26  import javax.xml.ws.ResponseWrapper;
27  import com.example.corp.AddressType;
28  import com.example.css.CustomerHistoryEntriesType;
29  import com.example.css.custinfo.CustomerInformationPort;
30
31  @WebService(name = "CustomerInformationPort",
32      targetNamespace = "http://www.example.com/css/custinfo",
33      wsdlLocation = " ... /CustomerInformation.wsdl")
34  public interface CustomerInformationPort {
35
36    @WebMethod
37    @WebResult(name = "address",
38        targetNamespace = "http://www.example.com/css/custinfo")
39    @RequestWrapper(localName = "getAddress",
40        targetNamespace = "http://www.example.com/css/custinfo",
41        className = "com.example.css.custinfo.GetAddress")
42    @ResponseWrapper(localName = "getAddressResponse",
43        targetNamespace = "http://www.example.com/css/custinfo",
44        className = "com.example.css.custinfo.GetAddressResponse")
45    public AddressType getAddress(
```

```
46      @WebParam(name = "custId",
47          targetNamespace = "http://www.example.com/css/custinfo")
48      String custId);
49
50   @WebMethod
51   @WebResult(name = "history",
52          targetNamespace = "http://www.example.com/css/custinfo")
53   @RequestWrapper(localName = "getCustomerHistory",
54          targetNamespace = "http://www.example.com/css/custinfo",
55          className = "com.example.css.custinfo.GetCustomerHistory")
56   @ResponseWrapper(localName = "getCustomerHistoryResponse",
57          targetNamespace = "http://www.example.com/css/custinfo",
58          className = "com.example.css.custinfo.GetCustomerHistoryResponse")
59   public CustomerHistoryEntriesType getCustomerHistory(
60      @WebParam(name = "custId",
61          targetNamespace = "http://www.example.com/css/custinfo")
62      String custId);
63
64   }
```

book-code/chap04/jaxwsworkaround/src/java/com/example/css/custinfo
/CustomerInformationPort.java

Looking at the code for this `CustomerInformationPort` interface, you can see that it implements the two methods `getAddress` and `getCustomer-History` as illustrated in Figure 4–4. What is most interesting, however, is the return type classes and the annotations that the `wsimport` tool created to implement the mapping from the WSDL.

The `getAddress` method, for example, has a return type of `com.example.corp.AddressType`. This is a class that has also been generated by `wsimport` from the schema definition for `corp:AddressType`. So, right away, you can see that mapping from the interface to the business logic in the two different classes, `Customer` and `CustomerHistory`, is not the only mapping challenge you need to overcome to implement this example. You are also going to have to translate between this generated `AddressType` class and the return type `samples.Address` used by the `Customer.getAddress()` method. I talk about this issue in detail in the next two sections. You'll notice that you have the same issue with the return type for `getCustomer-History()`—`com.example.css.CustomerHistoryEntriesType` is also a generated class that has to be mapped to the business logic return type: `samples.History`.

For a moment, let's look at some of the annotations generated in Example 4–18 and discuss what they do. Table 4–1 provides some explanation.

Table 4–1 Descriptions of the Java Annotations Appearing in Example 4–18

Annotation	Purpose	Comments
`@WebService`	Marks a Java class as implementing a Web service, or a Java interface as defining a Web service interface	The presence of the `wsdlLocation` value in this example indicates that the interface's service implementation bean is implementing a predefined WSDL contract (i.e., the "Start from WSDL" development mode).
`@WebMethod`	Indicates that a method is exposed as a Web service operation	The operation name defaults to the method name. In this case, you can see that these are the same as the `wsdl:operation` names.
`@WebResult`	Provides the local name and namespace for the return type—as defined in the WSDL	Since I am using document/literal wrapped, notice that the value for this annotation is the element defined in the `wsdl:types` section that is the child of the response wrapper element.
`@RequestWrapper`	Indicates the mapping between the WSDL request wrapper element and the JAXB-generated bean that implements it as a wrapper class	Notice that the `wsimport` tool has generated (via JAXB) a class named `com.example.cee.custinfo.GetAddress` that maps to the `custinfo:getAddress` type defined in the WSDL.
`@ResponseWrapper`	Same as `@Request-Wrapper` but for responses	Same as `@RequestWrapper` but for responses.

Continuing with this illustration, the code in Example 4–19 shows an implementation of the auto-generated service endpoint interface. This is the code that actually "splits" the `wsdl:portType` into two different classes.

Notice that the code for the `CustomerInformation` class contains `@Resource` annotations referencing two external resources—instances of the `Customer` and `CustomerHistory` classes. The `@Resource` annotation is defined in the Common Annotations specification [JSR-250]. When applied to a field, as in these examples, the Java EE 5 container will inject an instance of the requested resource (i.e., instances of `Customer` and `CustomerHistory`) when this service implementation bean is initialized. Of course, for this to work a corresponding valid JNDI resource must be defined in the application component environment where this service implementation bean is deployed. See the sections on JNDI and dependency injection found in the Java EE 5 specification [JSR-244] for more information on how injection works.

Example 4–19 Workaround for the JAX-WS `PortType` Mapping (i.e., the Service Implementation Bean)

```
28  @WebService(
29      endpointInterface="com.example.css.custinfo.CustomerInformationPort",
30      serviceName="CustomerInformationService")
31  public class CustomerInformation implements CustomerInformationPort {
32
33      @Resource
34      private Customer cust;
35
36      @Resource
37      private CustomerHistory custHist;
38
39      public AddressType getAddress(String custId) {
40          Address addr = cust.getAddress(custId);
41          AddressType addrType = convertAddressToAddressType(addr);
42          return addrType;
43      }
44
45      public CustomerHistoryEntriesType getCustomerHistory(String custId) {
46          History hist = custHist.getCustomerHistory(custId);
47          CustomerHistoryEntriesType entries =
48              convertHistoryToCustomerHistoryEntriesType(hist);
49          return entries;
50      }
```

book-code/chap04/jaxwsworkaround/src/java/samples/CustomerInformation.java

Continuing to look down through the code in Example 4–19, you can see that each method—`getAddress()` and `getCustomerHistory()`—uses the injected instances of the classes—`cust` and `hist`, respectively—that implement the business logic. You can also see that the code uses the static methods `convertAddressToAddressType` and `convertHistoryToCustomerHistory-EntriesType` to translate between the `wsimport`-generated return type classes and the classes used by the business implementation. This is the solution to the problem discussed along with Example 4–18. Not only do you need to make this service implementation bean a wrapper that splits the `portType` operations across two different classes, but you also need to translate between business-defined return type classes and the JAXB-generated implementations of the WSDL's XML Schema-defined return types.

The fact that you need multiple levels of wrapper code to implement this simple example is an indication that the JAX-WS 2.0 specification was not really designed with "Start from WSDL and Java" problems in mind. JAX-WS 2.0 and JAXB 2.0 are fine when you are doing "Start from Java" development. You can get by when you are doing "Start from WSDL" development. However, when you are doing "Start from WSDL and Java," the JWS specifications start to seem like they aren't really designed for the job. Strategies for handling "Start from WSDL and Java" are discussed in Chapter 5 where JAXB 2.0 capabilities are explored in depth. As discussed there, and in Chapters 6 and 7 where JAX-WS 2.0 is examined, the recommended approach is to do the best you can to create JAXB representations of the XML Schema types used in the WSDL that closely match your existing Java classes. That involves more work than simply running the schema compiler against the target WSDL. It involves writing your own annotations for your existing classes in an attempt to map them to the existing WSDL. Doing this will minimize the amount and complexity of the wrapper code required. Once you have created the JAXB classes to be deployed, you can work with the JAX-WS annotations (described in Chapters 6 and 7) to shape the generated WSDL to match the target.

4.5 SOA Often Requires "Start from WSDL and Java"

At this point, I think it is useful to pause for a moment and consider the challenge that faces architects and developers tasked with SOA Integration for the enterprise. SOA-style applications for enterprise integration typically include components from multiple systems. Each system has its own API. If a system is internally developed, that API was designed and is maintained by a particular group within the enterprise. If the system was purchased, the API is provided as part of the package. It may be customizable or it may not be. If it can be customized, that responsibility lies with a particular group within the enterprise.

Now consider the WSDL for the SOA components in an enterprise integration application. Where do the XML Schema building blocks for the WSDL come from? It is more than likely that for many of the common XML types (e.g., address), the enterprise has developed standards. Interoperability concerns require that an enterprise not have 15 different versions of the address type, for example. Similarly, if the SOA application is being used to integrate with external entities (e.g., suppliers or customers), it is likely that those entities have their own XML standards the SOA application must adhere. Perhaps an industry standard such as ebXML or Rosetta-Net is being used.

Even if, at one time, a firm had coherent information systems, it is likely that, as it grew, new departments and organizations were added and systems evolved in different directions. Now, as the firm struggles to consolidate systems and bring order so that its interfaces can be opened for Internet communication via Web services (either across departments or with external suppliers and customers), the need for adherence to standard schema is critical. As a result, it is likely that programmers implementing Web Services on top of existing applications will need to map such applications to standard WSDL and XML Schema interfaces. This is why the "Start from WSDL and Java" problem arises so frequently during the SOA application design process.

Figure 4–5 illustrates the typical situation for the SOA application designer. There are several source systems with APIs and several external standards for XML schema to be considered.

The important concept to grasp in considering Figure 4–5 is that none of the external inputs (APIs or Schema standards) is controlled by the SOA component designers. Nor are these external inputs likely to be controlled by the individuals responsible for exposing the system APIs as Web services.

So, suppose you are responsible for designing a Web service to expose part of System A's Java API. Say that you would like to annotate the Java classes/interfaces so that the WSDL generated by the Java EE 5 container is compliant with the organization's enterprise standards. For many reasons, you may not be able to do this. First, System A might be a third-party package that cannot be customized. Second, even if it can be customized, that responsibility probably resides in another organization. Third, even if it is an internally developed application, the customization process is probably not in your control. So, even in the best case, you probably have to make a

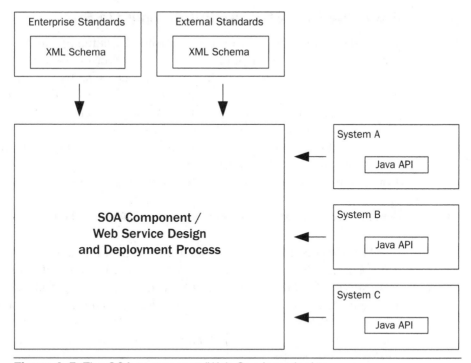

Figure 4–5 The SOA component/Web Services design process.

customization request and wait until it gets considered and implemented by the group that is responsible. Anyone who has worked in a large enterprise knows that this process can take months. If you have a deadline, it just isn't feasible.

Furthermore, there are good reasons why the organization responsible may not want to modify the API—even if it just involves some simple annotations. Most enterprises require unit testing, system testing, and integration testing for any change to a production system. That can be a showstopper right there. It might just be too much work or too expensive to modify that API.

As you can see from this discussion, the "Start from WSDL and Java" development mode is essential to SOA. Because the developers and architects who are deploying SOA components as Web services must work with externally defined APIs and XML schema, they need tools that enable them to map an existing API to a WSDL built from existing schemas.

The key to doing "Start from WSDL and Java" development is to have flexible tools for mapping Java to XML schema. In the next section, I look at this challenge in some more detail.

4.5.1 The Role of Java/XML Mapping in SOA

Java/XML mapping for SOA is accomplished by defining and implementing type mappings. A type mapping is simply a relationship between a Java class and an XML Schema type—for example, `corp:AddressType` and `samples.Address`. A type mapping is implemented by a *serializer* and a *deserializer*. The serializer converts instances of the Java class into XML instances that conform to the schema. The deserializer does the reverse.

When doing "Start from WSDL and Java" development, a large portion of the design process involves defining the type mappings and serializers. For example, suppose you have a Java method such as:

```
public void updateAddress(String custId, Address addr)
```

And suppose the corporate standard schema for `address` is a complex type: `corp:AddressType`. Then, the WSDL that is deployed to describe the Web service for `updateAddress` needs to include `corp:AddressType` as a message part. But furthermore, the serialization subsystem on the platform where the Web service is deployed must be able to access the deserializer for the type mapping `<corp:AddressType, samples.Address>`. When a SOAP request for the Web service arrives, the deserializer is used to convert the SOAP part to the Java method parameter. This process is illustrated in Figure 4–6.

As discussed in Section 4.3, the dispatching of this SOAP message is based on the wrapper element—`custinfo:updateAddress`. It gets mapped to the `updateAddress` method as shown. Below this wrapper element are the two message parts[8]—`custinfo:custId` and `custinfo:address`. These are mapped to the parameters `custId` (`String`) and `addr` (`Address`), respectively. This mapping, of the message parts to the method parameters, is not defined in the WSDL. The WSDL contains no information about the underlying Java implementation of the Web service. This property of the WSDL is consistent with the separation of concerns concept discussed in Section 4.2. After all, the consumer of the Web service shouldn't have to be concerned with such implementation details. All the consumer needs is the information necessary to construct the SOAP message and send it to the appropriate URL.

---

8. I refer to the children of the wrapper element as message "parts." This might be a little bit confusing, since these components of the SOAP message are not actually defined using the `wsdl:part` definitions in the document/literal wrapped style of WSDL. Nevertheless, the term "parts" seems to be the best characterization.

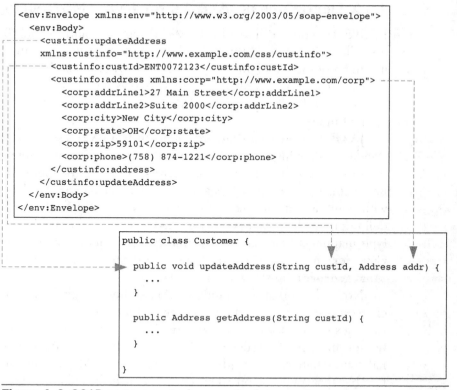

```
<env:Envelope xmlns:env="http://www.w3.org/2003/05/soap-envelope">
  <env:Body>
    <custinfo:updateAddress
      xmlns:custinfo="http://www.example.com/css/custinfo">
      <custinfo:custId>ENT0072123</custinfo:custId>
      <custinfo:address xmlns:corp="http://www.example.com/corp">
        <corp:addrLine1>27 Main Street</corp:addrLine1>
        <corp:addrLine2>Suite 2000</corp:addrLine2>
        <corp:city>New City</corp:city>
        <corp:state>OH</corp:state>
        <corp:zip>59101</corp:zip>
        <corp:phone>(758) 874-1221</corp:phone>
      </custinfo:address>
    </custinfo:updateAddress>
  </env:Body>
</env:Envelope>
```

```
public class Customer {

    public void updateAddress(String custId, Address addr) {
        ...
    }

    public Address getAddress(String custId) {
        ...
    }

}
```

Figure 4–6 SOAP parts map to Java method parameters.

So, the type mappings that link the SOAP/WSDL to the Java implementation are not defined in the WSDL, but rather are part of the internal—platform-specific—deployment information associated with the Web service. In the JWS model, these type mappings are defined by the JAXB standard mapping as customized by any annotations.

In Chapter 5, Sections 5.3 and 5.4, I look in detail at how to implement type mappings using JAXB 2.0. At this point, I just want to point out that the type mapping process is outside the scope of the WSDL and is a platform-specific issue. Furthermore, you should understand that being able to implement flexible type mappings is a key to the "Start from WSDL and Java" development model needed for SOA. As illustrated in Figure 4–6, the key to being able to deploy the `updateAddress()` method as a Web service with the desired WSDL is to be able to implement the type mapping `<corp:AddressType, samples.Address>`.

4.5.2 Limitations of JAXB 2.0 for Java/XML Mapping in SOA

JAXB 2.0 is a powerful tool for Java/XML binding, and Chapter 5 reviews its capabilities in detail. At this point, however, I am going to point out some of its limitations as a tool for doing "Start from WSDL and Java" development. This is not so much a criticism of JAXB 2.0 as much as it is another illustration of the difficulties presented by the "Start from WSDL and Java" development mode.

JAXB 2.0 defines a standard mapping from XML schema to Java. This standard mapping associates XML Schema element definitions with instances of `java.xml.bind.JAXBElement<T>`. At this point, I am not so much concerned with the specifics of the `JAXBElement<T>` class, but rather with pointing out that the one-to-one association of XML schema element definitions with instances of this class makes it impossible to implement type mappings that may split or merge elements to create Java instances. Consider, for example, the type mapping `<corp:AddressType, samples.Address>` illustrated in Figure 4–7.

Notice here that the standard XML Schema type for `address` has two elements—`addrLine1` and `addrLine2`—that must map into the `Address` variables `streetNum` and `streetName`. You can imagine a number of heuristics for implementing such a mapping. Probably some of the heuristics even fail for certain types of addresses (e.g., where do you put an apartment number that might be on `addrLine2`?). However, such heuristics cannot be easily implemented in JAXB 2.0.

Similarly, the phone number is represented in the standard XML schema as a single instance of `xs:string`. However, in the `Address` class it is an instance of `Phone`. As you can see in the diagram, the `Phone` class represents the phone number using three variables: area code, exchange, and number. Clearly, you could write a simple script to parse the phone element (`xs:string`) into these three variables. However, that type of mapping cannot be implemented within the JAXB standard mapping. To implement such a mapping within the JAXB framework, you need to implement your mapping heuristics as a Java class extending the `java.xml.bind.annotations.adapters.XmlAdapter<ValueType, BoundType>` class and annotate the `Address` class with `@XmlJavaTypeAdapter`. I go through an example of how to do this at the end of Chapter 5. As you will see there, it is a nontrivial exercise.

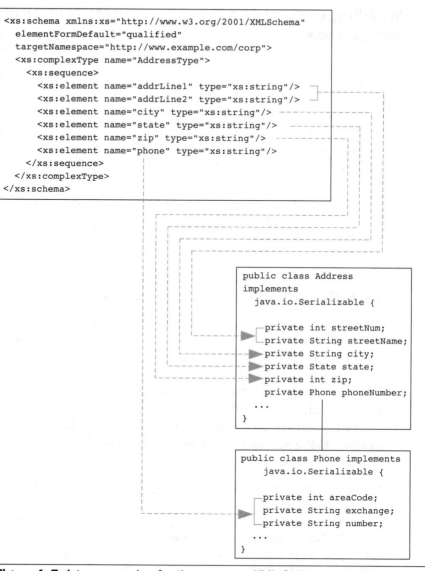

```
<xs:schema xmlns:xs="http://www.w3.org/2001/XMLSchema"
  elementFormDefault="qualified"
  targetNamespace="http://www.example.com/corp">
  <xs:complexType name="AddressType">
    <xs:sequence>
      <xs:element name="addrLine1" type="xs:string"/>
      <xs:element name="addrLine2" type="xs:string"/>
      <xs:element name="city" type="xs:string"/>
      <xs:element name="state" type="xs:string"/>
      <xs:element name="zip" type="xs:string"/>
      <xs:element name="phone" type="xs:string"/>
    </xs:sequence>
  </xs:complexType>
</xs:schema>
```

```
public class Address
implements
  java.io.Serializable {

  private int streetNum;
  private String streetName;
  private String city;
  private State state;
  private int zip;
  private Phone phoneNumber;
  ...
}
```

```
public class Phone implements
  java.io.Serializable {

  private int areaCode;
  private String exchange;
  private String number;
  ...
}
```

Figure 4–7 A type mapping for the `Address` XML Schema definition to the `Address` Java class definition.

4.6   Working around JAXB 2.0 Java/XML Mapping Limitations

Figure 4–7 shows an example of a type mapping that, although it could easily arise in practice, is nontrivial to handle within the JAXB framework. In this section, I show you a couple of practical alternatives for implementing such a type mapping using JAXB. The first approach uses the JAXB schema compiler and Java to map from the generated bean to the `Address` class. The second approach uses the JAXB schema generator and XSLT to map from `corp:AddressType` instances to the generated schema type.

The examples in this section can be found in chap04/sfwj. You can run them in batch mode by simply going to that directory and entering `ant run-both-deserializers`. Or, you can follow the instructions in the next section for running them individually step by step.

4.6.1 Using the Schema Compiler and Java

Here, I show how to augment JAXB—wrapping a standard JAXB binding inside additional code—to get the desired mapping. This approach takes advantage of the power of the JAXB framework without getting caught up in the difficulties associated with `XmlAdapter` and `@XmlJavaTypeAdapter`. It is a practical approach that forms the basis of the SOA-J Serialization Sub-System described in depth in Chapter 10.

To get started, let's examine the results of applying the JAXB schema compiler to the `corp:AddressType` listed in Figure 4–7 (see Example 4–20).

Example 4–20 The `AddressType` Class Generated by JAXB from `corp:AddressType`

```
60   @XmlAccessorType(AccessType.FIELD)
61   @XmlType(name = "AddressType", propOrder = {
62       "addrLine1",
63       "addrLine2",
64       "city",
65       "state",
66       "zip",
67       "phone"
68   })
69   public class AddressType {
70
```

```
71    @XmlElement(namespace = "http://www.example.com/corp")
72    protected String addrLine1;
73    @XmlElement(namespace = "http://www.example.com/corp")
74    protected String addrLine2;
75    @XmlElement(namespace = "http://www.example.com/corp")
76    protected String city;
77    @XmlElement(namespace = "http://www.example.com/corp")
78    protected String state;
79    @XmlElement(namespace = "http://www.example.com/corp")
80    protected String zip;
81    @XmlElement(namespace = "http://www.example.com/corp")
82    protected String phone;
```

book-code/chap04/sfwj/examples/AddressType.java

I'm showing only part of the com.example.corp.AddressType class in Example 4–20. But it is a simple bean and you can imagine the rest—it is all getters and setters for the fields shown here. Besides generating the fields and methods, JAXB has included annotations that are used to marshal/ unmarshal between instances of this class and instances of the corp:AddressType schema. Annotations are discussed in detail in Chapter 5, but so that you understand this example, I explain a little bit here.

The @XmlAccessorType annotation tells JAXB to map the fields (hence the value AccessType.FIELD) to schema element definitions. For example, the String field—addrLine1—gets mapped to an XML element named addrLine1. Likewise, the @XmlType annotation tells JAXB to map the class AddressType to an XML schema complex type. Finally, the @XmlElement annotations provide a namespace for the elements.

These annotations map this JAXB-generated Java class back to the corp:AddressType complex type (pictured in Figure 4–7) from which it was generated. To make this example a little more concrete, Example 4–21 shows an instance of the corp:AddressType schema.

Example 4–21 An Instance of corp:AddressType

```
4   <custinfo:address xmlns="http://www.example.com/corp"
5    xmlns:custinfo="http://www.example.com/css/custinfo">
6    <addrLine1>175 Main Street</addrLine1>
7    <addrLine2>Suite 200</addrLine2>
8    <city>New City</city>
```

```
 9      <state>OH</state>
10      <zip>59101</zip>
11      <phone>(758) 874-1221</phone>
12    </custinfo:address>
```

book-code/chap04/sfwj/src/xml/corp_address.xml

The entire process of deserializing an instance of `corpAddressType` to an instance of `samples.Address` using the JAXB schema compiler and Java is illustrated in Figure 4–8.

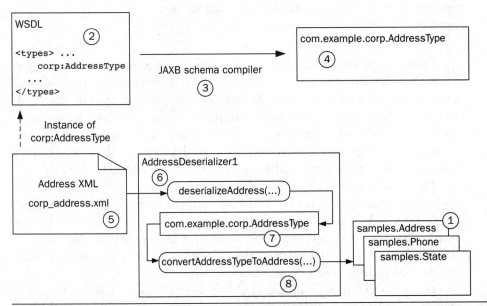

Figure 4–8 "Start from WSDL and Java" using the JAXB schema compiler and Java.

The following eight steps correspond to the labels in Figure 4–8 and describe how the process works:

1. The boxes in the lower right represent the "start from" Java. These classes include the `samples.Address` class. In order to solve the "Start from WSDL and Java" problem, you need to be able to map XML that conforms to the WSDL to these classes.

2. Steps 2–4 illustrate the use of the JAXB schema compiler. This happens prior to runtime. The box in the upper left of the figure

represents the "start from" WSDL. It contains the schema definition for `corp:AddressType` that you need to map to `samples.Address`.

3. Running the JAXB schema compiler against `corp:AddressType` creates a new class—`com.example.corp.AddressType`.

4. This new Java class, `com.example.corp.AddressType`, is used during runtime to implement the transformation.

5. Steps 5–8 illustrate the run-time transformation of an instance of `corp:AddresssType` (from the file `corp_address.xml`) in an instance of `samples.Address`.

6. The `AddressDeserializer.deserializeAddress()` method (listed in the top part of Example 4–24) takes the `corp_address.xml` file and uses JAXB to transform it into an instance of `com.example.corp.AddressType`.

7. Then, this instance of `com.example.corp.AddressType` is the input to the method `AddressDeserializer2.convertAddressTypeToAddress()` (listed in the bottom part of Example 4–24) that parses the Java properties into an instance of `samples.Address`.

8. Lastly, the resulting instance of `samples.Address` is returned.

So, as you can see, the goal of the deserialization process is to map the instance of `corp:AddressType` into the `samples.Address` class shown in Example 4–22. To get to that point, JAXB is used to create an instance of the intermediate class `com.example.corp.AddressType`.

Example 4–22 The Target Class: `samples.Address`

```
23  public class Address implements java.io.Serializable {
24    private int streetNum;
25    private String streetName;
26    private String city;
27    private State state;
28    private int zip;
29    private Phone phoneNumber;
30
```

book-code/chap04/sfwj/etc/java/samples/Address.java

As illustrated in Figure 4–7, part of the challenge here is to map the two address lines into the `streetNum` (`int`) and `streetName` (`String`) in this `samples.Address` class. Another challenge is to map the `phone` element into `phoneNumber`—which is an instance of `samples.Phone` shown in Example 4–23.

Example 4–23 The `samples.Phone` Class

```
21   public class Phone {
22       private int areaCode;
23       private String exchange;
24       private String number;
```

book-code/chap04/sfwj/etc/java/samples/Phone.java

As you can see, in this case the `phone` element must get parsed into three fields: `areaCode` (`int`), `exchange` (`String`), and `number` (`String`). In case you are wondering, I did not create these `samples.Address` and `samples.Phone` classes out of thin air just to come up with a tricky example. These classes are taken from the standard sample code that ships with IBM WebSphere Application Server (in the `WebServicesSamples` directory).

The first step in the deserialization process is to take the instance from Example 4–21 and unmarshal it into the JAXB schema-generated bean shown in Example 4–20. Once that is done, you use custom Java code to read values from the bean, parse them, and set values in the `samples.Address` class shown in Example 4–22. The code for this two-step process appears in Example 4–24.

Example 4–24 Deserialization Using the Schema-Generated Bean

```
61   public Address deserializeAddress(Source xml) throws Exception {
62
63     JAXBContext jc =
64       JAXBContext.newInstance("com.example.corp");
65     Unmarshaller u = jc.createUnmarshaller();
66     JAXBElement<com.example.corp.AddressType> addrJAXBElt =
67       u.unmarshal(xml, com.example.corp.AddressType.class);
68     com.example.corp.AddressType addrJAXB = addrJAXBElt.getValue();
69     return convertAddressTypeToAddress(addrJAXB);
70
71   }
72
73   private Address convertAddressTypeToAddress
```

```
74   (com.example.corp.AddressType addrJAXB) throws Exception {
75
76     Address addr = new Address();
77     String[] line1Parts = addrJAXB.getAddrLine1().split(" ",2);
78     int num = -1;
79     String street;
80     try {
81       num = Integer.valueOf(line1Parts[0]).intValue();
82     } catch (Exception e ) {}
83     if ( num > 0 ) {
84       addr.setStreetNum(num);
85       street = line1Parts[1];
86     } else {
87       street = addrJAXB.getAddrLine1();
88     }
89     String line2 = addrJAXB.getAddrLine2();
90     if (line2 != null && !line2.equals("") ) {
91       street += " - " + line2;
92     }
93     addr.setStreetName(street);
94     addr.setCity(addrJAXB.getCity());
95     addr.setState(State.valueOf(addrJAXB.getState()));
96     addr.setZip(Integer.valueOf(addrJAXB.getZip()).intValue());
97     String ph = addrJAXB.getPhone();
98     int areaStart = ph.indexOf("(");
99     int areaEnd = ph.indexOf(")");
100    String area = ph.substring(areaStart+1,areaEnd);
101    ph = ph.substring(areaEnd+1,ph.length());
102    String phoneSplit[] = ph.split("-", 2);
103    Phone phone = new Phone();
104    phone.setAreaCode(Integer.valueOf(area).intValue());
105    phone.setExchange(phoneSplit[0].trim());
106    phone.setNumber(phoneSplit[1].trim());
107    addr.setPhoneNumber(phone);
108    return addr;
109
110  }
```

book-code/chap04/sfwj/src/java/samples/deser/AddressDeserializer1.java

The first part of this process—unmarshalling to the generated bean—happens in the `deserializeAddress` method. The `corp:AddressType` instance is passed in to this method as an instance of `javax.xml.trans-form.Source`. The `JAXBContext` is created from the package (`com.example.corp`) containing the JAXB-generated beans. An `Unmarshaller` instance is created and used to unmarshal into an instance of `JAXBElement<com.example.corp.AddressType>`. This `JAXBElement` instance is a holder for an element instance of the generated bean. Lastly, you get an instance of the bean using the `JAXBElement.getValue` method.

That first step is the standard process for unmarshalling into a generated bean class. The next step, mapping the generated bean to `samples.Address`, takes place in the method named `convertAddressTypeToAddress` shown in Example 4–24.

Looking through the code in the `convertAddressTypeToAddress` method, you can see that it contains a bunch of confusing and ugly string parsing instructions. Unfortunately, there is no way to avoid having to write that type of code to implement the mapping pictured in Figure 4–7. Code like that is a fact of life when you are doing "Start from WSDL and Java" development. The real question is how to best manage and maintain that mapping code.

To run the example described earlier, follow these steps:

1. Go to `<book-code>/chap04/sfwj/modules/schema2java`.
2. To run the JAXB schema compiler on the schema containing `corp:AddressType` (found at http://soabook.com/example/corp/standardtypes.xsd), enter `mvn install`.
3. Go to `<book-code>/chap04/sfwj`.
4. To run the deserializer, enter `ant run-deserializer1`.

If you use JAXB for Java/XML mapping as illustrated in this section, you end up with this type of parsing code scattered around in various wrapper and utility classes. Maintenance is difficult. If a schema changes, you need to find all that parsing code and update it. Reuse is also difficult, because such parsing code has no clear description of its inputs and outputs. Without such descriptions, it is difficult to determine where the code can be reused, and developers just continue to write new parsing code for each situation they encounter.

An approach that helps to minimize the amount of ad hoc transformation and parsing code used in an SOA application is to do the transformations at the XML level, rather than at the Java class level. This can be done with XSLT, as described in the next section. One benefit of doing transformation at the XML level is that XML Schema can then be used to give precise descriptions of the input and output schemas—enabling reuse of the XSLT transformations.

4.6.2 Using the Schema Generator and XSLT

In this section, I illustrate a different approach to the mapping problem solved in the preceding section. Instead of generating a bean from the `corp:AddressType` schema, a schema is generated from the `samples.Address` class using the JAXB schema generator. XSLT is then used to map between the two schemas—the original and the JAXB-generated schema. Figure 4–9 illustrates how this process works.

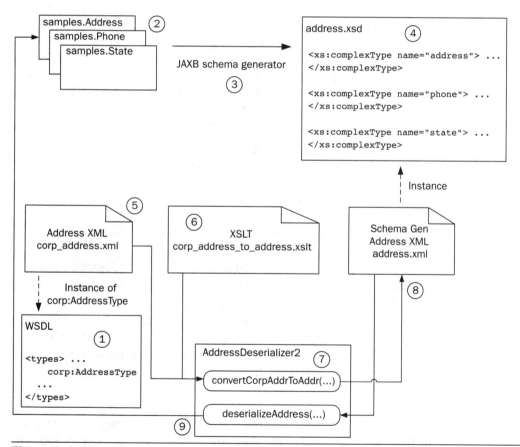

Figure 4–9 "Start from WSDL and Java" using the JAXB schema generator and XSLT.

The following nine steps correspond to the labels in Figure 4–9 and describe how the process works:

1. Steps 1–4 illustrate the use of the JAXB schema generator. This happens prior to runtime. The box in the lower left of the figure represents the "start from" WSDL. It contains the schema definition for `corp:AddressType`.

2. The boxes in the upper left represent the "start from" Java. These classes include the `samples.Address` class. In order to solve the "Start from WSDL and Java" problem, one mapping that needs to be implemented is from `samples.Address` to `corp:AddressType`. This example illustrates how to create a deserializer, using XSLT, that can convert instances of `samples.Address` into instances of `corp:AddressType`.

3. Running the JAXB schema generator against the `samples.Address` creates a new schema.

4. That schema, represented in the figure as `address.xsd`, contains a complex type—`address`. This generated address will be mapped to `corp:AddressType` by the XSLT.

5. The lower half of this figure (steps 5–9) illustrate the run-time transformation of the file `corp_address.xml` (an instance of `corp-AddressType`) into `address.xml` (an instance of `address` from `address.xsd`). `corp_address.xml` is an input to the `convertCorpAddrToAddr()` method from `AddressDeserializer2` (this method is listed in Example 4–27).

6. The XSLT stylesheet `corp_address_to_address.xslt` defines the transformation. It is listed in Example 4–26.

7. The method `AddressDeserializer2.convertCorpAddrToAddr()` invokes the transformation using XSLT and JAXP in the manner described in Chapter 3, Section 3.4.

8. The file `address.xml` is output. It is an instance of the complex type address defined by `address.xsd` (the JAXB schema-generated XSD).

9. The method `AddressDeserializer2.deserializeAddress()` (listed in Example 4–27) uses JAXB to unmarshal `address.xml` to an instance of `samples.Address`.

The key to this approach is to use the JAXB schema generator to create a schema that JAXB can bind to `samples.Address` so that the JAXB-based serialization is possible to and from the `samples.Address` class. Example 4–25 shows the schema that is generated from the `samples.Address` class.

Example 4–25 Schema Generated from `samples.Address`

```
4   <xs:schema version="1.0" xmlns:xs="http://www.w3.org/2001/XMLSchema">
5
6     <xs:complexType name="address">
7       <xs:sequence>
8         <xs:element name="city" type="xs:string" minOccurs="0"/>
9         <xs:element name="phoneNumber" type="phone" minOccurs="0"/>
10        <xs:element name="state" type="state" minOccurs="0"/>
11        <xs:element name="streetName" type="xs:string" minOccurs="0"/>
12        <xs:element name="streetNum" type="xs:int"/>
13        <xs:element name="zip" type="xs:int"/>
14      </xs:sequence>
15    </xs:complexType>
16
17    <xs:complexType name="phone">
18      <xs:sequence>
19        <xs:element name="areaCode" type="xs:int"/>
20        <xs:element name="exchange" type="xs:string" minOccurs="0"/>
21        <xs:element name="number" type="xs:string" minOccurs="0"/>
22      </xs:sequence>
23    </xs:complexType>
24
25    <xs:simpleType name="state">
26      <xs:restriction base="xs:string">
27        <xs:enumeration value="OH"/>
28        <xs:enumeration value="IN"/>
29        <xs:enumeration value="TX"/>
30      </xs:restriction>
31    </xs:simpleType>
32  </xs:schema>
```

book-code/chap04/sfwj/examples/address.xsd

As discussed in Chapter 2, the JAXB marshalling process is governed by the annotations on the classes. However, the `samples.Address` class (Example 4–22) does not have any annotations, so you may be wondering how JAXB can unmarshal instances of the preceding schema into that class. The answer is that the JAXB schema generator adds annotations to the class as it generates the schema. The original source code class definition is not affected, but compiled versions (.class files) are created that include the annotations. In this example, I use these compiled versions of `samples.Address` and `samples.Phone` rather than the ones generated by `javac`.

The next question is, how do you convert from instances of the `corp:AddressType` schema to the schema shown in Example 4–25? For that, you can use XSLT. An example of such an XSLT is shown in Example 4–26.

Example 4–26 XSLT for Transforming from `corp:AddressType` to the Generated Schema

```
4   <xsl:stylesheet version="1.0" xmlns:xsl="http://www.w3.org/1999/XSL/Transform"
5     xmlns:custinfo="http://www.example.com/css/custinfo"
6     xmlns:corp="http://www.example.com/corp">
7     <xsl:output method="xml" version="1.0" encoding="UTF-8"/>
8     <xsl:template match="custinfo:address">
9       <address>
10        <city><xsl:value-of select="corp:city"/></city>
11        <phoneNumber>
12          <areaCode><xsl:value-of
13          select="substring-before(substring-after(corp:phone,'('),')')"
14          /></areaCode>
15          <exchange><xsl:value-of select="normalize-space(
16          substring-before(substring-after(corp:phone,')'),'-'))"
17          /></exchange>
18          <number><xsl:value-of select="normalize-space(
19            substring-after(corp:phone,'-'))"/></number>
20        </phoneNumber>
21        <state><xsl:value-of select="corp:state"/></state>
22        <streetName><xsl:value-of select="substring-after(corp:addrLine1,' ')"
23        /> - <xsl:value-of select="corp:addrLine2"/></streetName>
24        <streetNum><xsl:value-of select="substring-before(corp:addrLine1,' ')"
25        /></streetNum>
26        <zip><xsl:value-of select="corp:zip"/></zip>
27      </address>
28    </xsl:template>
29  </xsl:stylesheet>
```

book-code/chap04/sfwj/src/xml/corp_address_to_address.xslt

This XSLT performs the same function as the Java parsing code in Example 4–24—except that here it is acting on an XML representation of an address rather than on a Java class instance of an address. There are several advantages to this approach. First, the XSLT is more readily reusable. Second, the process of transformation followed by unmarshalling into the `samples.Address` class is probably faster than the process outlined in the previous section.

Note that neither the XSLT nor the Java transformation is error-proof. They have been carefully crafted to work with the examples in this book! In the real world, you would need to get even more complicated to handle all the cases. And you would need good error handling to recover from the cases you didn't consider when designing the transformations.

The Java code that applies this transformation (using JAXP and XSLT) and then unmarshals into `samples.Address` is shown in Example 4–27.

Example 4–27 Applying the XSLT and Unmarshalling

```
66    public Address deserializeAddress(Source xml) throws Exception {
67
68       JAXBContext jc =
69          JAXBContext.newInstance(Address.class);
70       Unmarshaller u = jc.createUnmarshaller();
71       JAXBElement<Address> addrJAXBElt = u.unmarshal(xml, Address.class);
72       Address addr = addrJAXBElt.getValue();
73       return addr;
74
75    }
76
77    private Source convertCorpAddrToAddr(Source xml, Source xslt)
78    throws Exception {
79
80       Transformer transformer =
81          TransformerFactory.newInstance().newTransformer(xslt);
82       ByteArrayOutputStream ba = new ByteArrayOutputStream();
83       transformer.transform(xml, new StreamResult(ba));
84       return new StreamSource(new StringReader(ba.toString()));
85
86    }
```

book-code/chap04/sfwj/src/java/samples/deser/AddressDeserializer2.java

The method `convertCorpAddrToAddr` applies the XSLT. The result goes into a byte array and is returned as an instance of `StreamSource`. This `Stream-Source` can then be processed by the method `deserializeAddress()`, which simply unmarshals the transformed XML into an instance of `samples.Address`.

To run the preceding example, follow these steps:

1. Go to `<book-code>/chap04/sfwj`.
2. To run the JAXB schema generator on the Java classes (e.g., `samples.Address.java`) in the directory `etc/java/samples`, enter `mvn install`.
3. To run the XSLT and then the JAXB unmarshaller to deserialize the XML into an instance of `samples.Address` enter `ant run-deserializer2`.

4.7 Conclusions

This chapter was a quick tour of WSDL, SOAP, and Java/XML mapping. I looked at those topics from the perspective of SOA. The primary assumption is that you need to work with standards-compliant WSDL, XML Schema definitions, and Java classes as you build and deploy SOA components as Web services. This assumption is at odds with JWS in a few places. To demonstrate this, I showed a couple of examples of common integration problems that have no straightforward solution using JAX-WS 2.0 and JAXB 2.0.

The purpose of pointing out these limitations has less to do with criticizing JWS than with pointing out how difficult SOA can be. In the last chapter of this book, I cover the SOA-J Application Framework and outline a WSDL-centric approach to building SOA components from Java that might provide solutions to some of these limitations.

In the next four chapters, meanwhile, I look at the power of JWS and show lots of examples of SOA problems that it can handle effectively.

CHAPTER 5

The JAXB 2.0 Data Binding

This chapter describes how to use JAXB 2.0 for SOA. It is written for programmers and contains lots of details and code examples. JAXB 2.0 is critical to SOA because it supports *type mappings*. A type mapping is a map from a Java type (e.g., a class) to an XML Schema component (e.g., a complex type definition). *Serializers* are used to implement type mappings. A serializer converts an instance of a type mapping's Java type into an instance of its XML Schema component. A *deserializer* does the reverse.

The preceding chapter discusses the central importance of type mappings for SOA. Section 4.5 of that chapter discussed that the ability to implement type mappings—in other words, to do *serialization*—is critically important for a Web Services Platform Architecture that supports SOA. Within JWS, the tool for serialization is JAXB 2.0. This chapter teaches you how to use JAXB 2.0 to do the kinds of serialization needed for SOA. At the end, it examines how JAXB 2.0 can be used for data transformations (as an alternative to XSLT).

5.1 Binding versus Mapping

Chapter 2, Section 2.4, introduced JAXB 2.0 and briefly described the difference between binding and mapping. Before diving into the details of programming with JAXB 2.0, it is useful to look a little closer at that issue and emphasize that JAXB 2.0 is really more of a binding tool than a mapping tool. This has implications as to its usefulness for SOA. Figure 5–1 illustrates the difference between binding and mapping.

The top half of the figure illustrates the binding process. A binding tool converts Java types to XML types according to a standard mapping. That is, it implements a standard way of converting Java to XML (and vice versa). Most binding tools, like JAXB, map Java instances to XML documents, and map Java applications (e.g., class definitions) to XML Schema definitions. In this manner, a binding tool typically enables you to implement type mappings in two ways:

- Start from an existing Java application and use a *schema generator* to create a machine-generated XML schema (shaded gray in the top right corner of Figure 5–1).
- Start from an existing XML schema and use a *schema compiler* to create a machine-generated Java application (shaded gray in the middle left of Figure 5–1).

When you work with a binding tool, the type mappings you work with map between existing Java and generated XML schema definitions, or between existing XML schema definitions and generated Java program elements. In either case, at runtime, you will be working with machine-generated artifacts (either Java or XML schema). The type mappings you can use always include either machine-generated Java or machine-generated XML schema.

On the other hand, when you work with a mapping tool, the type mappings you work with are between existing Java and existing XML schema definitions. At runtime, you will not be working with any machine-generated artifacts.

The bottom half of Figure 5–1 illustrates the Java/XML mapping process. When working with a Java/XML mapping tool, you need to define the mappings between the XML and the Java. At runtime, the mapping tool uses your mapping definitions to serialize Java to XML or deserialize XML to Java.

JAXB 2.0 is primarily a binding tool. When starting from Java, a JAXB user writes Java code, and annotates it to map to a particular schema. Alternatively, when starting from XML, the JAXB user can begin with the schema and generate a Java code template, which can be customized and incorporated into an application. In either case, the annotations allow customization of the standard JAXB binding, so there is quite a bit of flexibility in terms of the schema to which you can map the Java code. In this respect, the annotations provide a mapping from the Java code to the schema. So, why isn't JAXB a mapping tool? The reason why I define JAXB as a binding tool, rather than a mapping tool, is twofold:

- The mappings that can be defined using the annotations are variations on the standard binding. So, while there is flexibility, there are lots of mappings that cannot be supported without resorting to custom coding using the `XmlAdapter` class (see Section 5.7).
- The mapping—as defined by the annotations—is static. You can't implement a different mapping without changing the annotations and recompiling the Java. In a true mapping tool, the mappings are defined separately from the schema and the Java. So, at runtime, you can change the mappings. True mapping tools can also support multiple

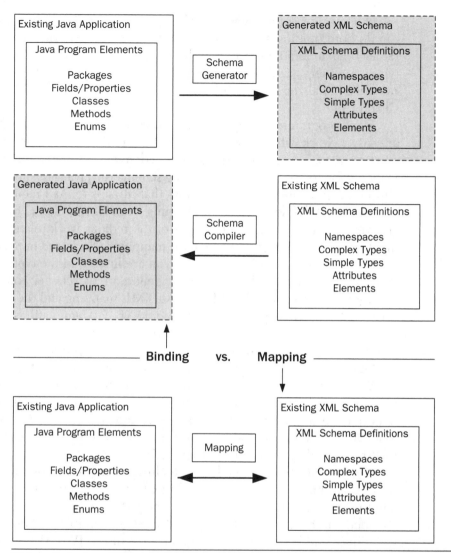

Figure 5–1 Java/XML binding versus Java/XML mapping.

mappings at runtime. This is impossible with JAXB because a Java class can have only one set of annotations.[1]

---

1. If Java were to support external annotation files—in other words, a format for placing annotations outside the Java class files—JAXB could be used more like a true mapping tool. This idea was discussed by the JAXB Expert Group, but was deemed a broader issue related to annotations in general, rather than a capability to be provided only within the context of JAXB 2.0.

One example of a mapping tool is Castor [CASTOR]. Actually, Castor can do both binding and mapping. Castor provides external mapping files rather than annotations to define the relationships between Java and XML types. Another example of a mapping tool (an experimental one) is the Adaptive Serializer Framework (ASF) included in SOA-J and discussed in Chapter 11.

Many programmers prefer binding tools to mapping tools. Binding tools are easy to work with because you don't have to define any mappings if you don't want to. You can use the schema compiler (or generator) to do the mapping for you. It looks at the existing schema (or Java class) and produces a machine-generated class (or schema) that it maps to. As I mentioned earlier, JAXB 2.0 defines a standard mapping from XML Schema to Java (and vice versa) that relieves programmers of the tedious work related to defining their own mappings. This standard mapping is discussed in Section 5.2.

So, when working with JAXB 2.0, you are limited to the type mappings that can be produced by the schema generator or schema compiler—in other words, the standard JAXB 2.0 Java/XML mapping and the customizations that can be expressed using the JAXB 2.0 annotations (with the schema generator) or the JAXB 2.0 binding language (with the schema compiler). And, as I showed in Chapter 4, Sections 4.5 and 4.6, there are limitations to the type mappings that can be implemented in this manner.

So, where does that leave us? In the first paragraph of this chapter, I reiterated the message from Chapter 4—that type mappings are centrally important to SOA. Now, I have just explained that JAXB 2.0 is a binding tool with limitations on the type mappings it can support. Does this mean that the JWS platform is not well suited for SOA?

No, it means that we need some techniques at our disposal to deal with those JAXB limitations. As discussed in Chapter 1, Section 1.1, it is important to remember that JWS is a toolset and JAXB 2.0 is the data binding tool included in that toolset. To implement SOA requires additional coding techniques and best practices layered on top of the JWS APIs. This means that in some situations, developers need to create their own Java/XML mapping framework on top of the Java/XML binding tool provided by JAXB 2.0. The good news is that JAXB 2.0 is an excellent binding tool and provides a good foundation for implementing type mappings.

In this chapter, I show you how type mappings can be implemented using JAXB 2.0 in an application-specific manner. That is, I illustrate techniques that can be used to implement the specific type mappings you need for a specific application.

The next section of this chapter provides an overview of the standard JAXB 2.0 Java/XML binding. You need to understand how this baseline binding works to effectively use JAXB 2.0. After that introduction, the remaining sections of this chapter look at the following four application-specific techniques for implementing type mappings with JAXB 2.0:

- Use custom Java code to map from an existing Java object to a JAXB 2.0 generated Java object, and then use JAXB 2.0 marshalling to create the XML instance.
- Use JAXB 2.0 annotations to influence the schema generator so that it produces a generated schema that matches the existing target schema.
- Use the JAXB 2.0 binding language to influence the schema compiler so that it produces generated Java classes that match the existing application.
- Use the JAXB 2.0 `XmlAdapter` class to implement custom marshaling from an existing Java class to an existing XML schema.

The last section in the chapter illustrates a related use of JAXB 2.0—implementing data transformations. In Chapter 3, Section 3.4, I showed how XSLT can be used for data transformation in an SOA context. In the last section of this chapter, I illustrate how such data transformations can be accomplished with JAXB 2.0 instead.

5.2   An Overview of the Standard JAXB 2.0 Java/XML Binding

Before taking you through the JAXB 2.0 code examples in this chapter, I provide a quick overview of the standard JAXB 2.0 Java/XML binding. This should be enough to give you the basic grounding you need to get started. For all the gory details, you should read the JAXB 2.0 specification [JSR-222].

Example 5–1 shows a schema for a simplified purchase order. This is the example that is used to illustrate the standard binding.

Example 5–1 The `simpleOrder` Schema

```
4   <schema targetNamespace="http://www.example.com/oms"
5     elementFormDefault="qualified" xmlns="http://www.w3.org/2001/XMLSchema"
6     xmlns:oms="http://www.example.com/oms">
7     <element name="simpleOrder">
```

```
8     <complexType>
9       <sequence>
10        <element name="billTo">
11          <complexType>
12            <sequence>
13              <element name="name" type="string"/>
14              <element name="street" type="string"/>
15              <element name="city" type="string"/>
16              <element name="state" type="string"/>
17              <element name="zip" type="string"/>
18              <element name="phone" type="string"/>
19            </sequence>
20          </complexType>
21        </element>
22        <element name="items">
23          <complexType>
24            <sequence>
25              <element name="item" type="oms:ItemType" maxOccurs="unbounded"/>
26            </sequence>
27          </complexType>
28        </element>
29      </sequence>
30    </complexType>
31  </element>
32  <complexType name="ItemType">
33    <sequence>
34      <element name="quantity" type="positiveInteger"/>
35      <element name="price" type="double"/>
36    </sequence>
37    <attribute name="productName" use="required" type="string"/>
38  </complexType>
39 </schema>
```

book-code/chap05/customjava/etc/simpleorder.xsd

Notice that the schema has a single global element named `simpleOrder`.
This element defines an anonymous purchase order type that is simply a
sequence of two elements: `billTo` and `items`. The `billTo` element represents the billing address, and defines an anonymous type—an address type.
The `items` element represents the list of items being purchased. The elements of the list are defined inside the `items` element's anonymous type—by
the element named `item`. This element has a named type—`ItemType`.

Toward the bottom of Example 5–1, you see the definition for `Item-Type`. It contains two elements—`quantity` (an `xs:positiveInteger`) and `price` (an `xs:double`). It also contains an attribute—`productName` (an `xs:string`).

The standard JAXB 2.0 binding for this schema is illustrated in Figure 5–2. As you can see, the standard binding defines two top-level classes from this `SimpleOrder` schema—`SimpleOrder` and `ItemType`. The class `SimpleOrder` also has two inner classes—`SimpleOrder.BillTo` and `SimpleOrder.Items`.

The numbered arrows in Figure 5–2 illustrate some of the important parts of the standard JAXB 2.0 binding. Here, I provide an overview of the standard binding by describing the binding concept called out by each arrow:

1. The namespace `http://www.example.com/oms` gets mapped to the Java package `com.example.oms`. If you want a different package mapping, you can use the `jaxb:package` declaration or the `@XmlSchema.namespace` annotation element.

2. The anonymous complex type defined by the element `simpleOrder` gets mapped to the top-level class (i.e., not an inner class), `Simple-Order`. In the default mapping, anonymous complex types get mapped to top-level classes only when they are defined by global element definitions.

3. The element `billTo` gets mapped to the property named `billTo` in the `SimpleOrder` class. By default, local element declarations are bound to properties.

4. The access method for the `billTo` property is, by default, Java-Beans style setter/getter methods. There is no standard JAXB binding language declaration for binding an element to a public or protected Java field (i.e., without the getter/setters). However, you can go the other way. That is, you can generate schema from Java where an element definition is bound to a Java field by using the `@XmlElement` annotation.

5. The anonymous complex type defined by the element `billTo` gets mapped to the inner class `SimpleOrder.BillTo`. The standard binding for anonymous complex types (that are not defined by global elements) is to make them inner classes. You can force all classes to be generated as top-level by using the `<jaxb:globalBindings localScoping="toplevel"/>` global declaration.

6. The element `item` gets mapped to a `List<ItemType>` property named `item`. This is the standard binding when the element definition has a `maxOccurs` value greater than 1. The Java type parameter for `List<T>` is equal to the Java type that is bound to the element definition's `type`

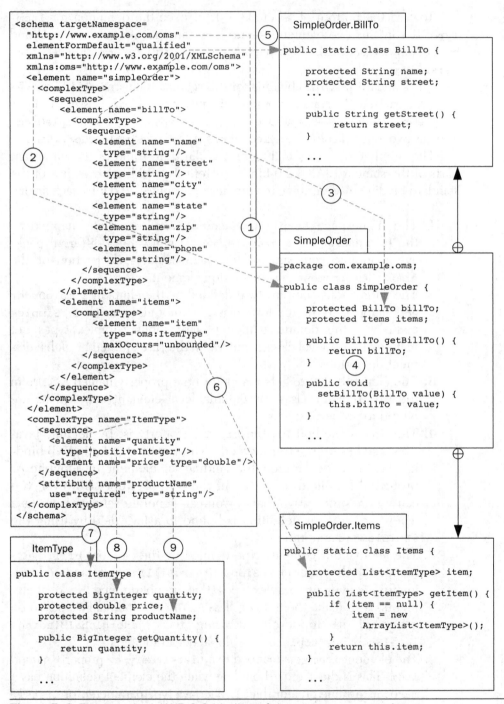

```
<schema targetNamespace=
  "http://www.example.com/oms"
  elementFormDefault="qualified"
  xmlns="http://www.w3.org/2001/XMLSchema"
  xmlns:oms="http://www.example.com/oms">
  <element name="simpleOrder">
    <complexType>
      <sequence>
        <element name="billTo">
          <complexType>
            <sequence>
              <element name="name"
                type="string"/>
              <element name="street"
                type="string"/>
              <element name="city"
                type="string"/>
              <element name="state"
                type="string"/>
              <element name="zip"
                type="string"/>
              <element name="phone"
                type="string"/>
            </sequence>
          </complexType>
        </element>
        <element name="items">
          <complexType>
            <element name="item"
              type="oms:ItemType"
              maxOccurs="unbounded"/>
          </sequence>
          </complexType>
        </element>
      </sequence>
    </complexType>
  </element>
  <complexType name="ItemType">
    <sequence>
      <element name="quantity"
        type="positiveInteger"/>
      <element name="price" type="double"/>
    </sequence>
    <attribute name="productName"
      use="required" type="string"/>
  </complexType>
</schema>
```

SimpleOrder.BillTo

```
public static class BillTo {

    protected String name;
    protected String street;
    ...

    public String getStreet() {
        return street;
    }

    ...
```

SimpleOrder

```
package com.example.oms;

public class SimpleOrder {

    protected BillTo billTo;
    protected Items items;

    public BillTo getBillTo() {
        return billTo;
    }

    public void
      setBillTo(BillTo value) {
        this.billTo = value;
    }

    ...
```

ItemType

```
public class ItemType {

    protected BigInteger quantity;
    protected double price;
    protected String productName;

    public BigInteger getQuantity() {
        return quantity;
    }

    ...
```

SimpleOrder.Items

```
public static class Items {

    protected List<ItemType> item;

    public List<ItemType> getItem() {
        if (item == null) {
            item = new
                ArrayList<ItemType>();
        }
        return this.item;
    }

    ...
```

Figure 5–2 The standard JAXB 2.0 binding of the simpleOrder schema.

attribute (or anonymous type); in this case, T = ItemType. The collection type (the default is java.util.List) can be customized using the binding language collectionType attribute at either the global or the property level.

7. The named complex type ItemType gets mapped to the top-level Java class ItemType. The standard mapping for named complexType definitions is to a top-level Java value class.

8. The default mapping for xs:positiveInteger (and xs:integer as well) is to java.math.BigInteger. This mapping can be customized using the binding language jaxb:javaType declaration or the @XmlElement.type annotation.

9. The default mapping for attribute declarations, like element declarations, is to properties with JavaBeans style setter/getter methods. Hence, the attribute productName gets mapped in the same manner as the element's children of ItemType.

A fragment of the JAXB-generated code for the SimpleOrder class is shown in Example 5–2. In the example, you can see the annotations that are introduced into the class to facilitate the run-time marshalling.

Example 5–2 The JAXB Value Class, SimpleOrder

```
88   @XmlAccessorType(AccessType.FIELD)
89   @XmlType(name = "", propOrder = {
90        "billTo",
91        "items"
92   })
93   @XmlRootElement(name = "simpleOrder")
94   public class SimpleOrder {
95
96        @XmlElement(namespace = "http://www.example.com/oms")
97        protected BillTo billTo;
98        @XmlElement(namespace = "http://www.example.com/oms")
99        protected Items items;
```

book-code/chap05/customjava/etc/schemacompiler_withcomments
/SimpleOrder.java

As discussed in Chapter 2, the annotations are the key to run-time marshalling and unmarshalling. Annotations are also how JAXB 2.0 achieves

Table 5–1 Descriptions of the Java Annotations Appearing in Example 5–2

Annotation	Purpose	Example
@XmlAccessorType	Tells the JAXB 2.0 runtime what parts (i.e., fields, properties, or both) of the Java class get mapped by default	In Example 5–2, the value `AccessType.FIELD` indicates that fields not explicitly annotated otherwise must be mapped, and properties (i.e., getter/setter pairs), unless explicitly annotated, must not be.
@XmlType	Tells the JAXB 2.0 runtime which schema type to map a class to and specifies some aspects of the mapping	The `name` attribute provides the name of the complex type definition. In Example 5–2, `name = ""` indicates that this is an anonymous type—in other words, it has no defined name (the global element name is defined elsewhere—see `@Xml-RootElement`). The `propOrder` attribute defines the order of the properties and fields. This ordering lines up with the ordering specified in the schema `<sequence>` definition from which this annotated class was generated.
@XmlRootElement	Tells the JAXB 2.0 runtime that this class maps to a global element definition	The `name` attribute provides the name of the global element. In Example 5–2, this name is `simpleOrder`. The target namespace, since it is not specified in this example, comes from the default package mapping.
@XmlElement	Tells the JAXB 2.0 runtime that a particular property or field maps to a schema element definition	In Example 5–2, it is used to map the `billTo` field to `oms:billTo` and the `items` field to `oms:items`. The `namespace` attribute, technically not needed in this case since the default is the package namespace, defines the target element's namespace. Technically, the `@XmlElement` is not needed to map theses fields either, because the default mapping has been set to `AccessType.FIELD` by the `@XmlAccessorType` annotation. For clarity, the schema generator sometimes includes annotations that are not strictly necessary.

portability across implementations. With JAXB 2.0, you can use the schema compiler from one implementation and use the generated classes on another implementation at runtime. This works because the run-time JAXB 2.0 engine does all the marshalling and unmarshalling based on introspection of the annotated classes. The annotations—together with the JAXB 2.0 standard mapping—tell the run-time engine how to map Java program elements to XML schema definition instances. Table 5–1 describes the runtime interpretation of the annotations from `SimpleOrder` that are in Example 5–2. I don't describe all the annotations here. For a complete description, see [JSR-222] and its associated Javadoc.

Example 5–3 shows a snippet of the generated code for `Simple-Order.BillTo`. This is an inner class. As discussed previously (see Figure 5–2), element definitions with anonymous complex types get mapped, by default, to inner classes.

Example 5–3 The JAXB Value Class, `SimpleOrder.BillTo`

```
176    @XmlAccessorType(AccessType.FIELD)
177    @XmlType(name = "", propOrder = {
178        "name"
179        "street",
180        "city",
181        "state",
182        "zip",
183        "phone"
184    })
185    public static class BillTo {
186
187      @XmlElement(namespace = "http://www.example.com/oms", required = true)
188      protected String name;
189      @XmlElement(namespace = "http://www.example.com/oms")
190      protected String street;
191      @XmlElement(namespace = "http://www.example.com/oms")
192      protected String city;
193      @XmlElement(namespace = "http://www.example.com/oms")
194      protected String state;
195      @XmlElement(namespace = "http://www.example.com/oms")
196      protected String zip;
197      @XmlElement(namespace = "http://www.example.com/oms")
198      protected String phone;
```

book-code/chap05/customjava/etc/schemacompiler_withcomments/SimpleOrder.java

Again, you can see, as in Example 5–2, that the `@XmlElement.propOrder` annotation element specifies the order in which the Java class properties map to the `<sequence>` definition of elements in the anonymous complex type. This is needed, because a Java class has no concept of ordering on its fields and properties (i.e., reflection provides no ordering information).

Example 5–4 shows the default mapping for the anonymous complex type defined by the `oms:item` element. This class, `SimpleOrder.Items`, is interesting because it illustrates the default mapping for elements that may occur multiple times (i.e., `maxOccurs > 1`). As you can see, the element `oms:item`, defined inside the anonymous complex type for the element `oms:items`, has been mapped to a property, `item`, with type `List<Item-Type>`. The default mapping for elements that occur multiple times is `java.util.List<T>`, where `T` is the default class mapped to the elements' type.

Example 5–4 The JAXB Value Class, `SimpleOrder.Items`

```
344    @XmlAccessorType(AccessType.FIELD)
345    @XmlType(name = "", propOrder = {
346        "item"
347    })
348    public static class Items {
349
350      @XmlElement(namespace = "http://www.example.com/oms")
351      protected List<ItemType> item;
352
353      /**
354       * Gets the value of the item property.
355       *
356       * <p>
357       * This accessor method returns a reference to the live list,
358       * not a snapshot. Therefore, any modification you make to the
359       * returned list will be present inside the JAXB object.  This is
360       * why there is not a <CODE>set</CODE> method for the item property.
361       *
362       * <p>
363       * For example, to add a new item, do as follows:
364       * <pre>
365       *    getItem().add(newItem);
366       * </pre>
367       *
368       *
```

```
369         * <p>
370         * Objects of the following type(s) are allowed in the list
371         * {@link ItemType }
372         *
373         *
374         */
375        public List<ItemType> getItem() {
376          if (item == null) {
377            item = new ArrayList<ItemType>();
378          }
379          return this.item;
380        }
381
382      }
```

book-code/chap05/customjava/etc/schemacompiler_withcomments/SimpleOrder.java

As you notice from looking at the code in Example 5–4, there is no setter for the `item` property. The getter returns a live list, not a copy. So, to update the `item` property, you need to get the live list and add, update, or delete individual elements. If you want to be able to set the entire collection, with JAXB 2.0, you will need to use the binding language to specify an alternative collection type. One way to do that is with a `<property>` declaration, such as:

```
<sequence>
  <annotation><appinfo>
    <jaxb:property collectionType="indexed"/>
  </appinfo></annotation>
  <element name="item" type="oms:ItemType" maxOccurs="unbounded"/>
</sequence>
```

Setting `collectionType="indexed"` in that manner will map the `item` element to an array property (i.e., `ItemType[ ]`), rather than a list. You will get a setter method such as:

```
public void setItem(ItemType[] values) { ... }
```

Another difference when using `collectionType="indexed"` is that the array returned from the getter is not "live"—it is a copy. See Section 5.5 of [JSR-222] for more details about mapping to collections.

Example 5–5 illustrates the default mapping for a named complex type (i.e., not anonymous). Named complex types do not get mapped to inner classes as their anonymous counterparts do. So, the type `oms:ItemType` gets mapped to `samples.ItemType`.

Example 5–5 The JAXB Value Class, `ItemType`

```
59   @XmlAccessorType(AccessType.FIELD)
60   @XmlType(name = "ItemType", propOrder = {
61       "quantity",
62       "price"
63   })
64   public class ItemType {
65
66       @XmlElement(namespace = "http://www.example.com/oms")
67       protected BigInteger quantity;
68       @XmlElement(namespace = "http://www.example.com/oms", type = Double.class)
69       protected double price;
70       @XmlAttribute(required = true)
71       protected String productName;
```

book-code/chap05/customjava/etc/schemacompiler_withcomments/ItemType.java

One thing to notice in Example 5–5 is the `@XmlAttribute` annotation. This annotation is very similar to `@XmlElement`, except that it maps its associated property (i.e., `productName`) to an attribute rather than an element. The `"required = true"` annotation element indicates that the XML definition should have the `"required"` attribute—indicating that the attribute is required for instances of the XML schema.

Another thing to notice is that the `quantity` property (with type `xs:positiveInteger`) is mapped to a property with class `java.math.BigInteger`.[2] This means that you could set the JAXB value of this property to a negative number, and marshal it out to XML. In such a scenario, no error is generated because the marshalling process does not, by default, validate its output against the source schema. JAXB 2.0 has delegated such validation to the JAXP 1.3 API. You can activate such validation by using the `setSchema(javax.xml.validation.Schema schema)` method on

---

2. See Section 6.2.2 of [JSR-222] for details on the default mappings for all atomic datatypes.

either a `Marshaller` or `Unmarshaller` instance. For more details on validation, see Section 3.5.2 of [JSR-222].

That wraps up this introduction to JAXB 2.0's standard mapping. The simple example presented here shows you the basics. Of course, the specification for the entire mapping is much more complex. [JSR-222] is more than 350 pages long and a great deal of that is devoted to describing the standard mapping and how to customize it using either annotations or binding language declarations. However, what you have seen in this section is enough to get started working with JAXB 2.0.

In the next section, I look at how to work with the standard mapping, without any customizations, to implement a type mapping.

5.3 Implementing Type Mappings with JAXB 2.0

This section shows how you can combine custom Java code with the JAXB standard mapping to implement any type mapping you desire. Many programmers like this approach because it does not require any understanding of the JAXB annotations. You simply work with the Java that gets generated and can ignore the annotations.

In the preceding section, I illustrated the default type mapping provided by JAXB 2.0. This is the notation I use to represent such a type mapping:

```
< {http://www.example.com/oms}simpleOrder,
     com.example.oms.SimpleOrder >
```

This notation has the form < `XML-Type`, `Java-Type` > where the `XML-Type` is the qualified name of an XML Schema-defined element or type. Likewise, `Java-Type` is the name of the Java class.

In this section, I illustrate how to implement the following type mapping:

```
< oms:simpleOrder, samples.MySimpleOrder >
```

In this case, `samples.MySimpleOrder` is not a JAXB-generated class. It is an existing Java class that I would like to map to `oms:simpleOrder`. Actually, `MySimpleOrder` is a representation, not of the element `oms:simpleOrder`, but of its anonymous complex type. So, with this custom type mapping, we are going to lose the element information (e.g., tag name) that is captured in JAXB by the `JAXBElement` representation. I implement this mapping by letting JAXB create an instance of `com.example.oms.SimpleOrder` and then mapping `SimpleOrder` to `MySimpleOrder`. Example 5–6 shows the Java class `MySimpleOrder`.

Example 5–6 The Existing Java Class, `MySimpleOrder`

```
24  public class MySimpleOrder {
25
26    private MyAddress billTo;
27    private List<MyItem> itemList;
28
29    public MySimpleOrder(String name, String street, String city, String state,
30        String zip, String phone) {
31      this(new MyAddress(name, street, city, state, zip, phone));
32    }
33
34    public MySimpleOrder(MyAddress addr) {
35      this.billTo = addr;
36      itemList = new ArrayList<MyItem>();
37    }
38
39    public MyAddress getBillTo() {
40      return billTo;
41    }
42
43    public List<MyItem> getItemList() {
44      return itemList;
45    }
46
47  }
```

book-code/chap05/customjava/modules/serializer/src/java/samples
  /MySimpleOrder.java

Two differences you can notice right away between this class and its JAXB-generated counterpart are as follows:

- The `billTo` variable, representing the billing address, has the Java type `MyAddress` rather than the JAXB-generated type `com.example.oms.BillTo`.

■ The items being purchased are represented by an instance of List<MyItem> rather than the JAXB-generated type, Simple-Order.Items.

So, to map samples.MySimpleOrder, to an instance of oms:simpleOrder, you need to map the billTo property (with Java type samples.MyAddress) to an oms:billTo element, and its itemList property (with Java type List<samples.MyItem>) to an oms:items element. Then, you combine those elements—oms:billTo and oms:items—to create an instance of oms:simpleOrder.

To understand the mapping code that implements this procedure, take a quick look at the samples.MyAddress and samples.MyItem classes. Example 5–7 shows the MyAddress class.

Example 5–7 The Existing Java Class, MyAddress

```
21  public class MyAddress {
22
23      protected String name;
24      protected String street;
25      protected String city;
26      protected String state;
27      protected String zip;
28      protected String phone;
29
30      public MyAddress(String name, String street, String city, String state,
31          String zip, String phone) {
32
33        this.name = name;
34        this.street = street;
35        this.city = city;
36        this.state = state;
37        this.zip = zip;
38        this.phone = phone;
39
40      }
41
42  }
```

book-code/chap05/customjava/modules/serializer/src/java/samples/MyAddress.java

As you can see, the `MyAddress` class is not a JavaBean, as it does not have setter/getter methods. It is simply a container for its constituent fields. It is not hard to imagine what the mapping from the `SimpleOrder.BillTo` class to `MyAddress` will look like. It will simply match up the corresponding properties with the `MyAddress` fields.

Example 5–8 shows the `samples.MyItem` class. The major differences between this class and the JAXB schema-generated class `com.example.oms.ItemType` concern the property types.

Example 5–8 The Existing Java Class, `samples.MyItem`

```
21   public class MyItem {
22
23     private int quantity;
24     private float price;
25     private String productName;
26
27     public MyItem(int quantity, float price, String productName)
28     throws Exception {
29       if (productName == null) {
30         throw new Exception("productName cannot be null");
31       }
32         this.productName = productName;
33         this.price = price;
34         this.quantity = quantity;
35     }
36
37     public float getPrice() {
38       return price;
39     }
40
41     public void setPrice(float price) {
42       this.price = price;
43     }
44
45     public String getProductName() {
46       return productName;
47     }
48
49     public void setProductName(String productName) {
50       this.productName = productName;
51     }
52
```

```
53     public int getQuantity() {
54        return quantity;
55     }
56
57     public void setQuantity(int quantity) {
58        this.quantity = quantity;
59     }
60
61  }
```

book-code/chap05/customjava/modules/serializer/src/java/samples/MyItem.java

MyItem.quantity has the primitive type int, whereas ItemType.quantity is a java.math.BigInteger. Similarly, the property price has the primitive type float here, but type double in the JAXB class. Lastly, the property productName is a java.lang.String in both classes.

Example 5–9 shows the mapping code that takes an instance of samples.MySimpleOrder and returns it as an XML document that is an instance of oms:simpleOrder. The XML document is returned as a javax.xml.transform.Source.

This mapping code works by creating an instance of the JAXB-generated class com.example.oms.SimpleOrder, populating it from the MySimpleOrder class, and marshalling the JAXB instance to get the XML document.

Example 5–9 The Mapping Code

```
67  public Source getXML(MySimpleOrder order) {
68
69     // create the JAXB SimpleOrder
70     SimpleOrder jaxbSimpleOrder = new SimpleOrder();
71     // map the addresses
72     MyAddress myAddress = order.getBillTo();
73     SimpleOrder.BillTo billTo = new SimpleOrder.BillTo();
74     billTo.setName(myAddress.name);
75     billTo.setCity(myAddress.city);
76     billTo.setPhone(myAddress.phone);
77     billTo.setState(myAddress.state);
78     billTo.setStreet(myAddress.street);
79     billTo.setZip(myAddress.zip);
80     jaxbSimpleOrder.setBillTo(billTo);
81     // map the items
```

```
82   jaxbSimpleOrder.setItems(new SimpleOrder.Items()); // needed to avoid NPE
83   List<ItemType> jaxbItemList = jaxbSimpleOrder.getItems().getItem();
84   for (MyItem myItem : order.getItemList()) {
85      ItemType jaxbItem = new ItemType();
86 //   jaxbItem.setPrice((double) myItem.getPrice());
87      jaxbItem.setPrice(Double.parseDouble(Float.toString(myItem.getPrice())));
88      jaxbItem.setProductName(myItem.getProductName());
89      jaxbItem.setQuantity(BigInteger.valueOf((long) myItem.getQuantity()));
90      jaxbItemList.add(jaxbItem);
91   }
92   try {
93      JAXBContext jaxbContext = JAXBContext.newInstance("com.example.oms");
94      Marshaller jaxbMarshaller = jaxbContext.createMarshaller();
95      SchemaFactory sf =
96         SchemaFactory.newInstance(XMLConstants.W3C_XML_SCHEMA_NS_URI);
97      Schema schema = sf.newSchema(
98         new URL("http://soabook.com/example/oms/simpleorder.xsd"));
99      jaxbMarshaller.setSchema(schema);
100     ByteArrayOutputStream baos = new ByteArrayOutputStream();
101     jaxbMarshaller.marshal(jaxbSimpleOrder, baos);
102     return new StreamSource(new StringReader(baos.toString()));
103  } catch (Exception e) {
104     throw new RuntimeException(e);
105  }
106
107 }
```

book-code/chap05/customjava/modules/serializer/src/java/samples
 /MySimpleOrderSerializerNonRecursive.java

The code shown in Example 5–9 starts by creating an instance of the JAXB-generated class SimpleOrder.BillTo—jaxbSimpleOrder—from the instance of the MyAddress obtained from order.getBillTo(). The properties are set using the BillTo.setXXX methods. This part is straightforward enough. Next, the oms:items property is set to an empty list using:

jaxbSimpleOrder.setItems(new SimpleOrder.Items());

This step is needed because oms:items does not get mapped to a List<T> by JAXB 2.0 and hence, without this initialization, jaxbSimpleOrder.getItems() would return a null. Following this initialization, a for loop is used to populate the members of the JAXB-generated

List<ItemType> from the members of order.getItemList()—which has type List<MyItem>.

Again, the setters of the form ItemType.setXXX are used. One interesting part of this code deals with how the property types are converted. The line:

```
jaxbItem.setPrice(Double.parseDouble(
  Float.toString(myItem.getPrice())));
```

converts the price property from float (in MyItem) to double (in ItemType). This technique—converting through string instances—is used to avoid the underflow/overflow issues that can occur when changes in precision occur.

If you instead use the more straightforward conversion (as shown in the commented-out line):

```
jaxbItem.setPrice((double) myItem.getPrice());
```

you end up with XML that looks like this:

```
<price>2.990000009536743</price>
```

instead of this:

```
<price>2.99</price>
```

Once the SimpleType instance—jaxbSimpleOrder—has been completely populated, it is marshaled out to XML. For this process, the JAXB-Context is created as follows:

```
JAXBContext jaxbContext = JAXBContext.newInstance("com.example.oms");
```

The String—com.example.oms—that gets passed to the factory method newInstance is the package name of the JAXB-generated classes.[3] From the JAXBContext, a Marshaller instance is created. Next, validation is activated by setting the schema on the Marshaller instance using these lines:

```
Schema schema = sf.newSchema(
    new URL("http://soabook.com/example/oms/simpleorder.xsd"));
jaxbMarshaller.setSchema(schema);
```

---

3. For more details on the JAXBContext and Marshaller APIs, I suggest you consult the JAXB Javadoc, which is very detailed.

If you take these lines out and run the example with some bad data (e.g., set a quantity to a negative number), the marshalling will succeed and give you XML that is invalid with respect to the original schema. However, if you set the validation as I have done here, and try to marshal with a negative quantity, you get a `SAXParseException` as validation fails.

Lastly, `jaxbSimpleOrder` is marshaled into memory (using a `ByteArray-OutputStream`) and returned as a `StreamSource`.

Example 5–10 shows the code I use for testing this mapping.

Example 5–10 Testing the Mapping Code

```
46    MySimpleOrderSerializerNonRecursive serializer =
47       new MySimpleOrderSerializerNonRecursive();
48    MySimpleOrder myOrder = new MySimpleOrder(
49       "John Doe",
50       "125 Main Street",
51       "Any Town", "NM", "95811",
52       "(831) 874-1123");
53    myOrder.getItemList().add(new MyItem(6, (float) 2.99, "Diet Coke"));
54    myOrder.getItemList().add(new MyItem(4, (float) 3.99, "Potato Chips"));
55    myOrder.getItemList().add(new MyItem(2, (float) 5.34, "Frozen Pizza"));
56    Transformer xform = TransformerFactory.newInstance().newTransformer();
57    xform.setOutputProperty(OutputKeys.INDENT, "yes");
58    xform.transform(
59       serializer.getXML(myOrder),
60       new StreamResult(System.out));
```

book-code/chap05/customjava/modules/serializer/src/java/samples
  /MySimpleOrderSerializerNonRecursive.java

As you can see, this code creates an instance of `MySimpleOrder` with three items. A `javax.xml.transform.Transformer` is used to write the XML source returned from the mapping method—`getXML()`—to `System.out`. You can run this code by following these steps:

1. Go to `chap05/customjava`.
2. To run the example enter `mvn install`.
3. The XML that is serialized from `MySimpleOrder` gets written to the console.

As you were reading through the code in this section, you probably noticed that in the process of mapping `MySimpleOrder` to `oms:simpleOrder`,

I had to write code that does a mapping of `MyItem` to `oms:item`. This code, however, is embedded in the parent type mapping and cannot be reused (other than by cut and paste). It would be nice if you had to write each type mapping only once, and then could reuse it whenever it appears as part of another type mapping.

The next section continues this discussion of implementing type mappings using JAXB. However, it gets a little more sophisticated by introducing a recursive pattern that can be used to make your type mapping code reusable.

5.4   A Recursive Framework for Type Mappings

In the preceding section, you may have noticed that to implement this mapping:

```
< oms:simpleOrder, samples.MySimpleOrder >
```

you had to implement the following mappings implicitly:

```
< oms:billTo, samples.MyAddress >
< oms:item, samples.MyItem >
```

In this manner, you can see that it is natural to define type mappings (and their implementations) recursively. For example, if you have an implementation of the submappings for `samples.MyAddress` and `sample.MyItem`, you can create a mapping implementation for `samples.MySimpleOrder` simply by running the submappings and using the results to set the corresponding properties on `samples.MySimpleOrder`.

In fact, all the Java/XML mapping (and binding) tools I am aware of use recursion to define and implement mappings.

To understand the recursion in JAXB 2.0, consider the following simple example, which marshals an instance of the `Foo` class:

```
package samples;

@XmlRootElement
Public class Foo {

   Bar1 p1
   Bar2 p2


}
```

JAXB recursively applies the standard mapping for class `Bar1` to the instance `p1`, and the standard mapping for class `Bar2` to the instance `p2`. JAXB then combines the results to create something like this:

```
<foo xmlns="http://samples">
  < result of marshalling p1 .... />
  < result of marshalling p2 ... />
</foo>
```

In this book, I refer to the code that implements a mapping from Java to XML as a *serializer* (and the code that does the reverse is a *deserializer*). I use this terminology to distinguish the general case from the specific JAXB 2.0 case where these operations are called *marshalling* and *unmarshalling*.

Figure 5–3 illustrates how serializers can be constructed recursively. The figure shows a serializer that maps a class `Foo` to a complex type named `X`. This serializer implements the type mapping <`X`, `Foo`>. Class `Foo` is composed of two properties: `P1` and `P2`. As defined by the type mapping <`Foo`, `X`>, the property `P1` (which has class `Bar1`) gets mapped to an element `E1` with type `Y`. Likewise, the property `P2` (which has class `Bar2`) gets mapped to an attribute `A2` with type `Z`. So, the serializer for <`X`, `Foo`> can be implemented in terms of the serializers for its property type mappings <`Y`, `Bar1`> and <`Z`, `Bar2`>.

In Figure 5–3, step 3 inside the box labeled `"Serializer for <X, Foo>"` describes how the element `E1` (of type `Y`) and attribute `A2` (of type `Z`) are assembled into the instance of complex type `X`. This is where the JAXB schema-generated classes get used.

The JAXB schema-generated class for complex type `X` (call it `XGen`) has setters/getters for the element `E1` and attribute `A2`. So, at this point, you need to set the element `E1` using the appropriate setter from `XGen` and likewise for attribute `A2`. Then, the last step is to use JAXB to marshal the instance of `XGen` out to an XML representation of the complex type `X`.

The recursive serialization process just described, and illustrated in Figure 5–3, is clearer and easier to understand if you look at a code example. So, in what follows, I show you a refactored version of the serializer for `SimpleOrder` illustrated in Example 5–9. As you walk through this example, you will see how to use JAXB to build a serializer for `SimpleOrder` from the serializers for its properties.

To get started, we need to define an interface for a recursive serializer. Example 5–11 shows the simple interface that is used here. As you can see, it has a single method—`getXML`—that takes an `Object` and returns its serialized form as an instance of `javax.xml.transform.Source`.

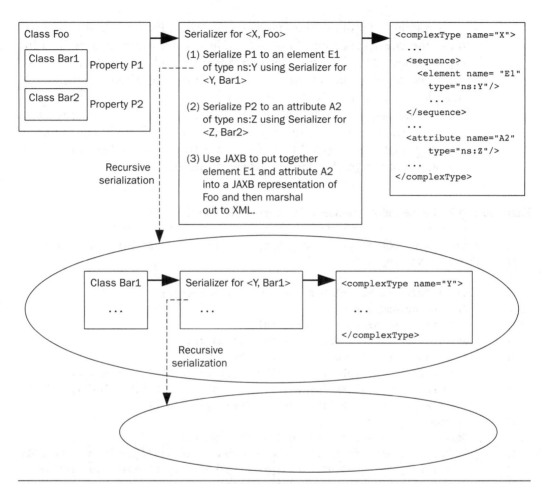

Figure 5–3 Custom mappings can be implemented recursively.

Example 5–11 The Serializer Interface

```
21   import javax.xml.transform.Source;
22
23   public interface Serializer {
24
25     public Source getXML(Object o);
26
27   }
```

book-code/chap05/customjava/modules/serializer/src/java/samples/Serializer.java

Example 5–12 shows the mapping code from Example 5–9 refactored to use the `Serializer` interface and serializers that have been defined for its properties: `billTo` (an instance of `MyAddress`) and `itemList` (an instance of `List<MyItem>`). One of the first things you notice when looking at this example is that it does not seem to include any mapping code. That is because the mapping code has mostly been refactored to the sub-serializers: `MyAddressSerializer` and `MyItemSerializer`. What is going on in the following code is the assembly of the results from those subserializers into an instance of the JAXB-generated class, `SimpleOrder`.

Example 5–12 The Serializer for `SimpleOrder`—Refactored

```
96    private SimpleOrder transformMySimpleOrderToJAXB(MySimpleOrder order)
97    throws JAXBException {
98
99      SimpleOrder jaxbSimpleOrder = new SimpleOrder();
100     // map the addresses
101     MyAddress myAddress = order.getBillTo();
102     Serializer myAddressSer = new MyAddressSerializer();
103     JAXBElement<SimpleOrder.BillTo> jaxbBillToElt =
104       (JAXBElement<SimpleOrder.BillTo>) jaxbUnmarshaller.unmarshal(
105         myAddressSer.getXML(myAddress),  SimpleOrder.BillTo.class);
106     jaxbSimpleOrder.setBillTo(jaxbBillToElt.getValue());
107     // map the items
108     Serializer myItemSer = new MyItemSerializer();
109     jaxbSimpleOrder.setItems(new SimpleOrder.Items()); // needed to avoid NPE
110     List<ItemType> jaxbItemList = jaxbSimpleOrder.getItems().getItem();
111     for (MyItem myItem : order.getItemList()) {
112       JAXBElement<ItemType> jaxbItemTypeElt =
113         (JAXBElement<ItemType>) jaxbUnmarshaller.unmarshal(
114           myItemSer.getXML(myItem),  ItemType.class);
115       jaxbItemList.add(jaxbItemTypeElt.getValue());
116     }
117     return jaxbSimpleOrder;
118
119   }
```

book-code/chap05/customjava/modules/serializer/src/java/samples
 /MySimpleOrderSerializer.java

As you can see, the preceding code creates an instance of `MyAddress-Serialzier`—a serializer that implements the type mapping `<oms:billTo, MyAddress>`. This serializer gets invoked—`myAddressSer.getXml(my-Address)`—and returns a `Source` instance representation of `oms:billTo` that is passed through the JAXB unmarshaller to produce a `JAXBElement<Simple-Order.BillTo>`. The value of this `JAXBElement` is then passed to the JAXB setter method, `SimpleOrder.setBillTo()`.

The code for serializing the items is similar, with the added twist of the `List<ItemType>` processing. First, the `SimpleOrder` instance gets its items properly initialized to an empty list using:

```
jaxbSimpleOrder.setItems(new SimpleOrder.Items())
```

Then, the `MyItemSerializer` class is used to serialize each instance of `MyItem` into a `Source` representation of `oms:ItemType`. Again, each `oms:ItemType` instance is passed through the JAXB unmarshaller to produce an instance of `JAXBElement<ItemType>`, and the value of that `JAXB-Element` (i.e., an instance of `ItemType`) is added to the JAXB list—`jaxbSimpleOrder.getItems()`.

Once this processing is completed, an instance of the JAXB schema-generated class `SimpleOrder` has been created from the original instance of `MySimpleOrder`. An XML form (i.e., `oms:simpleOrder`) can then be created by using the JAXB unmarshaller.

To understand this better, let's follow the recursion down a level and look at the implementation of the `MyAddressSerializer` class that implements the type mapping `<oms:billTo, MyAddress>`. The code for that serializer is shown in Example 5–13.

The mapping code is contained in the private method `transformMy-AddressToBillTo`. This code has been extracted from Example 5–9. It simply transforms an instance of `MyAddress` into an instance of the JAXB-generated class, `SimpleOrder.BillTo`.

Example 5–13 `MyAddressSerializer`: The Serializer for the `MyAddress` Class

```
39    public MyAddressSerializer() throws JAXBException {
40
41        jc = JAXBContext.newInstance("com.example.oms");
42        m = jc.createMarshaller();
43
44    }
45
46    public Source getXML(Object o) {
```

```
47
48      SimpleOrder.BillTo jaxbBillTo;
49      try {
50        jaxbBillTo = transformMyAddressToBillTo((MyAddress) o);
51        JAXBElement<SimpleOrder.BillTo> jaxbBillToElt =
52          new JAXBElement<SimpleOrder.BillTo>(
53              new QName("http://www.example.com/oms", "billTo"),
54              SimpleOrder.BillTo.class,
55              SimpleOrder.class,
56              jaxbBillTo);
57        ByteArrayOutputStream ba = new ByteArrayOutputStream();
58        m.marshal(jaxbBillToElt, ba);
59        return new StreamSource(new StringReader(ba.toString()));
60      } catch (JAXBException e) {
61        throw new RuntimeException(e);
62      }
63
64    }
65
66    private SimpleOrder.BillTo transformMyAddressToBillTo(MyAddress myAddr)
67    throws JAXBException {
68
69      SimpleOrder.BillTo jaxbBillTo = new SimpleOrder.BillTo();
70      jaxbBillTo.setName(myAddr.name);
71      jaxbBillTo.setCity(myAddr.city);
72      jaxbBillTo.setPhone(myAddr.phone);
73      jaxbBillTo.setState(myAddr.state);
74      jaxbBillTo.setStreet(myAddr.street);
75      jaxbBillTo.setZip(myAddr.zip);
76      return jaxbBillTo;
77
78    }
```

book-code/chap05/customjava/modules/serializer/src/java/samples/
MyAddressSerializer.java

The `Serializer` interface method—`getXML`—returns this `SimpleOrder.BillTo` instance as an XML `Source`. This is done by using a JAXB marshaller to marshal the `SimpleOrder.BillTo` into memory (i.e., as a `ByteArrayOutputStream`) and then return it wrapped as a `StreamSource`.

Notice the use of `JAXBElement`—the JAXB 2.0 representation of an XML element instance. `JAXBElement` is used to preserve element instance information such as the tag name. So, for example, if you have:

```
JAXBElement<com.example.oms.SimpleOrder> someElement = ....
```

the value of `some.Element.getName()` is the `QName` `{http://www.exam-ple.com/oms}simpleOrder`. To access the actual value of a `JAXBElement` representation, you need to use the `getValue()` method. For example, the following code accesses the street name of an instance of `oms:simpleOrder`:

```
JAXBElement<com.example.oms.SimpleOrder> someElement = ....
com.example.oms.SimpleOrder order = someElement.getValue();
String streetName = order.getBillTo().getStreet();
```

Lastly, I want to show you the `Serializer` implementation for `MyItem` in Example 5–14. You will notice that it does not use JAXB! I put this here to illustrate that this recursive serialization pattern works regardless of the style of serialization. This approach lets you combine different serialization styles—in this case, a JAXB-based serializer is used for `MyAddress`, and the simple text processing approach illustrated here is used for `MyItem`.

Example 5–14 `MyItemSerializer`: The Serializer for the `MyItem` Class

```
26  public class MyItemSerializer implements Serializer {
27
28    public Source getXML(Object o) {
29
30      MyItem myItem = (MyItem) o;
31      String xml =
32        "<?xml version=\"1.0\" encoding=\"UTF-8\"?>" +
33        "<item xmlns=\"http://www.example.com/oms\" productName=\"" +
34        myItem.getProductName() + "\">" +
35        "<quantity>" + myItem.getQuantity() + "</quantity>" +
36        "<price>" + myItem.getPrice() + "</price>" +
37        "</item>";
38      return new StreamSource(new StringReader(xml));
39
40    }
41
42  }
```

book-code/chap05/customjava/modules/serializer/src/java/samples
 /MyItemSerializer.java

In Example 5–14, you see that the XML for an instance of `oms:Item-Type` is created by simply building the `String` for an `oms:item` element. Then, this `String` is returned by wrapping it in a `StreamSource` instance.

You can run the code from this section by following these steps:

1. Go to `chap05/customjava`.
2. To run the example enter `mvn install`.
3. The XML that is serialized from `MySimpleOrder` gets written to the console.

In wrapping up this section, I would point out that the primary advantage of refactoring the mapping code from Example 5–9 like this is that it provides better code reuse. Now, for example, if you have another class with a property of type `MyAddress`, you can use the `MyAddressSerializer` to build its serializer.

You may have noticed that while I've called this approach to refactoring the code "recursive," I have not gone all the way with this example and shown how to build a truly recursive serialization system. All the recursion in this example has been done "by hand." That is, we have invoked the sub-serializers for the parent class manually by identifying the properties and hand-coding the references to their serializers. In Chapter 11, I take this example to the next level and walk you through a real implementation of a recursive serialization system based on JAXB 2.0. This section has been intended primarily to demonstrate how code reuse can be achieved and how JAXB schema-generated classes can be used to build serializers that work on non-JAXB (POJO) classes.

In the next section, I continue the overview of JAXB by exploring how the standard type mapping can be customized using annotations.

5.5 Implementing Type Mappings with JAXB 2.0 Annotations

The past two sections explored some techniques for implementing type mappings that use the classes created from an XML schema by the JAXB 2.0 schema generator. The basic idea behind these techniques is to map your existing POJOs to the Java representation of an XML schema created by the JAXB schema generator. Then, you can use the JAXB runtime to marshal/unmarshal between the JAXB classes and XML documents. So, to serialize your POJO, you run the mapping code to instantiate a JAXB-generated class, and then marshal the JAXB class out to XML.

In this section, I look at how you can eliminate the need for mapping code by using JAXB annotations to customize the JAXB 2.0 standard mapping. In many situations, you can annotate your POJOs so that they map directly to your target schema. When such a mapping is possible using annotations, you can use the JAXB 2.0 runtime to directly marshal/unmarshal your annotated POJOs to XML documents.

This section really shows off the power of the JAXB 2.0 annotations. As you will see, it is possible to achieve the entire mapping coded with custom Java in Sections 5.3 and 5.4 using annotations.

Of course, there are some drawbacks to this approach. Primarily, they are the following:

- Annotating the POJOs requires you to have access to the source code and the authority to recompile and deploy it in your organization. This is often not possible—particularly if the POJOs are owned by another department.
- It's often a trial-and-error process of implementing annotations, and then doing some testing to see whether they produce instances of the desired schema. This can be time-consuming and error-prone.
- Many type mappings cannot be implemented using annotations that simply customize the JAXB standard mapping. In such cases, you must fall back on the techniques outlined in Sections 5.3 and 5.4—or else use the JAXB 2.0 customization framework (i.e., the `@XmlJava-TypeAdapter` annotation that is discussed in Section 5.7).
- Each type mapping requires a different set of annotations—and therefore a new class. Let's say your POJO is a class named `Foo`. And let's say you want to support type mappings for two XML types: `oms:FooType` and `corp:BarType`. You will need to annotate `Foo` in two different ways to support `<oms:FooType, Foo>` and `<corp:BarType, Foo>`. So, that means two different versions of the `Foo` class must be created and supported.

One of the purposes of this book, with respect to JAXB, is to illustrate how to unlock the power of the annotations and work around some of these drawbacks. As alluded to in Chapter 3, wrapper classes can be used to handle situations where annotations cannot implement a mapping. You can also use wrappers as delegates in situations where you don't want to or cannot annotate your POJOs—or you need to provide multiple annotated versions of a class. The SOA-J framework discussed in Chapter 11 shows how to avoid wrapper classes altogether using a different approach to mapping that doesn't require user-defined annotations at all.

However, before focusing on these drawbacks and workarounds, I want to show how powerful JAXB annotations can be—in the situations where they can be used. Example 5–15 shows the annotated version of the MySimpleOrder class that you have been working with in the past two sections. Note that not all components of the JAXB mapping from MySimple-Order to its XML representation require annotations (e.g., the billTo property has no annotation—even though it maps to a billTo element). That is because explicit annotations are not needed when the JAXB standard default mapping is used for a component of the class definition.

Example 5–15 MySimpleOrder: The Annotated Version

```
28  @XmlRootElement(name="simpleOrder")
29  public class MySimpleOrder {
30
31    private MyAddress billTo;
32    private List<MyItem> itemList;
33
34    // must add a no-arg constructor
35    public MySimpleOrder() {}
36
37    public MySimpleOrder(String name, String street, String city, String state,
38        String zip, String phone) {
39      this(new MyAddress(name, street, city, state, zip, phone));
40    }
41
42    public MySimpleOrder(MyAddress addr) {
43      this.billTo = addr;
44      itemList = new ArrayList<MyItem>();
45    }
46
47    public MyAddress getBillTo() {
48      return billTo;
49    }
50
51    public void setBillTo(MyAddress billTo) {
52      this.billTo = billTo;
53    }
54
```

```
55   @XmlElementWrapper(name="items")
56   @XmlElement(name="item")
57   public List<MyItem> getItemList() {
58     return itemList;
59   }
60
61   public void setItemList(List<MyItem> itemList) {
62     this.itemList = itemList;
63   }
64
65 }
```

book-code/chap05/annotations/src/java/samples/MySimpleOrder.java

Here is a listing of the changes that have been made to the class, along with some explanation:

@XmlRootElement(name="simpleOrder")—The annotation has been added right before the class definition. The @XmlRootElement annotation maps a class to a global element definition. In this case, the name of the global element is specified by the name element as "simpleOrder". If this were not specified, the default value for name would be used—which is based on the class name. In this case, the default name would be "mySimpleOrder". @XmlRootElement also has a namespace optional element. Since namespace is not specified here, the global element's namespace is derived from the package (discussed later).

public MySimpleOrder() {}—A no arg constructor has been added to the class. User-authored types are required to provide a no arg constructor. This constructor is used by the JAXB 2.0 unmarshaller to create an instance.

@XmlElement(name="item")—Without this annotation, the property would be bound to an XML element named itemList—the property name the default mapping derives from the setter/getter method names. As you may notice, the other setter/getter pair (setBillTo/getBillTo) does not have an @XmlElement annotation. That is because it gets mapped to an XML element named billTo by default (see the note on @XmlAccessorType that describes the default mapping of properties).

@XmlElementWrapper(name="items")—This annotation specifies that the itemList property should be wrapped by an element named items. Without this annotation, by default, the Java type List<MyItem> would be mapped to a schema element definition like this:

```
<element name="item" type=... maxOccurs="unbounded"/>
```

and the serialized XML would look like this:

```
<item> ... </item>
<item> ... </item>
```

However, with the @XmlElementWrapper annotation, it gets mapped to this:

```
<element name="items">
  <element name="item" type=... maxOccurs="unbounded"/>
</element>
```

and the serialized XML looks like this:

```
<items>
  <item> ... </item>
  <item> ... </item>
</items>
```

This latter mapping is consistent with the schema for oms:simpleOrder. The @XmlElementWrapper is intended to be used with collections in this manner—to put a wrapper XML element around multiple occurrences of the same element.

In addition to these annotations, another annotation has a big impact on the mapping of this class to XML that does not appear here. That is the @XmlAccessorType annotation. It doesn't appear in this case because in Example 5–15, the default is used. If it were to appear, it would look like this:

@XmlAccessorType(AccessType.PUBLIC_MEMBER)—If present, this annotation would appear before the class definition. It specifies how the class properties get mapped to XML. AccessType.PUBLIC_MEMBER is the default. It indicates that every public getter/setter pair and every public field will be automatically bound to XML unless annotated by `XmlTransient`.

Looking at Example 5–15, you may be wondering how the namespace of the target XML is determined. By default, JAXB 2.0 derives the target namespace from the package name. In this case, the package name is `samples`, so the default namespace would be `http://samples`. However, JAXB provides a mechanism to specify a global mapping for the package: the `package-info.java` file.[4] Example 5–16 shows the `package-info.java` file used in this example.

Example 5–16 The JAXB 2.0 package-info.java File

```
19  @XmlSchema(
20      namespace = "http://www.example.com/oms",
21      elementFormDefault=XmlNsForm.QUALIFIED)
22  package samples;
23
24  import javax.xml.bind.annotation.XmlNsForm;
25  import javax.xml.bind.annotation.XmlSchema;
```

book-code/chap05/xprmnt_binder/src/java/samples/package-info.java

As you can see, this file consists of a package declaration and an annotation. The annotation provides the following mapping information:

`@XmlSchema(`
`    namespace = "http://www.example.com/oms",`
`    elementFormDefault=XmlNsForm.QUALIFIED)`—The `@XmlSchema` annotation is used only with a package declaration to define the mapping from a package to an XML schema. As you can see, in this case the `namespace` element maps this package to the target namespace `http://www.example.com/oms`. It also specifies that the `element-FormDefault` for the schema representation of this package should be `qualified`. This means that the element definitions mapped from

---

4. Actually, the use of `package-info.java` is recommended by [JSR-175], and that recommendation is followed by the GlassFish implementation of JAXB 2.0 used for the example in this book. The use of `package-info.java` is not strictly required for all JAXB implementations.

properties in the Java classes contained in this package are to be namespace-qualified. That is the same way `elementFormDefault` is specified in the schema for `oms:simpleOrder` shown in Example 5–1.

Example 5–17 shows the annotated version of the `MyAddress` class.

Example 5–17 `MyAddress`: The Annotated Version

```
26  @XmlAccessorType(XmlAccessType.FIELD)
27  @XmlType(name = "",
28      propOrder = {"name", "street", "city", "state", "zip", "phone"})
29  public class MyAddress {
30
31      @XmlElement(namespace = "http://www.example.com/oms")
32      protected String name;
33      @XmlElement(namespace = "http://www.example.com/oms")
34      protected String street;
35      @XmlElement(namespace = "http://www.example.com/oms")
36      protected String city;
37      @XmlElement(namespace = "http://www.example.com/oms")
38      protected String state;
39      @XmlElement(namespace = "http://www.example.com/oms")
40      protected String zip;
41      @XmlElement(namespace = "http://www.example.com/oms")
42      protected String phone;
43
44      // need a no-arg constructor
45      public MyAddress() {};
```

`book-code/chap05/annotations/src/java/samples/MyAddress.java`

In the target schema (see Example 5–1), this class maps to the anonymous complex type defined by the element definition for `oms:billTo`. Mapping to an anonymous type has some implications for the annotations, which are discussed here:

> `@XmlAccessorType(AccessType.FIELD)`—The `MyAddress` class does not have setter/getter methods. So, in this case, the access type specified by the annotation is `AccessType.FIELD`. This indicates that every nonstatic, nontransient field will be automatically bound to XML unless annotated by `XmlTransient`.

```
@XmlType(name = "",
    propOrder = {"name", "street", "city", "state",
    "zip", "phone"})
```
—The `@XmlType` annotation is used to map a class or an enum to a XML Schema type. This annotation does not appear in the `MySimpleOrder` class (Example 5–15) because the default mapping is used. However, in this case, the `MyAddress` class is mapped to an anonymous type—which is not the default—so an `@XmlType` annotation is needed. Setting the annotation element `name = ""` is how you indicate that this class should map to an anonymous type. Furthermore, the `propOrder` element specifies the ordering of the properties in the target XML schema `<sequence>` element. As you can see, the ordering here corresponds to the ordering specified in the schema shown in Example 5–1.

`@XmlElement(namespace = "http://www.example.com/oms")`—You may be wondering why the `@XmlElement` annotation is needed here. Since the `@XmlAccessorType` has specified that the access type is `FIELD`, the fields in this class are already mapped to XML elements. The reason is that the namespace of the target elements needs to be specified. The default JAXB 2.0 mapping indicates that the elements should inherit their namespace from the enclosing class. However, since this class is being mapped to an anonymous type, there is no namespace to inherit and one must be specified. A namespace must be specified because, as discussed in Example 5–16, the `elementForm-Default` attribute on the target schema has the value `qualified`.

The last annotated class I consider here is the `MyItem` class, shown in Example 5–18.

Example 5–18 `MyItem`: The Annotated Version

```
24  @XmlType(name = "ItemType", propOrder = {"quantity", "price"})
25  public class MyItem {
26
27    private int quantity;
28    private float price;
29    private String productName;
30
31    // need a no-arg constructor
32    public MyItem() {};
33
34    public MyItem(int quantity, float price, String productName)
```

```
35      throws Exception {
36        if (productName == null) {
37          throw new Exception("productName cannot be null");
38        }
39          this.productName = productName;
40          this.price = price;
41          this.quantity = quantity;
42      }
43
44      public float getPrice() {
45        return price;
46      }
47
48      public void setPrice(float price) {
49        this.price = price;
50      }
51
52      @XmlAttribute
53      public String getProductName() {
54        return productName;
55      }
56
57      public void setProductName(String productName) {
58        this.productName = productName;
59      }
60
61      public int getQuantity() {
62        return quantity;
63      }
64
65      public void setQuantity(int quantity) {
66        this.quantity = quantity;
67      }
68
69  }
```

book-code/chap05/xprmnt_binder/src/java/samples/MyItem.java

In the target schema (see Example 5–1), this class maps to the named complex type oms:ItemType. The salient aspects of this mapping are discussed here:

@XmlType(name = "ItemType", propOrder = {"quantity", "price"})—The MyItem class is mapped to the oms:ItemType complex type by specifying the annotation element name = "ItemType". In this case, the namespace for the XML schema type is provided by the @XmlSchema annotation at the package level (see Example 5–16).

@XmlAttribute—Since no @AccessorType annotation is specified for the MyItem class, the default mapping of properties is used—in the same manner as in Example 5–15. However, in this case, the property productName needs to be mapped to an attribute rather than an element. That is why the @XmlAttribute annotation gets used here. In contrast, the other two properties (i.e., quantity and price) get mapped to elements as specified by the default mapping.

Wrapping up this section, I next look at the code used to exercise the annotations illustrated earlier. Example 5–19 shows how I marshal and unmarshal an instance of MySimpleOrder in a "round-trip" fashion that validates the marshaled output against the schema shown in Example 5–1.

Example 5–19 Marshalling and Unmarshalling the Annotated Classes

```
36   public static void main(String[] args) throws Exception {
37
38       MySimpleOrder myOrder = new MySimpleOrder(
39           "John Doe",
40           "125 Main Street",
41           "Any Town", "NM", "95811",
42           "(831) 874-1123");
43       myOrder.getItemList().add(new MyItem(6, (float) 2.99, "Diet Coke"));
44       myOrder.getItemList().add(new MyItem(4, (float) 3.99, "Potato Chips"));
45       myOrder.getItemList().add(new MyItem(2, (float) 5.34, "Frozen Pizza"));
46       try {
47       JAXBContext jaxbContext = JAXBContext.newInstance(MySimpleOrder.class);
48         Marshaller jaxbMarshaller = jaxbContext.createMarshaller();
49         jaxbMarshaller.setProperty(Marshaller.JAXB_FORMATTED_OUTPUT,
50             Boolean.TRUE);
51         SchemaFactory sf =
52           SchemaFactory.newInstance(XMLConstants.W3C_XML_SCHEMA_NS_URI);
53         Schema schema = sf.newSchema(
54             new URL("http://soabook.com/example/oms/simpleorder.xsd"));
55         jaxbMarshaller.setSchema(schema);
56         ByteArrayOutputStream ba = new ByteArrayOutputStream();
57         jaxbMarshaller.marshal(myOrder, ba);
```

```
58          System.out.println(ba.toString());
59          Unmarshaller u = jaxbContext.createUnmarshaller();
60          MySimpleOrder roundTripOrder =
61            (MySimpleOrder) u.unmarshal(new StringReader(ba.toString()));
62          System.out.println("phone = " + roundTripOrder.getBillTo().phone);
63
64        } catch (Exception e) {
65          e.printStackTrace();
66        }
67      }
```

book-code/chap05/annotations/src/java/samples/MySimpleOrderSerializer.java

As you can see, this example starts by creating an instance of MySimple-Order. Next, a JAXBContext instance is created using the following version of the newInstance method:

JAXBContext.newInstance(java.lang.Class ...)

The context created in this manner will recognize the class(es) speci-fied, and any classes that are directly/indirectly referenced statically from the specified class(es). So, in Example 5–19, in addition to the MySimple-Order class, the MyAddress and MyItem classes will also be recognized by this context.

A Marshaller instance is created from the context, and the following method is used to turn on validation for this marshaller:

Marshaller.setSchema(javax.xml.validation.Schema)

As a result, all XML produced by this marshaller gets validated against the schema at the URL http://soabook.com/example/oms/simpleorder.xsd. This is the same schema as shown in Example 5–1.

As you can see, the output of the marshalling in this example is captured in a ByteArrayOutputStream. As a result, I can wrap a StringReader around this XML and use that to unmarshal the XML back into an instance of MySimpleOrder (i.e., the variable roundTripOrder). This "round trip," together with the schema validation, indicates that the annotations illustrated in this section accurately map the classes MySimpleOrder, MyAddress, and MyItem to the target XML schema.

You can run the code from this section by following these steps:

1. Go to `chap05/annotations`.
2. To run the example enter `mvn install`.
3. The XML that is serialized from `MySimpleOrder` and validated against the schema gets written to the console.

Once you spend some time working with these annotations and gain an intuitive understanding of the JAXB 2.0 standard mapping, it becomes fairly straightforward to create type mappings this way. So, while the JAXB 2.0 specification for these annotations is daunting, I highly recommend that you read it and then practice implementing some type mappings like the one illustrated here. After you spend some time with this technology, I think you will agree with me that annotations are a powerful tool for specifying type mapping when you are starting from a Java class.

In the next section, I look at how you use JAXB 2.0 to implement type mapping when you start from the other side—with an XML Schema definition.

5.6 Implementing Type Mappings with the JAXB 2.0 Binding Language

The preceding section looked at the "Start from Java" approach to implementing a type mapping with JAXB 2.0 annotations. In this section, I look at the "Start from XML Schema" (or "Start from XML" for short) approach.

In the end, the JAXB run-time implementation needs annotations for marshalling and unmarshalling. So, the "Start from XML" approach is based on adding binding language declarations to an XML schema that the JAXB schema generator interprets and uses to generate annotated Java code. In this manner, the binding language is a tool for customizing the default behavior of the schema compiler.

In this section, you again start with the `oms:simpleOrder` XML schema shown in Example 5–1. On the following pages, you will see how this schema can be customized by adding binding language declarations. My goal here is to get the schema generator to create annotated classes that come as close as possible to implementing the type mappings we looked at in the previous sections:

```
< oms:simpleOrder, samples.MySimpleOrder >
< oms:billTo, samples.MyAddress >
< oms:items, List<samples.MyItem> >
< oms:item, samples.MyItem >
```

In Section 5.3, I showed how to implement these type mappings using the JAXB 2.0 standard mapping and custom Java code. In Section 5.4, I showed how to do the same thing, but with a more elegant, recursive framework for serialization. Then, in Section 5.5, you saw how to implement these same type mappings using "Start with Java" by annotating the POJOs. In this section, you will see that it is not possible to implement these type mappings using the "Start from XML" approach. The binding language declarations are not as powerful as the annotations. You can get close to these type mappings, but not quite there. The mapping `< oms:items, List<samples.MyItem>>` is problematic because there is no way to "unwrap" the `oms:items` element to map its internal `oms:items` collection directly to a `List`.

To get started, look at Example 5–20, which shows the binding declarations that are needed at the global (top) level.

Example 5–20 The `jaxb:globalBindings` and `jaxb:schemaBindings` Declarations

```
4   <schema targetNamespace="http://www.example.com/oms"
5     elementFormDefault="qualified" xmlns="http://www.w3.org/2001/XMLSchema"
6     xmlns:jaxb="http://java.sun.com/xml/ns/jaxb" jaxb:version="2.0"
7     xmlns:oms="http://www.example.com/oms">
8     <annotation>
9       <appinfo>
10        <jaxb:globalBindings localScoping="toplevel"/>
11        <jaxb:schemaBindings>
12          <jaxb:package name="samples"/>
13        </jaxb:schemaBindings>
14      </appinfo>
15    </annotation>
```

book-code/chap05/bindinglang/etc/simpleorder_with_bindinglang.xsd

The binding declarations use the `<appinfo>` element specified by [XSD PART 1]. Inside the `<appinfo>` element, you can see a `jaxb:globalBind-ings` declaration and a `jaxb:schemaBindings` declaration.

The customizations specified inside the `jaxb:globalBindings` declaration have global scope. This means that they are customizations that affect the mapping of the entire schema—and any schemas that are included or imported. In general, the types of things you specify globally are the collection types used (e.g., `List` versus `Array`), whether to generate classes or interfaces, and whether to use inner classes. As you may recall from Section 5.2, the default JAXB 2.0 mapping generates inner classes from anonymous complex types. However, the target classes that are considered here (from the samples package) do not contain any inner classes. So, in this case, the `jaxb:globalBindings` element `localScoping` is set to `toplevel`, indicating that none of the generated classes should be inner classes.

Furthermore, the `jaxb:schemaBindings` declaration element provides customizations at the schema level (but unlike the global scope customizations, these do not apply to imported schemas). In this example, the `jaxb:package` declaration is used to specify that the package for the schema-generated classes should be `samples`.

So, these declarations move us a long way toward our goal by enabling us to specify that there should be no inner classes and that the package for all the classes should be `samples`. In Example 5–21, I illustrate how to get the exact class name you desire to map to.

Example 5–21 The `jaxb:class` Declaration

```
19    <element name="simpleOrder">
20      <annotation>
21        <appinfo>
22          <jaxb:class name="MySimpleOrder"/>
23        </appinfo>
24      </annotation>
25      <complexType>
26        <sequence>
27          <element name="billTo">
28            <complexType>
29              <annotation>
30                <appinfo>
31                  <jaxb:class name="MyAddress"/>
32                </appinfo>
33              </annotation>
34              <sequence>
35                <element name="name" type="string"/>
36                <element name="street" type="string"/>
37                <element name="city" type="string"/>
38                <element name="state" type="string"/>
39                <element name="zip" type="string"/>
40                <element name="phone" type="string"/>
41              </sequence>
```

```
42              </complexType>
43          </element>
```

book-code/chap05/bindinglang/etc/simpleorder_with_bindinglang.xsd

In this example, the `jaxb:class` declaration is used to specify the name of the target class to which a particular XML schema type or element definition should be mapped. Here, you can see that the declaration associated with the element `oms:simpleOrder` specifies that it gets mapped to a class named `MySimpleOrder`. Likewise, a little bit further down in the schema code, the anonymous complex type defined by the element `oms:billTo` is getting mapped to the `samples.MyAddress` class.

Example 5–22 shows a snippet from the `MySimpleOrder` class that is created by the schema generator from the `oms:simpleOrder` schema annotated with the previous binding language declarations. As you can see, it is similar to the `MySimpleOrder` class created "by hand" and illustrated in Section 5.5. However, the major difference here is that the `items` property has Java type `Items`—rather than `List<MyItem>`. Ideally, to implement the desired type mapping, you would like to have the schema generator add an `@XmlElementWrapper` annotation to the `items` property and make the type of the property `List<MyItem>`. But unfortunately, there is no way to specify this using the binding language.

Example 5–22 The `MySimpleOrder` Class Generated by the Schema Compiler

```
82   @XmlAccessorType(AccessType.FIELD)
83   @XmlType(name = "", propOrder = {
84       "billTo",
85       "items"
86   })
87   @XmlRootElement(name = "simpleOrder")
88   public class MySimpleOrder {
89
90       @XmlElement(namespace = "http://www.example.com/oms")
91       protected MyAddress billTo;
92       @XmlElement(namespace = "http://www.example.com/oms")
93       protected Items items;
```

book-code/chap05/bindinglang/etc/schemacompiler_withcomments/
  MySimpleOrder.java

Example 5–23 shows the `Items` class created by the JAXB schema generator. This class is not specified by any of the desired type mappings. As you can see, it is simply a wrapper class for the property `item`, which has Java type `List<MyItem>`.

Example 5–23 Generation of the `Items` Class Is Unavoidable

```
56  @XmlAccessorType(AccessType.FIELD)
57  @XmlType(name = "", propOrder = {
58      "item"
59  })
60  public class Items {
61
62      @XmlElement(namespace = "http://www.example.com/oms")
63      protected List<MyItem> item;
```

book-code/chap05/bindinglang/etc/schemacompiler_withcomments/Items.java

Example 5–24 shows how to handle datatype conversions when doing "Start from XML" with binding language declarations. As you recall from the discussion in Section 5.3, the `MyItem` class has a property named `quantity` with Java type `int` that maps to the schema element `quantity` with XML type `xs:positiveInteger`. Similarly, the `MyItem` class uses Java type `float` for the `price` property, whereas the XML type is `xs:double`.

Example 5–24 Datatype Conversion with the `jaxb:javaType` Declaration

```
57  <complexType name="ItemType">
58    <annotation>
59      <appinfo>
60        <jaxb:class name="MyItem"/>
61      </appinfo>
62    </annotation>
63    <sequence>
64      <element name="quantity" type="positiveInteger">
65        <annotation>
66          <appinfo>
67            <jaxb:property>
68              <jaxb:baseType>
69                <jaxb:javaType name="int"
```

```
70                        parseMethod="javax.xml.bind.DatatypeConverter.parseInt"
71                        printMethod="javax.xml.bind.DatatypeConverter.printInt"/>
72                 </jaxb:baseType>
73               </jaxb:property>
74             </appinfo>
75           </annotation>
76         </element>
77         <element name="price" type="double">
78           <annotation>
79             <appinfo>
80               <jaxb:property>
81                 <jaxb:baseType>
82                   <jaxb:javaType name="float"
83                      parseMethod="javax.xml.bind.DatatypeConverter.parseFloat"
84                      printMethod="javax.xml.bind.DatatypeConverter.printFloat"/>
85                 </jaxb:baseType>
86               </jaxb:property>
87             </appinfo>
88           </annotation>
89         </element>
90       </sequence>
91       <attribute name="productName" use="required" type="string"/>
92     </complexType>
93   </schema>
```

book-code/chap05/bindinglang/etc/simpleorder_with_bindinglang.xsd

In the binding language declarations in Example 5–24, you can see that the jaxb:javaType declaration is used to specify these datatype conversions. The jaxb:javaType declaration provides a way to customize the binding of an XML schema atomic datatype to a target Java datatype in a nonstandard way. The name attribute (int for the quantity property and float for the price property) specifies the Java datatype to be used for the property. Given this attribute, the JAXB schema generator should generate Java with a property having the type specified by the name attribute. Furthermore, the parseMethod and printMethod attributes specify static methods that provide the necessary datatype conversions to/from the Java type specified by the name attribute.

The parseMethod is applied during unmarshalling to convert a string (i.e., the lexical representation of the XML type coming from an XML document) into a value of the target Java datatype. Likewise, the printMethod is applied during marshalling to accomplish the reverse. As you can see in this example, the `print` and `parse` methods specified are static methods from the `javax.xml.bind.DatatypeConverter` class. This is a utility class provided to make it easier to do datatype conversions. Instead of having to understand the lexical representations of the XML Schema built-in types, you can simply use the `DatatypeConverter`. Consult the Javadoc for a detailed description of the `DatatypeConverter` class.

The mechanism by which the `print` and `parse` methods are invoked during marshalling and unmarshalling is the `@XmlJavaTypeAdapter` annotation. `@XmlJavaTypeAdapter` is discussed in detail in Section 5.7. For now, what you need to understand is that the `@XmlJavaTypeAdapter` annotation is used to specify a class that maps one datatype to another. When interpreting a `jaxb:javaType` declaration with `printMethod` and `parseMethod` attributes, the schema compiler annotates the target properties with `@Xml-JavaTypeAdapter` and generates an instance of `XmlAdapter` that invokes the `printMethod` and `parseMethod` static methods during marshaling and unmarshalling.

This mechanism will be a little clearer when you review the code generated by the schema compiler shown in Example 5–25.

Example 5–25 The `MyItem` Class with `@XmlJavaTypeAdapter` Annotations

```
58  @XmlAccessorType(AccessType.FIELD)
59  @XmlType(name = "ItemType", propOrder = {
60      "quantity",
61      "price"
62  })
63  public class MyItem {
64
65      @XmlElement(namespace = "http://www.example.com/oms", type = String.class)
66      @XmlJavaTypeAdapter(Adapter1.class)
67      protected Integer quantity;
68      @XmlElement(namespace = "http://www.example.com/oms", type = String.class)
69      @XmlJavaTypeAdapter(Adapter2.class)
70      protected Float price;
71      @XmlAttribute(required = true)
72      protected String productName;
```

book-code/chap05/bindinglang/etc/schemacompiler_withcomments/MyItem.java

In this example, you can see that the `quantity` element has the annotation `@XmlJavaTypeAdapter(Adapter1.class)`. This annotation tells the JAXB runtime that when it needs to marshal (or unmarshal) the `quantity` property, it should invoke the `@XmlJavaTypeAdapter` specified class, `Adapter1.class`. This class is shown in Example 5–26.

Example 5–26 An `XmlAdapter` Is Generated for Datatype Conversion

```
30   public class Adapter1
31       extends XmlAdapter<String, Integer>
32   {
33
34
35       public Integer unmarshal(String value) {
36           return (javax.xml.bind.DatatypeConverter.parseInt(value));
37       }
38
39       public String marshal(Integer value) {
40           return (javax.xml.bind.DatatypeConverter.printInt(value));
41       }
42
43   }
```

book-code/chap05/bindinglang/etc/schemacompiler_withcomments/Adapter1.java

As you can see, this `Adapter1` class has methods named `marshal` and `unmarshal`. The `marshal` method invokes the static method specified by the `jaxb:javaType printMethod` attribute. Likewise, the `unmarshal` method invokes the static method specified by the `jaxb:javaType parseMethod` attribute.

Example 5–27 shows the code that tests the classes the schema generator creates from the `oms:simpleOrder` schema together with the binding language declarations. As you can see from looking through this code, working with the versions of `MySimpleOrder`, `MyItem`, and `MyAddress` that are generated by the schema compiler is not as elegant as when working with the classes of the same name created by hand in the preceding section. Primarily, the reason is that the generated classes do not have any constructors other than zero argument (i.e., "no arg") constructors. So, instead of passing, for example, the `street`, `city`, `state`, `zip`, and `phone` to the `MyAddress` constructor, you have to first construct the class and then set all the properties.

Example 5–27 Exercising the Schema Generator-Produced Classes

```
38    public static void main(String[] args) throws Exception {
39
40        MySimpleOrder myOrder = new MySimpleOrder();
41        myOrder.setBillTo(new MyAddress());
42        myOrder.getBillTo().setName("John Doe");
43        myOrder.getBillTo().setStreet("125 Main Street");
44        myOrder.getBillTo().setCity("Any Town");
45        myOrder.getBillTo().setState("NM");
46        myOrder.getBillTo().setZip("95811");
47        myOrder.getBillTo().setPhone("(831) 874-1123");
48        Items items = new Items();
49        myOrder.setItems(items);
50        List<MyItem> itemList = items.getItem();
51        MyItem myItem = new MyItem();
52        myItem.setPrice((float) 2.99);
53        myItem.setQuantity(6);
54        myItem.setProductName("Diet Coke");
55        itemList.add(myItem);
56        myItem = new MyItem();
57        myItem.setPrice((float) 3.99);
58        myItem.setQuantity(4);
59        myItem.setProductName("Potato Chips");
60        itemList.add(myItem);
61        myItem = new MyItem();
62        myItem.setPrice((float) 5.34);
63        myItem.setQuantity(2);
64        myItem.setProductName("Frozen Pizza");
65        itemList.add(myItem);
66        try {
67          JAXBContext jaxbContext = JAXBContext.newInstance(MySimpleOrder.class);
68          Marshaller jaxbMarshaller = jaxbContext.createMarshaller();
69          jaxbMarshaller.setProperty(Marshaller.JAXB_FORMATTED_OUTPUT,
70              Boolean.TRUE);
71          SchemaFactory sf =
72            SchemaFactory.newInstance(XMLConstants.W3C_XML_SCHEMA_NS_URI);
73          Schema schema = sf.newSchema(
74              new URL("http://soabook.com/example/oms/simpleorder.xsd"));
75          jaxbMarshaller.setSchema(schema);
76          ByteArrayOutputStream ba = new ByteArrayOutputStream();
77          jaxbMarshaller.marshal(myOrder, ba);
78          System.out.println(ba.toString());
79          Unmarshaller u = jaxbContext.createUnmarshaller();
```

```
80        MySimpleOrder roundTripOrder =
81          (MySimpleOrder) u.unmarshal(new StringReader(ba.toString()));
82        System.out.println("phone = " + roundTripOrder.getBillTo().phone);
83
84      } catch (Exception e) {
85        e.printStackTrace();
86      }
87    }
```

book-code/chap05/bindinglang/modules/serializer/src/java/samples/
  MySimpleOrderSerializer.java

Another difference here, as mentioned in connection with Example 5–23, is that you have to create an instance of the extra class `Items`, and work with the `List<MyItems>` property through this wrapper class. So, it is a bit more awkward to work with these schema-generated classes than with the ones created by hand. However, the classes work perfectly, and as you can see from the code, the XML that is generated passes validation against the original schema.

You can run the code from this section by following these steps:

1. Go to `chap05/bindinglang`.
2. To run the example enter `mvn install`.
3. The XML that is serialized from `MySimpleOrder` and validated against the schema gets written to the console.

One advantage of working with the JAXB 2.0 binding language declarations, which we have not discussed, is the ability to place the binding declarations in an external binding file.[5] This approach is described in Appendix E of [JSR-222]. Basically, the external binding file contains the same declarations as appear in-line in a schema, but they are associated with the definitions in the schema using XPath 1.0 expressions. You can use this approach when you are not able to edit the schema directly, or you don't want to. One scenario where you wouldn't want to add in-line declarations to the schema is when it gets imported into other schemas or WSDL files that are published and you don't want the ultimate users of these schemas or WSDL to see the extra clutter produced by the binding language declarations. Furthermore,

---

5. For an example containing an external binding file, see Chapter 6, Section 6.4.2—the example involving the asynchronous invocation of a Web service.

you may want to define multiple type mappings on a single schema—in which case you cannot use in-line declarations.

In the past two sections, I showed you how to customize the JAXB 2.0 standard mapping through the use of annotations and binding language declarations. Although powerful, these approaches by themselves can't alter the basic structure of the JAXB 2.0 mapping. To implement type mappings that deviate from the JAXB 2.0 standard mapping more radically, you need to use the `@XmlJavaTypeAdapter` annotations along with the `XmlAdapter` class. That is the subject of the next section.

5.7 Implementing Type Mappings with the JAXB 2.0 XmlAdapter Class

As you saw in the preceding sections, annotations, and to a lesser extent, binding language declarations, are powerful tools for customizing the standard JAXB 2.0 Java/XML mapping. However, some structural limitations are imposed by the standard mapping that make it impossible to customize beyond a certain point without writing custom code.

Most of the time, the things you cannot do easily with JAXB 2.0 involve splitting, combining, or otherwise mixing together schema definitions to create Java properties where there is not a clear one-to-one correspondence. I call these sorts of mappings *multivariate type mappings*. In Chapter 4 (Sections 4.5 and 4.6), I introduced a multivariate type mapping. This mapping had two multivariate components:

- A two-line address in XML that mapped to a street number and street name in Java
- A single `xs:string` phone number that mapped to an area code, extension, and number in Java

In Chapter 4, I showed how to hand-code a workaround to implement such a mapping. In this section, I revisit this example and show how the `@XmlJavaTypeAdapter` annotation and the `javax.xml.bind.annotation.XmlAdapter` class can be used to encapsulate the hand-coded workaround and incorporate it into the JAXB 2.0 framework. In this manner, the `@XmlJavaTypeAdapter` annotation is a tool that can be used to incorporate custom code to extend the capabilities of the JAXB 2.0 runtime beyond the constraints of the standard JAXB 2.0 Java/XML mapping.

Example 5–28 shows the schema for `corp:AddressType`—the XML type involved in the multivariate mapping. As you can see, this is a straight-forward complex type definition where each element has the type `xs:string`.

Example 5–28 The `AddressType` Schema

```
4   <xs:schema xmlns:xs="http://www.w3.org/2001/XMLSchema"
5     elementFormDefault="qualified" targetNamespace="http://www.example.com/corp">
6     <xs:complexType name="AddressType">
7       <xs:sequence>
8         <xs:element name="addrLine1" type="xs:string"/>
9         <xs:element name="addrLine2" type="xs:string"/>
10        <xs:element name="city" type="xs:string"/>
11        <xs:element name="state" type="xs:string"/>
12        <xs:element name="zip" type="xs:string"/>
13        <xs:element name="phone" type="xs:string"/>
14      </xs:sequence>
15    </xs:complexType>
16  </xs:schema>
```

book-code/chap05/xmladapter/examples/standardtypes.xsd

The Java `Address` class that `corp:AddressType` is mapped to is shown in Example 5–29. As you can see, there is no way to define a one-to-one correspondence between the `corp:AddressType` elements and the `Address` class properties. This mapping is illustrated in Chapter 4, at the end of Section 4.5 (Figure 4–7).

Example 5–29 The `Address` Class Properties

```
23  @XmlJavaTypeAdapter(AddressAdapter.class)
24  public class Address {
25    private int streetNum;
26    private String streetName;
27    private String city;
28    private State state;
29    private int zip;
30    private Phone phoneNumber;
```

book-code/chap05/xmladapter/src/java/samples/Address.java

To implement the `<corp:AddressType,  Address>` type mapping, within the JAXB 2.0 framework, you need to use the `@XmlJavaTypeAdapter` annotation in three places:

1. Parsing the elements `addrLine1` and `addrLine2` to produce property values for `streetNum` and `streetName`, and vice versa
2. Implementing the nonstandard datatype conversion from the `zip` element (`xs:string`) to the `zip` property (`int`), and vice versa
3. Parsing the `phone` element into the constituent properties of the `Phone` class, and vice versa

As you can see from item 2, multivariate type mappings are not the only mappings that require the `@XmlJavaTypeAdapter` annotation. In many cases, nonstandard conversions of XML atomic types may also require an adapter.

Example 5–30 shows the `Phone` class's constituent properties. As you can see, mapping an `xs:string` to this class involves parsing out the area code, exchange, and number.

Example 5–30 The `Phone` Class Properties

```
23   @XmlJavaTypeAdapter(PhoneAdapter.class)
24   public class Phone {
25       private int areaCode;
26       private String exchange;
27       private String number;
```

book-code/chap05/xmladapter/src/java/samples/Phone.java

Figure 5–4 shows the marshalling procedure you are going to work through in the rest of this section. This diagram indicates how the type mappings are implemented using JAXB 2.0 and the `@XmlJavaTypeAdapter`. As you can see, the marshalling procedure makes use of an intermediate Java class named `AddressXML`.

As shown in the diagram, this marshalling procedure can be broken down into four steps:

1. The `Address` class instance is mapped to an instance of the `AddressXML` class. This first step parses the `streetNum` and `street-Name` into the `addrLine1` and `addrLine2` properties of `AddressXML`.

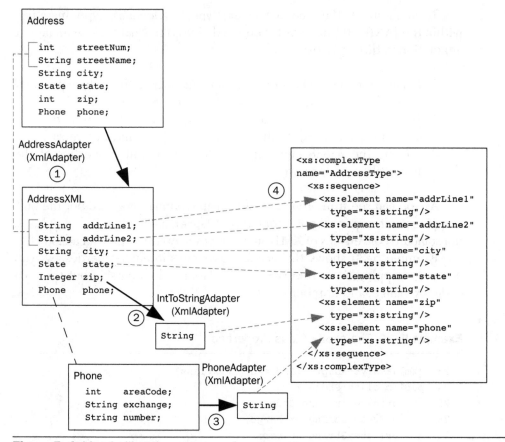

Figure 5–4 Marshalling the Address class to AddressType.

All the other properties of Address (i.e., city, state, zip, and phone) are mapped straight over to AddressXML. This transformation, from Address to AddressXML, is handled by the Address-Adapter class—an instance of XmlAdapter. The AddressAdapter class is specified as the value of the @XmlJavaTypeAdapter annotation on the Address class definition (see Example 5–29). Because of this @XmlJavaTypeAdapter annotation on the Address class definition, when you marshal an instance of Address, the JAXB 2.0 runtime automatically invokes the AddressAdapter to convert it to an instance of AddressXML, and then proceeds to marshal the AddressXML instance. This step takes care of the multivariate mapping of streetNum and streetName to addrLine1 and addrLine2.

2. The next step illustrated in Figure 5–4 occurs as the JAXB runtime proceeds to marshal the `AddressXML` instance. As you'll notice in Example 5–31, the `zip` property of `AddressXML` is annotated with an `@XmlJavaTypeAdapter` that references the `IntToStringAdapter` `XmlAdapter` implementation. This adapter class converts `zip` from an `Integer` to a `java.lang.String` so that the JAXB runtime can map it out to the target `xs:string` XML type for the `zip` element.

3. This step is invoked as the JAXB runtime marshals the `AddressXML` instance's `phone` property. This property is an instance of the `Phone` class (see Example 5–30) that is annotated with an `@XmlJavaType-Adapter` that references the `PhoneAdapter` class. `PhoneAdapter` is invoked by the JAXB runtime to process the `phone` property and implement the multivariate mapping that parses its three fields into a single `String`, for ultimate marshalling to `AddressType`'s phone element of XML type `xs:string`.

4. Once the `zip` and `phone` properties of `AddressXML` have been transformed by their respective `XmlAdapter` classes, the rest of the marshalling of this class instance follows the standard JAXB 2.0 run-time mapping to create an instance of `AddressType`.

Example 5–31 shows the `AddressXML` class that is used as an intermediary class for the marshalling of `Address` to an instance of the `AddressType` schema. As you can see, `AddressXML` has the same properties as `Address`, except that the `streetNum` and `streetName` properties have been replaced with `addrLine1` and `addrLine2`.

Example 5–31 The `AddressXML` Class Used As a Marshalling/Unmarshalling Intermediary

```
26  @XmlType(name="AddressType",
27        propOrder = {
28        "addrLine1",
29        "addrLine2",
30        "city",
31        "state",
32        "zip",
33        "phone"
34  })
35  @XmlAccessorType(XmlAccessType.FIELD)
36  public class AddressXML {
37
```

```
38   protected String addrLine1;
39   protected String addrLine2;
40   protected String city;
41   protected State state;
42   @XmlJavaTypeAdapter(IntToStringAdapter.class)
43   protected Integer zip;
44   protected Phone phone;
45
46 }
```

book-code/chap05/xmladapter/src/java/samples/AddressXML.java

Example 5–32 shows the `AddressAdapter` class that converts from `Address` to `AddressXML`, and vice versa. The `AddressAdapter` class extends the abstract class:

`javax.xml.bind.annotation.adapters.XmlAdapter<ValueType, BoundType>`

Extending `XmlAdapter` is a requirement for any class that is referenced by an `@XmlJavaTypeAdapter` annotation. The type parameters for `XmlAdapter` refer to the type JAXB doesn't know how to handle (`BoundType`) and the type JAXB knows how to handle (`ValueType`). When marshalling, the JAXB runtime invokes the marshal method from the `XmlAdapter` to convert the `BoundType` instance into a `ValueType` instance—which it then will marshal. (Note that the `ValueType` itself may contain `@XmlJavaTypeAdapter` references, so you can chain together `XmlAdapters` as we have done in this example.) Going the other way, the JAXB unmarshaller unmarshals an XML document into an instance of the `ValueType`, which then gets transformed by the `XmlAdapter.unmarshal` method to return an instance of `BoundType`.

Example 5–32 The `AddressAdapter` Class

```
23   public class AddressAdapter extends XmlAdapter<AddressXML, Address> {
24
25     public AddressXML marshal(Address addr) throws Exception {
26
27       System.out.println("entered AddressAdapter.marshal.");
28       AddressXML jaxbAddress = new AddressXML();
29       String[] streetParts = addr.getStreetName().split(" - ",2);
30       jaxbAddress.addrLine1 = addr.getStreetNum() + " " + streetParts[0];
31       if ( streetParts.length > 1 ) {
```

```
32        jaxbAddress.addrLine2 = streetParts[1];
33      } else {
34        jaxbAddress.addrLine2 = "";
35      }
36      // the rest is simple mapping
37      jaxbAddress.city = addr.getCity();
38      jaxbAddress.phone = addr.getPhoneNumber();
39      jaxbAddress.state = addr.getState();
40      jaxbAddress.zip = addr.getZip();
41      return jaxbAddress;
42
43    }
44
45    public Address unmarshal(AddressXML jaxbAddress)
46    throws Exception {
47
48      Address addr = new Address();
49      String[] line1Parts = jaxbAddress.addrLine1.split(" ",2);
50      int num = -1;
51      String street;
52      try {
53        num = Integer.valueOf(line1Parts[0]).intValue();
54      } catch (Exception e ) {}
55      if ( num > 0 ) {
56        addr.setStreetNum(num);
57        street = line1Parts[1];
58      } else {
59        street = jaxbAddress.addrLine1;
60      }
61      String line2 = jaxbAddress.addrLine2;
62      if (line2 != null && !line2.equals("") ) {
63        street += " - " + line2;
64      }
65      // the rest is simple mapping
66      addr.setStreetName(street);
67      addr.setCity(jaxbAddress.city);
68      addr.setState(jaxbAddress.state);
69      addr.setZip(jaxbAddress.zip);
70      addr.setPhoneNumber(jaxbAddress.phone);
71      return addr;
72    }
73
74  }
```

book-code/chap05/xmladapter/src/java/samples/AddressAdapter.java

As you can see in the code for AddressAdapter in Example 5–32, the parsing logic for converting between the two different formats for street address is the same as used in Chapter 4 (see Section 4.6). The only difference here is that I have bundled this logic inside an XmlAdapter instance so that it can be invoked by the JAXB runtime.

Example 5–33 shows another XmlAdapter implementation. This one is used in step 2 from Figure 5–4—to transform the zip property from an Integer to a String (and vice versa). As you can see, this is a very simple transformation, but it's necessary nonetheless because it is not a standard mapping supported by the JAXB runtime.

Example 5–33 The IntToStringAdapter Class

```
23  public class IntToStringAdapter extends XmlAdapter<String, Integer> {
24
25    public Integer unmarshal(String value) {
26      return new Integer(value); }
27
28    public String marshal(Integer value) {
29      return value.toString(); }
30
31  }
```

book-code/chap05/xmladapter/src/java/samples/IntToStringAdapter.java

Example 5–34 shows the PhoneAdapter implementation of XmlAdapter that is used in step 3 in Figure 5–4 to transform between the two different representations of phone number. Again, if you check back to Chapter 4 (Section 4.6), you will see that this code is the same as the parsing code used in that example. The only difference here is that it is bundled inside an instance of XmlAdapter so that it can be invoked by the JAXB runtime.

Example 5–34 The PhoneAdapter Class

```
22  public class PhoneAdapter extends XmlAdapter<String, Phone> {
23
24    public Phone unmarshal(String jaxbPhone) throws Exception {
25
```

```
26        Phone phone = new Phone();
27        int areaStart = jaxbPhone.indexOf("(");
28        int areaEnd = jaxbPhone.indexOf(")");
29        String area = jaxbPhone.substring(areaStart+1,areaEnd);
30        jaxbPhone = jaxbPhone.substring(areaEnd+1,jaxbPhone.length());
31        String phoneSplit[] = jaxbPhone.split("-", 2);
32        phone.setAreaCode(Integer.valueOf(area).intValue());
33        phone.setExchange(phoneSplit[0].trim());
34        phone.setNumber(phoneSplit[1].trim());
35        return phone;
36
37    }
38
39    public String marshal(Phone myPhone) throws Exception {
40
41      return "(" + myPhone.getAreaCode() + ") " + myPhone.getExchange() + "-" +
42      myPhone.getNumber();
43
44    }
45
46  }
```

book-code/chap05/xmladapter/src/java/samples/PhoneAdapter.java

---

To test the marshalling and unmarshalling of the Address class, I use the simple Order class shown in Example 5–35. Order has a single property—addr—with type Address.

Example 5–35 The Order Class: A Wrapper Used for Testing

```
26  @XmlRootElement(namespace="http://www.example.com/css/custinfo")
27  @XmlAccessorType(XmlAccessType.FIELD)
28  public class Order {
29
30    @XmlElement(namespace="http://www.example.com/css/custinfo")
31    protected Address addr;
32
33  }
```

book-code/chap05/xmladapter/src/java/samples/Order.java

The `Order` class is mapped by JAXB to the schema shown in Example 5–36. As you can see, this is a schema for an element named `order` that has a single child element named `addr`. The `addr` element has type `corp:AddressType`.

Example 5–36 The Schema Used for Validation Imports `corp:AddressType`

```
4   <xs:schema xmlns:xs="http://www.w3.org/2001/XMLSchema"
5     xmlns:corp="http://www.example.com/corp"
6     targetNamespace="http://www.example.com/css/custinfo"
7     elementFormDefault="qualified">
8     <xs:import namespace="http://www.example.com/corp"
9       schemaLocation="http://soabook.com/example/corp/standardtypes.xsd"/>
10    <xs:element name="order">
11      <xs:complexType>
12        <xs:sequence>
13          <xs:element name="addr" type="corp:AddressType"/>
14        </xs:sequence>
15      </xs:complexType>
16    </xs:element>
17  </xs:schema>
```

book-code/chap05/xmladapter/etc/orderElement.xsd

The code for testing the implementation of the type mapping `<corp:AddressType, Address>` using the `Order` class is shown in Example 5–37. This code implements a "round trip," marshalling out an instance of the `Order` class and unmarshalling the result back. During the marshalling, part of the process is validated against the schema shown in Example 5–36.

Example 5–37 Round-Trip Marshal, Unmarshal, and Validation

```
32  public class AddressSerializer {
33
34    public static void main(String[] args) throws Exception {
35
36      Address addr = new Address(
37          175,
38          "Main Street - Suite 200",
```

```
39          "New City", State.OH, 59101,
40            new Phone(758, "874","1221"));
41      Order order = new Order();
42      order.addr = addr;
43      try {
44        JAXBContext jaxbContext = JAXBContext.newInstance(Order.class);
45        Marshaller jaxbMarshaller = jaxbContext.createMarshaller();
46        jaxbMarshaller.setProperty(Marshaller.JAXB_FORMATTED_OUTPUT,
47            Boolean.TRUE);
48        SchemaFactory sf =
49          SchemaFactory.newInstance(XMLConstants.W3C_XML_SCHEMA_NS_URI);
50        Schema schema = sf.newSchema(new File(args[0])); // pass in the schema
51        jaxbMarshaller.setSchema(schema);
52        ByteArrayOutputStream ba = new ByteArrayOutputStream();
53        jaxbMarshaller.marshal(order, ba);
54        System.out.println(ba.toString());
55        Unmarshaller u = jaxbContext.createUnmarshaller();
56        Order roundTripOrder =
57          (Order) u.unmarshal(new StringReader(ba.toString()));
58        printAddress(roundTripOrder.addr);
```

book–code/chap05/xmladapter/src/java/samples/AddressSerializer.java

You can run this code by following these steps:

1. Go to `chap05/xmladapter`.
2. To run the example enter `mvn install`.
3. The XML that is serialized from `Order` and validated against the schema gets written to the console. In addition, the properties from the `Address` class instance that is created by the round-trip unmarshalling are printed to the console.

In this section, you saw how to take the custom code used for implementing type mappings in Section 5.3 and incorporate it into the JAXB 2.0 run-time framework using the `@XmlJavaTypeAdapter` annotation. The JAXB 2.0 runtime employs a recursive procedure for marshalling/unmarshalling—analogous to the process described in Section 5.4. The JAXB 2.0 runtime and the Section 5.4 process are analogous in that they both serialize a class instance by traversing the tree defined by its properties. To put that into the context of the example from this section, the `Address` class is serialized (or *marshaled* in the JAXB terminology), by recursively serializing each of its properties, and assembling the results together to create the XML document required by the type mapping to `corp:AddressType`.

As stated in Section 5.4, one of the goals of a recursive framework for serialization is to enable the reuse of type mapping implementations. In the JAXB 2.0 framework, implementing a type mapping as an `XmlAdapter` implementation makes it reusable. For example, the `AddressAdapter` class can be employed (via the `@XmlJavaTypeAdapter` annotation) anywhere you want to apply the `<corp:AddressType, Address>` type mapping. However, because `XmlAdapter` instances are invoked via annotations, they are not as flexible as you might like. For example, if you wanted to deploy a Java class with two different type mappings, encoded in two different `XmlAdapter` implementations, you would need to create and deploy two different versions of that class—since the `@XmlJavaTypeAdapter` annotation is part of the class definition itself. In Chapter 11, when I introduce the Adaptive Serializer Framework, you will see how we can work around that problem and provide a JAXB 2.0-based serialization subsystem that enables the clean reuse of type mappings and the application of multiple type mappings without requiring multiple versions of the same class.

5.8 JAXB 2.0 for Data Transformation (Instead of XSLT)

The previous sections of this chapter dealt with how to use JAXB 2.0 to implement type mappings—in other words, to map from Java to XML. JAXB 2.0 can also be used to map from one XML representation to another using similar techniques. This is called *data transformation*, and in Chapter 3, Section 3.5, I illustrated how to do it using XSLT.

Many Java programmers are not comfortable with XSLT. If that sounds familiar, this section is for you! Here, I show how to do data transformation with JAXB instead of XSLT. Using this approach, you write code to transform an instance of one JAXB-generated class into an instance of another JAXB-generated class. Such transformation code plays the same role as the XSLT stylesheet does in the example in Chapter 3, Section 3.5. Although easier to understand than XSLT for many Java programmers, one drawback of this approach is that the transformation code can be hard to understand and/or reuse. In general, the principle known as *separation of concerns* suggests that data transformation be handled separately from other code. As a result, if you're using this approach, it is a good idea to keep your transformation code separate from the business logic in well-commented modules.

The following example implements the same transformation as in Chapter 3, Section 3.5. The JAXB 2.0 data transformation process for this example is illustrated in Figure 5–5.

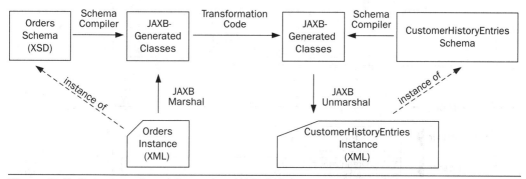

Figure 5–5 Data transformation using JAXB 2.0.

Prior to runtime, the JAXB 2.0 schema compiler is used to create Java classes that are bound to the Orders and CustomerHistoryEntries schemas.[6] These are represented as "JAXB Generated Classes" in Figure 5–5. Using these classes, you write the "Transformation Code" pictured as the arrow in the middle of the diagram. This code maps the fields and properties of the Orders-generated classes to the appropriate fields and properties of the CustomerHistoryEntries classes.

At runtime, an instance of the Orders schema is unmarshalled to its respective JAXB classes. Then, the transformation code is executed, to create instances of the CustomerHistoryEntries JAXB classes. The CustomerHistoryEntries JAXB class instances are then marshaled to an instance of the CustomerHistoryEntries schema to complete the data transformation.

Next, I am going to walk through the code that implements this data transformation. To make it easier to understand, I've reproduced the data mapping diagram from Chapter 3 that illustrates this transformation as Figure 5–6.

The Java code that implements this data transformation using the JAXB-generated classes is shown in Example 5–38. This is the same Web service

---

6. These schemas can be found at the beginning of Chapter 3. Alternatively, you can see the Orders schema at http://soabook.com/example/oms/orders.xsd and the CustomerHistory-Entries schema at http://soabook.com/example/css/custhistentries.xsd.

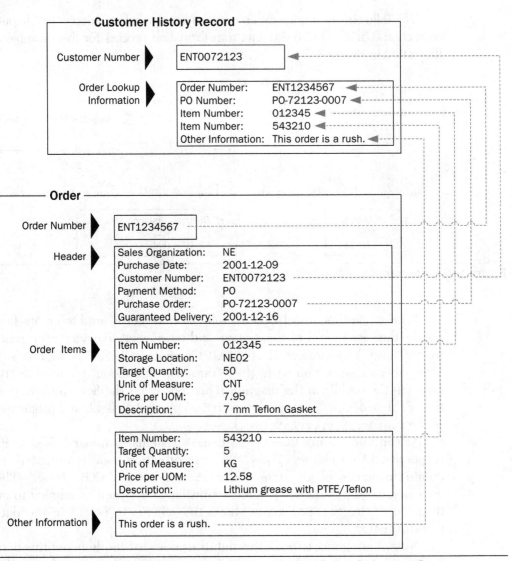

Figure 5–6 Data mapping for the transformation from a Sales Order to a Customer History Record (from Chapter 3).

example[7] used in Chapter 3, Section 3.4. Here, I am showing you how to get the same result using JAXB rather than XSLT. The Chapter 3 Web services

---

7. See Chapter 3, Section 3.4, for a detailed discussion of Web services used in this example. The service `GetNewOrders` returns instances of `oms:Orders`. Likewise, instances of `css:CustomerHistoryEntries` are posted to the Web service `UpdateCustomerHistory`.

being used in this example are RESTful,[8] so I am using `javax.xml.ws.Dis-`
`patch` to get an instance of `oms:Orders` as a `javax.xml.Source`. This
`oms:Orders` XML source is unmarshalled into an instance of `JAXBEle-`
`ment<OrdersType>`, from which an instance of the JAXB-generated class
`OrdersType` is extracted. From this, you get a list of the actual `OrderType`
instances (the JAXB-generated class representation of `oms:OrderType`) that
are transformed into customer history entries.

Example 5–38 Transforming Orders to Customer History Entries with Java

```
68   Dispatch<Source> getOrdersDispatch =
69     svc.createDispatch(orderQName, Source.class, Service.Mode.PAYLOAD);
70   Map<String, Object> requestContext = getOrdersDispatch.getRequestContext();
71   requestContext.put(MessageContext.HTTP_REQUEST_METHOD, "GET");
72   Source s =  (Source) getOrdersDispatch.invoke(null);
73   JAXBElement<OrdersType> newOrdersElt =
74     (JAXBElement<OrdersType>) u.unmarshal(s);
75   OrdersType newOrders = newOrdersElt.getValue();
76   List<OrderType> newOrderList = newOrders.getOrder();
77   CustomerHistoryEntriesType ch = new CustomerHistoryEntriesType();
78   CustomerHistoryEntryType che = null;
79   // for each order, create and add a customer history to the list
80   for (OrderType newOrder : newOrderList) {
81     che = new CustomerHistoryEntryType();
82     che.setCustomerNumber(newOrder.getOrderHeader().getCUSTNO());
83     CustomerHistoryEntryType.OrderLookupInfo orderLookupInfo =
84       new CustomerHistoryEntryType.OrderLookupInfo();
85     orderLookupInfo.setOrderNumber(newOrder.getOrderKey());
86     orderLookupInfo.setPURCHORDNO(newOrder.getOrderHeader().getPURCHORDNO());
87     orderLookupInfo.setOrderText(newOrder.getOrderText());
88     // add the item numbers
89     for (BUSOBJITEM boItem : newOrder.getOrderItems().getItem()) {
90       orderLookupInfo.getITMNUMBER().add(boItem.getITMNUMBER());
91     }
92     // add to the list history entries
93     ch.getCustomerHistoryEntry().add(che);
94   }
```

8. Some readers may be confused by the use of REST here, when I've said that SOAP is preferred for SOA. There are two reasons why this example uses REST: (1) to demonstrated
that JAXB mapping created here can directly replace the XSLT in the Chapter 3 example; (2)
so I don't have to introduce JAX-WS client code to handle SOAP—as JAX-WS is the subject
of the next chapter and hasn't been formally introduced yet.

```
95     JAXBElement<CustomerHistoryEntriesType> chElt =
96       new JAXBElement<CustomerHistoryEntriesType>(
97         new QName("http://www.example.com/css","CustomerHistoryEntries"),
98         CustomerHistoryEntriesType.class,
99         JAXBElement.GlobalScope.class,
100        ch);
```

book-code/chap05/transform/src/java/samples/OrderToCustHistJAXB.java

The Java class `CustomerHistoryEntriesType` is the JAXB-generated class bound to the `css:CustomerHistoryEntriesType` complex type—which is simply a sequence of `css:CustomerHistoryEntryType` elements. So, each customer history entry corresponds to an instance of the XML schema type `css:CustomerHistoryEntryType` and JAXB-generated Java class `CustomerHistoryEntryType`.

The transformation code starts by creating an instance of `CustomerHistoryEntryType` to hold the customer history entries that get created from the orders. Next, it iterates through the list of `OrderType` instances, transforming each into an instance of `CustomerHistoryEntryType` using the code inside the `for` loop.

For example, the `CustomerHistoryEntryType.setCustomerNumber()` setter is applied to the `OrderType.getOrderHeader().getCUSTNO()` property to map the customer number in the `oms:Order` to the customer number in the `css:CustomerHistoryEntry`.

Next, the transformation code creates a new instance of `CustomerHistoryEntryType.OrderLookupInfo`—the JAXB-generated representation of the anonymous type defined by the `OrderLookupInfo` element definition within `css:CustomerHistoryEntryType`. The properties of the `CustomerHistoryEntryType.OrderLookupInfo` instance are also set from the getters defined on the JAXB-generated `OrderType` class.

And so, the transformation proceeds in this manner, setting the properties on the `CustomerHistoryEntry` JAXB class by navigating the properties on the `OrderType` class. Once all its properties are set, each instance of `CustomerHistoryEntry` is added to the list property from `CustomerHistoryEntries`.

After the instance of the JAXB-generated class `CustomerHistoryEntries` has been completely constructed, there is one remaining step. You need to create an element instance from this class. This JAXB class is bound to the type `css:CustomerHistoryEntries`. The way an instance is created is with the `JAXBElement` constructor, as shown at the very end of Example 5–38.

An element is needed, because that is what gets POSTed to the REST-ful Web service to update the customer history records. The code for doing this RESTful POST is shown in Example 5–39.

Example 5–39 Using JAXB to Access a RESTful Service with `Dispatch`

```
105    svc.addPort(histQName, HTTPBinding.HTTP_BINDING, addCustHistUrl);
106    Dispatch<Object> postCustomerHistoryDispatch =
107      svc.createDispatch(histQName, jc, Service.Mode.PAYLOAD);
108    postCustomerHistoryDispatch.invoke(chElt);
```

book-code/chap05/transform/src/java/samples/OrderToCustHistJAXB.java

As shown in this code, you can invoke the RESTful service using the `JAXBElement` instance directly. This is accomplished by using a form of the `Dispatch` class with the `Object` type parameter—`Dispatch<Object>`—that works with JAXB-generated objects.[9]

You can run this code by following these steps. Just like in the example from Chapter 3, Section 3.4, after the code executes, the results (customer history entries) are written by the application to a temporary file of the form `${user.home}/tmp/soabook*.xml`. So, you can look to your `${user.home}/tmp` directory to verify that the example ran properly.

1. Start GlassFish (if it is not already running).
2. Go to `<book-code>/chap03/rest-post/endpoint-servlet`.
3. To deploy the CSS Web service enter `mvn install`, and then, `ant deploy`.
4. Go to `<book-code>/chap03/rest-get/endpoint-servlet`.
5. To deploy the OMS Web service, enter `mvn install`, and then `ant deploy`.
6. Go to `<book-code>/chap05/transform`.
7. To run the example, enter `mvn install`.
8. To undeploy the Web services, go back to `<book-code>/chap03/rest-post/endpoint-servlet` and enter `ant undeploy`. Do the same in the directory `<book-code>/chap03/rest-get/endpoint-servlet`.

---

9. See Section 4.3.3 of [JSR-224].

5.9   Conclusions

This chapter provided an overview of how JAXB 2.0 can be applied to implement type mappings. Type mappings are central to implementing SOA with Java, because they enable you to map your Java classes to standards-compliant WSDL interfaces. Those WSDL interfaces are built from enterprise or eBusiness standard XML Schema documents that provide agreed upon representations of business objects such as addresses and purchase orders. So, at a very basic level, SOA (in the Java world) is about mapping existing Java classes to standard XML Schema documents.

This chapter demonstrated a few approaches to type mapping. First, you saw an approach based on the standard JAXB 2.0 Java/XML mapping. This approach, introduced in Section 5.3, uses the JAXB schema generator to create Java representations of the XML schema side of the type mapping. The type mapping is implemented by writing custom code to transform the existing classes into the classes generated by the JAXB schema generator. Then, JAXB provides the run-time marshalling/unmarshalling for these generated classes.

In Section 5.4, I showed you how to get a little more sophisticated about this approach by introducing a `Serializer` interface that enabled you to bundle the type mapping code and reuse it. This approach also enabled you to build type mappings from other type mappings in a recursive manner.

Section 5.5 showed you how, in many cases, you can avoid writing custom mapping code by learning how to annotate your existing classes. You saw how these annotations could be used to customize the standard JAXB 2.0 Java/XML mapping to realize a wide variety of type mappings. I also discussed one drawback of annotations; namely, that despite their power, they are embedded in the class definitions, so to implement more than one type mapping means to keep more than one version of a class around. That is, one new class is needed for each type mapping.

Section 5.6 showed that you can also customize the standard JAXB Java/XML mapping by annotating your XML schema with JAXB binding language declarations. I showed how this approach modifies the output of the schema compiler to create classes with different annotations. You saw that one advantage of this approach is that the binding language declarations can be kept in a separate file from the schema. However, one disadvantage is that this approach is not as powerful as the "Start from Java" approach where existing Java classes are annotated to match a schema.

Section 5.7 looked at the limitations of the JAXB 2.0 standard Java/XML mapping and demonstrated how to work around them using the

`@XmlJavaTypeAdapter` annotation together with user-defined `XmlAdapter` class instances to implement custom type maps. You saw that this approach is powerful, but suffers from the same limitation as all annotation-oriented approaches to type mapping. You cannot have multiple type mappings for the same class because the annotations are part of the class definition.

Lastly, in Section 5.8, I showed how JAXB could be used for data transformation. The basic idea introduced in that section is that if you use the JAXB schema compiler to create Java representations of schemas, you can write Java code to transform between instances of those schemas by mapping one JAXB representation to the other.

That wraps up the basic tour of JAXB 2.0 as it applies to SOA. In the next section of the book, I begin to look at the JAX-WS 2.0 standard and focus on how it can be used to write SOA clients that are consumers of Web services.

CHAPTER 6

JAX-WS—Client-Side Development

JAX-WS 2.0 provides the Java Web Services standard for both deploying and invoking Web services. In this chapter, I look at the client-side invocation capabilities provided by JAX-WS. In particular, I focus on how to use JAX-WS as a client-side tool for creating SOA components that consume Web services.

6.1 JAX-WS Proxies

JAX-WS, like its predecessor, JAX-RPC, is designed so that programmers can invoke a Web service just as through they are invoking a Java method. In fact, in many respects, JAX-WS imitates Java Remote Method Invocation (Java RMI). Like Java RMI, JAX-WS enables the programmer to use a local method call to invoke a service on another host. Unlike Java RMI, however, the service on the other host does not need to be implemented as a Java application. In the JAX-WS case, the Web service on the remote host needs to provide a WSDL interface—a `wsdl:portType`[1] definition, to be precise. JAX-WS provides a standard WSDL to Java mapping that maps a `wsdl:portType` to a Java interface. Such an interface is called a *service endpoint interface* (SEI) because it is a Java representation of a Web service endpoint. At runtime, JAX-WS can generate an instance of a SEI that enables the programmer to invoke a Web service by invoking a method on the SEI.

The technology employed by JAX-WS to create a run-time instance of a SEI is the dynamic proxy class (for a quick overview of dynamic proxies, see the Javadoc for `java.lang.reflect.Proxy`). This technology enables JAX-WS to dynamically create (i.e., to create at runtime) an instance of a SEI

---

1. See Chapter 4 for a discussion of WSDL and its role as an interface definition language.

that can be used to invoke a Web service. The internal workings of a JAX-WS proxy are based on an instance of `java.lang.reflect.Invocation-Handler` that implements a standard WSDL to Java and Java to WSDL mapping. In essence, when you invoke a method on a proxy, the internal `InvocationHandler` converts the parameters into a SOAP message that is sent to the Web service endpoint. Likewise, the SOAP response message is converted into an instance of the SEI return type.

You don't need to understand the internal workings of dynamic proxies to create and use a SEI to invoke a Web services with JAX-WS. But if you are interested, it's a fascinating topic to explore.

JAX-WS proxies are dynamic—they are created at runtime. You do not need to generate stub classes that implement the SEI. However, you do need to generate the SEI prior to runtime. That is because the dynamic proxy technology employed by JAX-WS requires an interface definition in order to create a proxy class instance. JAX-WS implementations provide tools for creating a SEI from its corresponding `wsdl:portType`. In Glass-Fish, for example, this functionality is provided by the `wsimport` utility.

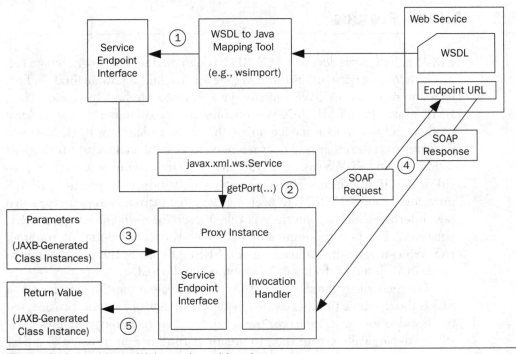

Figure 6–1 Invoking a Web service with a Java proxy.

Figure 6–1 illustrates the process of creating and using a SEI and its associated proxy instance.

1. A WSDL to Java mapping tool (e.g., the GlassFish `wsimport` utility) is used to read the target Web service's WSDL and generate a service endpoint interface (SEI). This step happens prior to compiling and running the client code that invokes the Web service.
2. At runtime, one of the `getPort()` methods from the `javax.xml.ws.Service` class is used to create a proxy instance that implements the SEI.
3. The Web service is invoked simply by invoking a method from the SEI. As indicated in Figure 6–1, the parameters that get passed to such a method are instances of JAXB-generated classes. That is because the SEI maps to its corresponding `wsdl:portType` using the standard JAXB XML Schema to Java mapping. Each method provided by the SEI corresponds to a `wsdl:operation` on the `wsdl:portType`.
4. The internals of the proxy instance convert the SEI method invocation parameters into a SOAP request and send it to the Web service's endpoint. In this diagram, I assume that the binding is SOAP over HTTP, but the JAX-WS architecture is designed to support other bindings.
5. Lastly, the proxy instance receives the SOAP response (or fault) and deserializes it into an instance of the SEI method's return type.

In what follows, I walk you through an example of how to invoke a Web service using a proxy instance in the manner just described. The example used here is a Web service for placing an order called the `RequestOrder` service. This service requires that the client send a customer number, a purchase order number (or credit card), and a list of items to be purchased. The Web service responds with a completed order, which serves as the customer's receipt. The order is represented as an instance of `oms:Order` (for an example of `oms:Order`, see Chapter 3, Example 3–1).

6.1.1 The JAX-WS WSDL to Java Mapping

As mentioned, the SEI is mapped from a Web service's `wsdl:portType` using the JAX-WS WSDL to Java mapping. So, to get started, I first illustrate how this mapping applies in this example.

Example 6–1 shows the WSDL types for the `RequestOrder` Web service. As with all the examples in this book, `RequestOrder` uses the document/literal wrapped style of WSDL (see Chapter 4 for a description of the WSDL styles).

The element `req:requestOrder` defined here is the wrapper element that contains the parameters `req:CUST_NO` (the customer number), `req:PURCH_ORD_NO` (the purchase order number), `req:ccard` (the credit card information), and one or more instances of `req:item` (the items being ordered). Likewise, `req:requestOrderResponse` is the wrapper element that contains the response parameter: `oms:Order` (the customer order).

Example 6–1 The WSDL Types Defined by the `RequestOrder` Web Service

```
10    <wsdl:types>
11      <xs:schema targetNamespace="http://www.example.com/oms">
12        <xs:include schemaLocation="http://soabook.com/example/oms/orders.xsd"/>
13      </xs:schema>
14      <xs:schema targetNamespace="http://www.example.com/faults">
15        <xs:include schemaLocation="http://soabook.com/example/faults/faults.xsd"
16        />
17      </xs:schema>
18      <xs:schema elementFormDefault="qualified"
19        targetNamespace="http://www.example.com/req">
20        <xs:import namespace="http://www.example.com/oms"/>
21        <xs:element name="requestOrder">
22          <xs:complexType>
23            <xs:sequence>
24              <xs:element name="CUST_NO">
25                <xs:simpleType>
26                  <xs:restriction base="xs:string">
27                    <xs:maxLength value="10"/>
28                  </xs:restriction>
29                </xs:simpleType>
30              </xs:element>
31              <xs:element name="PURCH_ORD_NO" minOccurs="0">
32                <xs:simpleType>
33                  <xs:restriction base="xs:string">
34                    <xs:maxLength value="35"/>
35                  </xs:restriction>
36                </xs:simpleType>
37              </xs:element>
38              <xs:element name="ccard" type="oms:BUSOBJ_CCARD" minOccurs="0"/>
39              <xs:element name="item" type="oms:BUSOBJ_ITEM"
40                maxOccurs="unbounded"/>
```

```
41                </xs:sequence>
42              </xs:complexType>
43            </xs:element>
44            <xs:element name="requestOrderResponse">
45              <xs:complexType>
46                <xs:sequence>
47                  <xs:element ref="oms:Order"/>
48                </xs:sequence>
49              </xs:complexType>
50            </xs:element>
51          </xs:schema>
52        </wsdl:types>
```

book-code/chap06/endpoint/modules/endpoint/src/webapp/WEB-INF/wsdl
  /RequestOrder.wsdl

The parameters contained in these wrapper elements get mapped to method parameters in the SEI using the JAXB 2.0 XML Schema to Java mapping. The method signatures in the SEI, on the other hand, get mapped from the operations defined on the `wsdl:portType`.

Example 6–2 shows the `wsdl:portType` for the `RequestOrder` Web service. The `wsdl:operation` named `requestOrder` is going to be mapped to a method on the SEI named `requestOrder`. The input parameters to that method will be taken from the `wsdl:input` message—in other words, `req:request`. As you can see, that message is a single `wsdl:part`, which is the `req:requestOrder` wrapper element discussed previously. So the parameters for the SEI method named `requestOrder` will be mapped from the child elements of the wrapper `req:requestOrder`. Similarly, the response type for the `requestOrder` method will map to `oms:Order` because `oms:Order` is the child element of the `wsdl:output` message. If this mapping seems confusing (which it can be!), please review the description of the document/literal wrapped style of WSDL found in Chapter 4.

Example 6–2 The `wsdl:portType` Defined by the `RequestOrder` Web Service

```
56      <wsdl:message name="request">
57        <wsdl:part name="parameters" element="req:requestOrder"/>
58      </wsdl:message>
59      <wsdl:message name="response">
60        <wsdl:part name="parameters" element="req:requestOrderResponse"/>
61      </wsdl:message>
```

```
62   <wsdl:message name="inputFault">
63     <wsdl:part name="parameters" element="faults:inputMessageValidationFault"/>
64   </wsdl:message>
65   <wsdl:portType name="RequestOrderPort">
66     <wsdl:operation name="requestOrder">
67       <wsdl:input message="req:request"/>
68       <wsdl:output message="req:response"/>
69       <wsdl:fault name="requestOrderInputFault" message="req:inputFault"/>
70     </wsdl:operation>
71   </wsdl:portType>
```

book-code/chap06/endpoint/modules/endpoint/src/webapp/WEB-INF/wsdl
  /RequestOrder.wsdl

In the example code, I used the GlassFish utility wsimport to generate the SEI classes from this WSDL. Example 6–3 shows how wsimport is invoked from inside Ant in my example code. It's a little confusing to read in this format, but you can get the basic idea.

Example 6–3 Invoking the wsimport WSDL to Java Mapping Tool from Ant

```
 7 <target name="wsdl2java">
 8   <mkdir dir="${basedir}/target/work/java"/>
 9   <mkdir dir="${basedir}/target/classes"/>
10   <exec executable="${wsimport}" failonerror="true">
11     <arg value="-d"/>
12     <arg value="${basedir}/target/classes"/>
13     <arg value="-s"/>
14     <arg value="${basedir}/target/work/java"/>
15     <arg value="-keep"/>
16     <arg value="http://${glassfish.host}:${glassfish.deploy.port}/chap06-
  endpoint-endpoint-1.0/requestOrder?wsdl"/>
17   </exec>
18 </target>
```

book-code/chap06/proxy/modules/wsdl2java/build.xml20

The wsimport utility is passed (the last argument) the URL of the RequestOrder service's WSDL. In this case, using the default values for the host and port, that URL is http://localhost:8080/oms/RequestOrder-Service?wsdl. The `wsimport` utility generates the SEI classes and places the source in the directory specified by the `-s` option (compiled classes go into the directory specified by `-d`).

Figure 6–2 shows the JAX-WS WSDL to Java mapping implemented by the `wsimport` utility. The box on the left-hand side labeled "RequestOrder WSDL" shows an edited snippet of the WSDL for the Web service. The five objects to the right of the WSDL represent classes that are generated by the `wsimport` utility. Some of these classes (e.g., `OrderType`) are purely the result of applying the JAXB XML Schema to Java mapping to the schemas defined in the `wsdl:types` section. Others (e.g., `RequestOrderPort`) are defined by the JAX-WS WSDL to Java mapping. These classes are all annotated with both JAXB and JAX-WS annotations. For the simplicity of this discussion, the annotations are omitted from Figure 6–2. Later in this section, I discuss the JAX-WS annotations.

In the following numbered list, each labeled mapping component in Figure 6–2 is explained. These are high-level explanations, intended to give you a good feel for how the WSDL to Java mapping is used in practice. For a detailed description of the mapping, you should read Chapter 2 of [JSR-224].

1. The `wsdl:portType` element is mapped to the service endpoint interface (SEI)—`RequestOrderPort`.
2. The `wsdl:operation` named `requestOrder` is mapped to a SEI method of the same name.
3. The `wsdl:input` message determines the parameters of the `requestOrder` method. As you can see, this message, `req:request`, has a single `wsdl:part`—the wrapper element `req:requestOrder` defined in the `wsdl:types` section. The children of this wrapper element (i.e., `CUST_NO`, `PURCH_ORD_NO`, `ccard`, `item`) define the method parameters. Notice that the `item` element gets mapped to a `List` because it has `maxOccurs > 1`.
4. Similarly, the `wsdl:output` message determines the response type—in other words, `OrderType`.
5. As defined by the JAX-WS mapping, each `wsdl:fault` gets mapped to a thrown exception. So here, the single `wsdl:fault` maps to the `"throws InputFault"` clause of the `requestOrder` method declaration.
6. The `wsdl:message` referred to by a `wsdl:fault` gets mapped to a class that extends `java.lang.Exception`. In this example, the `wsdl:message` named `inputFault` gets mapped to the `InputFault` class. This is a wrapper exception class for the fault bean (described next).

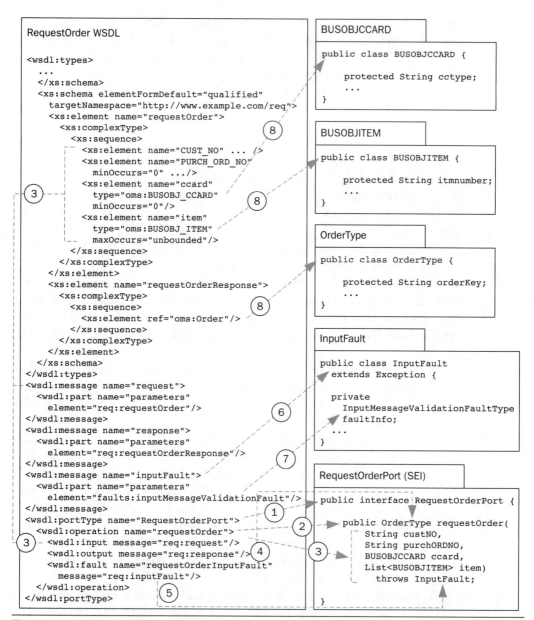

Figure 6–2 JAX-WS WSDL to Java mapping for `RequestOrder` Web service.

7. Furthermore, a `wsdl:fault` element refers to a `wsdl:message` with a single part. The global element declaration referred to by that part is mapped to a JavaBean that JAX-WS refers to as a fault bean. In this

example, the element `faults:inputMessageValidationFault` maps to the fault bean named `InputMessageValidationFaultType`. Fault beans like this are properties wrapped by an exception wrapper class (as described in the preceding item).

8. The types and global elements defined in the `wsdl:types` section get mapped to Java classes using the JAXB XML Schema to Java mapping described in Chapter 5. In this example, `oms:Order` gets mapped to `OrderType`, `oms:BUSOBJ_ITEM` gets mapped to `BUSOBJITEM`, and `oms:BUSOBJ_CCARD` gets mapped to `BUSOBJCCARD`.

This discussion provided an example of how JAX-WS maps WSDL to Java classes—and in particular, how a SEI is created from a `wsdl:port-Type`. Next, I discuss how the JAX-WS runtime converts a method invocation on a SEI into a SOAP message. The key to that process is the JAX-WS annotations.

6.1.2 Service Endpoint Interface Annotations

As you recall from Chapter 5, the JAXB runtime uses annotations to determine how to marshal/unmarshal a JAXB value class to/from XML. Analogously, the JAX-WS runtime uses annotations on the SEI to determine how to marshal a method invocation to a SOAP request message and unmarshal a SOAP response into an instance of the method's return type. For simplicity's sake, I only consider the example illustrated here—where the output message has a single part/wrapper child that maps to the SEI method's return value. If you are interested in all of the details of how operations with output messages that have multiple parts/wrapper children get mapped to annotated SEI operations, please see Chapters 2 and 7 of [JSR-224].

Figure 6–3 shows the annotated SEI, `RequestOrderPort`, and how it maps to the SOAP request and response messages. This is the annotated code produced by the `wsimport` utility as it generated the SEI from the `wsdl:portType` named `RequestOrderPort`. The annotations are discussed in detail in Table 6–1. Here, I highlight the aspects of the relationship between the SEI annotations and the SOAP messages that are numbered in Figure 6–3:

1. The `@RequestWrapper` annotation defines the wrapper element for the SOAP request message. In a document/literal wrapped style Web service, the SOAP request parameters appear as children of a wrapper element that is the only child of the SOAP body. The wrapper element is defined in the `wsdl:types` section as discussed in

Figure 6–3 JAX-WS SEI annotations and the corresponding SOAP request/response messages.

Example 6–1. So, as you can see in this example, the SOAP request message has a single child of its body—with the local name `request-Order` and namespace `http://www.example.com/req` as defined in the `@RequestWrapper` annotation.

2. The `@WebParam` annotations map the parameters of a SEI method to the parameters of the SOAP request message. In a document/literal wrapped style Web service, these parameters are children of the wrapper element, as discussed previously.

3. Analogous to the `@RequestWrapper` annotation, the `@ResponseWrapper` annotation defines the wrapper element for the SOAP response message. So, as you can see in Figure 6–3, the only child of the SOAP response body element is the wrapper element defined by this annotation.

4. The `@WebResult` annotation maps the return value of a SEI method to corresponding child of the response wrapper element contained in the SOAP response message's body. In this example, the annotation defines an element named `oms:Order`, and as you can see, that is the element appearing as the grandchild of the SOAP body in the response message.

Because the annotated Java interface (SEI) in Figure 6–3 is a little tough to read, I repeat the code listing for the `RequestOrderPort` class in Example 6–4.

Example 6–4 The Annotated Service Endpoint Interface

```
40  @WebService(name = "RequestOrderPort",
41      targetNamespace = "http://www.example.com/req",
42      wsdlLocation = "http://localhost:8080/oms/RequestOrderService?wsdl")
43  public interface RequestOrderPort {
44
45      @WebMethod
46      @WebResult(name = "Order", targetNamespace = "http://www.example.com/oms")
47      @RequestWrapper(localName = "requestOrder",
48          targetNamespace = "http://www.example.com/req",
49          className = "com.example.req.RequestOrder")
50      @ResponseWrapper(localName = "requestOrderResponse",
51          targetNamespace = "http://www.example.com/req",
52          className = "com.example.req.RequestOrderResponse")
53      public OrderType requestOrder(
54          @WebParam(name = "CUST_NO",
```

```
55                targetNamespace = "http://www.example.com/req")
56           String custNO,
57           @WebParam(name = "PURCH_ORD_NO",
58                targetNamespace = "http://www.example.com/req")
59           String purchORDNO,
60           @WebParam(name = "ccard", targetNamespace = "http://www.example.com/req")
61           BUSOBJCCARD ccard,
62           @WebParam(name = "item", targetNamespace = "http://www.example.com/req")
63           List<BUSOBJITEM> item)
64      throws InputFault
65      ;
66
67  }
```

book-code/chap06/proxy/edited/RequestOrderPort.java

Table 6–1 identifies and explains the use of annotations in the generated SEI interface appearing in Example 6–4. As you read through this table, notice that the "Purpose" column gives a general description of what the annotation is used for. The "Example" column, on the other hand, explains the role the annotation is playing in this particular example.

These annotations serve two purposes. As used here, they annotate a SEI and determine, at runtime, how to map a method invocation to SOAP request/response messages. However, these annotations are also used on the service side to deploy a Java class as a Web service. If you think about it, these two purposes are really the same—in either case, the annotations are mapping a `wsdl:operation` to a Java method. In fact, the mapping from the annotations to the SOAP request/response messages shown in Figure 6–3 is a byproduct of the WSDL SOAP Binding defined in Section 3 of [WSDL 1.1] and clarified in [WS-I BP 1.1]. Stated another way, the SEI annotations really define a mapping from the `wsdl:portType/wsdl:operation` to the Java interface/method. However, by following the WSDL SOAP Binding, we can also see the relationship between these annotations and the structure of the SOAP request/response messages.

I've covered the SEI annotations in a lot of detail here, because I feel it is useful for gaining some intuition about the interrelationships between the WSDL, the SOAP messages, and the mapped service endpoint interface (SEI). The better the grasp of these interrelationships you have, the easier it becomes to feel comfortable working with Web Services using the JAX-WS paradigm.

Table 6–1 Descriptions of the Java Annotations Appearing in Example 6–4

Annotation	Purpose	Example
`@WebService`	Identifies a Java class as implementing a Web service, or a Java interface as defining a Web service interface.	A mapped SEI (in this example, a SEI mapped from a `wsdl:portType`) must be annotated with `@WebService` per Section 2.2 of [JSR-224]. The `name` and `target-Namespace` attributes identify the `wsdl:portType`. The `wsdlLocation` attribute identifies the location of the WSDL containing the `wsdl:portType`.
`@WebMethod`	Identifies that the associated method has been mapped from a `wsdl:operation`.	A mapped SEI method (in this example, a SEI method mapped from a `wsdl:operation`) must be annotated with `@Web-Method` per Section 2.3 of [JSR-224].
`@WebResult`	Associates the SEI method's return value to a `wsdl:part` or the `wsdl:part`'s element definition.	For a document binding (as in this example), the `name` attribute corresponds to the local name of the XML element representing the return value, and the `targetName-space` attribute provides the namespace of the XML element. On the wire, in this example, this XML element corresponds to the wrapper child of the SOAP body (the grandchild of the SOAP body). For an rpc/literal binding, the `name` attribute can vary as the name of the response element is not defined and is not significant.[a]
`@RequestWrapper`	Identifies the request wrapper bean—a JAXB-generated class that maps to the request message's wrapper element.	For a document/literal wrapped style Web service (as in this example), the `class-Name` attribute specifies the fully qualified name of the JAXB-generated request wrapper bean. Likewise, the `localName` and `targetNamespace` attributes refer to the name and namespace of the `wsdl:types` defined wrapper element. The wrapper element appears as the only child of the SOAP request message's body. For an rpc/literal binding, this annotation is not used, as the wrapper element is not defined in the WSDL's schema.[a]

Continues

Table 6–1 Descriptions of the Java Annotations Appearing in Example 6–4 *(Continued)*

Annotation	Purpose	Example
@ResponseWrapper	Identifies the response wrapper bean—a JAXB-generated class that maps to the response message's wrapper element.	For a document/literal wrapped style Web service (as in this example), the class-Name attribute specifies the fully qualified name of the JAXB-generated response wrapper bean. Likewise, the localName and targetNamespace attributes refer to the name and namespace of the wsdl:types defined wrapper element. The wrapper element appears as the only child of the SOAP response message's body. For an rpc/literal binding, this annotation is not used, as the wrapper element is not defined in the WSDL's schema.[a]
@WebParam	Associates a SEI method's parameter with a particular wsdl:part (rpc style) or a wrapper child of a particular wsdl:part's element definition (document style). In either case, the @WebParam associates a Java representation of a parameter with the WSDL/SOAP representation.	For a document/literal wrapped style Web service (as in this example), the name and targetNamespace attributes refer to the name and namespace of a wrapper child of the wrapper element defined in the wsdl:types section. On the wire, these wrapper elements appear as the children of the request wrapper element, which is the only child of the SOAP request message's body. So, the @WebParam defined elements are the grandchildren of the SOAP request message's body. For an rpc/literal binding, the targetNamespace attribute is not used since parameters are unqualified in that case. Instead, the partName attribute is used indicating which part of the input message the parameter maps to.[a]

a. See Chapter 4, Section 4.3, for a discussion regarding the various styles of WSDL and the differences between document/literal, document/literal wrapped, and rpc/literal.

In the next section, I look at the nuts and bolts of invoking the example Web service using a JAX-WS client. After all this complicated discussion about mappings, you will be relieved to see that it is pretty easy to invoke a Web service with a JAX-WS proxy!

6.1.3 Invoking a Web Service with a Proxy

You can use several methods to get a proxy instance. In this section, we look at three of them. The most elegant approach involves dependency injection specified by an annotation, as illustrated in Example 6–5.

Example 6–5 Injecting a Proxy Instance with @WebServiceRef

```
31    @WebServiceRef(RequestOrderService.class)
32    public static RequestOrderPort port;
```

book-code/chap06/proxy/modules/client/src/java/samples/Client.java

The @WebServiceRef annotation defines a reference to a Web service. It follows the resource pattern exemplified by the javax.annotation.Resource annotation in Section 2.3 of [JSR-250]. When this annotation is applied on a field or method, the container will inject an instance of the requested resource into the application when the application is initialized.

In Example 6–5, it annotates the field port of type RequestOrderPort (the SEI used in this example). This is an example of dependency injection and the variable port is referred to as the injection target. Using the @WebServiceRef annotation in this way, the container will inject a proxy instance implementing the SEI into the injection target.

Of course, for such injection to work, this code must execute inside a container. For this example, I use the GlassFish Application Client Container (ACC)—appclient. The ACC is defined within Java EE 5 (see Chapter EE.9 of [JSR-244]) as a lightweight container required to provide only security and deployment services.

Getting back to the @WebServiceRef annotation, in this case I am using it to inject an instance of the SEI RequestOrderPort. When used in this manner, the value attribute of the annotation must refer to a generated service interface type (i.e., a subtype of javax.xml.ws.Service). The class specified here for the value attribute—RequestOrderService.class—was generated at the same time as the SEI by the wsimport utility. The RequestOrderService generated class provides a getRequestOrderPort() method that returns an instance of RequestOrderPort.

If you are not running inside a container, you cannot use the @WebServiceRef for injection, but you can still make use of the generated service class RequestOrderService, as shown in Example 6–6.

Example 6–6 Creating a Proxy Instance Using a Generated Service

```
63      RequestOrderService service = new RequestOrderService();
64      RequestOrderPort port = service.getRequestOrderPort();
65      (new Tester()).runTests(port);
```

book-code/chap06/proxy/modules/client/src/java/samples/Client.java

Finally, you can construct a proxy instance for the SEI dynamically by configuring an instance of the javax.xml.ws.Service class at runtime. This approach is shown in Example 6–7.

Example 6–7 Creating a Proxy Instance Using a Dynamically Configured Service

```
77    URL wsdlURL = new URL("http://"+hostName+":"+portVal+"/chap06-endpoint-
    endpoint-1.0/requestOrder?wsdl");
78    QName serviceQName =
79      new QName("http://www.example.com/req", "RequestOrderService");
80    QName portQName =
81      new QName("http://www.example.com/req", "RequestOrderPort");
82    Service service = Service.create(wsdlURL, serviceQName);
83    RequestOrderPort port =
84      (RequestOrderPort) service.getPort(portQName, RequestOrderPort.class);
85    (new Tester()).runTests(port);
```

book-code/chap06/proxy/modules/client/src/java/samples/Client.java

Using this approach, you make use of the Service.create() factory method to configure a Service instance using the WSDL's URL and QName of the wsdl:service. Technically, since the SEI is annotated with the WSDL's URL, you don't even need the URL parameter. However, in case the URL has changed since the SEI was generated, it is generally safer to specify the URL in this manner.

Having created the Service instance, you simply invoke the service.getPort() method passing in the QName of the wsdl:portType and the SEI (e.g., `RequestOrderPort.class`). The `Service` instance, using the dynamic proxy mechanism discussed at the beginning of Section 6.1, creates a proxy instance that you can cast to the SEI.

Example 6–8 shows how the proxy instance can be used and, in particular, how exceptions are handled.

Example 6–8 Exercising the Proxy Instance

```
46   public void runTests(RequestOrderPort port) throws Exception {
47
48     BUSOBJCCARD ccard = createCreditCard();
49     BUSOBJCCARD expiredCCard = createExpiredCreditCard();
50     ArrayList<BUSOBJITEM> itemList = createItemList();
51
52     OrderType order;
53     try {
54       System.out.println("Running test with expired credit card.");
55       order = port.requestOrder(
56           "ENT0072123", null, expiredCCard, itemList);
57     } catch (SOAPFaultException sfe) { // a run-time exception
58       processSOAPFault(sfe);
59     } catch (InputFault e) {   // a checked exception
60       System.out.println("Error - should have thrown SOAPFault");
61     }
62     try {
63       System.out.println("Running test with null customer number.");
64       order = port.requestOrder(
65           null, null, ccard, itemList);
66     } catch (InputFault ife) {
67       processInputFault(ife);
68     }
69     try {
70       System.out.println("Running test with a valid request.");
71       order = port.requestOrder(
72           "ENT0072123", null, ccard, itemList);
73       printReturnedOrder(order);
74     } catch (InputFault ife) {
75       processInputFault(ife);
76     }
```

book-code/chap06/proxy/modules/client/src/java/samples/Tester.java

The method `runTests`, shown in Example 6–8, receives as its single parameter a proxy instance, implementing the `RequestOrderPort` interface, that was created by one of the approaches discussed earlier. In the first few lines of this method, I create the JAXB instances that are passed as parameters to the proxy instance's SEI method. Since this example illustrates some exception handling, I created an "expired" credit card and a "good" credit card.

Inside the first try block, you can see how the dynamic proxy is invoked:

```
order = port.requestOrder("ENT0072123", null, expiredCCard, itemList);
```

It's that simple. You just invoke the `requestOrder` method on the `RequestOrderPort` interface. The return value has type `OrderType`—which is the JAXB binding of the `oms:Order` element specified by the `wsdl:output` message.

6.1.4 Fault Handling with Proxies

The WSDL for the `RequestOrder` Web service used in this example specifies a `wsdl:fault` in the `wsdl:operation` definition for `requestOrder`. As you can see in Example 6–4, this `wsdl:fault` gets mapped to the Java exception class `InputFault`. So, as you would expect, the code that exercises the `RequestOrderPort.requestOrder` method in Example 6–8 has catch blocks to handle any `InputFault` exceptions that might get thrown.

However, you may also have noticed that the code also catches and handles instances of `javax.xml.ws.soap.SOAPFaultException`. `SOAPFaultException` is the run-time exception the JAX-WS runtime uses to carry SOAP[2] protocol-specific fault information. So, if an invocation of the `RequestOrder` Web service returns a SOAP fault message that does not map to `InputFault` (i.e., the SOAP fault message's `detail` element isn't an instance of the `faults:inputMessageValidationFault` element specified by the `wsdl:fault`'s corresponding `wsdl:message`), JAX-WS converts this SOAP fault message to an instance of `SOAPFaultException`.

In an ideal world, all application-specific faults would be represented by a `wsdl:fault`. If this were true, the only `SOAPFaultException` you would get would be caused by system-level errors (e.g., a server error unrelated to the Web service's business logic). But in the real world, a Web service may return SOAP fault messages that are business-logic-related and not

---

2. As indicated in Chapter 4, "SOAP" refers to SOAP 1.1 unless specified otherwise.

represented by a `wsdl:fault`. That is why it is good practice, as shown in Example 6–8, to write catch blocks to handle `SOAPFaultException`.

As an example of this, the code in Example 6–8 first invokes the `requestOrder` method with an expired credit card. As I have set things up in this example, this causes the Web service to return a SOAP fault message that does not map to an `InputFault`. As a result, the `requestOrder` method throws the run-time exception `SOAPFaultException`. The `SOAP-ENV:Fault` element, from the SOAP message body, its shown in Example 6–9.

Example 6–9 The `SOAP-ENV:Fault` Element Resulting from an Expired Credit Card

```
3   <SOAP-ENV:Fault xmlns:SOAP-ENV="http://schemas.xmlsoap.org/soap/envelope/">
4     <faultstring>Business logic exception</faultstring>
5     <faultcode>SOAP-ENV:Client</faultcode>
6     <detail>
7       <expiredCC xmlns="http://www.example.com/req"> Credit card has
8       expired</expiredCC>
9     </detail>
10  </SOAP-ENV:Fault>
```

book-code/chap06/proxy/edited/soapfaultexception.xml

As you can see here, the `faultstring` element indicates that this is a business logic exception. The `detail` element tells you that this results from an expired credit card. The `detail` element is intended to provide more information than is conveyed by the `faultcode` element, because as you can see, in this example, the `faultcode` of `SOAP-ENV:Client` simply tells you there was a problem with the request message. Without the `detail`, you don't know what went wrong.

On the other hand, for application-specific faults that are represented by a `wsdl:fault`, the WSDL's `soap:fault` element specifies the contents of the SOAP fault message's `details` element. The `name` attribute relates the `soap:fault` to the `wsdl:fault` defined for the operation. So, from the WSDL (Example 6–1 and Example 6–2), you can see that for such messages, the `detail` element contains a single `faults:inputMessageValidationFault` child element. Per JAX-WS, that element gets mapped to the `FaultInfo` property of the `InputFault` exception wrapper class. Example 6–10 shows the sample code from this example that processes the `InputFault` instance.

Example 6–10 Processing an `InputFault` Exception

```
148    private void processInputFault(InputFault e) {
149
150      System.out.println("Mapped Exception (InputFault)");
151      System.out.println("InputFault.getMessage() =");
152      System.out.println(e.getMessage());
153      System.out.println("InputFault.getFaultInfo.getMsg() =");
154      System.out.println(e.getFaultInfo().getMsg());
155      System.out.println();
156
157    }
```

book-code/chap06/proxy/modules/client/src/java/samples/Tester.java

So, you can see that handling exceptions that get mapped from `wsdl:fault` declarations is relatively simple. You can just use the `get-FaultInfo()` method to get a JAXB representation of the fault message's `detail` element contents. This is a lot easier than using the SAAJ APIs to parse a `javax.xml.soap.SOAPFault` instance. Example 6–11 shows the results of running the code from Example 6–10 when a SOAP request message is sent to the Web service that contains a null customer number.

Example 6–11 `InputFault` Processing Output

```
3      [java] Running test with null customer number.
4      [java] Mapped Exception (InputFault)
5      [java] InputFault.getMessage() =
6      [java] Input parameter failed validation.
7      [java] InputFault.getFaultInfo.getMsg() =
8      [java] Customer Number cannot be null.
```

book-code/chap06/proxy/edited/inputfault.xml

To run the sample code in this section, do the following:

1. Go to `<book-code>/chap06/endpoint`.
2. To deploy the Web service, enter `mvn install`, and then enter `ant deploy`.

3. Go to `<book-code>/chap06/proxy`.

4. To run the example, enter `mvn install`,
and then enter `ant run-standalone`.

5. To run in the client container, enter `mvn install`,
and then enter `ant run-container`.

6. When you are done, go back to `<book-code>/chap06/endpoint`.

7. To undeploy the service, enter `ant undeploy`.

This section covered a lot of ground. You learned how to use JAX-WS proxies, and you learned a lot about the technology and standards behind the use of such proxies. To be comfortable working with JAX-WS, I think it is necessary to have some intuition about how the WSDL to Java mapping is defined. That is why I included so much information about the mapping, and the annotations that control its behavior at runtime. The JAX-WS API is designed to make it look like you can do Web services invocation simply by calling a method on a SEI. And with dynamic proxy technology, that is true. However, understanding how your software behaves—which is necessary when writing anything more sophisticated than a basic "Hello World" application—requires that you get a feel for the mappings and how SOAP fault messages get handled.

In the next section, I look at a less Java-centric approach to working with Web services. Instead of invoking SEI methods with JAXB-generated parameters, I show an example of how to send and receive XML messages using the JAX-WS client infrastructure.

6.2 XML Messaging

Although dynamic proxies make Web services invocations look like standard Java method calls, along with this simplicity comes many constraints that can make SOA difficult.

First, the proxy approach requires that you use a SEI that was generated, according to the standard JAX-WS WSDL to Java mapping, from the target Web service's WSDL. The parameters and return types of the methods on such a SEI are classes that are created by the JAXB schema compiler from the `wsdl:types` section of the WSDL. These are not going to be the same classes you are using in your business today. For example, if your business organization has a Java-based system for order management, you probably already have a credit card class you would like to use when invoking a Web service that requires credit card payment. Using the JAXB-generated

BUSOBJCCARD class from Section 6.1 (see Figure 6–2) to represent a credit card is problematic. You are going to be forced to write some custom middleware to translate between your existing credit card class and BUSOBJCCARD.

Second, it is often preferable to work with XML messages directly, rather than with JAXB schema-generated classes. One example of such a scenario is provided in Chapter 3, where I showed an example of an SOA Integration service that gets orders from one Web service and uses them to update a customer history system via another Web service. XSLT is used to transform the XML from the form used in the orders Web service to the form required by the customer history Web service. In that example, there was no need to bind the XML to a Java class. To do so would introduce a performance penalty and the potential for errors. So, when you are doing SOA Integration that involves chaining together multiple Web services, it often makes the most sense to work with XML directly rather than a Java binding.

Third, you may want to write code that can dynamically invoke a Web service. That is, invoke a Web service without having generated and compiled a SEI prior to runtime. Such an approach is required, for example, when the WSDL is not known prior to runtime. This can happen when a target Web service is looked up, using a registry, at runtime. It is not possible to invoke such "late binding" Web services using the SEI approach.

JAX-WS provides the `javax.xml.ws.Dispatch<T>` interface to handle these scenarios and provide support for XML messaging interactions with Web services. `Dispatch` provides support for the dynamic invocation of Web services.

6.2.1 XML Messaging with Raw XML

In this section, I provide an example of how to dynamically invoke a Web service using an XML message and the `Dispatch<T>` interface. The XML message used in this example appears in Example 6–12.

Example 6–12 The XML Message Used to Invoke a Web Service

```
4  <requestOrder xmlns="http://www.example.com/req"
5    xmlns:ns2="http://www.example.com/oms">
6    <CUST_NO>ENT0072123</CUST_NO>
7    <ccard>
8      <ns2:CC_TYPE>VISA</ns2:CC_TYPE>
9      <ns2:CC_NUMBER>01234567890123456789</ns2:CC_NUMBER>
```

```
10     <ns2:CC_EXPIRE_DATE>2009-10-31</ns2:CC_EXPIRE_DATE>
11     <ns2:CC_NAME>John Doe</ns2:CC_NAME>
12   </ccard>
13   <item>
14     <ns2:ITM_NUMBER>012345</ns2:ITM_NUMBER>
15     <ns2:STORAGE_LOC>NE02</ns2:STORAGE_LOC>
16     <ns2:TARGET_QTY>50</ns2:TARGET_QTY>
17     <ns2:TARGET_UOM>CNT</ns2:TARGET_UOM>
18     <ns2:PRICE_PER_UOM>7.95</ns2:PRICE_PER_UOM>
19     <ns2:SHORT_TEXT>7 mm Teflon Gasket</ns2:SHORT_TEXT>
20   </item>
21   <item>
22     <ns2:ITM_NUMBER>543210</ns2:ITM_NUMBER>
23     <ns2:TARGET_QTY>5</ns2:TARGET_QTY>
24     <ns2:TARGET_UOM>KG</ns2:TARGET_UOM>
25     <ns2:PRICE_PER_UOM>12.58</ns2:PRICE_PER_UOM>
26     <ns2:SHORT_TEXT>Lithium grease with PTFE/Teflon</ns2:SHORT_TEXT>
27   </item>
28 </requestOrder>
```

book-code/chap06/xmlmessaging/etc/requestOrder.xml

If this message looks familiar, it is because we worked with it—indirectly via JAXB—in the preceding section. This is an instance of the `req:request-Order` element defined by the `wsdl:types` section of the `RequestOrder` WSDL (see Example 6–1). This is the wrapper element that holds the parameters required by the Web service. Notice the parameters that are present in this example: customer number, credit card, and a list of items to be purchased. Notice also that this is not a SOAP message. It is the payload for a SOAP message that needs to be carried as the child of the SOAP `Body` element.

Example 6–13 shows how to create and use an instance of `Dispatch<T>` to invoke a Web service with the message in Example 6–12. The target is the `RequestOrder` Web service introduced in the previous section.

Example 6–13 Using `Dispatch<Source>` for XML Messaging

```
79   StreamSource xmlSource =
80     new StreamSource(new StringReader(xmlByteArray.toString()));
81   // create Service
82   URL wsdlURL = new URL("http://"+host+":"+port+
```

```
83      "/chap06-endpoint-endpoint-1.0/requestOrder?wsdl");
84   QName serviceQName =
85      new QName("http://www.example.com/req", "RequestOrderService");
86   Service service = Service.create(wsdlURL, serviceQName);
87   // create Dispatch<Source>
88   QName portQName =
89      new QName("http://www.example.com/req", "RequestOrderPort");
90   Dispatch<Source> dispatch = service.createDispatch(portQName,
91      Source.class, Service.Mode.PAYLOAD);
92   Source orderSource = dispatch.invoke(xmlSource);
93   JAXBContext jc = JAXBContext.newInstance(RequestOrderResponse.class);
94   Unmarshaller u = jc.createUnmarshaller();
95   RequestOrderResponse response =
96      (RequestOrderResponse) u.unmarshal(orderSource);
```

book-code/chap06/xmlmessaging/modules/client/src/java/samples/Client.java

Starting at the top of this code, you see that the XML message being used to invoke the service is encapsulated in the `StreamSource` variable named `xmlSource`. The `javax.xml.ws.Service` class acts as a factory for creating `Dispatch` instances. So, to create a `Dispatch`, we must first create a `Service` instance.

As you can see, the `Service` is created dynamically, as discussed in Example 6–7, using the WSDL's URL and the `QName` of the `wsdl:service`— `req:RequestOrderService`.

In the middle of this code block, the `Dispatch<T>` is created. The `Service.createDispatch()` method takes three parameters: the `QName` of the `wsdl:portType`, the `Class` of the type parameter `T`, and the service mode. The type parameter `T` specifies the `Class` used to encapsulate the XML message being sent. `Dispatch<T>` supports `javax.xml.transform.Source`, `Object` (for JAXB annotated classes), `javax.xml.soap.SOAPMessage`, and `javax.activation.DataSource` (for MIME-typed messages). In this example, I use `Source` to encapsulate the XML. In the next example, I illustrate how to use JAXB objects.

The service mode parameter can either be `javax.xml.ws.Service.Mode.MESSAGE` or `javax.xml.ws.Service.Mode.PAYLOAD`. With the former, you work with the entire SOAP message. With the latter, you use the `Dispatch<T>.invoke()` method with only the XML message—i.e., the payload that is contained in the SOAP `Body` element. As you can see, this example uses the `PAYLOAD` service mode. In `PAYLOAD` mode, the `Dispatch` instance is responsible for creating the SOAP message that contains the payload.

At the end of the code block from Example 6–13, `Dispatch<T>.invoke()` is called, and it returns the response XML message as a `Source` instance.

6.2.2 XML Messaging with Custom Annotated JAXB Classes

Another approach to XML messaging involves writing your own JAXB annotated classes to represent the XML messages that are sent and received from a Web service. That is the technique illustrated in this section.

The point here is that you can use JAXB without having to tie yourself to a JAX-WS-generated SEI. You can use JAXB annotations to map your existing Java classes to the message payloads a target Web service sends and receives.

Example 6–14 shows the code that sets up and uses the `Dispatch<Object>` instance along with the custom JAXB classes. Notice that the first thing I've done here is to create a `JAXBContext` using the custom classes—`MyRequestOrder` and `MyRequestOrderResponse`.

Example 6–14 Using `Dispatch<Object>` for XML Messaging with JAXB

```
124    JAXBContext ctxt = JAXBContext.
125    newInstance(MyRequestOrder.class, MyRequestOrderResponse.class);
126    QName portQName =
127       new QName("http://www.example.com/req", "RequestOrderPort");
128    Dispatch<Object> dispatchJAXB = service.createDispatch(portQName,
129        ctxt, Service.Mode.PAYLOAD);
130    // create the custom request order object
131    MyRequestOrder myReq = new MyRequestOrder();
132    myReq.ccard = createMyCreditCard();
133    myReq.item = createMyItemList();
134    myReq.CUST_NO = "ENT0072123";
135    myReq.PURCH_ORD_NO = "";
136    MyRequestOrderResponse resp =
137       (MyRequestOrderResponse) dispatchJAXB.invoke(myReq);
```

book-code/chap06/xmlmessaging/modules/client/src/java/samples/Client.java

The `Dispatch<Object>` instance is created by the `service` factory method as before, except this time we use the factory method that accepts a `JAXBContext` rather than a type parameter. This context is used by the underlying `Dispatch` implementation to marshal/unmarshal the Java objects to/from the message payloads.

Moving down the code, after the `Dispatch<Object>` instance is created, I configure an instance of the `MyRequestOrder` class—my custom JAXB annotated class that maps to the required SOAP request payload. This class is shown in Example 6–15. Lastly, the `Dispatch<Object>.invoke()` method is used to call the target Web service. The response message payload is marshaled to an instance of `MyRequestOrderResponse`—my custom JAXB annotated class for holding the response.

Example 6–15 The Custom JAXB Annotated Class: `MyRequestOrder`

```
26  @XmlAccessorType(XmlAccessType.FIELD)
27  @XmlType(namespace = "http://www.example.com/req")
28  @XmlRootElement(name = "requestOrder",
29      namespace = "http://www.example.com/req")
30  public class MyRequestOrder {
31
32      protected String CUST_NO;
33      protected String PURCH_ORD_NO;
34      protected MyCreditCard ccard;
35      protected List<MyItem> item;
36
37  }
```

book-code/chap06/xmlmessaging/modules/client/src/java/samples
/MyRequestOrder.java

Example 6–15 shows how simple it is to create a JAXB annotated object that maps to the XML message payload request wrapper. This `MyRequest-Order` class is simply a container for the four parameters contained as children of `req:requestOrder`. Likewise, Example 6–16 shows how I constructed a custom JAXB annotated class that maps to the credit card XML Schema type `oms:BUSOBJ_CCARD`.

Example 6–16 The Custom JAXB Annotated Class: `MyCreditCard`

```
26  @XmlAccessorType(XmlAccessType.FIELD)
27  @XmlType(name = "BUSOBJ_CCARD",
28      namespace = "http://www.example.com/oms")
```

```
29  public class MyCreditCard {
30
31      protected String CC_TYPE;
32      protected String CC_NUMBER;
33      protected String CC_EXPIRE_DATE;
34      protected String CC_NAME;
35      protected BigDecimal BILLAMOUNT;
36      protected String CHARGE_DATE;
37
38      @XmlAccessorType(XmlAccessType.FIELD)
39      @XmlType(name = "")
40      public static class OrderCcard {
41
42          @XmlElement(namespace = "http://www.example.com/oms")
43          protected MyCreditCard ccard;
44
45      }
46  }
```

book-code/chap06/xmlmessaging/modules/client/src/java/samples
/MyCreditCard.java

To run the sample code in this section, do the following:

1. Start GlassFish (if it is not already running).
2. Go to `<book-code>/chap06/endpoint`.
3. To deploy the Web service, enter `mvn install`,
   and then enter `ant deploy`.
4. Go to `<book-code>/chap06/xmlmessaging`.
5. To run the example, enter `mvn install`,
   and then enter `ant run`.
6. When you are done, go back to `<book-code>/chap06/endpoint`.
7. To undeploy the service, enter `ant undeploy`.

In this section, I illustrated how you can use `Dispatch<T>` to invoke a target Web service by working directly with the XML messages that are sent and received by the client. I also showed how you can create custom JAXB annotated classes that map to the messages sent and received by a Web service. These are powerful techniques to have at your disposal for situations where you can't, or don't want to, work with a SEI generated from WSDL.

In the next section, I take these ideas a step further and show how you can bypass JAXB entirely and use another Java/XML mapping tool to mediate between your existing Java classes and a target Web service.

6.3 Invocation with Custom Java/XML Mappings: An Example Using Castor Instead of JAXB

In this section, I show how you can use the Castor (www.castor.org) Java/XML mapping tool and the `Dispatch<T>` interface to map your existing Java classes to XML messages that can be used to interact with Web services. These same techniques can be applied to work with other Java/XML mapping tools as well. I have chosen Castor for this example simply because it is a relatively popular open source tool.[3]

Castor enables you to map existing Java classes to XML. Intead of using annotations, like JAXB, Castor uses an external mapping file. So, to map your classes to XML, you create a mapping file that associates each class and its properties with an XML type or element and its children. For some more background on the Castor Java/XML mapping process, read the section of www.castor.org titled "XML Mapping."

Using Castor, or another Java/XML mapping tool, makes sense if you need to work with existing Java classes and you can't or don't want to add JAXB annotations to them. If the classes are in production, you may not be able to modify them. Or it may require a lengthy process of modification, unit testing, system testing, and so on. to get annotated versions of the classes put into production. In such situations, it may be easier and faster to work with a tool like Castor than JAXB. In Chapter 11, I introduce SOA-J's "Adaptive Serializer" framework that takes this concept a step further to provide extremely flexible Java/XML mapping for production environments.

To get started with this Castor example, examine Example 6–17. It shows a portion of the class that represents a credit card. As you can see, it is a simple structure containing the properties of a credit card (e.g., card number, expiration date). It is actually similar to the custom JAXB credit card class shown in Example 6–16, except that the field names and types are different and there are no annotations.

---

3. Through the magic of Maven, you don't actually need to do anything to install Castor in order to run the examples in this section. When you follow the instructions at the end to run the examples, Maven downloads the Castor JAR for you.

Example 6–17 The CreditCard Class

```
20  public class CreditCard {
21
22      public String type;
23      public String num;
24      public String expireDate;
25      public String name;
26      public float amount;
27      public String chargeDate;
```

book-code/chap06/castor/src/java/samples/CreditCard.java

Likewise, Example 6–18 shows the MyRequestOrder class that is used to hold the request message parameters that need to be sent to the target Web service. Again, this class is similar to the JAXB version shown in Example 6–15, but it has no annotations.

Example 6–18 The MyRequestOrder Class: A Wrapper for the Request Parameters

```
24  public class MyRequestOrder {
25
26      protected String custno;
27      protected String purchordno;
28      protected CreditCard ccard;
29      protected List<MyItem> itemList;
```

book-code/chap06/castor/src/java/samples/MyRequestOrder.java

Example 6–19 shows a portion of the Castor mapping file used in this example. The top-level mapping element contains the relationships between classes and the XML they are mapped to. I also define the namespaces (i.e., req, oms) used in the target XML in the mapping element so that I can use their prefixes consistently throughout the file.

The children of the mapping element are class elements. These define the mappings from each Java class to their corresponding XML representations. The first class element maps the MyRequestOrder class to the req:requestOrder element.

Example 6–19 The Castor Mapping File

```
4  <!DOCTYPE mapping PUBLIC "-//EXOLAB/Castor Object Mapping DTD Version 1.0//EN"
5                         "http://castor.org/mapping.dtd">
6  <mapping xmlns:req="http://www.example.com/req"
7    xmlns:oms="http://www.example.com/oms">
8    <class name="samples.MyRequestOrder">
9      <map-to xml="requestOrder" ns-uri="http://www.example.com/req"/>
10     <field name="custno" type="java.lang.String">
11       <bind-xml name="req:CUST_NO" node="element"/>
12     </field>
13     <field name="purchordno" type="java.lang.String">
14       <bind-xml name="req:PURCH_ORD_NO" node="element"/>
15     </field>
16     <field name="ccard" type="samples.CreditCard">
17       <bind-xml name="req:ccard" node="element"/>
18     </field>
19     <field name="itemList" type="samples.MyItem" collection="collection">
20       <bind-xml name="req:item"/>
21     </field>
22   </class>
23   <class name="samples.CreditCard">
24     <map-to xml="BUSOBJ_CCARD" ns-uri="http://www.example.com/oms"/>
25     <field name="type" type="java.lang.String" direct="true">
26       <bind-xml name="oms:CC_TYPE" node="element"/>
27     </field>
28     <field name="num" type="java.lang.String" direct="true">
29       <bind-xml name="oms:CC_NUMBER" node="element"/>
30     </field>
31     <field name="expireDate" type="java.lang.String" direct="true">
32       <bind-xml name="oms:CC_EXPIRE_DATE" node="element"/>
33     </field>
34     <field name="name" type="java.lang.String" direct="true">
35       <bind-xml name="oms:CC_NAME" node="element"/>
36     </field>
37     <field name="amount" type="float" direct="true">
38       <bind-xml name="oms:BILLAMOUNT" node="element"/>
39     </field>
40     <field name="chargeDate" type="java.lang.String" direct="true">
41       <bind-xml name="oms:CHARGE_DATE" node="element"/>
42     </field>
43   </class>
```

book-code/chap06/castor/etc/mapping.xml

The children of the `class` element are `field` elements. These map the properties of the Java class to XML elements or attributes. For example, you can see that the `class` element for `MyRequestOrder` contains field elements for `custno`, `purchordno`, and so on. Lastly, the `field` element contains a child named `bind-xml` that specifies the XML the Java property gets mapped to. In Example 6–19, the `field` element for `custno` (at the top) has a `bind-xml` child that maps to the `req:CUST_NO` element.

That is a simple example of a Castor mapping file. If you are interested in a more detailed description of mapping files, check out the Castor Web site. Next, I show you how this mapping file can be used together with JAX-WS to invoke a Web service.

Example 6–20 contains the code that invokes the target Web service. At the beginning of this code, the mapping file is loaded into an instance of `org.exolab.castor.mapping.Mapping`. The Castor `Mapping` class plays a role similar to the `JAXBContext` class in that it is used to configure marshallers and unmarshallers. Next, I create an instance of `MyRequestOrder` and a `ByteArrayOutputStream` to marshal it into. The Castor `org.exolab.castor.xml.Marshaller` instance is constructed as a wrapper around the `ByteArrayOutputStream`. Then, the `Marshaller` is configured by loading in the `Mapping` instance using the `setMapping` method.

Example 6–20 Invoking the Web Service with the Castor Java/XML Mapping

```
48   String host = args[1];
49   String port = args[2];
50   // load Castor Mapping File
51   FileInputStream castorMappingFile = new FileInputStream(args[0]);
52   Mapping castorMapping = new Mapping();
53   castorMapping.loadMapping(new InputSource(castorMappingFile));
54   // Use Castor to marshal MyRequestOrder to XML
55   MyRequestOrder requestOrder = createRequestOrder();
56   ByteArrayOutputStream ba = new ByteArrayOutputStream();
57   Marshaller m = new Marshaller(new OutputStreamWriter(ba));
58   m.setMapping(castorMapping);
59   m.marshal(requestOrder);
60   Source xmlSource = new StreamSource(new StringReader(ba.toString()));
61   // create Dispatch<Source>
62   URL wsdlURL = new URL("http://"+host+":"+port+
63     "/chap06-endpoint-endpoint-1.0/requestOrder?wsdl");
64   QName serviceQName =
65     new QName("http://www.example.com/req", "RequestOrderService");
66   Service service = Service.create(wsdlURL, serviceQName);
```

```
67  QName portQName =
68    new QName("http://www.example.com/req", "RequestOrderPort");
69  Dispatch<Source> dispatch = service.createDispatch(portQName,
70    Source.class, Service.Mode.PAYLOAD);
71  // invoke Web service with Castor-generated XML
72  Source orderSource = dispatch.invoke(xmlSource);
```

book-code/chap06/castor/src/java/samples/Client.java

The method invocation

```
m.marshal(requestOrder);
```

marshals the `MyRequestOrder` instance to an XML document (stored in the `ByteArrayOutputStream`) according to the rules specified in the Castor mapping file that was loaded. From this point, the `Dispatch<Source>` instance is created and invoked as in the previous section of this chapter (see Example 6–13). The difference here is that the XML message being used for this invocation was generated using Castor, as described earlier.

To run the sample code in this section, do the following:

1. Start GlassFish (if it is not running already).
2. Go to `<book-code>/chap06/endpoint`.
3. To deploy the Web service, enter `mvn install`, and then enter `ant deploy`.
4. Go to `<book-code>/chap06/castor`.
5. To run the example, enter `mvn install`, and then enter `ant run`.
6. When you are done, go back to `<book-code>/chap06/endpoint`.
7. To undeploy the service, enter `ant undeploy`.

In this section, I illustrated some of the versatility that can be achieved using the `Dispatch<Source>` interface. Here, you have seen how a non-JAXB binding tool can be used together with `Dispatch<Source>` to invoke a Web service using your existing Java classes.

Up to this point, we have been discussing only the synchronous invocation of Web services. But JAX-WS also supports asynchronous invocation. That is the topic of the next section.

6.4 Asynchronous Invocation

JAX-WS provides easy-to-use APIs for asynchronous invocation. Using these APIs, along with the interface `java.util.concurrent.Future<T>`, you don't have to worry about thread use and other low-level concurrency issues in order to invoke Web services asynchronously.

Asynchronous invocation is a powerful tool for SOA programming because it helps you to manage the "impedance mismatch" between local execution and remote processing being handled by Web services. Typically, a Web services invocation executes significantly slower than the processing going on in your local address space. So, you can speed up your code considerably by running Web services invocations in separate threads, and having the locally executing code do something else while waiting for these invocations to complete.

In fact, the JAX-WS API provides two approaches to asynchronous processing: polling and callback. In the polling form of asynchronous invocation, your code is responsible for polling an instance of `java.xml.ws.Response<T>` (which extends `Future<T>`) to determine when a Web service invocation has completed. On the other hand, using the callback form of asynchronous invocation, your code supplies an instance of `javax.xml.ws.AsyncHandler` to process the results of the Web service invocation. When the Web service returns its results, they are automatically processed by the `AsyncHandler` instance you provided. In this manner, the `AsyncHandler` plays a role analogous to `javax.jms.MessageListener` on a JMS queue. Just as the `MessageListener` processes messages asynchronously as they arrive, so the `AsyncHandler` processes a Web service response asynchronously when it arrives. The major difference here, of course, is that whereas a `MessageListener` is configured once for a queue and handles many messages, an `AsyncHandler` must be specified with each asynchronous Web service invocation.

6.4.1 Polling

Example 6–21 shows an example of how to use the polling form of asynchronous invocation with a `Dispatch<T>` interface. As you can see, the `Dispatch<Source>` instance is configured in the same manner as in previous examples.

Example 6–21 Asynchronous Invocation with Polling

```
141   URL wsdlURL = new URL("http://"+host+":"+port+
142       "/chap06-endpoint-endpoint-1.0/requestOrder?wsdl");
143   QName serviceQName =
144       new QName("http://www.example.com/req", "RequestOrderService");
145   Service service = Service.create(wsdlURL, serviceQName);
146   QName portQName =
147       new QName("http://www.example.com/req", "RequestOrderPort");
148   Dispatch<Source> dispatch = service.createDispatch(portQName,
149       Source.class, Service.Mode.PAYLOAD);
150   Response<Source> responseSource = dispatch.invokeAsync(xmlSource);
151   long startTime = (new Date()).getTime();
152   while (!responseSource.isDone()) {
153       Thread.sleep(10);
154   }
155   long elapsed = (new Date()).getTime() - startTime;
156   Source orderSource = responseSource.get();
```

book-code/chap06/asynchronous/modules/client/src/java/samples/Client.java

In this case, however, the Web service is invoked using the `Dispatch<T>.invokeAsync(T msg)` method. Under the covers, this method uses the `java.util.concurrent.Executor`[4] associated with the `Service` instance that created the `Dispatch<T>` to invoke the Web service using a separate thread. The asynchronous invocation returns an instance of `Response<Source>`. The `javax.xml.ws.Response<T>` interface is a wrapper around `Future<T>` that provides an additional method—`getContext()`—to retrieve the response message context.

In this example, I use the `get()` method from `Future<T>` to retrieve the response message payload as an instance of `Source`. Notice that this example demonstrates the polling aspect of this form of asynchronous invocation. The polling can be seen in the `while` loop that polls the `isDone()` method to determine when the asynchronous invocation has completed. The variable `elapsed` captures the milliseconds required to complete the asynchronous invocation. To run this example,[5] do the following:

---

4. The `Executor` interface, along with `Future<T>` and the rest of the `java.util.concurrent` package, was introduced in J2SE 5.0. Implementations of `Executor` typically provide thread management services (e.g., pooling, scheduling). For more information, see [JSR-166].
5. This actually runs the code for all the examples in Section 6.4.

1. Start GlassFish (if it is not running already).
2. Go to `<book-code>/chap06/endpoint`.
3. To deploy the Web service, enter `mvn install`,
   and then enter `ant deploy`.
4. Go to `<book-code>/chap06/asynchronous`.
5. To run the example, enter `mvn install`,
   and then enter `ant run`.
6. When you are done, go back to `<book-code>/chap06/endpoint`.
7. To undeploy the service, enter `ant undeploy`.

In this section, I showed an example of asynchronous invocation using the `Dispatch<T>` client interface. It is also possible, however, to do asynchronous invocation with a proxy instance of a SEI, rather than a `Dispatch`.

6.4.2 Asynchronous Methods with Proxies

Before looking at how the callback form of asynchronous invocation works, I'm taking a little diversion to talk about how to enable asynchronous invocation when working with SEI proxies, rather than `Dispatch<T>`.

In addition to the asynchronous invocation methods on the `Dispatch<T>` interface, JAX-WS specifies that implementations must make it possible to generate service endpoint interfaces (SEIs) with client-side asynchronous methods. The generation of a SEI that includes asynchronous methods is optional at the user's discretion. JAX-WS also declares that the user must be able to specify the generation of these asynchronous methods using binding language declarations. See Chapter 5, Section 5.6, for a detailed discussion of JAXB 2.0 binding language declarations. The JAX-WS binding language works in a similar fashion, but is used to customize the WSDL to Java mapping (rather than the XML Schema to Java mapping that is customized by JAXB 2.0 binding declarations).

The asynchronous methods are generated as follows. Say that the synchronous mapping of the target `wsdl:operation` looks like this:

```
Xxx port.yyyZzz()
```

where `Xxx` is the return type and `yyyZzz` is the property name. Then, the polling form of the asynchronous mapping of that same `wsdl:operation` looks like this:

```
Response<Xxx> port.yyyZzzAsync()
```

and the callback form will look like:

```
Future<?> port.yyyZzzAsync(..., AsyncHandler<Xxx> asyncHandler)
```

The binding language declarations needed to generate these interfaces can be specified either inline with the WSDL or as a separate file. In my opinion, the inline specification of binding declarations seems rather impractical because usually the Web service will be deployed with its WSDL, and that WSDL is not going to contain, in general, custom binding language declarations that are used only by Java clients. Many would say that publishing WSDL with such annotations is actually bad practice because it introduces programming language specifics into the WSDL.

Example 6–22 shows how the necessary binding language specifications can be expressed in an external file. In this example, the `enableAsyncMapping` element (the innermost portion of the XML) is set to `true` to indicate that the WSDL to Java compiler that creates the SEI should enable the generation of the asynchronous methods.

Example 6–22 Binding Language Declarations for Enabling Asynchronous Methods

```
4   <bindings xmlns:wsdl="http://schemas.xmlsoap.org/wsdl/"
5       wsdlLocation="http://localhost:8080/chap06-endpoint-endpoint-1.0/
    requestOrder?wsdl"
6       xmlns="http://java.sun.com/xml/ns/jaxws">
7       <bindings node="//wsdl:portType[@name='RequestOrderPort']">
8         <bindings node="wsdl:operation[@name='requestOrder']">
9           <enableAsyncMapping>true</enableAsyncMapping>
10        </bindings>
11      </bindings>
12   </bindings>
```

book-code/chap06/asynchronous/modules/wsdl2java/etc
  /async-binding-customizations.xml

The `bindings` elements that surround this declaration use the `node` attribute to specify the part of the target WSDL that is to be modified by the enclosed binding declaration. The `node` attribute is set to an XPath expression to indicate the target location. As you can see from this example, `bindings` elements can be nested. Here, the outer `bindings` element specifies the `RequestOrderPort wsld:portType` of the target WSDL. Inside that, the second `bindings` element specifies the `requestOrder wsdl:operation`.

When using GlassFish to generate the SEI with the asynchronous methods, the external binding declarations file shown in Example 6–22 is passed to the `wsimport` utility with the `-b` option.

In the next section, I show an example of using the asynchronous methods on a SEI proxy generated in this manner. I also use the callback form of the asynchronous method to demonstrate that style of invocation.

6.4.3 Callback

Example 6–23 shows how to implement an asynchronous callback using a SEI. As you can see, the code for creating the `service` instance is the same as in Example 6–21. From the `service` instance, the `getPort()` method is used to create a proxy instance of the SEI `RequestOrderPort`. This is the same approach as used in Example 6–7.

Example 6–23 Asynchronous Invocation with Callback

```
103   URL wsdlURL = new URL("http://"+host+":"+portVal+
104       "/chap06-endpoint-endpoint-1.0/requestOrder?wsdl");
105   QName serviceQName =
106       new QName("http://www.example.com/req", "RequestOrderService");
107   Service service = Service.create(wsdlURL, serviceQName);
108   QName portQName =
109       new QName("http://www.example.com/req", "RequestOrderPort");
110   RequestOrderPort port = service.getPort(portQName, RequestOrderPort.class);
111   RequestOrderCallbackHandler cbh = new RequestOrderCallbackHandler();
112   cbh.setStartTime((new Date()).getTime());
113   Future<?> response1 = port.requestOrderAsync(
114       "ENT0072123", "", createCreditCard(), createItemList(), cbh);
115   Future<?> response2 = port.requestOrderAsync(
116       "ENT0072123", "", createExpiredCreditCard(), createItemList(), cbh);
117   try {
118   response1.get(2000, TimeUnit.MILLISECONDS);
119   } catch (TimeoutException te) {
120       response1.cancel(true);
121   }
```

book-code/chap06/asynchronous/modules/client/src/java/samples/Client.java

What is different here is the creation and use of the `AsyncHandler<T>` instance: `RequestOrderCallbackHandler`. This class, discussed later, is used to handle the response to the Web service invocation. It is invoked, by the thread handling the Web services call, when the response message is received.

Notice that the invocations themselves (there are two of them in Example 6–23)—port.requestOrderAsync()—contain the same four parameters as the synchronous versions (see Example 6–8), plus a fifth parameter—the AsyncHandler<T> instance. The asynchronous invocations return instances of Future<?> (i.e., response1 and response2). The Future<?> instance returned can be polled to determine when the operation has completed. However, this is not necessary since the response message is processed by the AsynchHandler<T> in a separate thread. In this example, I used the expression

```
response1.get(2000, TimeUnit.MILLISECONDS)
```

to poll the Future<?> instance that has been returned. This form of the Future<T>.get() method waits for, at most, 2,000 milliseconds for the operation to complete. If it has not completed in that amount of time, it throws a TimeoutException. In this example, I catch the TimeoutException and cancel the Web service invocation. In this manner, you can see that it is possible to use such an approach to place limits on the amount of time you will let an asynchronous invocation run.

Example 6–24 shows the implementation of AsyncHandler<T>—RequestOrderCallbackHandler—used in this section. The AsyncHandler<T> interface has a single method, handleResponse, which implements the action to be taken when the response message is received from a Web service invocation. The RequestOrderCallbackHandler implementation does two things. It calculates the elapsed time used by the asynchronous invocation, and it prints out the response message to the console.

Example 6–24 An AsyncHandler<T> Implementation

```
225  private static class RequestOrderCallbackHandler
226  implements AsyncHandler<RequestOrderResponse> {
227
228    private long startTime;
229
230    public void handleResponse (Response<RequestOrderResponse> response) {
231
232      long elapsed = (new Date()).getTime() - startTime;
233      Marshaller m;
```

```
234      try {
235        JAXBContext jc = JAXBContext.newInstance(RequestOrderResponse.class);
236        m = jc.createMarshaller();
237        m.setProperty(Marshaller.JAXB_FORMATTED_OUTPUT, Boolean.TRUE);
238        System.out.println();
239        System.out.println("=============================================");
240        System.out.println("Asynchronous Proxy Test");
241        System.out.println("with Callback and Dynamic Service");
242        System.out.println("Elapsed waiting time for Web service response:");
243        System.out.println(elapsed + " milliseconds.");
244        System.out.println("=============================================");
245        System.out.println();
246        System.out.println();
247        System.out.println("Response Message ============================");
248        if ( response != null ) {
249          RequestOrderResponse orderResponse = response.get();
250          m.marshal(orderResponse, System.out);
251        }
252      } catch (ExecutionException e) {
253        Throwable t = e.getCause();
254        if ( t instanceof SOAPFaultException ) {
255          processSOAPFault((SOAPFaultException) t);
256          return;
257        }
258        e.printStackTrace();
259      } catch (Exception e) {
260        e.printStackTrace();
261      }
262
263    }
264
265    public void setStartTime(long t) { startTime = t; }
266
```

book-code/chap06/asynchronous/modules/client/src/java/samples/Client.java

---

In addition, one other important function is performed by this handler—exception processing. As I illustrated in Section 6.1.4, it is very important to build fault handling into your Web services invocations. In this case, I show how to implement fault handling in a callback scenario, within an `AsyncHandler<T>` implementation. According to the JAX-WS specification, if a `wsdl:operation` asynchronous invocation fails, neither a SEI-specific exception nor a `SOAPFaultException` gets thrown directly; instead, it throws a `java.util.concurrent.ExecutionException` instance is returned from the `Response.get()` method. The cause of the `ExecutionException`, retrieved using the `getCause()` method, contains either the SEI-specific exception (e.g., `InputFault` from Example 6–4) or a protocol-specific exception such as `SOAPFaultException`.

In Example 6–24, I show the code to handle the `SOAPFaultException` case. In this case, I simply invoke the `processSOAPFault` method as in Example 6–8 to print out the contents of the SOAP fault message. You can run this example by following the same steps as shown in Example 6–21. The instructions there run both the polling and the callback invocations of the target Web service.

That concludes this discussion of client-side Web service invocation basics. I showed you how to use SEI proxies for Java style invocation, and how to use the `Dispatch<T>` interface for XML messaging. You saw both synchronous and asynchronous invocation styles. I also looked into some of the details of the JAX-WS WSDL to Java mapping and talked about the importance of fault processing when dealing with Web services invocation.

In the next section, I look at the topic of client-side handlers. Handlers enable you to do pre- and post-processing of the messages used to invoke Web services. Handlers can be used when doing SEI proxy style invocation or `Dispatch<T>` style XML messaging.

6.5 SOAP Message Handlers

The JAX-WS handler framework allows you to define message handlers that can process XML messages before and after a Web service invocation—either on the client side or on the server side. In this section, I focus on client-side handlers. Such handlers are commonly used to implement messaging functionality that is not specific to a particular Web service. For example, you might use a handler to add a `wsse:Security`[6] header or a `wsrm:Sequence`[7] header to a SOAP message. In fact, one of the primary uses envisioned for the JAX-WS handler framework is as a means to implement Web Services standards like WS-Security [WS-Security 1.1]

---

6. `wsse:Security` is a header block defined by the SOAP MessageSecurity 1.1 standard that is part of the OASIS WS-Security [WS-Security 1.1] specification.
7. `wsrm:Sequence` is a header block defined by the OASIS Web Services Reliable Messaging standard for reliable messaging [WS-RM].

and WS-ReliableMessaging [WS-RM] on top of the base invocation implementation.

To demonstrate the use of client-side message handlers, I created a simple example implementing message persistence using a handler. Message persistence is the process of saving a message to nonvolatile memory (e.g., disk) prior to sending it. It enables the user to recover the message and resend it in the event of a system failure (e.g., crash, network disruption, etc.). Message persistence can be used, for example, to help provide the type of delivery assurance specified in WS-ReliableMessaging.

Using JAX-WS, there are two approaches for configuring a message handler on a client: It can be done programmatically, or with the @javax.jws.HandlerChain annotation. In this section, I focus on the programmatic configuration of handlers. When I look at server-side handlers in the next chapter, I show examples that use the @HandlerChain annotation.

Interestingly, the JAX-WS specification does not define a standard deployment model for handlers. Such a model is provided by [JSR-109] and [JSR-181]. I discuss the deployment model for handlers in Chapter 8.

Example 6–25 shows how to programmatically configure handlers. Handlers are set up by configuring an instance of javax.xml.ws.handler.HandlerResolver on a Service instance. In this manner, any SEI proxy or Dispatch<T> created from such a Service instance will use the specified HandlerResolver to determine the handler chain defined for the particular wsdl:portType it implements. In the code example here, you can see that the Service.setHandlerResolver() method is used to set up an instance of the RequestOrderHandlerResolver—a class I have written that implements HandlerResolver (discussed further later).

Example 6–25 Programmatically Adding Handlers for a Web Service Invocation

```
55    private static void runPersistenceHandlerTest(File persistenceDir)
56    throws Exception {
57
58        RequestOrderService service = new RequestOrderService();
59        // add the handler to the service
60        service.setHandlerResolver(new RequestOrderHandlerResolver());
61        RequestOrderPort port = service.getRequestOrderPort();
62        // configure message request context
63        Map<String, Object> reqCtxt = ((BindingProvider) port).getRequestContext();
64        reqCtxt.put(PersistMessageHandler.PERSISTENCE_DIR_PROP, persistenceDir);
65        reqCtxt.put(AddMessageIdHandler.MSGID_PROP, "msg0001");
66        // add the callback handler
```

```
67    RequestOrderCallbackHandler cbh = new RequestOrderCallbackHandler();
68    cbh.setStartTime((new Date()).getTime());
69    Future<?> response = port.requestOrderAsync(
70        "ENT0072123", "", createCreditCard(), createItemList(), cbh);
71    response.get(2000, TimeUnit.MILLISECONDS);
72
73    }
```

book-code/chap06/handler/modules/client/src/java/samples/Client.java

It is important that the SEI proxy or `Dispatch<T>` (i.e., the `Binding-Provider`) be instantiated after the `Service` has been configured with the `HandlerResolver`. That is because the `BindingProvider` inherits the `HandlerResolver` that is configured at the time it gets instantiated. If, later on, you set a new `HandlerResolver`, `BindingProvider` instances created from that point on will use the new `HandlerResolver`. But those created previously will not be affected.

In the last half of the code in Example 6–25, you can see that I am configuring the request context of the `RequestOrderPort` SEI proxy. This is not generally required for handler configuration, but in the specific example I have created here, it is necessary for the simple persistence handler I implemented to operate. In this example, I am setting a property—`PERSISTENCE_DIR_PROP`—that specifies the directory where messages will be stored (i.e., persisted). At runtime, a handler has access to this request context. As you will see, my persistence handler reads that property to configure itself.

Example 6–26 shows my implementation of the `HandlerResolver` interface. This interface implements a single method—`getHandlerChain(PortInfo p)`—that returns a list of handlers.

Example 6–26 Implementing the `HandlerResolver` Interface

```
148   private static class RequestOrderHandlerResolver implements HandlerResolver {
149
150     public List<Handler> getHandlerChain(PortInfo arg0) {
151
152       List<Handler> handlerChain = new ArrayList<Handler>();
153       handlerChain.add(new AddMessageIdHandler());
154       handlerChain.add(new PersistMessageHandler());
155       return handlerChain;
```

```
156
157    }
158
159  }
```

book-code/chap06/handler/modules/client/src/java/samples/Client.java

At runtime, the `BindingProvider` (i.e., proxy or `Dispatch<T>`) uses this interface to get a list of handlers. Outbound messages are processed by the handlers in the order in which they appear in this list. Inbound messages (i.e., SOAP responses on the client side) are processed by the handlers in the reverse order.

As you can see here, the `List<Handler>` returned by `RequestOrder-HandlerResolver` contains two handlers: `AddMessageIdHandler` and `PersistMessageHandler`. The first of these, `AddMessageIdHandler`, adds a message ID (a unique identifier) header to the outgoing SOAP message. This ID is used by the subsequent handler, `PersistMessageHandler`, to create a unique filename under which the message gets persisted.

Both handlers implement the javax.xml.ws.handler.soap.SOAPHandler<T extends SOAPMessageContext> interface. Therefore, these are what the JAX-WS specification refers to as Protocol Handlers, which operate on protocol-specific messages (and message contexts). The protocol here is SOAP, so these handlers operate on SOAP messages. JAX-WS also defines Logical Handlers that operate only on the generic message payloads (and contexts). Logical Handlers implement javax.xml.ws.handler.LogicalHandler and are not able to manipulate protocol-specific parts of a message such as a SOAP header block.

Example 6–27 implements a Protocol Handler for SOAP that persists messages to a file system directory.

Example 6–27 A Message Handler for Client-Side Persistence

```
35  public class PersistMessageHandler implements SOAPHandler<SOAPMessageContext> {
36
37    public static final String PERSISTENCE_DIR_PROP =
38      "samples.persistence.directory";
39
40    public Set<QName> getHeaders() {
41      return null;
42    }
```

```
43
44    public boolean handleMessage(SOAPMessageContext ctxt) {
45
46      System.out.println("Entered PersistMessageHandler.handleMessage");
47      //  return if inbound message
48      if ( !((Boolean)ctxt.get(MessageContext.MESSAGE_OUTBOUND_PROPERTY)).
49          booleanValue()) { return true; }
50      SOAPMessage msg = ctxt.getMessage();
51      File persistenceDir = (File) ctxt.get(PERSISTENCE_DIR_PROP);
52      Iterator itr;
53      try {
54        itr = msg.getSOAPHeader().examineAllHeaderElements();
55        String msgId = null;
56        while (itr.hasNext() && msgId == null) {
57          SOAPHeaderElement headerElt = (SOAPHeaderElement) itr.next();
58          QName headerQName = headerElt.getElementQName();
59          if (headerQName.equals(AddMessageIdHandler.MSGID_HEADER)) {
60            msgId = headerElt.getAttribute("id");
61          }
62        }
63        if ( msgId == null ) {
64          System.out.println("No message ID header.");
65          return false;
66        }
67        File msgFile = new File(persistenceDir, msgId+".xml");
68        msgFile.createNewFile();
69        msg.writeTo(new FileOutputStream(msgFile));
70      } catch (Exception e) {
71        e.printStackTrace();
72        return false;
73      }
74      return true;
75
76    }
77
78    public boolean handleFault(SOAPMessageContext ctxt) {
79      return false;
80    }
81
82    public void close(MessageContext ctxt) {}
83
84
85  }
```

book-code/chap06/handler/modules/client/src/java/samples/PersistMessageHandler.java

As you can see, the `handleMessage()` method receives an instance of the `SOAPMessageContext`. The first thing that happens inside the `handle-Message()` method is that the context is examined to determine the value of `MessageContext.MESSAGE_OUTPUT_PROPERTY`. This handler only persists outgoing messages, so determining the direction of the message is the first thing that happens.

Assuming the message is outgoing, the next thing that happens is that the handler examines the `PERSISTENCE_DIR_PROP` (which got set in Example 6–25) to determine the directory into which the outgoing message should be saved. Next comes the SOAP header processing to find the header where the message's unique ID is contained. Such header processing is typical for a SOAP handler—although this example is extremely simple. If there were an authentication handler, for example, you might see code here that looked for a header containing an encrypted password to authenticate the user before sending his message over the wire. Having found the message ID, you can see that this code simply saves the message to a file using the `SOAPMessage.writeTo()` method. `SOAPMessage` and `SOAPHeader` are part of the SAAJ 1.3 API (SOAP with Attachments API for Java) for manipulating SOAP messages. SAAJ is the API that is typically used inside a handler to get access to the parts of a SOAP message. See [JSR-67] for more details on SAAJ.

To run the example from this section, do the following. After you run it, check the contents of `chap06/handler/persistedMessages` to see the SOAP message that has been saved there by the `PersistMessageHandler` handler.

1. Start GlassFish (if it is not running already).
2. Go to `<book-code>/chap06/endpoint`.
3. To deploy the Web service, enter `mvn install`,
   and then enter `ant deploy`.
4. Go to `<book-code>/chap06/handler`.
5. To run the example, enter `mvn install`,
   and then enter `ant run`.
6. When you are done, go back to `<book-code>/chap06/endpoint`.
7. To undeploy the service, enter `ant undeploy`.

That wraps up our discussion of handlers on the client side. I get into more depth with handlers in the next chapter, where I look at how to use them together with a Web service deployment.

6.6   Conclusions

In this chapter, you received a concise introduction to creating JAX-WS clients. In the first part, I focused quite a bit on explaining the JAX-WS WSDL to Java mapping. That is because I believe strongly that to use JAX-WS effectively, you need to understand how this mapping (along with the JAXB XML Schema to Java mapping) works. I encourage you to play around with the code examples in this chapter. For example, change the `RequestOrder.wsdl` file contained in the `<book-code>/chap06/endpoint` directory to modify the Web service interface. Of course, when you do this, you will need to also modify the `samples.RequestOrder` class in that same directory structure to comply with the new WSDL.

After doing this, run through the examples from each section in this chapter. Pay attention to how the SEI proxy method changes and how its parameters change. Doing this will start to develop your intuition for how the WSDL to Java mapping works and how changes to the WSDL ripple through your Java code.

In the next chapter, I provide a detailed look at how to create Web services using JAX-WS 2.0.

CHAPTER 7

JAX-WS 2.0—Server-Side Development

The preceding chapter looked at how JAX-WS can be used as a client-side tool to create consumers of SOA services. This chapter looks at the server-side capabilities provided by JAX-WS. I examine a variety of implementations, including examples that start from WSDL, integrate with existing (legacy) classes, and perform XML processing without any Java/XML binding. Deployment and packaging issues are discussed in the next chapter, where Web Services Metadata 2.0 (WS-Metadata) [JSR 181] and Web Services for Java EE 1.2 (WSEE) [JSR 109] are covered.

The key to understanding how to best use JAX-WS to develop and deploy useful SOA services is to look at and write lots of examples. So, that is what I give you in this chapter—lots of examples. However, before diving into the examples, it is good to step back for a minute and understand the big picture. Section 7.1 starts with an overview of the JAX-WS server-side architecture.

7.1 JAX-WS Server-Side Architecture

A Java EE 5 container provides deployment services for publishing Web services endpoints and run-time services for processing Web services requests, responses, and faults. This section looks at the run-time services architecture as specified primarily by JAX-WS [JSR 224] and to some extent by WSEE [JSR 109]. Deployment of security services and the run-time implementation of security are discussed briefly in the next chapter.

Figure 7–1 provides a high-level illustration of the run-time architecture for an endpoint deployed using the SOAP protocol binding. It shows the run-time components of a deployed Web service. The numbers label the steps of an invocation of the deployed Web service. On the far left, the Endpoint Listener and Dispatcher are components largely described by WS-Metadata and WSEE. The implementation of these components is platform specific and differs depending on whether the Web service is deployed as a stateless session bean (EJB) endpoint or as a servlet endpoint. A detailed discussion of these deployment options is deferred to the next chapter. In this chapter, I focus on the components and behavior that are common to both EJB endpoints and servlet endpoints.

The components of Figure 7–1 that are labeled "SOAP Protocol Binding" and "JAX-WS and JAXB Java/XML Binding" are largely described by the JAX-WS specification. The component labeled "Web Service" is described in all the specifications. For example, the `@WebServiceProvider` annotation is specified in JAX-WS, whereas the `@WebService` annotation is specified in WS-Metadata. The meta-data (e.g., deployment descriptors) that get packaged in a WAR or EJB-JAR is largely specified in WSEE.

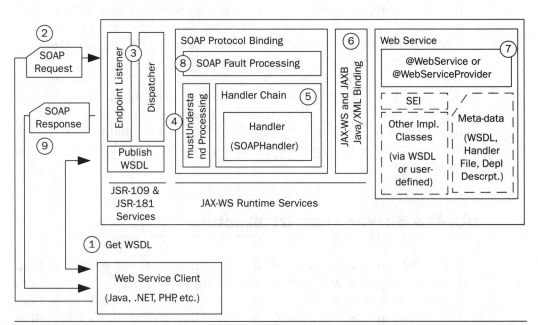

Figure 7–1 Server-side JAX-WS invocation sub-system.

To describe each component, I walk through an invocation by a client. The steps in the invocation follow the numbering in Figure 7–1. Note that the client can be written in any language (e.g., Java, C#, PHP, etc.).

1. The client starts by getting the WSDL for the Web service that has been deployed. WSEE requires that a JAX-WS provider support URL publication. In the examples supplied in this chapter, I use the WSDL that GlassFish publishes to the URL of the form http://<endpoint-address>?wsdl. Publishing the WSDL at a URL of that form is a common convention across Web Services providers, but is not mandated by any standard.

2. Based on the WSDL, the client composes a SOAP request and does an HTTP POST[1] to the URL specified by the `soap:address`'s `location` attribute.

3. The HTTP request containing the SOAP message is received by the Endpoint Listener. This listener is a servlet. The process by which the listener servlet is deployed or registered varies by Java EE container and even by type of deployment.[2] The listener servlet passes the HTTP request along to the Dispatcher. The Dispatcher may be implemented as a separate class from the Endpoint Listener, or the two may be combined, but the functionality is logically distinct. The Dispatcher's job is to look up the correct Web service endpoint implementation and dispatch the HTTP request to that endpoint.[3]

4. At this stage, the request processing transitions to the JAX-WS run-time system. Along with the request, the JAX-WS has received from the Dispatcher a description of the correct endpoint. A `javax.xml.ws.handler.MessageContext` is built from the contents of the HTTP request. In this case (since we are talking about SOAP), the message context is an instance of `javax.xml.handler.soap.SOAPMessageContext` and contains the SOAP request as a SAAJ `SOAPMessage`. This `SOAPMessageContext` is processed by the SOAP protocol binding before the actual Web service endpoint is invoked. The SOAP protocol binding is an example of a JAX-WS protocol binding. The primary responsibilities of such a JAX-WS protocol binding are to extract the message context from the transport protocol (e.g., SOAP/HTTP or XML/HTTP); process

---

1. HTTP GET is allowed when doing XML/HTTP, commonly called REST. See Chapter 3 for more details.

2. For example, in GlassFish, servlet endpoints have a listener (the `JAXWSServlet` class) that is deployed along with a provider-generated web.xml. SSB endpoints, on the other hand, use a different listener (the `EjbWebServiceServlet` class) that is registered at run-time when the SSB is started.

3. Chapter 4 contains a description of how SOAP over HTTP requests are dispatched to endpoints.

the message context through the handlers that have been configured for the Web service endpoint; and configure the result (either a response or an exception) to be sent back to the client using the appropriate transport. In this case, a SOAP protocol binding has the additional task of doing the `mustUnderstand` processing required by SOAP. If there are any "must understand" headers that are not understood, either a SOAP fault is dispatched or (if the endpoint is deployed as a one-way service) processing stops.

5. Next, the SOAP protocol binding invokes each handler in its associated handler chain. The handlers associated with the endpoint are defined by a deployment descriptor file that is specified by the `@HandlerChain` annotation on the service implementation bean. Handlers provide developers with the capability of preprocessing a message context before the endpoint gets invoked. Examples of the types of processing typically done by server-side handlers include persisting a message to provide recovery in the event of a server crash; encryption/decryption; sequencing (i.e., examining message header sequence IDs to ensure that messages are delivered in order); and so on. SOAP header processing is usually done by handlers, but the JAX-WS framework provides handlers with access to the SOAP body as well.

6. After the inbound handlers are finished, the SOAP message is unmarshalled into instances of the Java objects that are used to invoke the endpoint method. This unmarshalling process is governed by the JAX-WS WSDL to Java mapping and the JAXB 2.0 XML to Java mapping. The WSDL to Java mapping determines (from the `wsdl:operation`) which endpoint method to invoke based on the structure of the SOAP message. And the JAXB runtime serializes the SOAP message into the parameters required to invoke that method. If the deployed service implementation bean is an implementation of `javax.xml.ws.Dispatch<T>`, this process is much simpler. In that case, the message payload is simply passed to the `Dispatch.invoke()` method and the implementation processes the XML directly.

7. The last step of the inbound request processing is the invocation of the appropriate method on the deployed service implementation bean. After invocation, the process is reversed. The return value from the invocation (along with any parameters that have been declared OUT or IN/OUT) is marshaled to a SOAP response message of the appropriate form based on the JAX-WS WSDL to Java mapping and the JAXB 2.0 XML to Java mapping.

8. The outbound response processing invokes the handlers (in reverse order) again. If at any point, during inbound handler processing, endpoint invocation, or outbound handler processing, an unhandled exception is thrown, the SOAP Fault Processing component maps the exception to a SOAP fault message. In either case, SOAP fault or SOAP response message, the SOAP protocol binding formats the result for the appropriate transport (e.g., SOAP/HTTP).

9. Lastly, the Endpoint Listener servlet completes its processing and sends back the result received from the Dispatcher as an HTTP response to the client.

Those steps provide a high-level overview of the JAX-WS runtime as configured within a Java EE 5 container. Each Java EE provider implements things slightly differently, but the overview given here is largely dictated by the JWS specifications, so it should not vary enormously from one provider to the next. The most variation will be found in how the Endpoint Listener and Dispatcher components are implemented. Also, you should bear in mind that this overview assumes that the protocol binding is SOAP/HTTP. The process for a RESTful endpoint (i.e., XML/HTTP) is different in that the handlers do not implement the `SOAPHandler<T>` interface, and the (un)marshaling is greatly simplified because the endpoint processes XML directly. The JAX-WS runtime does not need to worry about the JAX-WS WSDL to Java mapping and the JAXB 2.0 XML to Java mapping for a RESTful service. Likewise, you can imagine that a SOAP/JMS deployment would also be different. Such a thing is not specified by JWS, but it is not hard to conceive of how it would work. To implement a SOAP/JMS protocol binding, you would need an Endpoint Listener on a JMS endpoint—that could be an instance of `javax.jms.MessageListener`. Likewise, a SOAP/JMS protocol binding would read/write the `SOAPMessageContext` from/to a `javax.jms.Message`.

So, as you can see from this discussion, the JAX-WS run-time architecture has been modularized so that it can be adapted to a variety of transports. The main focus of this chapter, however, is JAX-WS server-side processing of SOAP/HTTP.

Don't worry if this discussion seems a little bit confusing at this point. You don't need to understand the details of the JAX-WS invocation subsystem in order to create and deploy Web services. I include it here because, as you get more sophisticated about creating services with JAX-WS, you are likely to start wondering how all this stuff works. When you get to that point, come back and look at this section again.

In the next section, I walk through a detailed example of how to create, deploy, and invoke a JAX-WS endpoint using an existing WSDL contract and a service endpoint interface (SEI).

7.2 Start from WSDL Using a Service Endpoint Interface (SEI)

When starting from an existing WSDL document in JAX-WS, the most straightforward way to implement a Web service that conforms to the WSDL contract is to use a *service endpoint interface* (SEI). A SEI is a Java interface mapped from a `wsdl:portType` using the JAX-WS WSDL to Java mapping and JAXB XML to Java mapping. A SEI is specified using the `@WebSevice.endpointInterface` attribute, as shown in Example 7–1.

Example 7–1 The `@WebService` Annotation Defines a Web Service

```
47  @WebService(targetNamespace = "http://www.example.com/req",
48      endpointInterface="com.example.req.RequestOrderPort")
49  public class RequestOrder implements RequestOrderPort {
50
51      @Resource
52      WebServiceContext wscontext;
53
54      public OrderType requestOrder(String custNum, String poNum, BUSOBJCCARD ccard,
55          List<BUSOBJITEM> itemList) throws InputFault {
```

book-code/chap07/endpoint-sei/modules/endpoint/src/java/samples
  /RequestOrder.java

The class `RequestOrder`, shown in Example 7–1, implements the SEI `com.example.req.RequestOrderPort`. In the terminology of WS-Metadata, `RequestOrder` is a *service implementation bean* (SIB). A SIB contains the business logic of a Web service. It must be annotated with either `@WebService` or `@WebServiceProvider`. A service implementation bean is not required to reference a SEI. Later in this chapter, we will work with SIB that do not implement a SEI.

The SEI implemented by `RequestOrder` has a single method—`requestOrder`—shown at the bottom of Example 7–1. As you can see, this method, and the SEI, are the same as used in the preceding chapter to illustrate JAX-WS client development. The difference here is that whreas on the client side, you worked with dynamic proxy implementations of this SEI, on the server side, you are responsible for the actual implementation of this SEI.

Another thing to notice in Example 7–1 is the *dependency injection* defined by the `@Resource` annotation.[4] The `javax.xml.ws.WebService-Context` interface makes it possible for a SIB to access contextual information pertaining to the request being served. You can use the `WebServiceContext` to access the `javax.xml.soap.SOAPMessageContext`. This enables the SIB to access the results of processing that took place in the handler chain (e.g., the security profile for the user who sent the message).

Example 7–2 shows the `RequestOrderPort` SEI that has been generated from the WSDL. This SEI, its mapping to a SOAP message, and a detailed description of its annotations can be found in Chapter 6, Section 6.1.2. If you haven't read that section, please do so now so that you can understand everything that is going on with all these annotations.

Notice that the SEI, like the service implementation bean, is annotated with `@WebService`. A SEI is required by JAX-WS to have an `@WebService` annotation. If you glanced back at the illustration of this SEI in the preceding chapter, you may have noticed that the `wsdlLocation` attribute's value is different here. On the server side, you can use the `wsdlLocation` attribute to specify the location of a WSDL file deployed with the WAR or EJB-JAR containing the SIB. When you do that, the container uses the specified WSDL rather than generating WSDL. On the other hand, if `@WebService.wsdlLocation` is not specified, the WSDL file is generated from the annotations in the service implementation bean implementing the SEI. One reason to supply the WSDL inside the packaging like this is that it preserves all the detail. For example, some of the facets for XML Schema simple types (e.g., the `xs:maxLength` restriction for `xs:string`) are not captured by the standard JAXB mapping. So, if your WSDL started with such restrictions, and you try to recreate it from the annotated SEI, the resulting WSDL will no longer contain these restrictions. The WSDL used to generate the `RequestOrderPort` SEI is shown near the end of this chapter—in Example 7–29. The WSDL shown there contains such restrictions. Another benefit of using the `wsdlLocation` attribute like this is that it provides access to the

---

4. See Section 2.2 of [JSR 250] Common Annotations for the Java Platform for a description of the `@Resource` annotation.

original WSDL from inside the service implementation bean or its handlers. As I demonstrate in Section 7.5, this can be used as part of a mechanism to validate incoming SOAP messages against the WSDL and rejecting badly formed messages.

Example 7–2 The `@WebService` Annotation Used with a SEI

```
40  @WebService(name = "RequestOrderPort",
41      targetNamespace = "http://www.example.com/req",
42      wsdlLocation = "WEB-INF/wsdl/RequestOrder.wsdl")
43  public interface RequestOrderPort {
44
45    @WebMethod
46    @WebResult(name = "Order", targetNamespace = "http://www.example.com/oms")
47    @RequestWrapper(localName = "requestOrder",
48        targetNamespace = "http://www.example.com/req",
49        className = "com.example.req.RequestOrder")
50    @ResponseWrapper(localName = "requestOrderResponse",
51        targetNamespace = "http://www.example.com/req",
52        className = "com.example.req.RequestOrderResponse")
53    public OrderType requestOrder(
54        @WebParam(name = "CUST_NO",
55            targetNamespace = "http://www.example.com/req")
56        String custNO,
57        @WebParam(name = "PURCH_ORD_NO",
58            targetNamespace = "http://www.example.com/req")
59        String purchORDNO,
60        @WebParam(name = "ccard",
61            targetNamespace = "http://www.example.com/req")
62        BUSOBJCCARD ccard,
63        @WebParam(name = "item", targetNamespace = "http://www.example.com/req")
64        List<BUSOBJITEM> item)
65        throws InputFault
66    ;
67
68  }
```

book-code/chap07/endpoint-sei/examples/RequestOrderPort.java

When you use a SEI like this to implement a Web service, you end up working with the JAXB-generated classes produced by the mapping of the corresponding `wsdl:portType`. Example 7–3 gives you a flavor of what it is like to implement business logic with such JAXB-generated classes.

Example 7–3 Using JAXB to Implement Web Service Processing

```
77    //  generate a pseudo-unique 10-digit order ID
78    String orderId = Long.toString((new Date()).getTime());
79    orderId = orderId.substring(orderId.length()-10);
80    OrderType response = new OrderType();
81    response.setOrderKey(orderId);
82    //  create OrderHeader
83    BUSOBJHEADER hdr = new BUSOBJHEADER();
84    response.setOrderHeader(hdr);
85    hdr.setCUSTNO(custNum);
86    GregorianCalendar cal = new GregorianCalendar();
87    hdr.setPURCHDATE(dateAsString(cal));
88    cal.add(Calendar.DAY_OF_MONTH, 14);
89    hdr.setWARDELDATE(dateAsString(cal));
90    if ( poNum != null && poNum.length()>0 ) {
91      hdr.setPYMTMETH("PO");
92      hdr.setPURCHORDNO(poNum);
93    } else {
94      hdr.setPYMTMETH("CC");
95      // OrderType.OrderCcard
96      OrderType.OrderCcard ordCcard = new OrderType.OrderCcard();
97      ordCcard.setCcard(ccard);
98      response.setOrderCcard(ordCcard);
```

book-code/chap07/endpoint-sei/modules/endpoint/src/java/samples
/RequestOrder.java

In this particular case, the `requestOrder` method implements the business logic related to processing an order. If the order is successfully processed, this method returns a completed purchase order (implemented by the class `OrderType`). The snippet of code shown in Example 7–3 shows part of this processing and includes creating an order ID, setting the order date, defining the warrantee expiration date, and adding the payment information to the purchase order.

As you can see, this code constructs an instance of the JAXB-generated class, `OrderType`. The `setOrderKey` method is used to set the order's ID.

Next, an instance of the JAXB-generated class BUSOBJHEADER is created to hold the header information, like customer number and purchase date. All of this is pretty straightforward.

To run the sample code in this section, do the following:

1. Start GlassFish (if it is not already running).
2. Go to <book-code>/chap07/endpoint-sei.
3. Enter mvn install.[5]

Sometimes, however, you might not want to work with JAXB-generated classes. You might want to implement the business logic directly against the XML. XML processing can sometimes improve performance—especially if you can implement the business logic using an XSLT stylesheet. It also provides a degree of insulation from changes in the WSDL. When you use a SEI, as illustrated here, changes to the WSDL require that you regenerate the SEI and update all your code to accommodate the resulting changes to the JAXB-generated object. This can happen even when the changes to the WSDL are relatively minor and have nothing to do with the business logic you are implementing. For example, in this case, suppose the schema for addresses changes. Well, all we are really doing in the business logic of this example is copying the address from the request to the purchase order that gets returned. So, ideally, changes to the XML structure of an address shouldn't be a problem.

The next section shows how you can implement a Web service for an existing WSDL without having to use JAXB-generated classes.

7.3 Providers and XML Processing without JAXB

To deploy a Web service that enables you to work with XML messages directly—without the JAXB binding—you use the javax.xml.ws.Provider<T> interface. The Provider<T> interface defines a single method:

```
T invoke(T request)
```

---

5. This will build and deploy the service, run a client to invoke it, and undeploy the service when the client finishes running. The client is run as a JUnit test. Unlike in some of the examples in previous chapters, you do not need to deploy the service separately from running the client.

In this case, T, the type parameter, is the class used to represent the message or message payload. Provider supports two usage modes: Message and Message Payload. In Message mode, the service implementation bean works directly with protocol-specific message structures. For example, when used with a SOAP protocol binding, the invoke method receives and returns SOAP messages (as instances of the type parameter T). In Message Payload mode, the service implementation bean works with the payload of messages rather than the messages themselves. For example, when used with a SOAP protocol binding, the invoke method receives and returns the contents of the SOAP body rather than the entire SOAP message.

JAX-WS specifies the classes that must be supported as type parameters for Provider<T>. It requires that all implementations support javax.xml.transform.Source in payload mode with all the predefined bindings (i.e., SOAP/HTTP, XML/HTTP). Likewise, JAX-WS implementations must also support Provider<SOAPMessage> in message mode in conjunction with the predefined SOAP bindings.

Example 7–4 shows a snippet from a class declaration for RequestOrder-Endpoint—an implementation of Provider<Source>.

Example 7–4 The @WebServiceProvider Annotation Defines a Web Service Implemented Using Provider<T>

```
68  @WebServiceProvider(serviceName = "RequestOrderService",
69      portName="RequestOrderPort",
70      targetNamespace = "http://www.example.com/req",
71      wsdlLocation="WEB-INF/wsdl/RequestOrder.wsdl")
72  @ServiceMode(Service.Mode.PAYLOAD)
73  public class RequestOrderEndpoint implements Provider<Source> {
74
75    @Resource
76    WebServiceContext webServiceContext;
77
78    private static final String REQ_NS = "http://www.example.com/req";
79    private static final String OMS_NS = "http://www.example.com/oms";
80
81    public Source invoke(Source payload) {
82
```

book-code/chap07/endpoint-provider/modules/endpoint/src/java/samples
  /RequestOrderEndpoint.java

As you can see, this code uses the @WebServiceProvider annotation. A Provider-based service implementation bean must carry an @WebService-Provider annotation to tell the container that it is a service implementation bean. Unlike an @WebService annotated endpoint, a Provider implementation is not mapped to a WSDL interface by the JAX-WS WSDL to Java mapping. As a result, you must (per Section 5.3.2.2 of [JSR 109]) package a WSDL file with a Provider implementation. As shown in Example 7–4, the location of the WSDL file in this example is WEB-INF/wsdl/Request-Order.wsdl. In addition, as shown here, the @ServiceMode annotation is used to indicate whether the service should be deployed in Message mode or Message Payload mode. Table 7–1 summarizes the roles of these annotations.

Table 7–1 Descriptions of the Java Annotations Appearing in Example 7–4

Annotation	Purpose	Example
@WebServiceProvider	Identifies a Java class as a service implementation bean to be deployed as a Web service using the Provider<T> interface	A Provider-based service implementation bean (as in this example) must be annotated with @WebServiceProvider per Section 5.1 of [JSR-224]. The name and targetNamespace attributes identify the wsdl:portType. The wsdlLocation attribute identifies the location of the WSDL containing the wsdl:portType. The serviceName and portName identify the wsdl:service and wsdl:port local names.
@ServiceMode	Specifies the mode for a Provider<T> implementation; i.e., whether the Provider operates on messages or message payloads	In the example given here, the value Service.Mode.PAYLOAD indicates the Message Payload usage mode. The other option is Service.Mode.MESSAGE to indicate the Message usage mode.

You may be wondering what is the point of supplying a WSDL file for a Provider implementation when the JAX-WS runtime does not provide any binding for the incoming messages. One reason is that clients using the deployed service require a WSDL. By publishing a WSDL, you indicate the structure of the XML messages your Web service can process.

Unlike in the @WebService case, however, in the @WebServiceProvider case, it is your responsibility to do all the validation of the form of the incoming messages to ensure that they are compliant with the WSDL—at least compliant enough for your business logic to successfully process them.

This example uses javax.xml.transform.Source as the type parameter for Provider<T>. So, as you can see, it implements a method of the form:

```
public Source invoke(Source payload)
```

When the JAX-WS runtime receives a request that is dispatched to this Web service, it calls this invoke method and provides the message payload as the input parameter. To implement the business logic, it is up to you to process the raw XML. Example 7–5 shows how the Document Object Model (DOM) APIs are used in this example to do that processing. If you are not familiar with the DOM APIs, or you need a refresher, I suggest you take a second to look through one of the online tutorials, such as Chapter 6 of Sun's J2EE 1.4 tutorial found at http://java.sun.com/j2ee/1.4/docs/tutorial/doc/.

The DOM processing in Example 7–5 begins with the creation of a document to hold the payload request. This is necessary because the Source form of the payload is not accessible using the DOM APIs. You must transform it into a DOM representation. In this example, it is transformed into payloadDoc—an instance of org.w3c.dom.Document. The code creates another Document instance, referenced by respDoc, to hold the response message that is constructed. Next, an instance of javax.xml.transform.Transformer—xformer—is used to load the payload Source into the payloadDoc Document.

The WSDL for this service, shown toward the end of this chapter in Example 7–29, indicates that the response message should have the form:

```
<xs:element name="requestOrderResponse">
  <xs:complexType>
    <xs:sequence>
      <xs:element ref="oms:Order"/>
    </xs:sequence>
  </xs:complexType>
</xs:element>
```

As a result, using DOM to construct the response message in this example is done as follows:

```
Element responseElt =
  respDoc.createElementNS(REQ_NS, "requestOrderResponse");
```

The `Document.createElementNS` method is used here to create an element with the local name `requestOrderResponse` in the namespace defined by the `string` constant `REQ_NS` (the target namespace).

Example 7–5 Using DOM to Implement Web Service Processing

```
115    DocumentBuilderFactory dbfac = DocumentBuilderFactory.newInstance();
116    DocumentBuilder docBuilder = dbfac.newDocumentBuilder();
117    Document respDoc = docBuilder.newDocument();
118    Document payloadDoc = docBuilder.newDocument();
119   Transformer xformer = TransformerFactory.newInstance().newTransformer();
120    xformer.transform(payload, new DOMResult(payloadDoc));
121    Element responseElt =
122        respDoc.createElementNS(REQ_NS, "requestOrderResponse");
123    Element orderElt = respDoc.createElementNS(OMS_NS, "Order");
124    responseElt.appendChild(orderElt);
125    Element orderKeyElt = respDoc.createElementNS(OMS_NS, "OrderKey");
126    orderElt.appendChild(orderKeyElt);
127    // generate a pseudo-unique 10-digit order ID
128    String orderId = Long.toString((new Date()).getTime());
129    orderId = orderId.substring(orderId.length()-10);
130    orderKeyElt.appendChild(respDoc.createTextNode(orderId));
131    Element orderHeaderElt = respDoc.createElementNS(OMS_NS, "OrderHeader");
132    orderElt.appendChild(orderHeaderElt);
133    // items wrapper comes after header
134    Element orderItemsElt = respDoc.createElementNS(OMS_NS, "OrderItems");
135    orderElt.appendChild(orderItemsElt);
136    Element salesOrgElt = respDoc.createElementNS(OMS_NS, "SALES_ORG");
137    orderHeaderElt.appendChild(salesOrgElt);
138    salesOrgElt.appendChild(respDoc.createTextNode("WEB"));
139    Element purchDateElt = respDoc.createElementNS(OMS_NS, "PURCH_DATE");
140    orderHeaderElt.appendChild(purchDateElt);
141    purchDateElt.appendChild(
142        respDoc.createTextNode(dateAsString(new GregorianCalendar())));
143    Element custNoElt = respDoc.createElementNS(OMS_NS, "CUST_NO");
144    orderHeaderElt.appendChild(custNoElt);
145    // get CUST_NO from payload
146    NodeList nl = payloadDoc.getElementsByTagNameNS(REQ_NS, "CUST_NO");
147    custNoElt.appendChild(respDoc.createTextNode(
148        ((Text)((Element) nl.item(0)).getFirstChild()).getNodeValue()));
```

```
book-code/chap07/endpoint-provider/modules/endpoint/src/java/samples/
  RequestOrderEndpoint.java
```

As you can see, the code continues like that, using DOM APIs to build the response message tree. The `Document.createElementNS()` method is used to create elements, and the method `Node.appendChild()` is used to add them into the DOM tree.

To run the sample code in this section, do the following:

1. Start GlassFish (if it is not already running).
2. Go to `<book-code>/chap07/endpoint-provider`.
3. Enter `mvn install`.

This example should give you the sense that programming with the DOM API is tedious and error prone (but sometimes necessary). I used about 80 lines of DOM API code in this example (not all shown here). In contrast, the JAXB code from Example 7–3 to implement the same functionality requires about 20 lines. Of course, there are better ways to program with XML than working with the DOM APIs. I'm just using this example to make a point: It is significantly easier and less error prone for most Java programmers to work with JAXB-generated classes than to implement business logic by directly manipulating XML.

On the other hand, there are often good reasons not to use either XML programming techniques (e.g., DOM) or JAXB—particularly when doing SOA and you have existing Java classes that implement your business logic. For example, what happens if you already have a `PurchaseOrder` class and it contains a method named `processOrder` that already implements your company's business process for receiving an order, processing it, and returning a PO? Wouldn't you rather deploy that class? The problem you run into here is that the Java/WSDL mapping provided by JAX-WS and JAXB can't easily be coerced into mapping your existing `PurchaseOrder.processOrder()` method to the desired `wsdl:portType`. In such a situation, you may want to consider writing a JAX-WS service implementation bean that uses a custom Java/XML mapping to bind the WSDL types to your existing Java classes. The next section provides an example of how this can be done.

7.4   Deploying Web Services Using Custom Java/XML Mappings

In Chapter 6, I introduced Castor [CASTOR]—a Java/XML mapping tool that you can use to bind an existing Java class to an existing XML schema. In this section, I again use Castor to illustrate the techniques for using custom

Java/XML mappings in a JAX-WS context, but this time I focus on the server-side issues.

The first issue to consider in this example is how to get the Castor mapping file at runtime. In this case, I have packaged the mapping file inside the WAR at the location `/WEB-INF/castor/mapping.xml`. One way to get that file, illustrated in Example 7–6, is to use the instance of `WebService-Context` that has been injected using the `@Resource` annotation. The injection of the context, as shown in Example 7–1, happens at the time the endpoint is initialized. It is a live reference to the context, so changes the handlers made before the endpoint was invoked will be reflected.

In any event, I am using the context here simply to get to the `Servlet-Context` (via the `MessageContext`), as shown in the first few lines of the example. Once the `ServletContext` has been obtained, you can use the `getResourceAsStream` method to access the mapping file.

Example 7–6 Using Castor to Bind the Payload to Custom Classes

```
105    if ( webServiceContext == null ) {
106        throw new RuntimeException("WebServiceContext not injected.");
107    }
108    MessageContext mc = webServiceContext.getMessageContext();
109    ServletContext sc =
110        (ServletContext) mc.get(MessageContext.SERVLET_CONTEXT);
111    if ( sc == null ) {
112        throw new RuntimeException("ServletContext is null.");
113    }
114    InputStream castorMappingFile =
115        sc.getResourceAsStream("/WEB-INF/castor/mapping.xml");
116    if ( castorMappingFile == null ) {
117        throw new IOException("Castor mapping file not found.");
118    }
119    Mapping castorMapping = new Mapping();
120    castorMapping.loadMapping(new InputSource(castorMappingFile));
121    Unmarshaller u = new Unmarshaller(castorMapping);
122    DocumentBuilderFactory dbf = DocumentBuilderFactory.newInstance();
123    DocumentBuilder db = dbf.newDocumentBuilder();
124    Document payloadDOM = db.newDocument();
125    Transformer xf = TransformerFactory.newInstance().newTransformer();
126    xf.transform(payload, new DOMResult(payloadDOM));
127    MyRequestOrder reqOrder = (MyRequestOrder) u.unmarshal(payloadDOM);
```

book-code/chap07/endpoint-provider-castor/modules/endpoint/src/java/samples
 /RequestOrderEndpoint.java

Once you have obtained the Castor mapping file, you use a Castor `Unmarshaller` to instantiate your Java classes from the XML. As you can see, in this example, as in Example 7–5, I have used a `Transformer` to move the payload from a `Source` instance into a DOM `Document`. That is required simply because the Castor `Unmarshaller` cannot process a `Source` directly. Having done that, the following line instantiates the custom class `MyRequestOrder` from the payload:

```
MyRequestOrder reqOrder = (MyRequestOrder) u.unmarshal(payloadDOM);
```

The Castor mapping file tells the `Unmarshaller` how to map the XML into the `MyRequestOrder` instance. The Castor example in Section 6.3 of Chapter 6, illustrates how mapping files work and provides an example of a mapping file. Please have a look there, and examine the mapping file in this example (look in the directory `book-code/chap07/endpoint-provider-castor/modules/endpoint/src/webapp/WEB-INF/castor`) if you are interested in digging into the mechanics of the Castor mapping in this example.

Having applied the Castor mapping, you can now use the custom classes to implement the business logic. This is shown in Example 7–7.

Example 7–7 Implementing the Web Service with Custom Classes

```
132       MyRequestOrderResponse response;
133       try {
134         response = reqOrder.processOrder();
135       } catch (PaymentException pe) {
136         SOAPFactory fac = SOAPFactory.newInstance();
137         SOAPFault sf = fac.createFault(pe.getMessage(),
138           new QName("http://schemas.xmlsoap.org/soap/envelope/", "Client"));
139         throw new SOAPFaultException(sf);
140       }
```

book-code/chap07/endpoint-provider-castor/modules/endpoint/src/java/samples
  /RequestOrderEndpoint.java

So, instead of 20 lines of JAXB code, or 80 lines of DOM code, in this example I have implemented the business logic with one line of code:

```
response = reqOrder.processOrder();
```

Okay, so that is a little disingenuous, because the code that is hidden within the `processOrder` method here has about 20 lines—the same as the JAXB code. But in this case, I am reusing my existing code, instead of having to recreate business logic using the JAXB-generated classes. That is the big advantage of using your existing classes and a custom mapping tool like Castor. To do this, of course, you need to put in the work to create the Castor mapping file. See Section 6.3 of Chapter 6 to get an idea for how hard that is. What you will find is that there is a trade-off. If you have a lot of business logic code, it probably makes sense to use something like Castor in this manner to avoid rewriting your business logic with the JAXB-generated classes. An alternative approach is to use the JAXB-generated classes, and then write Java code to map them to your existing classes. Use the business logic in your existing classes, and then you have to map the results back to the JAXB classes to create the return value. This approach requires you to write custom mapping code in Java, instead of creating a Castor mapping file.

Getting back to the Castor example I've been working through, Example 7–8 demonstrates how to return the result value as a SOAP message. The custom class containing the result is `MyRequestOrderResponse`—referenced by the variable `response`. Again, the Castor mapping is used, but this time to marshal the `MyRequestOrderResponse` to XML that can be returned.

Example 7–8 Marshalling Custom Classes into the SOAP Response Payload

```
145        ByteArrayOutputStream ba = new ByteArrayOutputStream();
146        Marshaller m = new Marshaller(new OutputStreamWriter(ba));
147        m.setMapping(castorMapping);
148        m.marshal(response);
149        return new StreamSource(new StringReader(ba.toString()));
```

book-code/chap07/endpoint-provider-castor/modules/endpoint/src/java/
    samples/RequestOrderEndpoint.java

As you can see in this example, the Castor `Marshaller` uses the mapping file (`castorMapping`) to write XML into a `ByteArrayOutputStream`. These bytes are then wrapped in a `StreamSource` that is returned as the response message payload.

To run the sample code in this section, do the following:

1. Start GlassFish (if it is not already running).

2. Go to `<book-code>/chap07/endpoint-provider-castor`.

3. Enter `mvn install`.

As you were working through this section, you may have noticed in Example 7–7 that the code catches the `PaymentException` thrown by the business logic and transforms it into a `SOAPFaultException`. This is an example of how you can use the JAX-WS run-time infrastructure to return SOAP fault messages. In the next section, I look at the techniques for validation and fault processing in detail.

7.5 Validation and Fault Processing

Validation and fault processing are critical components of implementing a Web service that are often overlooked. Validation is critical because it is much more efficient to reject an XML message as invalid based on its structure than to allow an unpredictable failure to occur during the business logic processing of the bad data. Fault processing is important because any exception thrown by your Java code needs to potentially get translated into a SOAP fault that can be sent back to the client informing him of why the Web service invocation failed. If you had to write your own fault processing layer, you would be in for a lot of work. Fortunately, as depicted in Figure 7–1, JAX-WS provides SOAP fault processing in the SOAP/HTTP protocol binding. In this section, I show you how to implement validation and take advantage of the existing JAX-WS fault processing infrastructure.

7.5.1 Validation

When you develop a service implementation bean starting with a WSDL document, one of the things you often want to do is validate the incoming SOAP message against your WSDL types to make sure it is valid. When you are using JAXB outside of JAX-WS, you can turn on validation by using the `setSchema()` methods provided by `Marshaller` and `Unmarshaller`. You simply pass in the schema, as an instance of `javax.xml.validation.Schema`, and JAXB validates against it during marshalling or unmarshalling.

Unfortunately, in the 2.0 version of JAX-WS, you don't have the ability to turn on JAXB validation like that. So, you have to roll your own. The following example shows you how to do validation against WSDL. Note that this technique is particularly useful in those `Provider` endpoint cases, as in Sections 7.3 and 7.4, where you are not using JAXB at all.

The first thing you need to do to validate against your WSDL is to figure out how the service implementation bean code can access the associated WSDL. To accomplish that, you can use dependency injection to get an instance of the Web services context like this:

```
@Resource
WebServiceContext webServiceContext;
```

An example of this type of dependency injection occurs in Example 7–1 at the beginning of this chapter. Once you have included such a `WebServiceContext` field in your code, you proceed as shown in Example 7–9 to get the WSDL. From the `WebServiceContext`, you can get the `Message-Context`. Since we are deploying this as a servlet endpoint, the context property `MessageContext.SERVLET_CONTEXT` gives the `ServletContext`. From there, you can get the WSDL as packaged at the location `/WEB-INF/wsdl/RequestOrder.wsdl`.

Example 7–9 Using `WebServiceContext` to Access the WSDL

```
236    if ( webServiceContext == null ) {
237      throw new RuntimeException("WebServiceContext not injected.");
238    }
239    MessageContext mc = webServiceContext.getMessageContext();
240    ServletContext sc = (ServletContext) mc.get(MessageContext.SERVLET_CONTEXT);
241    if ( sc == null ) {
242      throw new RuntimeException("ServletContext is null.");
243    }
244    InputStream wsdlStream =
245      sc.getResourceAsStream("/WEB-INF/wsdl/RequestOrder.wsdl");
```

book-code/chap07/endpoint-provider/modules/endpoint/src/java/samples/
  RequestOrderEndpoint.java

Once you have the WSDL, you need to extract the XML schemas from its `<types>` section and use these for validation. The code in Example 7–10 shows how this can be done using the DOM API. First, the `InputStream` `wsdlStream`, obtained in Example 7–9, is loaded into a DOM `Document` instance. Then, the `getElementsByTagNameNS` method is used to extract the xs:schema nodes. After this, there is some DOM API code (inside the for loop) that copies these xs:schema nodes into an array. This step is necessary, because if you just pull the xs:schema nodes out of the WSDL's DOM tree, they will not have the necessary namespace prefix attributes. So, the code I wrote here takes all the namespace declarations from the WSDL and adds them to each xs:schema node copy to make each a valid stand-alone schema.

Example 7–10 Extracting Schema from the WSDL and Validating the SOAP Payload

```
252   DocumentBuilderFactory dbfac = DocumentBuilderFactory.newInstance();
253   DocumentBuilder docBuilder = dbfac.newDocumentBuilder();
254   Document wsdlDoc = docBuilder.newDocument();
255   Transformer xformer = TransformerFactory.newInstance().newTransformer();
256   xformer.transform(new StreamSource(wsdlStream), new DOMResult(wsdlDoc));
257   NodeList schemaNodes = wsdlDoc.getElementsByTagNameNS(
258       XMLConstants.W3C_XML_SCHEMA_NS_URI, "schema");
259   int numOfSchemas = schemaNodes.getLength();
260   Source[] schemas = new Source[numOfSchemas];
261   Document schemaDoc;
262   Element schemaElt;
263   for (int i=0; i < numOfSchemas; i++) {
264     schemaDoc = docBuilder.newDocument();
265     NamedNodeMap nsDecls = getNamespaces((Element) schemaNodes.item(i));
266     schemaElt = (Element) schemaDoc.importNode(schemaNodes.item(i), true);
267     for (int j=0; j<nsDecls.getLength(); j++) {
268       Attr a = (Attr) schemaDoc.importNode(nsDecls.item(j), true);
269       schemaElt.setAttributeNodeNS(a);
270     }
271     schemaDoc.appendChild(schemaElt);
272     schemas[i] = new DOMSource(schemaDoc);
273   }
274   SchemaFactory schemaFac = SchemaFactory.
275   newInstance(XMLConstants.W3C_XML_SCHEMA_NS_URI);
276   Schema schema = schemaFac.newSchema(schemas);
277   Validator validator = schema.newValidator();
278   if (!DOMSource.class.isInstance(payload) &&
279       !SAXSource.class.isInstance(payload) ) {
280     Document payloadDoc = docBuilder.newDocument();
281     xformer.transform(payload, new DOMResult(payloadDoc));
282     payload = new DOMSource(payloadDoc);
283   }
```

```
284    try {
285      validator.validate(payload);
286    } catch (SAXException se) {
```

book-code/chap07/endpoint-provider/modules/endpoint/src/java/samples
 /RequestOrderEndpoint.java

Having created an array of type `Source[]` to contain the schemas, I pass this array to an instance of `javax.xml.validation.SchemaFactory` to create an instance of `java.xml.validation.Schema`. From this, I get a JAXP Validator (`javax.xml.validation.Validator`). This `Validator` is used to validate the XML payload. One curious thing you may have noticed here is the check near the end to determine whether the payload is a `DOMSource` or a `SAXSource`. The reason for this check is that the `Validator` is only guaranteed to work on these types. In particular, it isn't guaranteed to work on a `StreamSource`. Hence, the possible transformation to a `DOMSource` becomes necessary.

The next logical question to wonder about is, what happens if the payload fails its validation? The answer is that you would probably like to return a SOAP fault message indicating why the validation failed. In the next section, I discuss this kind of fault handling and, more generally, the topic of JAX-WS fault processing.

7.5.2 Fault Processing

The WSDL specification provides a tag—`wsdl:fault`—for specifying fault messages. Ideally, all SOAP faults emitted by a Web service would conform to one of the WSDL's `wsdl:fault` message formats. Unfortunately, that is not necessarily the case, as many WSDL interface definitions do not even include `wsdl:fault` declarations, and just emit a SOAP fault of unspecified type when something goes wrong. Hence, in this section, I distinguish between Java exceptions that can reasonably be mapped to a `wsdl:fault` message (mapped exceptions) and those that have to be represented as generic SOAP faults (unmapped exceptions). As an example, it is likely that when an exception is thrown because input message validation fails, this would be a mapped exception because the WSDL writer could anticipate such an exception and define a `wsdl:fault` message for it. On the other hand, exceptions resulting from unanticipated run-time errors most likely will not have a corresponding `wsdl:fault` message and will need to be returned as generic SOAP faults.

The JAX-WS WSDL to Java mapping binds `wsdl:fault` messages to generate subclasses of `java.lang.Exception`. When you generate a SEI from a WSDL, these mapped exception classes are also generated. Section 6.1 of Chapter 6 describes this mapping and shows how mapped exceptions are generated. If you are still a little fuzzy on the WSDL to Java mapping, it's probably a good idea to quickly review that section.

So, if you have implemented your Web service using a SEI mapped from a `wsdl:portType`, one option for returning a SOAP fault is to throw a mapped exception, which the JAX-WS runtime will automatically translate into the appropriate `wsdl:fault` message, wrap in the SOAP body, and return. Example 7–11 illustrates this approach.

Example 7–11 Returning a `wsdl:fault` from within a SEI Implementation

```
61   InputMessageValidationFaultType ft = new InputMessageValidationFaultType();
62   if ( custNum == null ) {
63     ft.setMsg("Customer Number cannot be null.");
64     throw new InputFault("Input parameter failed validation.", ft);
65   }
66   if ( poNum == null && ccard == null ) {
67     ft.setMsg("Must supply either a PO or a CCard.");
68     throw new InputFault("Input parameter failed validation.", ft);
69   }
70   if ( itemList == null || itemList.isEmpty() ) {
71     ft.setMsg("Must have at least one item.");
72     throw new InputFault("Input parameter failed validation.", ft);
73   }
```

book-code/chap07/endpoint-sei/modules/endpoint/src/java/samples
  /RequestOrder.java

You can see two generated classes being used in Example 7–11: `InputMessageValidationFaultType` and `InputFault`. The first, `InputMessageValidationFaultType`, was mapped from the XML schema definition referenced by the `wsdl:fault` message. The second, `InputFault`, is mapped from the `wsdl:message` corresponding to this `wsdl:fault` itself. The name of this `wsdl:message` is `inputFault` and, hence, JAX-WS has generated a mapped exception named `InputFault`.

This fault mapping can be a little confusing, so I'm going to walk through it step by step, even though that is a little tedious. Example 7–12 shows a snippet of the WSDL, where the `wsdl:fault` is defined inside the `wsdl:portType` definition.

Example 7–12 The `wsdl:fault` Definition Inside the `wsdl:portType`

```
59  <wsdl:message name="inputFault">
60    <wsdl:part name="parameters" element="faults:inputMessageValidationFault"/>
61  </wsdl:message>
62  <wsdl:portType name="RequestOrderPort">
63    <wsdl:operation name="requestOrder">
64      <wsdl:input message="req:request"/>
65      <wsdl:output message="req:response"/>
66      <wsdl:fault name="requestOrderInputFault" message="req:inputFault"/>
67    </wsdl:operation>
68  </wsdl:portType>
```

book-code/chap07/endpoint-sei/modules/endpoint/src/webapp/WEB-INF/wsdl
  /RequestOrder.wsdl

Notice that the `wsdl:fault` (named `requestOrderInputFault`) references the message `req:inputFault`. The message `req:inputFault` is defined at the top of Example 7–12. This is the message JAX-WS maps to the mapped exception named `InputFault` used in Example 7–11. In Example 7–13, you can see the Java code generated by JAX-WS for `InputFault`. JAX-WS uses the `@WebFault` annotation to identify this class as a mapped exception. As you can see, this class is really a simple wrapper for the `InputMessageValidationFaultType` class. JAX-WS refers to this wrapped Java type as the *fault bean*. A `wsdl:fault` element inside a `wsdl:portType` always refers to a `wsdl:message` that contains a single `wsdl:part` with an `element` attribute. The global element declaration referred to by that `wsdl:part`'s `element` attribute is mapped by JAX-WS to a JavaBean called a fault bean.

Example 7–13 The Mapped Exception `InputFault` Generated by JAX-WS

```
25  @WebFault(name = "inputMessageValidationFault",
26      targetNamespace = "http://www.example.com/faults")
27      public class InputFault
28      extends Exception {
29
```

```
30   private InputMessageValidationFaultType faultInfo;
31
32   public InputFault(String message, InputMessageValidationFaultType faultInfo) {
33      super(message);
34      this.faultInfo = faultInfo;
35   }
```

book-code/chap07/endpoint-sei/examples/InputFault.java

The next step in understanding this fault mapping is to look at the schema from which the fault bean `InputMessageValidationFaultType` gets generated. In the WSDL used for this example, this schema is imported from http://soabook.com/example/faults/faults.xsd.[6] Example 7–14 shows that imported schema.

Example 7–14 The Imported Schema Referenced by the `wsdl:part` of the `inputFault` `wsdl:message`

```
4   <xs:schema targetNamespace="http://www.example.com/faults"
5      xmlns:faults="http://www.example.com/faults" elementFormDefault="qualified"
6      xmlns:xs="http://www.w3.org/2001/XMLSchema">
7      <xs:element name="inputMessageValidationFault"
8         type="faults:InputMessageValidationFaultType"/>
9      <xs:complexType name="InputMessageValidationFaultType">
10        <xs:attribute name="msg" type="xs:string"/>
11     </xs:complexType>
12  </xs:schema>
```

book-code/chap07/endpoint-sei/examples/faults.xsd

The name of the element mapped to the fault bean is `inputMessage-ValidationFault`. As you can see in this example, the schema is very simple—containing an attribute named `msg` that holds an `xs:string`, which is intended to hold a description of the fault. Of course, in the real world, the schema used might be much more complex to hold detailed information

---

6. The WSDL used in this example, shown in Example 7–29, is discussed along with a detailed explanation of WSDL in Chapter 4, Section 4.1. In that part of the book, you will also find a general discussion of how and why to import external schemas into your WSDL.

about the cause of a particular fault. In this case, the importance of using this `wsdl:fault` is not the information it carries, but the fact that its type (i.e., an instance of `InputMessageValidationFaultType`) tells the user receiving it that there was a validation failure and the SOAP message received by the Web service is not valid with respect to the WSDL.

Example 7–15 shows the fault bean generated from the imported schema.[7] This fault bean class contains a single property corresponding to the `msg` attribute in the schema from which it was generated.

Example 7–15 The Fault Bean `InputMessageValidationFaultType` Generated by JAX-WS

```
27   @XmlAccessorType(AccessType.FIELD)
28   @XmlType(name = "InputMessageValidationFaultType")
29   public class InputMessageValidationFaultType {
30
31     @XmlAttribute
32     protected String msg;
33
34     public String getMsg() {
35       return msg;
36     }
37
38     public void setMsg(String value) {
39       this.msg = value;
40     }
41
42   }
```

book-code/chap07/endpoint-sei/examples
  /InputMessageValidationFaultType.java

Putting these steps together, it should now make sense what is happening in Example 7–11. The code there identifies several input validation failures (i.e., null customer number, missing purchasing information, an empty item list) that might occur. In each case, the `msg` property of the fault bean (`InputMessageValidationFaultType`) is set with an appropriate message. Then, from the fault bean, an instance of `InputFault` is constructed with

---

7. The JAXB annotations used here are described in detail in Chapter 5.

the generic error message "Input parameter failed validation." When JAX-WS marshals this `InputFault` exception out to a SOAP 1.1 fault message, the `InputFault.getMessage()` and the `InputMessageValidationFault-Type.getMsg()` strings get mapped to different places. You will see exactly how these map into the SOAP fault in a minute, but before doing that, I am going to step back and discuss another way you can return a SOAP fault message from inside a service implementation bean.

In addition to using a fault bean, you can construct an instance of the SAAJ class `javax.xml.ws.soap.SOAPFaultException`. When you throw a `SOAPFaultException` from inside a service implementation bean, the JAX-WS runtime converts it to a SOAP fault message and returns it to the client.

Figure 7–2 shows how the various types of Java exceptions get mapped by JAX-WS to SOAP fault messages. The numbers in this illustration do not indicate steps in a process, but rather components of the mapping.

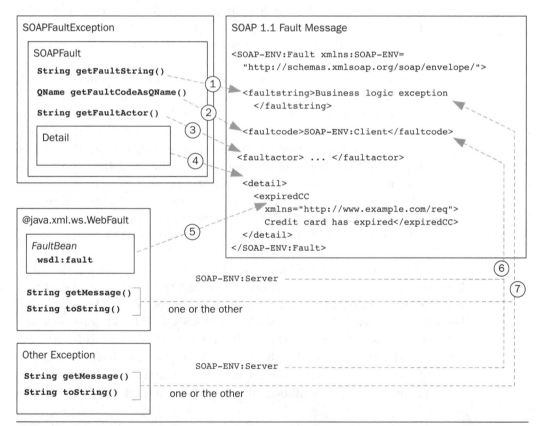

Figure 7–2 How JAX-WS maps exceptions to a SOAP 1.1 fault message structure.

The following describes each numbered component of the JAX-WS fault mapping:

1. A `SOAPFaultException` wraps a `javax.xml.soap.SOAPFault` that has a straightforward mapping to a SOAP 1.1 fault message. The `getFaultString` method maps to the `faultstring` element.
2. Similarly, the `getFaultCodeAsQName` method maps to the `faultcode`.
3. `getFaultActor` method maps to the `faultactor` element.
4. The `SOAPFault` class references an instance of `javax.xml.soap-.Detail`, which represents the `detail` element of a SOAP fault message. A `Detail` object is a container for `javax.xml.soap.Detail-Entry` instances—each of which maps to a child element of the SOAP fault's `detail` element.
5. The components labeled 5, 6, and 7 show how a mapped exception corresponds to a SOAP fault message. This is a visual illustration of the discussion surrounding Example 7–11 through Example 7–15. `@WebFault` annotates a mapped exception. The fault bean wrapped by the mapped exception corresponds to the `detail` element of the SOAP fault message.
6. The `faultcode` corresponding to a mapped exception is always `SOAP-ENV:Server`. This can be misleading, especially when the fault was generated by a poorly constructed SOAP request. Notice in the diagram that other exceptions (besides `SOAPFaultExceptions` and `@WebFault` mapped exceptions) are also transformed by JAX-WS into SOAP fault messages. In the case of a general exception, the `fault-code` also gets the default value of `ENV:Server`.
7. The `faultstring` corresponding to a mapped exception or a general exception is mapped from the `getMessage()` method, unless that returns null, in which case it is mapped from `getString()`.

Having gone through the JAX-WS SOAP fault message mapping in detail, it is now time to look at how you can use the SAAJ API to generate a `SOAP-FaultException` to send useful information back to the client. This approach is helpful in two cases: if you are not working with a SEI and don't have any mapped exceptions to take advantage of, and if you are working with a SEI but you have to handle an exception that doesn't correspond to a `wsdl:fault`.

Example 7–16 shows an example of the first variety. This snippet comes from a `Provider` implementation of the WSDL contract[8] that I have been

---

8. See Example 7–29 for the full WSDL document.

discussing throughout this section. This code can be used when the mapped `InputFault` is not available. It gets transformed by JAX-WS to a SOAP fault message with the same structure.

Example 7–16 Building and Returning a `wsdl:fault` Using `SOAPFaultException` within a `Provider<T>` Implementation

```
98      String errorMsg = validateAgainstWSDL(payload);
99      if ( errorMsg != null ) {
100       SOAPFactory fac = SOAPFactory.newInstance();
101       SOAPFault sf = fac.createFault(
102          "SOAP payload is invalid with respect to WSDL.",
103          new QName("http://schemas.xmlsoap.org/soap/envelope/", "Client"));
104       Detail d = sf.addDetail();
105       SOAPElement de = d.addChildElement(new QName(
106          "http://www.example.com/faults", "inputMessageValidationFault"));
107       de.addAttribute(new QName("", "msg"), errorMsg.replaceAll("\"",""));
108       throw new SOAPFaultException(sf);
109     }
```

book-code/chap07/endpoint-provider/modules/endpoint/src/java/samples
  /RequestOrderEndpoint.java

This code snippet starts by getting the results of the `validateAgainstWSDL()` method. This method contains the validation code illustrated in Example 7–10. If the method returns a non-null string, the validation failed and the string contains the error message. To turn that message into a SOAP fault, the first step is to get a `javax.xml.soap.SOAPFactory` and use it to construct a `SOAPFault`. As you can see here, the `faultstring` passed to the constructor is `"SOAP payload is invalid with respect to WSDL."`—explaining the general cause of failure (i.e., input validation failure). The other parameter passed to the constructor is the `faultcode` – `ENV:Client` (indicating that the client is responsible for the fault).

Having constructed a `SOAPFault`, the `detail` is added using the `addDetail()` method to create an empty `Detail` object. Next, a `SOAPElement` is created that will be added as a child to the `detail` element. This child is the `faults:inputMessageValidationFault` shown in Example 7–14. Here, instead of creating it using a fault bean (as in Example 7–11), I am constructing it by manipulating XML with the SAAJ API.

At this point, you may be wondering what happens when the client receives the SOAP fault message we have constructed in this manner. If the SOAP client is written with JAX-WS and uses the SEI generated from the WSDL, the client will map this SOAP fault to the `InputFault` mapped exception. This happens regardless of how the SOAP fault was created on the server side (i.e., from an `InputFault` instance or from a `SOAPFault-Exception`). Example 7–17 shows a log message printed by such a Java client after receiving the exception.

Example 7–17 The `wsdl:fault` Received by the Client As an `InputFault`

```
3   InputFault.getMessage( ) =
4
5      SOAP payload is invalid with respect to WSDL.
6
7   InputFault.getFaultInfo.getMsg( ) =
8
9      validation error: cvc-complex-type.2.4.a: Invalid content was found starting
10     with element 'ns1:ccard'. One of '{http://www.example.com/req:CUST_NO}'
11     is expected.
```

book-code/chap07/endpoint-provider/examples/wsdlfault_from_validation.xml

Looking at Example 7–17, you can see that the `InputFault.getFault-Info.getMsg()` returns the `detail` element with the error message from the server-side validation. In this case, the message received is a parse error telling you that the SOAP request did not contain the required element `req:CUST_NO`—in other words, no customer number was supplied. To run this example, do the following:

1. Start GlassFish (if it is not running already).
2. Go to `<book-code>/chap07/endpoint-provider`.
3. Enter `mvn install`.

Example 7–18 shows another snippet of code that will cause JAX-WS to return a SOAP fault message. In this case, the code throws a general `javax.xml.ws.WebServiceException`—the base exception class for all JAX-WS run-time exceptions. The error that occurred in this case is not a SOAP message validation error, but a business logic error: an expired credit card. In an ideal world, such an exception would map to one of the `wsdl:fault` messages. However, when you start from WSDL, it is often the case that not all your business logic exceptions are going to map neatly into a mapped exception. The code in Example 7–18 illustrates a simple way to get JAX-WS to produce a SOAP fault that conveys some of the information relevant to the business logic exception. In this case, you could simply construct a `WebServiceException` with the fault string `"Expired ccard."`

Example 7–18 A `WebServiceException` Is Mapped to a SOAP Fault by the Container

```
172        Element expireDateElt = (Element) ccardElt.getElementsByTagNameNS(
173            OMS_NS, "CC_EXPIRE_DATE").item(0);
174        String expireDateStr =
175          ((Text) expireDateElt.getFirstChild()).getNodeValue();
177        String today = dateAsString(new GregorianCalendar());
177        if (expireDateStr.compareTo(today) < 0 ) {
178          throw new WebServiceException("Expired ccard.");
179        }
```

book-code/chap07/endpoint-provider/modules/endpoint/src/java/samples
 /RequestOrderEndpoint.java

Example 7–19 shows the SOAP fault message the JAX-WS creates from this `WebServiceException`. When you follow the previous instructions to run the sample code, you will also see the client-side output for this SOAP fault message.

Example 7–19 The SOAP Fault Resulting from a `WebServiceException` Has No Detail Elements

```
3  <SOAP-ENV:Fault xmlns:SOAP-ENV="http://schemas.xmlsoap.org/soap/envelope/">
4    <faultstring>Expired ccard.</faultstring>
5    <faultcode>SOAP-ENV:Server</faultcode>
6  </SOAP-ENV:Fault>
```

book-code/chap07/endpoint-provider/examples
 /soapfault_from_webserviceexception.xml

You may have noticed that the `faultcode` in Example 7–19 is `SOAP_ENV:Server`. This is the default mapping for `WebServiceException`, but in this case it is misleading since the fault results from a client-side data problem—an expired credit card. So, if you want to produce a more accurate SOAP fault message, you have to again go to the trouble of using the SAAJ API to create a `SOAPFaultException`. A snippet of code for doing that is shown in Example 7–20.

Example 7–20 Mapping the Same Credit Card Error to a SOAP Fault with Detail Using `SOAPFaultException`

```
103    if ( hasExpired(ccard) ) {
104      try {
105        SOAPFactory fac = SOAPFactory.newInstance();
106        SOAPFault sf = fac.createFault("Business logic exception",
107          new QName("http://schemas.xmlsoap.org/soap/envelope/", "Client"));
108        Detail d = sf.addDetail();
109        DetailEntry de = d.addDetailEntry(
110          new QName("", "expiredCC"));
111        de.setValue("Credit card has expired");
112        throw new SOAPFaultException(sf);
113      } catch (SOAPException e) {
114        throw new RuntimeException(
115          "Failed to create SOAPFault: " + e.getMessage());
116      }
117    }
```

book-code/chap07/endpoint-sei/modules/endpoint/src/java/samples
  /RequestOrder.java

This will produce a more accurate fault code (i.e., `SOAP-ENV:Client`), and put the detailed explanation of the problem (expired credit card) in the `detail` element where it belongs. The SOAP fault message produced from this code is shown in Example 7–21.

Example 7–21 A Better SOAP Fault Explains the Credit Card Exception

```
3    <SOAP-ENV:Fault xmlns:SOAP-ENV="http://schemas.xmlsoap.org/soap/envelope/">
4      <faultstring>Business logic exception</faultstring>
5      <faultcode>SOAP-ENV:Client</faultcode>
```

```
6    <detail>
7      <expiredCC>Credit card has expired</expiredCC>
8    </detail>
9  </SOAP-ENV:Fault>
```

---

book-code/chap07/endpoint-sei/examples/soapfault_from_soapfaultexception.xml

---

To run this example, do the following:

1. Start GlassFish (if it is not running already).
2. Go to `<book-code>`/chap07/endpoint-sei.
3. Enter `mvn install`.

That wraps up a fairly detailed explanation of how to take advantage of the JAX-WS exception handling and SOAP fault mapping capabilities. If you have read through it all, congratulations—you have a lot of patience! The payoff is that you now have a good understanding of how to get JAX-WS to generate the SOAP faults required by high-quality Web services.

In the next section, I move on to another component of the JAX-WS runtime illustrated in Figure 7–1 from the beginning of this chapter: handler processing.

7.6 Server-Side Handlers

As I discussed briefly in Section 7.1, handlers are used to implement pre- and post-processing of a `MessageContext` before the invocation of the service implementation bean. In this section, I walk you through an example of how to write a server-side handler and configure a SIB with the handler. The handler I consider in this example encapsulates the WSDL validation illustrated in Example 7–10. In that example, the validation code is embedded in the SIB. Here, I show you how to configure that same code to do the validation in a handler. The advantage of this approach is that you can reuse such a handler across multiple endpoints.

In JAX-WS, server-side handlers are configured using the `@HandlerChain` annotation, which references a configuration file that describes the handlers that are included in the chain. Example 7–22 illustrates how the `@Handler-Chain` annotation is used. As you can see, this is a simple annotation that is included, along with `@WebService` or `@WebServiceProvider`, on the service implementation bean declaration.

Example 7–22 The `@HandlerChain` Annotation

```
44  @HandlerChain(file="handlerchain.xml")
45  @WebService(name = "targetNamespace = "http://www.example.com/req",
46      endpointInterface="com.example.req.RequestOrderPort",
47      wsdlLocation="WEB-INF/wsdl/RequestOrder.wsdl")
48  public class RequestOrder implements RequestOrderPort {
```

book-code/chap07/endpoint-sei-handler/modules/endpoint/src/java
  /samples/RequestOrder.java

The packaging location for the `@HandlerChain.file` attribute, which references the configuration file, is specified by the WSEE and WS-Metadata specifications. Basically, the `@HandlerChain.file` attribute can reference the configuration file as a URL or as a relative file location from the SIB class file. Alternatively, the configuration file can be packaged anywhere such that it is accessible as a resource from the classpath. I look at packaging issues like this in more detail in the next chapter.

Example 7–23 shows what the handler chain configuration file looks like. This is a simple XML file where the `handler-chain` element represents a handler chain, and its children, all `handler` elements, represent the handlers in the order they should be executed at runtime (reverse order for output SOAP responses). As per the JAX-WS specification (Section 9.2.1.2), however, if you have a mixture of Logical and Protocol Handlers, the Logical Handlers are executed before the protocol handlers, but the relative order within the two groups is preserved.

As described in the JAX-WS specification (Section 9 of [JSR 224]), Logical Handlers "only operate on message context properties and message payloads. Logical Handlers are protocol-agnostic and are unable to affect protocol specific parts of a message. Logical Handlers are handlers that implement `javax.xml.ws.handler.LogicalHandler`." Likewise, Protocol Handlers "operate on message context properties and protocol specific messages. Protocol Handlers are specific to a particular protocol and may access and change protocol specific aspects of a message. Protocol Handlers are handlers that implement any interface derived from `javax.xml.ws.handler.Handler` except `javax.xml.ws.handler.LogicalHandler`."

The `LogicalHandler` interface, for example, gives you access only to the payload via a `javax.xml.ws.LogicalMessage`. With respect to a SOAP binding, this would mean access to the SOAP `Body` element, but not its headers. A Protocol Handler (e.g., `SOAPHandler`), on the other hand, gives you access to the entire SOAP message.

Example 7–23 The `@HandlerChain` Configuration File

```
4   <handler-chains xmlns:jws="http://java.sun.com/xml/ns/javaee">
5     <handler-chain>
6       <handler>
7         <handler-class>samples.ValidationHandler</handler-class>
8       </handler>
9     </handler-chain>
10  </handler-chains>
```

book-code/chap07/endpoint-sei-handler/modules/endpoint/src/webapp/WEB-INF
/classes/samples/handlerchain.xml

Example 7–24 shows the implementation of the `ValidationHandler` class referenced in the preceding handler chain configuration file. Notice that this handler implements `javax.xml.ws.handler.soap.SOAPHandler<SOAP-MessageContext>`. That is the standard handler for the SOAP protocol binding, and the `javax.xml.ws.handler.soap.SOAPContext` is the standard extension of `MessageContext` used with the SOAP protocol binding.

The purpose of this handler is to validate the SOAP message against the WSDL. Since I want to do that only on the inbound SOAP message,[9] the first step in this handler is to check the direction of message flow using the `MessageContext.MESSAGE_OUTBOUND_PROPERTY`.

Example 7–24 The Validation Handler Implementation

```
55  public class ValidationHandler implements SOAPHandler<SOAPMessageContext> {
56
57    public boolean handleMessage(SOAPMessageContext context) {
58
```

---

9. Of course, there is no reason not to validate the outbound message, but that case is not shown in this example.

```
59     if ( ((Boolean)context.get(MessageContext.MESSAGE_OUTBOUND_PROPERTY)).
60        booleanValue() ) return true;
61     try {
62       SOAPMessage message = context.getMessage();
63       SOAPBody body = message.getSOAPBody();
64       SOAPElement requestElt =
65         (SOAPElement) body.getFirstChild();
66       String errMsg = validateAgainstWSDL(context, requestElt);
67       if ( errMsg == null ) {
68         return true;
69       }
70       SOAPFactory fac = SOAPFactory.newInstance();
71       SOAPFault sf = fac.createFault(
72           "SOAP payload is invalid with respect to WSDL.",
73           new QName("http://schemas.xmlsoap.org/soap/envelope/", "Client"));
74       Detail d = sf.addDetail();
75       SOAPElement de = d.addChildElement(new QName(
76           "http://www.example.com/faults", "inputMessageValidationFault"));
77       de.addAttribute(new QName("", "msg"), errMsg.replaceAll("\"",""));
78       throw new SOAPFaultException(sf);
79
80     } catch (Exception e) {
81       e.printStackTrace();
82       throw new WebServiceException(e);
83     }
84
85   }
```

book-code/chap07/endpoint-sei-handler/modules/endpoint/src/java/samples/
  ValidationHandler.java

Having determined that this is an inbound message, the next step is to use the SAAJ API to extract the payload from the SOAP body. Since I know that I'm using the document/literal wrapped style of WSDL,[10] I can cheat a little bit here and grab only the first child of the SOAP body. With that style, there is only one child. Having obtained the payload, the next step is to validate it and pass it to the `validateAgainstWSDL()` method. From this point, the processing is the same as the validation discussed in Example 7–10 and

---

10. See Chapter 4 for a detailed discussion of the different WSDL styles.

the fault processing discussed in Example 7–16. At the end of the validation processing, if there is an error, the handler throws a `SOAPFaultException`. Just as inside the service implementation bean, such exceptions thrown from the handler will be converted by the JAX-WS runtime to a SOAP fault message using the mapping described in the preceding section.

To run this example, do the following:

1. Start GlassFish (if it is not running already).
2. Go to `<book-code>/chap07/endpoint-sei-handler`.
3. Enter `mvn install`.

7.7   Java SE Deployment with javax.xml.ws.Endpoint

Up to this point, I have been discussing the server-side behavior of JAX-WS within a Java EE 5 container. Container-based deployment, however, is not the only means of implementing Web services supported by JAX-WS. The `javax.xml.ws.Endpoint` class is designed to enable you to deploy Web services from a Java SE application.

Java SE 5.0 does not include an implementation of `Endpoint`. To get such an implementation, and to run the example in this section, you need to download Java SE 6, and set the Maven property `jdk6.home` to point to the directory where you installed it.[11]

The amazing thing about working with `Endpoint` deployment is that you can use the same SEI and service implementation bean you would use for a Java EE deployment. Example 7–25 shows the SIB used in this example. It is basically the same one we have used throughout this chapter.

Example 7–25 The SEI Implementation to Be Published with `javax.xml.ws.Endpoint`

```
44   @WebService(name = "RequestOrder",
45       targetNamespace = "http://www.example.com/req",
46       endpointInterface="com.example.req.RequestOrderPort")
47   public class RequestOrder implements RequestOrderPort {
48
```

11. See Appendix B for a detailed explanation of how to install Java SE 6 and configure it for this example.

```
49   public OrderType requestOrder(String custNum, String poNum, BUSOBJCCARD ccard,
50       List<BUSOBJITEM> itemList) throws InputFault {
```

book-code/chap07/endpoint-endpoint/src/java/samples/RequestOrder.java

One slight difference between how the service implementation bean is annotated here versus the example in Section 7.2 is that here there is no wsdlLocation attribute specified in the @WebService annotation. As you will see, with an Endpoint instance, you can dynamically configure a pre-defined WSDL. Of course, you don't have to supply a WSDL to the Endpoint instance if you don't want to. Just like in the Java EE case, the Endpoint class can generate WSDL from SEI or SIB annotations. The JAX-WS and JAXB run-time annotation processing system is included in Java SE 6.

Example 7–26 shows the main class that creates and deploys the Endpoint instance used for this example. Deploying a Web service this way is a two-stage process. First, you create an Endpoint instance and then you publish it.

Example 7–26 Creating and Publishing a Web Service with `javax.xml.ws.Endpoint`

```
45   public static void main(String[] args) throws Exception {
46
47     Endpoint endpoint = Endpoint.create(new RequestOrder());
48     InputStream wsdlStream =
49       Client.class.getClassLoader().getResourceAsStream("RequestOrder.wsdl");
50     URL wsdlURL =
51       Client.class.getClassLoader().getResource("RequestOrder.wsdl");
52     if ( wsdlStream == null ) {
53       throw new RuntimeException("Cannot find WSDL resource file.");
54     }
55     ArrayList<Source> metadata = new ArrayList<Source>();
56     Source wsdlSource = new StreamSource(wsdlStream);
57     String wsdlId = wsdlURL.toExternalForm();
58     wsdlSource.setSystemId(wsdlId);
59     metadata.add(wsdlSource);
60     endpoint.setMetadata(metadata);
61     endpoint.publish("http://localhost:8680/oms");
```

book-code/chap07/endpoint-endpoint/src/java/samples/Client.java

As you can see here, all you have to do to create the `Endpoint` instance is:

```
Endpoint endpoint = Endpoint.create(new RequestOrder());
```

I think that is pretty cool. No deployment descriptors or even a container is needed! Of course, there is some sleight of hand going on here. Taking a peek at the Java SE 6 source code used to implement `Endpoint` reveals that a simple `HttpServer` class under the covers is instantiated when an `Endpoint` is created this way.

The next thing to notice in Example 7–26 is how you can set the meta-data to supply your own WSDL to the `Endpoint`. As mentioned, if you do not do this, the endpoint will return the JAX-WS-generated WSDL. If you do supply the WSDL, you need to use the `Endpoint.setMetadata()` method as shown. This method takes an instance of `List<Source>`. The meta-data included in this list can include XML schema and WSDL. As you can see in this code, when you supply a WSDL as a `Source` instance, you may also have to set its system ID. That step is required whenever the WSDL contains references (e.g., imported or included schema) that need to be resolved by an XML parser.

The last step in this process is to invoke the `Endpoint.publish()` method and supply an endpoint URL. It's that simple!

Example 7–27 shows the client code used to invoke the `Endpoint`. The first few lines of this code simply get the WSDL and print it out (using the `printWSDL()` method shown in Example 7–28). I have included this simply to demonstrate that the `Endpoint` we created publishes its WSDL correctly.

Example 7–27 Invoking the Published Endpoint

```
65   URL wsdlDeployURL = new URL("http://localhost:8680/oms/requestOrder?wsdl");
66   System.out.println("Endpoint Returns this WSDL");
67   System.out.println("===========================================");
68   printWSDL(wsdlDeployURL);
69   QName serviceQName =
70     new QName("http://www.example.com/req", "RequestOrderService");
71   QName portQName =
72     new QName("http://www.example.com/req", "RequestOrderPort");
73   Service service = Service.create(wsdlURL, serviceQName);
74   RequestOrderPort port =
75     (RequestOrderPort) service.getPort(portQName, RequestOrderPort.class);
```

```
76        BUSOBJCCARD ccard = createCreditCard();
77        ArrayList<BUSOBJITEM> itemList = createItemList();
78        OrderType order = port.requestOrder(
79            "ENT0072123", null, ccard, itemList);
80        System.out.println();
81        System.out.println();
82        System.out.println("Webservice Returns this Order");
83        System.out.println("=============================================");
84        printReturnedOrder(order);
85        endpoint.stop();
86
87    }
```

book-code/chap07/endpoint-endpoint/src/java/samples/Client.java

The second part of the code in Example 7–28 shows that you can create a JAX-WS client to invoke this `Endpoint` just as I illustrate in Chapter 6. You can get a `Service` built from the WSDL URL and create a dynamic proxy using the `RequestOrderPort` SEI. The process is exactly the same as for invoking any Web service. To run this example, do the following:

1. Go to `<book-code>/chap07/endpoint-endpoint`.[12]
2. Enter `mvn install`.

Example 7–28 Utility to Print the WSDL from the Published Endpoint

```
151    private static void printWSDL(URL wsdlURL) throws Exception {
152
153        HttpURLConnection con = (HttpURLConnection) wsdlURL.openConnection();
154        con.setRequestMethod("GET");
155        con.connect();
156        InputStream wsdlInput = con.getInputStream();
157        int b = wsdlInput.read();
158        while ( b > -1 ) {
159          System.out.print((char) b);
160          b = wsdlInput.read();
161        }
162        wsdlInput.close();
```

---

12. GlassFish does not need to be running for this example.

```
163        con.disconnect();
164
165    }
```

book-code/chap07/endpoint-endpoint/src/java/samples/Client.java

Example 7–29 shows the WSDL that is supplied to the `Endpoint` instance using the `setMetaData` method in Example 7–26. Even though it is a long listing, I include it here because it is referenced in a number of places in this chapter where I discuss WSDL. This is the WSDL used in most of the examples in this chapter.

Example 7–29 WSDL Supplied As Meta-data to the Endpoint

```
4   <wsdl:definitions xmlns:wsdl="http://schemas.xmlsoap.org/wsdl/"
5     xmlns:soap="http://schemas.xmlsoap.org/wsdl/soap/"
6     xmlns:xs="http://www.w3.org/2001/XMLSchema"
7     xmlns:oms="http://www.example.com/oms" xmlns:req="http://www.example.com/req"
8     xmlns:faults="http://www.example.com/faults"
9     targetNamespace="http://www.example.com/req">
10    <wsdl:types>
11      <xs:schema targetNamespace="http://www.example.com/oms">
12       <xs:include schemaLocation="http://soabook.com/example/oms/orders.xsd"/>
13      </xs:schema>
14      <xs:schema targetNamespace="http://www.example.com/faults">
15       <xs:include schemaLocation="http://soabook.com/example/faults/faults.xsd"
16       />
17      </xs:schema>
18      <xs:schema targetNamespace="http://www.example.com/req"
19        elementFormDefault="qualified">
20        <xs:element name="requestOrder">
21          <xs:complexType>
22            <xs:sequence>
23              <xs:element name="CUST_NO">
24                <xs:simpleType>
25                  <xs:restriction base="xs:string">
26                    <xs:maxLength value="10"/>
27                  </xs:restriction>
28                </xs:simpleType>
29              </xs:element>
30              <xs:element minOccurs="0" name="PURCH_ORD_NO">
```

```
31              <xs:simpleType>
32                <xs:restriction base="xs:string">
33                  <xs:maxLength value="35"/>
34                </xs:restriction>
35              </xs:simpleType>
36            </xs:element>
37            <xs:element type="oms:BUSOBJ_CCARD" minOccurs="0" name="ccard"/>
38           <xs:element type="oms:BUSOBJ_ITEM" name="item" maxOccurs="unbounded"
39            />
40          </xs:sequence>
41        </xs:complexType>
42      </xs:element>
43      <xs:element name="requestOrderResponse">
44        <xs:complexType>
45          <xs:sequence>
46            <xs:element ref="oms:Order"/>
47          </xs:sequence>
48        </xs:complexType>
49      </xs:element>
50    </xs:schema>
51  </wsdl:types>
52  <wsdl:message name="request">
53    <wsdl:part element="req:requestOrder" name="parameters"/>
54  </wsdl:message>
55  <wsdl:message name="response">
56    <wsdl:part element="req:requestOrderResponse" name="parameters"/>
57  </wsdl:message>
58  <wsdl:message name="inputFault">
59    <wsdl:part element="faults:inputMessageValidationFault" name="parameters"/>
60  </wsdl:message>
61  <wsdl:portType name="RequestOrderPort">
62    <wsdl:operation name="requestOrder">
63      <wsdl:input message="req:request"/>
64      <wsdl:output message="req:response"/>
65      <wsdl:fault message="req:inputFault" name="requestOrderInputFault"/>
66    </wsdl:operation>
67  </wsdl:portType>
68  <wsdl:binding type="req:RequestOrderPort" name="RequestOrderSOAPBinding">
69    <soap:binding style="document"
70      transport="http://schemas.xmlsoap.org/soap/http"/>
71    <wsdl:operation name="requestOrder">
72      <wsdl:input>
73        <soap:body use="literal"/>
74      </wsdl:input>
```

```
75        <wsdl:output>
76          <soap:body use="literal"/>
77        </wsdl:output>
78        <wsdl:fault name="requestOrderInputFault">
79          <soap:fault name="requestOrderInputFault"/>
80        </wsdl:fault>
81      </wsdl:operation>
82    </wsdl:binding>
83    <wsdl:service name="RequestOrderService">
84      <wsdl:port binding="req:RequestOrderSOAPBinding" name="RequestOrderPort">
85        <soap:address location="http://localhost:8680/oms/requestOrder"/>
86      </wsdl:port>
87    </wsdl:service>
88  </wsdl:definitions>
```

book-code/chap07/endpoint-endpoint/examples/generatedwsdl.xml

Example 7–30 shows the WSDL that is returned by the code in Example 7–27 when it queries the URL http://localhost:8680/oms/request-Order?wsdl. This is also a long listing, but I include it because I want you to notice some of the subtle differences between this and the WSDL that was included as meta-data supplied to the Endpoint instance. In particular, look at the schema import definitions and you will notice that the schemaLocation has changed in each case.

Example 7–30 WSDL Generated by JAX-WS within the Endpoint (When No Meta-data Is Supplied)

```
4   <definitions xmlns:tns="http://www.example.com/req"
5     xmlns:xsd="http://www.w3.org/2001/XMLSchema"
6     xmlns:soap="http://schemas.xmlsoap.org/wsdl/soap/"
7     xmlns="http://schemas.xmlsoap.org/wsdl/"
8     targetNamespace="http://www.example.com/req" name="RequestOrderService">
9     <types>
10      <xsd:schema>
11        <xsd:import namespace="http://www.example.com/req"
12          schemaLocation="http://localhost:8680/oms/requestOrder?xsd=1"/>
13      </xsd:schema>
14      <xsd:schema>
15        <xsd:import namespace="http://www.example.com/oms"
16          schemaLocation="http://localhost:8680/oms/requestOrder?xsd=2"/>
```

```
17      </xsd:schema>
18      <xsd:schema>
19        <xsd:import namespace="http://www.example.com/faults"
20          schemaLocation="http://localhost:8680/oms/requestOrder?xsd=3"/>
21      </xsd:schema>
22    </types>
23    <message name="requestOrder">
24      <part element="tns:requestOrder" name="parameters"/>
25    </message>
26    <message name="requestOrderResponse">
27      <part element="tns:requestOrderResponse" name="parameters"/>
28    </message>
29    <message name="inputMessageValidationFault">
30      <part xmlns:ns1="http://www.example.com/faults"
31        element="ns1:inputMessageValidationFault"
32        name="inputMessageValidationFault"/>
33    </message>
34    <portType name="RequestOrderPort">
35      <operation name="requestOrder">
36        <input message="tns:requestOrder"/>
37        <output message="tns:requestOrderResponse"/>
38        <fault message="tns:inputMessageValidationFault"
39          name="inputMessageValidationFault"/>
40      </operation>
41    </portType>
42    <binding type="tns:RequestOrderPort" name="RequestOrderPortBinding">
43      <soap:binding style="document"
44        transport="http://schemas.xmlsoap.org/soap/http"/>
45      <operation name="requestOrder">
46        <soap:operation soapAction=""/>
47        <input>
48          <soap:body use="literal"/>
49        </input>
50        <output>
51          <soap:body use="literal"/>
52        </output>
53        <fault name="inputMessageValidationFault">
54          <soap:fault use="literal" name="inputMessageValidationFault"/>
55        </fault>
56      </operation>
57    </binding>
58    <service name="RequestOrderService">
59      <port binding="tns:RequestOrderPortBinding" name="RequestOrderPort">
60        <soap:address location="http://localhost:8680/oms/requestOrder"/>
```

```
61     </port>
62   </service>
63 </definitions>
```

book-code/chap07/endpoint-endpoint/examples/originalwsdl.xml

The references to the corporate schema repositories[13] (e.g., `http://soa-book.com/example/oms/orders.xsd`) are missing and have been replaced by local references (e.g., `http://localhost:8680/oms/requestOrder?xsd=1`). The point I am making here is that, even if you provide a WSDL contract as meta-data to the `Endpoint`, you do not have a guarantee that it will be reproduced exactly.

7.8 Conclusions

This and the preceding chapter focused on the JAX-WS API and run-time behavior. Chapter 6 explored the client side uses of JAX-WS, and this chapter addressed the server side. My goal was to show you lots of examples so that you can experiment with them and modify them to create your own JAX-WS applications. You can read and reread this book, and even read the JAX-WS specification in depth, but you won't start to get an intuitive understanding for how JAX-WS works until you start writing your own code.

If you were familiar with JAX-RPC before reading this, you can probably see that JAX-WS is a big improvement. The JAXB framework is much more flexible than the old JAX-RPC Java/XML binding. Plus, it is great to have a single XML binding technology for all of Java. Now, you can write classes, using the JAXB (and JAX-WS) annotations, with deployment as Web services in mind. And there is no longer any need for the complex and confusing JAX-RPC type mapping deployment descriptor that was previously required.

Another big improvement is the `Provider<T>` interface for creating and deploying Web services that work directly with XML. As you might remember, in JAX-RPC to create something similar, you had to generate a SEI from a generic WSDL interface using the `<xs:any/>` element and then build the service implementation around that SEI.

---

13. Schema repositories are discussed in Chapter 4.

But the biggest improvement, in my mind, is the introduction of annotations to simplify the writing and deployment of services. In the preceding chapter and this one, I used annotations in the examples, and explained them as necessary, but didn't really discuss them in depth or push the limits of how they can be used. Related to annotations is the improvement in deployment descriptors. It is now possible, in many cases, to deploy a JAX-WS service implementation bean, as a servlet or an EJB endpoint, without any deployment descriptors.

In the next chapter, I discuss annotations and deployment in depth. The focus is on the two specifications that define most of the annotations and deployment methods: WS-Metadata [JSR 181] and WSEE [JSR 109].

CHAPTER 8

Packaging and Deployment of SOA Components (JSR-181 and JSR-109)

This chapter describes the nuts and bolts of packaging and deploying SOA applications with Java Web Services (JWS). The two specifications that provide most of the detail regarding packaging and deployment are Web Services Metadata for the Java Platform (WS-Metadata) [JSR 181] and Implementing Enterprise Web Services (WSEE) [JSR 109].

WS-Metadata defines a set of standard annotations programmers use to configure how the container will deploy a Java class as a Web service. During deployment, the JWS container interprets those annotations to generate artifacts and configure itself to deploy the specified Web service. For example, the container may construct a WSDL representation of a Web service based on the WS-Metadata annotations.

Java EE 5, through WS-Metadata, defines a much simpler programming model for the development and deployment of Web Services than J2EE.[1] J2EE requires the developer to use configuration files, particularly the `webservices.xml` file, to provide much of the information about how to configure a Java class as a Web service. In contrast, WS-Metadata uses annotations to declaratively specify the Web services a Java class provides and the `webservices.xml` file is no longer required. This simplifies the developer's life considerably, but it does create the same problems you always have when you use annotations—namely, that by encoding the definition of the Web service inside the Java class definition itself, if you want to deploy the same class, with different Web service representations, in different contexts, you need to override those annotations with deployment

---

1. J2EE means versions 1.4 and earlier of the J2EE specification.

descriptors.[2] For example, you are still free to use the `webservices.xml` file as, even though its use is optional, it continues to be supported. Section 7.4.2 of [JSR 181] defines the mapping of annotations to the `webservices.xml` file. If you choose to use both `webservices.xml` and annotations, the `webservices.xml` configuration information overrides the annotations. The JAX-RPC mapping file, required when using JAX-RPC in J2EE environments, is no longer needed since JAX-WS uses JAXB for all its data binding requirements.

WSEE defines a service architecture to ensure portability of Web Services applications across Java EE application server implementations. It defines requirements for each major integration point for Web services in Java EE, including client, server, and deployment models. WSDL bindings and security are also addressed. Whereas WS-Metadata specifies how to describe the Web service to be deployed from a Java class, WSEE clarifies how annotations must be used, and how the Java class and other artifacts must be packaged, to ensure proper deployment to any Java EE implementation. For this reason, WSEE is often referred to as the "portability specification"—compliance ensures that Web services are portable. It defines the types of objects that can be deployed as Web services, how to package those objects, and what annotations and/or deployment descriptors are required for deployment. For example, WSEE tells us that a Web service can be deployed either as a servlet endpoint or as an EJB endpoint.[3] WSEE describes the requirements for packaging either type of endpoint, and what deployment descriptors are necessary (if any). WSEE version 1.1 is included in J2EE, but has been extensively modified to work with WS-Metadata and JAX-WS in version 1.2. In this chapter, I use WSEE to refer to WSEE version 1.2.

To summarize the roles of these specifications, WS-Metadata simplifies the development and deployment of Web services through the use of annotations, and WSEE defines the proper use and packaging of WS-Metadata annotated classes. For many common deployment scenarios, no deployment descriptors are required. However, there are situations where you will want to use deployment descriptors, so it pays to understand how they

---

2. Only the WS-Metadata annotations can be overridden by deployment descriptors. The JAXB annotations, for example, that determine the XML Schema definitions in the deployed endpoint's WSDL, cannot be overridden.

3. Although stateless session beans are the only type of EJB that can be deployed as a Web service, in this book I follow common industry practice and refer to this as an EJB endpoint. Throughout this book, wherever you see EJB used to refer to a Web service implementation, I am writing specifically about the stateless session bean variety of EJB component. So, an EJB endpoint is always implemented using a stateless session bean.

work. In addition, it is important to realize that even though, as a developer, you may not have to deal much with deployment descriptors in JWS, your container is probably generating them (based on the annotations) and using them behind the scenes. So, understanding how annotations and deployment descriptors interact is important to understanding the behavior of Web Services deployment in general.

In the following sections, I provide examples that illustrate various types of deployment (e.g., servlet endpoint, EJB endpoint, with descriptors, without descriptors) and how the WS-Metadata annotations influence the behavior and WSDL contract definition of the Web service. But before diving into those details, I provide an overview of the JWS deployment process.

8.1 Web Services Packaging and Deployment Overview

WSEE defines the concept of a *port component* to refer to the component that gets packaged and deployed to the container to implement a Web service. A port component is an addition to the Java EE platform defined by WSEE and should be thought of in the same manner as other deployable components such as servlets and JSPs (Web container) or EJBs (EJB container). Like those other components, a port component depends on the functionality provided by the Web and EJB containers. WSEE does not specify how a Java EE container should implement port components. However, it is sensible for implementors to rely heavily on servlets, because that approach leverages the investment they have already made in developing servlet technology. The use of servlets for deployment in the GlassFish implementation is discussed in detail in Sections 8.1.1 and 8.1.2.

A port component defines the programming model artifacts that make up a portable Web service application. These components are defined in detail by the WSEE specification. A port component must include a *service implementation bean*. A service implementation bean (SIB) is a Java class that contains the business logic of a JAX-WS Web service. The SIB may also be a wrapper that invokes other classes containing the business logic. Either way, it is annotated with `@WebService` or `@WebServiceProvider` and its methods can be exposed as Web service operations. The service implementation bean is fully defined in the WS-Metadata specification. A SIB is the only required artifact in a port component.

However, a port component may also include a *service endpoint interface* (SEI), a WSDL document, *security role references*, and a Web Services deployment descriptor. a SEI is a Java interface that is mapped to a `wsdl:portType` according to the JAX-WS WSDL/Java Mapping.[4] When you include a SEI in a port component, the container uses that SEI (including its annotations) to generate the WSDL representation of the resulting Web service. If no SEI is present, the container generates the WSDL representation directly from the SIB.

A WSDL document can also be provided as part of the port component. In this case, the container does not generate WSDL, but rather uses the document supplied. When a WSDL is supplied, the endpoint address specified in the WSDL may be modified by the container to be consistent with the endpoint address where the resulting Web service is deployed. For example, the `soap:address` in the provided WSDL may be changed in the deployed WSDL to reflect the context root and path of the deployment.

Security role references are logical role names declared by the port component using the deployment descriptors for the Web or EJB component. Examples of how these descriptors are used for this purpose are discussed in Section 8.5.

The Web services deployment descriptor (`webservices.xml`) was required by JAX-RPC 1.1. It is no longer required, as the information it contains can be specified with annotations. However, you may want to use a `webservices.xml` descriptor if you need to deploy legacy classes that are not annotated or that override the value of some annotations.

Other deployment artifacts that may be used include `web.xml` (for deploying a servlet endpoint), `ejb-jar.xml` (for deploying an EJB endpoint), and implementation-specific descriptors (e.g., GlassFish's `sun-ejb-jar.xml` for specifying the context root of the endpoint URL for EJB deployment).

Per WSEE, port components may be packaged in a WAR file or EJB JAR file. Port components packaged in a WAR file are referred to in WSEE as *JAX-WS Service Endpoints*. These are simply service implementation beans that do not have the `@Stateless` annotation. "JAX-WS Service Endpoint" is a confusing term because it sounds a lot like "JAX-WS service endpoint interface (SEI)." In fact, a SEI can be implemented by either a JAX-WS Service Endpoint or a Stateless Session EJB in an EJB container.

Port components packaged in an EJB-JAR file must use a stateless session bean for the service implementation bean and be annotated `@Stateless`. Packaging is specified in Section 5.4 of [JSR 109]. I have always found packaging to be confusing, especially to programmers who

---

4. For a detailed discussion of the service endpoint interface, see Chapter 6, Section 6.1.

do not have a lot of experience writing and deploying EJBs. So, in the next two subsections, I provide a detailed explanation of how to package a Web service for deployment as either a WAR or an EJB-JAR.

8.1.1 Packaging a Servlet Endpoint Using a WAR

When you package a SIB for deployment as a servlet endpoint, your WAR is structured as shown in Figure 8–1. Each component of the package is numbered in this diagram and discussed.

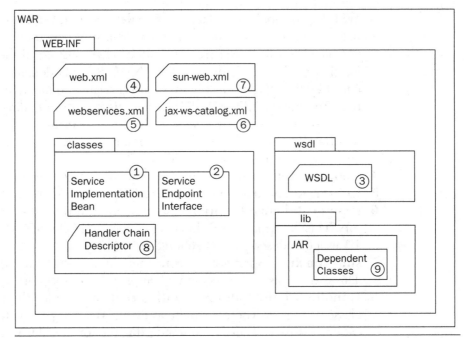

Figure 8–1 Servlet endpoint packaging.

1. **Service Implementation Bean [required]** is contained in the `WEB-INF/classes/<package-path>/`, where `<package-path>` is determined by the class's package name. This location is not mandatory, but customary. Alternatively, the SIB could be contained in a JAR under the `WEB-INF/lib` or even in an extension JAR installed in the Web container and referenced by the WAR's MANIFEST Class-Path. As long as the SIB is on the application classpath, the packaging will work. See Section 9.7 of Servlets 2.5 [JSR 154] for a complete description of

what locations are contained on the classpath of a WAR application. This class file must be annotated with `@WebService` or `@WebService-Provider`. Its methods contain the business logic that implements the Web service operations.

2. **Service endpoint interface [optional]** is contained in the `WEB-INF/classes/<package-path>/` where `<package-path>` is determined by the class's package name. This location is customary, but not mandatory. The SEI class file may be located anywhere on the application classpath (see classpath description in item 1). When used, the SIB's `@WebService.endpointInterface` attribute's value must equal the complete name of this SEI.

3. **WSDL [optional]** is contained in the `WEB-INF/wsdl` directory. This is not a mandatory location, but is customary. When used, the SIB's `@WebService.wsdlLocation` attribute's value must equal the relative location of this file.[5] Any files (e.g., XML Schema definitions) referenced by the WSDL must be referenced relative to the WSDL's location. For example, if the WSDL is in the `META-INF/wsdl` directory and it references a schema as `myschema.xsd`, then `myschema.xsd` should be in `META-INF/wsdl`. If the schema is referenced as `../myschema.xsd`, `myschema.xsd` should be in META-INF.

4. **web.xml [optional]** is contained in the `WEB-INF/` directory.

5. **webservices.xml [optional]** is contained in the `WEB-INF/` directory.

6. **jax-ws-catalog.xml [optional]** is contained in the `WEB-INF/` directory. This descriptor is used in connection with OASIS XML Catalog 1.1 usage as described in Section 8.6.

7. **sun-web.xml [optional]** is contained in the `WEB-INF/` directory. This is the GlassFish-specific Web application descriptor.

8. **Handler Chain File [optional]** is contained under the `WEB-INF/` classes directory where it will be available as a resource on the application classpath. There is no standard name for this file. This is not a mandatory location—it may also be specified as an external URL. Specifically, when used, the SIB's `@HandlerChain.file` attribute's value must equal either:
   - An absolute `java.net.URL` in external form (e.g., http://myhandlers.foo.com/handlerfile1.xml)
   - A relative path from the source file or class file (e.g., bar/handlerfile1.xml) specifying the location of this file

---

5. The `wsdlLocation` can also be an absolute URL, but for the WAR packaging shown here, you would use the relative path within the WAR.

9. **Dependent Classes [optional]** are bundled in a JAR and contained under the `WEB-INF/lib` directory where they are available on the application classpath. These are any classes the SIB or SEI depend on. This is not a mandatory location, but one possible approach when the SIB depends on a library of classes that may already be packaged in a JAR. The dependent classes may be located anywhere on the application classpath (see classpath description in item 1).

Most Java container implementations provide development tools that include packaging utilities to create and package a servlet endpoint WAR, as described earlier. However, you do not need to use such tools to create the WAR file if you do not want to. In fact, if you want WAR generation code that is portable across platforms, you may want to avoid vendor-specific utilities for packaging. That is because vendor-specific tools may include vendor-specific deployment descriptors or add vendor-specific features within the packaging. Many tools do not have such side effects, but some do. So, make sure you understand how your vendor's packaging tool works.

As an alternative, deployment packaging can be done in a portable manner using third-party, open source tools, such as Apache Ant or Apache Maven. In this book, all the packaging is done with Ant and Maven.

8.1.2 Packaging an EJB Endpoint Using an EJB-JAR

When you package a SIB for deployment as a stateless session bean endpoint, your EJB-JAR may be structured as shown in Figure 8–2. Each component of the package is numbered in this diagram and discussed.

1. **Service implementation bean [required]** is contained in the `<package-path>/` directory where `<package-path>` is determined by the class's package name. This location is not mandatory, but customary. Alternatively, the SIB could be contained in another JAR (e.g., bundled within an EAR with this same EJB-JAR) and referenced by the EJB-JAR's manifest file `Class-Path` attribute. You could even have the SIB located in an installed library and referenced by the EJB-JAR's manifest file `Extension-List` attribute. As long as the SIB is on the application classpath, the packaging will work. See Section EE.8.2 of the Java EE 5 specification [JSR 244] for a complete description of what locations are contained on the classpath of a portable application. This class file must be annotated with `@Stateless`, and `@WebService` or `@WebServiceProvider`. Its methods contain the business logic that implements the Web service operations.

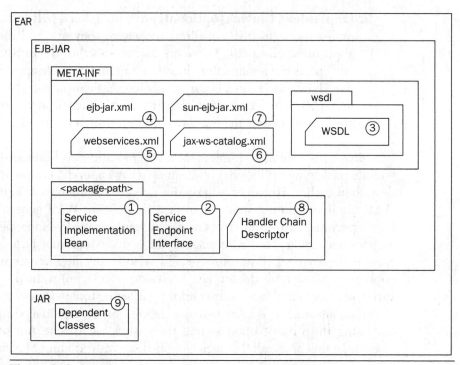

Figure 8–2 Stateless session bean endpoint packaging.

2. **Service endpoint interface [optional]** is contained in the `<pack-age-path>/` where `<package-path>` is determined by the class's package name. This location is customary, but not mandatory. The SEI class file may be located anywhere on the application classpath (see classpath description in item 1). When used, the SIB's `@WebService.endpointInterface` attribute's value must equal the complete name of this SEI.

3. **WSDL [optional]** is contained in the `META-INF/wsdl` directory. See the WSDL description in Section 8.1.1—WAR and EJB-JAR usage is the same.

4. `ejb-jar.xml` **[optional]** is contained in the `META-INF/`directory.

5. `webservices.xml` **[optional]** is contained in the `META-INF/`directory.

6. `jax-ws-catalog.xml` **[optional]** is contained in the `META-INF/` directory. This descriptor is used in connection with OASIS XML Catalog 1.1 usage as described in Section 8.6.

7. `sun-ejb-jar.xml` **[optional]** is contained in the `META-INF/`directory. This is the GlassFish-specific EJB deployment descriptor.

8. **Handler Chain File [optional]** is contained under the `<package-path>`/directory (`<package-path>` is determined by the SIB class's package name) where it is available as a resource on the application classpath. See the Handler Chain File description in Section 8.1.1—WAR and EJB-JAR usage is the same.

9. **Dependent Classes [optional]** are contained in a separate JAR file at the root of the enclosing EAR where they will be available on the application classpath. These are any classes the SIB or SEI depends on. This is not a mandatory location. The dependent classes may be located anywhere on the application classpath (see classpath description in item 1).

8.1.3 Auto-Deployment

WS-Metadata envisions, but does not require, an auto-deployment mechanism that provides "drag and drop" functionality.[6] The specification suggests that this could be a special server-side directory monitored by the container. When a WS-Metadata annotated class file is copied to this directory, the container examines the annotations, builds the WSDL, and configures the run-time machinery required for dispatching.

GlassFish implements such an auto-deployment mechanism. I provide an illustrative example of how to use it in Section 8.4.

8.1.4 Overview of the Container's Deployment Processing

This section provides an overview of the process by which a JWS container deploys a Web service. To some extent, this description delves into implementation issues that are outside the scope of the JSR specifications. In addition to the JSR specifications (particularly Section 8 of [JSR 109]), it is based on my review of the GlassFish V1 source code and discussions with developers at Sun. As GlassFish evolves, some of these details will become outdated. However, the general principles described here are applicable to all JWS containers.

A JWS deployable module is anything the container can deploy as a Web service. As described in the previous paragraphs of Section 8.1, it can be a WAR module or an EJB-JAR module. In the case of auto-deployment, it can be a single annotated class file. A JWS container includes a deployment subsystem that is responsible for deployment. This subsystem may contain some components (e.g., a command-line deployment utility) that are outside of the actual container. Note that the

---

6. Section 2.4 of [JSR 181].

actual deployment may involve an EAR that contains multiple deployable modules. For simplicity, I just focus on what happens during deployment of a single module.

First, the deployment subsystem validates the contents of the deployable module (e.g., checking that EJB Web service endpoints are deployed in EJB-JARs and not WARs). It may collect some binding information from the deployer (e.g., a context root for a WAR deployment may be provided as a command-line option). The deployment subsystem then deploys the components and Web services defined in the deployable module, publishes the WSDL documents representing the deployed Web services, deploys any clients using Web services, configures the server, and starts the application.

The deployment tool starts the deployment process by identifying the Web services using the Web service meta-data annotations or `webservices.xml` deployment descriptor file contained within the module. Per WSEE, deployment of services occurs before resolution of service references. This is done to allow deployment to update the WSDL port addresses before the service references to them are processed. This is necessary since the port addresses may be determined by information (e.g., context root) supplied at deployment time.

The processing of annotations is critical for an understanding of deployment, so I'm going to focus a bit on exactly how that works inside the GlassFish[7] [GLASSFISH] implementation. In GlassFish V1, the deployment subsystem loads all deployment descriptors (if any), and then the annotations are processed[8] by an annotation framework. On seeing an `@WebService`, for example, the annotation framework calls `WebServiceHandler`, which processes the annotation. While processing the annotation, the framework checks whether a deployment descriptor entry is already available (e.g., from `webservices.xml`), and if so, the annotation values will not override the equivalent defined in the descriptor.[9] At the end of the annotation

---

7. The discussion that follows, relative to the GlassFish internals, is based on GlassFish Version 1, UR1 (https://glassfish.dev.java.net/downloads/v1_ur1-p01-b02.html), that is used in Sun's Java System Application Server Platform Edition 9.0 Update 1 Patch 1. Class names and other details discussed here are subject to change in future versions of GlassFish.

8. The GlassFish classes that process Web Services annotations at deployment time are found in appserv-commons/src/java/com/sun/enterprise/deployment/annotation/handlers. For example, the `WebServiceHandler` class processes the `@WebService` annotation.

9. Per Section 5.3 of [JSR-109], "A deployment descriptor may be used to override or enhance the information provided in the service implementation bean annotation."

processing phase, all the information has been gathered that is required to generate the WSDL and other portable artifacts (if not packaged).[10]

For servlet endpoint deployment, GlassFish generates a `web.xml`,[11] which directs the HTTP request containing the payload (SOAP/HTTP, or just XML in the case of a RESTful service deployed with the XML/HTTP binding) to an instance of the `JAXWSServlet` class—a wrapper servlet class that dispatches requests to endpoints. More specifically, when you deploy a WAR with a servlet endpoint:

1. The GlassFish container creates a `web.xml` to deploy an instance of `JAXWSServlet`. If your WAR contained a `web.xml`, the generated `web.xml` is built from your original `web.xml`, but the `servlet-class` is replaced with `JAXWSServlet`. In addition, the `webservices.xml` deployment descriptor is generated (if it doesn't already exist) and the `service-endpoint-interface` references the class being deployed that you specified in your `web.xml`'s `servlet-class`. Note that `webservices.xml` is not required by JAX-WS, but generated for internal use by GlassFish.

2. When the `JAXWSServlet` instance is deployed, and initialized, the following happens:

   ▪ An instance of the endpoint implementation class (`com.sun-.enterprise.webservice.monitoring.JAXWSEndpointImpl`) is created from the port component as defined by the deployment descriptors and annotations. The description of this port component is represented internally as an instance of `com.sun.enter-prise.deployment.WebServiceEndpoint`. This `JAXWSEndpointImpl` instance is what processes the `MessageContext` containing the SOAP request/response.

   ▪ The deployment subsystem registers the endpoint implementation with the JAX-WS runtime. The registry is an instance of `com.sun.enterprise.webservice.JAXWSRuntimeEpiRegistry`. The endpoint object that gets registered is an instance of `com-.sun.xml.ws.spi.runtime.RuntimeEndpointInfo`, and it includes (among other things) an instance of the application-defined class

---

10. GlassFish can generate, for example, a `web.xml` or `ejb-jar.xml`, as needed for deployment. This is not required by the JSR specifications, but it is a sensible approach and other implementations will probably work similarly.

11. You can see the generated `web.xml` and other deployment artifacts if you look in `$GLASSFISH_HOME/domains/domain1/generated/xml/j2ee-modules/WEB-INF` after you have deployed an endpoint.

implementing the endpoint (i.e., the one class annotated with @Web-Service or @WebServiceProvider), a WebServiceContext instance, an associated WSDL file (either packaged or generated from annotations), an instance of the protocol binding (i.e., javax.xml-.ws.Binding), and the handler chain.

Once the endpoint has been deployed in this manner, the JAXWSServ-let wrapper is registered with the servlet container and is listening for requests. When the JAXWSServlet instance receives a SOAP/HTTP or XML/HTTP message (as HTTPServletRequest), it does the following:

1. Creates the MessageContext (including a reference to the Servlet-Context).
2. Passes the HTTP request/response objects, along with the Run-timeEndpointInfo, to an instance of com.sun.xml.ws.spi.run-time.Tie—the entry point for the JAX-WS run-time system.
3. The JAX-WS runtime decodes the SOAP request, applying the JAX-WS and JAXB XML/Java bindings, to get the parameters that are used to invoke the endpoint implementation class.
4. Then, the flow is reversed and the returned object is serialized back out to the HTTP response.

The internal deployment mechanism of GlassFish for servlet endpoints starts with the artifacts provided in the WAR and then creates (or modifies) the internally used descriptors. Figure 8–3 illustrates this process for the internally generated web.xml, webservices.xml, and WSDL files. These internally generated files (e.g., web.xml) are generated in an application specific location within the directory tree rooted at $GLASSFISH_HOME/domains/domain1/generated/xml. When you deploy a WAR, you can look in that directory to see the files that have been generated.

To some extent, the reason for this internal descriptor generation process[12] is to map the JAX-WS/WS-Metadata deployment model to the preexisting J2EE (i.e., JAX-RPC) deployment model that requires a webservices.xml file. It is also required in order to generate a web.xml that deploys the wrapper

---

12. Also, as Vijay Ramachandran at Sun explained to me, GlassFish generates these internal descriptors at deployment time so that "GlassFish can seamlessly support earlier Sun App Server implementations, keep changes low, and most importantly, avoid the costly process of annotation processing at the time of server restart. Once deployment is over, everything is available in descriptors" [Ramachandran] and GlassFish doesn't need to process the annotations again.

servlet (`JAXWSServlet`) discussed earlier. In any event, this approach allows GlassFish to support the JAX-WS/WS-Metadata deployment approach, and the legacy J2EE (i.e., JAX-RPC) approach. It is also consistent with the guidelines provided in Section 8 of [JSR 109].

In Figure 8–3, the numbered items illustrate how the generated artifacts are created either from annotations or from the `web.xml` supplied with the WAR (if any).

1. The `servlet-name` of the generated `web.xml` comes from the name of the class being deployed. This is because it is associated with the `servlet-link` element in the generated `webservices.xml` (see item 6). Furthermore, if you package a `web.xml` with the SIB, its `servlet-name` must also match the name of the SIB class.

2. The `servlet-class` of the generated `web.xml` is the `com.sun.enterprise.webservice.JAXWSServlet` wrapper class—as discussed earlier.

3. The `url-pattern` is the simple name of the endpoint class + "Service" (i.e., the default value of the `@WebService.serviceName` attribute), unless it is overridden by the `servlet-pattern` in a `web.xml` you provide—as shown here, `/Hello`. (The context root is a parameter provided to the deployer or a proprietary deployment descriptor.)

4. The generated `wsdl:service` name is specified by the `@WebService.serviceName` attribute, and

5. this also provides the value for the generated `webservices.xml` `wsdl-service` element. If you provided a `webservices.xml` (which is optional), the `wsdl-service` element's value would override the annotation to determine the `wsdl:service` name. But in this case, the `webservice.xml` is generated, so they are the same.

6. The `servlet-link` in the generated `webservices.xml` comes from the name of the class being deployed,[13] which is the same as the generated `web.xml` `servlet-name`.

7. The generated `wsdl-port` in the `webservices.xml` comes from the `@WebService.name` attribute. In this case, that attribute is not specified, so the default value (i.e., class name plus "Port") is used.

8. This `wsdl-port` provides the `wsdl:port` value. So, if you had provided a `webservices.xml`, the value you gave for `wsdl-port` would override the `@WebService.name` annotation.

---

13. See Section 5.3.2.1 of [JSR 109].

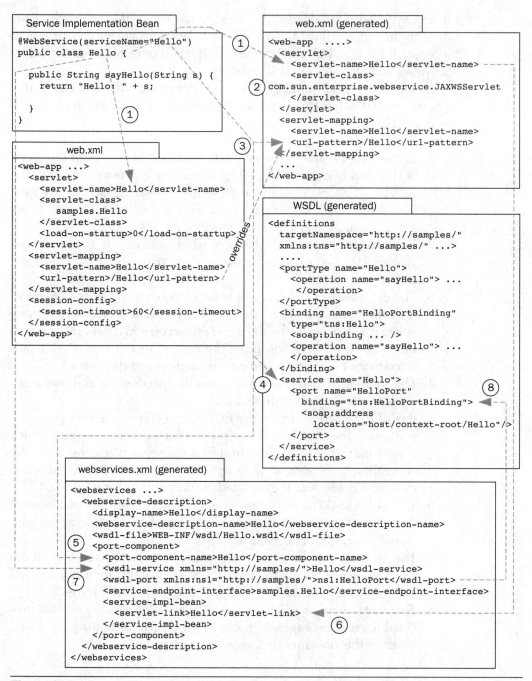

Figure 8–3 Internal descriptor generation for servlet endpoints.

WSEE [JSR 109] places an additional constraint on these mapping for the `@WebServiceProvider` case. It states that "For servlet based endpoints using this [`@WebServiceProvider`] annotation, the fully qualified name of the service implementation bean class must be used as the `<servlet-link>` element in the deployment descriptor to map the Port component to the actual servlet." As a consequence of this constraint, if you want to use a `web.xml` deployment descriptor with a `Provider<T>` implementation, the `<servlet-name>` must also equal the fully qualified name of the service implementation bean class. If you try to use another value for `<servlet-name>`, the results can be unpredictable. While this situation may seem like an arcane nuisance, I spent many hours pulling my hair out trying to debug such a service once, before realizing that the problem was with the `<servlet-name>`. It also means that you cannot deploy a `Provider<T>` implementation more than once (e.g., using different `url-patterns`). I mention it here in an effort to spare others from similar frustration.

8.1.5 EJB Endpoint Deployment and Dispatching

The deployment of stateless session bean (EJB) endpoints is similar, but has some differences, as discussed here. Like the servlet endpoint case, a wrapper servlet class—`EjbWebServiceServlet`[14]—is used to handle requests to services deployed as EJB endpoints. `EjbWebServiceServlet` uses an instance `EjbMessageDispatcher` to dispatch HTTP requests containing the payload (SOAP/HTTP, or just XML in the case of a RESTful service deployed with the XML/HTTP binding) requests to the appropriate endpoint.

At the time of deployment of an EJB-JAR, the Web service endpoint is registered. When the EJB Web service endpoint is registered, a listener (an instance of `EjbWebServiceRegistryListener`) registers the endpoint's path (i.e., the `endpoint-address-uri` from the generated deployment descriptor) as an ad hoc path with the Web container, along with the ad hoc servlet (i.e., `EjbWebServiceServlet`) responsible for servicing any requests on this path. An ad-hoc path is the `GlassFish` term for a servlet path that is mapped to a servlet not declared in the Web module's deployment descriptor.[15] GlassFish calls a Web module all of whose mappings are for ad hoc

---

14. The classes that handle the EJB endpoint's run-time behavior are found in the same place as the servlet endpoint classes: `appserv-core/src/java/com/sun/enterprise/webservice`.
15. The ad hoc registration of servlets is an internal GlassFish capability not prescribed by the Java EE 5 specifications.

paths an ad hoc web module. The `EjbWebServiceServlet` instance that receives SOAP or XML over HTTP on behalf of an EJB endpoint is deployed in an ad hoc Web module. As a result, you won't find a `web.xml` for this servlet or see it on the GlassFish Admin Console.

More specifically, when you deploy an EJB-JAR with an EJB endpoint, among other things, the following occur:

1. The GlassFish container creates the deployment descriptors necessary for deployment, including:

   - An `ejb-jar.xml` to deploy your service implementation bean (i.e., the class you have annotated with `@Stateless` and `@WebService`). If your EJB-JAR already contains an `ejb-jar.xml`, the generated `ejb-jar.xml` is built from your original `ejb-jar.xml` as a starting point. In the generated `ejb-jar.xml`, the `ejb-class` references your service implementation bean, and the `ejb-name` is the value specified by `@Stateless.name`.

   - A `webservices.xml` where the `service-endpoint-interface` references the service implementation bean unless the `@WebService.endpointInterface` annotation indicates a service endpoint interface. The `port-component-name` is the name of the Web service and it comes from the `@WebService.name` annotation (`wsdl:portType` for WSDL1.1). Note that `webservices.xml` is not required by JAX-WS, but is generated for internal use.

   - A `sun-ejb-jar.xml` (created from the one supplied with your EJB-JAR, if any). This is a GlassFish-specific descriptor. The `ejb-name` is the value specified by the `@Stateless.name`. The `endpoint-address-uri` specifies the endpoint path. You can change the default deployment path of an EJB endpoint by providing a `sun-ejb-jar.xml` with this information in your EJB-JAR. You can also configure security (see Section 8.5) using this deployment descriptor.

2. To handle security, an instance of `com.sun.enterprise.webservice.EjbContainerPreHandler` is created and inserted first in the handler chain for the endpoint.[16] This class performs the security authorization, prior to invoking any deployed handlers or the endpoint itself. This is a requirement specified by Section 9 of [JSR 109].

---

16. Once again, to emphasize the point made earlier about references to GlassFish classes, these class names and implementation details are GlassFish Version 1 UR1-specific. The details are subject to change in subsequent versions.

When the `EjbWebServiceServlet` instance receives a SOAP/HTTP or XML/HTTP message (as `HTTPServletRequest`), it does the following:

1. Looks up the endpoint descriptor (`EjbRuntimeEndpointInfo`) from the EJB endpoint registry (`WebServiceEjbEndpointRegistry`)
2. Performs authentication as described in JSR-109 Section 9
3. Passes the `HTTPServletRequest` and `HttpServletResponse`, along with the endpoint descriptor, to a dispatcher (`EjbMessageDispatcher`) for processing

The `EjbMessageDispatcher` processing is similar to the dispatching performed by `JAXWSServlet`, and includes the following steps:

1. Creates the `MessageContext` (without a reference to the `ServletContext`).
2. Passes the HTTP request/response objects, along with the `RuntimeEndpointInfo`, to an instance of `com.sun.xml.ws.spi.runtime.Tie`—the entry point for the JAX-WS run-time system.
3. The JAX-WS runtime decodes the SOAP request, applying the JAX-WS and JAXB XML/Java bindings, to get the parameters that are used to invoke the endpoint implementation class.
4. Then, the flow is reversed and the returned object is serialized back out to the HTTP response.

As with servlet endpoints, the internal deployment mechanism of Glass-Fish for EJB endpoints starts with the artifacts provided in the EJB-JAR and then creates (or modifies) the internally used descriptors. Figure 8–4 illustrates this process for the internally generated `ejb-jar.xml`, `webservices.xml`, and WSDL files. As in the servlet case, these internally generated files (e.g., `ejb-jar.xml`) are located within the directory tree rooted at `$GLASSFISH_HOME/domains/domain1/generated/xml`.

The numbered items in the figure illustrate how the various components of the generated artifacts are created from either annotations or the `sun-ejb-jar.xml` supplied with the EJB-JAR (if any).

1. The `ejb-name` of the generated `ejb-jar.xml` is taken from the `@Stateless.name`. If you are supplying a `sun-ejb-jar.xml` in order to specify the `endpoint-address-uri`, the `ejb-name` must match the `@Stateless.name`. Note also that the `ejb-link` of the generated `webservices.xml` is taken from this `@Stateless.name` value.

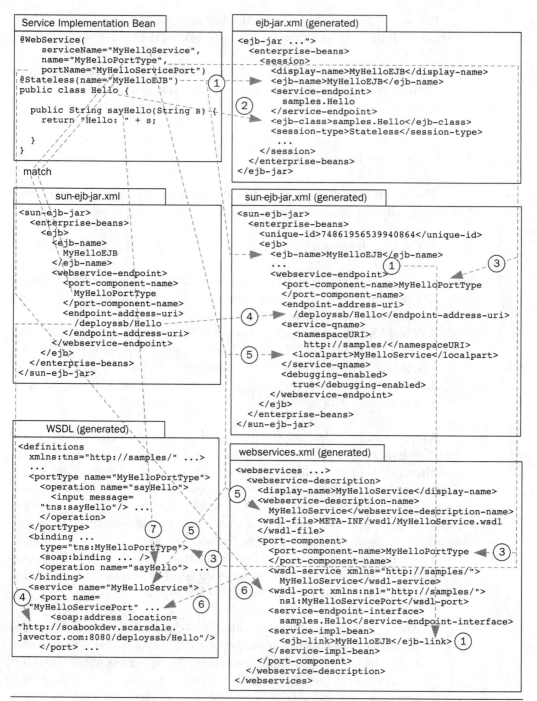

Figure 8–4 Internal descriptor generation for EJB endpoints.

2. The `ejb-class` of the generated `ejb-jar.xml` is the full name of the class annotated with `@WebService`.

3. The `@WebService.name` attribute's value becomes the `port-component-name` in the generated `sun-ejb-jar.xml`, and in the generated `webservices.xml`. Most important, however, it is the `wsdl:portType` name in the generated WSDL. Note that this value needs to match the `port-component-name` in the `sun-ejb-jar.xml` (if you supply one in order to specify the endpoint address).

4. As mentioned earlier, you can specify the endpoint address of your Web service by supplying a `sun-ejb-jar.xml` file with the `endpoint-address-uri` value set to the desired endpoint path. As you can see in this diagram, the WSDL `soap:address` location is taken from this value. If you do not supply an endpoint address, the default is composed from the `serviceName` / `portName`. As with anything related to the `sun-ejb-jar.xml` file, this behavior is GlassFish-specific, and other implementations may use different mechanisms for specifying the endpoint.

5. The `@WebService.serviceName` supplies the `wsdl:service` name for the generated WSDL file. It also corresponds to the `service-qname` in the generated `sun-ejb-jar.xml` and the `webservice-description-name` for the generated `webservices.xml`.

6. The `@WevService.portName` specifies the service port (`wsdl:port name` value) in the generated WSDL. It also corresponds to the `wsdl-port` in the generated `webservices.xml`.

7. The `operation name` in the generated WSDL corresponds to the method name in the `@WebService` annotated class.

That concludes a rather detailed overview of how deployment and descriptor generation works in the GlassFish implementation. If you got a little confused during that, don't worry about it. I provide these details for those readers who are curious about the internals of the deployment process. In the remaining sections of this chapter, I go through concrete examples that show how to deploy Web services in specific scenarios. If, after going through the examples, you are curious about how the internal implementation works, I suggest you come back and re-read this section. At that point, it will probably seem much less confusing.

8.2 Deployment without Deployment Descriptors

One of the great simplifications for Web Services in Java EE 5 is that you no longer need to use any deployment descriptors for a wide range of scenarios. In this section, I show examples of deploying a servlet endpoint without deployment descriptors using only a service implementation bean (SIB), using a service endpoint interface (SEI) with a SIB, and supplying your own WSDL (as when doing "Start from WSDL and Java" development of SOA integration services).

8.2.1 Using Only a Service Implementation Bean

The simplest possible deployment scenario is to use nothing but a SIB annotated with @WebService. Example 8–1 shows such a SIB.

Example 8–1 A SIB Deployed without Descriptors

```
23  @WebService
24  public class Hello {
25
26    public String sayHello(String s) {
27      return "Hello: " + s;
28    }
29
30  }
```

book-code/chap08/nodescriptor-sibonly/endpoint/src/main/java/samples/
    Hello.java

If you bundle this SIB in a WAR, without any descriptors (since the Servlet 2.5 specification, WARs do not require the web.xml descriptor), and deploy it, you get a Web service with the WSDL shown in Example 8–2. As you will notice, the key parameters in this WSDL are populated with the default values as follows:

- The wsdl:portType name (Hello) comes from the simple name of the SIB. This is the default value of @WebService.name.
- The wsdl:serviceName (HelloService) comes from the simple name of the SIB + "Service." This is the default value of @WebService.serviceName.

- The `wsdl:port` name (`HelloPort`) comes from the simple name of the SIB + "Port." This is the default value of `@WebService.portName`.
- The `soap:address location` (`http://soabookdev.scarsdale.ja-vector.com:8080/nodescriptor-sibonly-endpoint/HelloService`) is constructed from the name of the WAR file deployed (in this case, `nodescriptor-sibonly-endpoint.war`), plus the `wsdl:serviceName`. This default is not prescribed by WS-Metadata or WSEE, but rather is a GlassFish default. The form of the hostname used (in this case, `soabookdev.scarsdale.javector.com`) is also determined by GlassFish.[17]

Example 8–2 The WSDL Generated from a SIB without Deployment Descriptors

```
21   <portType name="Hello">
22     <operation name="sayHello">
23       <input message="tns:sayHello"/>
24       <output message="tns:sayHelloResponse"/>
25     </operation>
26   </portType>
27   <binding name="HelloPortBinding" type="tns:Hello">
28     <soap:binding transport="http://schemas.xmlsoap.org/soap/http"
29       style="document"/>
30     <operation name="sayHello">
31       <soap:operation soapAction=""/>
32       <input>
33         <soap:body use="literal"/>
34       </input>
35       <output>
36         <soap:body use="literal"/>
37       </output>
38     </operation>
39   </binding>
40   <service name="HelloService">
41     <port name="HelloPort" binding="tns:HelloPortBinding">
42       <soap:address
43         location="http://soabookdev.scarsdale.javector.com:8080/nodescriptor-
     sibonly-endpoint/HelloService"
```

---

17. At the time of this writing, there is no way in GlassFish to use a different hostname representation (e.g., `localhost`). But it is expected that such a capability will be provided in the near future.

```
44        xmlns:wsdl="http://schemas.xmlsoap.org/wsdl/"/>
45     </port>
46   </service>
```

book-code/chap08/nodescriptor-sibonly/examples/generated.wsdl

To run the sample code in this section, do the following:

1. Start GlassFish (if it is not already running).
2. Go to <book-code>/chap08/nodescriptor-sibonly.
3. Enter mvn install.[18]

8.2.2 Using a Service Endpoint Interface

You can modify the preceding example to use a SEI with the SIB. This approach is useful, for example, when you have a predefined Java interface you would like the Web service to implement, regardless of the other purposes the SIB is used for, or whether the SIB is deployed as an EJB or servlet endpoint. In this example, I implement the deployment as an EJB endpoint. You will notice that the SIB contains extra methods that are not deployed as Web service operations. Only the method defined on the SEI is deployed.

Example 8–3 shows a SIB that references a SEI using the @WebService.endpointInterface attribute. Notice that this SIB has two methods: sayHello and sayGoodbye.

Example 8–3 A SIB Using a SEI and Deployed without Descriptors

```
24   @WebService(endpointInterface="samples.HelloInf")
25   @Stateless
26   public class Hello {
27
28     public String sayHello(String s) {
29       return "Hello: " + s;
30     }
31
32     public String sayGoodbye(String s) {
```

18. This will build and deploy the service, run a client to invoke it, and undeploy the service when the client finishes running. The client that tests the endpoint is run as a JUnit test case.

```
33      return "Goodbye: " + s;
34   }
35
36 }
```

book-code/chap08/nodescriptor-sei/modules/endpoint/src/java/samples
/Hello.java

Example 8–4 shows the SEI that is referenced by the SIB shown in
Example 8–3. As you can see, the SEI also needs to be annotated with
@WebService. You can also see that this SEI implements only one
method—sayHello. This method is the only one from the corresponding
SIB that gets deployed as an operation on the resulting Web service.

Example 8–4 The Service Endpoint Interface (SEI)

```
24  @WebService
25  public interface HelloInf {
26
27    public String sayHello(String s);
28
29  }
```

book-code/chap08/nodescriptor-sei/modules/endpoint/src/java/samples
/HelloInf.java

If you bundle this SIB and SEI together in a WAR, without any descriptors, and deploy it, you get a Web service with the WSDL shown in Example 8–5. As you will notice, the key parameters in this WSDL are populated
with the default values as follows:

■ The wsdl:portType name (HelloInf) comes from the simple name
of the SEI. This is the default value of @WebService.name applied to
the SEI class, as opposed to the SIB. When a SEI is used, its annotations and their default values define the Web service, rather than the
annotations on the SIB. The exceptions to this are the @WebService
attributes serviceName and portName. Because these attributes are
not allowed on interfaces (per WS-Metadata), their values always
come from the SIB.

- The `wsdl:serviceName` (`HelloService`) comes from the simple name of the SIB + "Service." This is the default value of `@WebService.serviceName`.

- The `wsdl:port` name (`HelloPort`) comes from the simple name of the SIB + "Port." This is the default value of `@WebService.portName`.

- The `soap:address` location (`http://soabookdev.scarsdale.javector.com:8080/HelloService/Hello`) is constructed from the `serviceName` attribute value (in this case, the default `HelloService`), plus the simple name of the SIB Java class. This default is not prescribed by WS-Metadata or WSEE, but rather is a GlassFish default. Notice that it is different from the behavior described in Section 8.2.1. That is because in this example I am using an EJB-JAR to deploy the service as an EJB endpoint. In the previous example, I used a WAR to deploy the Web service as a servlet endpoint. GlassFish generates endpoint URLs differently for these two types of deployment.

Example 8–5 WSDL Generated from SIB and SEI without Deployment Descriptors

```
21    <portType name="HelloInf">
22      <operation name="sayHello">
23        <input message="tns:sayHello"/>
24        <output message="tns:sayHelloResponse"/>
25      </operation>
26    </portType>
27    <binding name="HelloPortBinding" type="tns:HelloInf">
28      <soap:binding transport="http://schemas.xmlsoap.org/soap/http"
29        style="document"/>
30      <operation name="sayHello">
31        <soap:operation soapAction=""/>
32        <input>
33          <soap:body use="literal"/>
34        </input>
35        <output>
36          <soap:body use="literal"/>
37        </output>
38      </operation>
39    </binding>
40    <service name="HelloService">
41      <port name="HelloPort" binding="tns:HelloPortBinding">
42        <soap:address
43        location="http://soabookdev.scarsdale.javector.com:8080/HelloService/
  Hello"
```

```
44                  xmlns:wsdl="http://schemas.xmlsoap.org/wsdl/"/>
45        </port>
46      </service>
```

book-code/chap08/nodescriptor-sei/examples/generated.wsdl

To run the sample code in this section, do the following:

1. Start GlassFish (if it is not already running).
2. Go to <book-code>/chap08/nodescriptor-sei.
3. Enter mvn install.

8.2.3 Including a WSDL Artifact

You can also bundle a WSDL file with your WAR or EJB-JAR, rather than have the container generate the WSDL description of the Web service for you. This can be done even when no deployment descriptors are used. In this section, I show an example of including a WSDL artifact in a WAR with a SIB only (no SEI is used).

Example 8–6 shows how to specify the use of a bundled WSDL file using the @WebService.wsdlLocation attribute. Notice that the location of the WSDL within the WAR package is WEB-INF/wsdl as discussed in Section 8.1.1.

Example 8–6 A SIB Deployed without Descriptors and Specifying a User-Defined WSDL

```
24   @WebService(wsdlLocation="WEB-INF/wsdl/hello.wsdl")
25   public class Hello {
26     @WebResult(targetNamespace="http://samples/")
27     public String sayHello(
28       @WebParam(targetNamespace="http://samples/") String arg0) {
29         return "Hello: " + arg0;
30       }
31   }
```

book-code/chap08/nodescriptor-wsdl/modules/endpoint/src/java/samples
  /Hello.java

The `hello.wsdl` file, specified by the `wsdlLocation` attribute, is shown in Example 8–7. This is pretty much the same as the WSDL generated previously (see Example 8–2), except for a couple of differences:

- The `<types>` section includes element definitions for the wrapper types required by this document/literal wrapped style WSDL. In the generated WSDL from Example 8–2, these element definitions do not appear because they are imported from a separate schema. In my opinion, that is a drawback of the generated WSDL—it causes it to be much less readable.
- The `soap:address location` attribute has the value "TBD" (to be determined). There is no need to specify a URL at this point, because it will be changed depending on how the Web service is deployed. In fact, as discussed in Example 8–8, when you query the Web service for its WSDL, this `soap:address location` gets replaced with a value created at deployment time.

Example 8–7 The WSDL Artifact Bundled in the WAR

```
8  <types>
9    <xs:schema elementFormDefault="qualified" targetNamespace="http://samples/">
10     <xs:element name="sayHello">
11       <xs:complexType>
12         <xs:sequence>
13           <xs:element name="arg0" type="xs:string" minOccurs="0"/>
14         </xs:sequence>
15       </xs:complexType>
16     </xs:element>
17     <xs:element name="sayHelloResponse">
18       <xs:complexType>
19         <xs:sequence>
20           <xs:element name="return" type="xs:string" minOccurs="0"/>
21         </xs:sequence>
22       </xs:complexType>
23     </xs:element>
24   </xs:schema>
25 </types>
26 <message name="sayHello">
27   <part name="parameters" element="tns:sayHello"/>
28 </message>
29 <message name="sayHelloResponse">
30   <part name="parameters" element="tns:sayHelloResponse"/>
```

```
31  </message>
32  <portType name="Hello">
33    <operation name="sayHello">
34      <input message="tns:sayHello"/>
35      <output message="tns:sayHelloResponse"/>
36    </operation>
37  </portType>
38  <binding name="HelloPortBinding" type="tns:Hello">
39    <soap:binding transport="http://schemas.xmlsoap.org/soap/http"
40      style="document"/>
41    <operation name="sayHello">
42      <soap:operation soapAction=""/>
43      <input>
44        <soap:body use="literal"/>
45      </input>
46      <output>
47        <soap:body use="literal"/>
48      </output>
49    </operation>
50  </binding>
51  <service name="HelloService">
52    <port name="HelloPort" binding="tns:HelloPortBinding">
53      <soap:address location="TBD"/>
54    </port>
55  </service>
```

book-code/chap08/nodescriptor-wsdl/modules/endpoint/src/webapp/WEB-INF/wsdl/
  hello.wsdl

When you bundle this SIB in a WAR, without any descriptors, and deploy it, you get a Web service with the WSDL shown in Example 8–7, except that the soap:address location gets changed as illustrated in Example 8–8. The new value, http://soabookdev.scarsdale.javector.com:8080/nodescriptor-wsdl-endpoint/HelloService, is the actual deployment URL, and its form is determined by the GlassFish defaults discussed in Section 8.2.1.

Example 8–8 The WSDL Generated from a SIB without Deployment Descriptors

```
51  <service name="HelloService">
52    <port name="HelloPort" binding="tns:HelloPortBinding">
```

```
53      <soap:address
54        location="http://soabookdev.scarsdale.javector.com:8080/nodescriptor-
   wsdl-endpoint/HelloService"
55        xmlns:wsdl="http://schemas.xmlsoap.org/wsdl/"/>
56    </port>
57  </service>
```

book-code/chap08/nodescriptor-wsdl/examples/generated.wsdl

When you package a WSDL in the module as described here, it is important to ensure that the annotation values for the `serviceName` and `portName` match those in the WSDL. If not, run-time errors will occur because of the mismatch.

To run the sample code in this section, do the following:

1. Start GlassFish (if it is not already running).
2. Go to `<book-code>/chap08/nodescriptor-wsdl`.
3. Enter `mvn install`.

8.3 Using Deployment Descriptors

As shown in the preceding section, Java EE 5 Web Services are a big improvement over J2EE in terms of ease of deployment and packaging. As illustrated, in many cases, no deployment descriptors are required. There are still situations, however, where you will want to use deployment descriptors. In this section, I provide examples for a number of these scenarios. Some of the use cases for deployment descriptors illustrated here include:

- Customizing the endpoint URL where a service gets deployed
- Passing deployment-specific environment information to the SIB or its handlers
- Overriding the value of an annotation

8.3.1 web.xml for Servlet Endpoints

This section focuses on how to use the `web.xml` file to customize the endpoint URL for a servlet-based Web service, and pass deployment-specific environment information to the SIB. The use of the `web.xml` descriptor for deploying

JAX-WS endpoints is described in the SRV.14.4.2 of [JSR 154] Java™ servlet 2.5 and further elaborated on in Section 5.3 of WSEE [JSR 109].

The most interesting deviation from its use for deploying servlets is that, when used for Web Services deployment, the `servlet-class` element references the SIB rather than a servlet class. As described in Section 8.1.4, inside GlassFish, this usage gets translated into a more traditional looking `web.xml` that is used internally when deployment occurs.

Section 8.1 of WSEE [JSR 109] provides an illustrative process of deployment that is not required, but is by and large followed by the Glass-Fish implementation and others. In Section 8.1, it states that "The WSDL port address for the Port component is the combination of the web app `context-root` and `url-pattern` of the servlet-mapping." In Example 8–9, you can see how I've used the `web.xml` in this example to specify a `url-pattern` of `/my-pattern`. Per WSEE, "no more than one servlet-mapping may be specified for a servlet that is linked to by a port-component. The url-pattern of the servlet-mapping must be an exact match pattern (i.e., it must not contain an asterisk ("*"))."

Example 8–9 Using `web.xml` to Specify a URL Pattern

```
4  <web-app xmlns="http://java.sun.com/xml/ns/javaee"
5    xmlns:j2ee="http://java.sun.com/xml/ns/javaee"
6    xmlns:xsi="http://www.w3.org/2001/XMLSchema-instance" version="2.5"
7    xsi:schemaLocation="http://java.sun.com/xml/ns/javaee
8    http://java.sun.com/xml/ns/javaee/web-app_2_5.xsd">
9    <servlet>
10     <servlet-name>Hello</servlet-name>
11     <servlet-class>samples.Hello</servlet-class>
12     <load-on-startup>0</load-on-startup>
13   </servlet>
14   <servlet-mapping>
15     <servlet-name>Hello</servlet-name>
16     <url-pattern>/my-pattern</url-pattern>
17   </servlet-mapping>
18   <env-entry>
19     <env-entry-name>appendedString</env-entry-name>
20     <env-entry-type>java.lang.String</env-entry-type>
21     <env-entry-value>ZipZapZang!</env-entry-value>
22   </env-entry>
23 </web-app>
```

book-code/chap08/descriptor-webxml/modules/endpoint/src/webapp/WEB-INF/web.xml

You may have noticed that the `url-pattern` provided in the `web.xml` does not completely determine the endpoint URL. The `context-root` and `hostname/port` must also be specified. The various JSRs do not provide a common approach for specifying these parameters. One method, which is Glass-Fish-specific, for specifying the `context-root` is to use the `--context-root` option with the `asadmin deploy` command.

Example 8–10 shows an alternative approach for specifying the `context-root`. In this case, I have used the GlassFish specific `sun-web.xml` descriptor. This descriptor is discussed in more detail in Section 8.3.4.

Example 8–10 The GlassFish-Specific `sun-web.xml` Deployment Descriptor Lets You Specify the Context Root

```
5   <sun-web-app>
6     <context-root>my-context</context-root>
7   </sun-web-app>
```

book-code/chap08/descriptor-webxml/examples/sun-web.xml

Unfortunately, I do not have any examples of how to manipulate the hostname that gets used by GlassFish to generate the `soap:address location` in the WSDL published with the deployed Web service. There does not seem to be any mechanism, at the time of this writing, to control that parameter. In my case, running on Debian Linux, I have a number of names defined in my `/etc/hosts`, and GlassFish picks `soabookdev.scarsdale.javector.com`. Example 8–11 shows what the WSDL generated for this example looks like after using the previous techniques for specifying the `context-root` and `url-parameter`.

Example 8–11 The `soap:address location` Specifies the Endpoint Address

```
40    <service name="HelloService">
41      <port name="HelloPort" binding="tns:HelloPortBinding">
42        <soap:address
43          location="http://soabookdev.scarsdale.javector.com:8080/my-context/
   my-pattern"
44          xmlns:wsdl="http://schemas.xmlsoap.org/wsdl/"/>
45      </port>
46    </service>
```

book-code/chap08/descriptor-webxml/examples/generated.wsdl

Wrapping up this discussion of the URL endpoint, Example 8–12 shows how the client code in this example looks. As you can see, the endpoint URL, plus the `?wsdl` suffix, is used to retrieve the WSDL. In this case, I've substituted the hostname `localhost` (via the system variable `glassfish.host`) for `soabookdev.scarsdale.javector.com`—and this works fine since I'm running the client on the same machine for these tests.

Example 8–12 The Client Code Uses the `soap:address` `Location` with the Specified `context-root` and `url-pattern`

```
44   String hostVal = System.getProperty("glassfish.host");
45   String portVal = System.getProperty("glassfish.deploy.port");
46   URL wsdlURL =
47     new URL("http://"+hostVal+":"+portVal+"/chap08-descriptor-webxml-
     endpoint/my-pattern?wsdl");
48   printWSDL(wsdlURL);
49   QName serviceQName = new QName("http://samples/", "HelloService");
50   QName portQName = new QName("http://samples/", "HelloPort");
51   Service service = Service.create(wsdlURL, serviceQName);
52   Hello port = (Hello) service.getPort(portQName, Hello.class);
53   String result = port.sayHello("Java Programmer");
54   System.out.println(result);
```

book-code/chap08/descriptor-webxml/modules/client/src/test/java/samples/
  TestClient.java

In addition to using the `web.xml` to modify the endpoint URL for a Web service, you can use it to pass environment information to the handlers. As you may have noticed, in Example 8–9, the `web.xml` supplies `env-entry` information. As described in Section 6.2.3 of WSEE [JSR 109], "With JAX-WS, a Handler may access the `env-entrys` of the component it is associated with by using JNDI to lookup an appropriate subcontext of `java:comp/env`. It may also access these if they are injected using the `@Resource` annotation."

Example 8–13 shows the handler (`HelloHandler`) used in this example. The `@Resource` annotation indicates that the variable `injected-String` receives the value `ZipZapZang!` specified in the `web.xml` `env-entry` element.

Example 8–13 The Handler Accesses `env-entry` Information Using the `@Resource` Annotation

```
29  public class HelloHandler implements SOAPHandler<SOAPMessageContext> {
30
31    public static final String APPEND_STRING = "samples.HelloHandler.appendStrg";
32
33    @Resource(name="appendedString")
34    String injectedString = "undefined";
35
36    public boolean handleMessage(SOAPMessageContext context) {
37
38      if ( ((Boolean)context.get(MessageContext.MESSAGE_OUTBOUND_PROPERTY)).
39          booleanValue() ) return true;
40      try {
41        context.put(APPEND_STRING, injectedString);
42        context.setScope(APPEND_STRING, MessageContext.Scope.APPLICATION);
43        System.out.println("HelloHandler has appendedString = " +
   injectedString);
44        return true;
45      } catch (Exception e) {
46        e.printStackTrace();
47        throw new WebServiceException(e);
48      }
49
50    }
```

book-code/chap08/descriptor-webxml/modules/endpoint/src/java/samples
  /HelloHandler.java

All this handler does is take the injected value and store it the message context so that it can be used by the SIB that implements the Web service. This is just a toy example, of course, but you could imagine use cases where it would be helpful to have deployment-specific information available to the endpoint's business logic. For example, this might be a file path used for logging.

Although, not strictly speaking a deployment descriptor, by using a handler in this example, I've introduced another configuration file—the Handler Chain Configuration File shown in Example 8–14. Handler configuration is described in more detail in Chapter 7, Section 7.6.

Example 8–14 Handler Chain Configuration File

```
4   <handler-chains xmlns:jws="http://java.sun.com/xml/ns/javaee">
5     <handler-chain>
6       <handler>
7         <handler-class>samples.HelloHandler</handler-class>
8       </handler>
9     </handler-chain>
10  </handler-chains>
```

book-code/chap08/descriptor-webxml/modules/endpoint/src/webapp/WEB-INF/classes/
  samples/myhandler.xml

Lastly, Example 8–15, shows what the SIB (`Hello.java`) does with the env-entry information received in this manner. In this case, it simply appends it to the message that is being echoed back to the client.

Example 8–15 The Endpoint SIB Accesses `env-entry` Information Stored in the `Web-ServiceContext`

```
26  @HandlerChain(file="myhandler.xml")
27  @WebService
28  public class Hello {
29
30    @Resource
31    WebServiceContext context;
32
33    public String sayHello(String s) {
34      String appendString =
35        (String) context.getMessageContext().get(HelloHandler.APPEND_STRING);
36      return "Hello: " + s + "[appended by handler: " + appendString + "]";
37    }
38
39  }
```

book-code/chap08/descriptor-webxml/modules/endpoint/src/java/samples/Hello.java

To run the sample code in this section, do the following:

1. Start GlassFish (if it is not already running).

2. Go to `<book-code>/chap08/descriptor-webxml`.

3. Enter `mvn install`.

8.3.2 ejb-jar.xml for Stateless Session Bean Endpoints

In this section, I show how you can use the `ejb-jar.xml` file to customize the deployment of annotated EJB endpoints. EJB 3.0 allows for partial deployment descriptors to augment or override the behavior of source code annotations. The use of such partial deployment descriptors can be helpful for adapting an annotated EJB for deployment-specific circumstances without having to edit its source code and annotations, recompile, and redeploy.

In the example shown here, I show how the `env-entry` element can be used to provide deployment-specific data to the endpoint (in the same manner as via the `web.xml` discussed in the preceding section). I also show how the `service-ref` element can be used to override the contents of an `@Web-ServiceRef` annotation within the endpoint EJB.

Example 8–16 shows the EJB endpoint used in this discussion (`Hello.java`). As you can see, it is similar to the servlet endpoint discussed in the preceding section (see Example 8–15), but with some additional functionality added to demonstrate different features and the removal of the handlers.[19] First, notice the `port` variable annotated with `@WebServiceRef`. This is a reference to a Web service—so this `Hello` Web service endpoint is calling another Web service. Second, notice the `goodbye` variable annotated with `@EJB`. This is a reference to a remote view of another EJB. The `Hello` Web service invokes another EJB using this reference. Third, notice the variable `injectedString` annotated with `@Resource`. This is a basic example of dependency injection used to provide deployment-specific information to the endpoint.

Example 8–16 The `Hello` EJB Endpoint

```
29    @WebService
30    @Stateless
31    @TransactionAttribute(TransactionAttributeType.NOT_SUPPORTED)
32    public class Hello {
33
34      @WebServiceRef(value = MyWebService.class,
35        wsdlLocation="http://someplace/myService?wsdl")
```

---

19. The `@TransactionAttribute` is used here simply to prevent certain implementations of JAX-WS 2.1 from generating WSDL that contains transaction assertions.

```
36     MyWeb port;
37
38     @EJB
39     Goodbye goodbye;
40
41     @Resource(name="myString")
42     String injectedString = "undefined";
43
44     public String sayHello(String s) {
45        String webServiceString = port.saySomething(s);
46        String goodbyeString = goodbye.sayGoodbye(s);
47        return "Hello: " + s + "[injectedString: " + injectedString + "]" +
48        System.getProperty("line.separator") + webServiceString +
49        System.getProperty("line.separator") + goodbyeString;
50     }
51
52  }
```

book-code/chap08/descriptor-ejbjar/modules/endpoint/src/java/samples/Hello.java

Consider the `@WebServiceRef` annotation that injects a proxy instance of the port component interface `MyWeb` into the `port` variable. Further down in the code, that Web service is invoked using the method `port.saySomething()`—and a `String` is returned. In this manner, the `Hello` EJB endpoint depends on another Web service, and as indicated in the `@WebServiceRef` annotation, the WSDL for that service is found at `http://someplace/myService?wsdl`. But what happens if the WSDL address changes? Then this reference will be invalid and the `Hello` endpoint will be broken. Example 8–17 shows how you can use the `ejb-jar.xml` descriptor to deal with such a change in the WSDL address.

Notice the `service-ref` element at the bottom of Example 8–17. That element is used to override the `@WebServiceRef.wsdlLocation` attribute from the annotated code. You can see that the `service-ref-name` refers to `samples.Hello/port`—in other words, the port variable annotated by `@WebServiceRef`. Furthermore, the `wsdl-file` element provides a URL for the Web service's WSDL (`http://localhost:8080/myweb/MyWebService.wsdl`). Using this deployment descriptor, the port variable will be instantiated with a proxy constructed from the WSDL at the location specified by `wsdl-file`, rather than by the `@WebServiceRef.wsdlLocation` annotation. In this manner, you can see that the `ejb-jar.xml` descriptor can be used as a change management tool to compensate when the references provided by annotations become out of date.

Example 8–17 The `ejb-jar.xml` Deployed with the `Hello` EJB Endpoint

```
 4    <ejb-jar xmlns="http://java.sun.com/xml/ns/javaee"
 5      xmlns:xsi="http://www.w3.org/2001/XMLSchema-instance"
 6      metadata-complete="false" version="3.0"
 7      xsi:schemaLocation="http://java.sun.com/xml/ns/javaee
 8      http://java.sun.com/xml/ns/javaee/ejb-jar_3_0.xsd">
 9      <enterprise-beans>
10        <session>
11          <ejb-name>Hello</ejb-name>
12          <service-endpoint>samples.Hello</service-endpoint>
13          <ejb-class>samples.Hello</ejb-class>
14          <session-type>Stateless</session-type>
15          <env-entry>
16            <env-entry-name>myString</env-entry-name>
17            <env-entry-type>java.lang.String</env-entry-type>
18            <env-entry-value>ZipZapZang!</env-entry-value>
19          </env-entry>
20          <service-ref>
21            <service-ref-name>samples.Hello/port</service-ref-name>
22            <service-interface>samples.MyWebService</service-interface>
23            <wsdl-file>http://localhost:8080/chap08-descriptor-ejbjar-
mywebservice-nowebxml/MyWebService?wsdl</wsdl-file>
24          </service-ref>
25        </session>
26      </enterprise-beans>
27    </ejb-jar>
```

book-code/chap08/descriptor-ejbjar/modules/endpoint/src/ejb/META-INF/ejb-jar.xml

Next, consider the `@EJB` annotation on the `goodbye` variable in Example 8–16. I've included this example simply to show how a remote view of an EJB can easily be invoked inside a Web service endpoint. Example 8–18 shows the EJB (`GoodbyeEJB`) that is invoked by using the `goodbye` variable. This EJB is deployed without any descriptors—simply using the `@Stateless` annotation.

Example 8–18 The EJB Invoked from within the `Hello` Web Service

```
23  @Stateless
24  public class GoodbyeEJB implements Goodbye {
```

```
25
26    public String sayGoodbye(String s) {
27      return "Goodbye: " + s;
28    }
29
30  }
```

book-code/chap08/descriptor-ejbjar/modules/goodbyebean/src/java/samples
/GoodbyeEJB.java

To provide the remote view for `GoodbyeEJB`, the interface `Goodbye` is annotated with `@Remote`, as shown in Example 8–19. Again, no deployment descriptor is used for this interface.

Example 8–19 The Interface that Provides the Remote View

```
23  @Remote
24  public interface Goodbye {
25
26    public String sayGoodbye(String s);
27
28  }
```

book-code/chap08/descriptor-ejbjar/modules/goodbyebean/src/java/samples/
Goodbye.java

So, in this `@EJB` example, no deployment descriptor information is required to deploy the `GoodbyeEJB` bean, or to reference it. You can see in Example 8–17 that there is no `ejb-ref` specifying the EJB reference. With the annotations, it is not required. However, if you look at the `ejb-jar.xml` that is generated by GlassFish at deployment time,[20] you will see that such an `ejb-ref` element is created from the annotations. Example 8–20 shows a snippet from the GlassFish-generated (internal use) descriptor that contains the `ejb-ref` element related to the `@EJB` annotation in this example.

---

20. The generation of internally used deployment descriptors by GlassFish is discussed in Section 8.1.

Example 8–20 GlassFish Generates an `ejb-ref` Element for Internal Use

```
25        <ejb-ref>
26          <ejb-ref-name>samples.Hello/goodbye</ejb-ref-name>
27          <ejb-ref-type>Session</ejb-ref-type>
28          <remote>samples.Goodbye</remote>
29          <injection-target>
30            <injection-target-class>samples.Hello</injection-target-class>
31            <injection-target-name>goodbye</injection-target-name>
32          </injection-target>
33        </ejb-ref>
```

book-code/chap08/descriptor-ejbjar/examples/generated-ejb-jar.xml

The final point I discuss in this example related to the use of the `ejb-jar.xml` deployment descriptor concerns the `env-entry` element as a mechanism for providing deployment-specific data to the endpoint and its handlers (if any). The use of `env-entry` illustrated in Example 8–17 is similar to the `web.xml` case discussed in the previous section (see Example 8–9). However, in the `web.xml` case, I showed how to use `env-entry` to inject a value into a handler, and here, I am using it to inject a value directly into the endpoint.

In Example 8–17, the `env-entry-name` value of `myString` corresponds to the `@Resource.name` attribute in the endpoint code (Example 8–16). When the endpoint is instantiated, and before it is invoked, the Java EE container injects the value provided in the `ejb-jar.xml` `env-entry-value` element (i.e., `ZipZapZang!`) into the `injectedString` variable.

To run the sample code in this section, do the following:

1. Start GlassFish (if it is not already running).
2. Go to `<book-code>/chap08/descriptor-ejbjar`.
3. Enter `mvn install`.

When you run the example, you will see a listing of the WSDL generated for this endpoint, along with the results from invoking the Web service implemented at this endpoint. Notice that the return value from the Web service contains information obtained through all the mechanisms discussed in this section: the `@WebServiceRef` referenced service, the `@EJB` referenced bean, and the `@Resource` dependency injection.

8.3.3 When to Use webservices.xml

The webservices.xml deployment descriptor file was introduced by the first version of [JSR 109] to define the set of Web services that are to be deployed in a container. However, with JAX-WS, the use of webservices.xml is optional since the annotations can be used to specify most of the information specified in this deployment descriptor. When you are deploying JAX-WS Web Services, the only reason you should use webservices.xml is to override or augment the annotation member attributes—or when you do not want to use annotations because you don't want to modify the Java source code.

One situation, illustrated in this section, where you might want to override or augment annotations, occurs when you want to deploy a handler with a Web service endpoint that hasn't been annotated for a handler. Alternatively, the endpoint may have been annotated for a handler, but you wish to use a different handler. One way to deal with this is to edit the source code to update or add the @HandlerChain annotation. But perhaps you do not have access or authority to modify the source code. Or perhaps you think it is a bad idea to have multiple versions of the same source code just so you can support using the endpoint with different handlers. In such a situation, you can deploy the endpoint with a custom webservices.xml to specify the handler chain.

Example 8–21 shows the Hello Web service endpoint with an @HandlerChain annotation that specifies the myhandler.xml handler configuration file.

Example 8–21 The Hello Web Service Endpoint with @HandlerChain

```
26   @HandlerChain(file="myhandler.xml")
27   @WebService
28   public class Hello {
29
30     @Resource
31     WebServiceContext context;
32
33     public String sayHello(String s) {
34       String appendString =
35         (String) context.getMessageContext().get(HelloHandler.APPEND_STRING);
36       return "Hello: " + s + "[appended by handler: " + appendString + "]";
37     }
38
39   }
```

book-code/chap08/descriptor-webservice/modules/endpoint/src/java/samples
/Hello.java

The myhandler.xml file is shown in Example 8–22. Notice that it specifies the handler class `samples.HelloHandler`.

Example 8–22 The `myhandler.xml` Handler Chain Configuration File

```
4   <handler-chains xmlns:jws="http://java.sun.com/xml/ns/javaee">
5     <handler-chain>
6       <handler>
7         <handler-class>samples.HelloHandler</handler-class>
8       </handler>
9     </handler-chain>
10  </handler-chains>
```

book-code/chap08/descriptor-webservice/modules/endpoint/src/webapp/WEB-INF
  /classes/samples/myhandler.xml

Now, suppose you would prefer to deploy this endpoint with the handler class `samples.ImprovedHelloHandler`. You could do that by bundling the `webservices.xml` file shown in Example 8–23 in the WEB-INF directory of the WAR module (or, if this were an EJB endpoint, in the META-INF directory).

Example 8–23 A `webservices.xml` to Override the `@HandlerChain` Annotation

```
4   <webservices xmlns="http://java.sun.com/xml/ns/javaee"
5     xmlns:xsi="http://www.w3.org/2001/XMLSchema-instance" version="1.2"
6     xsi:schemaLocation="http://java.sun.com/xml/ns/javaee
7     http://www.ibm.com/webservices/xsd/javaee_web_services_1_2.xsd">
8     <webservice-description>
9       <webservice-description-name>HelloService</webservice-description-name>
10      <port-component>
11        <port-component-name>Hello</port-component-name>
12        <wsdl-service xmlns:ns1="http://samples/">ns1:HelloService</wsdl-service>
13        <wsdl-port xmlns:ns1="http://samples/">ns1:HelloPort</wsdl-port>
14        <service-impl-bean>
15          <servlet-link>Hello</servlet-link>
16        </service-impl-bean>
17        <handler-chains>
18          <handler-chain>
19            <handler>
20              <handler-name>myhandler</handler-name>
```

```
21                <handler-class>samples.ImprovedHelloHandler</handler-class>
22              </handler>
23            </handler-chain>
24          </handler-chains>
25        </port-component>
26    </webservice-description>
27  </webservices>
```

book-code/chap08/descriptor-webservice/modules/endpoint/src/webapp/WEB-INF
  /webservices.xml

In this `webservices.xml` deployment descriptor, notice the `handler-chains` element in the bottom half of the listing. Here, the `handler-class` element specifies `samples.ImprovedHelloHandler`. To run this example, do the following:

1. Start GlassFish (if it is not already running).
2. Go to `<book-code>/chap08/descriptor-webservice`.
3. Enter `mvn install`.

In the output generated by the example, you will notice the text "NEW & IMPROVED!!!." This indicates that the `samples.ImprovedHelloHandler` class has been used as the handler, rather than the `samples.HelloHandler` class specified by the annotation.

When using the `webservice.xml` as discussed in this section, it is important to understand how the `port-component` names match up with the annotations. In other words, `port-component-name` relates to `@WebService.name`; `wsdl-service` relates to `@WebService.serviceName`; `wsdl-port` relates to `@WebService.portName`; and `service-endpoint-interface` relates to `@WebService.endpointInterface`. See Section 5.3.2.1 of [JSR 109] for all the details.

8.3.4 Platform-Specific Deployment Descriptors

Java EE 5 implementations each contain certain deployment descriptors that are not specified by the JSRs, but provide necessary or helpful deployment functionality in a nonportable manner. In this section, I take a quick look at how the `sun-web.xml` and `sun-ejb-jar.xml` files can be useful for Web services deployment with GlassFish. These descriptors are the GlassFish-specific files used for servlet and EJB endpoint deployment, respectively.

My recommendation is to use these platform-specific descriptors as little as possible, because they limit portability. One application that I have found where it is necessary to use them, however, is for the specification of a context root when not bundling modules inside an EAR package. When you deploy a Web service using SOAP over HTTP, its address has the following shape when deployed as a servlet endpoint:

```
http://<machine-name>:<port>/<context-root>/<url-pattern>
```

Using the `web.xml`, as discussed in Section 8.3.1, you can specify the `url-pattern`. Using the platform-specific descriptor `sun-web.xml`, you can specify the `context-root`. Consider the SIB shown in Example 8–24.

Example 8–24 Defining a Servlet Endpoint

```
24  @WebService(serviceName="MyHelloService")
25  public class Hello {
26
27    public String sayHello(String s) {
28      return "Hello: " + s;
29
30    }
31
32  }
```

book-code/chap08/descriptor-sunweb/modules/endpoint/src/java/samples/Hello.java

Without providing a `sun-web.xml` or a `web.xml`, the endpoint address is as shown in this snippet from the generated WSDL. As you can see, the `<context-root>` in Example 8–25 is `descriptor-sunweb-endpoint`. That happens to be the name of the module (WAR file) deployed, and is the default value for `<context-root>`. The `<url-pattern>`, on the other hand, is `MyHelloService`. That value is taken from the `@WebService.serviceName` attribute shown in Example 8–24.

Example 8–25 The WSDL Generated without a `sun-web.xml`

```
39   <service name="MyHelloService">
40     <port name="HelloPort" binding="tns:HelloPortBinding">
41       <soap:address
```

```
42            location="http://soabookdev.scarsdale.javector.com:8080/descriptor-
sunweb-endpoint/MyHelloService"
43             xmlns:wsdl="http://schemas.xmlsoap.org/wsdl/"/>
44      </port>
45    </service>
```

book-code/chap08/descriptor-sunweb/examples/generated-without-sunweb.wsdl

Now, consider what happens when you deploy this same SIB using the
`sun-web.xml` deployment descriptor shown in Example 8–26.

Example 8–26 Using sun-web.xml to Define the `context-root`

```
4  <sun-web-app>
5    <context-root>my-context</context-root>
6  </sun-web-app>
```

book-code/chap08/descriptor-sunweb/modules/endpoint/src/webapp/WEB-INF
  /sun-web.xml

In that case, you get an endpoint address where the `<context-root>` is
`my-context`. The results that illustrate this are shown in the snippet of generated WSDL in Example 8–27.

Example 8–27 WSDL Generated with a `sun-web.xml`

```
39    <service name="MyHelloService">
40      <port name="HelloPort" binding="tns:HelloPortBinding">
41        <soap:address
42          location="http://soabookdev.scarsdale.javector.com:8080/my-context/
MyHelloService"
43             xmlns:wsdl="http://schemas.xmlsoap.org/wsdl/"/>
44      </port>
45    </service>
```

book-code/chap08/descriptor-sunweb/examples/generated-with-sunweb.wsdl

To run the sample code in this section, do the following:

1. Start GlassFish (if it is not already running).
2. Go to `<book-code>/chap08/descriptor-sunweb`.
3. Enter `mvn install`.

Running this example will show you the WSDL and the results of an invocation of the Web service as deployed with the `sun-web.xml` shown in the preceding text. If you would like to deploy it without the `sun-web.xml`, you will need to go into the `chap08/descriptor-sunweb/modules/endpoint/src/webapp` directory and remove or rename the `sun-web.xml` file.

Next, I discuss the situation where the SIB is deployed as an EJB endpoint. Interestingly, the shape of the endpoint address is different in this case than for a servlet endpoint. When deployed as an EJB endpoint, the address for a Web service using SOAP over HTTP has the following shape:

```
http://<machine-name>:<port>/<endpoint-address-uri>
```

Using the platform-specific descriptor `sun-ejb-jar.xml`, you can specify the `endpoint-address-uri`. Consider the same SIB with the `@Stateless` annotation, as shown in Example 8–28.

Example 8–28 Defining an EJB Endpoint

```
24  @WebService(serviceName="MyHelloService")
25  @Stateless(name="MyHelloEJB")
26  @TransactionAttribute(TransactionAttributeType.NOT_SUPPORTED)
27  public class Hello {
28
29    public String sayHello(String s) {
30      return "Hello: " + s;
31
32    }
33
34  }
```

book-code/chap08/descriptor-sunejbjar/modules/endpoint/src/java
  /samples/Hello.java

When a `sun-ejb-jar.xml` descriptor is not provided, the endpoint address takes the form shown in the snippet of generated WSDL appearing in Example 8–29. As you can see, the `<endpoint-address-uri>` in this case is `MyHelloService/Hello`. That happens to be the value of `@WebSer-`

vice.serviceName (MyHelloService), followed by the value of @WebService.name (Hello—this defaults to the simple class name), which is also the wsdl:portType.

Example 8–29 WSDL Generated without a sun-ejb-jar.xml

```
40    <service name="MyHelloService">
41      <port name="HelloPort" binding="tns:HelloPortBinding">
42        <soap:address
43          location="http://soabookdev.scarsdale.javector.com:8080/
MyHelloService/Hello"
44          xmlns:wsdl="http://schemas.xmlsoap.org/wsdl/"/>
45      </port>
46    </service>
```

book-code/chap08/descriptor-sunejbjar/examples/generated-without-sunejbjar.wsdl

Now, consider what happens when you deploy this same SIB using the sun-ejb-jar.xml deployment descriptor shown in Example 8–30.

Example 8–30 Using sun-ejb-jar.xml to Define the endpoint-address-uri

```
4    <sun-ejb-jar>
5      <enterprise-beans>
6        <ejb>
7          <ejb-name>MyHelloEJB</ejb-name>
8          <webservice-endpoint>
9            <port-component-name>Hello</port-component-name>
10           <endpoint-address-uri>/my/endpoint/url</endpoint-address-uri>
11         </webservice-endpoint>
12       </ejb>
13     </enterprise-beans>
14   </sun-ejb-jar>
```

book-code/chap08/descriptor-sunejbjar/modules/endpoint/src/java/META-INF
/sun-ejb-jar.xml

In that case, you get an endpoint address where the <endpoint-address-uri> is my/endpoint/url. The results illustrating that are shown in the snippet of generated WSDL in Example 8–31.

Example 8–31 The WSDL Generated with a `sun-ejb-jar.xml`

```
39  <service name="MyHelloService">
40    <port name="HelloPort" binding="tns:HelloPortBinding">
41      <soap:address
42        location="http://soabookdev.scarsdale.javector.com:8080/my/endpoint/url"
43        xmlns:wsdl="http://schemas.xmlsoap.org/wsdl/"/>
44    </port>
45  </service>
```

book-code/chap08/descriptor-sunejbjar/examples/generated-with-sunejbjar.wsdl

To run the sample code in this section, do the following:

1. Start GlassFish (if it is not already running).
2. Go to `<book-code>/chap08/descriptor-sunejbjar`.
3. Enter `mvn install`.

Running this example will show you the WSDL and the results of an invocation of the Web service as deployed with the `sun-ejb-jar.xml` shown in the preceding text. If you would like to deploy it without the `sun-ejb-jar.xml`, you will need to go into the `chap08/descriptor-sunweb/ modules/endpoint/src/ejb` directory and remove or rename the `sun-ejb-jar.xml` file.

If you have read through this section, congratulations! You have just run through a fairly exhaustive explanation of the various Web service deployment scenarios defined by WS-Metadata and WSEE. If you just skimmed this section, that is fine also. I put all the detail here so that you can use it as a reference when writing and deploying your own Web Services. Hopefully, it will prove useful to you in your work.

8.4   Automatic Deployment with GlassFish

In this section, I look at a feature of GlassFish that is not required by WSEE, but is described in Section 2.4 (a) of WS-Metadata [JSR 181] as "Automatic deployment to a server directory—This is a 'drag and drop' deployment model, similar to that used by JSPs." GlassFish provides such "drag and drop" deployment. Using this mechanism to deploy a Web service, all you need to do is copy a class or module file to the GlassFish automatic deployment directory. The following example illustrates how it works.

Example 8–32 shows the (by now very familiar) `Hello.java` that is deployed in this example. In this auto-deploy scenario, it is deployed as a WAR without any descriptors. However, you can also deploy it with descriptors, and you can even deploy it simply as a class file without having to package it in a WAR.

Example 8–32 The Endpoint to Auto-Deploy

```
23  @WebService(serviceName="Hello")
24  public class Hello {
25
26    public String sayHello(String s) {
27      return "Hello: " + s;
28
29    }
30
31  }
```

book-code/chap08/autodeploy/modules/endpoint/src/java/samples/Hello.java

You can simply copy the compiled class file generated from Example 8–32 into the auto-deploy directory—that is all there is to it! In my examples, I always bundle the class files into a WAR, but it's not necessary. Example 8–33 shows the Ant script used to deploy the WAR. Notice that this script does not invoke the GlassFish `asadmin` utility. Instead, it simply copies the WAR file to the auto-deploy directory.[21]

Example 8–33 Script for Auto-Deployment

```
14  <target name="auto_deploy" depends="setenv">
15    <echo message="deploying: ${war}"/>
16    <copy file="${war}" todir="${autodeploy.dir}"/>
```

---

21. In this script, the WAR file's path is stored in the `${war}` property, and the path for the auto-deploy directory is stored in `${autodeploy.dir}`.

```
17    <waitfor maxwait="100" maxwaitunit="second" checkevery="100">
18      <or>
19        <available file="${autodeploy.dir}/${module}.war_deployed"/>
20        <available file="${autodeploy.dir}/${module}.war_deployFailed"/>
21      </or>
22    </waitfor>
23  </target>
```

book-code/chap08/autodeploy/modules/client/build.xml

In my GlassFish installation, the auto-deploy directory is located at $GLASSFISH_HOME/domains/domain1/autodeploy. Of course, your installation may be different, depending on the name of the domain you are using. I am using the default domain name—domain1—as described in Appendix B, Section B.3.

You have probably also noticed that the script in Example 8–33 contains a waitfor task. This is needed to give GlassFish time to process files copied into its auto-deploy directory. GlassFish polls this directory periodically to check for changes.[22] When it detects a new file, it attempts to process and deploy it. Hence, you need to include the waitfor task to prevent any other tasks from trying to use the Web service until GlassFish has had a chance to finish deploying it. In this example, the filename copied to the auto-deploy directory is ${service}.war. If it deploys successfully, GlassFish creates a file named ${service}.war_deployed. If deployment fails, GlassFish creates a file named ${service}.war_deployFailed. You can run this example by doing the following:

1. Start GlassFish (if it is not already running).
2. Go to <book-code>/chap08/autodeploy.
3. Enter mvn install.

I encourage you to play around with this auto-deploy capability and try different scenarios (e.g., deploy a class file, an EJB_JAR, etc.). This is a great tool for rapid prototyping of Web services.

---

22. The polling interval is determined by the autodeploy-polling-interval-in-seconds property in the domain's domain.xml configuration file.

8.5 Web Services Security

Security is treated very briefly in Section 9 of WSEE. The specification deals with authentication, authorization, and encryption (integrity and confidentiality). The security methods specified are HTTP-specific. There is no specification of how security should be supported for non-HTTP protocol bindings.

To support authentication, WSEE specifies that compliant servers must support both BASIC-AUTH and Symmetric HTTPS. Support for BASIC-AUTH is specified in Java servlet 2.5 [JSR 154] using the `login-config` element of the `web.xml` as illustrated in the snippet of a web.xml shown in Example 8–34.

Example 8–34 Specifying BASIC-AUTH Authentication

```
<web-app>

  <login-config>
    <auth-method>BASIC</auth-method>
    <realm-name>...</realm-name>
  </login-config>

</web-app>
```

When deploying a Web service using an EJB endpoint, you use a similar method for specifying BASIC-AUTH, except that you have to use the implementation-specific deployment descriptor for enterprise beans. Example 8–35 shows a snippet from a `sun-ejb-jar.xml`, the descriptor used with GlassFish.

Example 8–35 Specifying BASIC-AUTH Authentication Using `sun-ejb-jar.xml`

```
<sun-ejb-jar>
  <enterprise-beans>
    <ejb>
    ...
      <webservice-endpoint>
        <port-component-name>...</port-component-name>
        <endpoint-address-uri>...</endpoint-address-uri>
```

```
        <login-config>
          <auth-method>BASIC</auth-method>
        </login-config>
      </webservice-endpoint>
    </ejb>
    <webservice-description>
    ...
    </webservice-description>
  </enterprise-beans>
</sun-ejb-jar>
```

When a client calls a Web service using BASIC-AUTH, the basic authentication information is contained in the HTTP headers and is verified (using a server-specific method) by the container. WSEE requires that the EJB and Web containers support deploy time configuration of credential information to use for Web services requests using BASIC-AUTH. Again, the mechanism for this support is provider-specific.

Roles can also be specified to provide varying levels of security access. WSEE calls these "Security Role References," and they are contained in the provider-specific application deployment file (see Example 8–36).

Example 8–36 Specifying Security Role References Using `sun-application.xml`

```
<sun-application>
  <web>
  ...
  </web>
  <security-role-mapping>
    <role-name>User</role-name>
    <group-name>staff</group-name>
  </security-role-mapping>
  <security-role-mapping>
    <role-name>Admin</role-name>
    <group-name>staff</group-name>
    <group-name>eng</group-name>
    <group-name>mgr</group-name>
    <group-name>guest</group-name>
  </security-role-mapping>
</sun-application>
```

WSEE uses the term "Symmetric HTTPS" to refer to the scenario where authentication of both client and server using digital certificates is supported. Support for client authentication using a digital certificate in this manner is required by Java EE 5. WSEE is simply extending that to any other platform that claims to be WSEE-compliant.

Using encryption with a WSEE-deployed Web service is simply a matter of using HTTPS (HTTP over SSL) instead of HTTP. To do that, a WSEE server implementation must support using `https:` instead of `http:` to specify the WSDL port address. As you are probably aware, using an `https:` URL indicates that HTTP is to be used on a different default port (443) where the Web server provides support for Secure Sockets Layer (SSL) encryption/authentication layer between HTTP and TCP. In this manner, there is nothing special you need to do to deploy a Web service that supports encryption other than deploy it to an endpoint specified with `https:`. The specifics of specifying the endpoint address at deployment time are implementation-specific.

It is worth noting that there is a WS-Security [WS-Security] standard published by OASIS that handles security at the SOAP message level. This approach has the advantage that it can be used with non-HTTP bindings. However, WS-Security support is not required by WSEE or Java EE 5. (JAX-WS 2.1, however, is being designed with WS-Security support in mind.)

In addition, the upcoming [JSR 196] standardizes authentication for containers. One goal of this specification is to make Web service security completely portable.

8.6 OASIS XML Catalogs 1.1

In this section, I look at the OASIS XML Catalogs [XML Catalog 1.1] feature supported by JAX-WS. XML Catalogs let you map WSDL or XML references according to mapping rules defined in a catalog. This capability is useful if you are writing a Web service that will access WSDL at runtime, but you don't yet know where that WSDL will be deployed. Using XML Catalogs, you can use a placeholder WSDL when writing your service, and then resolve it at deployment time by including a catalog in your WAR or EJB JAR.

According to WSEE, "JAX-WS requires support for an OASIS XML Catalogs 1.1 specification to be used when resolving any Web service document that is part of the description of a Web service, specifically WSDL and XML Schema documents. Refer to Section 4.4 of the JAX-WS specification. The catalog file `jax-ws-catalog.xml` must be co-located with the module deployment descriptor (`WEB-INF/jax-ws-catalog.xml` for web modules and `META-INF/jax-ws-catalog.xml` for the rest)."

To understand how this works, consider the Web service shown in Example 8–37. Notice that the `@WebServiceRef.wsdlLocation` attribute refers to the URL `http://someplace/myService?wsdl`. That is a placeholder URL. It doesn't point to a real WSDL document, and will be mapped to a real WSDL address at deployment time.

Example 8–37 Web Service with WSDL Placeholder

```
27  @WebService
28  @Stateless
29  @TransactionAttribute(TransactionAttributeType.NOT_SUPPORTED)
30  public class Hello {
31
32    @WebServiceRef(value = MyWebService.class,
33        wsdlLocation="http://someplace/myService?wsdl")
34    MyWeb port;
35
36    public String sayHello(String s) {
37      String webServiceString = port.saySomething(s);
38      return "Hello: " + s +
39      System.getProperty("line.separator") + webServiceString;
40
41    }
42
43  }
```

`book-code/chap08/catalog/modules/endpoint/src/java/samples/Hello.java`

Example 8–38 shows the XML catalog that resolves the placeholder. As you can see, it maps the placeholder to `http://localhost:8080/chap08-catalog-mywebservice-nowebxml/MyWebService?wsdl`—which is the real location where the referenced service's WSDL is published.

Example 8–38 The XML Catalog That Resolves the Placeholder

```
3  <catalog xmlns="urn:oasis:names:tc:entity:xmlns:xml:catalog" prefer="system">
4    <system
5      systemId="http://someplace/myService?wsdl"
```

```
6      uri="http://localhost:8080/chap08-catalog-mywebservice-nowebxml/
MyWebService?wsdl"/>
7  </catalog>
```

book-code/chap08/catalog/modules/endpoint/src/ejb/META-INF/jax-ws-catalog.xml

To run the sample code in this section, do the following:

1. Start GlassFish (if it is not already running).
2. Go to <book-code>/chap08/catalog.
3. Enter mvn install.

XML Catalogs are extremely useful for change management. This is particularly true if you follow the best practices discussed in Chapter 4, and keep the XML Schema documents used in your WSDLs stored in a central repository. In such a case, when you deploy a Web service, the references to these XML Schema documents can be resolved using an XML Catalog. The XML Catalog gives you flexibility to change the published location of referenced documents without having to make changes to the code used to implement your Web services. All you need to do to implement the changed location is update the XML Catalog.

8.7 Wrapping Up

This chapter wraps up the overview of the JWS JSRs (i.e., JAXB, JAX-WS, WS-Metadata, and WSEE) presented in Chapters 5–8. In this chapter, I walked you through a detailed discussion of the packaging and deployment process used for JWS Web Services. I hope that all the examples presented here will help as you tackle the deployment challenges that will inevitably arise as you build and deploy your own JWS applications.

In the next two chapters, I show how to use JWS to develop an SOA-style application that integrates online shopping services from eBay, Yahoo! Shopping, and Amazon. The code examples in Chapters 9 and 10 are longer and more involved than the snippets used here to illustrate various features. But having mastered the JWS basics, at this point you should be ready to take on the development of a real application.

CHAPTER 9

SOAShopper: Integrating eBay, Amazon, and Yahoo! Shopping

This chapter pulls together the techniques from Chapters 3–8 and demonstrates how to develop a real SOA Integration application using JWS. The application—SOAShopper—is an online shopping system that integrates eBay, Amazon, and Yahoo! Shopping.[1] SOAShopper also demonstrates how to build an Ajax front-end that integrates with Java EE 5 Web Services. The topic of Ajax and JAX-WS is explored in depth in Chapter 10.

9.1 Overview of SOAShopper

Although SOAShopper is a demo application, the techniques it illustrates are powerful. If you understand how to build SOAShopper, you are ready to start building your own enterprise-quality SOA applications with Java Web Services. To summarize, the SOAShopper application uses the following technologies, APIs, and techniques discussed in preceding chapters:

- **Consuming RESTful Services** (Chapter 3): RESTful services are consumed from Yahoo! Shopping.
- **Deploying RESTful Services** (Chapter 3): A REST API is designed and deployed to enable integrated product search across eBay, Amazon, and Yahoo!.
- **Consuming WSDL/SOAP Services** (Chapter 4): WSDL/SOAP services are consumed from eBay and Amazon.

---

1. For instructions on how to build and run SOAShopper, see Appendix B, Section B.9.

- **Deploying WSDL/SOAP Services** (Chapter 4): A WSDL API is designed and deployed to enable integrated product search across eBay, Amazon, and Yahoo!.
- **JAXB 2.0 Type Mappings and Data Transformation** (Chapter 5): JAXB 2.0 is used to bind the eBay, Amazon, and Yahoo! Shopping APIs to a Java interface. Data transformation is used to map that interface to the SOAShopper data model.
- **JAX-WS 2.0 Client Development** (Chapter 6): JAX-WS 2.0 provides the client interface to consume Web services from eBay and Amazon.
- **JAX-WS 2.0 Service Development** (Chapter 7): JAX-WS 2.0 technology is used to provide the SOAP and REST services that consumers use to access SOAShopper. These services are also consumed by the Ajax front-end that provides a human interface for SOAShopper.
- **Packaging and Deployment with JSR-181 and JSR-109** (Chapter 8): SOAShopper is packaged using Java EE 5 standards so that it can be deployed on any application server supporting Java EE 5.
- **Ajax and JAX-WS** (Chapter 10): An Ajax front-end to SOAShopper provides the human interface that integrates with the services it provides using JAX-WS.

The use of all these different technologies and techniques is not contrived. Each has a useful and important role in the SOAShopper application. As a result, SOAShopper provides a good illustration of how the Java Web Services components work together to enable SOA Integration. Figure 9–1 provides a high-level illustration of the SOAShopper architecture.

SOAShopper runs inside a Java EE 5 container as shown by the shaded box in the center of Figure 9–1. The container running SOAShopper serves as an intermediary between clients, shown at the top of the diagram and the shopping services shown at the bottom. Three types of Web Services consumers are shown: Web Browser, REST-based, and WSDL/SOAP-based. The Web Browser provides a human client interface that uses Ajax technology to communicate with SOAShopper using POX.[2] The REST-based consumer is any other type of application that communicates using POX. The WSDL/SOAP-based consumer is an application that is WSDL-aware (i.e., can interpret the ports and bindings defined in the WSDL) and communicates using SOAP.

SOAShopper provides SOAP and REST style Web services to handle these consumers. On the other side, SOAShopper is also a consumer of

---

2. POX stands for "Plain Old XML" and refers to the XML/HTTP style of messaging used by REST. POX is described in detail in Chapter 3.

Web services. SOAShopper uses APIs generated by JAX-WS from the eBay and Amazon WSDLs to communicate with those services. In addition, a manually created API is used to communicate with the Yahoo! Shopping RESTful services.

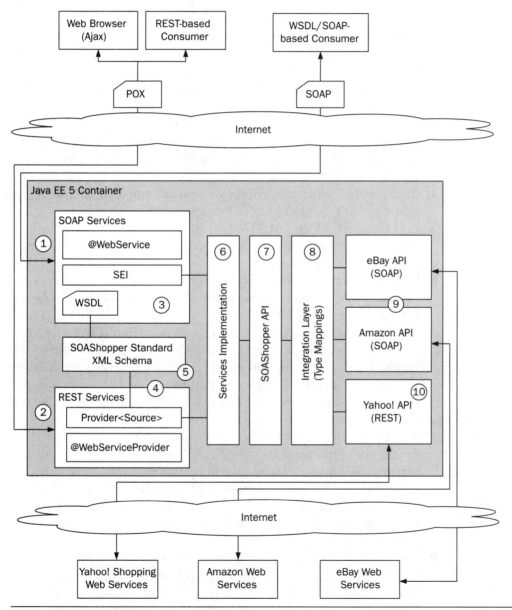

Figure 9–1 SOAShopper architecture.

To understand how SOAShopper works, consider a search request such as "find all Lenovo laptop computers costing less than $800.00." Such a request would be processed as follows:

1. If the request is sent from a WSDL/SOAP-based consumer, the search request is embedded in a SOAP message that is received at the URL where the SOAShopper SOAP Services have been deployed.

2. If the request is sent from an Ajax or other REST-based consumer, the search request is embedded in a plain XML message, or in the HTTP parameters or URL request string (or some combination of these), and it is received at the URL where the SOAShopper REST Services have been deployed.

3. In the SOAP case, the appropriate SEI (service endpoint interface) method is invoked. The method chosen is the one that corresponds to the port and operation from the SOAShopper WSDL that is specified by the SOAP message.

4. In the REST case, the `Provider<Source>` implementation at the center of SOAShopper's REST Services module is invoked.

5. In both the SOAP and REST cases, the request message and the ultimate response are built from XML that corresponds to the SOAShopper standard XML schema.

6. Within either the SEI deployment, or the `Provider<Source>` `invoke()` method, the request message is serialized into Java objects that are bound to the SOAShopper standard XML schema. These objects are passed as parameters to the Service Implementation. The Service Implementation provides the Web Services functionality by building the services on top of the baselevel SOAShopper API. In this case, the Service Implementation interprets the search request and invokes the proper SOAShopper API methods to make the search happen.

7. The SOAShopper API provides a common wrapper around the source shopping services. The SOAShopper methods invoke the Integration Layer to translate the operations into the syntax and semantics of the source systems: eBay, Amazon, and Yahoo!. A great deal of analysis of each source system is required in order to design and implement this wrapper and its corresponding Integration Layer.

8. The Integration Layer implements the interfaces defined by the SOAShopper API by invoking methods from the eBay, Amazon, and Yahoo! APIs. The business logic used to translate the semantics of SOAShopper into each source system is embedded here along with

the type mappings that translate SOAShopper instances into source system instances.

9. The eBay and Amazon APIs use SOAP to invoke the translated search request on their respective services. These APIs are bound to the WSDLs of the services and were automatically generated using JAX-WS tools.

10. The Yahoo! API uses REST to invoke the Yahoo! Shopping Web service. Since no WSDL is available for such RESTful services, this API was implemented by hand based on the description in the Yahoo! documentation.

Those steps provide a high-level overview of how the SOAShopper application is implemented. JWS provides all the tools necessary to deploy the SOAShopper services on the front-end and consume the eBay, Amazon, and Yahoo! services on the back-end. In particular, I was very impressed at how well the JAX-WS schema compiler handled the eBay and Amazon WSDLs. The eBay WSDL is more than 3 MB and compiles into more than 700 classes. But the SOAShopper application is able to use the classes generated from this WSDL with no problem. Admittedly, figuring out what all these classes are used for is difficult, but that is a problem related to the complexity of the eBay Web services themselves and not a reflection on the JAX-WS binding.

Being able to automatically generate Java bindings for the eBay and Amazon WSDLs points out one advantage of WSDL/SOAP versus REST. For the Yahoo! Shopping RESTful services, it was not possible to automatically generate Java binding classes. That is because there is no WSDL definition standard for REST. The approach I took was to use the JAXB schema compiler to generate Java classes that are bound to the XML responses. The requests, in the Yahoo! cases, are all specified using HTTP parameters. I mapped those parameters to message signatures to create a Java binding for the Yahoo! services. This approach is explained in full detail further along in this chapter. One immediate drawback of this approach that jumped out at me is change management. In the WSDL/SOAP case, if the services interface changes, that change is reflected in the WSDL. Such a change can be propagated into SOAShopper by recompiling the WSDL using the JAX-WS tools. Simply load the newly generated classes into your favorite IDE and you can see right away where the code no longer compiles and you need to refactor or write new code to accommodate the changes. In the REST case, there is no way to similarly automate the change management processes. Instead, you have to read the REST service documentation for each release, hope that all changes are noted, manually update the API code related to those changes, and then turn to your IDE to propagate the changes throughout the rest of SOAShopper.

One of the themes in this book is that when developing SOA-based applications, it is important to be able to integrate an existing WSDL with an existing Java API; in other words, the "Start from WSDL and Java" development mode. SOAShopper illustrates this theme because it provides a WSDL interface to its consumers that must be integrated with the Java representations of the shopping services provided by eBay, Amazon, and Yahoo!. Actually, as you will see, the WSDL is integrated with an internal SOAShopper Java model that integrates these three source shopping systems. Both the WSDL and the SOAShopper Java model must be able to change independently. The WSDL changes as new consumer requirements are identified and new features are added to the REST and WSDL/SOAP interfaces. The Java model changes independently as the source shopping systems change and as new features and capabilities are added. In SOAShopper, the Service Implementation (labeled 6 in Figure 9–1) handles the integration of the WSDL (and SOAShopper standard XML schema) with the SOAShopper API. Likewise, the SOAShopper API is mapped to the source system WSDL/XML interfaces via the Integration Layer.

To get started with the investigation of the SOAShopper details, I will first examine the WSDL and REST services provided by SOAShopper. Next, I'll show you how those services are exposed by the Java EE 5 container using JAX-WS. After that, the Service Implementation is explained. From there, we go back to the source systems and look at the different services provided by eBay, Amazon, and Yahoo!. In particular, I walk through some of the business analysis to identify commonality across these three systems. From this commonality, I show how the SOAShopper API is defined as a wrapper for these source systems. Finally, I wrap things up by showing how the Integration Layer links the SOAShopper API with the source systems using the Bridge design pattern defined in [Go4].

As I walk through these components of the SOAShopper application, I focus on only a small portion of the functionality. The idea is to illustrate how Java EE 5 Web Services can be used effectively, while not overwhelming you with the details of SOAShopper. For those who are interested in digging deeper into the workings of SOAShopper, the source code for the entire application can be found in the `<book-code>/chap09/soashopper` directory of the book example code.[3]

---

3. See Appendix B for detailed instructions on downloading and installing the book code.

9.2 SOAShopper SOAP Services

The SOAShopper application provides SOAP services that are defined by a WSDL document as described in items 1 and 3 in Figure 9–1. This WSDL document has been created by design—not generated from the SOAShopper API by JAX-WS. The reasons why this "Start from WSDL and Java" approach makes the most sense for SOAShopper are as follows:

- The SOAShopper WSDL should reuse standard XML schemas from existing libraries instead of generating unique schemas based on the JAX-WS binding. This is a best practice discussed in Chapter 4, Section 4.1.
- The SOAShopper WSDL should be insulated from the SOAShopper API so that each can be revised independently of the other.
- The SOAShopper WSDL should expose only certain operations as Web services—not the entire SOAShopper API.

Because the WSDL is independent from the SOAShopper API, a middle layer—labeled "Service Implementation" (item 6 in Figure 9–1)—is required to mediate between the JAX-WS service endpoint interface (SEI) and the SOAShopper API. In this section, the design and implementation of the WSDL and SOAP services are briefly discussed. Then, the next section looks at how the same services are made available using REST.

Example 9–1 shows the type definitions and one of the operations—offerSearch—defined by the WSDL. Notice that the wsdl:types section includes two standard schemas from the http://soabook.com/example library. The retail.xsd schema defines standard types (e.g., Currency-Type) used for online shopping. The faults.xsd schema, first discussed in Chapter 4, defines standard types that are used for SOAP faults.

Example 9–1 A Snippet of the SOAShopper WSDL Showing the xs:schema Definitions and wsdl:portType Defining the offerSearch Operation

```
11    <wsdl:types>
12      <xs:schema targetNamespace="http://www.example.com/faults">
13       <xs:include schemaLocation="http://soabook.com/example/faults/faults.xsd"
14       />
15      </xs:schema>
16      <xs:schema elementFormDefault="qualified"
```

```
17          targetNamespace="http://soabook.com/soashopper">
18          <xs:import namespace="http://www.example.com/retail"
19            schemaLocation="http://soabook.com/example/retail/retail.xsd"/>
20          <xs:element name="offerSearch">
21            <xs:complexType>
22              <xs:sequence>
23                <xs:element name="keywords" type="xs:string"/>
24                <xs:element name="category" type="retail:CategoryType"
25                  minOccurs="0"/>
26                <xs:element name="lowprice" type="retail:PriceType" minOccurs="0"/>
27                <xs:element name="highprice" type="retail:PriceType" minOccurs="0"/>
28              </xs:sequence>
29            </xs:complexType>
30          </xs:element>
31          <xs:element name="offerSearchReturn">
32            <xs:complexType>
33              <xs:sequence>
34                <xs:element ref="retail:offer" minOccurs="0" maxOccurs="unbounded"/>
35              </xs:sequence>
36            </xs:complexType>
37          </xs:element>
38        </xs:schema>
39      </wsdl:types>
40      <wsdl:message name="offerSearchRequest">
41        <wsdl:part name="parameters" element="tns:offerSearch"/>
42      </wsdl:message>
43      <wsdl:message name="offerSearchResponse">
44        <wsdl:part name="parameters" element="tns:offerSearchReturn"/>
45      </wsdl:message>
46      <wsdl:message name="inputFault">
47        <wsdl:part name="parameters" element="faults:inputMessageValidationFault"/>
48      </wsdl:message>
49      <wsdl:portType name="ShopperPort">
50        <wsdl:operation name="offerSearch">
51          <wsdl:input message="tns:offerSearchRequest"/>
52          <wsdl:output message="tns:offerSearchResponse"/>
53          <wsdl:fault name="offerSearchInputFault" message="tns:inputFault"/>
54        </wsdl:operation>
55      </wsdl:portType>
```

book-code/chap09/soashopper/soashopper-services-soap/src/main/webapp/WEB-INF
  /wsdl/soashopper.wsdl

Like the other WSDL documents defined in this book, the SOAShopper WSDL uses the document/literal wrapped style. The wrapper element for the request—`tns:offerSearch`—is defined in the `wsdl:types` section. As you can see there, it defines four parameters: `keywords` (for keyword search), `category` (e.g., Computers, Cellphones, etc.), `lowprice`, and `highprice` (defining a price range). The `keywords` parameter is simply a string—interpreted as space-delimited search keywords. The `category` parameter is an instance of `retail:CategoryType`—an `xs:simpleType` defined by an enumeration of valid categories, as shown in Example 9–2.

Example 9–2 The `CategoryType` Defines a List of Valid Categories (A Search Can Be Restricted to a Category)

```
75   <xs:simpleType name="CategoryType">
76     <xs:restriction base="xs:string">
77       <xs:enumeration value="COMPUTERS"/>
78       <xs:enumeration value="CELLPHONES"/>
79       <xs:enumeration value="MOVIES"/>
80     </xs:restriction>
81   </xs:simpleType>
```

book-code/chap09/soashopper/soashopper-services-soap/src/main/webapp/WEB-INF
/wsdl/retail.xsd

The `lowprice` and `highprice` parameters are instances of `retail:PriceType`—an `xs:complexType` that specifies an amount and a currency. An instance of `retail:PriceType` representing $9.89 (U.S. dollars) looks like this:

```
<lowprice currencyId="USD">9.89</lowprice>
```

The schema for `retail:PriceType` is shown in Example 9–3.

Example 9–3 The `PriceType` Defines a Price in Terms of a Decimal Amount (with Two Digits after the Decimal Place) and a Currency Identifier

```
50   <xs:complexType name="PriceType">
51     <xs:simpleContent>
52       <xs:extension base="tns:HundrethsType">
```

```
53            <xs:attribute name="currencyId" type="tns:CurrencyType"/>
54          </xs:extension>
55        </xs:simpleContent>
56      </xs:complexType>
57
58      <xs:simpleType name="HundrethsType">
59        <xs:restriction base="xs:decimal">
60          <xs:fractionDigits value="2"/>
61        </xs:restriction>
62      </xs:simpleType>
63
64      <xs:simpleType name="CurrencyType">
65        <xs:restriction base="xs:string">
66          <xs:enumeration value="USD"/>
67          <xs:enumeration value="GBP"/>
68          <xs:enumeration value="EUR"/>
69          <xs:enumeration value="JPY"/>
70        </xs:restriction>
71      </xs:simpleType>
```

book-code/chap09/soashopper/soashopper-services-soap/src/main/webapp/WEB-INF
/wsdl/retail.xsd

The SOAShopper WSDL in Example 9–1 also defines the SOAP
response for the offerSearch operation. Its wrapper element, tns:offer-
SearchReturn, contains a list of zero or more retail:offer element
instances. These are the online shopping offers found on eBay, Amazon, or
Yahoo! Shopping that satisfy the search criteria. The XML Schema definition of retail:offer is shown Example 9–4.

Example 9–4 OfferType Contains the Summary Information for an Online Shopping
Offer from eBay, Amazon, or Yahoo! Shopping

```
 7      <xs:element name="offerList">
 8        <xs:complexType>
 9          <xs:sequence>
10            <xs:element ref="tns:offer" minOccurs="0" maxOccurs="unbounded"/>
11          </xs:sequence>
12        </xs:complexType>
13      </xs:element>
14
```

```
15    <xs:element name="offer" type="tns:OfferType"/>
16
17    <xs:complexType name="OfferType">
18      <xs:sequence>
19        <xs:element name="offerId" type="xs:string" nillable="true"/>
20        <xs:element name="productId" type="xs:string" minOccurs="0"/>
21        <xs:element name="source" type="tns:SourceType"/>
22        <xs:element name="thumbnail" type="tns:PictureType" minOccurs="0"/>
23        <xs:element name="price" type="tns:PriceType"/>
24        <xs:element name="merchantName" type="xs:string" minOccurs="0"/>
25        <xs:element name="summary" type="xs:string"/>
26        <xs:element name="offerUrl" type="xs:anyURI"/>
27      </xs:sequence>
28    </xs:complexType>
```

book-code/chap09/soashopper/soashopper-services-soap/src/main/webapp/WEB-INF
/wsdl/retail.xsd

These schema definitions are all from `retail.xsd`, which is discussed further in the next section on the REST interface. Before going there, let's look at how this WSDL gets mapped to Java. Example 9–5 shows the interface `ShopperPort` that is generated from the `wsdl:portType` named `ShopperPort` (see Example 9–1).

Example 9–5 The SEI—`ShopperPort`—Is Generated from the WSDL by the JAX-WS WSDL Compiler

```
38    @WebService(name = "ShopperPort",
39      targetNamespace = "http://soabook.com/soashopper")
40    @XmlSeeAlso( { com.example.faults.ObjectFactory.class,
41      com.soabook.soashopper.ObjectFactory.class,
42      com.example.retail.ObjectFactory.class })
43    public interface ShopperPort {
44
45      @WebMethod
46      @WebResult(name = "offer", targetNamespace = "http://www.example.com/
retail")
47      @RequestWrapper(localName = "offerSearch",
48        targetNamespace = "http://soabook.com/soashopper",
49        className = "com.soabook.soashopper.OfferSearch")
50      @ResponseWrapper(localName = "offerSearchReturn",
```

```
51        targetNamespace = "http://soabook.com/soashopper",
52        className = "com.soabook.soashopper.OfferSearchReturn")
53    public List<OfferType> offerSearch(
54        @WebParam(name = "keywords",
55          targetNamespace = "http://soabook.com/soashopper")
56        String keywords,
57        @WebParam(name = "category",
58          targetNamespace = "http://soabook.com/soashopper")
59        CategoryType category,
60        @WebParam(name = "lowprice",
61          targetNamespace = "http://soabook.com/soashopper")
62        PriceType lowprice,
63        @WebParam(name = "highprice",
64          targetNamespace = "http://soabook.com/soashopper")
65        PriceType highprice) throws InputFault;
66
67    }
```

book-code/chap09/soashopper/soashopper-services-generated/edited
  /ShopperPort.java

To deploy a Web service corresponding to the `wsdl:portType` named `ShopperPort`, an `@WebService` annotated class that implements the `ShopperPort` SEI is created, and the code inside the `offerSearch()` method invokes methods from the Service Implementation Layer. This `@WebService` annotated class—named `ShopperPortImp`—is deployed to implement the SOAP endpoint corresponding to the `wsdl:portType` named `ShopperPort`. Using JAX-WS like this, to design and deploy a Web service with a SEI, is described in detail in Chapter 7, Section 7.2, and in Chapter 8, Section 8.2. The annotations appearing in Example 9–5 (e.g., `@WebService`), and the JAX-WS WSDL to Java mapping, are described in detail in Chapter 6, Section 6.1.

As you look through the generated code in Example 9–5, notice that the classes used for the parameters (e.g., `CategoryType`) and the return type (i.e., `OfferType`) are JAXB-generated classes compiled from the schemas included in the WSDL. Of course, these generated classes are different from those used in the SOAShopper API. So, one job of the Service Implementation Layer (item 6 in Figure 9–1) is to implement type mappings that translate from these generated types to the types used by the SOAShopper API.

To deploy the SOAP endpoint, an implementation of the SEI shown in Example 9–5 is created. That implementation, `ShopperPortImp`, is shown in Example 9–6.

Example 9–6 `ShopperPortImp` implements the `ShopperPort` SEI (This Class Gets Deployed by JAX-WS As the SOAP Endpoint)

```
32  @WebService(wsdlLocation = "WEB-INF/wsdl/soashopper.wsdl",
33      endpointInterface = "com.soabook.soashopper.ShopperPort")
34  public class ShopperPortImp implements ShopperPort {
35
36    public List<OfferType> offerSearch(String keywords, CategoryType category,
37        PriceType lowprice, PriceType highprice) throws InputFault {
38      return (new ShopperService()).offerSearch(keywords, category.toString(),
39        lowprice.getCurrencyId().toString(), lowprice.getValue().doubleValue(),
40        highprice.getValue().doubleValue());
41    }
42
43  }
```

book-code/chap09/soashopper/soashopper-services-soap/src/main/java/com/javector
  /soashopper/endpoint/soap/ShopperPortImp.java

As you can see, this implementation is simply a wrapper that invokes the `offerSearch()` method from the `ShopperServices` class. `ShopperServices` is part of the `ServicesImplementation` layer and serves as a go-between that insulates the WSDL and REST endpoint implementations from the SOAShopper API. As I discuss in the next section, this same `ShopperServices` class is used to service the REST endpoint requests.

9.3   An SOAShopper RESTful Service and the Standard XML Schema

Analogous to the SOAP services just discussed, the SOAShopper application provides RESTful services as described in items 2 and 4 of Figure 9–1. However, since REST (as defined and discussed in Chapter 3) has no standard interface definition language, there is no corresponding WSDL-like document from which a Java API can be generated by the JAX-WS compiler. Fortunately, in this case, the RESTful service's response messages can be defined by XML Schema. The schema instances used in this case are the same as those used in the SOAP/WSDL case—the SOAShopper Standard XML Schema labeled as item 5 in Figure 9–1. These standard schemas, `http://soabook.com/example/retail/retail.xsd` and `http://soabook.com/example/faults/faults.xsd`, are imported/included into the WSDL types section as shown in Example 9–1.

So, for RESTful services, instead of generating Java from a WSDL, we have to write our own endpoint classes based on a human-readable description of the services. Figure 9–2 shows the type of documentation that could be provided for the REST version of the `offerSearch` service.

Request URL
http://javector.com/soashopper/endpoint/rest/offerSearch

Summary
The SOAShopper `offerSearch` Web service lets you search for product offers across eBay, Amazon, and Yahoo! Shopping. The **keywords** request parameter is required and the rest are optional. Here is an example search that returns all product offers containing the keywords "laptop" and "thinkpad" with prices between 600.00 and 800.00 U.S. dollars:

```
http://javector.com/soashopper/endpoint/rest/offerSearch?
keywords=laptop%20thinkpad&
currencyId=USD&lowprice=600.00&highprice=800.00
```

Request Parameters

Parameter	Value	Description
keywords	string	A space-delimited list of keywords to search for. Offers containing all the keywords are selected.
category	string	Specifies the category to be searched (e.g., COMPUTERS, CELLPHONES, MOVIES).
currencyId	string	Specifies the currency for the `lowprice` and `highprice` parameters (e.g., USD, GBP, INR).
lowprice	double	Offers with price greater than `lowprice` are selected.
highprice	double	Offers with price less than `highprice` are selected.

Response Elements
The SOAShopper `offerSearch` REST response is an XML element named `offerList` defined by the schema located at:

```
http://soabook.com/example/retail/retail.xsd
```

Figure 9–2 The documentation for the REST `offerSearch` operation is provided in human-readable format.

As described in the Figure 9–2 documentation, for the `offerSearch` REST service, the request message parameters are provided as HTTP parameters. There is no XML specified for the request message. Furthermore, I assume the request parameters may be provided in URL-encoded format using either one of the following:

- A GET method (as indicated in the example provided within the Summary section of the Figure 9–2) with the URL-encoded parameters in the query string or
- A POST method with the URL-encoded parameters in the HTTP body

The response message, on the other hand, will be an HTTP response with the XML element named `offerList` in the body. Example 9–7 shows the XML Schema definition for the `offerList` element. This is the same XML Schema used by the SOAP endpoint and listed in Example 9–4.

Example 9–7 The XML Schema That Defines the `offerList` Response Element Used by the `offerSearch` REST Service

```
7    <xs:element name="offerList">
8      <xs:complexType>
9        <xs:sequence>
10         <xs:element ref="tns:offer" minOccurs="0" maxOccurs="unbounded"/>
11        </xs:sequence>
12      </xs:complexType>
13   </xs:element>
14
15   <xs:element name="offer" type="tns:OfferType"/>
16
17   <xs:complexType name="OfferType">
18     <xs:sequence>
19       <xs:element name="offerId" type="xs:string" nillable="true"/>
20       <xs:element name="productId" type="xs:string" minOccurs="0"/>
21       <xs:element name="source" type="tns:SourceType"/>
22       <xs:element name="thumbnail" type="tns:PictureType" minOccurs="0"/>
23       <xs:element name="price" type="tns:PriceType"/>
24       <xs:element name="merchantName" type="xs:string" minOccurs="0"/>
25       <xs:element name="summary" type="xs:string"/>
26       <xs:element name="offerUrl" type="xs:anyURI"/>
27     </xs:sequence>
28   </xs:complexType>
```

book-code/chap09/soashopper/soashopper-services-soap/src/main/webapp/WEB-INF
/wsdl/retail.xsd

In the SOAP case, JAX-WS provides a standard binding and tool for compiling the WSDL into a Java interface that can be used to deploy a service conforming to the WSDL. In the REST case, you must create your own Java interface that corresponds to the documentation provided for the service. Example 9–8 shows the Java interface definition that I created.

Example 9–8 The Java Interface Used to Define the REST Service Corresponding to the Documentation Given in Figure 9–2

```
22  public interface ShopperServiceREST {
23
24      public OfferList offerSearch(String keywords, String category,
25          String currencyId, Double lowprice, Double highprice);
26
27  }
```

book-code/chap09/soashopper/soashopper-services-rest/src/main/java
  /com/javector/soashopper/endpoint/rest/ShopperServiceREST.java

I have used certain conventions to define this ShopperServiceREST interface. These are not conventions that are specified by any standard (since no such standard is available). They are merely sensible conventions. First, the name of the method is the same as the REST operation, which is the last name in the URL path before the query string begins. Second, the parameters of the method are the same as the request parameters specified in the REST service documentation (see Figure 9–2). Lastly, the return type is the JAXB schema compiled class resulting from the offerList element defined by the schema located at http://soabook.com/example/retail/retail.xsd.

Now, if this were a SOAP service, the method implementing the service (i.e., offerSearch) would be annotated with the @WebMethod annotation (see Example 9–5). However, since this is a REST service, it is implemented using an instance of javax.xml.ws.Provider. When deploying a javax.xml.ws.Provider instance, its invoke() method is the only method that gets published as a service. So, the convention I use in this case is that the implementation class for a REST service should implement both the human-defined REST interface (e.g., ShopperServiceREST) and the javax.xml.ws.Provider interface. Using this convention, the invoke()

method calls the human-defined REST interface method (e.g., `Shop-perServiceREST.offerSeach()`). Example 9–9 shows the REST implementation class definition.

Example 9–9 The `ShopperServiceRESTImp` Class Implements the `offerSearch` REST Service by Implementing Both the `ShopperServiceREST` and the `Provider<Source>` Interfaces

```
43  @WebServiceProvider
44  @BindingType(HTTPBinding.HTTP_BINDING)
45  public class ShopperServiceRESTImp implements ShopperServiceREST,
46      Provider<Source> {
47
48      @Resource
49      WebServiceContext wsContext;
50
51      JAXBContext jaxbContext;
52
53      public ShopperServiceRESTImp() {
54        try {
55          jaxbContext = JAXBContext.newInstance(OfferList.class);
56        } catch (JAXBException je) {
57          throw new HTTPException(HttpServletResponse.SC_INTERNAL_SERVER_ERROR);
58        }
59      }
60
```

book-code/chap09/soashopper/soashopper-services-rest/src/main/java/com/javector
  /soashopper/endpoint/rest/ShopperServiceRESTImp.java

There are two other points worth noting from Example 9–9. First, the class contains a `WebServiceContext` (`wsContext`) variable that gets instantiated via dependency injection, and a `JAXBContext` (`jaxbContext`) variable that is instantiated in the constructor. The `wsContext` variable provides access to the HTTP request so that the HTTP parameters can be retrieved. Similarly, the `jaxbContext` variable provides the ability to create the HTTP response XML element, `offerList`, specified by the REST documentation in Figure 9–2.

Example 9–10 The RESTful Implementation of the `offerSearch()` Method Invokes `ShopperService.offerSearch()`—the Same Method Invoked by the SOAP Implementation

```
65    public OfferList offerSearch(String keywords, String category,
66        String currencyId, Double lowprice, Double highprice) {
67
68    ShopperService shopperService = new ShopperService();
69    List<OfferType> offers = shopperService.offerSearch(keywords,
70        category, currencyId, lowprice, highprice);
71    OfferList offerList = new OfferList();
72    List<OfferType> offerListOffers = offerList.getOffer();
73    offerListOffers.addAll(offers);
74    return offerList;
75
76    }
77
```

book-code/chap09/soashopper/soashopper-services-rest/src/main/java/com/javector
  /soashopper/endpoint/rest/ShopperServiceRESTImp.java

Example 9–10 shows the implementation of the `offerSearch()` method specified by the `ShopperServiceRESTImp`. The SOAShopper architecture has been designed so that the SOAP and REST implementations of `offerSearch` both invoked the same method from the Service Implementation Layer— `ShopperService.offerSearch()`. In this manner, the REST and SOAP endpoints are really just different APIs for invoking the same functionality.

Example 9–11 shows how the `invoke()` method, specified by the `Provider<Source>` interface, is implemented.

Example 9–11 The `invoke()` Method Specified by the `Provider<Source>` Interface Extracts the HTTP Parameters and Calls the `offerSearch()` Method

```
82    public Source invoke(Source source) {
83
84    MessageContext msgContext = wsContext.getMessageContext();
85    String httpMethod = (String) msgContext
86        .get(MessageContext.HTTP_REQUEST_METHOD);
87    Map<String, String[]> params = null;
88    if (httpMethod.equals("GET") || httpMethod.equals("POST")) {
89      HttpServletRequest httpReq = (HttpServletRequest) msgContext
90        .get(MessageContext.SERVLET_REQUEST);
```

```
91       params = httpReq.getParameterMap();
92     } else {
93       throw new HTTPException(HttpServletResponse.SC_METHOD_NOT_ALLOWED);
94     }
95     String keywords = getParam(params, "keywords");
96     if (keywords == null) {
97       throw new HTTPException(HttpServletResponse.SC_NOT_FOUND);
98     }
99     String category = getParam(params, "category");
100    String currencyId = getParam(params, "currencyId");
101    String lowpriceStr = getParam(params, "lowprice");
102    String highpriceStr = getParam(params, "highprice");
103    Double lowprice = lowpriceStr == null ? null : Double.valueOf(lowpriceStr);
104    Double highprice = highpriceStr == null ? null : Double
105        .valueOf(highpriceStr);
106    OfferList offerList = offerSearch(keywords, category, currencyId, lowprice,
107        highprice);
108    if (offerList == null) {
109      return null;
110    }
111    try {
112      return new JAXBSource(jaxbContext, offerList);
113    } catch (JAXBException e) {
114      throw new HTTPException(HttpServletResponse.SC_INTERNAL_SERVER_ERROR);
115    }
116
117  }
118
```

book-code/chap09/soashopper/soashopper-services-rest/src/main/java/com/javector
  /soashopper/endpoint/rest/ShopperServiceRESTImp.java

When the ShopperServiceRESTImp class is deployed, the JAX-WS run-time binds this invoke() method to the REST endpoint. So, XML/HTTP requests are passed to invoke(). The input parameter, of type Source, is ignored because this RESTful service takes no XML as input and instead uses the HTTP parameters contained in either the URL query string (for GET requests) or the HTTP body (for POST requests).

Instead, the code uses the WebServiceContext instance, wsContext, to get at the HttpServletRequest via the MessageContext. Then, the parameters are extracted using HttpServletRequest.getParameter-Map()—in the same manner in which such a process would happen within an

`HttpServlet` implementation. Once the parameters are extracted, the `offerSearch()` method gets invoked. The response—`offerList`—is a JAXB-generated class instance. As a result, we can wrap it as a `javax.xml.transform.Source` using `JAXBSource`, and return it.

The last issue to touch on related to the REST endpoint is deployment. Example 9–12 shows the web.xml deployment descriptor that is used.

Example 9–12 The web.xml Used to Deploy the REST Endpoint

```
4   <web-app xmlns="http://java.sun.com/xml/ns/javaee"
5     xmlns:j2ee="http://java.sun.com/xml/ns/javaee"
6     xmlns:xsi="http://www.w3.org/2001/XMLSchema-instance" version="2.5"
7     xsi:schemaLocation="http://java.sun.com/xml/ns/javaee
8     http://java.sun.com/xml/ns/javaee/web-app_2_5.xsd">
9     <display-name>soashopper-rest-endpoint</display-name>
10    <servlet>
11      <servlet-name>com.javector.soashopper.endpoint.rest.ShopperServiceRESTImp</servlet-name>
12      <servlet-class>com.javector.soashopper.endpoint.rest.ShopperServiceRESTImp</servlet-class>
13      <load-on-startup>0</load-on-startup>
14    </servlet>
15    <servlet-mapping>
16      <servlet-name>com.javector.soashopper.endpoint.rest.ShopperServiceRESTImp</servlet-name>
17      <url-pattern>/shopper</url-pattern>
18    </servlet-mapping>
19  </web-app>
```

book-code/chap09/soashopper/soashopper-services-rest/src/main/webapp/WEB-INF
/web.xml

Notice that the `<servlet-name>` is the fully qualified name of the REST endpoint implementation class. This is a GlassFish requirement that derives from the GlassFish implementation of WSEE [JSR 109]. Actually, the requirement, from Section 5.3.2.2 of [JSR 109], states that the `<servlet-link>` element in the `webservices.xml` deployment descriptor must use the fully qualified name of the `@WebServiceProvider` annotated class. But as discussed in Chapter 8, Section 8.1 (see Figure 8-3), in the GlassFish implementation, the `web.xml` `<servlet-name>` is used to generate the `webservices.xml` `<servlet-link>`, so the requirement carries back to the `web.xml`.

The `<url-pattern>`, toward the bottom of Example 9–12, determines the last part of the REST endpoint's URL. In this case, the endpoint is going to be `http://host-name/context-root/rest/shopper`. So, if you are deploying on your local machine (port 8080) and using `soashopper` as the context root, you end up with a REST service deployed at `http://localhost:8080/soashopper/rest/shopper`. So, to do a search for a `Thinkpad` laptop that costs less than $800, you could submit a `GET` request to the following URL:

```
http://localhost:8080/soashopper/rest/
   shopper&keywords=thinkpad&highprice=800.00
```

9.4 Service Implementation

The preceding two sections focused on how the SOAP and REST endpoints are designed. In this section, I turn my attention to the Service Implementation layer (item 6 in the SOAShopper architecture shown in Figure 9–1). The Service Implementation layer provides a set of classes and methods that handle both the SOAP and the REST requests. Essentially, the SOAP and REST endpoints are deployment wrappers around the basic Service Implementation functionality.[4]

Example 9–13 illustrates the wrapper functionality provided by the `ShopperService` class that is part of the Service Implementation layer. The method shown, `ShopperService.offerSearch`, has a signature comprising types used by the SOAP/REST endpoints: `String`, `Double`, and `OfferType`. As discussed in the previous sections, `OfferType` is the JAXB schema-derived class generated from `retail:OfferType`.

Example 9–13 The `ShopperService` Class Mediates between the REST/SOAP Endpoints and the SOAShopper API (The `ShopperService.offerSearch` Method Shown Here Processes Search Requests from the REST/SOAP Endpoints)

```
33    public List<OfferType> offerSearch(String keywords, String categoryId,
34        String currencyId, Double lowpriceVal, Double highpriceVal) {
```

---

4. For the REST case, this point is discussed in the text related to Example 9–10.

```
35
36      // convert from SOAP/REST request types to SOAShopper API types
37      TypeConverter tc = new TypeConverter();
38      Category category = tc.toCategory(categoryId);
39      Price lowprice = tc.toPrice(currencyId, lowpriceVal);
40      Price highprice = tc.toPrice(currencyId, highpriceVal);
41      // invoke the SOAShopper API
42      Shopper shoppingService = new Shopper();
43      List<Offer> offerList = shoppingService.offerSearch(keywords, category,
44          lowprice, highprice);
45      // convert from SOAShopper API return type to SOAP/REST response type
46      ArrayList<OfferType> offerTypeList = new ArrayList<OfferType>();
47      for (Offer o : offerList) {
48        offerTypeList.add(tc.toOfferType(o));
49      }
50      return offerTypeList;
51
52    }
```

book-code/chap09/soashopper/soashopper-servicesimp/src/main/java/com/javector
  /soashopper/services/ShopperService.java

So, as you can see in this example, the `ShopperService.offerSearch` method performs two functions: (1) It converts types between the SOAP/ REST services layer and the SOAShopper API; and (2) it invokes the SOAShopper API to perform the search. Notice the instance of a class named `TypeConverter` in this example. That is where the type mappings are implemented.

Example 9–14 shows how these type mapping are implemented. Essentially, this method implements the serialization portion of the type mapping:

```
<retail:OfferType, com.javector.soashopper.Offer>
```

The approach to type mapping used here is recursive in that the mapping from `Offer` to `retail:OfferType` is assembled using the mappings from the constituent parts of `retail:OfferType`. For example, the `toOfferType()` method shown invokes the methods that implement the type mappings for `<retail:PriceType, com.javector.soashopper.Price>` and `<retail:Pic-tureType, com.javector.soashopper.Picture>`.

Example 9–14 The `TypeConverter.toOfferType` Method Converts from the SOAShopper API's `OfferType` to the REST/SOAP Endpoint's JAXB Schema Compiled `OfferType`

```
194    /**
195     * Convert the SOAShopper API Offer type to the JAXB Generated OfferType used
196     * by the SOAP and REST endpoints.
197     *
198     * @param o
199     * @return
200     */
201    public OfferType toOfferType(Offer o) {
202
203        if (o == null) { return null; }
204        OfferType ot = new OfferType();
205        ot.setOfferId(o.getSourceSpecificOfferId());
206        ot.setProductId(o.getSourceSpecificProductId());
207        ot.setSource(toSourceType(o.getSource()));
208        ot.setThumbnail(toPictureType(o.getThumbnail()));
209        ot.setPrice(toPriceType(o.getPrice()));
210        ot.setMerchantName(o.getMerchantName());
211        ot.setSummary(o.getSummary());
212        ot.setOfferUrl(o.getUrl().toString());
213         return ot;
214
215    }
216
```

book-code/chap09/soashopper/soashopper-engine/src/main/java/com/javector/util
  /TypeConverter.java

The recursive framework for implementing type mappings used in this example is described in detail in Chapter 5, Sections 5.3 and 5.4. It is based on using the standard JAXB mapping along with recursion. Because this technique is used for the implementation of SOAShopper, there is no need for any customization of the JAXB standard mapping. This approach makes the code a little easier to understand and maintain for programmers who are not fluent in XML Schema or the JAXB annotations.[5]

---

5. For an alternative approach to implementing type mappings directly using JAXB annotations, binding language, and the `XMLAdapter` class, see Chapter 5, Sections 5.5–5.7. Using such an approach would enable us to dispense with the `TypeConversion` class and map the SOAShopper API directly to the SOAP/REST endpoint schema (`retail.xsd`) using annotations.

Having looked at the Services Implementation Layer that mediates between the SOAP/REST endpoints and the SOAPShopper API, in the next few sections, I am going to focus on how JAX-WS is used to access the source shopping systems: eBay, Amazon, and Yahoo! Shopping. Then, in the last section, I will come back and look at the SOAShopper API and the Integration Layer (items 7 and 8 in the SOAShopper architecture shown in Figure 9–1).

9.5   eBay and Amazon Services (SOAP)[6]

This section looks at the SOAP-based services provided by eBay and Amazon. Actually, the discussion focuses entirely on the eBay services. The Amazon implementation is structured similarly, however, and you can look at the code in `<book-code>/chap09/soashopper` to see the Amazon specifics.

Because the eBay and Amazon services provide WSDL descriptions, the JAX-WS WSDL/Java binding tool can generate the Java API used to invoke them. Section 9.2 shows how the WSDL/Java binding tool is used on the service side. In that section, the SOAShopper WSDL gets compiled to create the Java service endpoint interface (SEI) for our SOAP endpoint. In this section, I show how to use the same WSDL/Java binding tool[7] on the client side. Here, you will see how to generate proxies that use the client-side JAX-WS framework to invoke the eBay and Amazon Web services. Chapter 6 contains a detailed discussion of proxies and client-side JAX-WS, along with some simpler examples.

The SOAShopper build process uses Ant to invoke the WSDL/Java binding tool. The Ant target for compiling the eBay WSDL is shown in Example 9–15.

Example 9–15 The Apache Ant Target Used to Compile the eBay WSDL (The JAX-WS WSDL Compiler Tool `wsimport` Gets Invoked)

```
23    <target name="compile-ebay-wsdl">
24       <delete dir="${java.generated}/ebay" />
```

---

6. Some of the eBay-related code presented in this section was inspired by a JAX-WS 2.0 article [Eckstein] appearing on the Sun Web site.
7. The GlassFish tool is `wsimport`.

```
25      <exec executable="${wsimport}">
26        <!-- needed because ebay wsdl is huge -->
27        <env key="VMARGS" value="-Xmx512m" />
28        <!-- suppress the warning messages -->
29        <arg value="-quiet" />
30        <arg value="-keep" />
31         <arg line="-d target/junk" />
32        <arg line="-s ${java.generated}" />
33        <arg value="http://developer.ebay.com/webservices/479/eBaySvc.wsdl" />
34      </exec>
35     </target>
```

book-code/chap09/soashopper/soashopper-sources-generated/build.xml

This example shows the use of the GlassFish tool—wsimport. The last argument passed to wsimport in this Ant target is the URL of the WSDL to be compiled. As you can see, that URL is:

http://developer.ebay.com/webservices/479/eBaySvc.wsdl

Notice that this URL has a version number in it—479. The eBay WSDL changes fairly frequently, and each version increments that version number. You can find the latest version at:

http://developer.ebay.com/webservices/latest/eBaySvc.wsdl

I use a fixed version number for this example so that the code always compiles the same. A change in version means changes in the WSDL/Java-generated class definitions. This, in turn, can cause the modules of SOAShopper that depend on these generated classes to fail to compile.

Now, I consider where the WSDL/Java-generated classes fit into the big scheme of things. Figure 9–3 shows a diagram of the client-side invocation framework for eBay. The Amazon framework is similar. This client-side invocation framework is a version of the general JAX-WS approach to consuming Web services discussed in Chapter 6, Section 1.6, and illustrated in Figure 6–1. The framework shown here is a bit more elaborate, providing implementation-specific detail related to eBay.

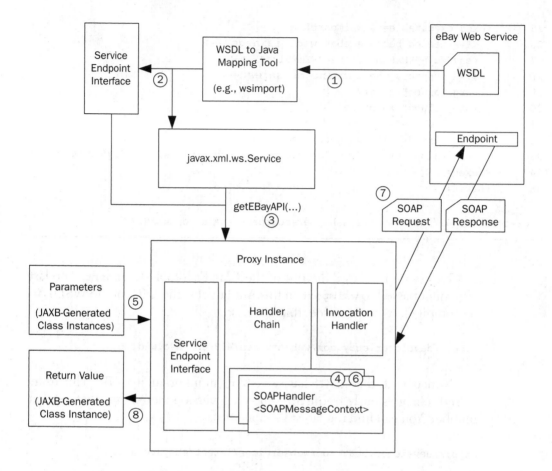

Client Component	Java Implementation
Service Endpoint Interface	`ebay.apis.eblbasecomponents.EBayAPIInterface`
javax.xml.ws.Service	`ebay.apis.eblbasecomponents.EBayAPIInterfaceService`
Parameters	`ebay.apis.eblbasecomponents.GetSearchResultsRequestType`
Return Value	`ebay.apis.eblbasecomponents.GetSearchResultsResponseType`
SOAPHandler	`com.javector.soashopper.ebay.RequesterCredentials`

Service Component	URL
Endpoint	`https://api.ebay.com/wsapi?` `    callname=XX&version=479&siteid=0&appid=YY&Routing=new`
WSDL	`http://developer.ebay.com/webservices/479/eBaySvc.wsdl`

Figure 9–3 The JAX-WS classes generated from the eBay WSDL are configured and used to invoke the eBay Web service.

The various components of this scenario are labeled 1–8, and each component is described:

1. The eBay WSDL is versioned, and different versions have different URLs. For this example, I used version 479.

2. The WSDL/Java mapping tool (`wsimport`) is used (as illustrated in Example 9–15) to generate the SEI (`ebay.apis.eblbasecomponents.EBayAPIInterface`) along with a `javax.xml.ws.Service` implementation that acts as a factory class that can generate instances of the SEI.

3. Items 1 and 2 are executed during the SOAShopper build. The remaining steps, including this one, are run-time steps. To invoke the eBay service, first you need to get a proxy class implementing the SEI. The `Service` class (`ebay.apis.eblbasecomponents.EBayAPIInterfaceService`) provides the factory method `getEBayAPI()` to provide an instance of that SEI (`ebay.apis.eblbasecomponents.EBayAPIInterface`).

4. The next component, 4, appears in the lower right of the diagram. Here, we need to do a little customization of the SEI proxy instance so that it conforms to the eBay invocation process. In this step, we add a `HandlerChain` instance to the proxy. The chain contains a single handler, `com.javector.soashopper.ebay.RequesterCredentials`, which adds some SOAP headers to outgoing request messages.

5. To send a SOAP request to the eBay service, the SEI method `getSearchResults` (see Example 9–17) is invoked with a single parameter of type `ebay.apis.eblbasecomponents.GetSearchResultsRequestType`. This parameter is a wrapper containing all the search parameters required by eBay (see Example 9–18). This parameter becomes the body of the SOAP message.

6. During invocation, the `SOAPHandler` that was added to the proxy instance in step 4 creates the SOAP header elements required by eBay.

7. Next, the `InvocationHandler` (see description in Chapter 6, Section 6.1), internal to the `Proxy` instance, sends the SOAP request to the eBay endpoint. Notice the representation of the SOAP endpoint URL shown in Figure 9–3: `https://api.ebay.com/wsapi?callname=XX&version=479&siteid=0&appid=YY&Routing=new`. This endpoint varies based on the name of the operation being invoked (i.e., `callname=XX`). It also contains URL encoded HTTP parameters in the query string for the version, site location (i.e., `siteid=0`), and so forth.

8. The SOAP response message from eBay is processed by the `Invoca-`
`tionHandler`, and the return value, of type `ebay.apis.eblbasecom-`
`ponents.GetSearchResultsResponseType`, specified by the WSDL,
is returned from the SEI method.

At this point, I walk through these eight steps in some more detail and
look at some of the code to better illustrate what is going on. Example 9–16
shows how we get the proxy instance (step 3) and configure it. As you can
see, an instance of the `javax.xml.ws.Service` generated by JAX-WS,
`EBayAPIInterfaceService`, is created and its `getEBayAPI()` method is
used to return an instance of the SEI, `EBayAPIInterface`, referenced by
the `port` variable.

Example 9–16 This Code from the `EBayShopperImp` Constructor Executes
Steps 3 and 4 from Figure 9–3

```
117     EBayAPIInterfaceService svc = new EBayAPIInterfaceService();
118     port = svc.getEBayAPI();
119     BindingProvider bp = (BindingProvider) port;
120     List<Handler> handlerChain = new ArrayList<Handler>();
121     handlerChain.add(new RequesterCredentials());
122     bp.getBinding().setHandlerChain(handlerChain);
```

book-code/chap09/soashopper/soashopper-engine/src/main/java/com
  /javector/soashopper/ebay/EBayShopperImp.java

Having obtained an instance of the SEI, it is configured (step 4) by adding
the `SOAPHandler`—an instance of `RequesterCredentials`. This is accomplished by calling the `BindingProvider.setHandlerChain()` method.

Example 9–17 shows the code that was generated by JAX-WS to define
the SEI method `getSearchResults`. This method is invoked in step 5.
Notice that the method has a single parameter, which eBay uses as a wrapper for its various search parameters.

Example 9–17 The `EBayAPIInterface.getSearchResults` Method That Is
Generated from the eBay WSDL

```
845     @WebMethod(operationName = "GetSearchResults")
846     @WebResult(name = "GetSearchResultsResponse",
```

```
847          targetNamespace = "urn:ebay:apis:eBLBaseComponents",
848          partName = "GetSearchResultsResponse")
849     public GetSearchResultsResponseType getSearchResults(
850          @WebParam(name = "GetSearchResultsRequest",
851             targetNamespace = "urn:ebay:apis:eBLBaseComponents",
852             partName = "GetSearchResultsRequest")
853          GetSearchResultsRequestType getSearchResultsRequest);
```

book-code/chap09/soashopper/soashopper-sources-generated/edited
  /EBayAPIInterface.java

The `GetSearchResults` operation from the eBay WSDL that produced this JAX-WS-generated `EBayAPIInterface.getSearchResults` method is this:

```
<wsdl:operation name="GetSearchResults">
  <wsdl:input message="ns:GetSearchResultsRequest"/>
  <wsdl:output message="ns:GetSearchResultsResponse"/>
</wsdl:operation>
```

Notice that the input message's name is `GetSearchResultsRequest`. That message is defined as follows in the WSDL:

```
<wsdl:message name="GetSearchResultsRequest">
  <wsdl:part name="GetSearchResultsRequest"
  element="ns:GetSearchResultsRequest"/>
</wsdl:message>
```

Here, you can see that this message has a single parameter—an element named `GetSearchResultsRequest`. You can see that name specified in Example 9–17 inside the `@WebParam` annotation.

From these snippets, we can conclude that the eBay WSDL appears to have the document/literal style[8] rather than document/literal wrapped. As discussed in Chapter 4, Section 4.3.5, in order to have the document/literal wrapped style, the message element (i.e., `ns:GetSearchResultsRequest`) would have to be named the same as the operation—`GetSearchResults`. This explains why the JAX-WS WSDL compiler created the SEI method `getSearchResults` (Example 9–17) with a single parameter. If the WSDL style had been document/literal wrapped, JAX-WS would have generated a

___
8. See Chapter 4 for a discussion of the WSDL styles.

SEI method that used the multiple elements contained within the `Get-SearchResultsRequest` element as a list of parameters.

Example 9–18 shows a snippet of the eBay WSDL containing the element definition for `GetSearchResultsRequest`. This type contains the parameters that must be mapped to the SOAShopper API search parameters.

Example 9–18 A Snippet from the eBay WSDL Showing the Search Request Type `Get-SearchResultsRequestType`

```
4  <!-- Version 479 -->
5  <!-- Copyright (c) 2003-2006 eBay Inc. All Rights Reserved. -->
6  <wsdl:definitions xmlns:wsdl="http://schemas.xmlsoap.org/wsdl/"
7    xmlns:xs="http://www.w3.org/2001/XMLSchema">
8    <wsdl:types>
9      <xs:schema targetNamespace="urn:ebay:apis:eBLBaseComponents">
10       <xs:element name="GetSearchResultsRequest"
11         type="ns:GetSearchResultsRequestType"/>
12       <xs:complexType name="GetSearchResultsRequestType">
13         <!-- .... / snip / ... -->
14         <xs:sequence>
15           <xs:element name="Query" type="xs:string" minOccurs="0"/>
16           <xs:element name="CategoryID" type="xs:string" minOccurs="0"/>
17           <xs:element name="PriceRangeFilter" type="ns:PriceRangeFilterType"
18             minOccurs="0"/>
19           <!-- .... / snip / ... -->
20         </xs:sequence>
21       </xs:complexType>
22       <!-- .... / snip / ... -->
23     </xs:schema>
24   </wsdl:types>
25   <!-- .... / snip / ... -->
26 </wsdl:definitions>
```

book-code/chap09/soashopper/soashopper-sources-generated/edited
  /eBaySvcSnippet.wsdl

As you can see, the schema definition for `GetSearchResultsRequest` contains a list of elements such as `Query`, `CategoryID`, and `PriceRangeFilter`. These subelements actually map to the SOAShopper API search parameters. For example, `Query` corresponds to `keywords`, and `PriceRangeFilter` corresponds to the `lowprice` and `highprice` parameters. This mapping is the job of the Integration Layer and is discussed in Section 9.7.

After the SEI method `getSearchResults` is invoked, the proxy instance builds the SOAP message to be sent to the eBay WSDL endpoint. However, a few more manipulations must be applied to the SOAP message before it is ready to send. Example 9–19 shows the code that executes step 6 from Figure 9–3. This code, from the `SOAPHandler RequesterCredentials`, adds the SOAP headers to the request message.

Example 9–19 The `RequesterCredentials SOAPHandler` Adds the SOAP Header Elements Required by the eBay SOAP Endpoint (This Code Executes Step 6 from Figure 9–3)

```
69    Boolean outboundProperty = (Boolean) smc
70        .get(MessageContext.MESSAGE_OUTBOUND_PROPERTY);
71
72    if (outboundProperty.booleanValue()) {
73      SOAPMessage message = smc.getMessage();
74      try {
75        SOAPHeader header = message.getSOAPHeader();
76        if (header == null) {
77          message.getSOAPPart().getEnvelope().addHeader();
78          header = message.getSOAPHeader();
79        }
80        SOAPElement heSecurity = header.addChildElement("RequesterCredentials",
81            "ebl", "urn:ebay:apis:eBLBaseComponents");
82        heSecurity.addChildElement("eBayAuthToken", "ebl",
83            "urn:ebay:apis:eBLBaseComponents").addTextNode(
84            ShopperCredentials.getEBayAuthToken());
85        SOAPElement userNameToken = heSecurity.addChildElement("Credentials",
86            "ebl", "urn:ebay:apis:eBLBaseComponents");
87        userNameToken.addChildElement("AppId", "ebl",
88            "urn:ebay:apis:eBLBaseComponents").addTextNode(
89            ShopperCredentials.getEBayAppID());
90        userNameToken.addChildElement("DevId", "ebl",
91            "urn:ebay:apis:eBLBaseComponents").addTextNode(
92            ShopperCredentials.getEBayDevID());
93        userNameToken.addChildElement("AuthCert", "ebl",
94            "urn:ebay:apis:eBLBaseComponents").addTextNode(
95            ShopperCredentials.getEBayCertID());
96
97      } catch (Exception e) {
```

```
98              e.printStackTrace();
99          }
100     }
```

book-code/chap09/soashopper/soashopper-engine/src/main/java/com/javector/
  soashopper/ebay/RequesterCredentials.java

This code adds a header named `RequesterCredentials`. As you can see, this header gets configured in this code with child elements such as `eBayAuthToken`, `Credentials`, and so on. These are the security credentials required by eBay. In the code, you can see that these security credentials are read from the `ShopperCredentials` object. `ShopperCredentials`, in turn, is populated by a set of properties stored in a file. It gets instantiated from the file when the SOAShopper application is loaded by the JVM.

The need for this SOAP header is specified in the WSDL. Here is the portion of the `wsdl:binding` that shows the SOAP binding for the `Get-SearchResults` operation:

```
<wsdl:operation name="GetSearchResults">
  <wsdlsoap:operation soapAction=""/>
  <wsdl:input>
    <wsdlsoap:header use="literal" message="ns:RequesterCredentials"
      part="RequesterCredentials"/>
    <wsdlsoap:body use="literal"/>
  </wsdl:input>
  <wsdl:output>
    <wsdlsoap:header use="literal" message="ns:RequesterCredentials"
      part="RequesterCredentials"/>
    <wsdlsoap:body use="literal"/>
  </wsdl:output>
</wsdl:operation>
```

As you can see, this SOAP binding specifies a header message (`ns:RequesterCredentials`) for the operation. The code in Example 9–19 implements the inclusion of this SOAP header in the request message sent to eBay.

You may be wondering why the JAX-WS WSDL/Java mapping tool did not simply bind the `ns:RequesterCredentials` message to a class and add it as a parameter to the `getSearchResults` method. As it turns out, this behavior is possible, but is described as optional by the JAX-WS 2.0 specification (see Section 2.6.2.1 of [JSR 224]). The mapping tool used in this example (i.e., GlassFish `wsimport`) does not implement this feature. As a result, we need to write our own SOAPHandler to take care of it.

The last step (step 7) that needs to be completed before the SOAP request can be sent to the eBay endpoint is to finalize the URL of that endpoint. Because the eBay WSDL uses the document/literal style (as opposed to rpc/literal or document/literal wrapped), the operation being invoked by the SOAP request is not the same as the wrapper element name of the child element in the SOAP body. So, if the eBay server is to determine which WSDL operation a given SOAP message invokes, it needs that additional piece of information. eBay asks us to provide that information, the operation name, as a URL-encoded parameter in the query string of the endpoint. So, in this case, the endpoint URL needs to include the parameter `callname=GetSearchRequest` in its query string. The code to accomplish that is shown in Example 9–20.

Example 9–20 The SOAP Endpoint for the eBay Service Contains URL-Encoded HTTP Parameters That Are Configured at Runtime

```
119    endpointURL = ebayURL + "callname=" + CALLNAME_TOKEN + "&siteid=0&appid="
120        + appid + "&version=" + WSDL_VERSION + "&Routing=new";
```

book-code/chap09/soashopper/soashopper-engine/src/main/java/com/javector
 /soashopper/ebay/EBayShopperImp.java

As you can see, the `endpointURL` has been set up with a `CALLNAME_TOKEN` string. This token gets replaced by the actual `callname` with each SOAP request. The code that accomplishes that is shown in Example 9–21. The URL-encoded HTTP parameter for `callname` (e.g., `GetSearchResults`) must be configured at runtime for each SOAP request. In JAX-WS 2.0, this can be accomplished by customizing the endpoint URL's query string and then setting it as the `BindingProvider.ENDPOINT_ADDRESS_PROPERTY`.

Example 9–21 The URL-encoded HTTP parameter for `callname`

```
160    private void configureEBayRequestType(AbstractRequestType art, String
 callname) {
161
162        art.setVersion(WSDL_VERSION);
163        art.setErrorLanguage(ERROR_LANGUAGE);
```

```
164    String endpointURL = eBayURLTemplate.replace(CALLNAME_TOKEN, callname);
165    ((BindingProvider) port).getRequestContext().put(
166        BindingProvider.ENDPOINT_ADDRESS_PROPERTY, endpointURL);
167    }
168
```

book-code/chap09/soashopper/soashopper-engine/src/main/java/com/javector/
  soashopper/ebay/EBayShopperImp.java

As you can see here, each method that invokes an eBay operation must first configure the call request object and the port using this method—`configureEBayRequestType`. This method sets necessary parameters (e.g., version and error language) on the request object.[9] It also customizes the endpoint URL to include the `callname` parameter as required by the eBay API. Using JAX-WS, we can set the newly modified `endpointURL` by setting the `BindingProvider.ENDPOINT_ADDRESS_PROPERTY` property in the `BindingProvider`'s request context.

That completes the discussion of how to invoke an eBay SOAP endpoint using JAX-WS. As you can see, it basically boils down to compiling the eBay WSDL and then working with the generated API classes within the JAX-WS client-side invocation framework. Some additional work needs to be done to handle the unusual endpoint query string conventions employed by eBay, and to add the security SOAP headers required. But all this is well within the capabilities provided by JAX-WS 2.0.

9.6 Yahoo! Services (REST)

Having completed the description of SOAP invocation, I now turn to the inner workings of invoking the Yahoo! Shopping services using REST. Although the invocation of REST services also uses the JAX-WS client-side framework, the process is not as automated as in the SOAP case. This is because a REST endpoint does not have a WSDL description or any other machine-readable interface definition.

As a result, to build a Yahoo! Shopping invocation subsystem for SOAShopper, I had to manually design the Java API rather than use a

---

9. The request type used as a parameter in this method is `AbstractRequestType`, the super type of `GetSearchResultsRequest`.

WSDL/Java mapping tool to generate an API. To the extent that the REST documentation includes XML Schema documents defining the XML requests and responses, however, the JAXB schema compiler can be used to create Java parameters and return types used by the methods that invoke the REST endpoints.

This is the case for Yahoo! Shopping—at least for the return types. The REST requests are simply HTTP parameters (passed, for example, as query strings). The responses, however, are instances of XML schemas that are referenced in the documentation. Example 9–22 shows the Ant build script used to invoke the JAXB schema compiler (i.e., the GlassFish `xjc` tool).

Example 9–22 The Apache Ant Target Used to Compile the Yahoo! Shopping Schemas (The JAXB Schema Compiler Tool `xjc` Gets Invoked)

```
8    <target name="compile-yahoo-schema">
9      <delete dir="${java.generated}/yahoo" />
10     <!-- product search schema -->
11     <exec executable="${xjc}">
12       <arg line="-d ${java.generated}" />
13       <arg value="http://api.shopping.yahoo.com/shoppingservice/v2/
productsearch.xsd" />
14       <arg value="http://api.shopping.yahoo.com/shoppingservice/v1/
merchantsearch.xsd" />
15       <arg value="http://api.shopping.yahoo.com/shoppingservice/v1/
cataloglisting.xsd" />
16       <arg value="http://api.shopping.yahoo.com/shoppingservice/v1/
catalogspecs.xsd" />
17       <arg value="http://api.shopping.yahoo.com/ShoppingService/v1/
userproductreview.xsd" />
18     </exec>
19   </target>
```

book-code/chap09/soashopper/soashopper-sources-generated/build.xml

As you can see in the example, the URLs of the Yahoo! Shopping schemas (e.g., `http://api.shopping.yahoo.com/shoppingservice/v2/prod-uctsearch.xsd`) are passed as parameters to the JAXB schema compiler.

The classes that get generated by this process (e.g., `yahoo.prods.Prod-uctSearch`) are used as the return types from the methods I designed to implement the REST service invocations. The process of designing and invoking these methods is illustrated in Figure 9–4.

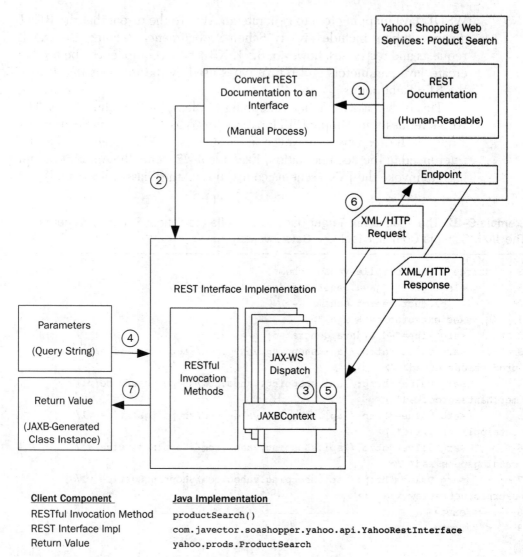

Client Component	Java Implementation
RESTful Invocation Method	`productSearch()`
REST Interface Impl	`com.javector.soashopper.yahoo.api.YahooRestInterface`
Return Value	`yahoo.prods.ProductSearch`

Service Component	URL

Endpoint	`http://api.shopping.yahoo.com/ShoppingService/V2/`
	`productSearch?appid=YahooDemo&category=Video%20Games&`
	`query=Doom&results=20`

REST Documentation	`http://developer.yahoo.com/shopping/V2/productSearch.html`

Figure 9–4 The JAXB classes generated from the Yahoo! Shopping response element schema are used, along with the JAX-WS run-time invocation framework, to invoke REST endpoints.

The various components of this process are labeled 1 through 7, and each component is described:

1. The Yahoo! Shopping REST documentation is available online at URLs that organize the services by type (e.g., Product Search) and version (e.g., V2).
2. The JAXB schema compilation tool (`xjc`) is used (as illustrated in Example 9–22) to generate the return types (`yahoo.prods.Product-Search`) used by the human-designed methods that invoke the REST service.
3. The JAXB schema compiler is executed during the SOAShopper build. The remaining steps, including this one, are run-time steps. To invoke the Yahoo! Shopping service, first a set of `javax.xml.ws.Dis-patch` objects is instantiated—one for each Yahoo! service. These `Dispatch` objects each used a `JAXBContext` that is capable of deserial-izing the XML response messages to a corresponding JAXB schema-compiled class instance.
4. To send an XML/HTTP request to the Yahoo! Shopping service, the `YahooRestInterface` method `productSearch()` (see Example 9–23) is invoked with parameters corresponding to those listed in the docu-mentation (e.g., `keywords`, `category`, `highestPrice`, and `lowest-Price`). These parameters and their values become the query string appended to the endpoint URL.
5. During invocation, a `Dispatch` instance is used to add the query string formulated from these parameters to the request message context.
6. Next, the `Dispatch` instance sends the XML/HTTP request to the Yahoo! endpoint (see Example 9–24). In this case, the request does not contain any XML—it is just a set of parameters represented in the query string.
7. The XML/HTTP response message from Yahoo! is processed by the `Dispatch` instance, where the XML is serialized by the JAXB run-time to an instance of `yahoo.prods.ProductSearch` and returned by the `productSearch()` method.

The next several examples walk through the specifics of these seven steps in more detail. Example 9–23 shows the Yahoo! Shopping Product Search (V2) API that I developed based on the Yahoo! documentation found at: `http://developer.yahoo.com/shopping/V2/productSearch.html`. This code configures a URL-encoded query string according to the parameters described there.

Example 9–23 The Java Code Used to Invoke the Yahoo! Shopping Product Search REST Endpoint Constructs a Query String of HTTP Parameters Derived from the Documentation

```
218    public ProductSearch productSearch(String keywords,
219        YahooShoppingTopLevelCategory category,
220        YahooShoppingCatalogListingClass catClass, YahooShoppingDepartment dept,
221        Double highestPrice, Double lowestPrice, Integer maxRefines,
222        String merchantId, Map<String, String> refinements, Integer results,
223        Boolean showNumRatings, Boolean showSubCategories,
224        YahooShoppingSortStyle sort, Integer start) {
225
226        if (keywords == null && category == null) {
227            throw new IllegalArgumentException(
228                "Both keywords and category cannot be null.");
229        }
230        String query = "appid=" + yahooShoppingAppId;
231        // query
232        if (keywords != null) {
233            query += "&query=" + keywords.replace(" ", "%20");
234        }
235        // category
236        if (category != null) {
237            query += "&category=" + category.getCategoryId();
382        }
239        // highestprice
240        Util util = new Util();
241        if (highestPrice != null) {
242            query += "&highestprice=" + util.floor(highestPrice, 2);
243        }
244        // lowestprice
245        if (lowestPrice != null) {
246            query += "&lowestprice=" + util.ceiling(lowestPrice, 2);
247        }
```

book-code/chap09/soashopper/soashopper-engine/src/main/java/com/javector
 /soashopper/yahoo/api/YahooRESTInterface.java

As you can see, each parameter passed to the method corresponds to a part of the query string. The code in the bottom portion of this listing shows how some of the familiar search parameters get mapped to the query string. For example, keywords gets mapped to the Yahoo! Product

Search parameter `query`. A few pages back in this chapter, Section 9.3 discusses the design of a similar REST endpoint Java API (for the SOAShopper REST endpoint), and Figure 9–2 provides an example of the style of documentation used by Yahoo! Shopping.

Once the query string is constructed, JAX-WS is used for invocation and the method returns an instance of the JAXB representation of Yahoo! Shopping's `{urn:yahoo:prods}ProductSearch` element.

Example 9–24 Setting the Query String on the JAX-WS `Dispatch` Instance and Invoking the REST Endpoint

```
326   productSearchDispatch.getRequestContext().put(MessageContext.QUERY_STRING,
327       query);
328   ProductSearch searchResults = null;
329   try {
330     searchResults = (ProductSearch) productSearchDispatch.invoke(null);
331   } catch (Exception e) {
332     throw new RuntimeException("YahooShopping Product Search: " + query
333         + " threw an Exception", e);
334   }
```

book-code/chap09/soashopper/soashopper-engine/src/main/java/com/javector
   /soashopper/yahoo/api/YahooRESTInterface.java

Example 9–24 shows how the `Dispatch` instance is configured. First, the query string is set using the `MessageContext.QUERY_STRING` property in the `Dispatch` instance's request context. Then, the `Dispatch` instance's `invoke()` method is called, and it is passed a `null` parameter since there is no XML to be sent to the REST endpoint. The results are cast to an instance of `ProductSearch`. The `Dispatch` instance is able to deserialize the response XML to an instance of `ProductSearch` because it has been configured with a `JAXBContext` as described.

I've now described, in detail, the design of the invocation layers for accessing SOAP and REST shopping system endpoints. In the next section, I look at how these layers are integrated to support the SOAShopper API that enables product search across eBay, Amazon, and Yahoo! Shopping.

9.7 SOAShopper API and the Integration Layer

As shown at the beginning of this chapter (Figure 9–1), the Integration Layer mediates between the SOAShopper API and the three source shopping systems: eBay, Amazon, and Yahoo!. Each source shopping system has its own object model, Java packages and classes that were generated by the JAXB schema compiler and/or the JAX-WS WSDL compiler. The SOAShopper API provides a common interface to all three of these source system object models.

The challenge here is to create an architecture that can bridge between the SOAShopper API and the source object models. The Integration Layer architecture needs to satisfy the following design criteria:

- Decouple the SOAShopper API from the source shopping system object models so that each can vary independently. The source WSDL and XML Schema change frequently,[10] and the Integration Layer needs to handle that without propagating those changes to the SOAShopper API.
- Be extensible so that new source shopping systems can easily be added.
- Isolate the type mapping code. It's important for the code that maps between the source system datatypes and the SOAShopper API datatypes to be isolated so that it can be maintained, enhanced, and debugged without disrupting the rest of the SOAShopper code base.

SOAShopper uses the Bridge Pattern, described in [Go4], to implement the Integration Layer. The intent of this pattern is to "decouple an abstraction from its implementation so that the two can vary independently."[11] The Bridge Pattern uses delegation, rather than inheritance, to relate the SOAShopping API to the source shopping systems. This enables the SOAShopping API and the source shopping systems to have separate class hierarchies. That is the key to decoupling the object models.

Figure 9–5 illustrates how the Bridge Pattern is implemented in SOAShopper.

On the left side of Figure 9–5 is a class hierarchy within the SOAShopper API. At the top of the hierarchy is the Shopper class—the base class that contains shopping functionality such as search. Subclasses of Shopper contain domain-specific shopping functionality. For example, the ComputerShopper

---

10. The eBay unified schema has been updated every two weeks throughout 2006. See http://developer.ebay.com/DevZone/XML/docs/WebHelp/ReleaseNotes.html.
11. Page 151 [Go4].

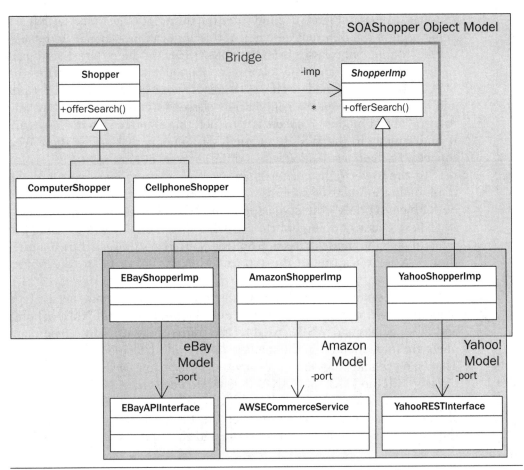

Figure 9–5 The Integration Layer is implemented using the Bridge Pattern.

class contains computer shopping-specific search criteria (e.g., memory, hard disk storage, CPU speed).

The right side of the figure shows the class hierarchies for the source shopping systems. `ShopperImp` is an abstract class that provides the methods used by `Shopper`. In this manner, all methods provided by `Shopper` and its subclasses are implemented by abstract methods on `ShopperImp`. Thus, the `Shopper` class hierarchy is decoupled from the domain-specific implementations related to eBay, Amazon, and Yahoo!. [Go4] uses the term *bridge* to describe this pattern because "it bridges the abstraction and its implementation, letting them vary independently."[12]

---

12. Page 152 [Go4].

The shading in Figure 9–5 indicates the different object models that are being used in the different domains of this application. Shopper and ShopperImp contain only classes from the SOAShopperAPI hierarchy. This area is shaded light gray and the classes contained within it comprise the SOAShopper object model. The YahooRESTInterface, EBayAPIInterface, and AWSECommerceService contain only classes from the Yahoo!, eBay, and Amazon object models, respectively. In fact, these source system classes are bound directly to the WSDL and/or XML Schema that define their Web services. Each area is shaded with a different tone of gray.

In the lower-right corner is an area of overlap where you find the implementation classes such as YahooShopperImp that use classes from both object models—the SOAShopper model and the source system models. These classes implement the SOAShopper model methods using the domain-specific model classes from the source systems. In this manner, these classes encapsulate the type mappings that relate to the object models.

The Integration Layer of the SOAShopper application contains the type mappings used to map between the SOAShopper standard XML schema and the schemas and WSDL used by the source systems. These type mappings are implemented in the manner described in Chapter 5, Section 5.3. That is, these mappings are implemented with custom Java code that works directly with the JAXB and JAX-WS generated classes.

The next few pages show some of the code and provide more details about how the Integration Layer uses the Bridge Pattern. Example 9–25 shows the code for one method—offerSearch—in the Shopper class.

Example 9–25 The Shopper Class Provides an Abstraction of an Online Shopping Interface

```
56    /**
57     * Search all the online stores.
58     *
59     * @param keywords
60     *         The keywords to search for. If category is null, then keywords
61     *         must not be null.
62     * @param category
63     *         The category to search in (e.g., Computers, Movies)
64     * @param lowprice
65     *         The low end of a price range to search. If null, then there is
66     *         no lower boundary.
67     * @param highprice
```

```
68     *            The high end of a price range to search. If null, then there
69     *            is no upper boundary.
70     * @return A list of offers meeting the search criteria.
71     */
72    public List<Offer> offerSearch(String keywords, Category category,
73        Price lowprice, Price highprice) {
74
75      ShopperImp yahooSvc = ShopperImp.newShopperImp(Store.YAHOO);
76      ShopperImp ebaySvc = ShopperImp.newShopperImp(Store.EBAY);
77      ShopperImp amazonSvc = ShopperImp.newShopperImp(Store.AMAZON);
78      List<Offer> offers = yahooSvc.offerSearch(keywords, category, lowprice,
79          highprice);
80      offers.addAll(ebaySvc.offerSearch(keywords, category, lowprice, highprice));
81      offers.addAll(amazonSvc
82          .offerSearch(keywords, category, lowprice, highprice));
83      return offers;
84
85    }
```

book-code/chap09/soashopper/soashopper-engine/src/main/java/com/javector
  /soashopper/Shopper.java

The offerSearch() method provides basic search capability based on keywords, product category, and price range. As you can see, the implementation of this method uses three *delegate* instances of ShopperImp—one for each source system. These delegates are instances of EBayShopperImp, AmazonShopperImp, and YahooShopperImp—as shown in Figure 9–5. As is typical in the Bridge Pattern, the delegates are created using a factory method—in this case, ShopperImp.newSOAShopperServiceImp().

In this example, the Shopper.offerSearch() method simply invokes the offerSearch() method on each delegate and then collects the results in a single List<Offer> instance. However, other methods defined by Shopper do more sophisticated processing using combinations of delegate method invocations. Typically, the implementor delegate classes (instances of ShopperImp) provide a lower level of functionality than the abstraction (Shopper). In such situations, the abstraction logic combines method calls to the delegate with internal code to implement its methods.

Example 9–26 shows a section from the implementation of the Shopper-Imp class. In particular, the code shows the factory method for creating new ShopperImp instances. As you can see, a switch statement handles the different cases—instantiating the right implementation of ShopperImp, depending on the source shopping system selected. The current code handles three cases: YAHOO, EBAY, and AMAZON. But you can see the pattern and how easy it is to extend the framework to handle additional source shopping systems.

Example 9–26 The ShopperImp.newShopperImp() Factory Method

```
31  public abstract class ShopperImp {
32
33    public static ShopperImp newShopperImp(Store src) {
34      if (src == null) {
35        throw new IllegalArgumentException("src may not be null.");
36      }
37      switch (src) {
38      case YAHOO:
39        return new YahooShopperImp(ShopperCredentials.getYahooAppID());
40      case EBAY:
41        return new EBayShopperImp(EBayShopperImp.EBAY_PRODUCTION_SERVER,
42            EBayShopperImp.SITE_ID_US, ShopperCredentials.getEBayAppID());
43      case AMAZON:
44       return new AmazonShopperImp(ShopperCredentials.getAmazonAccessKeyID());
45        default:
46          throw new RuntimeException("Unknown source: " + src.getName());
47      }
48    }
49
50    public abstract List<Offer> offerSearch(String keywords, Category category,
51        Price lowprice, Price highprice);
52
```

book-code/chap09/soashopper/soashopper-engine/src/main/java/com/javector/
  soashopper/ShopperImp.java

In addition to the factory method, the code snippet in Example 9–26 shows one of the methods specified by this delegate class's API—offer-Search(). Each implementation of ShopperImp, for each source system, must implement this method. So, when designing an SOA integration system like SOAShopper, the architects and developers must determine how to map the datatypes and semantics of each delegate method like offerSearch(), to the datatypes and semantics represented in the compiled WSDL and schema of each source system. Example 9–27 shows how the EBayShoppingImp class implements this method.

Example 9–27 The `EBayShopperImp.offerSearch()` Method

```
227    @Override
228    public List<Offer> offerSearch(String keywords, Category category,
229        Price lowprice, Price highprice) {
230
231      TypeConverter tc = new TypeConverter();
232      GetSearchResultsRequestType searchResultsRequest = new
  GetSearchResultsRequestType();
233      configureEBayRequestType(searchResultsRequest, "GetSearchResults");
234      List<DetailLevelCodeType> details = searchResultsRequest.getDetailLevel();
235      details.add(DetailLevelCodeType.RETURN_ALL);
236      if (category != null) {
237        EBayCategory eBayCategory = tc.toEBayCategory(category);
238        searchResultsRequest.setCategoryID(eBayCategory.getCategoryId());
239      }
240      searchResultsRequest.setQuery(keywords);
241      if (lowprice != null || highprice != null) {
242        PriceRangeFilterType prf = new PriceRangeFilterType();
243        if (lowprice != null) {
244          prf.setMinPrice(tc.toAmountType(lowprice));
245        }
246        if (highprice != null) {
247          prf.setMaxPrice(tc.toAmountType(highprice));
248        }
249        searchResultsRequest.setPriceRangeFilter(prf);
250      }
251      GetSearchResultsResponseType searchResultsResponse = null;
252      try {
253        searchResultsResponse = port.getSearchResults(searchResultsRequest);
254      } catch (Exception e) {
255        throw new RuntimeException(
256            "EBayAPIInterface.getSearchResults() threw an Exception", e);
257      }
258      List<SearchResultItemType> searchResultList = searchResultsResponse
259          .getSearchResultItemArray().getSearchResultItem();
260      List<Offer> retVal = new ArrayList<Offer>();
261      for (SearchResultItemType srit : searchResultList) {
262        retVal.add(new Offer(new EBayOfferImp(srit.getItem())));
263      }
264      return retVal;
265    }
266
```

book-code/chap09/soashopper/soashopper-engine/src/main/java/com/javector
  /soashopper/ebay/EBayShopperImp.java

`EBayShopperImp` is a wrapper factory class around the JAX-WS compiled classes which represent the eBay WSDL. It provides an intuitive interface for accessing eBay that shields the business application from the complexity of the underlying eBay WSDL. In addition, it provides for separation of concerns in that `EBayShopperImp` provides a consistent interface to business applications that does not need to be changed or recompiled each time the eBay WSDL changes. Business applications should use this class for integration with eBay instead of using the WSDL compiled classes generated by JAX-WS.

About two-thirds of the way down in Example 9–27, you can see a `try...catch` statement where the method `port.getSearchResults()` is invoked inside the `try` block. The variable `port` references an instance of `EBayAPIInterface` (`port` is initialized in the constructor). As discussed relative to Figure 9–5, `EBayAPIInterface` is the API to the eBay shopping services that is compiled from the eBay WSDL. The first two-thirds of the code in this example set up the Java instances necessary to invoke this eBay API method—`getSearchResults()`. This is the sort of code I was talking about early in this section where I wrote that "The Integration Layer of the SOAShopper application contains the type mappings used to map between the SOAShopper standard XML schema and the schemas and WSDL used by the source systems." The code shown in Example 9–27 takes care of the following semantic and datatype mappings:

- Maps the `offerSearch()` method from the SOAShopper object model to the `getSearchResults()` method in the eBay object model
- Maps the parameters of `offerSearch()`—`keywords`, `category`, `lowprice`, `highprice`—to the eBay request object of type `GetSearchResultsRequestType`
- Maps the eBay search results items (of type `SearchResultItemType`) into the SOAShopper object model search result item class— `Offer`

The eBay API is very rich and provides a powerful mechanism for full integration of third-party applications with the trading platform. It would require an entire book to explore all its capabilities in depth. The `getSearchResults()` method corresponding to the `GetSearchResults` operation from the `eBayAPIInterface portType` on the eBay WSDL[13] provides the primary search interface to eBay. This operation takes a single

---

13. The latest version of the eBay WSDL can be found at http://developer.ebay.com/webservices/latest/eBaySvc.wsdl. Be patient when trying to view it in a browser, as the WSDL is more than 3 MB of XML!

parameter, the XML element `GetSearchResults`. This parameter is a wrapper for lots of detailed information that can be used to specify conditions of the search, ranging from keywords, to category, payment method, auction type, and so forth.[14]

To invoke the `getSearchResults()` method, the code in Example 9–27 maps each parameter from `offerSearch()` (i.e., `keywords`, `category`, `lowprice`, `highprice`) to the appropriate content within the `GetSearchResults` element. For example, the `lowprice` and `highprice` parameters get mapped to a `PriceRangeFilterType` datatype that is used by eBay to hold a price range. To implement that mapping first requires a datatype conversion from the price datatype used in the SOAShopper model (i.e., `com.javector.soashopper.Price`) to the price datatype used by eBay (i.e., `ebay.apis.eblbasecomponents.AmountType`). Such simple type conversions are handled by a utility type mapping class—`com.javector.util.TypeConverter`. In this manner, you can see that the datatype mappings are contained in the source-system-specific implementations of the Bridge Pattern implementor classes like `EBayShopperImp`.

For some of the richer and more widely used datatypes, however, the datatype mapping is abstracted out of these implementor classes so that it can be used across the system. An example of this is the mapping from the eBay search result type (`SearchResultItemType`) to the SOAShopper search result type (`Offer`). In fact, the `Offer` datatype has been designed, after a careful analysis of the search results data modes for the three source systems (eBay, Amazon, and Yahoo!) to encapsulate basic functionality that is common across these systems. In this manner, `Offer` is part of the core SOAShopper API. Like the `Shopper` class, `Offer` is implemented using the Bridge Pattern. Figure 9–6 shows the implementation of `Offer`.

The parallel construction, as compared with the design of `Shopper` (see Figure 9–5), is obvious. Like `Shopper`, `Offer` is the root of a class hierarchy that defines specific domain-related subclasses for different types of search (e.g., `ComputerOffer` versus `CellphoneOffer`). In addition, like `Shopper`, the `Offer` implementor (i.e., `OfferImp`) has subclasses for each source system (i.e., `EBayOfferImp`, `AmazonOfferImp`, and `YahooOfferImp`). Each subclass contains the code specific to mapping the search results classes in its source system to the `Offer` datatype. In Example 9–27, this mapping code is invoked when the `Offer` constructor is called:

```
new Offer(new EBayOfferImp(srit.getItem()))
```

---

14. Documentation for the eBay operations like `GetSearchResults` is available online; for example, http://developer.ebay.com/DevZone/SOAP/docs/Reference/eBay/io_GetSearchResults.html.

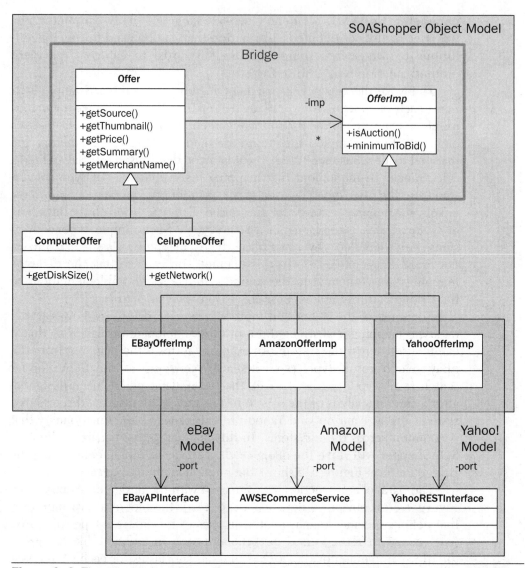

Figure 9–6 The `Offer` class hierarchy illustrates another Bridge Pattern in the SOAShopper implementation.

Example 9–28 shows a snippet from the abstraction `Offer` illustrating how the implementor, `OfferImp`, is used to implement the API. As shown, the `Offer.getPrice()` method is implemented differently depending on the type of offer that is encapsulated.

Example 9–28 Implementation of the `Offer.getPrice()` Method

```
81  /**
82   * @return The fixed price if this is not an auction, or else the minimum bid
83   *         allowed. Returns null if the offer is no longer available or if the
84   *         price cannot be determined by SOAShopper.
85   */
86  public Price getPrice() {
87    if (delegate.isAuction()) {
88      return delegate.minimumToBid();
89    }
90    return delegate.getPrice();
91  }
92
```

book-code/chap09/soashopper/soashopper-engine/src/main/java/com/javector
  /soashopper/Offer.java

If the offer is an auction (i.e., `delegate.isAuction()` returns true) the price returned is provided by the implementor method `minimumToBid()`. Otherwise, the price is returned by the method `getPrice()`. Notice that the implementor methods `isAuction()` and `minimumToBid()` are not represented in the abstraction class `Offer`. That is because the `Offer` class hides information about the mechanism for purchasing the product represented by its instance (e.g., auction versus simple purchase). These details, however, are needed in the implementor class, `OfferImp`, in order to correctly map the search results from eBay to the `Offer` datatype. In this manner, you can see that even if the SOAShopper API is relatively simple, as in the case with the `Offer` class, a great deal of more complex detail may be hidden under the covers in the implementor classes of the Bridge Pattern (e.g., `EBayOfferImp`).

That wraps up the discussion of the Integration Layer and SOAShopper API. The key points to take away are as follows:

- The Bridge Pattern is used to combine the different source systems into a single SOAShopper API.
- The semantic and datatype mappings from the Bridge Pattern are embedded in the concrete implementor classes (e.g., `EBayShopperImp`, `EBayOfferImp`).
- Significant business analysis is required to design good Bridge Pattern abstractions (e.g., `Shopper` and `Offer`) that encapsulate the common functionality provided by the source systems.

The next section summarizes the key points that are demonstrated by the SOAShopper case study examined in this chapter.

9.8   Conclusions about Implementing Real-World SOA Applications with Java EE

This chapter offered a detailed look at a real-world implementation of an SOA integration application based on Java Web Services. To really understand how it all fits together, I suggest that you read through the source code, and try to modify it or add features. A good exercise is to add another online shopping service as a source (in addition to eBay, Yahoo!, and Amazon).

In the next chapter, I demonstrate how this application (and its REST endpoint in particular) can be leveraged to build a user-friendly Ajax front-end that allows an end user to perform a cross-platform product search from a Web browser. Before leaving the world of back-end design and diving into the Ajax/REST interface, consider these conclusions as you contemplate designing your own SOA applications:

- REST endpoints are very common in the real world (e.g., Yahoo! Shopping). Learn how to use the JAX-WS `Dispatch` class to consume them and the `Provider` class to deploy them.
- JAX-WS 2.0 generates a Java API from WSDL very effectively—even a WSDL as large as eBay (> 3 MB). However, the results may not be usable "out of the box." As you saw in Section 9.5, the JAX-WS generated proxy instance may need to be tweaked by adding a query string to the SOAP endpoint, and/or adding a SOAPHandler to manage SOAP headers that either aren't supported by JAX-WS or aren't documented in the WSDL. One can argue that some of the commercial WSDLs out there (e.g., eBay) are cumbersome or non-compliant with various standards or best practices. But to be practical, if WSDLs like this are the ones you need to use to get your job done, you need to understand how to deal with their quirks within the JAX-WS framework.
- Design patterns like the Bridge Pattern [Go4] used in Section 9.7 can be a great help in designing the SOA Integration aspects of a Java EE 5 based Web Services application. Developers can benefit greatly by familiarizing themselves with the design patterns (e.g., Adapter, Bridge, Façade, and Proxy from [Go4]) most commonly associated with integration.

- Type mappings (see Section 9.4) are best isolated in a separate class or package, instead of embedding them in the code that deploys or consumes a Web service. This makes maintenance easier as schemas and WSDLs change and code must be modified to accommodate those changes. Having the type mapping code in one place, rather than scattered throughout the application, makes it easier to identify and implement the changes that are needed.

CHAPTER 10

Ajax and Java Web Services

In this chapter, I examine how Java Web Services can be used to support *Ajax* clients. Ajax, or Asynchronous JavaScript and XML, is a programming technique that enables you to create user interfaces for a Web browser that behave more like a local, stand-alone application than a collection of HTML pages.

Ajax is a good fit with Java Web Services. Using these two technologies together enables you to publish software components as services (via JAX-WS) and create great browser-based user interfaces on top of them (via Ajax). The entire application can then be packaged as an EAR or WAR and deployed on a Java EE application server.

To demonstrate this capability, I pick up here where I left off at the end of Chapter 9. In that chapter, I showed you how to build an online shopping application, SOAShopper, which can search across multiple Web-service-enabled sites (i.e., eBay, Yahoo! Shopping, and Amazon). In this chapter, I show how you can develop an Ajax front-end to SOAShopper. In particular, the code examined in this chapter demonstrates how to write an Ajax application that consumes RESTful Java Web Services endpoints.

In the second half of this chapter, I review the JavaScript code that implements the SOAShopper Ajax front-end in quite a bit of detail. For those of you who are familiar with Web front-end coding and JavaScript, this detail may seem tedious. I include it because my assumption is that many readers of this book are server-side Java programmers who do not usually do a lot of JavaScript development and, therefore, might be interested in the detailed code explanation.

10.1   Quick Overview of Ajax

Ajax is a well-documented technology, and my purpose here is not to write a detailed tutorial on Ajax programming.[1] However, I do want to go over some of the basics to set the stage for a discussion of the SOAShopper front-end and how it interacts with Java EE.

As many of you know, the major benefit of Ajax is that it allows a browser-based application to avoid the need for full-page refreshes each time new data is retrieved from the server. Ajax programmers use the JavaScript type `XMLHttpRequest` to exchange data with the server behind the scenes (i.e., without having to reload the entire HTML page being displayed by the browser). When new data (usually in XML format) is received by an `XMLHttpRequest` instance, JavaScript is used to update the *DOM* structure of the HTML page (e.g., inserting some rows in a table) without rebuilding the entire HTML page in memory.

To see what that means in practice, I walk you through some screen shots from the SOAShopper front-end. Then, in the rest of this chapter, I will show you how to write the code behind these screen shots.

If you build and deploy the SOAShopper application on your local machine[2] and point your browser to `http://<your-host>:<your-port>/shoashopper/ajax/search.html`, you should see something similar to what appears in Figure 10–1. This is the initial search screen for SOAShopper. The three labeled items in this figure are worth pointing out for discussion:

1. The URL where the application resides remains constant throughout its use. The search is performed and results are displayed without loading a new page. This is implemented by using JavaScript that updates the DOM residing in the browser's memory.
2. This search page offers you four search parameters: a set of keywords; a category to search; a low price; and a high price. These parameters correspond to the parameters supported by the SOAShopper `offerSearch` REST endpoint discussed in Chapter 9, Section 9.3 (see Figure 9–2). This search page contains JavaScript that converts these parameters into a query string that an `XMLHttpRequest` instance uses to invoke the `offerSearch` endpoint.

---

1. For a good introduction to Ajax, I recommend "Ajax in Action" [AIA].
2. For instructions, see Appendix B, Section B.9.

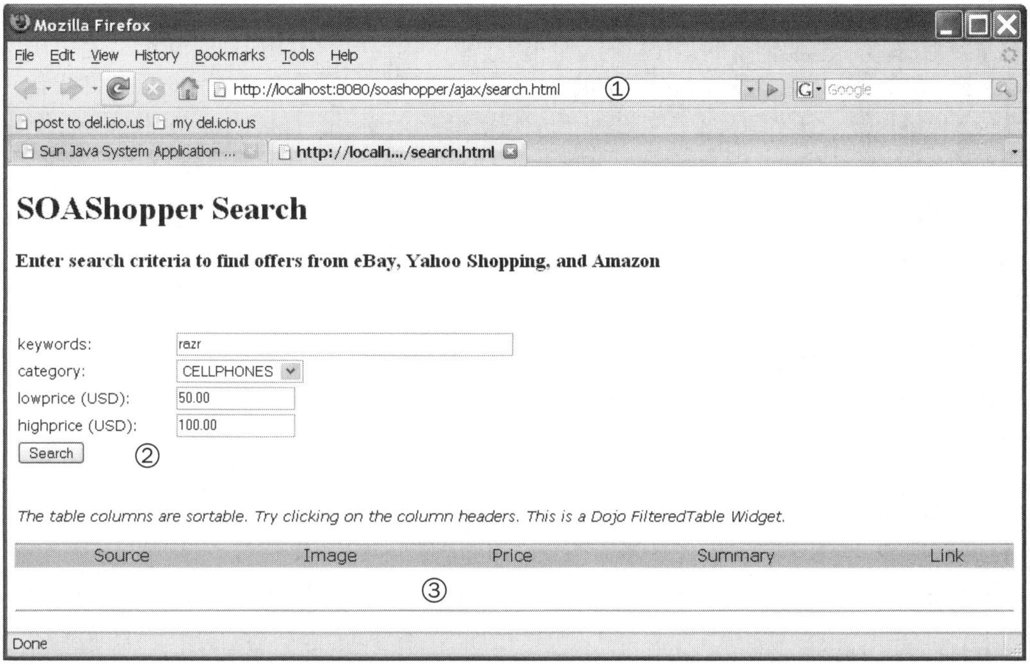

Figure 10–1 The initial SOAShopper search screen.

3. At the bottom of Figure 10–1 appear some column headings (i.e., Source, Image, Price, Summary) for an empty table. Once a search is performed and the XMLHttpRequest has received the results, a Java-Script function contained in this page processes those results and loads them into the table. This table is implemented using the Dojo Foundation's [DOJO] FilteredTable widget.

As you can see from Figure 10–1, a user has entered some criteria for a search. The keywords value is "razr." The search category is CELL-PHONES and the price range is $50.00–100.00. Figure 10–2 shows what happens to the screen when the user clicks on the Search button. The search takes a while to run (sometimes as long as a minute). This is not because the Java EE 5 application server is slow or because the JavaScript in the Web page is slow. Rather, it is because the shopping sites being searched (particularly eBay) can take quite a while to respond. To handle this, Ajax techniques are used to update the interface and let the user know the application is not broken.

There are two items labeled in Figure 10–2 that I want to point out:

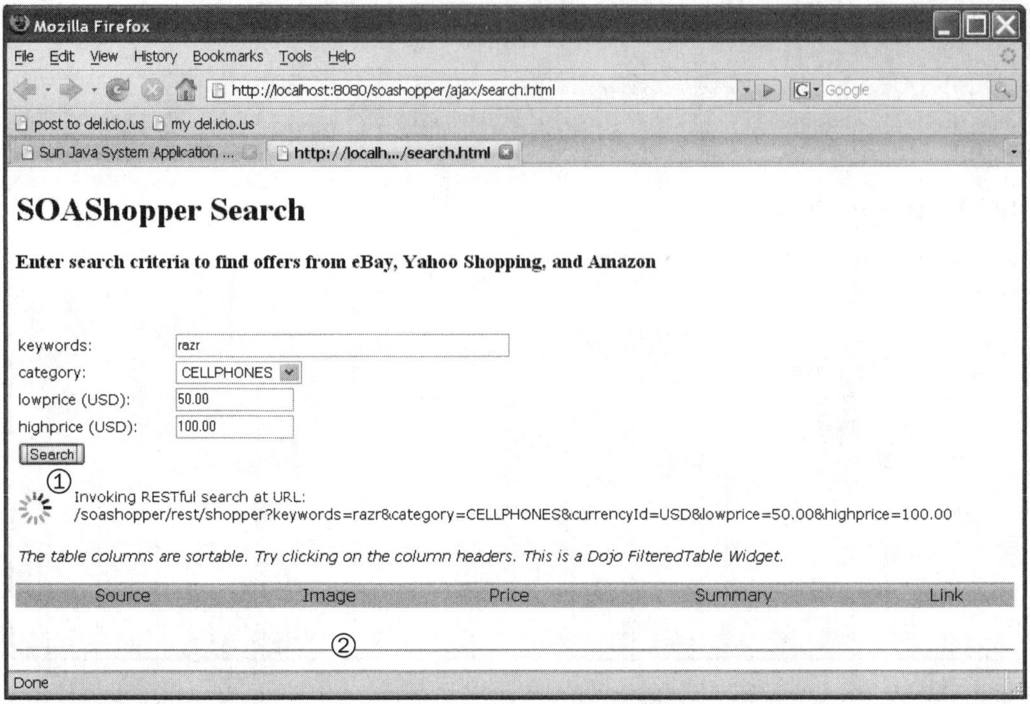

Figure 10–2 Screen shot showing asynchronous processing in progress.

1. First, notice that an icon and some text have appeared below the Search button. The icon is actually an animated GIF that indicates the application is working to retrieve data from the server. The text shows us the URL of the REST endpoint from which the data has been requested: `/soashopper/rest/shopper?keywords=razr&category =CELLPHONES&currencyId=USD&lowprice=50.00&highprice=100.00`. This is the URL and query string structure that are used in Chapter 9, Section 9.3, for the SOAShopper REST endpoint. This icon and message appear while the `XMLHttpRequest` request is happening asynchronously. The `search.html` page has not been reloaded either. Rather, the DOM representation of `search.html` that was loaded by the Web browser (Firefox in this case) has been changed by a JavaScript function that inserted the animated GIF and text into the appropriate place.

2. The search results table is still empty because the asynchronous request for data from the SOAShopper REST endpoint has not yet completed.

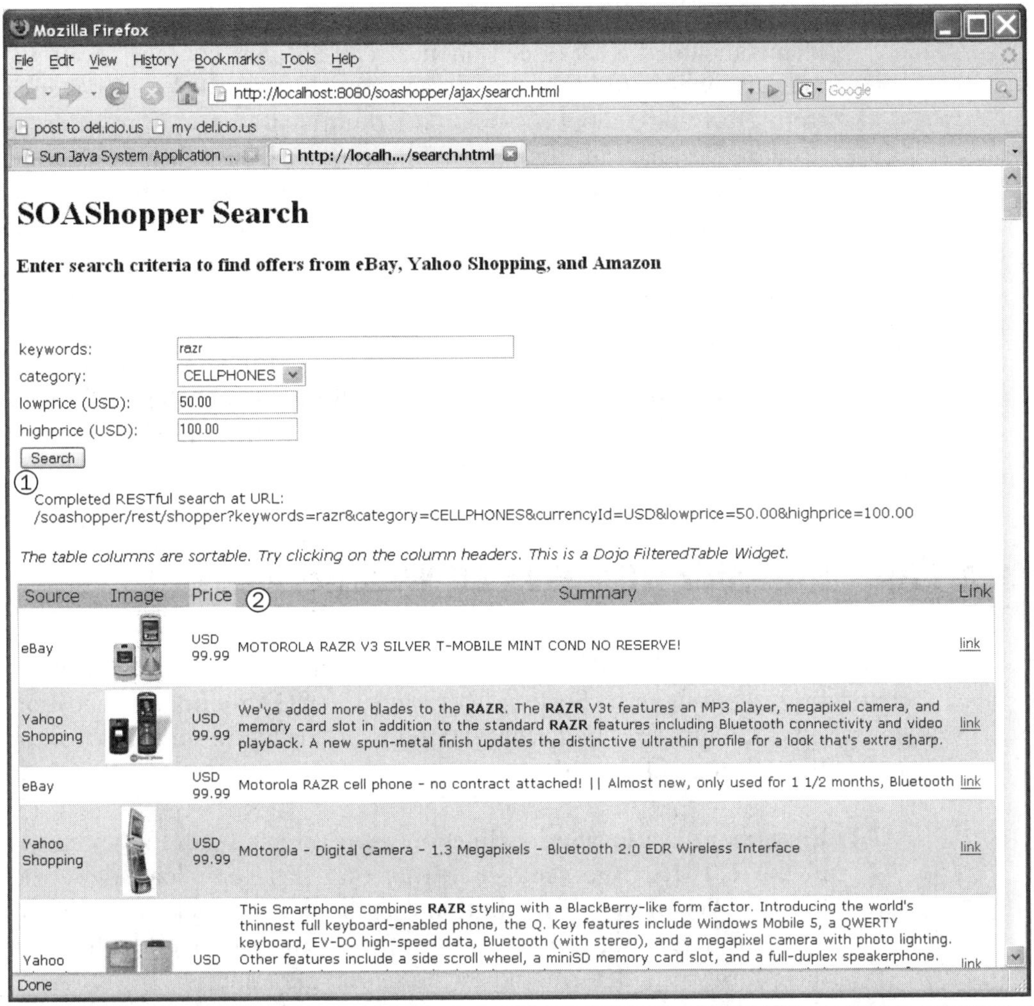

Figure 10–3 Screen shot showing search results displayed in the Dojo table widget.

Figure 10–3 shows the appearance of the SOAShopper search page after the search results have been returned from the server. At this point, the `XmlHttpRequest` object has received the search data from the REST endpoint and invoked a JavaScript function to load that data into the results table. Two other items, labeled in the figure, are worth pointing out:

1. The animated GIF has disappeared and the text below the Search button has changed to indicate that the results have been received.

2. The search results table has been populated. As you can see, these results included a list of cell phones. The leftmost column, "Source," indicates which site the offer came from (Figure 10–3 shows results from eBay and Yahoo! Shopping). A thumbnail image, if available, is displayed, along with the price and summary. The rightmost column contains a link to the page containing the offer. Clicking this link will take you to a page where you can purchase the cell phone that is listed.

One cool feature of the Dojo table widget used here is that the results can be sorted by column. Figure 10–3 shows the results sorted by price from high to low. Hence, the $99.99 phone appears at the top of the list.

That wraps up a quick overview of the SOAShopper search interface. In the next section, I look at the working relationship between Ajax and Java EE that has been demonstrated in these screen shots.

10.2   Ajax Together with Java EE Web Services

Figure 10–4 shows the interrelationship between the Ajax front-end illustrated by screen shots in Section 10.1, and the SOAShopper application described in Chapter 9. The numbered items in this figure trace the flow of events that implement the search:

1. First, there is a JavaScript function, `retrieveURL (url)`, contained in the HTML page (`search.html`), that has been loaded by the browser. When the Search button is pressed, this function is invoked with the parameter `url` set to the value of the REST endpoint with the query string determined by the search parameters.

2. Next, the `showSearchingMsg()` function is invoked to display the animated GIF and message illustrated in Figure 10–2.

3. Then, the `retrieveURL()` function instantiates an `XMLHttpRequest` object, which invokes the SOAShopper's REST endpoint asynchronously. It also configures a handler (the `processStateChange()` function used in step 7) on the `XMLHttpRequest` object.

4. The `XMLHttpRequest` object makes an HTTP GET request to the SOAShopper REST endpoint. This is an asynchronous request, and the main thread of execution returns to handle any other interactions that may occur while the search is going on.

5. Meanwhile, inside the Java EE container that has deployed the SOAShopper REST endpoint, processing of the `XMLHttpRequest`'s

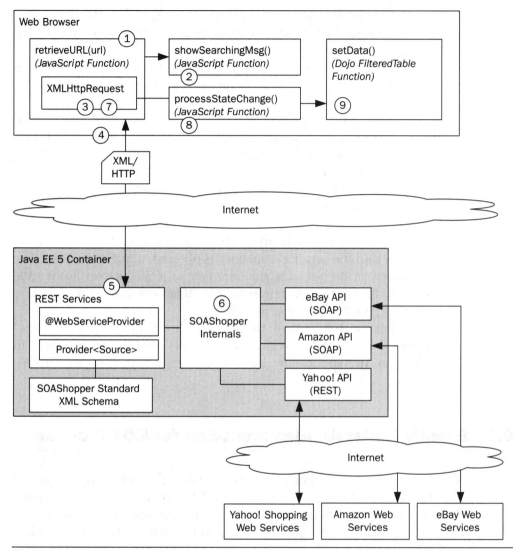

Figure 10–4 A typical Ajax client invokes REST endpoints asynchronously.

HTTP GET request is taking place. As described in Chapter 9, Section 9.3, query parameters are parsed from the query string and passed to the

6. SOAShopper internals. SOAShopper then translates the search request into the appropriate form for each online shopping service (eBay, Amazon, and Yahoo! Shopping), gets the results, and packages them into an XML document compliant with the `retail.xsd` schema

(see Chapter 9, Example 9–4, from Section 9.2). The XML document is then sent back to the `XMLHttpRequest` object over the HTTP response to its original GET request.

7. When the `XMLHttpRequest`'s state changes, indicating that the search response has been received, the `processStateChange()` handler (set in step 2) gets invoked.

8. The `processStateChange()` handler calls other functions that (i) change the message to indicate the search has finished, and (ii) process and format the XML data received from SOAShopper so that it can be displayed.

9. Lastly, the Dojo table widget's `setData()` function is invoked to display the search results.

One other relationship between the Ajax application running in the Web browser and the Java EE container is not shown in Figure 10–4. The Web container on the Java EE side also acts as a Web server hosting the Ajax application. So, the `search.html` page that contains the Ajax code is served by the Java EE container as well.

In the next section, I walk through the JavaScript code that implements steps 1–9. My goal is to give you a detailed understanding of how to implement an Ajax application that can interact with your Java EE REST endpoints.

10.3   Sample Code: An Ajax Front-End for SOAShopper

The code example discussion starts with the JavaScript function `retrieveURL()`, shown as step 1 in Figure 10–4. As you can see in Example 10–1, the first thing this code does is invoke the `showSearchingMsg()` function to display the message on the browser indicating that the search is underway.

Example 10–1 The `retrieveURL()` JavaScript Function Uses an `XMLHttpRequest` Object to Asynchronously Invoke the SOAShopper REST Endpoint

```
125    function retrieveURL(url) {
126      restURL = url;
127      showSearchingMsg(restURL);
128      if (window.XMLHttpRequest) { // Non-IE browsers
129        req = new XMLHttpRequest();
```

```
130          req.onreadystatechange = processStateChange;
131          try {
132            req.open("GET", url, true);
133            req.setRequestHeader('Content-type','text/xml');
134          } catch (e) {
135            alert(e);
136          }
137          req.send(null);
138        } else if (window.ActiveXObject) { // IE
139          req = new ActiveXObject("Microsoft.XMLHTTP");
140          if (req) {
141            req.onreadystatechange = processStateChange;
142            try {
143              req.open("GET", url, true);
144              req.setRequestHeader('Content-type','text/xml');
145            } catch (e) {
146              alert(e);
147            }
148            req.send();
149          }
150        }
151      }
```

book-code/chap09/soashopper/soashopper-ajax/src/main/webapp
  /search.html

Next, the code instantiates the `XMLHttpRequest` object and stores it in
the req variable. Actually, the code needs to handle two cases for Microsoft
and non-Microsoft browsers. In a non-Microsoft browser, it is created using:

```
new XMLHttpRequest()
```

However, in Internet Explorer, it is creating using:

```
new ActiveXObject("Microsoft.XMLHTTP")
```

Once the `XMLHttpRequest` object is instantiated, an HTTP GET
request is made to the specified `url` parameter using `req.open()` and
`req.send()` functions. The `setRequestHeader()` call is made to add the:

```
Content-type: text/xml
```

HTTP request header to the GET request. Strictly speaking, this should not be necessary. However, some REST endpoints require that the Content-type header be configured this way. For example, early versions of JAX-WS (including the first production release of GlassFish), required it.

Example 10–2 shows the code that implements step 2 from Figure 10–4. This code manipulates the Web browser's DOM representation of the search.html document.

Example 10–2 The JavaScript Method showSearchingMsg() Updates the Web Browser's DOM to Display an Animated GIF and Text Message

```
81    function showSearchingMsg(url) {
82       var messageTDElt = document.getElementById('searchingMessageId');
83       var loadingTDElt = document.getElementById('loadingId');
84       loadingTDElt.setAttribute('width','50');
85       var loadingNode = document.createElement('img');
86       loadingNode.setAttribute('src','images/bigrotation2.gif');
87       loadingNode.setAttribute('style', 'margin-right: 6px; margin-top: 5px;');
88       var existingLoadingNode = loadingTDElt.firstChild;
89       if (existingLoadingNode) {
90          loadingTDElt.removeChild(existingLoadingNode);
91       }
92       loadingTDElt.appendChild(loadingNode);
93       var msg = "Invoking RESTful search at URL: " + url;
94       var msgNode = document.createTextNode(msg);
95       var existingMsg = messageTDElt.firstChild
96       if (existingMsg) {
97          messageTDElt.removeChild(existingMsg);
98       }
99       messageTDElt.appendChild(msgNode);
100   }
```

book-code/chap09/soashopper/soashopper-ajax/src/main/webapp/search.html

First, this code gets a reference to a DOM element (stored in message-TDElt) where the text message should be displayed. The ID, 'searching-MessageId', refers to a cell in a table, halfway down the page. That cell is empty when the search.html page is loaded. However, the code here—in particular, the last line:

```
messageTDElt.appendChild(msgNode)
```

places the text "Invoking RESTful search at URL: ..." in that cell. Similarly, other parts of this code place an animated GIF reference (i.e., `images/bigrotation2.gif`) into another cell with the ID `'loadingID'`.

If you have done server-side Java DOM programming,[3] this type of HTML DOM programming in JavaScript should make sense. If you haven't seen any kind of DOM programming before, you might want to look at "Ajax in Action" [AIA] Chapter 2 for an introduction to manipulating HTML DOM.

Getting back to the HTTP GET request issued by the `XMLHttpRequest` object, this request is received by the Java EE container where SOAShopper is deployed—in particular, the request handled by the JAX-WS runtime where it ends up calling the `ShopperServiceRESTImp.invoke()` method,[4] which has been deployed at the endpoint invoked by the Ajax application. In Figure 10–4, this part of the process is labeled step 5. This Web service method, `ShopperServiceRESTImp.invoke()`, in turn invokes the SOAShopper API shown in Example 10–3.

Example 10–3 The Java Method `offerSearch` Is Bound to the REST Endpoint by JAX-WS (The Query String Parameters from the Browser's `XMLHttpRequest` Request End Up Getting Mapped to the Parameters of This Method)[5]

```
22   public interface ShopperServiceREST {
23
24     public OfferList offerSearch(String keywords, String category,
25         String currencyId, Double lowprice, Double highprice);
26
27   }
```

book-code/chap09/soashopper/soashopper-services-rest/src/main/java/com/javector
   /soashopper/endpoint/rest/ShopperServiceREST.java

At this point, the server-side SOAShopper application does the search of eBay, Yahoo! Shopping, and Amazon. This is step 6 in Figure 10–4. The internals of SOAShopper are described in detail in Chapter 9.

---

3. See, for example, the programming for WSDL processing and XML validation discussed in Chapter 7, Section 7.5—particularly Example 7–10.
4. See Chapter 9, Section 9.3, Example 9–11.
5. See Chapter 9, Section 9.3.

Of interest here, from the Ajax perspective, is what happens when the server-side SOAShopper application returns. As indicated by step 7 in Figure 10–4, a handler function—`processStateChange()`—is invoked.

Example 10–4 The JavaScript Function `processStateChange()` Is Invoked When the Asynchronous `XMLHttpRequest.send()` Function Returns (If the REST Query Returns "200 OK", the `processXML()` Function Is Invoked to Display the Search Results)

```
156    function processStateChange() {
157      if (req.readyState == 4) { // Complete
158        showFinishedMsg(restURL);
159        if (req.status == 200) { // OK response
160          processXML(req.responseXML);
161        } else {
162          alert("Problem invoking REST endpoint: " + restURL + " : "
163            + req.status + " " + req.statusText);
164        }
165      }
166    }
```

book-code/chap09/soashopper/soashopper-ajax/src/main/webapp
  /search.html

Example 10–4 shows the code for that handler function. It simply checks that an HTTP response code 200 was received (indicating success) and then invokes the `processXML()` function. For code clarity, it makes sense to keep such a handler function as simple as possible and organize the real work in another function. If the HTTP response is not 200 (indicating a problem), the code here simply sends an alert message. In a real production application, some diagnostics would take place together with an attempt to recover from the failure and maybe reissue the HTTP request.

Supposing that the HTTP response code is 200, the next step in this process is to parse the XML document returned by the SOAShopper service. As indicated by Example 10–3, the return type of the SOAShopper API is `OfferList`. `OfferList` is a JAXB schema-generated Java class compiled from the `retail:offerList` schema element in the `retail.xsd` schema shown in Example 10–5. This is the schema referenced in the REST endpoint documentation from Chapter 9.[6]

---

6. See Chapter 9, Section 9.3, Figure 9-2.

Example 10–5 The XML Schema Definition for the XML Document Received by the Ajax Application from the SOAShopper REST Endpoint

```
 7   <xs:element name="offerList">
 8     <xs:complexType>
 9       <xs:sequence>
10         <xs:element ref="tns:offer" minOccurs="0" maxOccurs="unbounded"/>
11       </xs:sequence>
12     </xs:complexType>
13   </xs:element>
14
15   <xs:element name="offer" type="tns:OfferType"/>
16
17   <xs:complexType name="OfferType">
18     <xs:sequence>
19       <xs:element name="offerId" type="xs:string" nillable="true"/>
20       <xs:element name="productId" type="xs:string" minOccurs="0"/>
21       <xs:element name="source" type="tns:SourceType"/>
22       <xs:element name="thumbnail" type="tns:PictureType" minOccurs="0"/>
23       <xs:element name="price" type="tns:PriceType"/>
24       <xs:element name="merchantName" type="xs:string" minOccurs="0"/>
25       <xs:element name="summary" type="xs:string"/>
26       <xs:element name="offerUrl" type="xs:anyURI"/>
27     </xs:sequence>
28   </xs:complexType>
```

book-code/chap09/soashopper/soashopper-services-soap/src/main/webapp/WEB-INF
/wsdl/retail.xsd

This schema was used as a guide for writing the `processXML()` function appearing in Example 10–6. In this function, the response XML document from SOAShopper is passed in as the parameter `searchDoc`. As indicated by the schema, each individual offer[7] returned is contained in an `<offer>` element. Hence, the line:

```
var listOffers = searchDoc.getElementsByTagName('offer');
```

---

7. An "offer" is a product offered for sale on one of eBay, Yahoo! Shopping, or Amazon.

returns an array[8] of `<offer>` elements. The `processXML()` function then proceeds to iterate through that array, using the DOM API to extract the following information:

- `source`—the source of the offer (i.e., eBay, Yahoo!, or Amazon)
- `thumbnailHtml`—a fragment of HTML referencing a thumbnail image of the product offered (e.g., `<img src="http:// ..." width=".." height=".."/>`)
- `priceStr`—the price of the offer (e.g., USD 19.95)
- `summary`—a string containing a description of the offer
- `urlHtml`—a fragment of HTML referencing the page where the offer can be purchased (e.g., `<a href="http:// ....">link</a>`)

Example 10–6 does not show the code used to extract each variable, but it contains enough to give you an idea of how the DOM API is used to process the returned XML.

Example 10–6 The Function `processXML()` Walks the DOM of the XML Returned by the REST Endpoint to Extract the Data That Gets Displayed

```
173    function processXML(searchDoc) {
174    try {
175    var listOffers = searchDoc.getElementsByTagName('offer');
176    for (var i=0; i<listOffers.length; i++) {
177      var item = listOffers.item(i);
178      var sourceStr =
179        item.getElementsByTagName('source').item(0).firstChild.data;
180      var thumbnailElts = item.getElementsByTagName('thumbnail');
181      var thumbnailElt;
182      var thumbnailUrl = "";
183      var thumbnailHtml = "";
184      if (thumbnailElts && thumbnailElts.item(0)) {
185        thumbnailElt = thumbnailElts.item(0);
186        thumbnailUrl =
187         thumbnailElt.getElementsByTagName('url').item(0).firstChild.data;
188        thumbnailHtml = "<img src='"+thumbnailUrl+"'";
189        var h = thumbnailElt.getElementsByTagName('pixelHeight');
190        if (h && h.item(0)) {
191          thumbnailHtml += " height='"+h.item(0).firstChild.data+"'";
192        }
```

---

8. Technically a `NodeList`.

```
193        var w = thumbnailElt.getElementsByTagName('pixelWidth');
194        if (w && w.item(0)) {
195          thumbnailHtml += " width='"+w.item(0).firstChild.data+"'";
196        }
197        thumbnailHtml += "/>";
198      }
```

book-code/chap09/soashopper/soashopper-ajax/src/main/webapp/search.html

Next, the values that have been extracted need to be put into a format that can be loaded into the Dojo table widget. The widget accepts data in *JSON* format,[9] so the `processXML()` function creates a new variable, `json-Data`, to hold the data in that form. Each offer, in JSON format, is loaded into a global array named `theSOAShopperLiveData` (see Example 10–7).

Example 10–7 Search Results Data Is Converted to JSON Format for Display by the Dojo Table Widget

```
215        var jsonData = {
216          Id:i,
217          source:sourceStr,
218          thumbnail:thumbnailHtml,
219          price:priceStr,
220          summary:summaryStr,
221          url:urlHtml
222        };
223        theSOAShopperLiveData.push(jsonData);
224      } // end for
225      populateTableFromLiveSOAShopperData();
```

book-code/chap09/soashopper/soashopper-ajax/src/main/webapp/search.html

Finally, when all the offer data has been converted to JSON and loaded into the array, the function `populateTableFromLiveSOAShopperData()` is called to load the Dojo table widget.

---

9. JSON is a text-based data interchange format used as a serialization alternative to XML. It is commonly used in Ajax programming because it works well with JavaScript. See the Glossary. See also www.json.org.

Example 10–8 shows the code that loads the table.

Example 10–8 The JSON Data Is Loaded into the Dojo Table Widget

```
234  function populateTableFromLiveSOAShopperData() {
235  try {
236    var w = dojo.widget.byId("fromSOAShopperData");
237    if(w.store.get().length > 0){
238      alert("you already loaded SOAShopper data :)");
239      return;
240    }
241    w.store.setData(theSOAShopperLiveData);
242  } catch(e) {
243    alert(e);
244  }
245  }
```

book-code/chap09/soashopper/soashopper-ajax/src/main/webapp/**search.html**

Note that the first step is to invoke a Dojo function (`dojo.widget.byId`) to get a reference to the Dojo table widget. The Dojo functions are loaded using script elements such as:

```
<script type="text/javascript" src="scripts/dojo.js"></script>
```

in the HTML `<head>` element. Once we have a reference to the table widget, it is loaded with the JSON data by calling the `store.setData()` method. Note that `w.store` is the data store associated with the table widget referenced by `w`.

Example 10–9 The Dojo `FilteringTable` Widget Is Used to Display the Search Results

```
300  <table dojoType="filteringTable" id="fromSOAShopperData" multiple="true"
301    alternateRows="true" cellpadding="0" cellspacing="0" border="0"
302    style="margin-bottom:24px;">
303    <thead>
304      <tr>
305        <th field="source" dataType="String">Source</th>
306        <th field="thumbnail" dataType="html" align="center">Image</th>
307        <th field="price" dataType="String">Price</th>
```

```
308          <th field="summary" dataType="String">Summary</th>
309          <th field="url" dataType="html">Link</th>
310       </tr>
311    </thead>
312 </table>
```

`book-code/chap09/soashopper/soashopper-ajax/src/main/webapp/search.html`

Wrapping up this tour of the SOAShopper JavaScript, Example 10–9 shows the HTML for the Dojo table widget. Notice that it contains the attribute `dojoType` that identifies it as a `FilteringTable`. The `<th>` header cells in this table contain field attributes that map each column to the corresponding JSON field name (see Example 10–7).

10.4 Conclusions about Ajax and Java EE

In this chapter, I presented a brief overview of Ajax programming by focusing on how to create a front-end for the SOAShopper application constructed in Chapter 9. I hope you have enjoyed this little detour from Java programming and found it helpful for understanding one type of consumer of Java EE Web services. Some of the more important takeaways from this chapter are as follows:

- Ajax and Java EE support a nice separation of concerns, where server-side Java EE handles the hard-code SOA integration and deployment of Web service endpoints, and Ajax provides an attractive and user-friendly front-end.
- The entire application, Ajax front-end, and Java EE back-end can be bundled as a single EAR for painless deployment to any Java EE application server.
- Creating Ajax applications requires a mastery of JavaScript and HTML DOM that may not be familiar to most server-side Java EE programmers. However, as I illustrated in the SOAShopper search example presented here, it is not too difficult to pick up those skills.
- When creating and deploying Java EE service endpoints, it is probably good practice, at least for the more complex services, to create a simple Ajax front-end to go along with the service. An Ajax front-end makes it easy for the consumers of a service you have written

to visually experience the data your service returns. The ability to "play" with a Web service in such a manner can give a developer a much better intuitive sense for the service interface than a WSDL or XML schema.

In the next and final chapter, I look at an alternative to the Java Web Services framework that is WSDL-centric, rather than Java-centric. This SOA-J framework, first mentioned at the end of Chapter 1, leverages JWS, but provides an alternative paradigm for Web services development and deployment.

CHAPTER 11

WSDL-Centric Java Web Services with SOA-J

This chapter introduces the Service Oriented Architecture for Java (SOA-J) Application Framework. SOA-J is a Web Services publishing framework that is WSDL-centric. It enables you to construct WSDL defined services from Java POJOs and EJBs. The Web Services published by SOA-J can be used as components within a Service Oriented Architecture (SOA). In this manner, SOA-J can be used to map existing Java applications into an SOA framework.

The goal of SOA-J is to leverage the Java Web Services (JWS) standards to create a framework that facilitates WSDL-centric construction of Web Services. Using SOA-J, you create a Web service by building its WSDL and annotating that WSDL document with references to the Java elements that implement it. Unlike with the JWS "Start from WSDL" development mode, there is no need to compile the WSDL and work with machine-generated classes.[1] Instead, you set up a configuration file, having the same structure as your target WSDL but with additional information about the Java implementation, and the SOA-J framework publishes the WSDL and maps SOAP requests to the implementation at runtime.

Such a WSDL-centric approach is perfect for situations where you need to create Web services that integrate into a standard corporate or eBusiness framework (i.e., where there are standard schemas and message descriptions). This scenario is described in Chapter 4.

As of this writing, SOA-J is a prototype application. I created it as a proof-of-concept to explore the viability of WSDL-centric SOA development in Java. So, don't plan to build your next enterprise SOA application with SOA-J! However, if you are interested in learning how to create an application framework to enhance JWS, SOA-J is a great learning tool.

---

1. See Chapter 9 for a detailed example of an application developed using "Start from WSDL."

The source code for SOA-J is included with the code examples you can download with this book[2] at `<book-code>/chap11/soaj`. You can also find the latest version of SOA-J at http://soa-j.org.

I have three purposes for including a detailed discussion of SOA-J in this book. First, for readers who want to gain a deep understanding of Java Web Services, I believe the best approach is to examine an implementation of a Web Services platform in detail. SOA-J serves that purpose because it includes a basic implementation of the Web Services Platform Architecture (WSPA) introduced in Chapter 1. Instead of examining SOA-J, I could have described an existing open source server like Apache Axis [AXIS] [AXIS2]. However, such a discussion of a full-featured product like Axis would have required an entire book unto itself. Instead, I favored illustrating the concepts of WSPA implementation using a relatively simple application prototype. SOA-J provides a clear and simple implementation of the WSPA using JWS technologies. Once you understand the design principles behind SOA-J, you will have no trouble understanding other WSPA frameworks such as Apache Axis and XFire [XFIRE].

My second purpose it to illustrate how some of the limitations of JWS can be overcome. For example, SOA-J offers more flexible change management, because it allows you to describe a Web service without using annotations (that are tied to source) or deployment descriptors (that are packaged in modules). Instead, SOA-J uses configuration files that can be updated dynamically at runtime. In this manner, SOA-J Web services can be created, changed, and deleted without touching Java source code, undeploying modules, or restarting containers.

Third, and most important, I am hoping to stimulate thought and debate on how to enhance future versions of JWS with WSDL-centric development features. As SOA infrastructures move beyond the prototyping phase and become corporate standards, it is going to become increasingly important for Java developers to easily integrate their work with existing WSDL and XML Schema standards.

In his book *Service Oriented Architecture* [Erl], Thomas Erl writes, "if a product, design, or technology is prefixed with 'SOA,' it is something that was (directly or indirectly) created in support of an architecture based on service-orientation principles."[3] This is exactly the case with SOA-J. It is designed to support service orientation for Java applications.

---

2. See Appendix B for instructions on how to download, install, and configure the book software.
3. Page 41 [Erl].

In what follows, I give an overview of SOA-J and use it to illustrate how a Web Services Platform Architecture can be implemented. At the end of the chapter, I look at how SOA-J measures up against Erl's standards for "service orientation."

11.1 SOA-J Architecture

SOA-J is designed to run inside a Java EE container and to leverage the Web Services infrastructure provided by JAX-WS, JAXB, WS-Metadata, and WSEE.[4] Unlike Apache Axis, XFire and other standalone Web Services server solutions, SOA-J does not replace the internal Web Services capabilities of the Java application server, but enhances them. Figure 11–1 provides a high-level illustration of the SOA-J architecture.

As illustrated here, SOA-J is deployed as a Web module (WAR). SOA-J is packaged as a port component implementing the JAX-WS `Provider<T>`[5] interface and therefore can be deployed (per WSEE and WS-Metadata) as a servlet endpoint.[6] In this manner, you can see that SOA-J is built on top of the JAX-WS implementation provided by the Java EE container. SOA-J also takes advantage of WSEE and WS-Metadata for packaging and deployment, and JAXB for serialization. Because it is built on these portable technologies, SOA-J can be deployed and run on any Java application server that supports Java EE .

As shown in Figure 11–1, SOA-J binds Web services to endpoints. Each endpoint published by SOA-J has an associated URL where SOAP requests can be posted. A WSDL document is also associated with an endpoint to describe the Web services available at that URL. Endpoints are dynamically configured and can be created and removed at runtime. You do not need to undeploy the SOA-J module, or restart the Java EE server, in order to create, change, or delete an endpoint.

SOA-J can receive SOAP requests at any of the endpoints that have been configured by the user. When SOA-J receives a SOAP request at a

---

4. These acronyms refer to Java standards for Web Services discussed throughout this book. For JAX-WS (The Java™ Architecture for XML-Based Web Services) [JSR 224], see Chapters 6 and 7. For JAXB (The Java™ Architecture for XML Binding) [JSR 222], see Chapter 5. For WS-Metadata (Services Metadata for the Java™ Platform) [JSR 181] and WSEE (Implementing Enterprise Web Services) [JSR 109], see Chapter 8.
5. See Chapter 7, Section 7.3, for a discussion of the JAX-WS `Provider<T>` interface.
6. See Chapter 8, Section 8.1, for a discussion of the deployment options for JAX-WS port components.

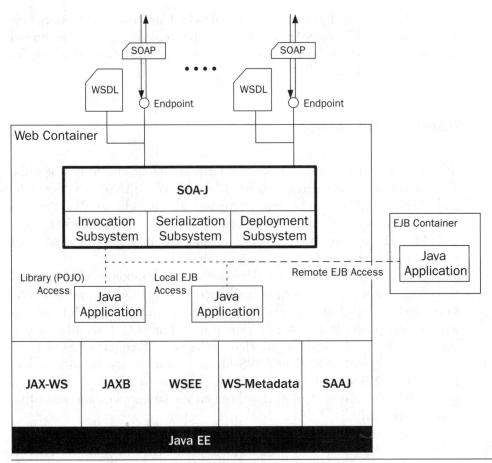

Figure 11–1 SOA-J server-side architecture.

configured endpoint, it invokes all the components of the Web Services Platform Architecture[7] to process that request: the deployment subsystem, the invocation subsystem, and the serialization subsystem. The deployment subsystem determines which Java class and method to invoke—based on the structure of the SOAP request and how the endpoint has been configured. The invocation subsystem invokes the proper class and method, using the serialization subsystem to translate between XML and Java objects. This process is discussed in detail in the remainder of this chapter. For now, consider how SOA-J is configured to publish its endpoints. Figure 11–2 provides a high-level illustration of the configuration process.

---

7. See Chapter 1, Section 1.3.

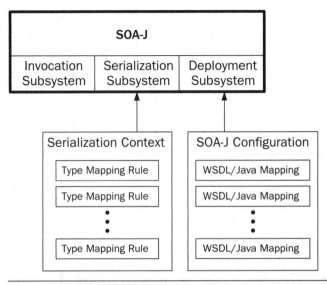

Figure 11–2 SOA-J configuration involves a Serialization Context and an Operation Map.

An endpoint is configured using a WSDL/Java mapping. The set of WSDL/Java mappings that is used to configure SOA-J is called the *SOA-J Configuration*. Each WSDL/Java mapping defines pairings of Java class/methods with `wsdl:operation` instances from a particular `wsdl:port` defined in a WSDL document. The Java class/method associated with a `wsdl:operation` gets invoked when a SOAP message is received that references that `wsdl:operation`.

Configuration of SOA-J also requires a *Serialization Context*. The Serialization Context is a set of type mapping rules. Each type mapping rule tells SOA-J how to either (i) serialize instances of a particular Java class to instances of a particular XML type; or (ii) deserialize instances of a particular XML type into instances of a particular Java class. The serialization subsystem uses this Serialization Context to deserialize SOAP parameters into Java parameters, and to serialize the Java return type instance (resulting from invoking the target Java class/method) into a SOAP parameter. The type mapping rules are written in a declarative XML language defined by the Adaptive Serialization Framework. I go through an example of some rules in Section 11.4.

Both the SOA-J Configuration and the Serialization Context are dynamic XML documents. They can be updated at runtime to dynamically reconfigure the behavior of SOA-J. Contrast this style of configuration with the JWS approach where the annotations that define the WSDL and Java/XML bindings are compiled into `.class` files and packaged into deployment modules. Changing the behavior of a deployed JWS Web service requires undeployment, Java source code changes, recompilation, repackaging, and redeployment. Changing the behavior of an SOA-J deployed Web service simply involves editing an XML file.

The SOA-J invocation subsystem manages the sequence of events from receiving the SOAP request, to dispatching it to the correct Java class/method, to invoking the serialization subsystem, and do on, as described in Chapter 1.

That is a very high-level sketch of SOA-J architecture and configuration. In the rest of this chapter, I go through an example of how a Web service is configured and invoked using SOA-J. These sections also describe in detail how SOA-J is implemented.

11.2 WSDL-Centric Development with SOA-J

As discussed in the preceding section, SOA-J is configured using an SOA-J Configuration file. This is the heart of the WSDL-centric development philosophy of SOA-J. You construct a Web service by creating its WSDL via the SOA-J Configuration. The structure of the SOA-J Configuration file mirrors the WSDL structure.

Example 11–1 shows an example of such a configuration file for deploying a single `wsdl:port`, `POSystemPort`, with two `wsdl:operations`: `retrieveAddress` and `updateAddress`. As you look through this listing, notice how it parallels the construction of a WSDL document. In essence, when writing an SOA-J Configuration file, you are creating a WSDL along with the information needed to map it to Java classes and methods. The SOA-J elements `soajWSDL`, `soajService`, `soajPort`, and `soajOperation` used in this configuration file correspond to the WSDL elements, respectively, `wsdl:definitions`, `wsdl:service`, `wsdl:port`, and `wsdl:operation`.

Example 11–1 An Example of the SOA-J Configuration File

```
4   <soajConfiguration xmlns:xsi="http://www.w3.org/2001/XMLSchema-instance"
5     xsi:schemaLocation="http://javector.com/soaj/config ../../../../../../../
    provider/src/main/resources/config/soaj-config.xsd"
6     xmlns:po="http://javector.com/ser/adaptive/po"
7     xmlns:xs="http://www.w3.org/2001/XMLSchema"
8     xmlns="http://javector.com/soaj/config">
```

```
9    <soajWSDL wsdlName="POSystem"
10     wsdlNamespace="http://javector.com/soaj/provider/posystem">
11     <soajService serviceName="POSystemService">
12       <soajPort portName="POSystemPort"
13         endpoint="http://localhost:8080/posystem/soaj/updateService">
14       <soajOperation operationName="retrieveAddress">
15         <soajPOJOMethod javaMethod="getPOfromDatabase"
16         javaClass="com.javector.soaj.wsdlgentest.po.PurchaseOrderProcessing">
17           <paramClass>java.lang.String</paramClass>
18         </soajPOJOMethod>
19         <parameterMapping>
20           <javaClass>java.lang.String</javaClass>
21           <xmlElement>
22             <eltName>poNum</eltName>
23             <eltType>xs:string</eltType>
24           </xmlElement>
25         </parameterMapping>
26         <returnMapping>
27           <javaClass>com.javector.soaj.wsdlgentest.po.PurchaseOrder</
     javaClass>
28           <xmlElement>
29             <eltRef>po:billTo</eltRef>
30           </xmlElement>
31         </returnMapping>
32       </soajOperation>
33       <soajOperation operationName="updateAddress">
34         <soajPOJOMethod javaMethod="updateAddress"
35       javaClass="com.javector.soaj.wsdlgentest.po.PurchaseOrderProcessing">
36           <paramClass>com.javector.soaj.wsdlgentest.po.Address</paramClass>
37           <paramClass>java.lang.String</paramClass>
38         </soajPOJOMethod>
39         <parameterMapping>
40           <javaClass>com.javector.soaj.wsdlgentest.po.Address</javaClass>
41           <xmlElement>
42             <eltName>po:billTo</eltName>
43             <eltType>po:BillToType</eltType>
44           </xmlElement>
45         </parameterMapping>
46         <parameterMapping>
47           <javaClass>java.lang.String</javaClass>
48           <xmlElement>
49             <eltName>string</eltName>
50             <eltType>xs:string</eltType>
51           </xmlElement>
```

```
52              </parameterMapping>
53              <returnMapping>
54                <javaClass>void</javaClass>
55                <xmlElement>
56                  <eltRef>xs:void</eltRef>
57                </xmlElement>
58              </returnMapping>
59            </soajOperation>
60          </soajPort>
61        </soajService>
62      </soajWSDL>
63      <mappingXml>config/adaptivemap.xml</mappingXml>
64      <userDefinedSchemas>
65        <userDefinedSchema>
66          <targetNamespace>http://javector.com/ser/adaptive/po</targetNamespace>
67          <schemaLocation>http://localhost:8080/posystem/config/purchaseOrder.xsd
68          </schemaLocation>
69        </userDefinedSchema>
70      </userDefinedSchemas>
71    </soajConfiguration>
```

book-code/chap11/soaj/provider-javaeetesting/provider-javaeetesting-
  generatedwsdl-testartifacts/posystem/src/main/resources/config/SoajConfig.xml

The core components of an SOA-J Configuration file are the soajOperation elements. Such operation elements define a mapping from a Java class/method to a wsdl:port and wsdl:operation. The wsdl:operation is specified by the operationName attribute. The wsdl:port is defined by the surrounding soajPort element.

The soajOperation elements are grouped under soajPort elements to define a wsdl:port. Hence, SOA-J can create a wsdl:port using a variety of Java classes and methods. This is more flexible than the JWS model, where all the operations on a single wsdl:port must be implemented by methods from the same Java class.

Following the structure of a WSDL document, the soajPort elements are contained within an soajService element to define a wsdl:service. And the soajService elements are contained within an soajWSDL element to define a WSDL document (since a WSDL document can contain multiple wsdl:service elements). The entire operation map is contained in a single soajConfiguration element, which can contain multiple soajWSDL elements. In this manner, the operation map can define multiple WSDL documents, and each instance of an SOA-J server can support an unlimited number of WSDL documents.

Now, take a closer look at the `soajOperation` element in Figure 11–1 with the attribute `operationName="retrieveAddress"`. It has an `soaj-POJOMethod` as the child element that defines the Java class and method for implementation. The `soajPOJOMethod` element is used for deploying a POJO. SOA-J also supports deployment of EJBs (3.0 and 2.1). Here, you can see that this operation is implemented using the `com.javec-tor.soaj.wsdlgentest.po.PurchaseOrderProcessing` class and the `get-POfromDatabase` method. That method has this signature:

```
PurchaseOrder getPOfromDatabase(String poNum)
```

After the `soajPOJOMethod` element comes the `parameterMapping` elements. These map the parameters of the `getPOfromDatabase()` method to the XML types or elements supported by the Web service being implemented. In this case, there is only one parameter of Java type `string`. As you can see, it is mapped to an element with the name `poNum` and the XML type `xs:string`.

Next, the `returnMapping` element maps the return type of the `getPO-fromDatabase` (`com.javector.soaj.wsdlgentest.po.PurchaseOrder`) to the element `po:billTo`. The element `po:billTo` is defined in one of the schemas listed at the very bottom of this `soajConfiguration`—under the `userDefinedSchemas` element. The `userDefinedSchemas` element lets you reuse standard schemas within your SOA-J configurations. This is the best practice discussed in Chapter 4, Section 4.1, where I describe the concept of a schema library.

In this manner, the `soajOperation` elements are defined, along with the Java program elements necessary to implement them. These `soajOper-ation` elements are then organized into `soajPort` and `soajService` elements to define a WSDL.

You may also have noticed the `mappingXml` element appearing just after the `</soajWSDL>` tag. This references the location of the Serialization Context definition, which is discussed in Section 11.4.

The information contained in this SOA-J configuration serves two purposes. First, it provides SOA-J with the type mappings (e.g., `PurchaseOrder` to `po:billTo`) for serializing and deserializing. Second, it provides SOA-J with all the information needed to construct the WSDL documents representing the Web services that are configured by the operation map. WSDL documents constructed by the current SOA-J prototype always use the document/literal wrapped style.[8] The WSDL that is generated from the `soaj-Configuration` shown in Example 11–1 is listed in Example 11–2.

---

8. See Chapter 4, Section 4.3, for a description of the various WSDL styles.

Example 11–2 WSDL Generated from the SOA-J Configuration

```
 6  <definitions xmlns="http://schemas.xmlsoap.org/wsdl/"
 7    xmlns:tns="http://javector.com/soaj/provider/posystem"
 8    xmlns:soaj1="http://javector.com/ser/adaptive/po"
 9    xmlns:xsd="http://www.w3.org/2001/XMLSchema"
10    xmlns:soap="http://schemas.xmlsoap.org/wsdl/soap/" name="POSystem"
11    targetNamespace="http://javector.com/soaj/provider/posystem">
12    <types>
13      <xsd:schema targetNamespace="http://javector.com/ser/adaptive/po">
14        <xsd:include
15          schemaLocation="http://localhost:8080/posystem/config/
purchaseOrder.xsd"
16        />
17      </xsd:schema>
18      <xsd:schema xmlns="http://www.w3.org/2001/XMLSchema"
19        targetNamespace="http://javector.com/soaj/provider/posystem"
20        elementFormDefault="qualified">
21        <xsd:import namespace="http://javector.com/ser/adaptive/po"/>
22        <element name="retrieveAddress">
23          <complexType>
24            <sequence>
25              <element name="poNum" type="xsd:string"/>
26            </sequence>
27          </complexType>
28        </element>
29        <element name="retrieveAddressResponse">
30          <complexType>
31            <sequence>
32              <element ref="soaj1:billTo"/>
33            </sequence>
34          </complexType>
35        </element>
36        <element name="updateAddress">
37          <complexType>
38            <sequence>
39              <element name="billTo" type="soaj1:BillToType"/>
40              <element name="string" type="xsd:string"/>
41            </sequence>
42          </complexType>
43        </element>
44        <element name="updateAddressResponse">
45          <complexType>
46            <sequence/>
```

```
47              </complexType>
48            </element>
49          </xsd:schema>
50        </types>
51        <message name="request_retrieveAddress">
52          <part name="parameters" element="tns:retrieveAddress"/>
53        </message>
54        <message name="response_retrieveAddress">
55          <part name="parameters" element="tns:retrieveAddressResponse"/>
56        </message>
57        <message name="request_updateAddress">
58          <part name="parameters" element="tns:updateAddress"/>
59        </message>
60        <message name="response_updateAddress">
61          <part name="parameters" element="tns:updateAddressResponse"/>
62        </message>
63        <portType name="POSystemPortType">
64          <operation name="retrieveAddress">
65            <input message="tns:request_retrieveAddress"/>
66            <output message="tns:response_retrieveAddress"/>
67          </operation>
68          <operation name="updateAddress">
69            <input message="tns:request_updateAddress"/>
70            <output message="tns:response_updateAddress"/>
71          </operation>
72        </portType>
73        <binding name="POSystemPortBinding" type="tns:POSystemPortType">
74          <soap:binding transport="http://schemas.xmlsoap.org/soap/http"
75            style="document"/>
76          <operation name="retrieveAddress">
77            <soap:operation soapAction=""/>
78            <input>
79              <soap:body use="literal"/>
80            </input>
81            <output>
82              <soap:body use="literal"/>
83            </output>
84          </operation>
85          <operation name="updateAddress">
86            <soap:operation soapAction=""/>
87            <input>
88              <soap:body use="literal"/>
89            </input>
90            <output>
```

```
91          <soap:body use="literal"/>
92        </output>
93      </operation>
94    </binding>
95    <service name="POSystemService">
96      <port name="POSystemPort" binding="tns:POSystemPortBinding">
97        <soap:address location="http://localhost:8080/posystem/soaj/
   updateService"
98        />
99      </port>
100   </service>
101 </definitions>
```

book-code/chap11/soaj/provider-javaeetesting/provider-javaeetesting-
  generatedwsdl-testartifacts/posystem/edited/POSystem.wsdl

This WSDL is constructed entirely from the SOA-J configuration. So, you do not need to write WSDL documents when working with SOA-J. They are created naturally from the configuration shorthand in a straightforward manner. Notice that, in this case, the SOA-J Configuration is about 70 percent of the length of the WSDL. And in addition to containing the information necessary to construct the WSDL, the configuration contains the type mapping information necessary for the Java deployment. To see how this works, I will walk through the process by which this WSDL was constructed.

The `wsdl:definition` element's `name` and `targetNamespace` attributes come from the `soajWSDL` element's `wsdlName` and `wsdlNamespace` attributes, respectively. For each `userDefinedSchema` in the SOA-J configuration, the WSDL has an `xsd:schema` element inside the `wsdl:types` section that uses `xsd:include` to bring the `userDefinedSchema` into the WSDL. This implements the schema library strategy from Chapter 4.

The last `xsd:schema` element in the WSDL does not have an `xsd:include` element. Rather, it defines the request/response wrappers for the `soajOperation` elements from the configuration. As you can see in Example 11–2, the wrapper elements `retrieveAddress` and `retrieveAddressResponse` are created for the `operationName retrieveAddress`. This follows the convention for document/literal wrapped style WSDL. The wrapper names are taken from the operation name, with "Response" appended for the response element name. Inside the `retrieveAddress` wrapper element is the `poNum` element—taken from the `parameterMapping` element in the `soajOperation`. Likewise, the `retrieveAddressResponse` wrapper element in the WSDL contains the `soaj1:billTo` reference from the `returnMapping` in the SOA-J configuration. Notice that in the original SOA-J configuration, a different prefix—po—was used. The SOA-J prototype does not preserve prefixes, but simply generates them from scratch.

The WSDL messages `request_retrieveAddress` and `response_retrieveAddress` are defined in the document/literal wrapped style by referencing the respective wrapper elements. The WSDL `portType` for the `soajPort` in the configuration with `portName="POSystemPort"` is named by appending "Type," and its operation has the name of the `soajOperation`'s `operationName` attribute. The `wsdl:binding` and `wsdl:port` elements then follow naturally as you would expect, with the `wsdl:port`'s `name` attribute provided by the `soajPort portName` attribute. The `soap:address` of the `wsdl:port` comes from the `soajPort endpoint` attribute.

The WSDL generated by SOA-J follows naturally from the SOA-J configuration. That is a key design element of the SOA-J framework. Once you have gone to the trouble of defining the parameter and return type mappings in the SOA-J configuration, the WSDL should flow naturally. SOA-J does not aim for ease of use by shielding the user from the type mapping definitions, as does the annotated approach with JWS. That is because a primary goal of SOA-J is to make it easy for you to deploy applications against WSDLs you construct from standard schemas—to facilitate SOA Integration. The ease of use SOA-J aims for is making it easy to do integration based on standard WSDL and XML Schema libraries. That makes it a little harder to do the configuration than when using WS-Metadata [JSR 181]. On the other hand, the good news is that by forcing you to define the type mappings, the SOA-J configuration process has done all the work that is needed to generate the WSDL.

So, you can see from this discussion that the configuration of SOA-J is entirely WSDL-centric. The next section looks at how the invocation subsystem works—in other words, how SOAP messages are processed and dispatched.

11.3 Invocation Subsystem

The invocation subsystem is responsible for receiving SOAP messages and processing them according to the model described in Chapter 1, Section 1.3.1. As implemented in SOA-J, the invocation subsystem is responsible for:

1. Receiving a SOAP message
2. Determining the message's target service—i.e., which WSDL operation is the message intended to invoke

3. Given the target WSDL operation, dispatching the message to the correct Java class/method to invoke
4. Handing off the SOAP message to the Serialization subsystem to deserialize it into Java objects that can be passed to the Java target as parameters
5. Invoking the Java target using the parameters generated by the Serialization subsystem and getting the Java object returned by the target method
6. Handing off the returned object to the Serialization subsystem to serialize it into an XML element conformant with the return message specified by the target WSDL operation
7. Wrapping the returned XML element as a SOAP message response conforming to the target WSDL operation and, if an exception has occurred, mapping it to a SOAP Fault that will be the response
8. Sending the SOAP response

Figure 11–3 provides a static class UML diagram showing the high-level implementation of the SOA-J invocation subsystem. SOAP requests are first received by the `SoajDispatcher`. The `SoajDispatcher` is an `HttpServlet` that simply provides a base context root for all SOA-J endpoints managed within a single SOA-J configuration. For example, the `SoajDispatcher` may receive all HTTP requests for endpoints matching `http://myserver/posystem/soaj/*`. In this case, an individual SOA-J endpoint, like the one described for the `POSystemPort`, may get deployed to something like `http://myserver/posystem/soaj/updateService`.

The `SoajDispatcher` passes the SOAP request on to the `SoajProvider`—which implements the JAX-WS `Provider<Source>` interface discussed in Chapter 7. The `Provider<Source>` processing implemented by the underlying JAX-WS 2.0 runtime gives SOA-J three advantages here. First, it provides access to the `WebServiceContext` that contains the HTTP endpoint information necessary for dispatching. Second, it hands us the SOAP message as a `javax.xml.transform.Source`. Third, it enables the invocation subsystem to return SOAP Faults simply by throwing instances of `javax.xml.ws.soap.SOAPFaultException` as described in Chapter 7, Section 7.5.

For each SOAP request received, the `SoajProvider` instantiates a `RequestController`—the class that handles SOA-J request processing. The `RequestController` contains an `InputDataProcessor` instance for processing the SOAP request and creating an instance of `WSRequest`—the SOA-J internal representation of a SOAP request message and its context. In addition, the `RequestController` contains a `FlowInterpreter` instance, which is responsible for instantiating the appropriate SOA-J operation (i.e., dispatching), invoking it, and creating a `WSResponse` instance to contain the results. `WSResponse` is the SOA-J internal representation of a SOAP response message.

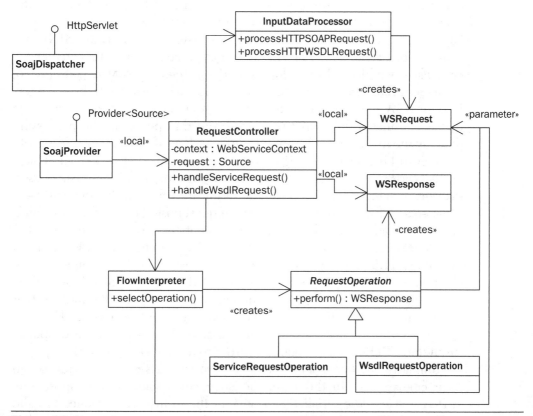

Figure 11–3 SoajProvider uses RequestController to manage the invocation process.

You may have noticed that in the class diagram in Figure 11–3, the `RequestOperation` (an abstract class) has two subclasses: `ServiceRequestOperation` and `WsdlRequestOperation`. That is because this invocation subsystem handles WSDL requests and SOAP requests. SOA-J follows the convention that HTTP GET requests posted to the endpoint suffixed with "`?wsdl`" result in HTTP responses containing the target WSDL. Such WSDL requests also get processed by the invocation subsystem. However, in such cases, the `FlowInterpreter` creates an instance of `WsdlRequestOperation` to handle the request. In the SOAP case, an instance of `ServiceRequestOperation` is created.

Currently, SOA-J handles only SOAP over HTTP. To extend it to handle other transport protocols, such as JMS, would simply be a matter of extending the `RequestController` class to service JMS messages carrying SOAP payload (i.e., SOAP over JMS). Of course, there would be no `WebService-Context` parameter in this case—in other words, the target endpoint for the JMS message would need to be determined by another mechanism, perhaps by JMS meta-data or using WS-Addressing [WS-ADDRESSING 1.0 Core]. Along with extending the `RequestController`, the `InputDataProcess` class would need to add a method—`processJMSSOAPRequest()`. So, the `RequestController` and `InputDataProcessor` form the transport interface for SOA-J. These classes are used to generate the `WSRequest` instance that encapsulates the SOAP request. From that point on, the processing done by the invocation subsystem is independent of the transport protocol.

Figure 11–4 shows the high-level structure of the `WSRequest` and `WSResponse` classes. Focusing on `WSRequest` first, notice that it has two subclasses: `WsdlRequest` for encapsulating a request for the WSDL document, and `ServiceRequest` for encapsulating a SOAP request posted to a Web service endpoint. In addition, the `WSRequest` contains a reference to the `SoajConfiguration`—in other words, the SOA-J Configuration file discussed in Section 11.2. The `ServiceRequest` contains the XML parameters—the children of the wrapper element in the SOAP request body. These will be deserialized to become the Java parameters used to invoke the method that implements the target service. In addition, the `ServiceRequest` class contains the `operationName` (the wrapper element's name) and the `endpoint` (from the HTTP request headers) in order to dispatch the request.

Similarly, the `WSResponse` class has two subclasses: `WsdlResponse` and `ServiceResponse`. In this case, the `ServiceResponse` has, at most, one `XmlParameter`—the serialized instance of the return type produced by the target Java class/method.[9] The `WsdlResponse` contains the SOA-J-generated WSDL.

Figure 11–5 shows the class structure, related to `ServiceRequestOperation`, that handles the processing of the `ServiceRequest` (`WSRequest`) to invoke a Web service. Recall from Figure 11–3 that the `FlowInterpreter` creates an instance of the `ServiceRequestOperation` class to process the `WSRequest`. As illustrated in Figure 11–5, the `perform()` method implements invocation using locally created instances of `SoajOperation` and `ServiceInvoker`. `SoajOperation` is created from the SOA-J configuration

---

9. SOA-J does not support IN/OUT parameters. So, either zero or one parameter is returned. This is another simplifying assumption (like supporting only document/literal wrapped style WSDL). In practice, I've not found IN/OUT parameters particularly useful.

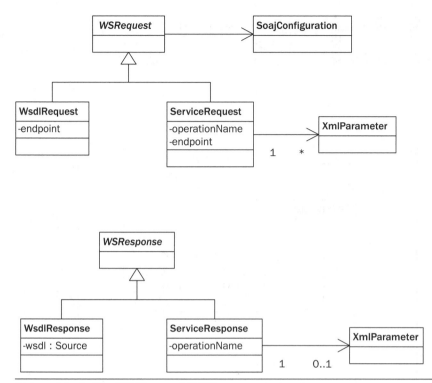

Figure 11–4 The WSRequest/WSResponse structures.

file information accessed through the `ServiceRequest` (`WSRequest`). It is an encapsulation of the Java class/method to be invoked.

As indicated, `SoajOperation` is a parameter to the `ServiceInvoker`, and the `ServiceInvoker` actually invokes the `SoajOperation`. To do that, the `ServiceInvoker` uses the `SerializationMappingRules` (illustrated as the Type Mapping Rules comprising the Serialization Context in Figure 11–2) and `Schema` (containing the type and element definitions for the XML parameters) to construct an instance of the `AdaptiveContext` interface. The `AdaptiveContext` instance handles the deserialization of the XML parameters and the serialization of the return type instance.

At this point, it helps to look at some sequence diagrams to understand how these classes work together to handle invocation. Figure 11–6 shows the sequence of events by which a SOAP/HTTP request is processed. The HTTP request is processed by the `SoajDispatcher`, which passes along the SOAP request and HTTP context to the `SoajProvider`. `SoajProvider` instantiates a `RequestController` and invokes its `handleServiceRequest()` method—which eventually returns a response (as a

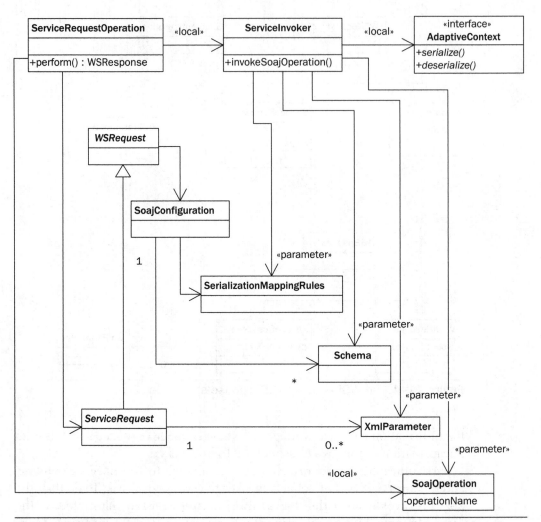

Figure 11–5 ServiceRequestOperation creates a ServiceInvoker that invokes the SoajOperation.

javax.xml.transform.Source) that the SoajProvider can put out on the wire as a SOAP response.

Within the handleServieRequest() method, the InputDataProcessor instance's createWSRequest() method is invoked to instantiate a WSRequest from the SOAP request and HTTP context. Then, that wsRequest instance is passed to the FlowInterpreter's createOperation() method to instantiate the ServiceRequestOperation. The RequestController invokes the ServiceRequestOperation's perform() method to process the request

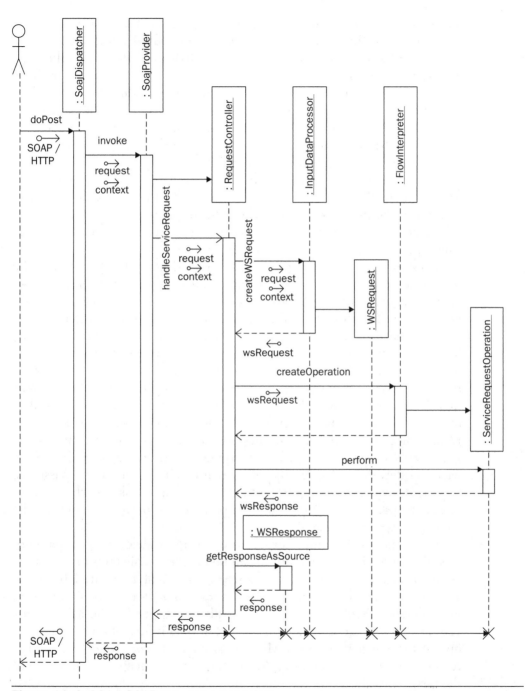

Figure 11–6 SOA-J SOAP request processing.

and get back the `WSResponse` instance. Calling the `getResponseAsSource()` method returns the XML that can be used to create the SOAP response.

Figure 11–7 shows a sequence diagram that drills down into the `ServiceRequestOperation`'s `perform()` method (appearing at the far right of Figure 11–6). As you can see, what happens here is that the `WSRequest`'s reference to the `SoajConfiguration` is used to get some of the parameters needed for invocation. These include the `rules` (`SerializationMappingRules`), `schema` (`Schema`), `parameters` (`XmlParameter` instances as a `List<Source>`), and `op` (`SoajOperation`).

The rules and schema are used to create an instance of `ServiceInvoker`. Then, the `params` and `op` are passed to the `invokeOperation()` method of the `ServiceInvoker`. The `invokeOperation()` method returns the response XML as a `java.xml.transform.Source` that gets encapsulated in the `WSResponse` that is returned.

Continuing to drill down into the details, Figure 11–8 illustrates the `ServiceInvoker`'s role in the invocation subsystem. When the `ServiceInvoker` is constructed, it uses the `AdaptiveContextFactory` to create a new `AdaptiveContext` from the type mapping rules (serialization context) and schema provided by the SOA-J configuration. Note that the SOA-J implementation should cache this `AdaptiveContext` so that it is not reconstructed for every SOAP request, but rather only when the configuration or serialization context files have changed. The `AdaptiveContext` then becomes the interface to the serialization subsystem—discussed in more detail in the next section. The `ServiceInvoker`'s `invokeOperation()` method then uses that `AdaptiveContext`, passing it to the `DeserializerHelper` along with the parameters and `SoajOperation`, to get back the deserialized Java objects (`paramObjects`) that will be passed to the target Java class/method. The `SoajOperation` is passed to the `DeserializerHelper`, along with these other parameters, because it contains the parameter type mappings.

Once the XML parameters have been deserialized to Java parameters, the target Java class/method can be invoked. This target is encapsulated in an instance of the `SoajMethod` class that is created from the `SoajOperation` by the `SoajMethodFactory`. `SoajMethod` is discussed in more detail in Section 11.5. It is basically a wrapper for the `java.lang.reflect.Method` class that contains additional information necessary to invoke the method in cases where it is an EJB. `SoajMethod` also takes responsibility for instantiating (or getting a reference to) an instance of the target class.

`SoajMethod`'s `invoke()` method returns the Java response to the `ServiceInvoker`, where the next step executed by the `invokeOperation()`

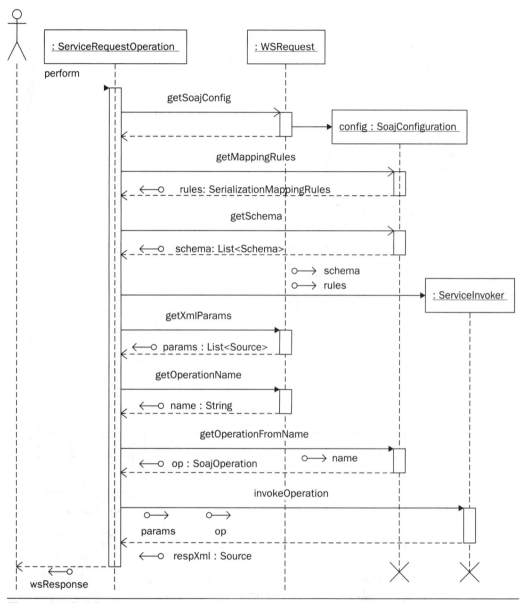

Figure 11–7 SOAJ Web service invocation process.

method is to serialize this into an XML response using the `Serializer-Helper`. `SerializerHelper` and `DeserializerHelper` are simply convenience classes that provide serialization and deserialization services by delegating to the supplied `AdaptiveContext` parameter.

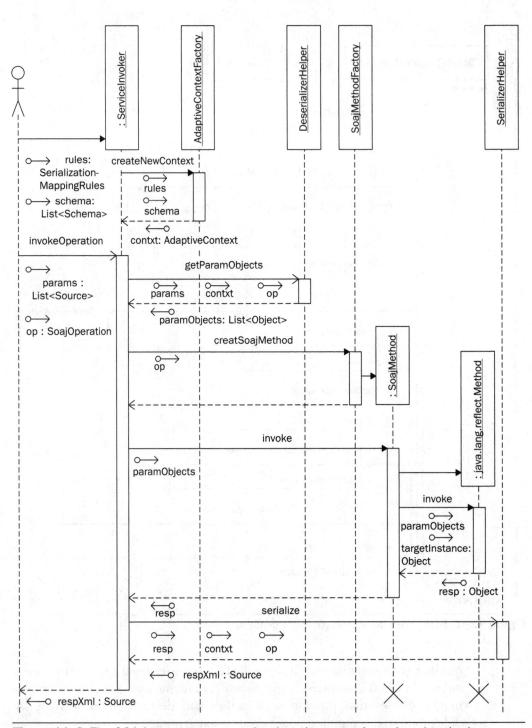

Figure 11–8 The SOA-J `ServiceInvoker` invokes the target Java class/method.

From this description of SOA-J, you should have a pretty good idea how a SOAP server implements an invocation subsystem. The details will vary from implementation to implementation, but the basic outline remains the same. All SOAP servers have to receive the SOAP message, dispatch it to the correct WSDL operation, deserialize the parameters, invoke the target class/method, and serialize the response. How this is done, however, can have a big impact on the performance of the system. More recent implementations of SOAP servers like Axis 2.x [AXIS2] and XFire [XFIRE] use pull parser technology like StAX [JSR 173] to minimize the amount of memory and processing used by avoiding reading the entire SOAP message into a DOM instance. Earlier implementations, such as Axis 1.x [AXIS], suffer from performance problems because they are not able to manage memory as carefully.

SOA-J is built on top of Java EE, so it does not have complete control over the processing of the SOAP message. If the underlying Java EE 5 implementation hands the `SoajProvider` the SOAP message as a `javax.xml.transform.Source` that has been implemented as a `DOMSource`, the DOM instance has already been created. If the `Source` received is a `StreamSource` and no DOM processing has taken place, SOA-J could take steps to optimize performance. It is interesting to point out, however, that concern about such issues might not matter all that much for processing small SOAP requests. Performance is a complex topic, with many variables. By studying SOA-J, you can get an appreciation for how SOAP servers are implemented and understand how they implement different strategies to attempt to improve performance.

The next section looks at the serialization subsystem. SOA-J uses a unique serialization implementation that is designed to facilitate SOA Integration where you start from both existing Java objects and existing XML schemas. This "Start from WSDL and Java" approach is described in Chapter 4, Section 4.5.

11.4 Serialization Subsystem

When working with JAX-WS 2.0 and JAXB 2.0, I was impressed with how easily Java classes could be annotated and deployed as Web services. However, I was also very frustrated to discover how difficult it was to deploy existing Java classes against an existing schema. With JAXB 2.0 and JAX-WS 2.0, you basically get WSDL based on the schema JAXB 2.0 generates from your classes and annotations. You can try to map your

Java class to a target schema by manipulating the annotations. However, for reasons described in detail in Chapter 4, annotations are not a good way to implement such type mappings. To summarize, here are some of the shortcomings:

1. To change a type mapping, you need to edit the source, recompile, and redeploy.
2. Annotations are a very unintuitive way to create type mappings. You have to fiddle with them, keep regenerating the resulting schema (via JAXB), and try to see whether you can "come close" to the target schema. This approach kills your productivity.
3. Many type mappings are impossible to generate with JAXB annotations. See Chapter 4 for some examples.
4. Good design practice (i.e., separation of concerns) dictates that a mapping layer should insulate the XML (WSDL) representation of your Web services from the Java implementation.[10] JAXB annotations, although convenient, bury that mapping layer inside the Java source code. This makes it difficult to understand and maintain.

For these reasons, I decided to implement a serialization subsystem, on top of JAXB 2.0, that enables developers to maintain type mappings as rules defined in XML. I named it Adaptive Serializers, because it enables you to easily maintain and adapt your system to changes in Java classes and XML schema. This section gives you an idea how Adaptive Serializers work by walking through a specific example.

The example starts by looking at the code from some simple Java classes that are going to be used to implement a Web service. These are the `MyPurchaseOrder`, `Address`, and `Phone` classes—snippets of which are shown in Example 11–3, Example 11–4, and Example 11–5, respectively.

The `PurchaseOrder` class contains two attributes: a "bill to" address (of type `Address`) and a `List` of items. The `retrieveAddress` operation discussed in Section 11.2 simply returns the `Address` attribute of the `PurchaseOrder` instance.

---

10. See Chapter 9, Section 9.4, to see how this sort of mapping layer is implemented in the SOAShopper application. In that system, there is no attempt to use annotations to map the WSDL and XML schemas to the SOAShopper API. Instead, a layer of Java code is used, the Service Implementation layer, to map from the classes generated from the WSDL to the SOAShopper API. The SOA-J serialization system includes that sort of mapping layer in its framework.

Example 11–3 PurchaseOrder

```
25    public class PurchaseOrder {
26
27      private Address billTo = new Address();
28      private List items;
29      private String ponum;
30
31      public void setBillTo(Address billTo) {
32        this.billTo = billTo;
33      }
34
35      public void setItems(List items) {
36        for (Object item : items) {
37          addItem((Item) item);
38        }
39      }
40
41      public Address getBillTo() {
42        return billTo;
43      }
44
45      public List getItems() {
46        return items;
47      }
48
49      public void addItem(Item item) {
50        if ( items == null ) {
51          items = new ArrayList();
52        }
53        items.add(item);
54      }
55
56      public String getPonum() {
57        return ponum;
58      }
59
60      public void setPonum(String ponum) {
61        this.ponum = ponum;
62      }
63
64    }
```

book-code/chap11/soaj/provider-javaeetesting/provider-javaeetesting-
  generatedwsdl-testartifacts/posystem/src/main/java/com/javector/
  soaj/wsdlgentest/po/PurchaseOrder.java

The `Address` and `Phone` classes, with snippets shown next, are the same classes introduced in Chapter 4, Section 4.6, where I discussed some of the difficulties related to mapping these classes to an XML schema using JAXB 2.0.

Example 11–4 Address

```
21    public class Address implements java.io.Serializable {
22        private int streetNum;
23        private java.lang.String streetName;
24        private java.lang.String city;
25        private StateType state;
26        private int zip;
27        private Phone phoneNumber;
28
```

book-code/chap11/soaj/provider-javaeetesting/provider-javaeetesting-
  generatedwsdl-testartifacts/posystem/src/main/java/com/javector/
  soaj/wsdlgentest/po/Address.java

Example 11–5 Phone

```
21    public class Phone {
22         private int areaCode;
23        private String exchange;
24        private String number;
25
```

book-code/chap11/soaj/provider-javaeetesting/provider-javaeetesting-
  generatedwsdl-testartifacts/posystem/src/main/java/com/javector/
  soaj/wsdlgentest/po/Phone.java

To briefly summarize one of the problems, it relates to the structure of the `Phone` class. In order to map it to the schema shown in Example 11–6, the three Java properties (`areaCode`, `exchange`, and `number`) must get mapped to the single `phone` element (inside of `po:BillToType`) of type `xs:string`. Another problem relates to the `Address` class itself. Again, to map it to the schema in Example 11–6 (`po:BillToType`), the Java properties `streetNum` and `streetName` must get mapped to the elements `addrLine1` and `addrLine2`. In both these cases, the Java properties must be significantly transformed, split, and recombined to map them to/from the target XML elements. I call these kinds of mappings multivariate type mappings. They arise commonly in practice—particularly when doing SOA integration—and cannot be handled with JAXB 2.0 annotations.

Example 11–6 `PurchaseOrder` Schema

```
4   <xs:schema targetNamespace="http://javector.com/ser/adaptive/po"
5     xmlns:xs="http://www.w3.org/2001/XMLSchema"
6     xmlns:po="http://javector.com/ser/adaptive/po"
7     elementFormDefault="qualified" attributeFormDefault="unqualified">
8     <xs:element name="purchaseOrderList">
9       <xs:complexType>
10        <xs:sequence>
11          <xs:element ref="po:purchaseOrder" maxOccurs="unbounded"/>
12        </xs:sequence>
13      </xs:complexType>
14    </xs:element>
15    <xs:element name="purchaseOrder">
16      <xs:complexType>
17        <xs:sequence>
18          <xs:element ref="po:billTo"/>
19          <xs:element ref="po:items"/>
20        </xs:sequence>
21        <xs:attribute name="ponum" type="xs:string" use="required"/>
22      </xs:complexType>
23    </xs:element>
24    <xs:complexType name="BillToType">
25      <xs:sequence>
26        <xs:element name="company" type="xs:string"/>
27        <xs:element name="street" type="xs:string"/>
28        <xs:element name="city" type="xs:string"/>
29        <xs:element name="state" type="xs:string"/>
30        <xs:element name="zip" type="xs:string"/>
31        <xs:element name="phone" type="xs:string"/>
32      </xs:sequence>
33    </xs:complexType>
34    <xs:element name="billTo" type="po:BillToType"/>
35    <xs:element name="items">
36      <xs:complexType>
37        <xs:sequence>
38          <xs:element ref="po:item" maxOccurs="unbounded"/>
```

```
39          </xs:sequence>
40        </xs:complexType>
41      </xs:element>
42      <xs:element name="item">
43        <xs:complexType>
44          <xs:sequence>
45            <xs:element name="quantity" type="xs:positiveInteger"/>
46            <xs:element name="price" type="xs:double"/>
47          </xs:sequence>
48          <xs:attribute name="productName" type="xs:string" use="required"/>
49        </xs:complexType>
50      </xs:element>
51    </xs:schema>
```

book-code/chap11/soaj/provider-javaeetesting/provider-javaeetesting-
  generatedwsdl-testartifacts/posystem/src/main/webapp/config/purchaseOrder.xsd

---

As described in Chapter 4, Section 4.6, one approach to dealing with multivariate type mappings is to write helper code that translates from the classes a JAXB schema compile creates from the `po:BillToType` to our `Address` class. Similar helper code can be written to deal with the `Phone` mapping. Although this approach works, it boils down to embedding the Java to XML mapping logic inside of helper Java classes. These helper classes are difficult to maintain and understand. It is definitely not a good approach to managing type mappings and it will not scale.

A slightly better solution is offered in Chapter 5, Section 5.7, where I show how to implement these multivariate type mappings using JAXB 2.0 `XmlAdapterClass` instances. This approach essentially embeds the helper classes inside of the JAXB framework so that the JAXB runtime can use annotations to recognize when the helper code should be invoked to help it with a given serialization or deserialization. This approach is slightly better because it at least provides some organization and a standard interface for the helper Java classes. But it still has the major problem that the type mappings are embedded inside Java classes. Again, this approach creates major change management headaches and violates basic separation-of-concerns design principles.

These problems can be avoided by separating the type mappings from the code by foregoing annotations and instead using an expressive type mapping language that lets you easily define and maintain the logic for converting between a Java class and an XML Schema component.

This is the approach taken by Adaptive Serializers. Type mappings are written in XML as shown in Example 11–7. An individual type mapping implementation is represented by the `strategy` element. One type mapping can have multiple strategies, and the Adaptive Serializer implementation can choose the most appropriate one based on the context. For now, I will keep it simple and just talk in terms of one strategy per type mapping.

Example 11–7 shows the `strategy` for the type mapping between `PurchaseOrder` and `po:PurchaseOrder`. The Java class and XML type for the type mapping are represented as attributes of the `strategy` element. The actual implementation of the strategy is defined by its children—the `rule` elements.

Example 11–7 Defining the Serialization Rule for `PurchaseOrder`

```
78    <strategy javaClass="com.javector.soaj.wsdlgentest.po.PurchaseOrder"
79      xmlType="po:purchaseOrder">
80      <rule javaName="ponum" xmlName="ponum" xmlType="xs:string"
81        xmlNodeType="ATTRIBUTE" javaClass="java.lang.String"/>
82      <rule javaName="billTo" xmlName="po:billTo" xmlType="po:billToType"
83        xmlNodeType="ELEMENT"
84        javaClass="com.javector.soaj.wsdlgentest.po.Address"/>
85      <rule javaName="items" xmlName="po:item"
86        xmlNodeType="ELEMENT" javaClass="com.javector.soaj.wsdlgentest.po.Item">
87        <wrap>
88          <javaWrap name="items" type="java.util.List"/>
89          <xmlWrap name="po:items"/>
90        </wrap>
91      </rule>
92    </strategy>
```

book-code/chap11/soaj/provider-javaeetesting/provider-javaeetesting-
  generatedwsdl-testartifacts/posystem/src/main/resources/config/adaptivemap.xml

For example, the second rule defined in this strategy maps the `billTo` property of the Java class `PurchaseOrder` to the `po:BillTo` element. The `xmlNodeType` attribute (=`"ELEMENT"`) indicates that the `xmlName` refers to an element as opposed to an attribute. This rule does not tell us how the Java property (an instance of `Address`) should be converted to an instance of the `po:billTo` global element. That is another type mapping, and is defined by a separate strategy. In this manner, a type mapping strategy is defined recursively.

The third rule shown in Example 11–7 maps the Java property `items` (a `List`) to the global element `po:item`. Since this is a rule for a collection, the `javaClass` attribute is specified to indicate how the members of the collection should be treated. Here, they are being serialized/deserialized as instances of `Item`. Inside this rule, you see the `wrap` element. This tells the Adaptive Serializer that the `po:item` elements generated from the members of the `List` should be wrapped inside a container element. In this case, the wrapper has the name `items`.

Returning to the rule for the `billTo` Java property, Example 11–8 shows the strategy for the type mapping from `Address` to `po:BillToType`, which the rule requires. Examining the first rule in this strategy, you can begin to see how multivariate type mappings are handled. This rule applies to the element `po:street`. The `javaName` is "."—indicating that the rule maps some transformation of the entire `Address` class to the element `po:street`. This rule is one-way—it applies only to serialization (since it is a transformation, it doesn't naturally define a deserialization back to any one Java property)—hence the attribute `restrictTo="SERIALIZATION"`. Inside the rule is a `script` element. This element holds some Groovy [GROOVY] script that is applied to the `Address` instance to obtain the `po:street` value. You can see that it is a simple concatenation of the street number and street name. This is how the Adaptive Serializer framework enables type mappings that cannot be handled by binding frameworks like JAXB. It lets you put scripting fragments in the type mapping rules like this where they can be easily managed and updated as necessary.

But how do we do the reverse, and deserialize the `po:street` element? The second and third rules down show how it can be done using XPath expressions. The first of these rules deserializes the `xs:string` value of `po:street` by parsing out the substring before the ' ' (space). That should be the street number. The second of these rules deserializes the `xs:string` value of `po:street` by parsing the substring after the ' ' (space). That should be the street name.

Example 11–8 Defining the Serialization Rule for `Address`

```
26    <strategy javaClass="com.javector.soaj.wsdlgentest.po.Address"
27      xmlType="po:billToType" xmlName="po:billTo">
28      <rule javaName="." xmlName="po:street" xmlType="xs:string"
29        xmlNodeType="ELEMENT" restrictTo="SERIALIZATION">
30        <script><![CDATA[
31          return source.getStreetNum()+" "+source.getStreetName();
32        ]]></script>
```

```
33    </rule>
34    <rule javaName="streetNum" javaClass="int" xmlName="po:street"
35      xmlType="xs:string" xmlNodeType="ELEMENT" restrictTo="DESERIALIZATION">
36      <script><![CDATA[substring-before(.,' ')]]></script>
37    </rule>
38    <rule javaName="streetName" javaClass="java.lang.String" xmlName="po:street"
39      xmlType="xs:string" xmlNodeType="ELEMENT" restrictTo="DESERIALIZATION">
40      <script><![CDATA[substring-after(.,' ')]]></script>
41    </rule>
42    <rule javaName="city" xmlName="po:city" xmlType="xs:string"
43      xmlNodeType="ELEMENT"/>
44    <rule javaName="state" xmlName="po:state" xmlType="xs:string"
45      xmlNodeType="ELEMENT"/>
46    <rule javaName="zip" xmlName="po:zip" xmlType="xs:string"
47      xmlNodeType="ELEMENT"/>
48    <rule javaName="phoneNumber"
49      javaClass="com.javector.soaj.wsdlgentest.po.Phone" xmlName="po:phone"
50      xmlType="xs:string" xmlNodeType="ELEMENT" restrictTo="DESERIALIZATION"/>
51    <rule javaName="phoneNumber" xmlName="po:phone" xmlType="xs:string"
52      xmlNodeType="ELEMENT" restrictTo="SERIALIZATION">
53      <script><![CDATA[
54        String area = Integer.toString(source.getAreaCode());
55        return "("+area+")"+" "+source.getExchange()+"-"+source.getNumber();
56      ]]></script>
57    </rule>
58  </strategy>
```

book-code/chap11/soaj/provider-javaeetesting/provider-javaeetesting-
  generatedwsdl-testartifacts/posystem/src/main/resources/config/adaptivemap.xml

So, you can see that the Adaptive Serializer type mapping language enables you to use Groovy scripts and XPath to handle the kinds of type mappings that JAXB 2.0 is unable to deal with without resorting to the complexities of the `xmlAdapter` class. In addition to this benefit, however, the real advantage is that the helper code is maintained in the type mapping layer and does not have to be embedded in the deployed Java classes. So, changing it is easier and can be accomplished without having to recompile and redeploy. Also, by breaking the helper code down into small manageable chunks, it is easier to maintain and manage as an integral part of the XML mapping layer.

The preceding example gives you an idea of how the Adaptive Serializer type mapping language works. Figure 11–9 shows how the Adaptive

Serializer framework plugs into SOA-J. As indicated in the preceding sequence diagram (Figure 11–8), the invocation subsystem serializes and deserializes via the `AdaptiveContext` interface with the help of the `DeserializerHelper` and `SerializerHelper` classes. In Figure 11–9, you can see these helper classes and the `AdaptiveContext` interface. The `AdaptiveContext` interface is implemented by an abstract class named `BaseSoajContext` that holds references to the XML schemas and the `AdaptiveMap`. The `AdaptiveMap` contains the strategies (like those illustrated in Example 11–7 and Example 11–8) that implement the type mappings. The `BaseSoajContext` is the Java implementation of the Serialization Context described in Section 11.2 that is provided in the SOA-J configuration. `BaseSoajContext` cannot perform any serialization or deserialization. It only contains the context and implements the `AdaptiveContext` interface with abstract methods.

The `AdaptiveJaxbContext` class provides the serialization context and infrastructure needed to implement the `AdaptiveContext` interface. This class has `Jaxb` as part of its name because it uses JAXB 2.0 to implement the serialization logic. I have also worked on implementations that use other Java/XML binding technologies (e.g., Apache XMLBeans [XMLBeans]). For this implementation of SOA-J, I used JAXB 2.0 because it is provided as part of the Java EE 5 run-time implementation. `AdaptiveJaxbContext` provides a couple of important pieces of functionality. First, it reads the instances of Schema (i.e., the XML Schema definitions used in the type mappings), and compiles them using the JAXB schema compiler. It is these JAXB-generated classes that the serialization subsystem uses to implement the type mappings. `AdaptiveJaxbContext` creates a class loader that contains these JAXB-generated classes. This is the class loader used by the serialization subsystem. Second, the `AdaptiveJaxbContext` class provides `newSerializer()` and `newDeserialzer()` methods for creating serializers and deserializers.

The classes that implement serializers and deserializers follow a similar pattern, so I will describe only the serializers here. The serializer classes derive from `BaseAdaptiveSerializer`. An instance of `BaseAdaptiveSerializer` corresponds to a particular `strategy` element like the one shown in Example 11–8 for serializing `Address`. The `BaseAdaptiveSerializer` contains the logic for executing the `rule` elements that implement the `strategy`.

Executing a rule typically involves serializing a Java property to an XML element or attribute that is part of the target XML. This gets done recursively, as the instance of `BaseAdaptiveSerializer` finds a strategy (from the `AdaptiveMap`) that implements the rule's type mapping, and creates a new instance of `BaseAdaptiveSerializer` to execute the strategy. The

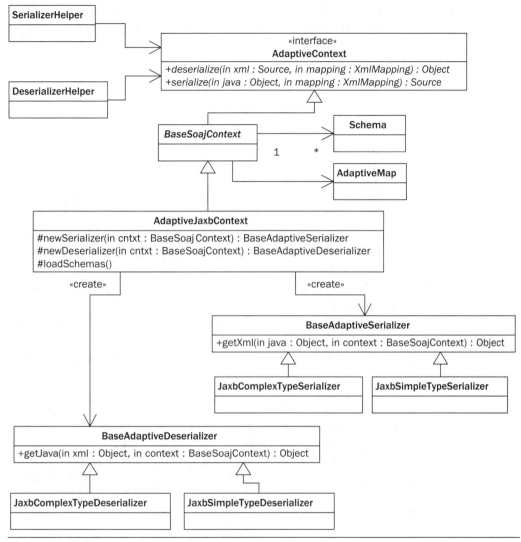

Figure 11–9 Top-level serialization classes.

recursion stops when a strategy can be implemented without any rules (e.g., mapping a `String` to an `xs:string`). Usually, this happens when the `BaseAdaptiveSerializer` is an instance of `JaxbSimpleTypeSerializer`—the serializer class used to create instances of simple XML types (e.g., `xs:string`).

`BaseAdaptiveSerializer` also is extended by `JaxbComplexTypeSerializer`—the serializer class used to create instances of complex XML types.

When choosing a serializer to execute a strategy, the Adaptive Serializer framework looks at the target XML component. If it represents a simple type, `JaxbSimpleTypeSerializer` is used. Otherwise, `JaxbComplexType-Serializer` is used.

To wrap up this discussion of the serialization subsystem, the most important points to remember about the Adaptive Serializer Framework (ASF) are as follows:

- The ASF facilitates SOA Integration by allowing you to define type mappings between existing Java classes and existing XML schema.
- The ASF facilitates separation of concerns by keeping serialization separate from the Java code. This contrasts with annotations, which store the serialization instructions directly in the Java classes. With ASF, type mappings are stored separately from the Java code and XML schema using the ASF mapping language illustrated in Example 11–7 and Example 11–8.
- The ASF mapping language defines type mappings with `strategy` elements. A strategy element can contain child rule elements that tell the ASF how to implement the strategy. A rule implicitly defines a type mapping that can be implemented with a strategy. In this manner, the ASF mapping language defines type mappings recursively.
- The recursive structure of the type mapping definitions is mirrored in the recursive algorithm used by the ASF to execute serialization and deserialization.
- The ASF implementation distributed with SOA-J is built using JAXB so that it can run directly in a Java EE 5 container without additional Java/XML binding libraries. However, it is also possible to implement the ASF using other Java/XML binding tools such as XML-Beans [XMLBeans].

In the next section, I look at how the SOA-J deployment subsystem is designed.

11.5 Deployment Subsystem

To some extent, this section picks up where Section 11.2, covering the WSDL-centric SOA-J configuration, left off. It drills down into some of the implementation details describing how the configuration is realized in

the Java code for SOA-J. In Section 11.2, I described the `soajOperation`
element as the core component of an SOA-J configuration. Likewise, the
corresponding Java class—`SoajOperation`—is the core Java class in the deployment subsystem.

Figure 11–10 shows the static class diagram for the structure of `Soaj-`
`Operation`. An `SoajOperation` contains a single `JavaMethodType`—a class
that encapsulates a target Java class/method. Its attributes include the name
of the Java class, and the method signature. The purpose of the `Java-`
`MethodType` class is to provide SOA-J with an instance of `java.lang-`
`.reflect.Method` that can be invoked. However, the mechanism for creating such an instance depends on the type of Java class encapsulated by `Java-`
`MethodType`.

As you can see in Figure 11–10, `JavaMethodType` is extended by
`EJB21MethodType`, `EBJ30MethodType`, and `POJOMethodType`. Each class provides the capability to create the appropriate `java.lang .reflect.Method`
based on the procedures used to obtain an instance of the corresponding
class. If it is an EJB, either `EJB21MethodType` or `EJB30MethodType` gets
used to request an instance from the container (it can be either remote or
local). If it is a POJO, the `POJOMethodType` class simply loads the encapsulated class and uses `Class.newInstance()` to get a target `Object` for invocation of the method.

In addition to providing a target `Object` and instance of
`java.lang.reflect.Method` that can be invoked, the other function of the
`SoajOperation` class is to provide SOA-J with the type mappings to serialize
and deserialize the parameters, returned `Object`, and exceptions.[11] These
mappings are contained within the `SoajOperation` as instances of the
`WSDL2JavaMappingType` class. This class, so named because it is used to
capture the SOA-J type mappings that are used to construct the WSDL (as
described in Section 11.2), represents a mapping from a `Class` to either an
XML Schema element or a type.

As the basic deployment unit, `SoajOperation` instances are grouped
into `SoajPort` instances (representing `wsdl:port`), which are grouped into
`SoajService` instances (representing `wsdl:service`), which are grouped
into `SoajWSDL` instances (representing a WSDL document). This hierarchy is
illustrated in Figure 11–11.

As you probably recognize, this hierarchy parallels the SOA-J configuration hierarchy discussed in Section 11.2. And in fact, the top-level

---

11. For simplicity of description, I have not described the mapping of `Exception` instances,
but it is handled the same as the return type. When thrown, mapped exceptions get serialized according to the type mapping rules and returned inside a SOAP Fault.

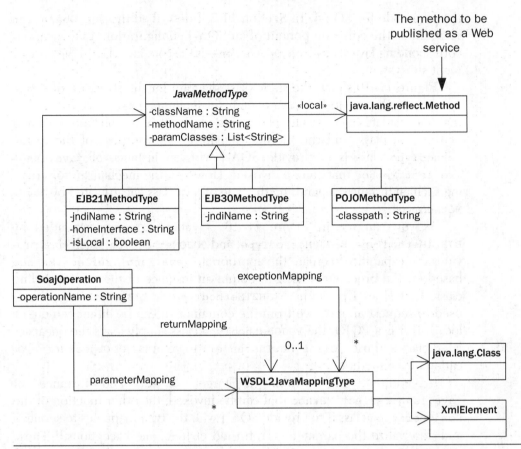

Figure 11–10 Class diagram for SoajOperation—the basic unit of deployment.

configuration class, SoajConfiguration, contains multiple SoajWSDL instances—one for each WSDL document that has been configured. But the SoajConfiguration class also contains additional components. The Schema instances are simply the userDefinedSchema elements from the SOA-J configuration file (illustrated at the beginning of this chapter in Example 11–1) that reference the schemas used in the WSDLs deployed by the SOA-J configuration. Likewise, the Mapping class simply encapsulates the ASF mapping strategies (illustrated in Example 11–7 and Example 11–8) that implement the WSDL2JavaMappingType type mappings defined at the SoajOperation level.

The ClasspathType, however, has not been discussed yet. This corresponds to a JAR file that can be uploaded by SOA-J to load a particular class that is used by an SoajOperation. In particular, the POJOMethodType

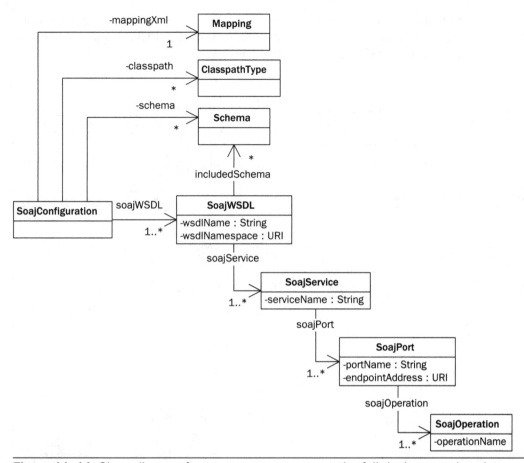

Figure 11–11 Class diagram for SoajConfiguration—the full deployment descriptor defining WSDL and Context.

(illustrated in Figure 11–10) contains a property named classpath. This is a reference to a URL that contains a JAR containing the class definition of the POJO. Of course, if the class is contained in the WAR used to deploy SOA-J, the reference to this JAR is not needed. But SOA-J provides the capability to upload classes that are not deployed with the SOA-J WAR. This is an important part of keeping the configuration dynamic. If you add an soajOperation to the configuration file, you need to be able to tell SOA-J where to find its class definition. Otherwise, you would have to repackage the SOA-J WAR to contain the new JAR.

Figure 11–12 shows an object diagram of a deployment subsystem instance for a hypothetical purchase ordering system. The SoajConfiguration instance—PDconfig—contains references to two `ClasspathType` instances: `purchasingCP` and `inventoryCP`. These represent JARs containing the purchasing system classes and the inventory system classes.

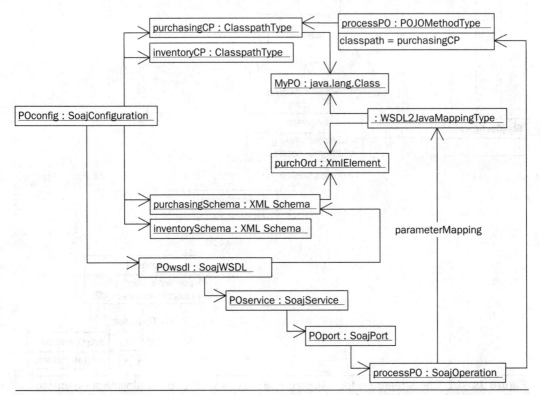

Figure 11–12 Object diagram illustrating the deployment of a purchase order system.

On the XML side, the `POconfig` instance references the `purchaseSchema` and `inventorySchema`. These are enterprise standard schemas used to represent purchasing and inventory components with standard XML types and elements. For simplicity, this diagram shows only one WSDL (although the real configuration for a purchasing system would probably have many)—the `POwsdl` instance. Within this WSDL, only one `wsdl:operation` is shown (again for simplicity)—the `processPO` operation. Notice that the `POwsdl` instance references the `purchasingSchema`, because its `types` section includes that schema (its types are used by the `processPO` operation).

The `processPO` operation references the `processPO` `POJOMethodType`. Here, you can see also the reference from this `POJOMethodType` back to the purchasingCP ClasspathType so that SOA-J knows where to find the POJO's class definition (assuming it is not deployed with the SOA-J WAR). The processPO operation also contains a parameterMapping linking the MyPO Java class (the parameter processed by the processPO POJOMethod-Type) with the purchOrd element from the purchasingSchema. This is a nice illustration of how the WSDL2JavaMappingType (type mapping) provides the bridge between the XML side of an SOA-J configuration and the Java side.

11.6 Conclusions

This chapter provided an overview of how SOA-J implements the Web Services Platform Architecture introduced in Chapter 1. I created SOA-J to provide an illustration of how the JWS technologies can be leveraged to create an Application Framework that is useful for doing SOA Integration. In designing SOA-J, I kept in mind the requirements for building SOA-based applications outlined in Thomas Erl's book, titled *Service Oriented Architecture* [Erl].

In Chapter 3, Section 3.2, of his book Erl identifies a number of characteristics that are common to a contemporary SOA. SOA-J specifically addresses a number of those characteristics:

1. Service orientation through the use of Web Services
2. Autonomy
3. Open standards
4. Interoperability and federation
5. Reusability
6. Loose coupling and organizational agility

In particular, a production-quality system, based on the principles illustrated by SOA-J, would enable you to use your existing Java applications within what [Erl] defines as a contemporary SOA[12] much faster, better, and less expensively than with JWS alone. In this manner, SOA-J is a framework, leveraging the power of JWS, which enables you to quickly and easily incorporate Java applications in a contemporary SOA. Table 11–1 examines how SOA-J enables each of the six SOA characteristics and how it enhances some of the JWS features.

---

12. Page 40 [Erl].

Table 11–1 How SOA-J Implements Erl's Contemporary SOA

Contemporary SOA Characteristic	SOA-J Capability	How It Enhances JWS
Service orientation through the use of Web Services	Publishes existing Java applications as Web services via WSDL-centric development. There is no need to edit source code or descriptors, recompile, repackage, or redeploy.	Eliminates some of the work required to deploy existing Java classes in the JWS framework; for example, annotation, recompilation, repackaging, and redeployment.[a]
Autonomy	Separates the Java code (business logic) from the Web service interface (WSDL).	Eliminates the need for a layer of "mapping code" between the Java API that is bound to the WSDL and the Java that implements the business logic.
Open standards	Enables you to create and deploy Web services by working directly with WSDL. A wide variety of WSDL and XML to Java type mappings can be supported.	Introduces flexibility into the WSDL to Java mapping process. Allows you to go beyond the type mappings supported by JAXB.
Interoperability and federation	Promotes interoperability and federation by enabling Java interfaces to be mapped to existing WSDL interfaces defined by other, preexisting, federated applications.	Enables programmers to avoid the custom coding currently required to map Java interfaces to other existing WSDL interfaces (see Chapter 4).
Reusability	Enables Java code to be reused in multiple SOA components without changing code. A single Java class can support multiple WSDL component representations.	Currently, when reuse requires changes to the WSDL representation, the Java code's annotations or deployment descriptors must be changed.
Loose coupling and organizational agility	Loosely couples the SOA component interface to the underlying Java code. Change is easily accommodated by modifications to the type mapping infrastructure.	Can help reduce the change management maintenance burden by decoupling the WSDL representation from the Java annotations.

a. It is possible to use JWS without annotations (via deployment descriptors, as described in Chapter 8), but this approach is not the focus of the "ease-of-use" features in Java EE 5. Furthermore, even without annotations, you will still need to repackage and redeploy to publish existing classes as Web services.

As you can see by reading through Table 11–1, the areas where the WSDL-centric approach of SOA-J can enhance JWS are primarily related to the tight coupling of Java source code to the WSDL/XML representation of a Web service. SOA-J helps by providing a layer of abstraction, the type mapping layer, between the Java source code and the WSDL representation of a Web service. This type mapping layer enhances both flexibility (allowing a wider range of XML representations of Java types) and change management. Changes to the WSDL representation can be mapped to the underlying Java code simply by editing the type mapping layer. Likewise, the WSDL representation can be insulated from changes to the Java code by tweaking the type mapping layer.

I'm hopeful that by providing this illustration of my prototype implementation of the SOA-J framework, I will help others working on building SOA frameworks come up the learning curve. Toward this end, this explanation of SOA-J is intended to remove some of the mystery related to how SOAP servers are implemented. By removing some of this mystery, and pointing out some of the useful components needed in an Application Framework for SOA Integration, this discussion aims to aid those developers working on the next generation of SOA frameworks for Java.

Java, XML, and Web Services Standards Used in This Book

The XML and Java standards used by developers to implement SOA applications are a moving target. For this book, I have chosen to cover the standards that are either closely related to Java EE 5 and Java SE 6, or are most commonly used by developers today. For this reason, for example, the book discusses WSDL 1.1 and not WSDL 2.0. WSDL 1.1 is supported by Java EE 5, whereas WSDL 2.0 is not. This appendix provides some explanation of why certain standards are discussed and others are not.

Web Services Description Language (WSDL) 1.1

A core component of JAX-WS 2.0 [JSR 224] is the mapping between WSDL 1.1 and Java. There is no mapping defined for WSDL 2.0. Furthermore, on page 2 of [JSR 224], it states that "The expert group for the JSR decided against [support for WSDL 2.0] for this release. We will look at adding support in a future revision of the JAX-WS specification." Also, at the time of this writing, WSDL 2.0 has not progressed to a "Recommendation" of the W3C. It is still a "Candidate Recommendation." Perhaps by the time of publication, it will have become a "Recommendation." But even so, it is my feeling that WSDL 2.0 is not widely used for SOA development. As a result, I decided not to focus on WSDL 2.0 in this book, but instead to concentrate on WSDL 1.1.

The following versions of WSDL have been circulated. Interestingly, as you can see, none of them—as of yet—has made it to the level of a full W3C Recommendation.

- WSDL 1.1 [WSDL 1.1] was published as a W3C Note on March 15, 2001. The publication of a Note does not imply any endorsement by the W3C.

- WSDL 1.2 was published in Working Draft form by the W3C during 2001–2003. It never became a Recommendation.
- WSDL 2.0 [WSDL 2.0] is currently a Candidate Recommendation.

SOAP Version 1.1

In this book, SOAP means SOAP Version 1.1 [SOAP 1.1], unless a specific reference is made to SOAP Version 1.2 [SOAP 1.2]. As they relate to the topics discussed in this book, the differences between SOAP 1.1 and SOAP 1.2 have little impact. The reasons for focusing on SOAP 1.1 are:

- At the time this is being written, SOAP 1.1 is still much more widely implemented than SOAP 1.2.
- Web service endpoints implemented using JAX-WS use SOAP 1.1/ HTTP as the default binding.

XSL Transformations (XSLT) Version 1.0

XSLT 1.0 became a W3C Recommendation in November 1999. So, it is a little old by industry standards. But it is still doing the job and is more than sufficient for the data transformation tasks encountered in many SOA integration applications. In any event, its successor, XSLT 2.0, has just reached the W3C Recommendation stage (as of Januray 23, 2007). As of this writing, XSLT 2.0 has not yet been widely adopted. So, in this book, XSLT 1.0 is used.

XML Schema Version 1.0

XML Schema 1.0 was approved as a W3C Recommendation on May 2, 2001, and a second edition incorporating many errata was published on October 28, 2004. XML Schema 1.1 is in W3C Working Draft status at the time of this writing.

JAX-WS 2.0 and JAXB 2.0

At the time of this writing, JAX-WS 2.0 has already been superseded by JAX-WS 2.1, for which a maintenance draft was published in November 2006. JAX-WS adds support for WS-Addressing. Likewise, JAXB 2.0 has been super-seded by JAXB 2.1. JAXB 2.1 includes a variety of ease-of-use features, but no major changes to the specification. Since the Java EE 5 and Java SE 6 specifi-cations include support for JAX-WS 2.0 and JAXB 2.0, not the 2.1 versions of these specifications, this book covers only JAX-WS 2.0 and JAXB 2.0.

Software Configuration Guide

In addition to reading this guide, please check `http://soabook.com` for the latest information about configuring and running the code examples in this book. Because the software used in these examples is relatively new, the configuration guidelines are subject to frequent change. For that reason, it's very important that, in addition to this appendix, you read the instructions at `http://soabook.com` before configuring your environment to run the examples.

This appendix provides an overview of how to set up your software environment to run the sample code provided with this book. If you are going to follow along with the example code and run it (which is highly recommended), you need to have installed the following:

- J2SE 5 (Java 2 Platform, Standard Edition 5) or later
- Java EE 5 (Java Platform, Enterprise Edition 5) or later
- Apache Ant 1.7.*x*
- Apache Maven 2.0.*x*
- Book Example Code

In addition, one section of the book (Chapter 7, Section 7.7) requires version 6 of Java SE. Installation of this is optional—required only if you want to run the `java.xml.ws.Endpoint` example from that section:

- Java SE 6 (Java Standard Edition 6)—OPTIONAL

Instructions for installing and configuring this software for your Windows or Linux environment are provided here.

B.1 Install Java EE 5 SDK

You need both J2SE 5 (Java 2 Platform, Standard Edition 5) and Java EE 5 (Java Platform, Enterprise Edition 5) to run the code examples in this book. I recommend you get them both from Sun by installing the Java EE 5 SDK, which you can download at http://java.sun.com/javaee.

Java EE 5 SDK contains the Sun Java Systems Application Server Platform Edition 9.*x*—an implementation of the Java EE 5 standards built around the GlassFish[1] open source application framework. Sun refers to its application server as SJSAS PE 9.*x*, but throughout this book, I just call it GlassFish.

The examples in this book have been tested on version 9.1 which, at the time of this writing is a Beta product, scheduled for final release in August 2007. As I was writing this book, GlassFish was the only available implementation of the Java EE 5 standard, so it's the only application server the code examples have been tested with. However, all the code examples should work with other application servers that implement the Java EE 5 standards. There is no GlassFish specific code in my examples. However, the scripts for deploying and undeploying Web services make use of the GlassFish utilities (e.g., `asadmin`). So, if you are using something other than GlassFish, you will need to edit my Maven and Ant scripts to change the way the deployment works.

1. Download and install the Java EE 5 SDK. The following application server defaults are used during installation. If you change these, remember the values because you will need them later when configuring Ant and Maven to build and run the book example code.

Admin User Name:	admin
Admin Password:	adminadmin
Admin Port:	4848
HTTP Port:	8080
HTTPS Port:	8181

    The directory where you installed the application server will be represented in the remaining instructions as `<AppServer>`. (For Windows, the default value of `<AppServer>` is `C:/Sun/AppServer`.[2] For Linux, it is `/home/username/SUNWappserver`).

---

1. You can download the source code and learn more about the GlassFish server at https://glassfish.dev.java.net/. The GlassFish community is very friendly and the mailing lists are very helpful for finding answers to all sorts of Java EE 5-related questions. Plus, whenever you really want to dig in and see how things work, you can browse through the GlassFish source code.
2. The path separator symbol I use is always "/" (forward slash)—even when referring to Windows environments where the backslash "\" character is actually used. This is consistent with Apache Ant and Maven usage.

2. Add the `<AppServer>/bin` directory to the `PATH` environment variable.
3. Set the `JAVA_HOME` environment variable to the path where you installed J2SE 5 (or J2SE 6). For example, on my desktop, I have JAVA_HOME set to `C:\Program Files\Java\jdk1.5.0_10`.
4. Add the `$JAVA_HOME/bin`[3] directory to the `PATH` environment variable.

B.2 Install Apache Ant 1.7.x

To run some of the code examples, you need to use Ant 1.7.x. I use Ant 1.7.0 in my environment. For instructions on downloading and installing Ant 1.7.x, see http://ant.apache.org/.

1. Download and install Ant 1.7.*x*. The directory where you installed Ant 1.7.*x* will be represented in the remaining instructions as `<Ant1.7.x>`.
2. Add the `<Ant1.7.x>/bin` directory to the `PATH` environment variable.

B.3 Install Apache Maven 2.0.x

To build and run the code examples, you need to use Maven 2.0.*x*—*not* Maven 1.*x*. I use Maven 2.0.4 in my environment. For instructions on downloading and installing Maven 2.0.*x*, see http://maven.apache.org/download.html.

1. Download and install Maven 2.0.*x*. The directory where you installed Maven 2.0.*x* will be represented in the remaining instructions as `<Maven2.0.x>`.
2. Add the `<Maven2.0.x>/bin` directory to the `PATH` environment variable.

---

3. For Windows, the value of this environment variable is `%JAVA_HOME%`, and in Linux it is `$JAVA_HOME`. Throughout these instructions, I use the $ notation from Linux. If you are installing on Windows, you just need to remember to convert to the % notation.

B.4 Install the Book Example Code

The examples are provided in a ZIP file that you can unzip wherever you like. Download and unzip the examples from `http://soabook.com`. The directory where you extract the examples is referred to throughout this book as `<book-code>`.

B.5 Configure Maven

The book code you downloaded in Section B.4 contains configuration files you need to modify in order to build the examples in your environment.[4] The following steps walk you through the configuration process:

1. Start by renaming the file `<book-code>/pom.xml.sample` to `<book-code>/pom.xml`. This is the base Maven project file that configures the Maven build environment. It contains a `<profiles>` section that defines a set of properties needed to run the examples in your environment. Using a text editor, open the file `<book-code>/pom.xml`. Starting at line 12 of `pom.xml`, you will see the following text:

```
<profile>
  <id>mark.hansen.desktop</id>
  <activation>
    <file>
      <exists>c:/mark.homepc</exists>
    </file>
  </activation>
  <properties>
    <glassfish.home>c:/bin/glassfish-v2-b28</glassfish.home>
    <glassfish.host>localhost</glassfish.host>
    <glassfish.domain>domain1</glassfish.domain>
    <glassfish.admin.port>4848</glassfish.admin.port>
    <glassfish.deploy.port>8080</glassfish.deploy.port>
    <glassfish.admin.user>admin</glassfish.admin.user>
    <glassfish.admin.password.file>c:/soabook/code/book-code/
glassfish.password</glassfish.admin.password.file>
```

---

4. To learn more about Maven build profiles, see http://maven.apache.org/guides/introduction/introduction-to-profiles.html.

```
<jdk6.home>c:/Program Files/Java/jdk1.6.0</jdk6.home>
   </properties>
</profile>
```

The items highlighted in **bold** are the ones you may need to modify. First, change the `<id>` tag value to something other than `mark.hansen`. This is the ID of your profile.[5] Next, change the `<exists>` tag value to the pathname of a file that exists on your development environment. In my case, I have created an empty file named `c:/mark.homepc` on my desktop that Maven uses to determine that it is running on my desktop. When Maven runs in your environment, it will look for the file pathname you specify inside the `<exists>` tag. If it finds the specified file, Maven will proceed to set the properties as defined in the `<properties>` section of the profile.

You need to edit this properties section of your profile—starting with the `<properties>` tag—to conform to your environment. Make sure to use FORWARD SLASHES "/"—even in Windows (i.e., `C:/Sun/AppServer`—*not* `C:\Sun\AppServer`). In Linux, do not use the "~" abbreviation for `/home/username`, as it can cause problems inside Maven scripts. Table B–1 describes the meaning of the various properties.

Table B–1 Maven Configuration Properties

`glassfish.appsrvr`	The path to the GlassFish application server home. This should be the same as `<AppServer>` described in Section B.1, step 1.
`glassfish.host`	The hostname of the machine running the application server; e.g., when running on a standalone machine, this can be `localhost`.
`glassfish.domain`	The name of the GlassFish domain you want to use to deploy and run the code examples. The default domain created when GlassFish is installed is `domain1`.
`glassfish.admin.port`	The port used for GlassFish administration. The default port used when GlassFish is installed is `4848`.
`glassfish.deploy.port`	The port used by GlassFish to listen for application requests. The default port used when GlassFish is installed is `8080`.

Continues

---

5.   A Maven project can have more than one profile so that the build can be portable to run on (for example) your desktop and your laptop. Each profile has its own ID.

Table B–1 Maven Configuration Properties *(Continued)*

`glassfish` `.admin.user`	The GlassFish administrator username. By default, this is `admin`.
`glassfish.` `admin.password.file`	This references a password file you create in the next step. It should be set to `<book-code>/glassfish.password`.
`jdk6.home`	(Optional) This is the path to the directory where the Java SE 6 SDK is installed. See Section B.11.

2. Rename the file `<book-code>/glassfish.password.sample` to `<book-code>/glassfish.password`. Open the file `<book-code>/glass-fish.password` and check that the value for `AS_ADMIN_PASSWORD` agrees with the password you provided during installation of GlassFish. The default is "adminadmin."

3. Open a console window (DOS or XTerm) and change to the `<book-code>` directory. Enter the following command to install the `<book-code>/pom.xml` to Maven's repository:

```
mvn install
```

This is important, because in order to build and run the code samples, the top-level `pom.xml` must be loaded in the repository.

B.6   Configure Ant

In addition to requiring configuration for Maven, the book code you downloaded in Section B.4 contains configuration files you need to modify for Ant to work properly in your environment. The following steps describe how to configure for Ant:

1. Copy the file `<book-code>/common-build.xml.sample` to `<book-code>/common-build.xml`.

2. Using a text editor, open the file `<book-code>/common-build.xml`. At the top of the file, right after the `<project ...>` tag, is a section that contains a group of property definitions that looks like this:

```
<property environment="env"/>
<property name="glassfish.appsvr"
  value="${env.GLASSFISH_HOME}"/>
```

```
<property name="glassfish.host" value="localhost"/>
<property name="glassfish.domain" value="domain1"/>
<property name="glassfish.admin.port" value="4848"/>
<property name="glassfish.deploy.port" value="8080"/>
<property name="glassfish.admin.user" value="admin"/>
<property name="glassfish.admin.password.file" value=
  "c:/soabook/code/book-code/glassfish.password"/>
<property name="jdk6.home" value=
  "c:/Program Files/Java/jdk1.6.0"/>
```

Just as you did in Section B.5 for Maven, you need to modify many of these properties to conform to your environment. In fact, many of these properties are the same as those used in the Maven environment. Those property values highlighted in **bold** may need to be changed. As in Section B.5, Table B–2 describes how the property values should be set.

Table B–2 Ant Configuration Properties

`glassfish.appsrvr`	The path to the GlassFish application server home. This should be the same as `<AppServer>` described in Section B.1, step 1.
`glassfish.host`	The hostname of the machine running the application server; e.g., when running on a stand-alone machine, this can be `localhost`.
`glassfish.domain`	The name of the GlassFish domain you want to use to deploy and run the code examples. The default domain created when GlassFish is installed is `domain1`.
`glassfish.admin.port`	The port used for GlassFish administration. The default port used when GlassFish is installed is `4848`.
`glassfish.deploy.port`	The port used by GlassFish to listen for application requests. The default port used when GlassFish is installed is `8080`.
`glassfish.admin.user`	The GlassFish administrator username. By default, this is `admin`.
`glassfish.admin.password.file`	This references a password file that you create in the next step. It should be set to `<book-code>/glassfish.password`.
`jdk6.home`	(Optional) This is the path to the directory where the Java SE 6 SDK is installed. See Section B.11.

B.7   Starting and Stopping the GlassFish Server

To **START** the GlassFish application server, enter the following at a command-line prompt:

```
asadmin start-domain
```

To **STOP** the GlassFish application server, enter the following at a command-line prompt:

```
asadmin stop-domain
```

For the `asamin` command to work, you must have `<AppServer>/bin` on your `$PATH` as described in Section B.1.

B.8   Test the Installation by Running an Example

Following is an excerpt from the instructions to run an example found in Chapter 3. Follow these instructions, and if the environment is set up properly, it should run.

Running the examples requires opening a command prompt (Windows) or XTerm (Linux). The term "Go to" means to change directories to the one specified.

1. Start GlassFish (if it is not already running).
2. Go to `<book-code>/chap03/rest-get/endpoint-servlet`.
3. To build and deploy the Web service, enter:

```
mvn install
```

... and when that command finishes, then enter:

```
ant deploy
```

4. Go to `<book-code>/chap03/rest-get/client-http`.
5. To run the client, enter:

```
mvn install
```

6. To undeploy the Web service, go back to `<book-code>/chap03/rest-get/endpoint-servlet` and enter:

```
ant undeploy
```

After running the client (step 5), you should see some output to the console that looks like this:

```
<?xml version="1.0" encoding="UTF-8"?><Orders
  xmlns="http://www.example.com/oms"
 xsi:schemaLocation="http://www.example.com/oms   http://soabook.com/
  example/oms
/orders.xsd" xmlns:xsi="http://www.w3.org/2001/XMLSchema-instance">
  <Order>
    <OrderKey>ENT1234567</OrderKey>
    <OrderHeader>
      <SALES_ORG>NE</SALES_ORG>
      <PURCH_DATE>2001-12-09</PURCH_DATE>
      <CUST_NO>ENT0072123</CUST_NO>
      <PYMT_METH>PO</PYMT_METH>
      <PURCH_ORD_NO>PO-72123-0007</PURCH_ORD_NO>
      <WAR_DEL_DATE>2001-12-16</WAR_DEL_DATE>
    </OrderHeader>
    <OrderItems>
      <item>
        <ITM_NUMBER>012345</ITM_NUMBER>
        <STORAGE_LOC>NE02</STORAGE_LOC>
        <TARGET_QTY>50</TARGET_QTY>
        <TARGET_UOM>CNT</TARGET_UOM>
        <PRICE_PER_UOM>7.95</PRICE_PER_UOM>
        <SHORT_TEXT>7 mm Teflon Gasket</SHORT_TEXT>
      </item>
      <item>
        <ITM_NUMBER>543210</ITM_NUMBER>
        <TARGET_QTY>5</TARGET_QTY>
        <TARGET_UOM>KG</TARGET_UOM>
        <PRICE_PER_UOM>12.58</PRICE_PER_UOM>
        <SHORT_TEXT>Lithium grease with PTFE/Teflon</SHORT_TEXT>
      </item>
    </OrderItems>
    <OrderText>This order is a rush.</OrderText>
  </Order>
  <Order>
    <OrderKey>ENT1234568</OrderKey>
    <OrderHeader>
      <SALES_ORG>NE</SALES_ORG>
      <PURCH_DATE>2001-12-09</PURCH_DATE>
```

```
      <CUST_NO>ENT0098211</CUST_NO>
      <PYMT_METH>PO</PYMT_METH>
      <PURCH_ORD_NO>PO-98211-00147</PURCH_ORD_NO>
      <WAR_DEL_DATE>2001-12-19</WAR_DEL_DATE>
    </OrderHeader>
    <OrderItems>
      <item>
        <ITM_NUMBER>087321</ITM_NUMBER>
        <STORAGE_LOC>NE05</STORAGE_LOC>
        <TARGET_QTY>2</TARGET_QTY>
        <TARGET_UOM>CNT</TARGET_UOM>
        <PRICE_PER_UOM>598.49</PRICE_PER_UOM>
        <SHORT_TEXT>Acme Air Handler</SHORT_TEXT>
      </item>
    </OrderItems>
  </Order>
</Orders>BUILD SUCCESSFUL
```

B.9   Build and Deploy the SOAShopper Case Study (Chapters 9 and 10)

SOAShopper is online shopping search tool discussed in Chapters 9 and 10. It provides an Ajax front-end that runs in a browser. Because Ajax is based on JavaScript, and all browsers do not implement JavaScript the same way, the SOAShopper front-end renders differently on different browsers. On some browsers, it may not work at all. I have tested it with Firefox 2.0.0.1 and Microsoft IE 6.0.2900.*x*. For both of these browsers it works fine.

The code for SOAShopper can be found at `<book-code>/chap09/` `soashopper` in the book example code download. (See Section B.4 for instructions for downloading and installing the book example code.)

Before attempting to build and run SOAShopper, please make sure you have completed the configuration steps outlined in Section B.1 through Section B.8. Once you have completed the configuration, follow these steps to build SOAShopper and open the Ajax front-end:

1. Open a console window and go to the directory `<book-code>/` `chap09/soashopper`.
2. Enter `mvn clean`.
3. Enter `mvn install`.
4. Enter `ant deploy`.

5. Open your browser at the following URL: `http://${glass-fish.host}:${glassfish.deploy.port}/soashopper/ajax/search.html`. For example, using the default values, the URL would be `http://localhost:8080/soashopper/ajax/search.html`.

6. To undeploy the application, return to the console window and enter `ant undeploy`.

B.10   Build and Deploy the SOA-J Application Framework (Chapter 11)

Please check `http://soabook.com` for instructions on building and running SOA-J and the code examples from Chapter 11. The source code can be found at `<book-code>/chap11/soaj`.

B.11   Install Java SE 6 (Optional)

You need to install Java SE 6 only if you want to run the `javax.xml.ws.Endpoint` example from Chapter 7, Section 7.7. But I recommend you do so, because the `Endpoint` API is very cool and you will enjoy seeing how it works. You can get it from `http://java.sun.com/javase/downloads`.

1. Download and install the Java SE Development Kit (JDK) 6. When you are doing the installation, and following along with the wizard, I recommend you do not install the JRE (unless you want to run Java SE 6 as your default JRE)—particularly if you are using Windows. I've seen Windows get confused when JREs are installed for both Java SE 6 and Java SE 5.

2. Review the instructions for Sections B.5 and B.6 (configuring Maven and Ant) to make sure you have set the property named `jdk6.home` to be the location of the JDK 6 installation.

B.10. Build and Deploy the SOA Application Framework (Chapter 14)

B.11. Install Java SE 6 (Optional)

Namespace Prefixes

To simplify the XML used in examples and figures, namespace prefix definitions are not always provided. Where namespace prefixes are not explicitly defined, they conform to standard usage in the Java EE, Java SE, and W3C specifications, or the standard usage in this book, as summarized here.

env1	http://schemas.xmlsoap.org/soap/envelope	SOAP 1.1
env2	http://www.w3.org/2003/05/soap-envelope	SOAP 1.2
jaxb	http://java.sun.com/xml/ns/jaxb	JAXB 2.0
jaxws	http://java.sun.com/xml/ns/jaxws	JAX-WS 2.0
soap	http://schemas.xmlsoap.org/wsdl/soap	WSDL 1.1 SOAP Binding
wsdl	http://schemas.xmlsoap.org/wsdl/	WSDL 1.1
xsl	http://www.w3.org/1999/XSL/Transform	XSLT 1.0
wsrm	http://docs.oasis-open.org/wsrm/200510	WS-RX
wsse	http://docs.oasis-open.org/wss/2004/01/oasis-200401-wss-1.0.xsd	WS-Security
xmime	http://www.w3.org/2005/05/xmlmime	Binary Data in XML
xop	http://www.w3.org/2004/08/xop/include	XOP 1.0
xs	http://www.w3.org/2001/XMLSchema	XML Schema 1.0

Glossary

The glossary provides definitions for many of the technical terms specific to Java Web Services. Definitions often reference other definitions, and terms appearing in *italics* are defined within the glossary.

Ajax   A Web browser-based user interface development technique that is short for *Asynchronous JavaScript and XML*. Ajax is primarily used to create Web browser user interfaces that do not require full-page refreshes each time new data is retrieved from the server. Ajax programmers use the JavaScript type *XMLHttpRequest* to exchange data with the server behind the scenes (i.e., without having to reload the entire HTML page being displayed by the browser). When new data (usually in XML format) is received by an *XMLHttpRequest* instance, JavaScript is used to update the *DOM* structure of the HTML page (e.g., inserting some rows in a table) without rebuilding the entire HTML page in memory.

annotations   Annotations are program elements added to the Java programming language starting with J5SE to enable a declarative style of programming. Within a Java source file, annotations are indicated by the "@" symbol. For example, the `@WebService` annotation is used to declare that a class should be deployed as a Web service.

anonymous type   An XML Schema type that is not defined explicitly, but rather implicitly as part of an element definition. Such types are called anonymous because they do not have qualified names.

AOP   See *aspect oriented programming*.

aspect oriented programming   The programming paradigm of aspect-oriented programming (AOP) provides for the encapsulation and modularization of cross-cutting concerns.[1] The basic idea is that concerns such as security, which cut across an application, should not have to be "reimplemented" in each place they are needed. Instead, a single security

---

1. See www2.parc.com/csl/groups/sda/publications/papers/Kiczales-ECOOP97/for-web.pdf.

implementation should be referenced as needed. Java EE 5 implements AOP concepts using *annotations*.

binding   See *Java/XML binding*.

binding declaration   An instruction, written in the *binding language*, that maps a particular XML Schema or WSDL component to its Java representation. JAXB 2.0 binding declarations are specified as instances of the `<jaxb:bindings>` element. JAX-WS 2.0 binding declarations use the `<jaxws:bindings>` element.

binding language   An XML-based language that uses the XML Schema elements to embed JAXB and/or JAX-WS binding customization instructions into WSDL and/or XML Schema documents. The binding language is used to customize the default WSDL/XML to Java mappings defined by JAX-WS and JAXB. The binding language is used to express *binding declarations*.

binding runtime framework   The run-time part of a JAXB 2.0 implementation. It provides the *marshal* and *unmarshal* operations.

data transformation   The process of changing the format of an XML document from one schema representation to another. Data transformation is used when getting data from a source system (e.g., an Order Management System) and using it to update a target system (e.g., a Customer History database). In this example, an order record goes through data transformation to create a customer history record that is used to update the database.

datatype mapping   A datatype mapping is a transformation from one representation of a datatype to another. For example, an XSTL transformation from one XML Schema representation of a product to another can be referred to as a datatype mapping. A datatype mapping is similar to a *type mapping*, except that the term *datatype mapping* is usually used when both types are represented in the same language (e.g., both Java or both XML). The term *type mapping* is typically used when the transformation applies to types represented in different forms (e.g., Java to XML).

declarative (programming language)   A language is said to be *declarative*, rather than *procedural*, if it defines a set of rules that are applied to an input to create an output.

delegate   See *delegation*.

delegation   As described in [Go4], page 20, "Delegation is a way of making composition as powerful for reuse as inheritance." In delegation, a class implements a method by invoking methods on a delegate instance.

This is like inheritance, where a class can defer implementation of a method to the implementation defined in a parent class. However, it is more flexible than inheritance because the delegation relationship can change at runtime by using delegates of different types.

dependency injection   A programming design pattern whereby an instance of an object (the *Injection Target*) can be "injected" at runtime so that a program may use the instance without having to programmatically construct it or locate it. Java implements dependency injection with the `@Resource` annotations, for example.

derived schema   See *schema generator*.

deserialization   Converting a sequential byte (serial) representation of an object to an in-memory (which may be stored as a tree, graph, etc.) representation.

deserializer   A programming component that implements *deserialization*.

dispatching   Dispatching is part of the invocation process. Given a SOAP message, determining its target WSDL operation and the corresponding Java method to invoke is referred to as dispatching.

Document Object Model   A standard, in memory, representation of an HTML or XML document. The standard is maintained by the W3C—see [DOM]. A DOM structure represents a document as a tree. Web browsers typically represent HTML using the DOM. XML is commonly manipulated using DOM within Java programs.

DOM   See *Document Object Model*.

ECMAScript   A scripting language standard defined by Ecma International in its ECMA-262 specification. *JavaScript* is an implementation of ECMAScript.

EJB   See *Enterprise Bean*.

endpoint listener   A component of the deployment subsystem of a Web Services Platform Architecture. The endpoint listener is responsible for listening for request messages at a certain address and transport (e.g., HTTP). When a Web service is deployed, it is associated with a particular endpoint listener.

Enterprise Bean   An Enterprise Bean or Enterprise JavaBean (EJB) is a Java class whose instances are managed at runtime by an Enterprise JavaBean container.

Enterprise JavaBean container   The component of a Java EE 5 implementation that hosts EJBs. The EJB container provides services such as persistence, transaction processing, concurrency control, security, and so on.

Extensible Stylesheet Language Transformations Abbreviated XSLT, Extensible Stylesheet Language Transformations is an XML-based language used to describe transformations of XML documents. Using an XSLT, for example, you can transform an XML document into a human-readable HTML page. XSLT can be used within an SOA framework to transform data representations from one format to another. This can be very useful for facilitating integration where, for example, Company A's representation of a Purchase Order needs to be transformed into Company B's representation.

fail-fast validation A form of JAXB 2.0 validation whereby each manipulation (e.g., setting a property) of a JAXB-annotated program element is checked against the associated schema. An unchecked exception is thrown whenever a manipulation would result in the underlying XML Infoset becoming invalid with respect to the schema.

fault bean See *JAX-WS fault bean*.

flexible unmarshalling mode Contrasted with *structural unmarshalling*, when using the JAXB 2.0 flexible unmarshalling mode, certain types of validation errors are ignored, such as out-of-order elements or missing attributes.

HTTP parameter A set of parameter/value pairs may be passed to a program deployed at a URL endpoint using HTTP parameters in the form `p1=v1&p2=v2&...&pn=vn`, where `p1 ... pn` are parameters and `v1 ... vn` are the corresponding values. Such parameters are *URL encoded* and can be passed either in the HTTP body (e.g., when an HTTP form is submitted) or in a *query string*.

IDL See *Interface Definition Language*.

Injection Target See *dependency injection*.

interceptor An *aspect oriented programming* (AOP) concept. An interceptor program element can be used to intercept, and take action, before or after a method's invocation. A common example involves security. A security interceptor could be associated with all the methods in a particular application that need to check credentials before being executed.

Interface Definition Language (IDL) An Interface Definition Language is a computer language that provides a standard method for describing how to invoke a software component.

Java content interface JAXB 1.0 binds complex types to content interfaces rather than *value classes*. Implementations of these interfaces are generated by object factories. This type of binding is still available in

JAXB 2.0 as an alternative to value classes. *Structural unmarshalling* requires the use of Java content interfaces.

Java dynamic proxy class   A Java dynamic proxy class is a class, created at runtime, that implements a list of interfaces that are also specified at runtime.

Java program elements   Java program elements include the components of a Java data model for an application: package, field, property (i.e., JavaBean property), and types (classes and enum construct).

Java Remote Method Invocation (Java RMI)   Java Remote Method Invocation (Java RMI) is a technology for distributed Java to Java applications, in which the methods of remote Java objects can be invoked from other Java virtual machines, possibly on different hosts. RMI uses object serialization to marshal and unmarshal parameters.

JavaScript   JavaScript is an implementation of the `ECMAScript` standard. It is a scripting language commonly used to do client-side programming for Web applications. Most Web browsers support JavaScript. JavaScript programs can read to and write from a browser interface by manipulating the browser's *DOM* representation of an HTML page. JavaScript is not a variant of Java. The two languages are very different. See *Ajax*.

JavaScript Object Notation   A text-based data interchange format used for serialization. Often referred to as JSON, it is lightweight and easier to read than XML. For these reasons, it is considered by some to be preferable to XML for the exchange of simple data structures often encountered in *Ajax* programming.

Java/XML binding   A Java/XML binding is a one-to-one *Java/XML map* between a set of Java program elements and XML Schema components and a set of rules that are used to convert an instance of a Java program element (e.g., a class) into an instance of its corresponding XML Schema component (e.g., an XML Schema type).

Java/XML map   A Java/XML map is a set of pairs <J, X>, where J is a Java program element and X is an XML Schema component. Each pair <J, X> is referred to as an individual *type mapping*.

JAXB-annotated Java program elements   *Java program element* definitions that have been annotated with *mapping annotations*.

JAXB 2.0 schema-derived program elements   Java program elements that are created by the JAXB 2.0 *schema compiler* when it compiles a schema. These program elements are said to be "bound" to their respective schema components.

JAXB 2.0 standard Java/XML mapping   The standard mapping defined by JAXB 2.0 that associates XML Schema components with JAXB-annotated Java program elements.

JAXB value class   Generated by a *schema compiler*, a JAXB value class provides JavaBeans-style access (i.e., get and set) methods to the content of its corresponding *schema component*.

JAX-WS fault bean   A Java class generated by the JAX-WS mapping to represent the contents of a fault message described by a WSDL document. JAX-WS maps `wsdl:fault` elements to Java exceptions that wrap fault beans containing the contents of the fault. More specifically, a `wsdl:fault` element inside a `wsdl:portType` always refers to a `wsdl:message` that contains a single `wsdl:part` with an `element` attribute. The global element declaration referred to by that `wsdl:part`'s `element` attribute is mapped by JAX-WS to a Java bean called a fault bean.

JAX-WS port component   A JAX-WS port component defines the programming model artifacts that make up a portable Web service application. These components are defined by WSEE 1.2 [JSR 109]. A port component must include a *service implementation bean*. It may also include a *service endpoint interface* (SEI), a WSDL document, *Security Role References*, and a Web Services deployment descriptor.

JAX-WS Service Endpoint   A WSEE [JSR 109] term for a Web *service port component* deployed as a WAR in the Web container. This is a confusing term because it sounds a lot like JAX-WS service endpoint interface (SEI). In fact, a SEI can be implemented by either a JAX-WS Service Endpoint or a Stateless Session EJB in an EJB container.

JAX-WS service endpoint interface (SEI)   A Java interface that is mapped to a `wsdl:portType` according to the JAX-WS WSDL/Java mapping. A SEI must include an `@WebService` annotation. Other annotations may be used to influence the mapping of the interface to the WSDL.

JAX-WS service implementation bean (SIB)   A service implementation bean contains the business logic of a JAX-WS Web service. It is annotated with `@WebService` or `@WebServiceProvider` and its methods can be exposed as Web Service operations. The service implementation bean is fully defined in WS-Metadata [JSR 181].

JSON   See *JavaScript Object Notation*.

JSR-181 processor   WS-Metadata 1.0 (JSR-181) implementations provide a processor that reads the annotations on a Java Web service source file to create the deployment descriptors and other artifacts needed to create a runnable Web service.

mapping annotations   Java language *annotations* that are used to control how Java program elements are mapped to either XML Schema components or WSDL components. JAXB 2.0 provides mapping annotations for Java to XML Schema. JAX-WS 2.0 and WS-Metadata provide mapping annotations for Java to WSDL.

marshal   The JAXB 2.0 process of converting instances of JAXB-annotated classes to an *XML Infoset representation* according to the *JAXB 2.0 standard Java/XML mapping* as customized by the mapping annotations.

mock object   A mock object is a Java class used for *test-driven development*. The mock object implements the API of a real object, but its return value(s) are hard-coded with test data. Mock objects are used to test the run-time behavior of interface definitions without requiring the business logic implementations.

multivariate type mapping   A multivariate type mapping is a *type mapping* in which there is no one-to-one correspondence between schema elements and attributes and Java properties. Such mappings involve combining and/or splitting schema elements and attributes to create a Java property or set of properties. An simple example of such a mapping is when you have a phone number represented as a single `xs:string` in an XML schema, but as two properties—an area code and a number— in a Java class.

MTOM   See *MTOM/XOP*.

MTOM/XOP   The W3C standard titled "SOAP Message Transmission Optimization Mechanism" (see www.w3.org/TR/soap12-mtom/). It describes a standard procedure for content out of the XML Infoset, compressing it, packaging it as a MIME attachment, and replacing it with a reference in the Infoset. The packaging encoding used with MTOM is XOP, another W3C standard titled "XML-binary Optimized Packaging" (see www.w3.org/TR/xop10/). XOP replaces base64-encoded content with an `xop:include` element that references the respective MIME part encoded as a binary octet stream. If data is already available as a binary octet stream, it can be placed directly in an XOP package.

noun (REST)   Within the REST context, the word *noun* refers to a *resource*—for example, a purchase order. Nouns are contrasted with *verbs*, which define actions.

POJO   Plain Old Java Object. This term is usually used to distinguish a regular Java class from an *EJB*.

port component   See *JAX-WS port component*.

POX   Plain Old XML. POX is used to describe XML when it is used as a stand-alone message format (e.g., without a SOAP layer). POX is the style of message used by *RESTful* Web services that communicate using XML/HTTP.

predicate   Predicates are code fragments that apply schema validation rules to program element properties. They are used by JAXB 2.0 implementation to implement *fail-fast validation*.

procedural (programming language)   A language is said to be *procedural*, rather than *declarative*, if it consists of a set of instructions to be executed sequentially in a stateful environment.

program element   See *Java program elements*.

QoS   See *Quality of Service*.

Quality of Service   A Quality of Service requirement refers to a Web service's capability to meet a specific *Service Level Agreement* (SLA) standard such as network reliability. For example, a "guaranteed processing order" QoS might be a requirement that a Web service process messages in the order they are received.

query string   A query string is the part of a URL, following the "?" character, that contains a list of HTTP parameters to be passed to a program that is deployed at an endpoint. A URL containing a query string as the format `http://host/path/program?p1=v1&p2=v2&...&pn=vn`, where `p1 ... pn` are parameters and `v1 ... vn` are the corresponding values. Since some characters cannot be part of a URL (e.g., a space), these are represented using special codes defined by the *URL encoding* specification (RFC 1738). For example, the URL-encoding for a white space is `%20`. Query strings are often used as a mechanism to pass parameters to RESTful endpoints (e.g., Yahoo! Shopping APIs).

Remote Procedure Call (RPC)   A protocol that enables a client program to invoke a procedure (e.g., Java method) on a remote server (i.e., a different address space).

Representational State Transfer   An architectural style of networked systems usually referred to by its acronym: REST. The REST style was first formalized in [Fielding]. As used in this book, REST refers to an architectural approach using simple XML over HTTP interfaces without SOAP or any of the additional complexities introduced by the Web Services stack.

representation (REST)   In the REST context, a representation is defined to be a particular formatting of a REST *resource*. For example, the representation of the purchase order at http://myserver.com/oms/po could an XML file—po.xml.

request bean   A Java class that represents a WSDL request. JAX-WS 2.0 defines a mapping from WSDL to Java. This mapping defines a request bean corresponding to the input message for a `wsdl:operation`. Likewise, a response bean is defined corresponding to the output message for a `wsdl:operation`. Together with JAXB 2.0, the JAX-WS runtime can serialize a request bean instance into a properly constructed SOAP message payload corresponding to the `wsdl:operation` input message. Likewise, the message payload of a SOAP response can be deserialized into the response bean, from which the Java representation of the `wsdl:operation` response can be extracted.

response bean   See *request bean.*

resource (REST)   In the REST context, a resource is defined to be a piece of information (e.g., a purchase order) that can be referred to using a URI.

REST   See *Representational State Transfer.*

RESTful   A Web service designed and deployed using the REST approach is referred to as a *RESTful* service.

reusable schema   The SOA Integration architectural concept of having standard, reusable XML Schema definitions for the XML messages that are exchanged between SOA components. This concept implements the goal of having well-defined interface definitions between SOA components, because the XML schemas that are standardized are the building blocks of the WSDL interface definitions.

RPC   See *Remote Procedure Call.*

SAAJ   The Java APIs used for creating and manipulating SOAP messages. It is an acronym for SOAP with Attachments API for Java. See [JSR 67] Java™ APIs for XML Messaging: SOAP with Attachments API for Java™ (SAAJ).

schema compiler   A JAXB 2.0 schema compiler takes an XML Schema instance as input and generates a set of schema-derived *Java program elements* according to the standard Java/XML mapping.

schema component   See *XML schema component.*

schema-derived program elements   See *JAXB 2.0 schema-derived program elements.*

schema generator   A JAXB 2.0 schema generator takes a set of existing program elements and generates an XML Schema instance referred to as the *derived schema*. The JAXB runtime can (un)marshal instances of the program elements to instances of the derived schema.

Security Role References   The Java EE 5 mechanism for providing Web Services security, Security Role References are logical role names declared by a *port component*'s deployment descriptors. Roles such as "User" and "Admin" can be used to provide varying levels of access to Web services.

semantic mapping   A semantic mapping is similar to a *datatype mapping*, except it is concerned with mapping the meaning of a type (e.g., schema definition, class) rather than just its structure. Although the boundary between semantic mappings and datatype mappings is a little fuzzy, it is most common to see mappings of Java method implementations from one API to another referred to as semantic mapping. For example, the mapping of a shopping search API from a generic model to the Amazon and Yahoo! shopping services would be described as a semantic mapping (see Chapter 9).

Separation of Concerns   The software architecture principle which holds that separate concerns (i.e., features) should not share overlapping code. For example, the code for the user interface should not, in general, contain code that makes database updates. The use of the term, as applied to computer science, is explained in detail in [Disjkstra].

serialization   Converting an in-memory representation of an object (which may be stored as a tree, graph, etc.) to a sequential byte (serial) representation.

serializer   A programming component that implements *serialization*.

service endpoint interface   See *JAX-WS service endpoint interface*.

service implementation bean   See *JAX-WS service implementation bean*.

Service Level Agreement   An agreement between a Web service consumer and a Web service provider that guarantees certain properties of performance. Examples include quantifiable measures like guaranteed response time and guaranteed reliability (i.e., if a message is sent it is guaranteed to be delivered).

Service Oriented Architecture   A style of software architecture that is based on the use of services to create applications. Abbreviated SOA, it implies a style of systems development whereby applications are composed by linking together individual services in a loosely coupled manner.

SLA   See *Service Level Agreement*.

SOA   See *Service Oriented Architecture*.

SOA Component   A single service that can be part of an SOA application. When doing SOA based on Web Services, an SOA component corresponds to a `wsdl:port`. Sometimes, *SOA Component* is also used to refer to an individual `wsdl:operation` within a `wsdl:port`.

SOA-style loosely coupled systems integration   An approach to systems integration that involves deploying the applications to be integrated as sets of SOA-style services. The integration is accomplished by aggregating the resulting services and applying workflow techniques to create loosely coupled applications built on the underlying services.

SOA-style systems integration   See *SOA-style loosely coupled systems integration*.

SOA Integration   See SOA-style *loosely coupled systems integration*.

SOAP   A protocol for exchanging XML-based messages across a network. SOAP is the messaging standard for Web Services. See [SOAP 1.1] and [SOAP 1.2].

SOAP body   A SOAP message must contain a `<Body>` element. It is used to carry the payload of the SOAP message.

SOAP header block   A SOAP message may contain an optional `<Header>` element. It is used to pass application-related information intended to be processed by SOAP nodes along the path the message travels—so-called metadata. The immediate children of the `<Header>` element are called header blocks. A header block usual contains some logical grouping of metadata such as its security information.

SOAP Messages with Attachments   SOAP Messages with Attachments (SwA) (www.w3.org/TR/SOAP-attachments) was the industry's first attempt to standardize an approach to treating binary data as SOAP message attachments. SwA defines a binding for a SOAP 1.1 message within a MIME multipart/related message. The MIME multipart mechanism for encapsulation of compound documents is used to bundle attachments with the SOAP message.

Standard Java/XML mapping   See *JAXB 2.0 Standard Java/XML mapping*.

"Start from Java" development mode   A Java EE approach to the development of Java Web Services where the programmer starts with a Java class (or classes) he wishes to deploy as a Web service. The class is annotated using WS-Metadata and JAXB annotations that describe how it should map to a WSDL interface definition. Tools are invoked (e.g., a

JAXB schema generator) to generate the WSDL and XML Schema used in the interface definition.

"Start from WSDL and Java" development mode   A combination of the "Start from Java" and "Start from WSDL" development modes. In this case, you have both an existing WSDL that defines a set of Web services to be deployed, and a set of existing Java classes you need to use to implement those Web services. The challenge is to map between the existing WSDL and Java to implement the Web services. This development mode is most commonly encountered when doing *SOA-style loosely coupled systems integration*.

"Start from WSDL" development mode   A Java EE approach to the development of Java Web Services where the programmer starts with a WSDL document he wishes to implement as a Web service. The WSDL (and the XML Schema type definitions it includes) may be annotated using WS-JAX-WS and JAXB *binding declarations* that describe how it should map to a set of Java classes. Tools are invoked (e.g., a JAXB schema compiler) to generate the Java classes that get deployed as Web services. These generated classes provide the deployment structure for the Web service, and the programmer must add the business logic to them.

stateless   An application that does not keep a persistent set of data between transactions.

structural unmarshalling mode   Contrasted with *flexible unmarshalling*, this is the unmarshalling mode where strict validation of XML data against schema is enforced.

SwA   See *SOAP Messages with Attachments*.

test-driven development   Test-driven development is a software development methodology that focuses on writing tests first (as a means of specification), and then implementing the software to make the tests pass.

type mapping   A type mapping defines a relationship between a Java programming element and an XML Schema component—for example, `corp:AddressType` and `samples.Address`. A type mapping is implemented by a *serializer* and a *deserializer*. The serializer converts instances of the Java class into XML instances that conform to the schema. The deserializer does the reverse.

unmarshal   The JAXB 2.0 process of converting an *XML Infoset representation* to a tree of *content objects*. The conversion is defined by the Infoset's associated XML schema together with the *JAXB 2.0 standard*

Java/XML mapping as customized by any *mapping annotations* specified in the program element definitions of the target content objects. The content objects' *Java program elements* are either *JAXB 2.0 schema-derived program elements* or existing program elements mapped to the schema by the *schema generator*.

URL-encoded   See *query string*.

value class   See *JAXB value class*.

verb (REST)   Within the REST context, the word *verb* refers to a protocol operation—for example, the HTTP GET operation. *REST* emphasizes a minimal use of verbs, as contrasted with *RPC*, where a great diversity of operations may be implemented and specified with an interface definition language such as WSDL.

W3C   See *World Wide Web Consortium*.

Web Services   A Web service is a programmatic interface for application-to-application communication that is invoked by sending and receiving XML. The term "Web Services" refers to the discipline of writing, deploying, and using Web services. A "Web service" is different from a "service" as defined within a *Service Oriented Architecture*. As the term is used in this book, a "Web service" is a "service" that has an XML interface and is defined using WSDL or REST.

Web Services Definition Language   An interface definition language, written in XML, used for describing Web services. WSDL 1.1 is currently the most commonly used (www.w3.org/TR/wsdl)—but it is not an official W3C recommendation. WSDL 2.0 (www.w3.org/TR/wsdl20/) is on track to become a W3C Recommendation.

Web Services protocol stack   A layered collection of protocols used to define, implement, locate, and invoke Web services. At the bottom layer of the stack is a service transport (e.g., HTTP, SMTP) responsible for transporting messages. On top of that is an XML messaging layer (e.g., SOAP 1.2) used to encode messages in a common XML format. A service description protocol (e.g., WSDL) is often used to describe the public interface of a service. There may also be a service discovery protocol (e.g., UDDI) involved to provide access to a central directory (or registry) of Web services. In addition, there are *Quality of Service* (QoS) layers that can be used together with SOAP such as WS-Addressing (for service transport independent addressing), WS-Security (for security), and WS-ReliableMessaging (for message reliability).

Web Services stack   See *Web Services protocol stack*.

World Wide Web Consortium A standards body that provides many of the most important Web Services specifications (e.g., XML, XML Schema, SOAP, WSDL). See www.w3.org.

wrapper-based integration An approach to the *"Start from WSDL and Java"* development mode where the WSDL/*schema compiler* is used to create Java wrapper classes that can be deployed to implement the Web services specified in a particular WSDL. These wrapper classes are then edited to invoke the actual classes that implement the business logic behind a Web service.

wrapper element See *WSDL wrapper element*.

WSDL See *Web Services Definition Language*.

WSDL compiler A JAX-WS 2.0 WSDL compiler takes a WSDL instance as input and generates a set of schema-derived *Java program elements* according to the standard WSDL/Java and XML/Java mappings. A WSDL compiler delegates the compilation of the XML schema elements within the source WSDL to a JAXB *schema compiler*.

WSDL wrapper element An element defined in the `<wsdl:types>` section of a document/literal wrapped style WSDL that "wraps" the parameter types of the input and/or output messages used by the Web service. The parameters appear as child elements of the wrapper element.

WS-I Attachments Profile Version 1.0 The WS-I Attachments Profile Version 1.0 (see www.ws-i.org/Profiles/AttachmentsProfile-1.0.html)—WSIAP—clarifies SOAP Messages with Attachments (SwA). See *SOAP Messages with Attachments*. SwA was the industry's first attempt to standardize an approach to treating binary data as SOAP message attachments. The industry now seems to be converging on *MTOM/XOP*, rather than SwA, as the primary standard for handling binary data with SOAP.

WSIAP See *WS-I Attachments Profile Version 1.0*.

XMLHttpRequest A JavaScript API used to transfer data (often XML) to and from a Web server over HTTP. See *Ajax*.

XML Information Set A W3C Recommendation that provides a set of definitions used to refer to the information contained in an XML document (www.w3.org/TR/xml-infoset/). Commonly referred to as an XML Infoset, an Information Set can include up to 11 different types of information items, including documents, elements, attributes, processing instructions, and so on.

XML Infoset See *XML Information Set*.

XML Infoset representation   A programming language representation of an XML Infoset. One example is the W3C's Document Object Model (DOM) (www.w3.org/DOM/) that provides an object-oriented API for accessing an XML document as a tree structure. Alternatively, an XML Infoset can be represented as a stream of events. This approach is used by the Simple API for XML (SAX) (www.saxproject.org/). There are many other representations of XML Infosets—each suited to a particular programming language or style of XML processing. Of particular importance in this book is JAXB, which represents an XML Infoset as instances of Java classes that are bound to XML Schema components.

XML Path Language   Often abbreviated XPath, the XML Path Language is a W3C defined syntax for addressing portions of an XML document (www.w3.org/TR/xpath). For example, XPath enables you to specify a particular child element of an element defined in an XML document.

XML Schema   A W3C Recommendation that defines an XML schema language (www.w3.org/XML/Schema). Other schema languages include Document Type Definition (DTD) and RELAX NG. An XML schema is a description of a type of XML document. It constrains the structure and contents of conforming documents. XML Schema provides a language for expressing such constraints, effectively enabling the definition of XML types.

XML schema component   A schema defined in the XML Schema language is composed of a variety of components, including complex and simple type definitions, element declarations, attribute declarations, model groups, and so on. These are formally defined in the W3C document "XML Schema Part 1: Structures Second Edition" (www.w3.org/TR/2004/REC-xmlschema-1-20041028/structures.html).

XPath   See *XML Path Language*.

XSLT   See *Extensible Stylesheet Language Transformations*.

References

[AIA] Crane, David, Eric Pascarello, and Darren Jones. *Ajax in Action*. Manning Publications. ISBN 0201633612, January 1995.

[AXIS] Apache Axis 1.*x*.
http://ws.apache.org/axis

[AXIS2] Apache Axis 2.*x*.
http://ws.apache.org/axis2

[CASTOR] The Castor Project.
www.castor.org/

[DIJKSTRA] Dijkstra, E. "On the Role of Scientific Thought," *Selected Writings on Computing: A Personal Perspective*. Springer-Verlag, 1982, pp. 60–66.

[DOJO] The Dojo JavaScript toolkit, The Dojo Foundation.
http://dojotoolkit.org/

[DOM] Document Object Model (DOM) Level 3 Core Specification Version 1.0, W3C Recommendation April 7, 2004.
www.w3.org/TR/DOM-Level-3-Core/

[Eckstein] Eckstein, and Robert Rajiv Mordani. "Introducing JAX-WS 2.0 with the Java SE 6 Platform, Part 2," November 2006.
http://java.sun.com/developer/technicalArticles/J2SE/jax_ws_2_pt2/

[Fielding] Fielding, Roy Thomas. "Architectural Styles and the Design of Network-based Software Architectures." Doctoral dissertation, University of California, Irvine, 2000.
www.ics.uci.edu/~fielding/pubs/dissertation/top

[GLASSFISH] GlassFish Open Source Java EE 5 Application Server.
https://glassfish.dev.java.net/

[Go4] Gamma, Erich, Richard Helm, Ralph Johnson, and John Vlissides. *Design Patterns: Elements of Reusable Object-Oriented Software*. Addison-Wesley Professional Computing Series. ISBN 1932394613, October 2005.

[GROOVY] The Groovy Java Scripting Language.
http://groovy.codehaus.org/

[Hunt] Hunt, Andrew, and David Thomas. *The Pragmatic Programmer: From Journeyman to Master.* Addison-Wesley Professional; 1st edition, ISBN 020161622X, October 1999.

[Hunter] Hunter, David, et al. *Beginning XML.* Wrox (Third Edition), ISBN 0764570773, September 2004.

[JSON] Crockford D. "The application/json Media Type for JavaScript Object Notation (JSON)." The Internet Engineering Task Force (Network Working Group) RFC-4627, July 2006.
http://tools.ietf.org/html/rfc4627

[JSR 109] Web Services for Java EE 1.2. JSR, JCP, May 11, 2006.
http://jcp.org/en/jsr/detail?id=109

[JSR 152] JavaServer Pages™ 205. JSR, JCP, November 24, 2003.
http://jcp.org/en/jsr/detail?id=152

[JSR 154] Java™ Servlet 2.5. JSR, JCP, May 11, 2006.
http://jcp.org/en/jsr/detail?id=154

[JSR 166] Concurrency Utilities. JSR, JCP, September 30, 2004.
http://jcp.org/en/jsr/detail?id=166

[JSR 173] Streaming API for XML. JSR, JCP, March 25, 2004.
http://jcp.org/en/jsr/detail?id=173

[JSR 175] A Metadata Facility for the Java™ Programming Language. JSR, JCP, September 30, 2004.
http://jcp.org/en/jsr/detail?id=175

[JSR 181] Web Services Metadata for the Java™ Platform 2.0. JSR, JCP, May 1, 2006.
http://jcp.org/en/jsr/detail?id=181

[JSR 196] Java™ Authentication Service Provider Interface for Containers. JSR, JCP, in progress.
http://jcp.org/en/jsr/detail?id=196

[JSR 206] Java™ API for XML Processing (JAXP) 1.3. JSR, JCP, September 30, 2004.
http://jcp.org/en/jsr/detail?id=206

[JSR 222] The Java™ Architecture for XML Binding (JAXB) 2.0, JSR, JCP, May 11, 2006
http://jcp.org/en/jsr/detail?id=222

[JSR 224] The Java™ Architecture for XML-Based Web Services (JAX-WS) 2.0. JSR, JCP, May 11, 2006.
http://jcp.org/en/jsr/detail?id=224

[JSR 244] Java™ Platform, Enterprise Edition 5 (Java EE 5) Specification. JSR, JCP, May 8, 2006.
http://jcp.org/en/jsr/detail?id=244

[JSR 250] Common Annotations for the Java Platform. JSR, JCP, May 11, 2006.
http://jcp.org/en/jsr/detail?id=250

[JSR 52] A Standard Tag Library for JavaServer Pages™ 1.2 (Maintenance Release 2). JSR, JCP, May 11, 2006.
http://jcp.org/en/jsr/detail?id=52

[JSR 67] Java™ APIs for XML Messaging: SOAP with Attachments API for Java™ 1.3 (SAAJ). JSR, JCP, April 12, 2006.
http://jcp.org/en/jsr/detail?id=67

[JSR 914] Java™ Message Service (JMS) API. JSR, JCP, December 2, 2003.
http://jcp.org/en/jsr/detail?id=914

[Monson-Haefel] Monson-Haefel, Richard. *J2EE Web Services*. Addison-Wesley Professional, ISBN 0130655678, October 2003.

[Namespaces in XML] Namespaces in XML 1.0 (Second Edition). W3C Recommendation August 16, 2006.
www.w3.org/TR/REC-xml-names/

[Ramachandran] Personal e-mail communication from Vijay Ramachandran. Sun Microsystems, January 15, 2007.

[SOAP 1.1] Simple Object Access Protocol (SOAP) 1.1. W3C Note, May 8, 2000.
www.w3.org/TR/soap11/

[SOAP 1.2] SOAP Version 1.2 Part 0: Primer. W3C Recommendation, June 24 2003.
www.w3.org/TR/soap12-part0

[STRUTS] Apache Struts.
http://struts.apache.org

[SwA] SOAP Messages with Attachments. W3C Note, December 11, 2000.
www.w3.org/TR/SOAP-attachments

[SYSTINET] Systinet Server for Java.
www.systinet.com/products/ssj/overview

[Walmsley] Walmsley, Priscilla. *Definitive XML Schema*. Prentice-Hall PTR, ISBN 0321146182, December 2001.

[WS-ADDRESSING 1.0 Core] Web Services Addressing 1.0—Core. W3C Recommendation, May 9, 2006.
www.w3.org/TR/ws-addr-core/

[WSDL 1.1] Web Services Description Language (WSDL) 1.1. W3C Note, March 15, 2001.
www.w3.org/TR/wsdl

[WSDL 2.0 Part 2] Web Services Description Language (WSDL) Version 2.0 Part 2: Adjuncts. W3C Working Draft, August 3, 2005.
www.w3.org/TR/wsdl20-adjuncts

[WSDL 2.0] Web Services Description Language (WSDL) Version 2.0 Part 1: Core Language. W3C Working Draft, August 3, 2005.
www.w3.org/TR/wsdl20/

[WS-I BP 1.1] Basic Profile Version 1.1, Final Material. August 24, 2004.
www.ws-i.org/Profiles/BasicProfile-1.1.html

[WSIAP] XML Attachments Profile Version 1.0, WS-I Final Material. April 20, 2006.
www.ws-i.org/Profiles/AttachmentsProfile-1.0.html

[WS-RM] Web Services ReliableMessaging (WS-ReliableMessaging). OASIS Web Services Reliable Exchange (WS-RX) Technical Committee, Committee Draft 03, March 14, 2006.
http://docs.oasis-open.org/ws-rx/wsrm/200602/wsrm-1.1-spec-cd-03.pdf

[WS-Security 1.1] Web Services Security (WS-Security). OASIS Web Services Security (WSS) Technical Committee, OASIS Standard Specification, February 1, 2006.
www.oasis-open.org/committees/tc_home.php?wg_abbrev=wss#technical

[WS-Security] Web Services Security OASIS Standard 1.1.
www.oasis-open.org/committees/tc_home.php?wg_abbrev=wss#technical

[XFIRE] Codehaus XFire Java SOAP Framework.
http://xfire.codehaus.org

[XJ] XML Enhancements for Java, IBM Alphaworks.
www.alphaworks.ibm.com/tech/xj

[XMIME] Describing Media Content of Binary Data in XML. W3C Working Group Note, May 4, 2005.
www.w3.org/TR/xml-media-types/

[XML 1.0] Extensible Markup Language (XML) 1.0 (Second Edition). W3C Recommendation, October 6, 2000.
www.w3.org/TR/2000/REC-xml-20001006.

[XML Catalog 1.1] XML Catalogs. OASIS Standard V1.1, October 7, 2005.
www.oasis-open.org/committees/download.php/14810/xml-catalogs.pdf

[XMLBeans] Apache XMLBeans.
http://xmlbeans.apache.org

[XML-Infoset] XML Information Set, John Cowan and Richard Tobin, eds. W3C, March 16, 2001.
www.w3.org/TR/2001/WDxml-infoset-20010316/

[XOP] XML-binary Optimized Packaging. W3C Recommendation, January 25, 2005.
www.w3.org/TR/xop10/

[XPath], XML Path Language, James Clark and Steve DeRose, eds. W3C, November 16, 1999.
www.w3.org/TR/1999/RECxpath-19991116

[XSD Part 0] XML Schema Part 0: Primer. W3C Recommendation, May 2, 2001.
www.w3.org/TR/xmlschema-0/

[XSD Part 1] XML Schema Part 1: Structures. W3C Recommendation, May 2, 2001.
www.w3.org/TR/xmlschema-1/

[XSD Part 2] XML Schema Part 2: Datatypes. W3C Recommendation, May 2, 2001.
www.w3.org/TR/xmlschema-2/

[XSLT 1.0] XSL Transformations (XSLT), Version 1.0. James Clark. W3C Recommendation, November 16, 1999.
www.w3.org/TR/1999/REC-xslt-19991116

Index

informIT